Research Anthology on Agile Software, Software Development, and Testing

Information Resources Management Association
USA

Volume II

Published in the United States of America by
   IGI Global
   Engineering Science Reference (an imprint of IGI Global)
   701 E. Chocolate Avenue
   Hershey PA, USA 17033
   Tel: 717-533-8845
   Fax: 717-533-8661
   E-mail: cust@igi-global.com
   Web site: http://www.igi-global.com

                    Library of Congress Cataloging-in-Publication Data

Names: Information Resources Management Association, editor.
Title: Research anthology on agile software, software development, and
   testing / Information Resources Management Association, editor.
Description: Hershey, PA : Engineering Science Reference, [2022] | Includes
   bibliographical references and index. | Summary: "This reference book
   covers emerging trends of software development and testing, discussing
   the newest developments in agile software and its usage spanning
   multiple industries, covering topics such as global software
   engineering, knowledge management, and product development"-- Provided
   by publisher.
Identifiers: LCCN 2021040441 (print) | LCCN 2021040442 (ebook) | ISBN
   9781668437025 (h/c) | ISBN 9781668437032 (eISBN)
Subjects: LCSH: Agile software development. | Computer programs--Testing.
Classification: LCC QA76.76.D47 R468 2022 (print) | LCC QA76.76.D47
   (ebook) | DDC 005.1/112--dc23/eng/20211021
LC record available at https://lccn.loc.gov/2021040441
LC ebook record available at https://lccn.loc.gov/2021040442

British Cataloguing in Publication Data
A Cataloguing in Publication record for this book is available from the British Library.

The views expressed in this book are those of the authors, but not necessarily of the publisher.

For electronic access to this publication, please contact: eresources@igi-global.com.

List of Contributors

Table of Contents

Volume I

Section 1
Fundamental Concepts and Theories

Section 2
Development and Design Methodologies

Volume II

Section 3
Tools and Technologies

Volume III

Section 4
Utilization and Applications

Section 5
Organizational and Social Implications

Section 6
Managerial Impact

Section 7
Critical Issues and Challenges

Preface

As organizations grow to require new and innovative software programs to improve processes, there is a need for the science of software development to constantly evolve. Agile practices have shown great benefits for improving the effectiveness of software development and its maintenance due to their ability to adapt to change. It is essential for organizations to stay current with the developments in agile software and software testing to witness how it can improve business operations.

Staying informed of the most up-to-date research trends and findings is of the utmost importance. That is why IGI Global is pleased to offer this four-volume reference collection of reprinted IGI Global book chapters and journal articles that have been handpicked by senior editorial staff. This collection will shed light on critical issues related to the trends, techniques, and uses of various applications by providing both broad and detailed perspectives on cutting-edge theories and developments. This collection is designed to act as a single reference source on conceptual, methodological, technical, and managerial issues, as well as to provide insight into emerging trends and future opportunities within the field.

The *Research Anthology on Agile Software, Software Development, and Testing* is organized into seven distinct sections that provide comprehensive coverage of important topics. The sections are:

1. Fundamental Concepts and Theories;
2. Development and Design Methodologies;
3. Tools and Technologies;
4. Utilization and Applications;
5. Organizational and Social Implications;
6. Managerial Impact; and
7. Critical Issues and Challenges.

The following paragraphs provide a summary of what to expect from this invaluable reference tool.

Section 1, "Fundamental Concepts and Theories," serves as a foundation for this extensive reference tool by addressing crucial theories essential to understanding the concepts and uses of agile software, software development, and testing in multidisciplinary settings. The first chapter of this section, "Challenges and Trends of Agile," by Prof. Jorge Marx Gómez of Carl von Ossietzky Universität Oldenburg, Germany and Prof. Fayez Salma of Carl von Ossietzky Universität Oldenburg, Germany, studies agile methodologies and different challenges with suggested solutions generated from agile philosophy itself. The last chapter of this section, "A Historical and Bibliometric Analysis of the Development of Agile," by Profs. Sathiadev Mahesh, Kenneth R. Walsh, and Cherie C. Trumbach of University of New Orleans, USA, summarizes the traditional approaches and presents the conditions that led to agile approaches such as product complexity, shortened life cycle of the market, and eventually to the widespread acceptance of Scrum.

Section 2, "Development and Design Methodologies," presents in-depth coverage of the design and development of agile software for their use in different applications. The first chapter of this section, "Software Effort Estimation for Successful Software Application Development," by Prof. Syed Mohsin Saif of Islamic University of Science and Technology, India, explains different types of software applications, software estimation models, the importance of software effort estimation, and challenges faced in software effort estimation. The last chapter of this section, "A Simulation Model for Application Development in Data Warehouses," by Prof. Nayem Rahman of Portland State University, Portland, USA, presents a simulation model of a data warehouse to evaluate the feasibility of different software development controls and measures to better manage a software development lifecycle and improve the performance of the launched software.

Section 3, "Tools and Technologies," explores the various tools and technologies used in the implementation, development, and testing of agile software for various uses. The first chapter of this section, "Use of Qualitative Research to Generate a Function for Finding the Unit Cost of Software Test Cases," by Prof. Mark L. Gillenson of University of Memphis, Memphis, USA; Prof. Thomas F. Stafford of Louisiana Tech University, Ruston, USA; Prof. Yao Shi of University of Memphis, Memphis, USA; and Prof. Xihui "Paul" Zhang of University of North Alabama, Florence, USA, demonstrates a novel use of case research to generate an empirical function through qualitative generalization. This innovative technique applies interpretive case analysis to the problem of defining and generalizing an empirical cost function for test cases through qualitative interaction with an industry cohort of subject matter experts involved in software testing at leading technology companies. The last chapter of this section, "Metastructuring for Standards: How Organizations Respond to the Multiplicity of Standards," by Prof. Ronny Gey of Friedrich Schiller University Jena, Germany and Prof. Andrea Fried of Linköping University, Sweden, focusses on the appearance and implementation of process standards in software development organizations.

Section 4, "Utilization and Applications," describes how agile software is used and applied in diverse industries for various technologies and applications. The first chapter of this section, "Social Capital and Knowledge Networks of Software Developers: A Case Study," by Prof. VenuGopal Balijepally of Oakland University, Rochester, USA and Prof. Sridhar Nerur of University of Texas at Arlington, Arlington, USA, examines the structural and relational dimensions of developers' knowledge networks, identifies the specific actionable knowledge resources accessed from these networks, and explores how entry-level and more experienced developers differ along these dimensions. The findings from the qualitative analysis, backed by limited quantitative analysis of the case study data, underpin the discussion, implications for practice, and future research directions. The last chapter of this section, "A Game Theoretic Approach for Quality Assurance in Software Systems Using Antifragility-Based Learning Hooks," by Profs. Vimaladevi M. and Zayaraz G. of Pondicherry Engineering College, India, proposes an innovative approach which uses a fault injection methodology to perform the task of quality assurance.

Section 5, "Organizational and Social Implications," includes chapters discussing the impact of agile software on society and shows the ways in which software is developed in different industries and how this impacts business. The first chapter of this section, "Media Richness, Knowledge Sharing, and Computer Programming by Virtual Software Teams," by Profs. Idongesit Williams and Albert Gyamfi of Aalborg University, Denmark, concludes, based on the case being investigated, that rich media does not fit the task characteristics of a software programmer. It further concludes that media richness does affect knowledge sharing in these virtual teams. This is because the current lean media actually enables knowledge sharing as it fits the core characteristics of the software programming process. The last chapter of this section, "On the Rim Between Business Processes and Software Systems," by Profs. Ricardo J. Machado and Maribel Yasmina Santos of Universidade do Minho, Portugal and Prof. Maria Estrela Ferreira da Cruz of Polytechnic Institute of Viana do Castelo, Portugal, uses the information existing in business process models to derive software models specially focused in generating a data model.

Section 6, "Managerial Impact," presents the impact of agile software within an organizational setting. The first chapter of this section, "Boosting the Competitiveness of Organizations With the Use of Software Engineering," by Prof. Mirna Muñoz of CIMAT, A. C. Unidad Zacatecas, Mexico, provides a research work path focused on helping software development organizations to change to a continuous software improvement culture impacting both their software development process highlighting the human factor training needs. Results show that the implementation of best practices could be easily implemented if adequate support is provided. The last chapter of this section, "Measuring Developers' Software Security Skills, Usage, and Training Needs," by Prof. Daniela Soares Cruzes of SINTEF Digital, Norway; Prof. Tosin Daniel Oyetoyan of Western Norway University of Applied Sciences, Norway; and Prof. Martin Gilje Gilje Jaatun of SINTEF Digital, Norway, presents a survey instrument that can be used to investigate software security usage, competence, and training needs in agile organizations.

Section 7, "Critical Issues and Challenges," presents coverage of academic and research perspectives on challenges to using agile software in different methods, technologies, and techniques in varied industry applications. The first chapter of this section, "Towards a Security Competence of Software Developers: A Literature Review," by Prof. Nana Assyne of University of Jyväskylä, Finland, utilises a literature review to identify the security competences of software developers. Thirteen security competences of software developers were identified and mapped to the common body of knowledge for information security professional framework. The last chapter of this section, "Open Source Software Development Challenges: A Systematic Literature Review on GitHub," by Prof. Abdulkadir Seker of Sivas Cumhuriyet University, Turkey; Prof. Banu Diri of Yıldız Technical University, Turkey; Prof. Halil Arslan of Sivas Cumhuriyet University, Turkey; and Prof. Mehmet Fatih Amasyalı of Yıldız Technical University, Turkey, reviews the selected 172 studies according to some criteria that used the dataset as a data source.

Although the primary organization of the contents in this multi-volume work is based on its seven sections, offering a progression of coverage of the important concepts, methodologies, technologies, applications, social issues, and emerging trends, the reader can also identify specific contents by utilizing the extensive indexing system listed at the end of each volume. As a comprehensive collection of research on the latest findings related to agile software, the *Research Anthology on Agile Software, Software Development, and Testing* provides software developers, software engineers, computer engineers, IT directors, students, managers, faculty, researchers, and academicians with a complete understanding of the applications and impacts of agile software and its development and testing. Given the vast number of issues concerning usage, failure, success, strategies, and applications of agile software in modern technologies and processes, the *Research Anthology on Agile Software, Software Development, and Testing* encompasses the most pertinent research on the applications, impacts, uses, and development of agile software.

Chapter 26
Software Release Planning Using Grey Wolf Optimizer

Vibha Verma
University of Delhi, India

Neha Neha
University of Delhi, India

Anu G. Aggarwal
(iD) https://orcid.org/0000-0001-5448-9540
University of Delhi, India

ABSTRACT

This chapter presents the application of grey wolf optimizer in software release planning considering warranty based on the proposed mathematical model that measures reliability growth of software systems. Hence, optimal release and warranty time is determined while minimizing the overall software development cost. The software cost model is based on failure phenomenon modelled by incorporating fault removal efficiency, fault reduction factor, and error generation. The model has been validated on the fault dataset of ERP systems. Sensitivity analysis has been carried out to study the discrete changes in the cost parameter due to changes in optimal solution. The work significantly contributes to the literature by fulfilling gaps of reliability growth models, release problems considering warranty, and efficient ways for solving optimization problems. Further, the grey wolf optimizer result has been compared with genetic algorithm and particle swarm optimization techniques.

INTRODUCTION

In recent times IT-based firms focus on developing reliable software systems without bearing any financial or goodwill losses during the post-implementation phase. The technology advancements in Medical, Defence, Space, Transportation, banks, universities, homes appliances, etc. have increased the demand for qualitative software products. These products facilitate day to day task handling by reducing

DOI: 10.4018/978-1-6684-3702-5.ch026

the efforts and time required at both the individual and organizational level and any failure encountered during the software operations may lead to heavy financial losses and sometimes may prove hazardous to human lives also (Yamada and Tamura, 2016).

Due to the ever-increasing importance of software systems, the researchers and IT firms are continuously working to improve their reliability and hence the quality. For this, it is very necessary to assess the reliability of a software system during its development phase. The software development process, also known as the software development life cycle, through this phase developers try to enhance the software quality. Here the development process comprises of few steps i.e., planning, analysis, design, implementation, testing and maintenance. Among all these steps, testing is considered as the most decisive and essential task for improving the quality of the software by detecting and removing the faults. Faults detectability influences software reliability growth which results in the development of Software Reliability Growth Models (SRGMs).

Since 1970 numerous SRGMs have been developed for the assessment of software reliability. These models incorporate various aspects related to software development for e.g. the code size and complexity, the skill of tester, developer and programmer, testing tools and methodology, resources allocated, etc. A number of researchers and IT practitioners have proposed Non-Homogenous Poisson Process (NHPP) based SRGMs to assess the reliability of the software system (Aggarwal et al., 2019; Anand et al., 2018; Kapur et al., 2011). These models help to predict the number of faults and the time for the next failure on the basis of observed failure data.

These time-dependent SRGMs are divided into two classes: one is perfect debugging where it has been assumed that whenever a new failure occurs the faults causing it is removed immediately and no new faults are introduced in the meantime. The other one is imperfect debugging which further can be split into two types: (a) whenever originally detected faults are removed that do not remove completely this phenomenon is known as imperfect fault removal and (b) it takes several attempts to remove a fault and also some new faults which were previously non-existent may also get generated. This phenomenon re-introduction of faults is known as Error generation (Yamada et al., 1984). In this chapter, we model the failure phenomenon of software incorporating error generation.

Previously it was assumed that faults initiating the failure are removed with complete efficiency but later it was observed that all the encountered faults are not removed i.e. fault removal process is not 100% efficient (Zhang et al., 2003) i.e. only few number of faults are removed out of the overall faults spotted. It can be defined as the ability or effectiveness in the fault removal process. This measure helps the developer to predict the effectiveness of the fault detection and further effort needed. In our study, we have considered Fault Removal Efficiency (FRE) because it is immensely correlated with fault removal process i.e., as the FRE escalates fault removability escalates as well.

Also, it was stated that in practice the number of faults experienced is not the same as the faults removed during the process. Musa (1975) defined Fault Reduction Factor (FRF) as "the ratio of a number of faults removed to the number of failures experienced". This indicates that for the reliability evaluation FRF plays an important role. Experimentally, FRF takes values between zero and one. It has been discovered that FRF could be affected by issues like fault dependency, complex code, human nature, etc. This, in turn, affects the FRF curves which can be increasing, decreasing or constant. Here we consider that FRF follows Weibull distribution while error generation and FRE are considered to be constant. FRF, FRE and error generation all these factors have been incorporated because of their significant impact on the failure process.

In the development phase software engineers also face the challenge to develop a reliable product at the lowest possible cost. In this direction, several release time problems have been formulated to find optimal software release time that incurs a minimum cost of software development to developers (Gautam et al., 2018; Kapur et al., 2012). Based on the failure phenomenon and requirements, developers have to determine the optimal testing time period for which they will perform testing. Infinite testing until all the faults are removed is not feasible for developers since it incurs an enormous cost. On the other hand, inadequate testing may result in catastrophic failures and loss of willingness among the users for the product. To tackle these researchers have devised cost optimization problems that minimize cost along with attaining a level of reliability for the system. In our proposed optimization problem, we consider various costs influencing the development process such as testing and warranty cost, opportunity cost and penalty cost of failures after the warranty expires.

In today's age of competition, companies use product differentiation techniques to mark existence of their product into the market. One of the value-added services that are used widely by the companies is warranty. Software systems are getting complex day by day that creates insecurities among the buyers. In these situations warranty acts as marketing tool. By providing warranty, developer guarantees the user to remove all the faults causing failure during usage for a specified period of time. It benefits the developers by creating a sense of product quality among its users but also incurs some additional cost to developers. Hence they have to maintain balance so that they can gain profits and avoid losses. Market Opportunity cost is dependent on testing time which tends to increase with an increase in testing time. Hence appropriate time to release the software is very necessary. It is defined as loss to the firm due to loss of opportunity caused due to delay in release in monetary terms.

The model is validated using a real fault dataset to obtain optimal release and warranty time. Several methods have been used in the past to solve the software release time optimization problems considering warranty and reliability requirements of the system. One of the most recognized and efficient ways is using soft computing techniques. These techniques became popular because they are simple, flexible, derivation-free and avoids local minima (Mohanty et al., 2010). We have discussed the approach in detail in the future section.

The objective of this study is to use the swarm inspired Metaheuristic Grey Wolf Optimizer (GWO) algorithm to solve the software release time problem. In this study, we obtain optimal release time and optimal warranty time period based on development cost criteria incurred during various phases based on mathematical model that estimates the reliability of software system. The advantage of using GWO over other techniques is that here the optimization problem is continuously controlled by the leader which is not the case of other algorithms. GWO comprises of less number of parameters thus is less cumbersome to deal with. Also this algorithm is versatile in nature because it can be implemented to most of the optimization problems without changing much in the mechanism. Figure 1 presents the research approach followed in this chapter. The main focus of the proposed study is,

- To model the failure process of the software system incorporating FRF, FRE and error generation.
- To examine the model's goodness of fit using real-life software fault dataset.
- To find optimal release time and optimal warranty period based on reliability and cost components using the Grey Wolf optimization algorithm.
- To study the impact of different cost components via sensitivity Analysis on
  ◦ Release time
  ◦ Warranty time period

  ◦ Overall Development Cost
- To identify key cost components affecting the cost.
- To test the significance of error generation and fault removal efficiency on software development cost.

Figure 1. Research Methodology

A number of SRGMs and its concerned release planning problems have been proposed in the literature. None of the studies discuss the failure tendency of software systems under the impact of Weibull FRF, FRE and error generation together. Many meta-heuristic techniques such as Genetic Algorithm have been used for solving optimization problems in the field of software reliability. But recently some new techniques with better convergence properties have been proposed which have not been employed to solve the software release time problems. Therefore we have made an attempt to utilize the GWO technique to determine the when to release the software into market and for what duration warranty should be given for the software product. This is so because GWO overcomes many limitations of previous techniques.

Due to the impact of different environmental factors on the SRGMs and also in the urge of making high reliable software consisting of all possible functions and features, this situation motivates us to develop a model through this impact and also the different costs involved in developing it. This research is an attempt to provide software engineers an SRGM which can estimates the faults more accurately as it involves different factors that affect the estimation. Also the cost function comprising of opportunity cost, penalty cost and warranty cost, is optimized using GWO. Previously, to obtain the optimal value many soft computing techniques have been used here we have used GWO due to its flexible nature and high performance than the other algorithms.

The study contributes to the literature by using a better optimization technique to solve the software development cost minimization problem. The overall cost of the software system is based on the failure phenomenon modelled by incorporating Weibull FRF, FRE and error generation. The inclusion of practical factors into the models helps in better fault prediction. Therefore incorporating these environmental factors makes the model more accurate and realistic. The proposed study used GWO technique to determine the optimal release and warranty time for the software system. Using of more realistic mathematical model for assessing reliability of software system and one of the latest meta-heuristic techniques GWO for solving optimization problems helps to achieve the best possible results of the release planning problem.

The chapter is organized as follows; in the next section, we have discussed the related concepts and its literature followed by the modelling of SRGM and optimization problem formulation with detailed methodology. Further, we have briefly explained GWO used for the optimization. In the next section application of the proposed approach is illustrated and compared with two standard meta-heuristic techniques along with discussion of the results. Further, we conclude the work and give the limitations and future scope of our study.

BASIC TERMINOLOGIES AND LITERATURE REVIEW

In this section, we will discuss the past and contemporary research being done in the relevant area. Studying literature, in brief, helps to identify the importance of the problem under consideration and find the research gap. All the concepts and terms used are discussed to elaborate and highlight the significance of software release planning by maintaining the reliability under resource constraints. Reliability for a software system is defined as the "probability of failure-free operation for a fixed period of time under the same conditions" (Yamada and Tamura, 2016). This area came more into light when there was a tremendous increase in software demand in almost every. The developers and firms deal with the challenge of providing the best products to end-user.

SRGMs

The reliability of software systems is measured by observing the failure phenomenon. Many SRGMs are based on NHPP assuming the number of failures to be counting process. These models represent the relationship between a number of faults removed or detected with time. The failure process for a general NHPP based SRGMs is modelled by the following differential equations,

$$\frac{dm(t)}{dt} = b(t)\big(a(t) - m(t)\big) \tag{1}$$

Where,

    $a(t)$ is fault content,

    $b(t)$ is the rate of detecting faults and

    $m(t)$ is a measure of a cumulative number of faults detected or removed up to time t.

Solving the differential equation (1), we obtain the expression for Mean Value Function (MVF) $m(t)$. Different expressions are obtained by representing $a(t)$, $b(t)$, as different functions (representing curves) based on the assumptions as well as the dataset. In the past various NHPP based SRGMs have been developed by researchers. One of the very initial SRGM given by Goel andOkumoto (1979) considered finite failure model with constant parameters whose intensity function is exponentially distributed. Many times S-shaped curve for MVF has been observed rather than exponential. This implies an improvement in testing efficiency as the testing progresses with time. This 2-stage model given by Yamada et al. (1984) consists of fault detection and fault isolation phases of the testing process. The model considers delay or time lag between the fault detection and removal assuming that all the detected faults are removed. Kapur andGarg (1992) developed an SRGM assuming that detection of a fault leads to detection of some more faults in the system. They considered that there was some kind of mutual dependence between the faults.

FRF

This factor is defined as "the net number of faults removed is only a proportion of the total number of failures experienced" or as "the net number of faults detected proportional to the number of failures experienced". It was first defined and proposed by Musa (1975). The FRF forms discussed in the literature have been listed in Table 1.

Table 1. Expressions for FRF

References	Explanation	Mathematical Expression for FRF ($0 < F \pounds 1$)
Musa (1975), Musa (1980), Musa et al. (1987),	FRF was modelled as the proportion of failures experienced to the number of faults removed.	$F = \dfrac{n}{m}$ m be the number of failures experienced n is the number of faults removed.
Malaiya et al. (1993), Naixin andMalaiya (1996), Musa (1991)	Based on observations the value of FRF can be modelled by fault exposure ratio (at time$t$).	$F = \dfrac{\lambda_0}{kfm}$ $\lambda 0$ is the initial failure intensity, k: is the faults exposure ratio, f: is the linear execution frequency of the program.
Friedman et al. (1995),	FRF has also defined in the form of detectability, associability and fault growth ratio The Detectability ratio is defined as the number of faults whose resulting failures could be detected. The value of D is near 1, the value of A is near 0 and the value of G lies between 0 and 0.91.	$F = D(1+A)\,(1-G)$, D is the detectability ratio, A is the associability ratio, G is the fault growth ratio.

There may be variation in FRF under different situations and environmental factors. There is a noticeable relationship between environmental factors and FRF. Some of the factors influencing FRF are:

- Time difference between detection and removal of faults.
- Imperfection in debugging causes reintroduction or an increase in a number of latent faults. Also sometimes it requires more than one attempt to remove a particular fault. The value of FRF decreases when new faults are introduced.
- Change in efficiency to remove faults due to the introduction of some new faults. Efficiency is affected because all faults are of different severity and require different effort levels to be eliminated.
- Resources allocated for testing and debugging.
- Dependence of fault on some factors or on each other.

Table 2 presents the SRGMs consisting of FRF as the key parameter.

Table 2. SRGMs based on FRF

Researchers	FRF ($0<F\pounds1$)	Model
Musa (1975), Musa (2004)	Musa in his basic Execution time model assumed FRF to be Proportional to the hazard rate function.	$\frac{dm(t)}{dt} = Fz(t) = F\varphi[a - m(t)]$ $z(t)$ is the hazard rate function φ be the per fault hazard rate. *The mean value function is:* $m(t) = a(1 - e^{-F\varphi t})$
Hsu et al. (2011)	FRF is defined as constant as well as the time variable. Considering that scenario Hsu et. al. defined it to be constant, decreasing and increasing for software with a single release • Constant: $F(t) = F$ • Decreasing curve: $F(t) = F_0 e^{-kt}$ • Increasing curve: $F(t) = 1 - (1 - F_0) e^{-kt}$ F_0 represents initial FRF while k is a constant	$\frac{dm(t)}{dt} = r(t)(a - m(t))$, $r(t) = rF(t)$ $m(t)$ for the three cases is given as: $m(t) = a(1 - e^{-Frt})$ $m(t) = a\left(1 - e^{-\left(\frac{(F_0-1)(1-e^{-kt})}{k} + t\right)}\right).$ $m(t) = a\left(1 - e^{-\left(\frac{F_0(1-e^{-kt})}{k}\right)}\right).$ where r is FDR.
Pachauri et al. (2015)	Pachauri et. al. considered Inflexion S-shaped FRF for the multiple versions of the software system under perfect and imperfect debugging environment. In total 3 models were proposed.	$\frac{dm(t)}{dt} = rF(t)(a(t) - m(t))$, $F(t) = \frac{\alpha}{1 + \beta e^{-\alpha t}}$ *Model1:* $m(t) = a\left(1 - \left(\frac{1+\beta}{1+\beta e^{-\alpha t}}\right)^r e^{-\alpha rt}\right)$ *Model 2:* $\frac{da(t)}{dt} = \alpha \frac{dm(t)}{dt}$ $m(t) = \frac{a}{1-\alpha}\left(1 - \left(\frac{1+\beta}{1+\beta e^{-\gamma t}}\right)^{r(1-\alpha)} e^{-\gamma r(1-\alpha)t}\right)$ *Model 3: Extended 2ⁿᵈ model for M-R software.* *α: fault introduction rate* *γ and β are shape and scale parameters resp.*
Aggarwal et al. (2017)	Aggarwal et. al. considered the successive releases of the OSS based on Exponentiated Weibull FRF along with the effect of change point and error generation.	$m_{ir}(t) = \begin{cases} \left(\frac{a_i}{(1-\alpha_{i1})} + a_{i-1}^*\right) F_{i1}(t)\tau_i \\ \left(\frac{a_i}{(1-\alpha_{i1})} + a_{i-1}^*\right)\left(1 - \frac{(1-F_{i1}(\tau_i))(1-F_{i2}(\tau_i))}{(1-F_{i2}(\tau_i))}\right) \\ \frac{\alpha_{i1} - \alpha_{i2}}{(1-\alpha_{i1})} F_{i1}(\tau_i) \\ \tau_i T_i \end{cases}$

Error Generation

SRGMs formulated assuming that the fault content remains the same throughout is not a practical approach. There is a possibility that faults get generated due to some reasons. This is known as the error generation phenomenon(Goel, 1985; Yamada et al., 1992). The accuracy of the models can be improved by considering the practical issues encountered during fault detection and removal process. This may be the result of several environmental factors that affect the testing process such as tester's skill, code complexity, erroneous code, availability of resources, the severity of faults, etc. The functional form of error generation is considered to be linearly or exponentially increasing with time.

Goel (1985) extended J-M (Jelinski and Moranda, 1972) model considering the imperfect fault removal process. Pham et al. (1999) integrated the imperfect debugging with delayed S-shaped fault detection rate. In later years Kapur and Younes (1996) introduced the imperfect debugging SRGM considering faults removal process to be exponentially distributed. Jain et al. (2012) proposed the imperfect debugging SRGM with fault reduction factor and multiple change points. Apart from these many other researchers considered imperfect environment conditions of debugging and testing (Chatterjee and Shukla, 2017; Kapur et al., 2011; Li and Pham, 2017a; Sharma et al., 2018; Williams, 2007). Recently many considered FRF factor and error generation together (Anand et al., 2018; Chatterjee and Shukla, 2016; Jain et al., 2012; Kapur et al., 2011)

FRE

During the process of detecting and removing faults, it is not possible to completely remove all the faults latent in the system. This signifies that the testers and debuggers involved in the process are not 100% efficient in removing faults. This efficiency can be measured in percentages. Therefore there was a need to develop a model incorporating a factor representing the efficiency of removing faults. This measure helps the development team to analyze the effectiveness of fault removal process. FRE and faults removed are correlated because higher is the efficiency higher will be the fault removal rate and vice versa. Jones (1996) defined FRE as "percentage of faults removed by review, inspections, and tests." He also briefly described its importance and range for different testing activities. The range is as follows:

1. The efficiency of unit testing ranges from 15% to 50%.
2. The efficiency of integration testing ranges from 25% to 40%.
3. The efficiency of system testing ranges from 25% to 55%.

Liu et al. (2005) proposed an NHPP based SRGM where FRE was defined as the function of debugging time. They assumed the bell-shaped fault detection rate. Later Huang andLyu (2005) considered improvements in testing efficiency with time to give release policy based on reliability. Kremer (1983) proposed the birth-death process in the reliability growth model, assuming imperfect fault removal (death process) and fault generation (birth process). Li andPham (2017b) gave the SRGM model incorporating FRE. He analyzed the accuracy of the model when testing coverage concept is taken together with FRE and error generation parameter.

Release Time Problems

The planning software release is a crucial part of the software development process. The time of release is based on several factors like the failure phenomenon followed by the system, reliability, the cost of testing and debugging during testing, and various kinds of cost the developers have to bear after the release. Three kinds of release problems have been mainly formulated in literature. One is maximizing reliability subject to the resource constraints, second is minimizing development cost subject to reliability constraint and last can be a multi-objective problem with the objective of minimizing cost and maximizing reliability.

Goel andOkumoto (1979) gave a release policy based on reliability and cost criteria. Leung (1992) obtained optimal release time under the constraint of a given budget. Pham (1996) proposed a release planning problem by optimizing cost consisting of penalty cost for failures occurring in the operational phase. Huang andLyu (2005) also proposed a release policy considering improvements in testing efficiency based on reliability and cost criteria. Inoue andYamada (2008) extended existing release policies by incorporating change-point in the SRGM. Li et al. (2010) carried out release time sensitivity analysis by considering a reliability model with testing effort and multiple change points. Kumar et al. (2018) proposed a reliable and cost-effective model considering patching to determine optimal release time.

While planning release policies, firms do not take into account the goodwill loss due to failures after release. This plays a major role in influencing demand. To overcome customer discontent due to failures during the execution of software, the developers offer warranties assuring their users to maintain the software for a time period pre-specified by them. These plans cover all kinds of failures under some specified conditions of usage. This increases the cost burden on firms, hence they need to decide a period length that does not take them into monetary losses. In this direction, Kimura et al. (1999) proposed an optimal software release policy by considering a Warranty policy. Pham and Zhang (1999) proposed a cost optimization model considering warranty cost and risk costs. Dohi (2000) proposed a cost minimization model to determine the optimal period for warranty. Rinsaka andDohi (2005) also proposed a cost model to minimize the development cost and find an optimal warranty period. These optimization problems consider cost component for providing warranty and cost of removing fault during that period. Kapur et al. (2013) developed a cost model to find optimal release and warranty time considering testing and operational cost. Luo and Wu (2018) optimized warranty policies for different types of failures. They considered that failure could occur due to software failure, hardware failure or due to any human factor.

Software Development is a time-consuming and costly process. Developers aim to achieve desirable reliability, minimizing the cost of development along with satisfying the customer requirements. On the other hand, users demand a reliable product at less cost and good customer service. As already discussed that there are some existing cost models in the literature to challenge the above concern, still, release policies considering warranty plan have not been given much concern. Still, researchers are working to improve the policies due to fast-changing technologies and stipulations from customers

Soft Computing Techniques in Software Reliability

Soft Computing is an optimization technique used to find solutions to real-world problems. These techniques are inspired by nature. It can be categorized into fuzzy logic (FL), Evolutionary, Machine Learning and Probabilistic. This chapter focuses on evolutionary algorithms and more specifically meta-heuristic technique. These techniques are developed based on some animal behavior. With time a number of techniques have been developed like Genetic Algorithm (GA) (Holland, 1992) inspired by the evolutionary mechanism of living beings, Ant Colony Optimization (ACO) (Dorigo and Di Caro, 1999) inspired from the colony of real ants, Particle Swarm Optimization (PSO) (Eberhart and Kennedy, 1995) was inspired from social interactions and many more. Recently also some techniques have been devised to improve the optimization process. These techniques have been widely applied in various areas like engineering, actuarial, process control, etc. The application of soft computing techniques can be extensively seen in the field of hardware reliability for solving various optimization problems (Garg, 2015; Garg and Sharma, 2013). These techniques can be used to solve multi-objective problems (Garg and Sharma, 2013) and for analyzing the performance of industrial systems (Garg, 2017). Recently many models have been developed by integrating two different soft computing techniques to solve optimization problems. Garg (2016) proposed hybrid PSO-GA approach for solving constrained optimization problems. Later, Garg (2019) proposed hybrid (Gravitational Search Algorithm) GSA-GA for solving the constrained optimization problem. In this study, focus is on the applications in the area of software reliability. Table 3 recollects some of the work done in the literature using these techniques.

Table 3. Soft Computing Application in Software reliability

Reference	Technique Used	Explanation
Pai (2006)	Support Vector Machine and GA	Reliability Forecasting
Sheta and Al-Salt (2007)	PSO	Parameter Estimation
Fenton et al. (2008)	Bayesian Network	For predicting software reliability and a failure rate of defects
Kapur et al. (2009)	GA	Testing resource allocation for modular software under cost and reliability constraints
Aljahdali and Sheta (2011)	FL	SRGM development using FL
Al-Rahamneh et al. (2011)	Genetic Programming	To develop SRGM
Saed and Kadir (2011)	PSO	Performance Prediction
Aggarwal et al. (2012)	GA	Testing Effort Allocation
AL-Saati et al. (2013)	Cuckoo Search	Parameter Estimation
Nasar et al. (2013)	Differential Evolution	Software Testing Effort Allocation
Shanmugam and Florence (2013)	ACO	To determine the accuracy of software reliability growth models
Tyagi and Sharma (2014)	Adaptive Neuro-Fuzzy	To estimate the reliability of a component-based software system.
Kim et al. (2015)	GA	Parameter Estimation
Mao et al. (2015)	ACO	To generate test data for structural testing
Choudhary et al. (2017)	GSA	Parameter Estimation
Choudhary et al. (2018)	Firefly Optimization	Parameter Estimation
Gupta et al. (2018)	Differential Evolution	Test case optimization: Selection and prioritization of test cases for wide-ranging fault detection
Chatterjee and Maji (2018)	Bayesian Network	For software reliability prediction in the early phase of its development
Chaudhary et al. (2019)	Crow Search Optimization	Parameter Estimation
Ahmad and Bamnote (2019)	Whale-Crow Optimization	Software Cost Estimation
Proposed Work	GWO	Software Release planning; determining optimal release, warranty time, the overall cost of software development.

After conducting the comprehensive literature survey suggest the gap in using of latest and better techniques for optimizing software development cost and obtain optimal release and warranty time period. The above Table 3 clearly highlights the breach.

PROPOSED MODELLING FRAMEWORK

In this section, we develop a mathematical model for software release planning. The approach can be divided into two steps. In the first step, an NHPP based modelling framework is developed by taking into consideration various factors affecting the failure process and then in the second step cost minimization model is developed by taking into consideration different cost components of testing and operational phase. Release planning of the software is largely affected by the testing conditions and tools; financial and goodwill losses due to failures after release and the warranty cost. The notations used in the subsequent sections are given in Table 4.

Table 4. Notations

t	Time
$m(t)$	Cumulative number of faults detected up to time t
$b(t)$	Rate of Fault Detection
$a(t)$	Fault content at time t
a	Faults Initially present in the software system
α	Constant Rate of Error generation
P	Constant, Fault removal Efficiency
$F(t)$	Time-variable Fault Reduction Factor
y,k	Constant parameters of Weibull function
R	Learning Rate as the testing progresses
C_t	Unit Cost of performing testing
C_{tr}	Per unit cost of removing faults during the testing phase
C_w	Unit Cost of providing Warranty time
C_{wr}	Per unit cost of fault removal during the warranty
C_{opp}	Market Opportunity cost
C_{pw}	Per unit cost of removing faults after the warranty has expired
$Z(t)$	Software development Cost Function
T	Software Release Time
W	: Warranty Time

Model Assumptions

The proposed SRGM is based on the following assumptions:

1. The failure process is based on general assumptions of a Non-Homogenous Poisson Process.
2. As testing progresses, there is an increase in the fault content of the system at a constant rate. Mathematically it is given as $a(t) = a + \alpha m(t)$.
3. The development team is not 100% efficient in fault removal. Software testing team efficiency is represented by a constant parameter p.
4. Time variable FRF is modelled using Weibull function. Mathematically it is expressed as $F(t) = yt^k$. FRF is modelled using Weibull function because of its property to restore the constant, increasing, decreasing trends.

Based on the above assumptions the mathematical model for Fault Removal Process is developed as follows:

$$\frac{dm(t)}{dt} = b(t)\big(a(t) - pm(t)\big) \tag{2}$$

Where,

$$b(t) = F(t)r; \tag{3}$$

$$F(t) = yt^k; \tag{4}$$

$$a(t) = a + \alpha m(t) \tag{5}$$

Using Equations (3), (4) and (5) in Equation (2), we get;

$$\frac{dm(t)}{dt} = yt^k r\big(a + \alpha m(t) - pm(t)\big) \tag{6}$$

Solving the above differential equation using initial condition; at $t=0$; $m(t)=0$, the Mean value function is obtained as follows;

$$m(t) = \frac{a}{p-\alpha}\left[1 - \exp\left(-\frac{yr(p-\alpha)}{k+1}t^{k+1}\right)\right] \tag{7}$$

Software Development Cost Optimization

Next, we develop the optimization model to minimize the overall cost of software development. Some cost is incurred during every phase of development. In our model, we have considered two phases namely; testing and operational phase of SDLC. The operational phase is further divided into warranty and post-warranty phases (Figure 2).

Figure 2. Software Product's Life Cycle

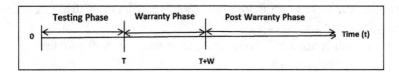

After the software code has been developed, it is tested for a limited time aiming to remove maximum possible faults from the system before it is released to the market.

Though the developers strive hard to achieve the maximum reliability of the product through testing but too much testing may not be economically viable for them. Apart from the economic considerations, the developer is also interested in early release to have the 'first entry edge' in the market. There is a strong conflict between the economic and quality aspiration levels. For this optimization, the theory provides valuable tools to look for appropriate release planning while creating a balance between the cost and quality considerations. To differentiate their products in the market the IT firms also provide warranties for support during the post-implementation phase. During warranty, the developer assures the user that any failure / unusual behavior occurring during this time will be fixed by the developer and all the cost will be borne by the developer only. After the warranty expires, if a failure occurs then it leads to goodwill loss of the firm and detrimental to its image. Therefore the developer considers penalty cost for any failure occurring after the warranty expires during the operational phase.

Cost Components

The optimization model considers the costs involved during the two major phases of the development process. These costs components are part of the testing and operational phase.

The testing phase consists of the following three costs:

1. Fixed cost of testing: This cost is incurred due to resources and time spent on testing.
2. Per unit cost of removing faults during the testing phase.
3. Market Opportunity cost

The operational phase consists of three cost components related to Warranty and post Warranty phase:

1. Fixed cost of warranty
2. Per unit cost of dealing with faults encountered during the warranty period.
3. The penalty cost of faults that occur after the warranty expires. This cost is taken into account because these faults result in goodwill loss and may hamper further purchases. Hence the developer needs to control the cost they have to bear due to this.

Cost Model Assumptions

Our proposed software development cost model for release planning is based on the following set of assumptions.

1. Testing (Warranty) cost is linearly related to testing (warranty) time.
2. The cost of removing faults during the testing (warranty) phase is a linear function of the number of faults detected during testing (warranty).
3. FRP is modelled by NHPP based SRGM given by Equation (7).
4. The software cost takes into consideration testing cost; opportunity cost; warranty cost; error removal during the testing phase; error removal during the warranty and after the warranty expires.
5. Any failure post-warranty period may lead to penalty costs to developers.

Cost Model

Considering all the above discussions we obtain total expected software cost and formulate optimization problem with the objective of minimizing the total expected cost of development with two decision variables T(Testing Time) and W(Warranty Time).

$$MinZ = C_t T + C_{tr} m(T) + C_{opp} T^2 + C_w W + C_{wr} \left(m(T+W) - m(T) \right) + C_{pw} \left(m(\infty) - m(T+W) \right) (O_1)$$

where

$T, W > 0$

Where $m(.)$ is given by equation (7)

The optimization problem (O_1) is solved using a soft computing technique called Grey wolf Optimizer (Mirjalili et al., 2014) in MATLAB. In the next section, we discuss the relevance of using this technique for optimization.

Now, we summarize all the steps of the study:

1. Formulate the MVF incorporating the factors affecting the FRP. Here we have considered imperfect debugging due to error generation, the efficiency of the testing team and FRF
2. Estimation of SRGM parameters using a real-life fault dataset of web-based ERP systems.
3. Determine cost components for the optimization model based on the life cycle of a software product.
4. Formulate the cost minimization problem with two decision variables T and W i.e. release time and warranty time period.
5. Apply GWO in MATLAB to obtain the optimal values for T and W and then evaluate the costs.
6. To determine the key cost component, sensitivity analysis is done on each cost component. This helps to visualize the impact of the increase/decrease in cost by 10% on the release time, warranty time and total cost.

GREY WOLF OPTIMIZER

Metaheuristics represent "higher level" heuristic-based soft computing algorithms that can be directed towards a variety of different optimization problems by instantiating generic schema to individual problems, needing relatively few modifications to be made in each specific case. Meta-heuristic techniques have become popular due to four major reasons. Firstly it's easy to understand the concepts inspired by natural phenomena. Secondly, it can be applied to various problems without actually making modifications to the algorithm. These algorithms solve the problem as black boxes. Thirdly these techniques are stochastically computed by starting optimization with a random solution, without having to calculate derivatives of each search space. Hence they are derivative-free. Lastly, it avoids the local optimal solution. This is probably due to their stochastic nature, which helps them to move from local to global solutions.

GWO (Mirjalili et al., 2014) is a meta-heuristic algorithm inspired by the social hierarchy and hunting behavior of Grey Wolves. The solution convergence of this technique explores search space as a multi-level decision mechanism and does not require gradient for the search path. GWO is versatile for optimization problems because of its easy implementation process and few parameters in the algorithm. This is a powerful method to avoid premature convergence by expanding the search area and speeds up the optimization process. This has been applied in quite a few areas like economic dispatch problems (Jayabarathi et al., 2016), parameter estimation (Song et al., 2015), etc. This method is better in convergence than other methods because of following advantages:

1. It has a good procedure for conveying and sharing the information.
2. It considers three solutions (α,β,δ) to get the best optimization results considering a random function. This helps to fasten the process of moving from local to global optimal values.
3. There are only two main parameters that need to be adjusted for the transition between exploration and exploitation.

Grey Wolves follow a very strict social leadership hierarchy and policy for chasing prey. These are generally found in packs consisting of 5-12 wolves. Further, they are divided into four levels of hierarchy (Figure 3). Level one i.e. the one at the top of the hierarchy corresponds to the pack leader alpha (α), which can be either male or female. All the important decisions like the sleeping place, hunting, etc. are taken by alphas and dictated to other members. The power and role of the grey wolf decrease as we move down the hierarchy. The next level is of subordinates that help leaders in making decisions. These are known as beta (β). Betas help to maintain discipline and implement the decisions taken by the leaders. In case alpha gets old or dies untimely, beta takes its place. Delta (δ) dominates the omegas (ω) at the lowest level and report to the betas. Omegas are allowed to eat.

Figure 3. Social Hierarchy of Grey Wolves (In Decreasing order of Dominance)

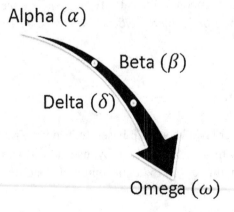

This hierarchy also represents the level of solutions i.e. alpha (α) is considered to be the best solution, beta (β) is the second-best solution and deltas (δ) is the third-best solution. The rest of the solutions are leftover and taken as omegas (ω). The alpha, beta and delta guide the optimization process while omegas follow them.

Grey wolves are not only social because of their hierarchy but their group hunting is also a special interesting social behavior. Broadly the whole process can be categorized into two phases:

1. Exploration: Here the possible areas where the prey could be located are identified.
2. Exploitation: The areas identified are searched thoroughly and attacking is done.

The hunting process of grey wolves is divided into the following steps:

1. Search for prey (Exploration)
2. Approaching the prey by tracking and chasing
3. Encircling the prey
4. Harassing the prey till it stops its movement
5. Attaching prey (Exploitation)

The mathematical model and algorithm have been broadly explained by Mirjalili et al. (2014). The whole process followed by the GWO algorithm is depicted through a flow chart (Figure 4).

We will discuss the step by step process thoroughly.

1. Initialization of GWO parameters such as maximum number of Iterations, Population size, number of search agents and vectors d, A and C. These vectors are initialized using a random function. (Equations 8 and 9)

$$\vec{A} = 2\vec{d}.rand_1 - \vec{d} \tag{8}$$

$$\vec{C} = 2.rand_2 \tag{9}$$

Where d linearly decreases from 2 to 0 as iteration proceeds

2. Random generation of wolves based on their pack sizes.
3. The fitness value of each search agent is calculated using the below-mentioned equations;

$$\vec{D} = \left| \vec{C}.\vec{H}_p\left(t\right) - \vec{H}\left(t\right) \right| \tag{10}$$

$$\vec{H}\left(t+1\right) = \left| \vec{H}_p\left(t\right) - \vec{A}.\vec{D} \right| \tag{11}$$

Where, $\vec{H}_p(t)$ is the position of prey and $\vec{H}(t)$ is the wolf position. Equation (10) calculates the distance between the prey and wolf and then accordingly the wolf updates his/her position using equation (11).

Figure 4. Flowchart for Optimization using Grey Wolf Optimizer

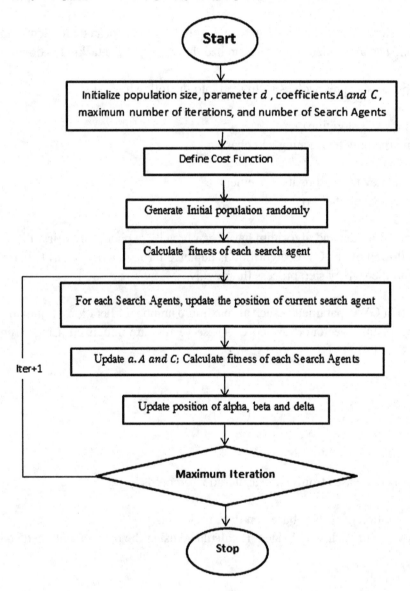

4. Obtain the best search agent (α), the second-best one (β) and the third-best search agent (δ) using equations (11-16);

$$\vec{D}_\alpha = \left| \vec{C}_1.\vec{H}_\alpha - \vec{H} \right| \tag{12}$$

$$\overrightarrow{D_{\beta}} = \left| \overrightarrow{C_1} . \vec{H}_{\beta} - \vec{H} \right| \tag{13}$$

$$\overrightarrow{D_{\delta}} = \left| \overrightarrow{C_1} . \vec{H}_{\delta} - \vec{H} \right| \tag{14}$$

$$\overrightarrow{H_1} = \vec{H}_{\alpha} - \overrightarrow{A_1} . (\overrightarrow{D_{\alpha}}) \tag{15}$$

$$\overrightarrow{H_2} = \vec{H}_{\beta} - \overrightarrow{A_2} . (\overrightarrow{D_{\beta}}) \tag{16}$$

$$\overrightarrow{H_3} = \vec{H}_{\delta} - \overrightarrow{A_3} . (\overrightarrow{D_{\delta}}) \tag{17}$$

5.   Based on the locations of three beast search agent the location of the current one is updated using equation (18);

$$\vec{H}(t+1) = \frac{\overrightarrow{H_1} + \overrightarrow{H_2} + \overrightarrow{H_3}}{3} \tag{18}$$

6.   Again the fitness values of all the agents are calculated
7.   The values of $\vec{H}_{\alpha}$, $\vec{H}_{\beta}$, and $\vec{H}_{\delta}$ are updated accordingly.
8.   When stopping condition reaches print the solution, otherwise repeat step 5 for all the iterations

GWO algorithm consists of a few parameters, but they are a very important role in convergence. Hence we discuss the significance of these parameters in detail. The grey wolves diverge to search for prey (exploration) and converge to attack (exploitation). Mathematically this is achieved through the parameter $\vec{A}$. Its value is influenced by $\vec{a}$. To model a wolf approaching towards the prey, the value of $\vec{a}$ is decreased up to zero from two. If |A|>1 then the wolf moves away from the prey in hope to find a better prey otherwise if |A|<1 then wolf moves towards the prey for attacking.

Component $\vec{C}$ also helps in exploration. It provides random weights to acknowledge the impact of prey in defining the distance. If $C>1$ then it emphasizes its effect otherwise it deemphasizes the effect of prey. C is deliberately decreased randomly throughout the process from first to last iterations which are definitely not a linear decrease. Thus it is helpful in bringing the local solutions to halt. On studying these parameters thoroughly we can sum the process of searching the prey into steps as:

1.   The random population of wolves (candidate solutions) is generated.
2.   The wolves at the top three levels of hierarchy determine the position of prey.
3.   All the candidates update their position from prey.
4. $\vec{a}$ decreased from 2 to 0 to emphasize exploration and exploitation.
5. $\vec{A}$ value tends the wolves to either converge or diverge form prey.

6.   Hence after satisfaction, the algorithm is terminated.

NUMERICAL RESULTS AND DISCUSSIONS

Data Description

The proposed SRGM needs to be validated on a real-life fault dataset before employing it for optimal release planning. For this, we have used the fault data set obtained from web-based integrated ERP systems. The data was collected from August 2003 to July 2008 (SourceForge.net, 2008). The data has been used in literature to validate the MVF (Hsu et al., 2011; Li and Pham, 2017a). The data set consists of 146 faults observed in 60 months. 60 observations in a dataset to validate the model is quite a large time series. Before estimating the parameters of the model we need to ensure that the dataset is appropriate for the considered model. Hence we have applied *Laplace Trend* analysis. This helps to analyze the trend depicted by the dataset, which can be increasing, decreasing or stable. This test was given and described by Ascher andFeingold (1978). Later it was extended by Ascher andFeingold (1984) and Kanoun (1989).

The method calculates the Laplace factor for each time unit as the testing progress. The value of the factor including the sign determines the trend. Negative Laplace factor implies growth in reliability, positive one implies decay whereas if the Laplace factor value is between -2 to +2 and it is stable. For the dataset considered in our study, we observed the decay in reliability at the end of 60 months of testing. The Laplace factor value obtained using equation (19) is 4.444 which implies that there is decay in reliability.

$$k\left(t\right) = \frac{\sum_{i=1}^{t}\left(i-1\right)h\left(i\right) - \frac{t-1}{2}\sum_{i=1}^{t}h\left(i\right)}{\sqrt{\frac{t^2-1}{12}\sum_{i=1}^{t}h\left(i\right)}} \qquad (19)$$

The decay trend (Figure 5) shown by the data can only be encountered using a distribution that can capture the S-Shaped failure phenomenon. Hence the proposed fault removal process is appropriate for the fault dataset as it depicts the S-Shaped failure curve.

Parameter Estimation and SRGM Validation

Using the above-mentioned dataset, we estimate the unknown parameters of the model in SPSS using the LSE method. The estimates are given in Table 5.

The goodness of fit curve (Figure 6) shows that the model has a good fit to the data. The values of performance criteria (Table 6) evaluated goes well with the values reported in the literature. The table compares the obtained results with the results presented in Li andPham (2017a) The various performance measures used are the Coefficient of determination (R^2) which is the outcome of regression analysis that shows how much variance of the dependent variable is being explained by the independent variables and Mean square error (MSE).

Figure 5. Reliability Growth Trend depicted by data

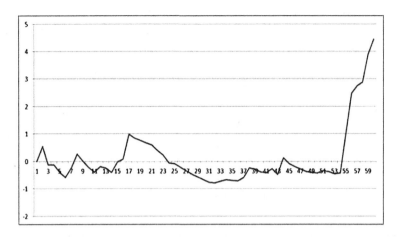

Table 5. Estimated Parameters

Parameter	Estimated Value
a	147
α	0.623
P	0.377
K	0.096
Y	0.196
R	0.054

Figure 6. Goodness-of-fit Curve

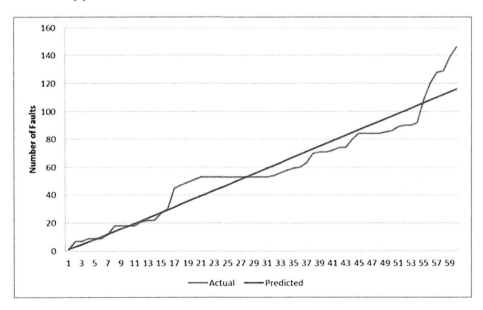

Table 6. Model Performance Analysis

Model	R^2	MSE	PP	PRR
Li andPham (2017a)	0.934	85.955	5.0095	4.428
Chang et al. (2014)	0.927	94.451	2.898	1.795
Pham (2014)	0.883	151.356	2.491	4.827
Roy et al. (2014)	0.928	90.462	2.274	2.213
Zhang et al. (2003)	0.922	101.947	$4.99e^{+4}$	5.093
Proposed Model	0.927	86.627	1.151	1.374

Boxplot

Boxplot is a graphic representation of spread in the data by dividing it into quartiles. It is also termed as whiskers plot since whiskers are present at upper and lower ends of the box representing the top and bottom 25% of values respectively. The last data point at the lower end of the whisker is the minimum value while the topmost value at the whisker is the maximum value. This data excludes the outliers that may be present in the data which are plotted separately as the single data points. The interquartile range i.e. the area covered by the box consists of 50% data with median lying within the box depicted using a line. In this study, we have plotted the boxplots for absolute errors between the observed faults during testing and the predicted faults using the proposed model for each calendar time

Figure 7. Boxplot for ERP software

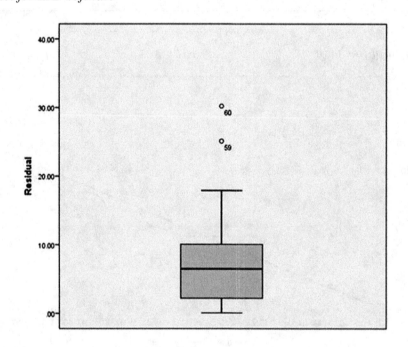

From Figure 7 we can observe that most of the data points lie at the lower end of the boxplot forming a short box implying a good fit. This suggests that the difference between the observed and predicted faults is less here.

Optimization Using GWO

Now we do release planning for the software system considering the optimization problem O_1 discussed in the previous section. Firstly need to assign values to all the unknown parameters. The parameters of MVF are replaced with values obtained from estimation (Table 4) and cost components are assigned values based on the literature (Kapur et al., 2013; Pham and Zhang, 1999).

Considering the cost components values as:

C_t=2, C_{tr}=3, C_w=2.5, C_{rw}=2.75, C_{opp}=0.5, C_{pw}=5

The optimization problem to be solved using GWO in MATLAB is

$$MinZ = 2T + 3m\left(T\right) + 0.5T^2 + 2.5W + 2.75\left(m\left(T + W\right) - m\left(T\right)\right) + 5\left(m\left(\infty\right) - m\left(T + W\right)\right)\left(O_2\right)$$

where

$T, W > 0$

Where $m(t)$ is given by equation (7).

The parameters of the mathematical model have been estimated in SPSS. The cost parameters of the software cost model have been assumed based on the literature and industrial practices. The number of search agents and maximum number of iterations required for carrying out GWO was assumed on the basis of previous studies. The number of search Agents was initialized to be 30 and the maximum number of iterations was set to be 150. Alpha, Beta and Delta solutions were initialized with zeros based on the number of variables in the optimization problem. The vector d is initialized using maximum number of iteration given by equation (20) and it tends to decrease from 2 to 0. The vector $A's$ are initialized through d and random variable between 0 and 1 (Equation 8). The vector $C's$ are generated through random variable between 0 and 1 (Equation 9).

$d = 2 - 1 * ((2)/\text{Max\_iter})$ (20)

The results obtained are given in Table 7. Figure 8 shows the convergence curve followed by GWO for solving the optimization problem O_2.

From the results we can observe that:

1. Cost components of the testing phase are the major part of the total cost.
2. Timely release of the software is very important otherwise it increases the loss due to the increase in market opportunity cost.

3. The penalty cost due to failures in the post-warranty phase must be controlled by properly analyzing the software during testing.
4. Providing a warranty helps to reduce the penalty cost by taking responsibility for early failures. If the developer does not give warranty cover for its product then any failure after release adds up to penalty cost. This leads to goodwill loss among the users.

Table 7. GWO Results

Optimal Warranty Time Period		12 Months
Optimal Software Release Time		64 Months
Cost ($)		
Testing Phase Cost	Testing Cost	788
	Opportunity Cost	1352
Operational Phase Cost	Warranty Cost	188
	Post-Warranty Cost	1936
Total Cost		4258

Figure 8. GWO Convergence Curve

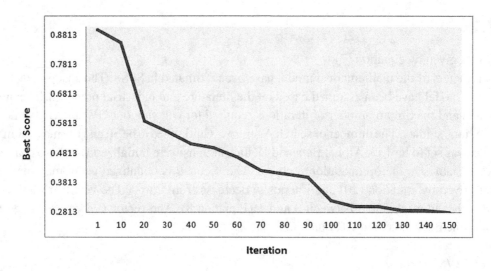

To establish stability and feasibility of GWO, its performance has been compared with standard and well-known GA and PSO. GA and PSO are very commonly used and widely accepted algorithm in Software Reliability Engineering (Al-Rahamneh et al., 2011; Saed and Kadir, 2011; Srivastava and Kim, 2009; Windisch et al., 2007). Optimization results are given in Table 8. The results show that GWO gives better fitness value (Minimum cost of development) for optimization. In future we may use other meta-heuristic techniques for doing optimization.

Table 8. Comparison Results

Algorithm	Optimal Testing Time	Optimal Warranty Time	Optimal Development Cost
GWO	64	12	4258
PSO	60	24	4526
GA	60	30	4518

Cost Sensitivity Analysis

Next, we study the effect of each cost component on the overall cost of software development. Sensitivity analysis is a very helpful way to understand the importance of cost components. It studies the impact of the independent variable on the dependent variable under the same conditions. It helps the developers to decide about the cost that they to focus on most since it has maximum influence on the overall cost. Hence it helps to identify the key inputs that extensively affect the outcome.

In our study, we have studied the effect of a change in each cost component on the optimal release time of the software, warranty time period and the corresponding total cost of software development. Firstly each cost factor is increased by 10% then decreased by 10% and observe the relative change. Relative Change can be defined as "determine the percentage change in the dependent quantity with a change in an independent variable". Mathematically is expressed as:

$$Relative\,Change = \frac{new\,value - old\,value}{old\,value} \quad (21)$$

Tabular representation of the values obtained on sensitivity analysis is given in Table 9. Figures 9 and 10 give the graphical view of relative changes in release time, warranty time and cost on increase and decrease respectively.

Following observations can be made from Table 9:

1. An increase in testing removal cost persuades the developers to reduce testing time and provide warranty cover for the larger period and vice versa. Hence the testing duration decreases and warranty duration increases with increases in testing cost.
2. An increase in market opportunity costs leads to the early release of the software with an increased warranty time period. Releasing quickly forces the developers to provide a warranty for more time than usual.
3. Also, it is observed that an increase in warranty costs leads to a maximum relative change in the warranty period. In such cases, the developer spends more time on testing to reduce the risk of faults after release and hence control the cost due to warranty.
4. Whereas the increase in penalty cost leads to longer warranty and testing time periods allotted for the software product and vice-versa. Developers can't afford losses due to failures during the operational phase. So to avoid the situation firms test the software for longer time periods and provide a bit larger warranty coverage.

5. Testing Cost is the key cost component that majorly affects the overall cost. The developer needs to focus on this particular component to control the total cost incurred.

Table 9. Cost Sensitivity Analysis

Cost Factor	Cost		Warranty Time (W^*) (Months)	Relative Change in Warranty Time	Testing time (T^*) (Months)	Relative Change in Testing Time	Relative Change in Total Cost
	Original Cost	Modified Cost					
Increase by 10%							
C_t	2	2.2	14	0.166667	62	-0.03125	0.009629
C_{opp}	0.5	0.55	13	0.083333	62	-0.03125	0.03241
C_{rt}	3	3.3	15	0.25	61	-0.04688	0.00775
C_w	2.5	2.75	10	-0.16667	67	0.046875	0.002114
C_{rw}	2.75	3.025	9	-0.25	68	0.0625	0.00047
C_{pw}	5	5.5	13	0.083333	65	0.015625	0.042978
Decrease by 10%							
C_t	2	1.8	11	-0.08333	67	0.047619	-0.01174
C_{opp}	0.5	0.45	11	-0.08333	65	0.015873	-0.03171
C_{rt}	3	2.7	10	-0.16667	68	0.063492	-0.0108
C_w	2.5	2.25	15	0.25	63	-0.01587	-0.00493
C_{rw}	2.75	2.47	16	0.333333	62	-0.03175	-0.00423
C_{pw}	5	4.5	11	-0.08333	63	-0.01587	-0.04415

Figure 9. Relative Change on 10% Increase in Cost Component

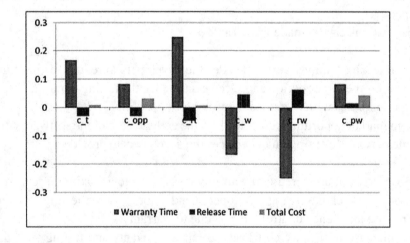

Impact of Parameters on Total Cost

In order to study the effect of error generation (α) on total development cost, we have calculated the total development cost when the error generation parameter is decreased by 10% each time. The gradual decrease results in a decrease in overall cost. Similarly, by increasing the testing efficiency (p) by 10%, we see a decrease in the total cost. The observations are very clear from Figure 11. If the developer is able to control these parameters then it is also possible to control the cost. Figure 11 provides two important observations:

1. that even a small decrease in the rate of error generation, makes the cost to fall drastically. This is because if the fewer errors are generated and the faults are removed with the same rate then the same effort is consumed to remove a fewer number of faults. Hence there is a sudden decrease in the cost.
2. On the other hand, if testing capabilities improve but error generation also increases then decrease is cost is less as compared to the previous case.

Figure 10. Relative Change on 10% Decrease in Cost Component

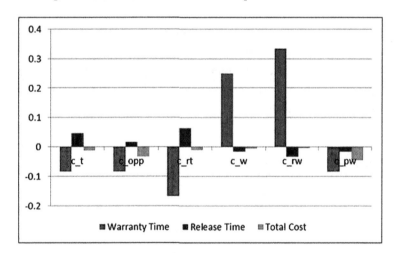

CONCLUSION AND FUTURE SCOPE

Due to the size and complexities of software systems, detection and correction of faults are challenging and costly. Even after the release of the software, penalty cost is increased and finally loss of goodwill. Thus during the testing phase engineers focus on the maximum removal of the faults to develop a reliable product. Thus it is important to discuss a trade-off between the release time and the reliability of software before release. Here in this chapter, we have discussed the optimal release planning by using GWO. We have also discussed the cost sensitivity analysis and showed the importance of the cost parameters in the software development process.

Initially, we developed an SRGM considering the Error Generation, Fault Removal Efficiency and Fault Reduction Factor, where FRF follows Weibull distribution. For the validation of our model, we have used a real-life dataset of faults from a web-based ERP system and applied Laplace Trend Analysis to check if the data is appropriate for the proposed SRGM. In our study, Laplace factor is 4.444 which is positive in sign and thus indicates decay in the reliability. We have considered the s-shaped model that can fit any dataset following any trend and hence it can capture the failure occurrence of the data with decay trend.

Now we have estimated the parameters of the SRGM using non-linear regression and to analyze its performance we have used different performance measures such as Mean Square Error, Predictive Power and Predictive Ratio Risk. We calculated the Coefficient of determination that gives the variance explained by the independent variable. The goodness of the fit curve is also being plotted which indicates good predictive power of the model.

Once the model is validated release planning problem is discussed for the software system. For this, we formulated a cost optimization function involving testing cost, warranty cost, penalty cost, opportunity cost with two decision variables testing time and warranty time. We solved the problem using the GWO technique to obtain the optimal release time and optimal warranty time by minimizing the total expected cost and the results obtained are shown in Table 7. The results of GWO was compared to some well known meta-heuristic techniques to show its stability and feasibility with the existing models. We also carried out a cost sensitivity analysis to analyze different cost parameters (Table 9). Through the cost sensitivity, we have discussed the cost which has a large impact on the overall cost.

Our study is significant for assessing the reliability and optimizing the release time and warranty with the help of GWO, a meta-heuristic technique. It assists the developer in the testing process with detecting and removing faults while some factors impacting the testing. it also helps the developer to focus on the cost influencing the overall cost.

Figure 11. Impact of error generation parameter and FRE

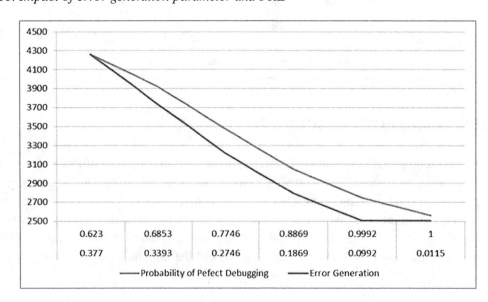

LIMITATIONS AND FUTURE SCOPE

The limitations of the current study can be overcome by working on the following perspectives of the proposed study:

- We may integrate the model using a multi-release context as it analyses the release time for a single release of the software.
- In the given chapter we carried out two factors FRF, FRE that control failure process but this research can further be extended with other factors such as testing coverage, resource consumptions.
- Instead of using GWO to obtain the optimal release time and warranty time, we can also use other meta-heuristic approaches and can make a comparison among the results.
- We have validated our proposed model using a single dataset but in future more datasets can also be included in the discussion.
- The proposed release problem involves warranty cost, penalty cost and opportunity cost whereas other costs influencing the total cost may be included in the objective function.
- Here we have taken a single objective function of cost minimization but we can also consider the problem when there is a multi-objective optimization function.

REFERENCES

Aggarwal, A. G., Dhaka, V., & Nijhawan, N. (2017). Reliability analysis for multi-release open-source software systems with change point and exponentiated Weibull fault reduction factor. *Life Cycle Reliability and Safety Engineering, 6*(1), 3–14. doi:10.100741872-017-0001-0

Aggarwal, A. G., Gandhi, N., Verma, V., & Tandon, A. (2019). Multi-Release Software Reliability Growth Assessment: An approach incorporating Fault Reduction Factor and Imperfect Debugging. *International Journal of Mathematics in Operational Research., 15*(4), 446. doi:10.1504/IJMOR.2019.103006

Aggarwal, A. G., Kapur, P., Kaur, G., & Kumar, R. (2012). Genetic algorithm based optimal testing effort allocation problem for modular software. *Bharati Vidyapeeth's Institute of Computer Applications and Management (BVICAM)*, 445.

Ahmad, S. W., & Bamnote, G. (2019). Whale–crow optimization (WCO)-based Optimal Regression model for Software Cost Estimation. *Sadhana, 44*(4), 94. doi:10.100712046-019-1085-1

Al-Rahamneh, Z., Reyalat, M., Sheta, A. F., Bani-Ahmad, S., & Al-Oqeili, S. (2011). A new software reliability growth model: Genetic-programming-based approach. *Journal of Software Engineering and Applications, 4*(8), 476–481. doi:10.4236/jsea.2011.48054

AL-Saati, D., Akram, N., & Abd-AlKareem, M. (2013). *The use of cuckoo search in estimating the parameters of software reliability growth models.* arXiv preprint arXiv:1307.6023

Aljahdali, S., & Sheta, A. F. (2011). *Predicting the reliability of software systems using fuzzy logic.* Paper presented at the 2011 Eighth International Conference on Information Technology: New Generations. 10.1109/ITNG.2011.14

Anand, S., Verma, V., & Aggarwal, A. G. (2018). 2-Dimensional Multi-Release Software Reliability Modelling considering Fault Reduction Factor under imperfect debugging. *INGENIERIA SOLIDARIA, 14.*

Ascher, H., & Feingold, H. (1978). *Application of Laplace's test to repairable system reliability.* Paper presented at the Actes du 1er Colloque International de Fiabilité et de Maintenabilité.

Ascher, H., & Feingold, H. (1984). *Repairable systems reliability: modeling, inference, misconceptions and their causes.* M. Dekker.

Chanda, U., Tandon, A., & Kapur, P. K. (2010). Software Release Policy based on Change Point Considering Risk Cost. *Advances in Information Theory and Operations Research,* 111-122.

Chang, I. H., Pham, H., Lee, S. W., & Song, K. Y. (2014). A testing-coverage software reliability model with the uncertainty of operating environments. *International Journal of Systems Science: Operations & Logistics, 1*(4), 220–227.

Chatterjee, S., & Maji, B. (2018). A bayesian belief network based model for predicting software faults in early phase of software development process. *Applied Intelligence,* 1–15.

Chatterjee, S., & Shukla, A. (2016). Modeling and analysis of software fault detection and correction process through weibull-type fault reduction factor, change point and imperfect debugging. *Arabian Journal for Science and Engineering, 41*(12), 5009–5025. doi:10.100713369-016-2189-0

Chatterjee, S., & Shukla, A. (2017). An ideal software release policy for an improved software reliability growth model incorporating imperfect debugging with fault removal efficiency and change point. *Asia-Pacific Journal of Operational Research, 34*(03), 1740017. doi:10.1142/S0217595917400176

Chaudhary, A., Agarwal, A. P., Rana, A., & Kumar, V. (2019). *Crow Search Optimization Based Approach for Parameter Estimation of SRGMs.* Paper presented at the 2019 Amity International Conference on Artificial Intelligence (AICAI). 10.1109/AICAI.2019.8701318

Choudhary, A., Baghel, A. S., & Sangwan, O. P. (2017). An efficient parameter estimation of software reliability growth models using gravitational search algorithm. *International Journal of System Assurance Engineering and Management, 8*(1), 79–88. doi:10.100713198-016-0541-0

Choudhary, A., Baghel, A. S., & Sangwan, O. P. (2018). *Parameter Estimation of Software Reliability Model Using Firefly Optimization. In Data Engineering and Intelligent Computing* (pp. 407–415). Springer.

Dohi, T. (2000). The age-dependent optimal warranty policy and its application to software maintenance contract. *Proceedings of 5th International Conference on Probabilistic Safety Assessment and Management.*

Dorigo, M., & Di Caro, G. (1999). Ant colony optimization: a new meta-heuristic. *Proceedings of the 1999 congress on evolutionary computation-CEC99.* 10.1109/CEC.1999.782657

Eberhart, R., & Kennedy, J. (1995). A new optimizer using particle swarm theory. *Proceedings of the Sixth International Symposium on Micro Machine and Human Science.* 10.1109/MHS.1995.494215

Fenton, N., Neil, M., & Marquez, D. (2008). Using Bayesian networks to predict software defects and reliability. *Proceedings of the Institution of Mechanical Engineers, Part O: Journal of Risk and Reliability, 222*(4), 701–712.

Friedman, M. A., Tran, P. Y., & Goddard, P. I. (1995). *Reliability of software intensive systems*. William Andrew.

Garg, H. (2015). An efficient biogeography based optimization algorithm for solving reliability optimization problems. *Swarm and Evolutionary Computation, 24*, 1–10. doi:10.1016/j.swevo.2015.05.001

Garg, H. (2016). A hybrid PSO-GA algorithm for constrained optimization problems. *Applied Mathematics and Computation, 274*, 292–305. doi:10.1016/j.amc.2015.11.001

Garg, H. (2017). Performance analysis of an industrial system using soft computing based hybridized technique. *Journal of the Brazilian Society of Mechanical Sciences and Engineering, 39*(4), 1441–1451. doi:10.100740430-016-0552-4

Garg, H. (2019). A hybrid GSA-GA algorithm for constrained optimization problems. *Information Sciences, 478*, 499–523. doi:10.1016/j.ins.2018.11.041

Garg, H., & Sharma, S. (2013). Multi-objective reliability-redundancy allocation problem using particle swarm optimization. *Computers & Industrial Engineering, 64*(1), 247–255. doi:10.1016/j.cie.2012.09.015

Gautam, S., Kumar, D., & Patnaik, L. (2018). *Selection of Optimal Method of Software Release Time Incorporating Imperfect Debugging*. Paper presented at the 4th International Conference on Computational Intelligence & Communication Technology (CICT). 10.1109/CIACT.2018.8480133

Goel, A. L. (1985). Software reliability models: Assumptions, limitations, and applicability. *IEEE Transactions on Software Engineering, SE-11*(12), 1411–1423. doi:10.1109/TSE.1985.232177

Goel, A. L., & Okumoto, K. (1979). Time-dependent error-detection rate model for software reliability and other performance measures. *IEEE Transactions on Reliability, 28*(3), 206–211. doi:10.1109/TR.1979.5220566

Gupta, V., Singh, A., Sharma, K., & Mittal, H. (2018). *A novel differential evolution test case optimisation (detco) technique for branch coverage fault detection. In Smart Computing and Informatics* (pp. 245–254). Springer.

Holland, J. H. (1992). Genetic algorithms. *Scientific American, 267*(1), 66–73. doi:10.1038cientificamerican0792-66

Hsu, C.-J., Huang, C.-Y., & Chang, J.-R. (2011). Enhancing software reliability modeling and prediction through the introduction of time-variable fault reduction factor. *Applied Mathematical Modelling, 35*(1), 506–521. doi:10.1016/j.apm.2010.07.017

Huang, C.-Y., & Lyu, M. R. (2005). Optimal release time for software systems considering cost, testing-effort, and test efficiency. *IEEE Transactions on Reliability, 54*(4), 583–591. doi:10.1109/TR.2005.859230

Inoue, S., & Yamada, S. (2008). *Optimal software release policy with change-point*. Paper presented at the International Conference on Industrial Engineering and Engineering Management, Singapore. 10.1109/IEEM.2008.4737925

Jain, M., Manjula, T., & Gulati, T. (2012). Software reliability growth model (SRGM) with imperfect debugging, fault reduction factor and multiple change-point. *Proceedings of the International Conference on Soft Computing for Problem Solving (SocProS 2011)*.

Jayabarathi, T., Raghunathan, T., Adarsh, B., & Suganthan, P. N. (2016). Economic dispatch using hybrid grey wolf optimizer. *Energy, 111*, 630–641. doi:10.1016/j.energy.2016.05.105

Jelinski, Z., & Moranda, P. (1972). *Software reliability research. In Statistical computer performance evaluation* (pp. 465–484). Elsevier. doi:10.1016/B978-0-12-266950-7.50028-1

Jones, C. (1996). Software defect-removal efficiency. *Computer, 29*(4), 94–95. doi:10.1109/2.488361

Kanoun, K. (1989). *Software dependability growth: characterization, modeling, evaluation*. Doctorat ès-Sciences thesis, Institut National polytechnique de Toulouse, LAAS report (89-320).

Kapur, P., Aggarwal, A. G., Kapoor, K., & Kaur, G. (2009). Optimal testing resource allocation for modular software considering cost, testing effort and reliability using genetic algorithm. *International Journal of Reliability Quality and Safety Engineering, 16*(06), 495–508. doi:10.1142/S0218539309003538

Kapur, P., & Garg, R. (1992). A software reliability growth model for an error-removal phenomenon. *Software Engineering Journal, 7*(4), 291–294. doi:10.1049ej.1992.0030

Kapur, P., Pham, H., Aggarwal, A. G., & Kaur, G. (2012). Two dimensional multi-release software reliability modeling and optimal release planning. *IEEE Transactions on Reliability, 61*(3), 758–768. doi:10.1109/TR.2012.2207531

Kapur, P., Pham, H., Anand, S., & Yadav, K. (2011). A unified approach for developing software reliability growth models in the presence of imperfect debugging and error generation. *IEEE Transactions on Reliability, 60*(1), 331–340. doi:10.1109/TR.2010.2103590

Kapur, P., & Younes, S. (1996). Modelling an imperfect debugging phenomenon in software reliability. *Microelectronics and Reliability, 36*(5), 645–650. doi:10.1016/0026-2714(95)00157-3

Kapur, P. K., Yamada, S., Aggarwal, A. G., & Shrivastava, A. K. (2013). Optimal price and release time of a software under warranty. *International Journal of Reliability Quality and Safety Engineering, 20*(03), 1340004. doi:10.1142/S0218539313400044

Kim, T., Lee, K., & Baik, J. (2015). An effective approach to estimating the parameters of software reliability growth models using a real-valued genetic algorithm. *Journal of Systems and Software, 102*, 134–144. doi:10.1016/j.jss.2015.01.001

Kimura, M., Toyota, T., & Yamada, S. (1999). Economic analysis of software release problems with warranty cost and reliability requirement. *Reliability Engineering & System Safety, 66*(1), 49–55. doi:10.1016/S0951-8320(99)00020-4

Kremer, W. (1983). Birth-death and bug counting. *IEEE Transactions on Reliability, 32*(1), 37–47. doi:10.1109/TR.1983.5221472

Kumar, V., Singh, V., Dhamija, A., & Srivastav, S. (2018). Cost-Reliability-Optimal Release Time of Software with Patching Considered. *International Journal of Reliability Quality and Safety Engineering*, *25*(04), 1850018. doi:10.1142/S0218539318500183

Leung, Y.-W. (1992). Optimum software release time with a given cost budget. *Journal of Systems and Software*, *17*(3), 233–242. doi:10.1016/0164-1212(92)90112-W

Li, Q., & Pham, H. (2017a). NHPP software reliability model considering the uncertainty of operating environments with imperfect debugging and testing coverage. *Applied Mathematical Modelling*, *51*, 68–85. doi:10.1016/j.apm.2017.06.034

Li, Q., & Pham, H. (2017b). A testing-coverage software reliability model considering fault removal efficiency and error generation. *PLoS One*, *12*(7). doi:10.1371/journal.pone.0181524 PMID:28750091

Li, X., Xie, M., & Ng, S. H. (2010). Sensitivity analysis of release time of software reliability models incorporating testing effort with multiple change-points. *Applied Mathematical Modelling*, *34*(11), 3560–3570. doi:10.1016/j.apm.2010.03.006

Liu, H.-W., Yang, X.-Z., Qu, F., & Shu, Y.-J. (2005). *A general NHPP software reliability growth model with fault removal efficiency*. Academic Press.

Luo, M., & Wu, S. (2018). A mean-variance optimisation approach to collectively pricing warranty policies. *International Journal of Production Economics*, *196*, 101–112. doi:10.1016/j.ijpe.2017.11.013

Malaiya, Y. K., Von Mayrhauser, A., & Srimani, P. K. (1993). An examination of fault exposure ratio. *IEEE Transactions on Software Engineering*, *19*(11), 1087–1094. doi:10.1109/32.256855

Mao, C., Xiao, L., Yu, X., & Chen, J. (2015). Adapting ant colony optimization to generate test data for software structural testing. *Swarm and Evolutionary Computation*, *20*, 23–36. doi:10.1016/j.swevo.2014.10.003

Mirjalili, S., Mirjalili, S. M., & Lewis, A. (2014). Grey wolf optimizer. *Advances in Engineering Software*, *69*, 46–61. doi:10.1016/j.advengsoft.2013.12.007

Mohanty, R., Ravi, V., & Patra, M. R. (2010). The application of intelligent and soft-computing techniques to software engineering problems: A review. *International Journal of Information and Decision Sciences*, *2*(3), 233–272. doi:10.1504/IJIDS.2010.033450

Musa, J. D. (1975). A theory of software reliability and its application. *IEEE Transactions on Software Engineering*, *SE-1*(3), 312–327. doi:10.1109/TSE.1975.6312856

Musa, J. D. (1980). The measurement and management of software reliability. *Proceedings of the IEEE*, *68*(9), 1131–1143. doi:10.1109/PROC.1980.11812

Musa, J. D. (1991). Rationale for fault exposure ratio K. *Software Engineering Notes*, *16*(3), 79. doi:10.1145/127099.127121

Musa, J. D. (2004). *Software reliability engineering: more reliable software, faster and cheaper*. Tata McGraw-Hill Education.

Musa, J. D., Iannino, A., & Okumoto, K. (1987). *Software reliability: Measurement, prediction, application. 1987.* McGraw-Hill.

Naixin, L., & Malaiya, Y. K. (1996). Fault exposure ratio estimation and applications. *Proceedings of ISSRE'96: 7th International Symposium on Software Reliability Engineering.*

Nasar, M., Johri, P., & Chanda, U. (2013). A differential evolution approach for software testing effort allocation. *Journal of Industrial and Intelligent Information, 1*(2).

Pachauri, B., Dhar, J., & Kumar, A. (2015). Incorporating inflection S-shaped fault reduction factor to enhance software reliability growth. *Applied Mathematical Modelling, 39*(5-6), 1463–1469. doi:10.1016/j.apm.2014.08.006

Pai, P.-F. (2006). System reliability forecasting by support vector machines with genetic algorithms. *Mathematical and Computer Modelling, 43*(3-4), 262–274. doi:10.1016/j.mcm.2005.02.008

Pham, H. (1996). A software cost model with imperfect debugging, random life cycle and penalty cost. *International Journal of Systems Science, 27*(5), 455–463. doi:10.1080/00207729608929237

Pham, H. (2014). A new software reliability model with Vtub-shaped fault-detection rate and the uncertainty of operating environments. *Optimization, 63*(10), 1481–1490. doi:10.1080/02331934.2013.854787

Pham, H., Nordmann, L., & Zhang, Z. (1999). A general imperfect-software-debugging model with S-shaped fault-detection rate. *IEEE Transactions on Reliability, 48*(2), 169–175. doi:10.1109/24.784276

Pham, H., & Zhang, X. (1999). A software cost model with warranty and risk costs. *IEEE Transactions on Computers, 48*(1), 71–75. doi:10.1109/12.743412

Rinsaka, K., & Dohi, T. (2005). Determining the optimal software warranty period under various operational circumstances. *International Journal of Quality & Reliability Management, 22*(7), 715–730. doi:10.1108/02656710510610857

Roy, P., Mahapatra, G., & Dey, K. (2014). An NHPP software reliability growth model with imperfect debugging and error generation. *International Journal of Reliability Quality and Safety Engineering, 21*(02), 1450008. doi:10.1142/S0218539314500089

Saed, A. A., & Kadir, W. M. W. (2011). *Applyisng particle swarm optimization to software performance prediction an introduction to the approach.* Paper presented at the 2011 Malaysian Conference in Software Engineering. 10.1109/MySEC.2011.6140670

Shanmugam, L., & Florence, L. (2013). *Enhancement and comparison of ant colony optimization for software reliability models.* Academic Press.

Sharma, D. K., Kumar, D., & Gautam, S. (2018). Flexible Software Reliability Growth Models under Imperfect Debugging and Error Generation using Learning Function. *Journal of Management Information and Decision Sciences, 21*(1), 1–12.

Sheta, A., & Al-Salt, J. (2007). Parameter estimation of software reliability growth models by particle swarm optimization. *Management, 7,* 14.

Song, X., Tang, L., Zhao, S., Zhang, X., Li, L., Huang, J., & Cai, W. (2015). Grey Wolf Optimizer for parameter estimation in surface waves. *Soil Dynamics and Earthquake Engineering*, *75*, 147–157. doi:10.1016/j.soildyn.2015.04.004

SourceForge.net. (2008). *An Open Source Software Website*. Author.

Srivastava, P. R., & Kim, T.-h. (2009). Application of genetic algorithm in software testing. *International Journal of Software Engineering and Its Applications*, *3*(4), 87–96.

Tyagi, K., & Sharma, A. (2014). An adaptive neuro fuzzy model for estimating the reliability of component-based software systems. *Applied Computing and Informatics, 10*(1-2), 38-51.

Williams, D. P. (2007). Study of the warranty cost model for software reliability with an imperfect debugging phenomenon. *Turkish Journal of Electrical Engineering and Computer Sciences*, *15*(3), 369–381.

Windisch, A., Wappler, S., & Wegener, J. (2007). Applying particle swarm optimization to software testing. *Proceedings of the 9th annual conference on Genetic and evolutionary computation.* 10.1145/1276958.1277178

Yamada, S., Ohba, M., & Osaki, S. (1984). S-shaped software reliability growth models and their applications. *IEEE Transactions on Reliability*, *33*(4), 289–292. doi:10.1109/TR.1984.5221826

Yamada, S., & Tamura, Y. (2016). *Software Reliability. In OSS Reliability Measurement and Assessment.* Springer. doi:10.1007/978-3-319-31818-9

Yamada, S., Tokuno, K., & Osaki, S. (1992). Imperfect debugging models with fault introduction rate for software reliability assessment. *International Journal of Systems Science*, *23*(12), 2241–2252. doi:10.1080/00207729208949452

Zhang, X., Teng, X., & Pham, H. (2003). Considering fault removal efficiency in software reliability assessment. *IEEE Transactions on Systems, Man, and Cybernetics. Part A, Systems and Humans*, *33*(1), 114–120. doi:10.1109/TSMCA.2003.812597

This research was previously published in Soft Computing Methods for System Dependability; pages 1-44, copyright year 2020 by Engineering Science Reference (an imprint of IGI Global).

Chapter 27
A Survey on Different Approaches to Automating the Design Phase in the Software Development Life Cycle

Sahana Prabhu Shankar
https://orcid.org/0000-0001-8977-9898
Ramaiah University of Applied Sciences, India

Harshit Agrawal
https://orcid.org/0000-0003-3515-0474
Ramaiah University of Applied Sciences, India

Naresh E.
https://orcid.org/0000-0002-8368-836X
M. S. Ramaiah Institute of Technology, India

ABSTRACT

Software design is a basic plan of all elements in the software, how they relate to each other in such a way that they meet the user requirements. In software development process, software design phase is an important phase as it gives a plan of what to do and how to do it during the implementation phase. As the technology is evolving and people's needs in the technological field are increasing, the development of software is becoming more complex. To make the development process somewhat easy, it is always better to have a plan which is followed throughout the process. In this way, many problems can be solved in the design phase, for which a number of tools and techniques are present. One is known as Design Patterns. In software engineering, a design pattern is a general solution to commonly occurring problems in software design. A design pattern isn't a finished design that can be transformed directly into code.

DOI: 10.4018/978-1-6684-3702-5.ch027

INTRODUCTION

For any software to be built, it is highly important that it satisfies the client's needs. In order to completely understand what the client wants from the software, Requirement Analysis phase plays a vital role as in this phase, the analyst tries to gain as much about the domain, functioning and basic plan of the system to be designed. Once the requirement analysis phase is completed, next is the Design phase. In design phase, a basic outline/plan is made for the software to be built which includes all the elements which will be used in the implementation phase. If there is any ambiguity in the analysis phase, the design following the requirements collected, will also have the same ambiguity. Thus, it is very important to collect and interpret all the user requirements carefully, correctly and completely.

It is suggested to always first define a basic design of the software to analyse its behaviour and also to identify the short-term risks, so that informed design decisions can be made before the system goes in the implementation phase. Not only this, but designing prior to the implementation phase can also be helpful to breakdown the complex problems in simple sub-problems and thus making the implementation part easier. From a good design phase, the software gains higher productivity, better code maintainability, higher adaptability, and Quality. Thus, a good design is recommended for success of any software project.

The advantages of having a well-defined architecture in the software development process is that it helps in making the software safer, more reliable, easy to implement and maintain. Since a well-defined software architecture breaks down the software in smaller components, it also helps in reducing the problems generally occurring while developing complex softwares. Software architecture's influence is on engineering principle and it focusses on code, object design, boxes-and-arrows and GUI of the software.

DIFFERENT PHASES IN SOFTWARE DEVELOPMENT LIFE CYCLE

But software development lifecycle (SDLC) is not only about the design phase it consists of a total of five phases:

1. Requirement Engineering
2. Design
3. Implementation
4. Integration and Testing
5. Operations and Maintenance

We already have learned so much about the design phase. Before going to the automation techniques which are used in design phase let us first have a brief introduction about the rest of the phases.

REQUIREMENT ENGINEERING

The requirement phase of software engineering serves as the architecture of the software development. It consists of analysing the needs of the stakeholders, discussing the proper approach to develop and maintain the software and finally documenting each and every process required. This is known as requirement engineering.

Figure 1. Phases of Software development lifecycle

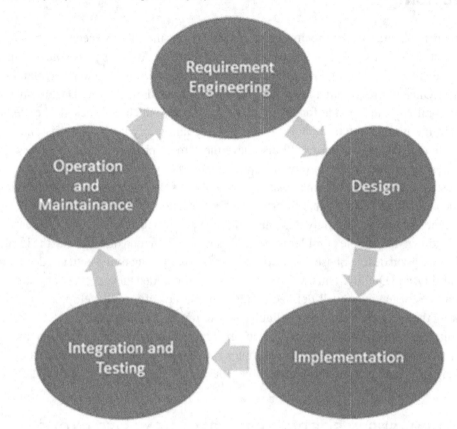

There are mainly two types of requirements:-

- **Functional Requirements:** These include all the requirements which are essential in the designing of the software. They are the first hand requirements which clearly states the working of the developed software.
- **Non-Functional Requirements:** These are the requirements which are not essential for the system working but are needed to make the software more usable and ensure better results. Example - security, maintainability, reusability etc.

The process involved in requirement engineering are:

- Requirements elicitation
- Requirements specification
- Requirements verification and validation
- Requirements management

The first step in the requirement engineering phase is the requirement elicitation.

REQUIREMENT ELICITATION

Consists of collecting information about the design of the software from the stake holders. This could be tricky if there is any problem in interaction with the customer's needs as it could create errors due to less understanding about the software. Thus, to avoid such situations the following two main methods are generally practised:

- **Discussion and Brainstorming Sessions** Groups involving of the stakeholders, developers and software engineers are set for discussing about the development and needs of the software. Everyone is welcomed to give their views and ideas and each of the ideas are documented. Finally, the important requirements are selected.
- **Quality Function Deployment:** It gives the customer the highest concern and act according to the likes of the customer.

The requirement of the customers is separated into three categories-

- **Normal Requirements:** As the name indicates, these requirements tell us about the basic goals and objective of the software. These requirements are collected by the requirement analysts from the stakeholders of the client company or the client himself.
- **Expected Requirements**: While collecting the normal requirements, as the client may not belong to the technical field, and sometimes they just assume some of the requirements to be so much obvious that they do not think it is really important to even state them to the requirements analyst. Such type of requirements are expected by the client and in many cases, requirements analysts just have to assume these on their own.
- **Exciting Requirements**: After collecting the normal requirements and assuming some expected requirements, there are still some of the requirements, that the client could not think of and the requirements analysts feel that they should be added to make the system more convenient and better. And when the software is presented to the client along with those some exciting requirements, they prove to be very satisfying.

REQUIREMENT SPECIFICATION

It is the elaboration of the requirements and their implementation by proper software requirement models. In this level of requirements engineering phase, the analysts go through the requirements collected in the elicitation phase in deep, understand them and then with the use of various existing models like Entity Relationship Diagram, Data Flow Diagrams, Function Decomposition Diagram, Data Dictionaries and many more, they elaborate those requirements in a document, so that they appear to be more clear and understandable in the upcoming phases of the software development lifecycle.

REQUIREMENT VERIFICATION AND VALIDATION

It involves verifying the requirements documented with the initial customer's needs to ensure all the criteria given by the stake holders are fulfilled.

Also, the verification of the requirements consists of checking if there is any conflict between any two requirements or if there is any non-feasible requirement, in such cases again the elicitation process is triggered.

The last and most crucial stage of requirement engineering is the **requirement management**. The SRS document made by verifying and analysing the customer's requirement should be able to change if there is any change required by the customer or the developer. All, the changes and documentation regarding the changes should be properly managed.

DESIGN

Software design phase is meant to be the most important phase of the development, as the decisions made in this phase are the bases on which the software is built. The role of a software design engineer is not only to identify the design patterns for the problem but also to identify the various types of architecture which can be used in it. A software design engineer first has to make a clear understanding of the software to be developed, who will be the end user? What will be the target audience of the software? What other competing softwares are already present in the market? And how to make the software better than other competing softwares? These are some basic questions a software design engineer must be clear about in his mind

IMPLEMENTATION

As the name of the phase itself indicates, in this phase whatever design has been made in the design phase for the given problem statement, it is implemented via coding into a real software system. In this phase, programmers including web-developers, backend engineers, frontend engineers, network engineers, object oriented developers, come together and work on the problem statement while following same design which came out as the result of the design phase. In the implementation phase, the selection of the correct software design pattern is very crucial as if chosen wrong, the design pattern will not only become the reason for a large number of bugs but will also lead to the failure in the implementation of the required software. Because, in the implementation phase, all the classes, their relationships with each other and the outside environment are all defined in the objects identified in the design pattern only. In the implementation phase, the frontend developers write the code to design the user interface (UI), so that the user can interact with the system. The backend developers write the required database code and connect it to the frontend of the system. The developers not only write codes for the system but also perform unit testing along with the development of the unit codes. Since the designing of the test cases starts right after the requirement analysis phase, the developers do test the units of codes they write on the basis of the designed test cases for that particular unit and the developer cannot move on to the next piece of code until the current unit does not satisfies all (or a minimum number of) test cases. This process known as Test Driven Development.

INTEGRATION AND TESTING

Testing is the most important phase in the software development process since it helps to review on the entire work done until now and point the critical, major or minor defects in the software, thus reducing the loss of money and compromise with the quality of the software.

The benefits of testing can be stated as follows:

- To point out the defects and faults that arises in the software.
- To ensure that the customer's requirements were fulfilled. Often contracts may include monetary penalties for the product's timing and performance. Where sufficient code testing can also avoid monetary losses in such cases.
- Testing also helps to maintain the quality of the software which gradually wins the customer trusts and makes the software more worth for money.

Defects or errors in a software arises when the expected outcome of a function does not match with the actual outcome. The types of defects in a software can be stated as follows:

- **Functionality Errors:** These occurs when there is a fault in the function of any part of the software which results in the difference in the expected outcome. Example - If the cancel button of a software does not shutdown the software as expected.
- **Communication Errors:** These occurs if there is an error in the communication between the software and the end-user. Example - If the user cannot find the help option in a software or cannot use the proper method to perform any function they desire.
- **Error handling Errors:** Any errors that occur while the user interacts with the software must be dealt with in a clear and meaningful way. If not, it is called Error Handling Error.
- **Calculation Errors:** The errors arises in the software due to wrong formula used in any calculation in the main code or due to use of wrong logic in the functionality of any part of the software.
- **Control flow Errors:** Control flow describes the next step that the software will take if any command is given to it, if the software fails to follow the flow as required this is known as the control flow error.

The process of testing can be broadly divided into types. First is the static testing and next is dynamic testing.

Static testing deals like non-functional testing where the functionality of the software and the code is not tested and only the documents are verified. It is mostly done in the verification phase. It includes reviewing, walkthrough, and inspection.

Dynamic testing deals with the functional aspects of the system. It is done by running the code and performing the different test cases on the software. It includes integration testing, system testing.

Like this, for every new unit that is developed, it is first **Unit Tested** and then integrated with the existing partial system to perform **Integration Testing**. As a conclusion of this, the fully working required system is obtained.

System testing consists of three different kinds of testing process stated as follows:

- α-testing is when the developers or development team tests the system in their environment and also the code is visible to them so that they can make the required changes instantly.
- β-testing is when some few users are selected and are provided the α-tested version of the system, so that they can test the system in their environment. This testing is very important, as the final or end users' opinion is very important and may differ largely from that of the development team. Also the users do not care about how the implementation is done, so their reviews about the system are purely concerned with the functionality and the user experience.
- **Acceptance Testing:** This testing is when the software is released to all the users, the users perform an acceptance testing which is nothing but did they really get, what they were expecting from the software and also whether they accept to use the software or not.

There is no fixed pattern to how a software must be tested thus, there are many different types of testing with each type focussing on any one of the frequent errors to detect and correct effectively. Some of the important testing methods are as follows:-

Black Box Testing: In this type of testing, the system is considered to be a black box i.e. the whole system is seen as one box only, where the user interface only is visible and available to interact with and the implementation of the software i.e. the code part or how the system is doing its functioning is hidden. Black Box testing only concerns with, whether the system is satisfying the features, functionalities and the requirements stated by the user or not.

Boundary Value Testing: From the statistics of the available old data of testing in the software companies, it can be said that most of the faults or bugs occur at the boundary values of the input fields. So in order to avoid them, a boundary value analysis is performed, in which the inputs are taken as only the values close to the boundary values of the input fields and then check whether the system is responding correctly according to the input given to it or not.

Example: If in a system, an input field is there to enter the marks of the students they got in an exam. Minimum marks what a student can get is 0 as there is no negative marking in the exam and the exam contains maximum marks as 100. This means, the marls input field must take the values only between 0-100 and reject any others. For such systems, we perform boundary value analysis. First, we need to identify the boundary values of the input field, which are clear from the above explanation i.e. 0 and 100. So, we take the values around these values like -1, 0, 1, 99, 100, 101 and test if the system is accepting only 0, 1, 99, 100 and rejecting -1, 101 or not.

Compatibility Testing: As indicated by the name only, in this testing, the testers perform the system testing of the software in different conditions like, on different hardware, using different web servers, changing the network connection and many other factors. Performing this testing, the testers ensures that the system is compatible with multiple environments and will run just fine on some other configurations too.

Gorilla Testing: As understood by the name itself, it is mainly done to check for the robustness of the system. In this testing, the testers and sometimes even the developers perform a thorough and heavy check on the functioning of a particular piece of code, so that it does not lead to any kinds of bugs, when once integrated with the system.

Regression Testing: Regression testing is performed whenever any particular piece of code in system is changed, added, deleted or just modified. In this testing, an integration test is performed on the system in order to check whether the modified code is correctly integrated with the system or not. Before performing the integration test, the modified code is separately unit tested. Since, it can be very hectic to perform the complete system integration testing again and again just after changing a little piece of code, this testing is mainly done with the help of the automation tools.

OPERATIONS AND MAINTENANCE

Software maintenance is a very important aspect of the software development process. It takes care of all the updates and modifications regarding the software after it has been created and delivered. It is varied depending on the system and client usage. Example- The maintenance of the software made for online banking is crucial and require more work while the maintenance of the software for library book keeping is less and require less work.

Based on the amount of work required by the client the maintenance is of the following types:-

- **Corrective Maintenance:** After the system is released to the users, it may happen that they encounter some issues or bugs in it. After the reports of these bugs are reached to the developer, they look into it and correct them and provide an update to the system. This type of maintenance of the system is known as the corrective maintenance of the system.
- **Adaptive Maintenance:** Once the software is released in the market to the users, the technologies change, so in order that the system does not gets outdated, the developers update the system to the newest technology and trends, this type of maintenance is known as adaptive maintenance of the system.
- **Perfective Maintenance:** With time, it may happen that the user requirements from the system changes, may happen that some features that were previously very needed and important may become redundant with time and some other new features get added. So, in order that the users keep using the system, the developers must keep track of the changing user requirements and keep the system up to date according to them, this type of maintenance is known as the perfective maintenance.
- **Preventive Maintenance:** Maintaining the system only according to the present needs and requirements will not be a wise idea to do, as it will lead to the frequent updating of the software as the requirements change, which may lead to lagging behind from the competing softwares in the market. So, it is always better to have a guess of what may be required in the future and what problems may be required to be solved in the future. Having a guess of such factors and updating the software by keeping these things in mind is known as preventive maintenance,

The process of maintenance involves seven crucial steps stated as follows:-

- **Identification and Tracing:** It includes identification of the modification or maintenance required by the system. Sometimes, the modifications are required by the client and sometimes they are required by the system by notifying the client. There could be maintenance for removal of bugs or updating required in the software.
- **Analysis:** In the analysis phase the impact of the modification or updating is analysed on the software i.e. there should be no problem or fault occurring in the previous system due to the introduction of new features also, the cost of the maintenance is analysed.
- **Design:** The new features are designed and their respective test cases are created at this phase.

- **Implementation:** It includes the implementation of the code for the new modules mostly with the same language as the original software.
- **System testing and Acceptance testing**: After the new modifications are added to the original system there is integration testing of the new modules separately and along with the original modules. Also, there is testing done in the real time environment with the users.
- **Delivery:** It includes the delivery of the new modules to all the original software and their installation. Sometimes, there is a separate cost for the installation of the new modules and sometimes it is free of cost.
- **Maintenance Management:** It deals with any problems faced at any phase of the maintenance of the software. It is aided with version control tools to control versions, semi-version or patch management.

SOFTWARE DESIGN IN PRACTICE

Software design patterns are the representations of some of the best practices followed by good and experienced professionals in software development field. Design patterns include the explanation of the basic outline of the system to be designed. It describes the problem, its solution, how to implement the solution and also what will be the consequences of following a particular design pattern. Unified Modelling Language (UML) is a collection of graphical notations which is useful to describe and design the software systems. It addresses almost all the views needed to develop such systems.

UML is a language for:

- **Visualizing:** UML models things graphically
- **Specifying:** Building models that are precise, unambiguous, and complete
- **Constructing:** Its models can be directly connected to a number of programming languages
- **Documenting:** UML addresses the documentation of a system architecture, expresses requirements and tests, models the activities of project planning and release management, etc.

It is important to keep maintaining the updated design-documents, not only in the initial phases of development, but also in the later phases in order to make the software maintainable. But often times, these design documents aren't well managed and are lost or damaged. Along with which, the design info of the software is also lost.

Traditionally, till now, all the design information was kept in the documents only. But after a number of cases, where these documents are compromised, people are trying to automate the detection of design patterns using machine learning algorithms and Artificial Neural Networks. So that, even if the design documentation was poor or compromised in any way, design pattern information can be retrieved and the software is easy to maintain. As this information is about the responsibilities of various classes and also their relationships and interactions with each other.

The automation of design pattern recognition is broadly divided into two phases. In the first phase, set of candidate classes according to their roles is identified and then the search space is reduced. In the second phase, all possible combinations of the classes identified in the first phase are made with the related candidate roles and checked if it matches with any valid instances of a DP or not. All this is done by using existing recognition tools and by training an Artificial Neural Network engine which recognises different roles and instances of a DP. The motivation behind using this two phase method to automate the design pattern recognition is that it fully utilizes the capabilities of machine learning techniques and Artificial Neural Network (ANN), which despite being so highly successful, haven't yet been used in the Design Pattern recognition completely. By using this method, an approach to completely learn the rules and regulations of DP recognition techniques from DP instances implemented in real world is developed. Since, there are many different DP present and all of them have different rules, features and implementation techniques, training an ANN proves to be useful in increasing the accuracy of design pattern recognition.

Drawback of using full capabilities of machine learning (ML) methods in Design Pattern recognition is that there is no large standard benchmark available by which the ML models can be trained. Thus, to overcome this disadvantage, a large training dataset with an acceptable level of validity and reliability should be prepared.

Figure 2. Overall Design Pattern Recognition Process

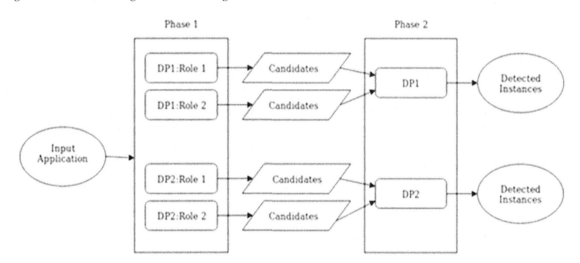

TRADITIONAL WORKING OF DESIGN PHASE

Traditionally till now, to identify a design pattern during the design phase of development of a software, one must have a string knowledge about all the 25+ design patterns which are currently present. Since some of the design patterns are closely interrelated and don't differ much from each other, it is very important and difficult at the same time to have complete and clear knowledge about all the existing design patterns. After acquiring a profound knowledge about the software design patterns one has to follow certain steps to identify the correct design pattern:

- **Understanding the Problem:** It is very important to first understand the problem statement correctly as if there is even a small misinterpretation in the problem understanding, it leads to the selection of a wrong design pattern which will lead to the origin of new problems in the implementation phase.

- **Understanding the Intent of the Design Pattern:** Intent of a design pattern tells us 'What does the design pattern do?' It also has the information of what specific design problem or issue does the design pattern addresses. Thus, after understanding the problem statement, one has to look through the Intents of all the existing design patterns and then choose the design patterns which seem to be relevant to the problem statement.
- **Understanding the Inter-Relation Between the Design Patterns:** As more than one design patterns may seem relevant from the Intent view point. It is important to understand how different design patterns inter-relate to each other in order to direct us to the selection of the right pattern or group of patterns. It may happen that one design pattern seems relevant, when seen by intent point of view is just because of its relation with the right design pattern and it really isn't relevant to the problem.
- **Understanding The Cause Of Redesign:** Redesigning a system affects many parts of it and some changes are proved to be expensive. Design patterns are helpful in avoiding these changes as much as possible by only changing the specific parts of the system. So while redesigning a system, one must first look at the cause of redesign and then accordingly choose the design pattern that is relevant according to the intent of the problem and also helps to minimize the changes.

After going through all the above steps, one may recognize the software design pattern correctly. But if there is any mistake in any of the step, the chosen design pattern will not be right and will lead to an error in the implementation phase. Not only in choosing the design pattern correctly, but also if one makes a mistake in the documentation, it again leads to error(s) in the implementation phase. If chosen and documented the design pattern correctly, it is very important to maintain that document with care. As, if in future the software needs to be upgraded, the information of the applied software design pattern is very crucial. Thus, after following so many steps, providing so much caution, and spending a lot of time, there's always a possibility that things may go wrong at some point.

ROLE OF DESIGN ENGINEER IN DESIGN PHASE

In software development life cycle, software design phase is meant to be the most important phase of the development, as the decisions made in this phase are the bases on which the software is built.

The role of a software design engineer is not only to identify the design patterns for the problem but also to identify the various types of architecture which can be used in it. A software design engineer first has to make a clear understanding of the software to be developed, who will be the end user? What will be the target audience of the software? What other competing softwares are already present in the market? And how to make the software better than other competing softwares? These are some basic questions a software design engineer must be clear about in his mind. After being cleared about the above questions, the software design engineer tries to identify the architecture of the software which includes system architecture, application architecture, functional architecture, UI architecture.

Apart from architectural design, one more design i.e. Interface design is there which is important. As the name indicates, in this level of software design phase, the design engineer creates the design of the interaction medium between the system and the user. While designing the interface of any system, the design engineer must not think about how the design will be implemented in the coding section and must treat the system like a black box. Interface design also includes how the system receives and responds to the messages sent or events triggered by the user. Specification of data and its format and the order of the messages or events received and the output messages. Software development process is very similar to constructing a building. Only designing will not be sufficient, one also has to have an idea about the time, money and effort estimation of the process. In software development process this also is the job of the software design engineer only. This includes estimating efforts where in this step, the software design engineer estimate how much amount of work will be required which helps in finishing the work within the given deadline and also helps to estimate the required financial resources.

AUTOMATION OF THE DESIGN PHASE

As previously we read about how manual functioning in the design phase can be very time and effort consuming along with chances of having many errors which lead to delay in the development process. In the current era of Artificial Neural Networks and Machine Learning, after automating the testing phase, using the machine learning techniques engineers are now moving to develop algorithms to automate the design phase too. Benefits of automating the design phase in software development life cycle are that it reduces the amount of both the time and efforts required as compared to that of in manual techniques. Apart from the time and efforts, automating the design also leads to less number of errors and precise documentation of the design phase.

The Figure 4 depicts the various phases involved in automating the design phase. The main role of any software design engineer is to design a software architecture that provides a solution to the given problem statement along with the one which also follows both the functional requirements and non-functional requirements of the system collected in the requirement analysis phase to the fullest possible extent. However sometimes, the Software requirements specifications document which is the resultant document of the requirement analysis phase which contains all the information about the functional and non-functional requirements may lack some important details of some requirements. For example: If a software requirement specification document consists a requirement as "All transaction notifications should be sent to the user." In the given requirement, major details are from the architectural point of view are missing like, 'What type of notifications would it be?' because in case of popup notification, event driven architecture has to be implemented but for the email notification, event driven architecture won't be good enough as email notifications require real-time notifications for which a publish-subscribe architecture would be the right choice. Missing of some crucial details can impact the architectural decisions and if wrong architectural decisions are made, it may happen that the requirements, as a result of missing data in which, such wrong architectural decisions are made will not be implemented or correctly satisfied in the final developed system. In such situations, the software design engineer or the software architect on the basis of their knowledge and experiences make some unconfirmed choices about the missing details, or sometimes even have an eliciting session with the stakeholders of the client company. But these assumptions, if not made with proper knowledge and experience often get incorrect, which may lead to expensive and time consuming refactoring efforts at the later stages.

But the above process to make unconfirmed choices on the missing data on the basis of knowledge and experience of a single or small group of software design engineers and software architects can be inefficient and also very time consuming making the software development process not only expensive but also delayed. A better solution to this problem can be using **Data Mining** techniques.

Figure 3. Steps to automate the design phase in SDLC

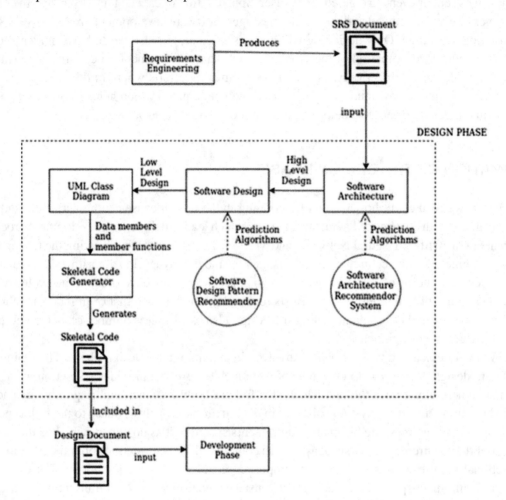

DATA MINING

The process of looking at large collection of information to generate new information is termed as Data Mining. Intuitively, "data mining" is about deducing patterns and gathering or generating new information from the collected data. It is also known as knowledge discovery process, knowledge mining from data, knowledge extraction or data /pattern analysis.

The aim of data mining is create/search new patterns which are yet unknown. Once such patterns are found then they can be used to make certain decisions for development of their businesses.

The steps are:

- Exploration
- Pattern identification
- Deployment

Exploration: Data is cleaned and then transformed into another form and important variables and nature of data based on the problem are determined.

Pattern Identification: Identification of pattern which provide best prediction.

Deployment: New patterns are generated to desired outcome.

DATA MINING TECHNIQUES

Various data mining techniques are used for various kind of problems:-

- **Tracking Patterns:** Basic technique used in data mining. It is learning to recognize the patterns in the data sets. It is finding some absurdity in the data happening at fixed intervals, or an ebb and flow of a certain variable over time.

- **Classification:** It is complex data mining technique which requires collection of different attributes together to form discernible categories, which then can be used to serve some function or to conclude.

- **Association:** Association is data mining technique which is used to track patterns. In other words it is dependently linking variables. In such case, attributes and events which are correlated or dependent on other attribute or event is taken into consideration.

- **Outlier Detection:** In many cases, clear understanding of the data set cannot be given just by recognizing the overarching pattern. But to do that identification of anomalies is necessary, or outliers of the data.

- **Clustering:** Clustering technique is almost same as Classification technique. But it also contains grouping a large data into chunks of smaller data according to their similarities.

- **Regression:** Primarily, it is used for modelling and planning. Used to find out the likelihood of particular variables, when there is presence of other related variables.

- **Prediction:** Prediction data mining technique is one most important techniques, it is used to show the data which may be required in the future. It charts the previous events and on the basis of that it predicts the possible outcome.

DATA MINING TOOLS

Rapid Miner

It provides an integrated environment for data preparation, deep learning, machine learning, predictive analysis and text mining too. One of the apex leading open source platform this. It uses java programming language for programs. It gives an opportunity to try a good amount of arbitrarily nestable operators which are made by graphical user interfaces of rapid miner and details are given in XML files.

Oracle Data Mining

Oracle represents Oracle's Advanced Analytics Database. Most of the leading companies maximize their potential of the data results in more accurate results. The algorithm used in this system for data is very powerful to target customers. It is helpful in identification of anomalies and cross selling opportunities also and allow the users create a new prediction model as per their requirements. It is very helpful in customisation of the customer profile in the way the user requires.

Python

It is free and open source language. It is mostly compared to R. As compared to R, Its learning curve is very easy to understand and use. Many users also use it to do complex analysis in very less time and to build datasets. It's also provide very basic concepts like variables, functions, loops and conditions and data type also as any other languages like JAVA, C++,etc.

Application of Data Mining in Automating Design Phase

Data mining is the process of looking at a huge amount of data and generate new data by extrapolating the existing patterns in the dataset, we can create a large dataset of of all the available information, "Missing details of a requirement in a Software requirement specification" and their correct unconfirmed choices and also add some more possible data provided by well experienced and knowledge software design engineers and software architects. Then, for the same types of situations occurring in future software developments, this dataset, data mining tools and algorithms can be used to predict an unconfirmed guess in less amount of time as compared to the manual one, and also using this automated process would give a choice which is more likely to be correct as it is based upon the unconfirmed choices which proved to be correct in the past problems.

ASSOCIATION RULE MINING

Association rules are the conditional statements which are useful in showing the estimations of the relationship between two or more data items in different large datasets in various types of databases.

Working of Association Rules

At a basic level, association rule mining includes analysing the data to find any kinds of patterns, especially **if-then** condition types, or finding any co-occurrences in the data i.e. finding if with the occurrence of one data value, is some other value co-occurring? These analysis are made using machine learning algorithms.

An association rule can be divided into two parts:

1. **Antecedent**: This part represents the **if** part of the association rule.
2. **Consequent**: This part represents the **then** part of the association rule.

Thus, we can say that whenever an antecedent data element is found in the data, it will be followed or combined with a consequent item, representing the **if-then** relationship. [Agrawal et Al. 1992]

Using the above two parts, one can easily identify the if-then patterns in a dataset. But, to find some of the most important patterns, some criteria must be used. Two important criteria, which are used in association rule mining are:

1. **Support**: If two itemset A and B are given, then an *association rule* **A ->B** will have a support *s*, if *s*% of the transaction in the transaction database do contain **A È B** (A union B). In general words, Support is a metric that shows how frequently the data items appear in the dataset.
2. **Confidence**: If two itemset A and B are given, then an *association rule* **A ->B** will have a confidence *c*, if *c*% of the transaction in the transaction database do contain **A** and **B**. In general words, Confidence is a metric that shows how many times the if-then pattern is followed by the elements in the dataset. (Geng & Hamilton, 2006)

Using the above two criteria and the two parts i.e. antecedent and consequent in a dataset, one can recognize the patterns and can also identify the association rules between the data items. Association rules can be identified from two or more itemset. But the problem starts if there are large number of itemset and one tries to make association rules with all the possible elements in the itemset. It will lead not only to consumption of high amount of time but also then, we will be having so many rules, each with a very little meaning which isn't good for the analysis, as we need a strong base for the pattern recognition. Thus, association rules are often created by the rules which are well defined in the data.

ASSOCIATION RULE MINING ALGORITHMS

Some of the most popular algorithms which use association rules are Automatic Identification System **AIS, SETM, Apriori.**

Automatic Identification System AIS

In this algorithm, itemset of the data are automatically generated and are counted as the data is scanned. The AIS algorithm identifies that which are all the large itemset that contain an association rule following and pattern matching candidates also known as transactions. And then, it creates new candidates by extending the large itemset with the items of the transactions data identified previously. [Agrawal et Al. 1992]

SETM

This algorithm was introduced in order to make use of SQL databases, so that large bulky itemset could be handled. All the members of the large bulky itemset in this algorithm 'Lk' are represented by <TID, itemset> form where TID is the unique identification id of a transaction. Similarly, the candidate itemset, 'Ck' is represented by <TID, itemset>. Being somewhat same as the previous algorithm i.e. Automatic Identification System AIS, this algorithm also iterates through the itemset few times, identifying the association rules and the relationship patterns but, this algorithm accounts for the itemset in the last iteration. Also the method of generating new candidates is same but, their transaction id are stored in a sequential manner. In the last iteration of scanning, algorithm calculates the support and confidence using the sequential structure developed in the previous iterations. (Houtsma & Swami, 1995)

Apriori

As the name indicates, in this algorithm, we already gather a prior knowledge of information about the previous itemset. The large itemset of only the previous iteration is considered for the current iteration and if any itemset of previous iteration is not large enough, it is simply neglected or deleted and all the remaining itemset are treated as the candidates in the current iteration. This algorithm follows a property which is known as **apriori property** which states that "**All subsets of a frequent itemset must be frequent. If an itemset is infrequent, all its supersets will be infrequent.**" Thus, in this algorithm, we generate level-wise itemset and check for whether they are frequent or not along with their size, so that they follow apriori property and can be used as candidates in the next level. (Geng & Hamilton, 2006)

CLASSIFICATION

Let's understand this with an example. Take Gmail, so how do you think the mail is getting classified as a spam or not? Classification is the process of dividing the data set into different categories or groups by adding label to it. In other way you can say that it is a technique of categorizing the observation into different category. So basically you are taking the data, analysing it and on the basis of some condition and finally divide it into various categories. (Han, n.d)

But Why to Classify the Data?

We classify the data to perform productive analysis on it. Like when you get the mail the machine predicts it to be a spam or not and on the basis of that prediction it adds that mail to the respective folder. In general this classification algorithm handled questions like Does this data belongs to category A or B? You can also use this for protection or to check whether the transaction is genuine or not in case of bank transactions or to classify different items like fruits on the basis of its taste, colour and size.

Types of Classification

There are several different ways to perform a same task like, in order to predict whether a given person is a male or a female, the machine had to be trained first. But there are multiple ways to train the machine and you can choose any one of them. Just for predictive analytics there are many different techniques -

1. Decision Tree
2. Random Forest
3. Naive Bayes
4. K Nearest Neighbour (KNN)

And others like logistic regression, linear regression, support vector machines etc.

Decision Tree

Decision tree is a graphical representation of all the possible solution to a decision. It can be explained very easily. For example here is a task which says that should I go to a restaurant or should I buy a hamburger? You are confused on that so for that what you'll do is you will create a decision tree for it. Starting with the root node, first of all you'll check whether you are hungry or not. If you are not hungry then just go back to sleep. If you are hungry and you have $25 then you will decide to go to restaurant and if you are hungry and you don't have $25 then you will just go and buy a hamburger.

Figure 4. Decision tree: Hamburger example

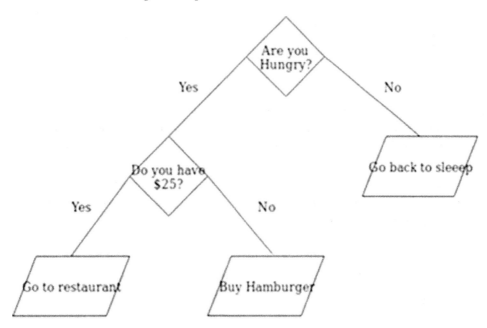

A decision tree is a graphical representation of all the possible solution to a decision based on certain conditions. Well it is called so because it starts with a root and then branches off to a number of solution just like a tree and even the tree starts from a root and it starts growing its branches once, it gets bigger and bigger similarly in a decision tree it has a root which keeps on growing with increasing number of decision and the conditions. In a decision tree, each branch represents an outcome of a condition or decision and each leaf node represents a label class. (Han, n.d)

Clustering

Clustering means grouping of objects based on the information found in the data describing the objects or their relationships. So, we have a dataset and then we try to group or classify them. For example: we have people residing and there is a cable connection going on. If you want to increase your chance of people subscribing for this cable connection you better understand the demography there. So that you can provide the channels required to those people. And target those people, which means if there is a particular community which has particular language preference, if you think that this set of community has more of a Spanish people or Spanish-speaking people and this community has more of a French-speaking people and so-on, it is better to understand these classifiers in order to target them better. So, because you can have your set of channels completely tied to them, those set of people can pick those and subscribe. Else your competitor gains a foothold there. So this is one of the reason we go for something like a clustering. So the goal is that the objects in one group should be similar to each other but it has to be different from objects in another group. So clustering deals with finding a structure in a collection of unlabelled data. Initially, all the data seems to be the same and then you try to find the structure of collections within the data. Some of the examples of clustering methods are:

1. k-means clustering
2. Fuzzy or C means clustering
3. Hierarchical clustering

k-Means Clustering

k-means clustering is one of the simplest algorithms which uses **unsupervised learning** method to solve known clustering issues. First start with cluster of two for the entire population. It tries to split the entire population into two clusters. Then we try to see it with three clusters. Then we try to see it with four plus clusters. So we increase the number of clusters which is the **K** value here so that is how this clustering is done. We do iterative models in order to find which/where the appropriate cluster is. k-means clustering means clustering in terms of inputs. It needs a number of clusters under the training set so that is what it requires. (Han, n.d)

APPLICATION OF DATA MINING AND MACHINE LEARNING TECHNIQUES FOR AUTOMATING THE DESIGN PHASE

In (Liu et al, 2018), the authors talk about the ways the pattern recognition algorithms can be employed for detecting the various design patterns. These design patterns include behavioural, state, observer and strategy. They have developed a framework that combines the execution data with source code to do the job. This combined approach produces results that have greater recall and precision than static approaches. In addition, this framework also identifies missing roles that is not available with the present approach.

In (Wang et al., 2018) authors talk about machine learning driven approach for architectural designs. Having a self-adaptive architecture in place is very important, consider the kind of applications being developed in internet of things. In order to achieve this dynamic nature of architecture, we make use of machine learning techniques. The proposed approach is mainly meant for IoT applications and it does continuous monitoring of quality parameters defined on the applications. It also does prediction of the possible deviation based on the acceptable quality parameters. It also proposes a way to prevent the deviation by generating a list of alternative solutions. It then does selection of the best possible solution from the list. Finally verification of whether the new solution selected satisfies the quality of requirements.

In (Muccini and Vaidhyanathan, 2019), authors say that detection of software design patterns help to accelerate the activities in software architecture and design, coding as well as operations and maintenance phase. The authors do an analysis of the available tools in the past decade and record the results in terms of language used for development, techniques used. They conclude by telling that there is scarcity of comprehensive detection tools and that the tools should be language independent. The development of such a comprehensive tool can be of research interest.

In (Almuammar & Fasli, 2017), authors talk about the challenge of extracting design patterns from streams of data with high velocity, volume, variety and varsity. The authors also comment that the growth in the use and applications of IoT devices is responsible for data explosion. This paper aims to discover patterns from such heterogeneous data streams. The experiment was conducted on a car parking lot with a heterogeneous environment consisting of a car parking mobile application, sensors and automated payment machines. The researchers suggest that it is extremely challenging to mine patterns in a dynamic environment. The mining was carried out using multi-support thresholds. A hybrid algorithm of FP-growth with Naïve Bayes is used. The results show only interesting patterns when the naïve Bayes classifier is used without multiple database scans. This helps to reduce the time required for multiple scans, thus improving the efficiency.

In (Dwivedi et al. 2016), authors say that design patterns provide reusable solutions to commonly occurring problems. The first case why design patterns came up was because a pattern was discovered by observing the way two or more classes were combined. It is as well appreciated if reverse engineering could be applied on already written piece of code to identify the design pattern behind it. This further helps to improve the maintainability of the code. The authors make use of software metrics to build the training database for experiments. They use machine learning algorithms like decision tree and recurrent neural network for pattern recognition. An open source software jhotdraw has been used for recognition of design patterns. The dataset is built using 67 object oriented approaches. The patterns under consideration were abstract factory and adapter design patterns. They say that this can be extended for identification of other patterns also in the object oriented system.

In (Anish 2016), the author states that the details required to formulate the software architectural design are sometimes missing directly from the software requirements specification document. Hence, often the software architects go back to stake holders for clarifications before proceeding with the design. The results are based on interviews with the software architects, where they were questioned regarding how they would manage with the missing requirement information in huge software projects, use the knowledge of these software architecture experts so that we can aid the business analysts do their job better and elicit the requirements in a better manner. It uses the machine learning techniques to automate the process of gathering requirements.

In (Osman et al. 2013), author talks about the reverse engineering techniques for obtaining design patterns from source code. This paper proposes an automated approach for combining various diagrams obtained by reversed engineering approach with the one's that would have been obtained by actual forward engineering approach as the UML diagrams. The training set consists of both forward engineered diagram as well as reverse engineered one's. The supervised machine learning algorithm makes use of the training set to identify the classes to be included in the class diagram. A comparative study is done with nine different algorithms to see which one outperforms the other.

In (Chaturvedi et al. 2018), authors are mainly focussed on extracting the design patterns from object oriented based projects. A dataset consisting of a total of 71 object oriented projects which are java based is considered. First, Feature Extraction phase, in which the authors have used Source Monitor Tool which extracts the features of the project i.e. number of lines, percent branch statement, classes etc. Then Dimensionality Reduction phase, in which the dataset is reduced in size by only taking the relevant components. Then Classification and Exponential parameterization. Classification method is also known as supervised learning in which authors have used angular distance method to classify the data. From this classified data, to extract pattern data, exponential parameterization is performed on it. Then Machine Learning Algorithms Applied in which a total of four machine learning algorithms Linear Regression, polynomial regression, support vector regression model and neural network are applied to minimize the root mean square error values.

In (Gupta et al. 2019), authors have focussed on the code smell concentration to detect the need of change requirement in the code. The dataset considered is a collection of 629 open source projects. Using the software metrics as input, the code smell of each software experiment is estimated. Wilcoxon sign rank is used to test statistical significance between the smelly and non-smelly software experiments. Then, cross correlation analysis is used to select uncorrelated feature. Then, classification method is applied in which three different kernels are separately used to train the model. Then, three techniques downward sampling, random sampling and upward sampling are used to balance the imbalanced data.

In (Dwivedi et al. 2016), authors have focussed on a mining technique for the software design pattern, which is based on supervised learning and software metrics. The selected dataset in the experiment consists of five number of design patterns which are Abstract Factory, Adapter, Bridge, Singleton, and Template Method for the mining of the design pattern available in the source code of a project. Then software metrics are selected, as the object oriented approach is mostly used by pattern-base solutions and it also contains an optimum number of software metrics, 67 such metrics are chosen in the experiment. At last, Layer Recurrent Neural Network and Random forest methods are used for the mining of the prepared dataset.

In (Jahan et al. 2019), authors applied a machine learning approach to remove Emergent Behaviour in the early phases of the development cycle only, as it can create a severe damage during execution. First, Pre-processing, in this the scenarios are converted into events and then these events are converted into symbolic words and sentences. Then Training, a recurrent neural network called as LSTM is trained over possible sentences. Then Detection, using LSTM, some events are verified with their next events to check whether it will lead to generation of Emergent Behaviour or not. And a detailed report is produced for the same.

CONCLUSION

Software Engineering can be considered to be the backbone of computer science and engineering. All phases are equally important for successful execution of a software project. The design phase provides the skeleton for the software system. Having a good design in place is important for the further phases. Hence having an unbiased and more accurate way of designing the system is needed. This can be easily achieved by making use of advancements in the field of data mining techniques which has been highlighted in this chapter. Also the various algorithms are discussed with their relevance to their application to the design phase.

REFERENCES:

Agrawal, R., Imieliński, T., & Swami, A. (1993, June). Mining association rules between sets of items in large databases. ACM. *SIGMOD Record*, *22*(2), 207–216. doi:10.1145/170036.170072

Almuammar, M., & Fasli, M. (2017, October). Pattern discovery from dynamic data streams using frequent pattern mining with multi-support thresholds. *Proceedings 2017 International Conference on the Frontiers and Advances in Data Science (FADS)* (pp. 35-40). IEEE. 10.1109/FADS.2017.8253190

Anish, P. R. (2016, September). Towards an Approach to Stimulate Architectural Thinking during Requirements Engineering Phase. *Proceedings 2016 IEEE 24th International Requirements Engineering Conference (RE)* (pp. 421-426). IEEE. 10.1109/RE.2016.30

Chaturvedi, S., Chaturvedi, A., Tiwari, A., & Agarwal, S. (2018, August). Design Pattern Detection using Machine Learning Techniques. *Proceedings 2018 7th International Conference on Reliability, Infocom Technologies, and Optimization (Trends and Future Directions)(ICRITO)* (pp. 1-6). IEEE. 10.1109/ICRITO.2018.8748282

Dwivedi, A. K., Tirkey, A., & Rath, S. K. (2016, December). Applying software metrics for the mining of design pattern. *Proceedings 2016 IEEE Uttar Pradesh Section International Conference on Electrical, Computer, and Electronics Engineering (UPCON)* (pp. 426-431). IEEE. 10.1109/UPCON.2016.7894692

Dwivedi, A. K., Tirkey, A., Ray, R. B., & Rath, S. K. (2016, November). Software design pattern recognition using machine learning techniques. *Proceedings 2016 IEEE Region 10 Conference (TENCON)* (pp. 222-227). IEEE.

Geng, L., & Hamilton, H. J. (2006). Interestingness measures for data mining: A survey. [CSUR]. *ACM Computing Surveys*, *38*(3), 9. doi:10.1145/1132960.1132963

Gupta, H., Kumar, L., & Neti, L. B. M. (2019, March). An Empirical Framework for Code Smell Prediction using Extreme Learning Machine. In *Proceedings 2019 9th Annual Information Technology, Electromechanical Engineering, and Microelectronics Conference (IEMECON)* (pp. 189-195). IEEE. 10.1109/IEMECONX.2019.8877082

Han, J. (n.d.). *Data Mining: Concepts and Techniques* (3rd ed.). Morgan Kaufmann Publishers.

Houtsma, M., & Swami, A. (1995, March). Set-oriented mining for association rules in relational databases. *Proceedings of the eleventh international conference on data engineering* (pp. 25-33). IEEE. 10.1109/ICDE.1995.380413

Jahan, M., Abad, Z. S. H., & Far, B. (2019, May). Detecting emergent behaviors and implied scenarios in scenario-based specifications: a machine learning approach. *Proceedings of the 11th International Workshop on Modelling in Software Engineering* (pp. 8-14). IEEE Press. 10.1109/MiSE.2019.00009

Liu, C., Van Dongen, B., Assy, N., & Van Der Aalst, W. M. (2018, May). Poster: A General Framework to Detect Behavioral Design Patterns. *Proceedings 2018 IEEE/ACM 40th International Conference on Software Engineering: Companion (ICSE-Companion)* (pp. 234-235). IEEE.

Muccini, H., & Vaidhyanathan, K. (2019, March). A Machine Learning-Driven Approach for Proactive Decision Making in Adaptive Architectures. *Proceedings 2019 IEEE International Conference on Software Architecture Companion (ICSA-C)* (pp. 242-245). IEEE. 10.1109/ICSA-C.2019.00050

Osman, M. H., Chaudron, M. R., & Van Der Putten, P. (2013, September). An analysis of machine learning algorithms for condensing reverse engineered class diagrams. *Proceedings 2013 IEEE International Conference on Software Maintenance* (pp. 140-149). IEEE. 10.1109/ICSM.2013.25

Wang, Y., Zhang, C., & Wang, F. (2018, December). What Do We Know about the Tools of Detecting Design Patterns? *Proceedings 2018 IEEE International Conference on Progress in Informatics and Computing (PIC)* (pp. 379-387). IEEE. 10.1109/PIC.2018.8706318

This research was previously published in the Handbook of Research on Engineering Innovations and Technology Management in Organizations; pages 350-372, copyright year 2020 by Engineering Science Reference (an imprint of IGI Global).

Chapter 28
Expert Group Knowledge Triggers:
When Knowledge Surfaces

Hanna Dreyer
University of Gloucestershire, UK

Gerald Robin Bown
University of Gloucestershire, UK

Martin George Wynn
ⓘ https://orcid.org/0000-0001-7619-6079
University of Gloucestershire, UK

ABSTRACT

Specialised knowledge is a key component of success in an organisational context that resides in the expertise of the organisation's personnel. To explore this situation, an ethnographic case study was chosen in which data was collected from a software development project. Extempore verbal exchanges occur through the interplay of project team members in weekly meetings, as the software was tested, analyzed, and altered in accordance with the customer's needs. Utilizing tacit knowledge from the project members as well as the group, new tacit knowledge surfaces and spirals, which allows it to build over time. Five extempore triggers surfaced during the research generated through explicit stimuli, allowing project members to share and create new knowledge. Through the use of ideas developed by Husserl and Heidegger, this study has cast some light on verbal exchanges that, through their interjection, allow significant learning to take place. The theoretical development places these learning triggers in an interpretive framework, which can add value to other software development projects.

DOI: 10.4018/978-1-6684-3702-5.ch028

INTRODUCTION

Project management assumes a rational approach to decision-making by project managers, but recent empirical studies (Wynn, 2018) support the view that managerial judgment is the preferred mode of decision selection in many projects. Managerial judgment is based on situational assessment, and thus on time-constrained knowledge rather than on more prescriptive rational decision-making (Taylor, 2004). The surfacing of knowledge in projects has been conceptualised as emanating from a combination of improvisation, project management and knowledge management activities (Leybourne & Kennedy, 2015). The issue of improvisation, however, can be seen to be at odds with established best practice. Prescriptive, probabilistic and objective based project management systems are no guarantee of success and in some cases they can create an illusion of control that is not always justified (Hodgson & Drummond, 2009). All projects have a temporal focus and the dominant logic in this field is structured planning to achieve workable projects on time. Knowledge sharing is at the core of meetings where different forms of expert knowledge are required.

Tacit knowledge is a difficult form of knowledge to share and acquire during a project due to its intangible nature. Tacit knowledge is at the core of a knowledge based society and its exchange is still of great interest to researchers. How tacit knowledge is exchanged and used within the different project teams plays a vital role in project success. Banacu (2013) stresses the importance of tacit knowledge transfer due to companies needing it to obtain a competitive advantage. This research analyses a project team's tacit knowledge exchange within a software development meeting environment.

White and Perry (2016) argue that there has not been enough focus on the expert knowledge of software developers and their influence on the production of information systems. This is an area where software work is highly socialized but careers were highly individualized (Benner, 2008). Their mutual standing in the work overcomes the set of partial knowledge that they each possess. Being able to manage different knowledge sources through coordination and integration is a significant challenge during such a project (de Souza et al., 2006). The focus of the research lies in exploring knowledge exchange in software development projects and sheds light on how this expert group knowledge actualises and thus contributes to theory. Embedded observation in a particular project provided the empirical material for this research.

This article discusses the findings of a research project (Dreyer, 2018) which aimed to understand how tacit knowledge surfaces within the software development process. It examines how the group knowledge generated through expert interaction can be recognised in a software development project, and used to improve project implementation (Clancy, 2006). The paper consists of five sections. After this introductory section, theories relevant to the area of study are identified and discussed. The following section then outlines the research methodology deployed in the study. There then follows an evaluation of the data and a discussion of findings, and in the concluding section, the main outcomes of the research are summarised and implications are discussed.

THEORETICAL BACKGROUND

Project teams, and in particular those involved in software development, exist to provide workable solutions that incorporate and create new knowledge from the separate expertise held within the team. In discussing the idea of knowledge creation, the theory of tacit knowledge has been influential since the work of Nonaka and Takeuchi (1995). This created a protocol for a knowledge generating company using a Socialisation, Externalisation, Combination and Internalisation (SECI) model. In the same volume, three of the model elements are presented in a recursive pathway, as more available knowledge is created in the transfer from tacit to explicit knowledge. Internalisation is the counter flow in this model and it occurs across and counter to the other three modalities.

The concept of tacit knowledge arises from the observation by Polanyi (1962) that "our personal knowing of a thing is unspecifiable" (p.343) to the extent that it is more than the articulated fact. Importantly, this tacit knowledge is seen as the form of knowledge that is *not* routinely articulated and embodied in human action (Scharmer, 2001; Riain, 2009). This leaves open the question of whether the knowing is not, or cannot be articulated. Personal knowledge communication contains both these elements in ways that are difficult to separate. This will apply to knowledge from an expert who, as such, is considered to have expertise. Importantly, Nonaka and Takeuchi (1995) see the process to convert tacit knowledge to explicit knowledge as essentially context dependent, which entails physical proximity and interaction.

In this view, a shared reality and face-to-face interactions are the root of knowledge creation (Berger & Luckmann, 1967). These interactions are seen as "the key to conversion and transfer of tacit knowledge and, thus, are the triggers for the whole knowledge creation process" (Bartolacci et al., 2016, p.795). This process is holistically contained in the context, but often needs disjunctions to crystallise the knowledge available. Having several groups of experts involved moderates the flow of knowledge substantially, and hence developing a shared understanding is essential, as it is a group effort to develop software (Fischer & Ostwald, 2001). This shared reality is a form of "putting oneself into work" (Heidegger, 2001, p.160).

There have been a number of difficulties in implementing such a knowledge creation project in a timely manner, particularly in software projects (Marouf & Khalil, 2015). A Husseralian approach to phenomenology is one that derives the essence of an idea. Husserl (2012, p. 255) considers that a thought can emerge as a vague thought that is, in its initial stages "an inarticulate grasp". Polanyi's (1962) use of the term "strenuous groping" and the view that "any science is grounded in a tacit ontology of its object domain" indicates the "unspoken assumption about the objects in use" (p.301). Knowledge we acquire and own is not entirely specifiable and therefore gives rise to the articulate grasping as we seek to extend our articulation of what we know. Triggers add value in a group context by enabling this process. Triggers can be seen as unique events that start a process, initiating something new. They are an initiation of a phase change in the knowledge development process that enables articulation. Accepting that there are some dynamic effects, the process of knowledge exchange will not be self-generating without interventions. These situations are not always easy to recognize, as they are not routinely articulated, and therefore the opportunity for the identification of a new understanding may be missed. Engeström, Kerosuo, and Kajamaa (2007) see these discontinuities as either mundane or directional. Directional changes can seem an anathema to the idea of continuity but continuity is not the same for all participants. These triggers or "discontinuities" in the existing situation, can be created from outside the group, and can "trigger micro-processes of organizational learning" (Berends & Lammers, 2010, p. 1060). Through the recognition of tacit knowledge triggers and the creation of an analytical framework, the group as well as the individual knowledge sources are assessed. This analysis builds upon existing theories, discussed below, which were used to understand and extract tacit knowledge.

Others have developed the idea of a shared space as the forum for knowledge development. It is possible to share knowledge through different channels; however, a shared space reinforces the relationship between colleagues allowing knowledge creation to take place (Dreyer & Wynn, 2017). These spaces are formed in different ways, such as through informal discussions during a break, emails or meetings.

Developing the view of shared reality, the environment where knowledge can be exchanged and is able to build up has been called "Ba". This concept, developed by Nonaka and Teece (2001), gives a basis for knowledge to be shared and created. Nonaka and Konno (1998) see "Ba" as a mental flexibility and an ongoing dynamic process that allows new insights to be constantly generated. The space of "Ba" provides for a continuous flow of knowledge exchange, where the knowledge is able to transform and change. Knowledge is not tangible, but is able to evolve and build up tacitly through its self-transcendence. This view recognizes that this knowledge forum is a shared space where relationships can emerge (Nonaka & Teece, 2009). Knowledge is thus not a set of facts and figures; it is not a set of statistics or applied conceits, but a "space" in which processes are constantly iterative, marked by close communication, by modelling, by mentoring, and by incessant experiential inputs that lead to outputs. Given the creation of a knowledge generating space, they recognize the need for dynamic effects. This space is not tangible, but is a fluid continuum wherein there is constant change and transformation resulting in new levels of knowledge. Knowledge is a process and never becomes finalised, which is paralleled in the software development process, where databases are built and then later updated over time with more information. However, both need knowledge or information, which is captured and put into context. It is a self-transcending and ever-spiraling evolution. Embracing the concept of "Ba" is essentially arguing for a learning culture, which has the advantage of promoting the concept of presence to each other. However, it seems that the proximity entailed in knowledge creation needs further exploration. In Heidegger's terms, this space can be seen as a "clearing" or a "shedding of light". (Heidegger, 2015, p.133).

Further work has been done on the knowledge exchange dynamic. Group tacit knowledge is the focus of Ryan and O'Connor's (2013) Theoretical Model for the acquisition and sharing of Tacit Knowledge in Teams (TMTKT). They note, "individuals draw from the team tacit knowledge and create their own tacit knowledge. This is a background process which is dynamic and reciprocal relying on constructivist situated learning" (Ryan & O'Connor, 2013, p.1618). Looking at knowledge flow, their approach allows the analysis of knowledge movement within a group. The model (Figure 1) was constructed by using a qualitative approach and the focus is to explore the flow of team tacit knowledge. The cycle of the model begins with the current state of knowledge within the team; through constructive learning, an essential part of knowledge creation and sharing which greatly develops individual knowledge. Constructive learning is, at its essence, the process of an individual assimilating new facts and experiences into a pre-existing web of knowledge and understanding (Ryan & O'Connor, 2013). The gained individual knowledge - expert knowledge - can then be shared with the team, allowing "transactive memory" to build up. In the context of this model, the "transactive memory" is defined as team tacit knowledge, where the expert knowledge from each individual in the team is stored and a common understanding is developed. Transactive memory is thus the combination of specialization, credibility and coordination of knowledge within the group (Ryan & O'Connor, 2012). Once the team has established common team tacit knowledge, which can be influenced by other human factors such as emotions or outside influences, the spiral begins anew in a continuous cycle. Team tacit knowledge and its flow allows the social analysis of the project group during the meetings. This model proposes that individual constructive learning precedes the development of transactive memory. Given the discussion above, any team tacit knowledge must be present but individualized; the transactive memory becomes focused on the project outcomes and therefore allows a team to progress in the project.

Clarke (2010) proposes a model evaluating tacit knowledge from an individual point of view (Figure 2). Incorporating the idea of triggers, knowledge input begins the process; tacit knowledge is then created through reflection; and triggers, such as group discussions and breakdowns, influence reflection on the newly gained knowledge. There are both tacit and explicit elements of this new knowledge. The tacit knowledge triggers in Clarke's model are used as a form of sensitization during this research, and are then further developed to be utilized in a group setting.

Figure 1. Theoretical model for the acquisition and sharing of tacit knowledge in teams

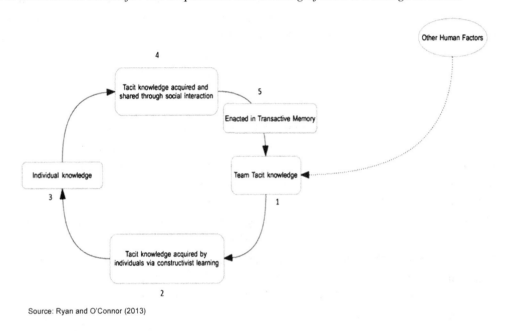

Source: Ryan and O'Connor (2013)

Figure 2. The tacit knowledge spectrum model

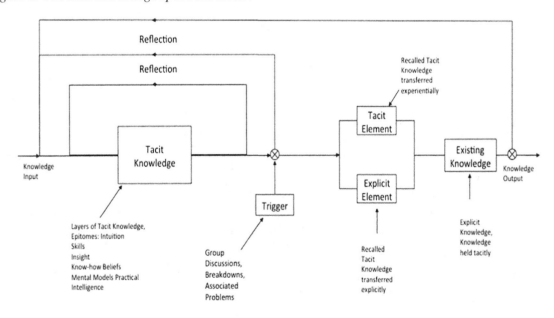

Source: Clarke (2010)

The benefit of this model (Figure 2) is the manner in which it incorporates the idea of triggers and the cycle of reflection by team members. The literature discussed above provides the theoretical basis for the analysis of tacit knowledge within teams as well as the flow of tacit knowledge and its environment. Nonaka and Teece (2009) established the "Ba" environment for tacit knowledge exchange; the SECI model allows the classification and evaluation of knowledge exchange and associated learning; Ryan and O'Connor's (2012) model provides a team view of tacit knowledge exchange, complemented by Clarke's (2010) individual perspective of tacit knowledge. Knowing more about the operation of these triggers will help develop an understanding of expert team knowledge creation.

RESEARCH METHOD

The goal of the research is to show what influenced the surfacing of expert knowledge and the articulated interaction surrounding the occurrence of triggers. The aim is to provide insight into which triggers allow tacit, expert, knowledge to surface to aid teams to achieve project success. Using the theoretical ideas discussed above, a strategy of analytic generalization (Yin, 2009) was adopted to develop theory.

As noted above, an embedded case study was chosen to analyse the interactions in a potential group knowledge space. Therefore, this research used an organization and a specific software project as a single ethnographic case study which "remains firmly grounded in the ethnographer being there" (Riain, 2009, p. 303). A case study approach allows a "detailed investigation of one or more organizations, or groups within organizations, with a view to providing an analysis of the context and processes involved in the phenomenon under study" (Hartley, 1994, p.323). They "provide the opportunity to place research into a certain context due to the selection of specific sectors, institutions, countries, etc." (Cunningham, Menter & Young, 2017, p. 923). This approach can generate a great deal of detail, and Silverman (2013) has pointed out how case studies can provide a complex and rich understanding of change projects across a period of time.

The chosen case study allowed an inside, participant, view of a software development project, where experts discussed the content needed for the development of the software product. By electing to pursue participant observation and an inductive research approach, the aim was to let the findings emerge over time. The research was conducted over a three-month period, focusing on approximately 30 hours of recorded meetings, with ten team members involved. The software environment was geared to a fast-paced project, there being a clear launch date for the new software. One of the authors was an embedded member of the software team, and an active participant in the work of that team. To develop a software product, multiple groups of experts are needed to achieve a productive knowledge flow (Fischer & Ostwald, 2001). These sessions were project meetings, which took place several times a week. Four of the team members were core, attending most of the meetings and therefore had the most influence on the project. According to Valente and Davies (1999), key actors play a central role in groups through the creation of new ideas and their understanding. The core team consisted of human resource consultants, later referred to as HR A and HR B, as well as software developers, SD A and SD B. In addition, the end user or client - CL A - was often involved in the process. Other experts from the companies joined in when their knowledge was needed, and their input is represented by the prefix HR, CL or SD depending on the company from which they come.

The focus lies within the times the meetings took place, shedding light on the expert knowledge exchanged during face-to-face formal interaction, aiming to highlight the importance of meetings. The extensive researcher involvement created a developed appreciation of the interactions at work in these meetings. The recordings of the meetings were coded through contextualization, and then systematically reviewed. First, the meetings were generally evaluated by date, which then allowed topics discussed during the meetings to surface. These transactional topics were then pulled together to find tacit knowledge, its triggers, expert and team knowledge, knowledge creation as well as the exchange over time, through the previously discussed theories. Different themes started to surface, which were previously found in the literature, such as constructive learning, individual and group tacit knowledge, as well as tacit knowledge triggers. Focusing on tacit knowledge triggers, a more in-depth analysis through a narrative, inductive approach was undertaken using the ideas of individual noemic knowledge and the interactions from being present in the discussion.

The case study and the focus on being with others allows a greater appreciation of the knowledge exchange that can develop. Using the phenomenology of Husserl (2012, pp. 86-7) which emphasizes the indutiablity of internal perception and the tenuousness of outer perceptions. The internal perceptions are noetic but they are influenced by the social environment. This interaction between what is personally known and sharing space with others should become manifest in expert project meetings. Rabanaque (2010) quotes Husserl to note that the living body is "the connecting bridge (verbindende Brucke) between subjectivity in the world and physical thinghood in the world" (p.47). Noting this standpoint has enabled the study to develop the connection between personal knowledge and contextual interaction. Thus, a cumulative picture emerged from the findings and allowed theoretical generalization in order to create new knowledge. Focusing on one project, each team member plays a crucial role in passing on tacit knowledge to his or her colleague. Knowledge elements are then passed on to other project team members through one or multiple triggers, which allows knowledge to surface. Each team member passes on his or her currently articulated knowledge. This then encourages or triggers the creation of new knowledge in the other team members. The knowledge is dragged from the tacit to the articulate in this process. This key assumption was evaluated and examined in the software development context. The triggers are related to extracts in the data where evidence of each trigger was found and established. As the research focuses on one project, knowledge passed on over time can be put into context and evaluated against knowledge that has been previously exchanged.

In the following section, the data is evaluated to highlight knowledge generating episodes. Using the knowledge exchanged in the different companies, the interplay of knowledge exchange helps further understand how the knowledge spirals within the project. Five main triggers were found, which are discussed in detail below. A combination of theory and data will be demonstrated.

RESULTS AND DISCUSSION

The knowledge within the project was spread between the different participants, and a group effort was needed to achieve success. Within each collected extract, triggers were observed which allowed tacit knowledge to surface. The goal during the analysis was first, to find evidence of tacit knowledge, and then to understand what kind of tacit knowledge was found, and lastly, to determine what made tacit knowledge surface. During this analysis phase, five main triggers were identified which are discussed below with collected extracts from the research. Clarke (2010) identified tacit knowledge triggers, but they were not identified in types. The trigger types emerged through the data as well as their impacts.

Following the transcription and analysis of the meetings, 45 extracts were selected and used to demonstrate evidence of tacit knowledge and its triggers. In this initial phase, the SECI model was used as a sensitizing approach. Within these extracts, Socialization, Internalization and Group tacit knowledge were always found; externalization was found 28 times, and combination nine. These findings were used as the basis to show tacit knowledge exchange. Then, tacit knowledge triggers were analyzed from the data. Visual triggers were found 18 times, conversational triggers 39, constructive learning triggers 19, anticipation triggers two and recall triggers seven times (Figure 3). These triggers and their operation are the focus of the following discussion.

Visual Triggers

Visual triggers allow an individual to utilize previously gained knowledge to surface by reading or seeing information. During the research, this trigger mainly surfaced when the software was looked at and edited by the team. The knowledge is gained tacitly, becomes processed, thus triggering a socialization within the group. In these scenarios, the software development company would present the developed software pages (i.e. screen design and content) to the human resource consultancy. The pages in the software were analyzed by the team and changed according to their needs when possible. This mainly focused on wording, the layout or process in which the pages were to be found and structured within the software. Visual triggers were found on numerous occasions, one example is the following:

SD A: Multiple Pensions. Order of priority. So, when they run out of money, this one comes first, this one comes next... Say you are on 500 GBP a week and you get an attachment of earning because you failed to pay your child support. So, the attachment will have top priority. There is a level at which deductions should stop.

HR A: Sorry can you just go back to the pensions type.

SD A: yea.

HR A: Just wanted to see where I can attach the file.

SD A: I think this needs a real thorough look; I am just skimming through it.

In this extract, SD A explained the pensions pages. Through constructive learning, the HR consultants learned how the pensions pages functioned; during the explanations, HR A stops the discussion to refer back to a previously seen page. SD A had moved on, HR A was still processing the visually gained knowledge in the previous page and asked to go back to see if a feature was available. In another extract, one specific part of a page - the payroll ID - triggered a conversation within the group. The work reference and the ID were confused by SD A, thinking two references were used by the HR company; this triggered HR A to further explain their system of referencing employees. This visual trigger allowed conversational triggers to surface by starting socialization between the project members.

Visual triggers can also be more simplistic. In another extract, the team looks at the salary screen, and needs to rearrange the display order to fit the requirements of the HR consultants. The visual stimuli of the software triggers work and process knowledge of the HR team, which is to be combined with the software engineering environment. Similar situations were found in other extracts, where the 360 feedback is being assessed. HR A says changes within the structure of the pages will need to be done to fit the requirements of the client. HR A's tacit knowledge base of the customer as well as experience are combined with the knowledge visually gained through the software.

Throughout the data analysis there have been several extracts demonstrating how visual mediums trigger knowledge within an individual. This triggered knowledge enables the project team to further conversations, complete gaps of knowledge within the group' and thus allows group tacit knowledge to prosper. Visual triggers launch an internal process within an individual, where the tacit knowledge base is used to combine the current tacit knowledge of an individual with the new visually gained knowledge.

Conversational Triggers

Conversational triggers occur frequently during meetings. Knowledge surfaces explicitly, which is then processed by a team member. The individual will then use the newly gained knowledge, add it to their existing knowledge and create new tacit knowledge. This interaction continues within the group and allows knowledge gaps to be addressed. Due to conversations being at the center of the research, conversational triggers are one of the most frequent and are found throughout the research. The following extract demonstrates a conversational trigger:

HR A: In an unrelated topic, we talked about sick pay, policies and rules last week. I do not have any up to date paper work from you guys. Could you send me the most recent copy?

CL A: I can send you the policies, because we did update them about 6 weeks ago, when we changed the sickness payroll for the organization.... So I can send that over to you. Could you copy in SD A as well? Thank you.

SD A: So Payroll, while you mention that...

The analyzed extract demonstrated a conversational trigger, where HR A discusses the pay policies, this then triggers SD A's tacit knowledge, where the topic is changed to payroll. SD A listens to HR A and CL A discussing a finance related topic and this enables the recall of an unsolved issue with payroll. Later in the discussion, seen during another extract HR A furthers the topic of payroll by building on the knowledge SD A shared. Through explicit exchange within the group, knowledge spirals and builds individual knowledge within each individual. Topics of discussion are altered and enhanced by using the tacit knowledge gained from the previous group member. Their similarities trigger socialization and externalization such as in another conversation, where the discussion allows knowledge to spiral and prosper within the group. Externalized knowledge is used by several members of the project, processed and complemented by the knowledge of each individual taking part in the discussion.

Conversational triggers are one of the most frequent triggers found in the analysis of the data. Explicit communication within the group allows group tacit knowledge to build and each individual to utilize the knowledge to work to achieve project success. This trigger is often in combination with visual or constructive learning, where an external verbal medium allows an individual to take in information, process and reflect the knowledge to then externalize the new processed knowledge. This greatly supports group tacit knowledge and the core objective of a meeting - 'to get everyone on the same page'.

Constructive Learning Triggers

A constructive learning trigger occurs when a project member explains to the others a specific topic of the project. The knowledge is passed on from one person explicitly to the group as a whole, which tacitly utilizes and combines the knowledge. During the project, learning was crucial due to the software being tailored to the company. Each project group, the HR consultants, software developers as well as the customer exchanged knowledge through learning and integrating the knowledge in the software as well as its usage. This trigger also results in socialization, where questions are raised to clarify and add to the subject. An example of a constructive learning trigger can be found in the following extract:

SD A: Is it a standard wage? You can have multiple standard wages such as London living wage. You can put pay on hold. So you know when the customer.... just going to get SD B up to speed.

HR A: So that is going to be the annual basic pay, sorry, the FTA (in full) isn't it? Oh no, it's going to be FTM (in full).

SD A: Yea.

HR A: Because over here you have the percentage haven't you. So will it work out?

SD A: I don't know, we need to ask SD B.

HR A: Because otherwise there is a lot of room for error.

SD A: The pro rata bit didn't work, the rest did. The standard hours need to be calculated to see hourly rate by default (on screen).

When SD A explains the pay by period page to the HR consultants, constructive learning takes place. This allowed HR A to process the gained knowledge and externalize what had not yet been understood. Externalization of knowledge can also confirm newly gained knowledge. SD A explains payments, which then triggers HR A to confirm the name of annual basic pay, FTM.

Constructive learning can also be task related; another extract shows the customer as well as the HR team are trying to understand what data can be fed into the system and how it should be structured. This allows an interplay between constructive learning and conversational triggers, which can also be found in the extract above, where knowledge surfaces by teaching as well as learning and ultimately an understanding of an issue of the project is achieved.

Visual, conversational and constructive learning triggers interplay in some of the extracts. While the software pages are being shown, conversations are being triggered and furthered within the group. This also allows constructive learning to take place. Conversational triggers can also often be triggered by visual triggers. During another meeting, the recruitment page in the software triggers a conversation on how the employees are ordered, by usage or alphabetically. Here, the visually, explicitly gained knowledge triggers a thought process within each individual, which is then turned into a conversation where knowledge surfaces through discussion.

Anticipation Triggers

An anticipation trigger allows an individual to raise a topic within the group, which he or she had waited or hesitated to address. The trigger surfaces through a similar topic of discussion and allows a change of topic. In this case, the project member plans to talk about a subject during the meeting, and waits for a moment to bring it up. This is not to be put in direct comparison to a "to-do-list" or minutes, where the subjects of discussion are being listed before a meeting and discussed one after the other, but rather allows another issue to emerge through its similarity. It can surface during externalization or socialization.

During the extract shown in the conversation trigger section, SR A was anticipating discussing payroll during the meeting, but a conversational trigger allowed the finance topic to emerge. Another example of an anticipation trigger is demonstrated in an extract, which builds on a previous meeting where HR A asks to run through the 360 feedback. Here an email was sent to the group about the topic. It was not necessarily planned to discuss the topic; however, HR A specifically asks CL A to explain and run through the process. This built on the previous meeting between SD A and HR A found in the extract below:

SD A: Now we are getting into linked records - we have done the core records. We talked about name changing, to be the item type: appraisal type; standard appraisal; 360 appraisals; and scoring appraisal. So this is something to look at with SD B tomorrow.

HR A: My thoughts on the whole are that we will probably have to change some of that, but I am not quite sure to what yet, until we start building the form, and then work through every stage of the process. I think it will become clearer.

SD A: Is there something from the old software that could make it clearer?

HR A: No, because they currently don't use it. I've got draft one of the questionnaire done now, which I would be happy to send to you but it hasn't even been checked by CL A yet. While we're at it, you know we talked about the summary of the feedback and SD B asked what kind of format you wanted it in? We just got some off the internet that CL A quite likes - do you want them now or should I give them to SD B?

SD A: To SD B -the feedback is in the process engine, so that's his / her part.

Anticipation triggers are the least commonly found triggers within the data. The meetings were usually structured around a specific topic of the software, which was addressed. Unlike recall triggers, where knowledge pops up, anticipation triggers build around the notion of waiting to discuss a topic when the meeting allows the subject to come up.

Recall Triggers

Recall triggers surface when a topic of discussion or a visual trigger allows an individual to remember knowledge related to the subject which seemed forgotten or not shared in its entirety. This trigger can occur during any stage of the tacit knowledge process. New gained knowledge is processed through several steps, when it is initially heard or seen, and combined with existing knowledge; or when it is transformed into explicit knowledge and shared with the group, recall triggers can emerge. This can change previously shared knowledge and alter the conversation. These triggers are of significance due to the knowledge almost being forgotten and often not being able to surface, as well as the knowledge being at risk of not being shared in its entirety or differently; this could change the outcome of parts of the project:

SD A: So they might have a monthly London weighting allowance. What do you pay by period?

HR A: They have a clothing allowance and a first aid allowance.

SD A: So those sort of things. So it has a name, pay by period name, it has a pay type, it has a period it can fall into. It has to be authorized.

HR A: Every period?

SD A: Every payment has to be authorized. Sorry yes, it is authorized on their account and then it's generated into weekly or monthly payroll as it gets signed off.

HR A: Would you only put in payments for that month or put in something for future months?

SD A: ...you put it in as a go ahead, so when you set it up you select if it is set up for just once or if it runs every month.... For example, season tickets run over 10 or 12 months.

During the above extract, SD A explains the monthly allowance page to the HR consultants and during this discussion, HR A asks how allowances are authorized. SD A first replies quickly, but then goes into more detail when recalling that the short answer was not sufficient to understand the authorization process. This internalisation process allowed SD A to clarify and further the discussion. Recall triggers can also be minimal, where an individual mistakes one thing for another. In another extract, validating recall triggers, HR A recalls a conversation from the day before and combines the current topic and processes with the previously gained bureau knowledge to fill in gaps of knowledge.

In addition, more evidence was found in an incident where HR A confuses FTA with FTM, which is a tacit process where, through knowledge recall, the initial thought is corrected. In the extract above HR A recalls previously gained work knowledge and shares it with the project members. The conversation focuses on recruitment, where HR C is the recruitment expert within the group. HR A's knowledge is triggered through HR C's uncertainties and is able to add valuable knowledge, having previously worked in the field.

Recall triggers are quite frequent throughout the meetings and they are often found in combination with conversations, constructive learning and visual stimuli. Recall triggers are an internal tacit process where knowledge 'pops up' at random. This might be related, as well as unrelated, to the discussed topic. This trigger allows an individual to communicate knowledge, which is recalled in order to further the knowledge exchange within the group, and thereby enhance group tacit knowledge. Figure 3 shows the number of triggers (left–hand 'y' axis) by category ('x' axis) found in the analysed conversational data. Conversational triggers were the most frequent, meaning that within a conversation newly gained knowledge allowed new knowledge to surface. This is followed by constructive learning triggers, visual triggers, recall triggers and anticipation triggers.

The triggers found through the research demonstrate the need to allow the creation of a knowledge-sharing place within a company as well as teams. These spaces should help teams find a safe environment which supports knowledge exchange and allows the experts within the team to share and build on each other's knowledge. Using different means throughout the meetings can also help trigger expert knowledge to surface, allowing more knowledge to spiral and build.

In Figure 4, the creation of knowledge and its relationship to trigger points is shown. It is evident that, in absolute terms, conversational triggers allow group tacit knowledge (Group TK) to surface the most. Constructive learning and visual triggers are the second and third respectively. It can also be seen that knowledge combination is the least likely to surface via these triggers, whereas socialization, internalization and group tacit knowledge were the strongest tacit knowledge exchange factors. The model helps understand the trigger points and their importance to tacit knowledge exchange.

Figure 3. Tacit knowledge triggers found in the analysed data

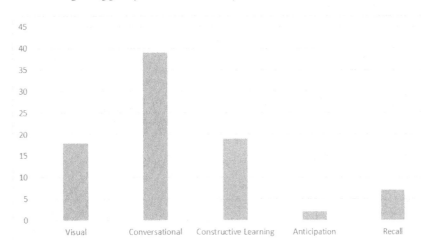

Figure 4. Knowledge creation and its relationship to trigger points

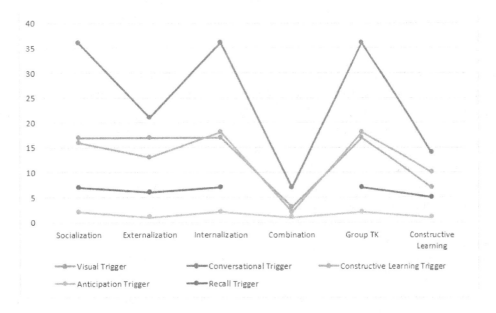

Tacit knowledge triggers allow the exchange of expert knowledge in an organization. In the five-phase model of Nonaka and Takeuchi (1995), the process of tacit knowledge in relation to the market can be seen (Figure 5). This allows a view of the continuous cycle of sharing tacit knowledge within a company. From sharing tacit knowledge, creating concepts, justifying concepts, building an archetype and cross-levelling knowledge, the internalization process is shown. This process helps the triggers find their place in the knowledge creation process.

Figure 5. Five phase model of the organisation knowledge creation process

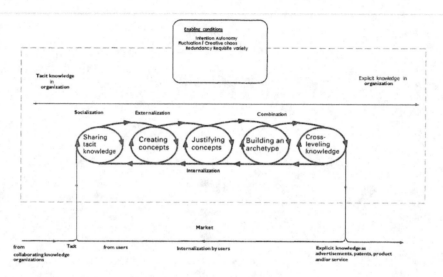

Source: Nonaka and Takeuchi (1995, p.84)

In summary, this research project discovered and described the development of five types of triggers that are episodic moments for tacit knowledge conversion. The different triggers that emerged through the research were:

1. **Visual Triggers:** Tacit knowledge surfacing through visual stimuli;
2. **Conversational Triggers:** Tacit knowledge surfaces through a conversation held within the team;
3. **Constructive Learning Triggers:** Tacit knowledge is enabled through a team member explaining and the others learning from them;
4. **Anticipation Triggers:** Tacit knowledge was exchanged by an individual in the group by waiting for the topic to come up or the meeting to take place;
5. **Recall Triggers:** Tacit knowledge resurfaces through discussions or visual aids, which seemed forgotten or not present by an individual.

Appreciating the role of triggers in the situated learning of software teams is a significant contribution to the understanding of how group knowledge emerges. This will also help researchers further understand the impact tacit knowledge has on project success. It is important to interpret and analyse knowledge adequately in software projects to prevent misconceptions (McAfee, 2003). Using an appreciation of a developed theory of triggers can help project teams focus on exchanging and exploring knowledge from different perspectives. Constructive learning within the group, as well as discussions to further understand the software and exploring the knowledge input from each individual are crucial for a project to succeed.

However, these moments can only be created within a dynamic environment in which an exchange of knowledge is supported by the project team. Spending time together as a team and working together is at the core of knowledge creation and transfer. Seeing the project develop over time allows strategies to surface and be applied during the software development process (Vitalari & Dickson, 1983). Bouncing ideas off one another, and subsequent mutual learning, furthers the knowledge creation process. This allows each individual to take in more knowledge and provide a better, more complete view of the subject and enables the prospect of more complete software to emerge.

In relation to categorizing these triggers, Heidegger (1992) notes that Aristotle identifies five modes bringing things into "truthful safekeeping" (p. 377). So anticipation triggers, for example, are self-reflective, in that becoming aware of them allows their incorporation into group discussion. The modes are detailed below (Table 1) and it is possible to map the triggers against these modes. It should be noted that these modes are not mutually exclusive; some modes are combinations of others.

Table 1. Phenomenology of trigger types

routine-directive-productive operating	Conversational triggers are those that become involved with productive operating towards the work
observing-discussing-revealing determination	Constructive learning triggers are those where there is merit in further discussion about the issue.
solicitous circumspecting (circumspection)	Anticipation triggers are those where an issue needs to be brought out in advance from the work.
authentic-seeing understanding	Visual Triggers that stem from the productive observation of the material at hand.
pure beholding	Recall Triggers occur when knowledge is retained and becomes part of intelligent application.

CONCLUSION AND IMPLICATIONS

The aim of the paper was to further understand and progress the field of knowledge transfer and its triggers within a software development environment. This initial objective gave rise to a new theoretical idea. The conversion of tactile skills is not the crucial element in the development of group knowledge. From the empirical data conducted for this study, the process of externalisation can be considered as being with Mitsein and the joint presence of the expert group allows their presence to be a noematic bridge. The basis of expert meetings is not therefore one of discussion but the emergence of new presentations by the participants. This emergent expertise is the refinement of the phenomenological essences of what is needed to deliver the combined knowledge. This framework, based on a phenomenological approach, will aid the implementation of managerial judgement in expert group sessions. Possessing an awareness of these distinctions will facilitate knowledge capture. How they emerge opens the way to further research into what makes tacit knowledge surface within groups. Appreciating them as breaks in the flow of the project that generate knowledge is important; together with this, they are an opportunity to understand in a better way the mind of the other. Heidegger indicates that practical revealing is "a factical relationship of concern with respect to the world which is just encountered" (Heidegger, 1992, p.382). His further work resonates with this theme where the Scientist, Scholar, and Guide continue to discuss the relationship between determination, speculation, and authentic seeing (Heidegger, 2010, pp.5-6). This structure provides for valuing the unexpected, and what Berends and Antonacopoulou (2014) call "surprises", as they are not always in accord with the espoused aims of the project. This allows managers the opportunity to create environments, in which this personal knowledge can surface and be shared within the teams.

This research highlights how interaction (seen as a "noematic bridge" in terms of a shared learning conversation) with the knowledge triggers can be productive. Taylor (2004) sees triggers as risk factors, and whilst they may delay project completion, an appreciation of the operation of triggers will enable the team learning to be incorporated within an appropriate timescale. Varying the context of the project team as well as testing the triggers on day-to-day working groups can shed light on tacit knowledge triggers. This study has found that recognizing phase changes in project temporality allows managers to appreciate the knowledge gained from extempore interjections. The development of awareness of triggers in a dynamic environment helps the comprehension of expert knowledge exchange in software projects. Understating the knowledge a team has, and aiding its emergence through exchange, can ultimately lead to more productive outcomes for software development teams, and will contribute to successful and well-functioning products. The value of such an approach to the creation of knowledge is to see the concept of truth not as correctness towards the object, because in this situation it remains indeterminate. The alternative view is to see truth as non-concealment - it brings forward that which remains hidden. Using the framework to identify triggers, in the form of modes of knowing, is an approach that reveals the personal knowledge that indicates and reveals the unspoken assumptions about the objects in use discussed above. Further investigation into knowledge sharing and interaction between software project groups will help to validate the triggers.

REFERENCES

Banacu, C. S., Busu, C., & Nedelcu, A. C. (2013). Tacit Knowledge Management – Strategic Role in Disclosing the Intellectual Capital. *Proceedings of the International Management Conference*, *7*(1), 491-500, November.

Bartolacci, C., Cristalli, C., Isidori, D., & Niccolini, F. (2016). Ba virtual and inter-organizational evolution: A case study from an EU research project. *Journal of Knowledge Management*, *20*(4), 793–811. doi:10.1108/JKM-09-2015-0342

Benner, A. (2008). *Work in the New Economy: Flexible Labor Markets in Silicon Valley.* DOI: doi:10.1002/9780470696163

Berends, H., & Antonacopoulou, E. (2014). Time and Organizational Learning: A Review and Agenda for Future Research. *International Journal of Management Reviews*, *16*(4), 437–453. doi:10.1111/ijmr.12029

Berends, H., & Lammers, I. (2010). Explaining Discontinuity in Organizational Learning: A Process Analysis. *Organization Studies*, *31*(8), 1045–1068. doi:10.1177/0170840610376140

Berger, P., & Luckmann, T. (1967). *The Social Construction of Reality*. New York: Anchor.

Clancy, T. (2006). *The Standish Group Report Chaos*. New York: ACM.

Clarke, T. (2010). *The development of a tacit knowledge spectrum based on the interrelationships between tacit and explicit knowledge*. Retrieved March 9 2019 from https://repository.cardiffmet.ac.uk/bitstream/handle/10369/909/T%20Clarke.pdf

Cunningham, J. A., Menter, M., & Young, C. (2017). A review of qualitative case methods trends and themes used in technology transfer research. *The Journal of Technology Transfer*, *42*(4), 923–956. doi:10.100710961-016-9491-6

De Souza, K., Awazu, Y., & Baloh, P. (2006). Managing Knowledge in Global Software Development Efforts, Issues and Practices. *IEEE Software*, *23*(5), 30–37. doi:10.1109/MS.2006.135

Dreyer, H. (2018). *Tacit Knowledge in a Software Development Project* (PhD Thesis). University of Gloucestershire. Available at: http://eprints.glos.ac.uk/6441/1/PhD%20Thesis_Tacit%20Knowledge%20in%20a%20Software%20Development%20Project_Hanna%20Dreyer_redacted_personal_information.pdf

Dreyer, H., & Wynn, M. (2016). Tacit and Explicit Knowledge in Software Development Projects: A Combined Model for Analysis. *International Journal on Advances in Software*, *9*(3&4), 154–166.

Engeström, Y., Kerosuo, H., & Kajamaa, A. (2007). Beyond discontinuity: Expansive organizational learning remembered. *Management Learning*, *38*(3), 319–336. doi:10.1177/1350507607079032

Fischer, G., & Ostwald, J. (2001). Knowledge management: Problems promises realities and challenges. *IEEE Intelligent Systems*, *16*(1), 60–72. doi:10.1109/5254.912386

Hartley, J. (2004). *Case Study Research*. London: Sage.

Heidegger, M. (1992). Phenomenological interpretations with respect to Aristotle: Indication of the hermeneutical situation. *Continental Philosophy Review*, *25*(3–4), 355–393.

Heidegger, M. (2001). *Zollikon Seminars: Protocols - Conversations – Letters*. Evanston: Northwestern University Press.

Heidegger, M. (2010). *Country Path Conversations*. Bloomington: Indiana University Press.

Heidegger, M. (2015). *Being and Truth*. Bloomington: University Press.

Hodgson, J., & Drummond, H. (2009). Learning from fiasco: What causes decision error and how to avoid it? *Journal of General Management*, *35*(2), 81–92. doi:10.1177/030630700903500206

Husserl, E. (2012). Ideas. London: Routledge. (Original publication 1931)

Langford, T., & Poteat, W. (1968). Upon first sitting down to read Personal Knowledge: an introduction. In Intellect and Hope: Essays in the thought of Michael Polanyi, (pp. 3-18). Academic Press.

Leybourne, S., & Kennedy, M. (2015). Learning to Improvise, or Improvising to Learn: Knowledge Generation and Innovative Practice. *Knowledge and Process Management, 22*(1), 1–10. doi:10.1002/kpm.1457

Marouf, L., & Khalil, O. (2015). The Influence of Individual Characteristics on Knowledge Sharing Practices Enablers and Barriers in a Project Management Context. *International Journal of Knowledge Management, 11*(1), 1–27. doi:10.4018/IJKM.2015010101

McAfee, A. (2003, Winter). When too much IT knowledge is a dangerous thing. *MIT Sloane Management Review*, 83-89.

Nonaka, I., & Konno, N. (1998). The concept of 'Ba': Building a foundation for knowledge creation. *California Management Review, 40*(3), 40–54. doi:10.2307/41165942

Nonaka, I., & Takeuchi, H. (1995). *The Knowledge Creating Company*. Oxford: Oxford University Press.

Nonaka, I., & Teece, D. (2001). *Managing Industrial Knowledge*. London: Sage.

Polanyi, M. (1962). *Personal Knowledge*. London: Routledge.

Rabanaque, L. R. (2010). The Body as Noematic Bridge Between Nature and Culture. In P. Vandevelde & S. Luft (Eds.), *Epistemology, archaeology, ethics: current investigations of Husserl's Corpus* (pp. 41–52). London: Continuum.

Riain, S. O. (2009). Extending the Ethnographic Case Study. In D. Byrne & C. C. Ragin (Eds.), *The Sage Handbook of Case Based Methods* (pp. 289–306). London: Sage. doi:10.4135/9781446249413.n17

Ryan, S., & O'Connor, R. V. (2013). Acquiring and sharing tacit knowledge in software development teams: An empirical study. *Information and Software Technology, 55*(9), 1614–1624. doi:10.1016/j.infsof.2013.02.013

Scharmer, C. (2001). Self-transcending knowledge: Sensing and organizing around emerging opportunities. *Journal of Knowledge Management, 5*(2), 137–150. doi:10.1108/13673270110393185

Silverman, D. (2013). *Doing Qualitative Research*. London: Sage.

Taylor, H. A. (2004). *Risk management and tacit knowledge in IT projects: making the implicit explicit* (PhD thesis). Queensland University of Technology. Retrieved March 8 2019 from http://eprints.qut.edu.au/15907/

Valente, T. W., & Davies, R. (1999). Accelerating the diffusion of innovations using opinion leaders. *The Annals of the American Academy of Political and Social Science, 566*(1), 55–67. doi:10.1177/000271629956600105

Vitalari, N., & Dickson, G. (1983). Problem solving for effective systems analysis: An experiential exploration. *Communications of the Association for Information Systems, 26*(11), 948–956.

White, G., Parry, G., & Puckering, A. (2016). Knowledge acquisition in information system development: A case study of system developers in an international bank. *Strategic Change, 25*(1), 81–95. doi:10.1002/jsc.2048

Wynn, M. (2018). Technology Transfer Projects in the UK: An Analysis of University-Industry Collaboration. *International Journal of Knowledge Management, 14*(2), 52-72.

Yin, R. K. (2009). *Case Study Research Design and Methods*. London: Sage.

This research was previously published in the International Journal of Knowledge Management (IJKM), 16(2); pages 1-17, copyright year 2020 by IGI Publishing (an imprint of IGI Global).

Chapter 29
A Customized Quality Model for Software Quality Assurance in Agile Environment

Parita Jain

Amity Institute of Information Technology, Amity University, Noida, India

Arun Sharma

Department of Information Technology, Indira Gandhi Delhi Technical University for Women, Delhi, India

Laxmi Ahuja

Amity Institute of Information Technology, Amity University, Noida, India

ABSTRACT

The agile approach grew dramatically over traditional approaches. The methodology focuses more on rapid development, quick evaluation, quantifiable progress and continuous delivery satisfying the customer desire. In view of this, there is a need for measurement of the agile development process. In this respect, the present research work investigates the inter-relationships and inter-dependencies between the identified quality factors (QF), thereby outlining which of these QF have high driving power and dependence power, working indirectly towards the success of agile development process. This paper proposes a new agile quality model, utilizing an interpretive structural modeling (ISM) approach and the identified factors are classifies using Matriced' Impacts Croise's Multiplication Applique'e a UN Classement (MICMAC) approach. The research findings can significantly impact agile development process by understanding how these QF related to each other and how they can be adopted.

DOI: 10.4018/978-1-6684-3702-5.ch029

INTRODUCTION

From the past few years, the focus is more on to enhance software development practices by improving reusability, understandability of requirements, software delivery time and cost-effectiveness and many other characteristics. Quality being the most important aspect either in discrete production process or continuous production process, needs to be focused more to deliver a product that is acceptable by customers. According to International Standard Organization ISO 9000, quality is defined as the totality of characteristics of a product as a whole to satisfy the stated and implied needs in accordance with its capability. Here the stated needs mean the requirements that are given by the customer at the time of an agreement, and the implied needs are the needs that are identified by the developers as the necessary needs to be included while developing the product. Definition of quality has been perceived differently by various persons, but the one that has been given by the customer is the definition that counts the most. Quality corresponds to standards, cost of the product, conformance to requirements and value for performance (Juran & Gryna, 2010; Weinberg, 1992).

Overall quality is the much more complicated term than it appears. There are varieties of perspectives for consideration, for example, customer's perspective, developer's perspective, tester's perspective, specification based perspective, manufacturing based perspective, quality assurance based perspective and many more. In every single domain, quality is one of the most important factors for a product to survive in the market. Many more definitions are given by different researchers from the perspective of manufacturing the product and engineering the product respectively. Definition of quality has a contextual bias towards these two industries. A general definition is possible for all the areas; however, when applying to IT software products the context is slightly different. Some of the authors named as Meyer (2000), Pressman (2011), and Sommerville (2015) states' software quality differently but from the same perspective towards software product. The quality of the development process significantly affects the value received by customers and development teams. Hence, for high quality product it's important to concentrate more on development process as development of good quality software is usually an organizational effort, "something of higher quality has more value than of low quality".

Need of Quality Model for Agile

Over the years, developers found that for development the traditional software development methodologies proving to be a, "well defined process for development" work poorly in practice. Moreover, from the literature, it appears that developers are not more interested to adopt traditional processes and are finding ways to reduce efforts to adopt them either intentionally or unintentionally. With the escalation in quality software's, specifying relevant development process is a necessity. Assimilating agile methodology process for development is a good option to counter ever escalating software complexity. Software organizations are ready to accept the quick approach for developing software with the availability of resources, unable to do so due to uncertainty of proving agile process quality. Initially, when introduced agile methodology was applicable on small-scale projects where the methodology proved as a best practice for software development but with the increase in utility the agile methodology also applicable on large-scale projects.

It has been observed that agile methodology is the best practice so far for developing quality software but quantification of quality parameters is still a major challenge. Besides this, in current scenario, expectations of customers, stakeholders and need of quality changed significantly. The agile methodology emerged because of two significant characteristics, as follows: firstly, it can handle customer changing needs throughout the software development life cycle (SDLC). Secondly, it can release software in shorter time with right delivery strategy within the defined cost.

The paper proposes a quality model, derived using a two stage approach. Firstly, critical quality factors (QF) are identified through a survey of literature and expert opinions from the industry, working within the field of agile development from last many years. Furthermore, the methodology interpretive structural modeling is used to develop a structural model to identify how each QF interacts with each other. Thereafter, an analysis based on driving power and dependence power is done and the QF are further categorized according to the MICMAC approach. Present study attempts to find inter-relationships and inter-dependencies between QF in agile development process which will help in identifying which QF have greater driving or dependence power than others and are thus critical quality factors towards agile development process success.

LITERATURE REVIEW: THE FOUNDATION OF ANALYSIS

As software industry adopted agile software development methodology, it becomes inevitable to *distinctly* outline its characteristics, benefits and organizational ramifications. The agile methodology emerged as a lightweight methodology for development. It offers many benefits, such as customer involvement, greater reusability, iterative and incremental perspective of software. Various approaches are proposed and had some extent of success in improving software quality, usability, efficiency, maintainability and helping many organizations to develop large complex software's on different platforms. However, still organizations face enormous problems while developing software's.

Timperi (2004) focused on quality assurance practices of different agile methodologies providing study towards lack of balance in quality assurance activities for producing good-quality software. He found that an agile methodology proposes various quality assurance practices, excluding testing as an important factor for quality assurance. Furthermore, he concluded that none of the agile practices had any pragmatic evidence for quality assurance work in the process itself. Mnkandla and Dwolatzky (2006) in their paper stated that in existing literature, there has not been any evidence that provides an aspect of software quality improvement as the basis of any software quality characteristics. For this purpose, an innovative technique in the form of a tool has been introduced and tested on two agile methodologies' XP and lean development, determining which factors of software quality they improve. Hashmi and Baik (2007) provided an overview on quality assurance practices of the agile processes. The study reveals that still there are ongoing debates on the flexibility to change, productivity and quality of agile methodology processes. In depth, they compare XP practices with traditional spiral model from the perspective of ensuring product quality, built in QA practices in SDLC of XP and productiveness.

A literature reviewed up to 2009 given by Sfetsos and Stamelos (2010) identified 535 studies of which 46 were found to be empirical studies regarding agile practices as a quality process. They classified their study into three clusters to evaluate quality perspective in agile methodologies. The findings from the study show that if agile practices have implemented in a correct manner, they can improve product quality. In addition, they reported wide range of improvements in various phases of agile practices in order to provide good-quality software. Based on the existing literature, the authors Imreh and Raisinghani (2011) found that not much research has been done in the field of quality of agile software development. Some of the IT organizations found the new practices that are successful, but some of the experiences showed them as less successful. The paper provided a study that focuses more on the quality aspects rather than the technical aspects of agile development.

Besides the several recent studies claiming very less work for quality of agile approaches, sufficient studies are there that proves popularity of different practices within agile methodologies and comparison between them showing again the lack of quality aspects in all of them. Galvan et al. (2015) presented a study that provides an overview of at what ratio SCRUM and XP agile methodologies coping up with ISO/IEC 2911 standard. The study shows that software developers are more interested in acceptance with project management in SCRUM and XP practices and less care about software implementation, which will indirectly, affects the quality of the software product. The work done by Torgeir and Lassenius (2016) focused on emerging practices in agile software development. There is an increase in interest on continuous integration from 2006 to 2015 in usage of some of the practices. The Scrum being the most popular practices; more research has been done on the Scrum practices in comparison to Extreme programming and other agile practices. They also identified some of the key research areas that can be taken up in the future as a significant area of study such as focus on an organization processes, product value and many more.

A systematic review of large-scale agile transformations from traditional to agile practices conducted by Dikert et al. (2016) identifying 35 reported challenges grouped into nine categories and 29 success factors grouped into 11 categories. The study presents that still agile methodology lacks behind in some of the categories that reported as most important ones and research is seriously lagging behind with the growing adoption of agile practices for software development. Another paper presented by Papadopoulos (2015) focuses on how well light weight agile methodologies perform better than heavy weight software development methodologies. With the analysis of a case study author found evidence for the same. With the effectiveness of agile over traditional, he also observed that still there is a scope of improvement in the quality aspect and customer perception aspect of the end product in agile practices. Indicating on growing need of agile practices within the software industry for the development of software rather than adopting heavy weight traditional practices, review of an ample number of research papers presented by Jain et al. (2016) discussed that the traditional development incorporates a QA (quality assurance) factors in the process while in agile methodologies, there is no separate QA factor that must be taken care of, they just rely on routine activities of the development team for QA of the process and product. Hence, still there is a need to deal with backlogs of quality assurance for agile practices.

Focusing on lack of quality aspects, various studies have been carried out to overcome with this problem. For this Opelt and Beeson (2008) provided steps to integrate QA into the agile process. As the study shows that agile processes did not include QA into practices because of the reason that QA might slow down the software development process. They further discussed why the role of QA is important for balancing quality of product with the needs of the business. Some of the researchers in addition presented a quality evaluation scheme that focuses on the reliability aspect of software quality in iterative agile development based on traditional metrics. Jinzenji et al. (2013) presented this scheme due to the lack of management of software quality in agile methodologies. At the end with the experimental results, they showed that traditional metrics quality evaluation scheme can be applicable on iterative development from the aspect of conventional reliability metrics only.

Olszewska et al. (2016) presented a metrics model to measure quantitatively the influence of agile methodologies' adoption for software development in organizations. The study done, also showed that lot of research has been done on the adoption of agile practices but in the form of success stories and case studies, mostly of qualitative in nature. Hence, there is a need to prove the impact of growing agile software development empirically. They used goal question metric approach providing a quantitative metrics model declaring significant improvements in 6 of the metrics and decline in one of the metrics taken in study. Finding the limitations of agile practices in industry subjectively Agarwal et al. (2016) applied ANNOVA test based on the online survey provided by agile experienced professionals to satisfy the literature quantitatively. According to the literature, they found out one of the major flaws in adopting agile methods, lacked of upfront planning which overall effects the process quality and product quality both.

Among the literature that exists, very few agile quality models are presented and evaluated in a universal manner for agile practices. Sanghoon Jeon et al. (2011) focused on the roadblocks of SCRUM methodology. With the literature, they found fall in the use of SCRUM practices in the aspect that it only concentrates on functional features rather it should also target on software quality aspects. Due to this reason they presented a new quality attribute driven agile development method named ACRUM that is derived from SCRUM practices including quality aspects as well. The model proposed proves to be efficient, but it can only be used on behalf of SCRUM practice. One cannot take the proposed quality model on behalf of all the agile practices that are used for software development in industries.

Bajnaid et al. (2012) addressed the shortcomings of agile practices of not including quality assurance as a part of their process to ensure whether the quality assurance process has been followed and quality assurance standards have been met or not. To overcome the disadvantages, they proposed a process driven e-learning system that senses developer's activities and guides them through required software quality assurance practices while development of the software. Another framework proposed by Sagheer et al. (2015) as a solution to an issue of analyzing whether quality has been assured in the software which is being developed using agile software development methodology and recapitulate that how quality can be assured in agile practices using different quality factors. Discussing the limitations of various quality models proposed previously in the paper, Jain et al. (2016) presented a new framework for measuring agile process quality using an interpretive structural modeling approach so that developers can focus their efforts on the identified attributes for deploying higher-quality products. The model identified the most critical factors important for agile quality development but did not provide any empirical solution for evaluating the quality. That is, there is a need to measure the proposed model. Additionally, the model did not include factors on which agile practices actually depends upon.

Various quality models have been proposed taking quality perspective into account as a whole for software development but still organizations are in a way for finding out a solution for agile quality assurance. Hence, there is a need for a quality model that includes all the important factors of the agile development process on which distinct practices of agile development depend, verifying the model to be holistically substantiated for all the defined agile practices.

Approaches for Decision Making

Interpretive Structural Modeling is a well establish methodology used for depicting interrelationship among varied variables that define the problem to be solved. It is one of the popular techniques that have been used for multi-criteria decision making in different fields of research. The literature, in the contrary presents different other approaches like analytic network process (ANP), analytic hierarchy process (AHP), decision making trial and evaluation laboratory (DEMATEL) and many more techniques that are useful in almost all problems related to decision making. Several review papers are present in the literature which elaborate distinctive methods of multi-criteria decision making. However, these papers mainly include the comparison between different multi-criteria decision making methods, as well as their applications in various fields of research.

Velasquez and Hester (2013) provide an analysis of commonly used multi-criteria decision making (MCDM) methods, identifying their advantages and disadvantages and explaining how these methods can be used, in particular, applications. Majumder (2015) focuses on basic working principle of different MCDM methods and specifically identifies limitations of AHP method. Gayatri and Chetan (2013) also provide the comparison of varying MCDM methods, which are gaining importance for solving a specific problem. Thakkar et al. (2008) have compared three MCDM techniques, ISM, ANP and AHP and extract various advantages of ISM in unusual areas for modeling and solving decision making problems over other two techniques. Many researchers reviewed and compared different MCDM methods and found ISM as a method of solving problems, which are subjective in nature, has higher ability for capturing dynamic complexities, proving ISM approach better than other decision making approaches.

PROPOSED AGILE QUALITY MODEL

The quality model proposed for agile development refers to all the agile quality attributes or factors that must be included within the model to assure quality of the agile practices, and the product deployed after processing. With the identified quality factors based on literature review and experts' opinions from the software industry, working within the field of agile development from last many years, a new quality model based on ISO 9126-1 is proposed in the present paper. The model proposed after specifying the quality factors and applying ISM approach to establish interrelationships among these recognized factors and extracting an overall tree-like structure, which further portrays a hierarchical structure model. After that, a MICMAC analysis approach is applied that provides insight on the impact of quality factors in a holistic way. The step by step procedure for developing a model is shown in Figure 1.

Figure 1. Step by step procedure

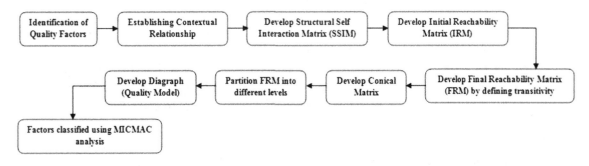

For the present work, ISO/IEC 9126-1 standard quality model introduced by ISO and IEC in 2001 is taken as a basis. The model includes six quality factors, identifying both internal and external characteristics of the software product. Factors that are taken as important factors for quality assurance are functionality, reliability, usability, efficiency, maintainability and portability. ISO/IEC 25010:2011 is a quality model that replaces ISO/IEC 9126-1:2001 quality model, which has been technically revised after ISO/IEC 9126:1991. This model is also a part of SQuaRE series of international standards. In comparison with ISO/IEC 9126, the model ISO/IEC 25010:2011 incorporates security and compatibility with the existing characteristics as amendments in the model (Al-Qutaish & Al-Sarayreh, 2008; Idri et al., 2013; Samadhiya et al., 2010).

The proposed agile quality model specifically based upon ISO/IEC 9126-1 quality model, as when analyzed, it has been identified that only four of the quality characteristics can be taken up, for solving the defined problem or issue, validating the process quality of agile methodologies. For this, ISM is applied on the identified 19 quality factors and at the end a customized agile quality model is proposed in the form of a hierarchal structural model. ISM is an interactive learning process used to identify the structural model that illustrates inter-relationships among identified 19 quality factors (Jain et al., 2016).

Step 1: It starts with an identification of QF, which are applicable to the defined problem or issue (Sohani & Sohani, 2012). Then the contextual relationship between the QF is determined with respect to which inter-relationships and inter-dependencies are chosen. Initially, literature survey and brainstorming with industry expert's opinion was used to develop the initial matrix Structural Self Interaction Matrix (SSIM) as depicted in Figure 2, where each symbol has some meaning to it according to the symbol interpretation as shown in Table 1.

Step 2: Replacing each cell in SSIM by binary numbers' 0s or 1s, an Initial Reachability Matrix (IRM) is developed based on the rules defined in Table 2.

Step 3: Then Final Reachability Matrix (FRM) is obtained, defining the transitivity which states that, if any variable A is related to variable B and variable B is related to variable C then A is related to C. The FRM for the given QF is depicted in Figure 3 where the value 1* depict transitivity.

Step 4: Thereafter, Driving Power and Dependence of QF are calculated. The Driving Power of the factors' is derived by summing the entries of one in the rows and the Dependence of the factors' is derived by summing the entries of 1's in the columns. The matrix obtained called as Conical Matrix as shown in Figure 4.

Step 5: To achieve Level Partitioning of the QF in agile development process, the Final Reachability Matrix undergoes recurrent iterations. In Agile Development Process, it was achieved in five iterations thus; partitioning of the QF in five levels is depicted in Table 3.

Step 6: Then according to the levels identified, a diagraph is developed showing the hierarchal dependence of quality factors. The QF having minimum influence gets isolated first and is placed at the top of the diagraph. While on the other hand, the QF having the maximum influence hold till the last and placed at the bottom of the diagraph. The diagraph illustrates how the QF influence each other and how QF are influenced by others. The diagraph portrays an "Agile Quality Model" describing the hierarchal inter-dependence between the quality factors in agile development process. This is represented in Figure 5.

Step 7: After structuring QF in levels, MICMAC analysis is performed based on Driving Power and Dependence of QF in agile development process. The analysis is based on cross-impact matrix multiplication and classifies the critical agile quality factors into four clusters, named as Autonomous, Dependent, Linkage and Driving.

Table 1. SSIM symbol interpretation

Symbol	Meaning	Interpretation
V	$i \longrightarrow j$	variable i influence variable j
A	$j \longrightarrow i$	variable j influence variable i
X	$i \longleftrightarrow j$	variable i and j influence each other
O	$i \longleftrightarrow j$	variable i and j will not influence each other

Table 2. Rules for converting SSIM to IRM

Symbol	Rules for replacement
V	(i, j)th entry becomes 1 and (j, i)th entry becomes 0
A	(j, i)th entry becomes 1 and (i, j)th entry becomes 0
X	(i, j)th entry becomes 1 and (j, i)th entry also becomes 1
O	(i, j)th entry becomes 0 and (j, i)th entry also becomes 0

Figure 2. Structural self interaction matrix for QF in agile development process

		QF1	QF2	QF3	QF4	QF5	QF6	QF7	QF8	QF9	QF10	QF11	QF12	QF13	QF14	QF15	QF16	QF17	QF18	QF19
Functionality	QF1	1	O	A	A	A	X	A	V	A	A	V	A	A	V	A	O	O	A	A
Committed Story Points	QF2		1	X	O	V	O	X	O	V	O	O	V	O	V	V	V	O	O	O
Total Numbers of User Stories	QF3			1	V	V	O	V	O	V	V	O	V	O	O	O	V	O	V	O
Functional Completeness	QF4				1	A	O	A	A	A	A	X	V	O	O	O	X	O	A	O
Sprint Stretch Factor	QF5					1	V	A	V	X	V	V	V	V	V	A	O	A	V	O
Efficiency	QF6						1	O	O	A	X	O	O	O	A	X	A	X	X	X
User Stories Planned	QF7							1	O	O	X	O	V	O	O	V	V	V	X	O
Post Delivery Defects	QF8								1	X	A	X	O	A	X	O	O	O	O	X
Defect Removal Efficiency	QF9									1	V	V	X	A	O	O	O	O	O	X
User Stories Delivered	QF10										1	O	X	A	O	A	X	A	X	A
Maintainability	QF11											1	X	A	X	O	O	O	O	O
Functional Correctness	QF12												1	X	X	O	A	O	A	A
Pre Delivery Defects	QF13													1	O	O	O	A	O	A
Reliability	QF14														1	O	A	O	O	O
Planned Effort	QF15															1	O	V	X	O
Earned Story Points	QF16																1	A	O	O
Actual Effort	QF17																	1	V	O
User Stories Delivered per Sprint	QF18																		1	A
Defects Removed per Sprint	QF19																			1

VALIDATION OF THE PROPOSED MODEL

After identifying the factors and structuring them at different levels, MICMAC analysis is used for analysis purpose. It is a validation method that provides insight on the impact of factors on the total system. That is, the analysis is mainly to identify key variables or factors that are important to overall system changes. It is basically a cross-impact matrix multiplication applied to classification. MICMAC method was given by Godet (1986), which is based on cross-impact matrix multiplication used in the analysis of indirect and hidden relationships among the factors of the agile quality model obtained using ISM technique.

Figure 3. FRM for QF in agile development process

	QF1	QF2	QF3	QF4	QF5	QF6	QF7	QF8	QF9	QF10	QF11	QF12	QF13	QF14	QF15	QF16	QF17	QF18	QF19
QF1	1	0	0	0	0	1	0	1	0	0	1	0	0	1	0	0	0	0	0
QF2	1	1	1	0	1	0	1	0	1	1*	1*	1	1*	1	1	1	0	1*	0
QF3	1	1	1	1	1	1*	1	1	1	1	1*	1	1*	1*	0	1	1*	1	0
QF4	1	0	0	1	0	0	0	0	0	0	1	1	0	1*	0	1	0	0	0
QF5	1	0	0	1	1	1	0	1	1	1	1	1	1	1	0	1*	0	1	1*
QF6	1	0	0	1*	0	1	0	1*	0	1	0	0	0	0	0	1	0	1	1
QF7	1	1	0	1	1*	1*	1	0	0	1	1*	1	0	1*	1	1	1	1	0
QF8	0	0	0	1	0	0	0	1	1	0	1	0	0	1	0	0	0	0	1
QF9	1	0	0	1	1	1	0	1	1	1	1	1	0	1*	0	0	0	1*	1
QF10	1	0	0	1	0	1	1	1	0	1	1*	1	0	1*	0	1	0	1	0
QF11	1	0	0	1	0	0	0	1	0	0	1	1	0	1	0	0	0	0	0
QF12	1	0	0	0	0	1*	0	1*	1	1	1	1	1	1	0	0	0	0	0
QF13	1	0	0	1*	0	0	0	1	1	1	1	1	1	1*	0	1*	0	1*	0
QF14	0	0	0	0	0	0	0	1	0	0	1	1	0	1	0	0	0	0	0
QF15	1	0	0	1*	1	1	0	1*	1*	1	1*	1*	1*	1	1	1*	1	1	1*
QF16	1*	0	0	1	0	1	0	0	0	1	1*	1	0	1	0	1	0	0	0
QF17	1*	0	0	1	1	1	0	1*	1*	1	1*	1*	1	1	0	1	1	1	1*
QF18	1	0	0	1	0	1	1	1	0	1	1*	1	0	1*	1	1*	0	1	0
QF19	1	0	0	0	0	1	0	1	1	1	1*	1	1	1*	0	1*	0	1	1

All the quality factors have been classified into four clusters based on their Driving Power and Dependence Power as depicted in Figure 6 (Sohani & Sohani, 2012) named as:

- Autonomous or Excluded variables: The cluster includes those variables having weak driving power and weak dependence power.
- Dependent variables: The cluster includes those variables having weak driving power but strong dependence power.
- Linkage or Relay variables: The cluster includes those variables having strong driving power as well as strong dependence power.
- Independent variables: The cluster includes those variables that influence the most. That is, the variables having strong driving power but weak dependence power.

In this research work, an MICMAC software tool named as MICMAC (Identification of Keys Variables) has been used for MICMAC analysis on the proposed new agile quality model, which was developed by French Computer Innovation Institute 3IE (Institute d'Innovation Informatique pour l'Entreprise), given by LIPSOR Prospective (foresight) Strategic and Organizational Research Laboratory.

Figure 4. Conical matrix for QF in agile development process

	QF1	QF2	QF3	QF4	QF5	QF6	QF7	QF8	QF9	QF10	QF11	QF12	QF13	QF14	QF15	QF16	QF17	QF18	QF19	Driving Power
QF1	1	0	0	0	0	1	0	1	0	0	1	0	0	1	0	0	0	0	0	5
QF2	1	1	1	0	1	0	1	0	1	1*	1*	1	1*	1	1	1	0	1*	0	14
QF3	1	1	1	1	1	1*	1	1	1	1	1*	1	1*	1*	0	1	1*	1	0	17
QF4	1	0	0	1	0	0	0	0	0	0	1	1	0	1*	0	1	0	0	0	6
QF5	1	0	0	1	1	1	0	1	1	1	1	1	1	1	0	1*	0	1	1*	14
QF6	1	0	0	1*	0	1	0	1*	0	1	0	0	0	0	0	1	0	1	1	8
QF7	1	1	0	1	1*	1*	1	0	0	1	1*	1	0	1*	1	1	1	1	0	14
QF8	0	0	0	1	0	0	0	1	1	0	1	0	0	1	0	0	0	0	1	6
QF9	1	0	0	1	1	1	0	1	1	1	1	1	0	1*	0	0	0	1*	1	12
QF10	1	0	0	1	0	1	1	1	0	1	1*	1	0	1*	0	1	0	1	0	11
QF11	1	0	0	1	0	0	0	1	0	0	1	1	0	1	0	0	0	0	0	6
QF12	1	0	0	0	0	1*	0	1*	1	1	1	1	1	1	0	0	0	0	0	9
QF13	1	0	0	1*	0	0	0	1	1	1	1	1	1	1*	0	1*	0	1*	0	11
QF14	0	0	0	0	0	0	0	1	0	0	1	1	0	1	0	0	0	0	0	4
QF15	1	0	0	1*	1	1	0	1*	1*	1	1*	1*	1*	1	1	1*	1	1	1*	16
QF16	1*	0	0	1	0	1	0	0	0	1	1*	1	0	1	0	1	0	0	0	8
QF17	1*	0	0	1	1	1	0	1*	1*	1	1*	1*	1	1	0	1	1	1	1*	15
QF18	1	0	0	1	0	1	1	1	0	1	1*	1	0	1*	1	1*	0	1	0	12
QF19	1	0	0	0	0	1	0	1	1	1	1*	1	1	1*	0	1*	0	1	1	12
Dependence	17	3	2	14	7	13	5	15	10	14	18	16	8	18	4	13	4	12	7	

Figure 5. Diagraph depicting QF levels in agile development process/ agile quality model

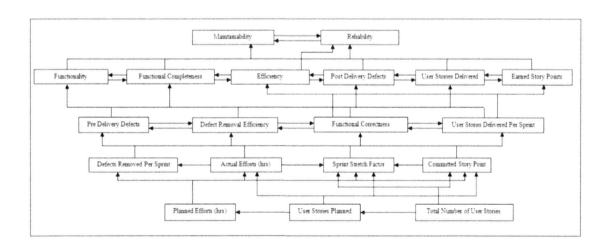

Table 3. Level segregation of QF in agile development process

	Quality Factors	Level
1	Functionality	II
2	Committed Story Points	IV
3	Total Numbers of User Stories	V
4	Functional Completeness	II
5	Sprint Stretch Factor	IV
6	Efficiency	II
7	User Stories Planned	V
8	Post Delivery Defects	II
9	Defect Removal Efficiency	III
10	User Stories Delivered	II
11	Maintainability	I
12	Functional Correctness	III
13	Pre Delivery Defects	III
14	Reliability	I
15	Planned Effort	V
16	Earned Story Points	II
17	Actual Effort	IV
18	User Stories Delivered per Sprint	III
19	Defects Removed per Sprint	IV

Figure 6. MICMAC analysis for QF in agile development process

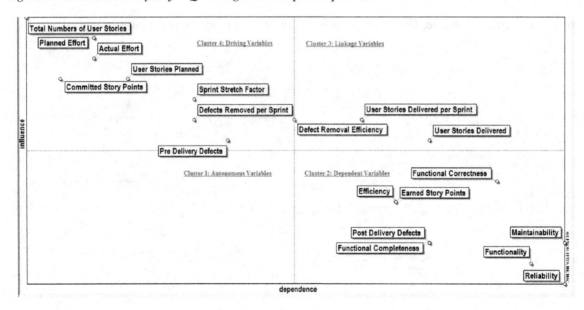

RESULTS AND DISCUSSIONS

In this research work, on performing MICMAC analysis in Figure 6, based on Driving Power and Dependence of QF in agile development process. It has been found that no quality factor is emerging in 3rd cluster as an Autonomous variable, thus depicting that none of the QF are autonomous and hence all the selected 19 QF are contributing towards the success of agile development process. In the 4th cluster, QF 1,4,6,8,11,12,14 and 16 are emerging as dependent variables having high Dependence Power and low Driving Power and hence are dependent upon other QF having high Driving Power. Analyzing the first cluster, three QF emerged as linkage variables and are considered as powerful factors having both high Driving Power as well as high Dependence Power. Focusing more on these variables will lead to increase success rates for agile development process.

On the analysis of the 2nd cluster, it has been found that eight QF emerged as independent variables, i.e QF 2, 3, 5, 7, 13, 15, 17 and 19. They have high Driving Power and low Dependence Power. These factors should be handled carefully as they highly affect the agile development process as a whole. Quality factors having high driving and dependent power are the strongest QF as they overall define the quality of the whole development process. Both the powers provide valuable insight about the importance and inter-dependence of quality factors on each other.

Thus, with this MICMAC analysis, all the 19 QF have been segregated into different levels based on their Driving Power and Dependence Power. Also, QF has been categorized into four clusters as Linkage, Independent, Autonomous and Dependent. Focusing more on Independent QF by development team members during agile process, together with Linkage QF leads to success of agile development process. Also, the model proposed has been validated as both the hierarchal structure obtained with ISM approach and the analysis done through MICMAC giving almost the same results as discussed in Table 4. Hence, the new proposed customized agile quality model can be used for empirically evaluating the agile process quality in a holistic manner.

Table 4. Results of validation

Classification of Quality Factors	MICMAC Validation Approach	ISM Modeling Approach
Autonomous Variables	No quality factor (QF) is emerging in 1st cluster as an autonomous variable	Using ISM, in the model no quality factor (QF) emerged as a variable that can be excluded or not important.
Dependent Variables	In this cluster, QF- 1,4,6,8,11,12,14 and 16 are emerging as dependent variables having high dependence power and low driving power.	Within the quality model, QF- 1,4,6,8 and 16 emerged at level II depending on other factors for evaluation. Within this, QF-11, 14 emerged at level I having highest dependence power. Also, QF-12 emerged at level III defining less dependency with some driving power.
Linkage Variables	QF- 9, 10 and 18 are emerging as linkage variables in 3rd cluster and are considered as powerful factors.	QF- 9 and 18 emerged at level III. The variables overall link the dependent and driving variables by providing moderate behavior. The QF- 10 emerged at level II.
Driving Variables	In 4th cluster, large number of quality factors emerged as independent variables. QF- 2, 3, 5, 7, 13, 15, 17 and 19. They have high driving power and low dependence power.	QF- 3, 7 and 15 emerged at level V, providing the highest influence or driving power on other factors. The QF- 2,5,17 and 19 emerged at level IV and QF-13 emerged at level III.

CONCLUSION

To access the quality of agile development process is still a major challenge for software practitioners though very few studies have been carried out on accepting agile process quality and deploying a quality product however, still the process quality for agile methodologies has not been proven quantitatively. The research work aims to find out the impact of different quality factors in agile development process of software development. A customized new agile quality model based on ISO/IEC 9126-1 is proposed using interpretive structural modeling approach for modeling of identified quality factors and analyzing the model with MICMAC analysis. With this, inter-relationships and inter-dependencies between the quality factors in agile development process were identified thereby improving the agile process quality and proving it quantitatively in a holistic manner. In the present research work, total 19 quality factors have been identified and analyzed, proving to be important at different levels through their hierarchical structure. Prior knowledge of quality factors, having high influence on the success of agile development process would help agile project development team members to provide their focus more towards these quality factors in order to get a quality product as an outcome. Thus, focusing more on limited quality factors, success of agile development process can be ensured. The scope of the present research work is limited with a theoretical validation and proving it with the real life projects. Further, we are working on the limitation by implementing proposed quality model on some real life application developed with agile methodology.

REFERENCES

Agrawala, A., Atiq, M. A., & Maurya, L. S. (2016). A Current Study on the Limitations of Agile Methods in Industry Using Secure Google Forms. *Procedia Computer Science*, *78*, 291–297. doi:10.1016/j.procs.2016.02.056

Al-Qutaish, R. E., & Al-Sarayreh, K. (2008). Software Process and Product ISO Standards: A Comprehensive Survey. *European Journal of Scientific Research*, *19*(2), 289–303.

Bajnaid, N., Benlamri, R., & Cogan, B. (2012). An SQA e-Learning System for Agile Software Development. In R. Benlamri (Ed.), *Networked Digital Technologies. NDT 2012. Communications in Computer and Information Science* (Vol. 294, pp. 69–83). Springer; . doi:10.1007/978-3-642-30567-2_7

Dikert, K., Passivaara, M., & Lassenius, C. (2016). Challenges and success factors for large-scale agile transformations: A systematic literature review. *Journal of Systems and Software*, *119*, 87–108. doi:10.1016/j.jss.2016.06.013

Dingsøyr, T., & Lassenius, C. (2016). Emerging themes in agile software development: Introduction to the special section on continuous value delivery. *Information and Software Technology*, *77*, 56–60. doi:10.1016/j.infsof.2016.04.018

Galvan, S., Mora, M., O'Connor, R. V., Acosta, F., & Alvarez, F. (2015). A Compliance Analysis of Agile Methodologies with the ISO/IEC 29110 Project Management Process. *Procedia Computer Science*, *64*, 188–195. doi:10.1016/j.procs.2015.08.480

Gayatri, S., & Chetan, S. (2013). Comparative Study of Different Multi-criteria Decision-making Methods. *International Journal on Advanced Computer Theory and Engineering*, 2(4), 9–12.

Godet, M. (1986). Introduction to La Prospective: Seven Key Ideas and One Scenario Method. *Futures*, *18*(2), 134–157. doi:10.1016/0016-3287(86)90094-7

Hashmi, S. I., & Baik, J. (2007). Software Quality Assurance in XP and Spiral - A Comparative Study. In *Proceedings of the International Conference on Computational Science and Applications* (pp. 367-374).

Idri, A., Moumane, K., & Abran, A. (2013). On the Use of Software Quality Standard ISO / IEC 9126 in Mobile Environments. In *Proceedings of the 20th Asia-Pacific Software Engineering Conference (APSEC)*, (pp. 1-8). Bangkok, Thailand

Imreh, R., & Raisinghani, M. S. (2011). Impact of Agile Software Development on Quality within Information Technology Organizations. *Journal of Emerging Trends in Computing and Information Sciences*, 2(10), 460–475.

Jain, P., Ahuja, L., & Sharma, A. (2016). Current State of the Research in Agile Quality Development. *Proceedings of the International Conference on Computing for Sustainable Global Development* (pp. 1877-1879). Delhi, India.

Jain, P., Sharma, A., & Ahuja, L. (2016). ISM Based Identification of Quality Attributes for Agile Development. In *Proceedings of the 5th International Conference on Reliability, Infocom Technologies and Optimization (Trends and Future Directions) (ICRITO)* (pp. 615-619). Noida, India. doi:10.1109/ICRITO.2016.7785028

Jeon, S., Han, M., Lee, E., & Lee, K. (2011). Quality Attribute driven Agile Development. *Proceedings of the Ninth International Conference on Software Engineering Research, Management and Applications (SERA)* (pp. 203-210). Baltimore, Maryland, USA.

Jinzenji, K., Hoshino, T., Williams, L., & Takahashi, K. (2013). An Experience Report for Software Quality Evaluation in Highly Iterative Development Methodology Using Traditional Metrics. *IEEE 24th International Symposium on Software Reliability Engineering (ISSRE)* (pp. 310-319). Southern California, United States.

Juran, J. M., & Gryna, F. M. (2010). *Juran's Quality Control Handbook*. New York: McGraw-Hill.

Majumdar, M. (2015). Multi Criteria Decision Making In: *Impact of Urbanization on Water Shortage in Face of Climatic Aberrations*, Part of the series Springer Briefs in Water Science and Technology (pp. 35-47). Singapore. doi:10.1007/978-981-4560-73-3_2

Meyer, B. (2000). *Object-Oriented Software Construction*. New Jersey: Prentice Hall PTR.

Mnkandla, E., & Dwolatzky, B. (2006). Defining Agile Software Quality Assurance. *Proceedings of the International Conference on Software Engineering Advances (ICSEA'06)* (pp. 36-42). Papeete, Tahiti.

Olszewska, M., Heidenberg, J., Weijola, M., Mikkonen, K., & Porres, I. (2016). Quantitatively measuring a large-scale agile transformation. *Journal of Systems and Software*, *117*, 258–273. doi:10.1016/j.jss.2016.03.029

Opelt, K., & Beeson, T. (2008). Agile Teams Require Agile QA: How to make it work, an experience report. Paper presented at the International Conference on Practical Software Quality and Testing (PSQT 2008 West), Las Vegas, Nevada.

Papadopoulos, G. (2015). Moving from traditional to agile software development methodologies also on large, distributed projects. *Procedia: Social and Behavioral Sciences*, *175*, 455–463. doi:10.1016/j.sbspro.2015.01.1223

Pressman, R. S. (2011). *Software Engineering a Practitioner's Approach*. New York: McGraw-Hill.

Sagheer, M., Zafar, T., & Sirshar, M. (2015). A Framework For Software Quality Assurance Using Agile Methodology. *International Journal of Scientific & Technology Research*, *4*(2), 44–50.

Samadhiya, D., Wang, S. H., & Chen, D. (2010). Quality models: Role and value in software engineering. In *Proceedings of the 2nd International Conference on Software Technology and Engineering* (pp. 320–324). San Juan, Puerto Rico: ICSTE; . doi:10.1109/ICSTE.2010.5608852

Sfetsos, P., & Stamelos, I. (2010). Empirical Studies on Quality in Agile Practices: A Systematic Literature Review. In *Proceedings of the Seventh International Conference on the Quality of Information and Communications Technology,* Porto, Portugal (pp. 44-53). doi:10.1109/QUATIC.2010.17

Sohani, N., & Sohani, N. (2012). Developing Interpretive Structural Model for Quality Framework in Higher Education: Indian Context. *Journal of Engineering, Science &. Management in Education*, *5*(2), 495–501.

Sommerville, I. (2015). *Software Engineering*. California: Addison-Wesley.

Thakkar, J., Kanda, A., & Deshmukh, S. G. (2008). Interpretive Structural Modeling (ISM) of IT enablers for Indian Manufacturing SMEs. *Information Management & Computer Security*, *16*(2), 113–136. doi:10.1108/09685220810879609

Timperi, O.P. (2004). An Overview of Quality Assurance Practices in Agile Methodologies. T76.650 Seminar in Software Engineering.

Velasquez1, M. & Hester, P.T. (2013). An Analysis of Multi-Criteria Decision Making Methods. *International Journal of Operations Research, 10(2),* 56-66.

Weinberg, G. M. (1992). *Quality Software Management* (Vol. 1). New York: Dorset House Publishing.

This research was previously published in the International Journal of Information Technology and Web Engineering (IJITWE), 14(3); pages 64-77, copyright year 2019 by IGI Publishing (an imprint of IGI Global).

Chapter 30
An Empirical Study on the Network Model and the Online Knowledge Production Structure

Quan Chen

Zhongshan Institute, University of Electronic Science and Technology of China, Zhongshan, China & School of Business Administration, South China University of Technology, Guangdong, China

Jiangtao Wang

Zhongshan Institute, University of Electronic Science and Technology of China, Zhongshan, China

Ruiqiu Ou

Zhongshan Institute, University of Electronic Science and Technology of China, Zhongshan, China

Sang-Bing Tsai

Zhongshan Institute, University of Electronic Science and Technology of China, Zhongshan, China

ABSTRACT

Mass production has attracted much attention as a new approach to knowledge production. The R software system is a typical product of mass production. For its unique architecture, the R software system accurately recorded the natural process of knowledge propagation and inheritance. Thus, this article established a dynamic complex network model based on the derivative relationship between R software packages, which reflects the evolution process of online knowledge production structure in R software system, and studied the process of knowledge propagation and inheritance via the dynamic complex network analysis method. These results show that the network size increases with time, reflecting the tendency of R software to accelerate the accumulation of knowledge. The network density and network cohesion decrease with the increase of scale, indicating that the knowledge structure of R software presents a trend of expansion. The unique extension structure of R software provides a rich research foundation for the propagation of knowledge; thus, the results can provide us a new perspective for knowledge discovery and technological innovation.

DOI: 10.4018/978-1-6684-3702-5.ch030

1. INTRODUCTION

The concept of mass production (peer production) is described as "the pattern of knowledge product production that is distributed together by the distributed users and jointly owned by the users." A typical feature of this new mode of production is that of non-central control: the producer voluntarily chooses the production content and result sharing, the producer is the user, and the output knowledge product is public (Benkler, 2006). All of these aspects are based on the Internet. The mass production project mode is mainly divided into 2 categories: Free Open Source Software Mode and Online Encyclopedia Mode. Open source software and online encyclopedias belong to the knowledge product area of online production, but the participants in the open source software need to have the ability to program. Because of this need for programming ability, the requirements for the participants are better than those for participants in online encyclopedias. The corresponding participation group is relatively stable, and the cooperation relationship between the knowledge producers in the community is more stable and persistent. In 2009, Black Duck reported that the cost of open source software development was estimated at 387 billion US dollars. Increasing numbers of software companies are involved in the development of open source software; one such example is that of Oracle's purchase of Sun's open source project for $7.4 billion in 2010. Google investment has created the open source community Google Code and the open source database MySQL. In the open source community, subsequent developers can create innovations based on the creations of earlier developers. This type of piggy-backing is a derivative of the anonymous cooperation model. It has not only greatly improved the efficiency of the creations of the developers but also promotes the development of knowledge products; that is, the speed of the development of open source software. The open source development mode provides a new way for the transformation of the industrial mode. Openness and transparency in the open source community can help to quickly gather public wisdom and effectively promote the formation and development of a new knowledge ecosystem.

Since it is a new approach to knowledge production, the mass production mode has attracted significant attention. Benkler and Nissenbaum (2006) examined how production cooperation can lead to knowledge innovation and communication in strange communities from an ethical perspective. The collaborative production mode in the open source community is usually described as a "virtual team" (Cohendet et al., 2001; Wellman, 1997). The research on the open source community can be summed up in 3 aspects: the participants' motivation for research, type of community the participants belong to, and network analysis of the community relations.

The research on the participants' motivations can be roughly classified into 3 categories: external motivation, intrinsic motivation, and internalized external motivation. External motivation includes career development (Hann et al., 2002; Hars & Ou, 2001; Orman, 2008; Hann et al., 2004), intrinsic motivation includes an interest in sharing (Ghosh, 1998) or learning opportunities (Shah, 2006; Ye & Kishida, 2003), and internalized motivation includes the development of the developer's own use requirements (Lakhani & Von Hippel, 2003; Lerner & Tirole, 2002). Henkel (2006) studied companies' participation in Linux open source community discovery and found that companies' desire to get external technology support was the main motivation for participation in open source. The motivation for individual participation is not only related to internal motivation (such as personal needs or prestige) but also related to the project community (such as leadership efficiency, interpersonal relationships, and community ecology) (Xu et al., 2009). Developers in different regions have different dominant motives (Subramanyam & Xia, 2008). Some studies also identified the motivation of dynamic participation (Shah, 2006; Wu et al., 2007).

The literature about the characteristics of community participants is mainly focused on the role characteristics of the participants in the community. For example, Mockus et al. (2000) indicated that the community had 3 types of contributors: source code providers, program error correctors, and error reporters. The number of contributors reporting problems was the greatest, error correctors came next, and the source code providers had the lowest number of participants. Only a few source contributors provided most of the source code, while the error correction amount of the program error correctors was relatively average. Ye and Kishida (2003) divided the open source community participants into 8 categories (project leader, core developer, developer, active developer, peripheral developer, error reporter, modifier, and reader) according to the core degree of the participant's position in the community. Crowston and Howison (2005) divided the participants in the open source community into 4 groups (founders and coordinators, developers, active users, and inactive users) from the perspective of management and compared the community structure to onions to reflect the differences and hierarchical characteristics of the developer community. Crowston and Howison (2006) suggested that the participation of open source community members generally has an onion-type hierarchy, the core of which is the programmer; the outermost layer belongs to the error reporter. The transition from outer layer to inner layer involves a high cost, and the number of personnel in the core layer is very small. Barcellini et al. (2009) divided the role of the community into 4 categories: the first category is the project leader, generally the initiator of the project; the second category is the project manager or the core developer, who is responsible for the maintenance of the code database and the files; the third is the initiator, and this person is involved in the process of software improvement; and the fourth category is users, including contributing users.

The literature on the relationships in the community focuses on the analysis of the collaborative structure characteristics in the community. For example, Hunt and Johnson (2002) studied the activity distribution of about 4,000 projects in the SourceForge community. The activity of these projects follows the Pareto distribution, which the authors attributed to "the winner takes all" attitude in the software production process. Madey et al. (2002) studied the cooperative network discovery in the open source community of SourceForge and found that of the total number of participants, the number of participants actually involved in the project and size of the connected graph all followed the power law distribution. Therefore, the power law distribution is 1 piece of evidence for the self-organizing production mode of the open source community. Gao et al. (2003) studied the network structure of 50,000 projects in the SourceForge open source community by using the dynamic 2-division network. The study found that the degree of the nodes and the size of the connected graph in the community were all subordinate to the power law distribution, with an aggregation coefficient of 0.7. Xu (2007) and his colleagues (2006) also found power-law distribution characteristics and small-world characteristics when studying the SourceForge open source community cooperation network. Stol and Babar (2009) gave a comprehensive summary and analysis of researches on open source software. Wang et al. (2012) established a cooperative social network through the use of developer partnerships and explored the impact of social networks on project performance in the open source community.

Although literature studied the mass production from various perspectives, few papers paid attention to knowledge production structure and its evolution process in mass productions. To fill this gap, we take R software system for example to study the evolution process of online knowledge production structure in mass production. R software is a typical knowledge product that was developed in the mass production mode. R software relies on its modularity, software package system, and eco-friendly environmental characteristics, enabling it to develop rapidly as open source software (Koch, 2005). The unique architecture of the R software package mode (Fox, 2009) makes the R software system more like a naturally growing organic software body. The system allows other developers to develop software packages independently without the intervention of the core developers of the software and allows any individual to exploit the new software package derived from the predominant feature code of the previous software package without the need for the conformance vote of other types of open source software. These software packages provide not only the process of knowledge dissemination and inheritance but also the process of human beings operating in the field of scientific exploration and engineering, on the basis of the continuous accumulation of previous algorithms and programming innovations.

Specifically, in this paper, we use dynamic complex network model to study the production process of R software system and reveal its evolution process of online knowledge production structure. The basic structure of this paper is as follows: the second section describes the extension process of the R software package. The third section uses the dynamic complex network model to describe the evolution characteristics of the derivative relationship of the R software package. The fourth section studies the expansion characteristics of the knowledge production structure of the software package. The final section summarizes our study.

2. R SOFTWARE

R software became open source in 1997 and is one of the most important tools in data science. The typical characteristics of R software are its interface, interactions, functions, object-oriented programming language, modularity, and global open source collaboration. In the list of programming software released by TIOBE in May 2013, R software surpassed SAS software for its use in statistics (TIOBE, 2013)[1]. At present, R software has more than 4,600 software packages and more than 6,700 official registered developers. The unique architecture of the R software package enables developers to use the functions of the existing software packages to reduce technical difficulties and technical barriers to development when developing new software packages with their own unique technology and ideas (Fox, 2009). New software is not subject to the intervention of the core developer of R software. Therefore, the developer only needs to use the advantages and characteristic codes of the previous software packages and reintegrate them into new functional software packages. The growth and utilization of R software is a naturally-growing organic software body. Different software package management systems reflect different software development control ideas and evolve different development paths.

The R software package system defines 3 relationships to organize and coordinate its development: (1) the dependency relationship, that is, the new software package calls the existing software package, then the new software package must be declared in the description file (description.txt) to automatically load the dependent software package at runtime; (2) importing the relationship, that is, importing the relationships through the introduction of the name space (Name Space) coordinates and the conflicts of the same functions between different packages; and (3) recommended relationships (suggests), which recommends that the developer use multiple software packages in the completion of complex problems. Dependency is the motivating force behind R software expansion, and the import relationship only solves the conflict problem of the name of the developer's function package. The recommendation relationship helps the software users make better decisions.

The software packages developed using R software contains unique knowledge. The technological background of this knowledge is accumulated knowledge and knowledge involved in solving the natural and social problems during scientific research. These knowledge structures are combined by programming technology, forming the knowledge structure of R software. In the R software package, there are substantial dependencies and recommendation relationships. R software is an organic combination of a large number of software packages. This organic combination of its internal structure provides a rich foundation for network analysis.

3. METHOD

The study was reviewed and approved by an institutional review board Zhongshan Institute, University of Electronic Science and Technology of China (ethics committee).

The resources of R software are stored in the R software master station (r-project.org), the package software's storage and downloading station CRAN (cran.r-project.or) and its mirrors around the world, the official Developer Platform (r-forge.r-project.org), and other important developer platforms (such as bioconductor.org and omegahat.org). In particular, the software package storage and download station CRAN contains authoritative and comprehensive package data. Therefore, the data of the software package mainly comes from CRAN. The data mining method from the software package description file of CRAN includes the name of the software package, earliest release time of the software package, and name of the software package that the software package depends on. It has collected 4,712 software packages and 10,868 groups of dependencies, of which 837 software packages do not have dependencies. We obtained effective data for 3,875 software packages and 10,868 sets of dependency relations.

4. DISCUSS

The dependency structure between the R software packages reflects the process of R software's extension and the derivative relationship between the software packages, that is, the knowledge propagation and inheritance. Therefore, based on the derivative relationship between the software packages, we constructed the network structure of the software package and described the dynamic network description of the dynamic network based on the time-associated edge. The time section is shown in Figure 1.

4.1. The Speed of Increase in the Number of Software Packages

In reality, the scale of the network has been changing dynamically. Figure 2 shows the function image of the number of nodes. The number of nodes increases with time, and the growth rate is increasing. The nodes in the R software package network correspond to the software packages. The growth of the nodes means the growth of the number of software packages, that is, that new software packages are being developed. The emergence of the new software package means the entry of new technologies, as well as the enrichment and extension of its peripheral applications. The right fitting of Figure 2 shows that the growth of the R software network shows a power law growth mode, with a power index of 0.165. The growth of the R software package is consistent with the expansion of its application scope. Since R software has rapidly gained popularity in scientific computing, it has been intently sought after by those in that industry due to the increasing demands to utilize big data. The number of people who have joined the R software development team has grown rapidly, and the number of R software packages has been growing exponentially in accordance with the power law.

Figure 1. Representative sections of the R software dynamic-directed network

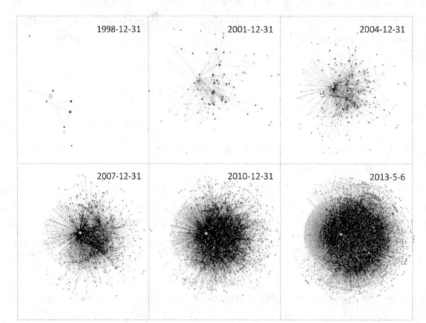

Figure 2. The size of the R software network

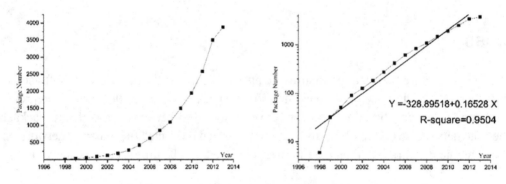

4.2. The Evolution Order of the Network Density

There are 2 ways to measure network density: One is density and the other is via the average degree. Density is defined as the number of connected nodes of a network divided by the maximum possible number of connected edges, and the average degree is defined as the average number of the connected sides of the nodes. The density is measured by the relative density of the network, and the average degree is the absolute density of the network. In the R software package on the network, the density and the average degree of K are a function of time, and these can be respectively denoted as $P(T)$ and $K(t)$. Figure 3 shows the $P(T)$ and $K(T)$ trends. The average output of R software has been stable at 2.7-2.8 since 2009, that is, on average, 2.7-2.8 new software packages can be derived from every software package. As the average degree of departure tends to be constant, the network density tends to be sparse as the number of nodes N increases.

Figure 3. The evolution of the density (left) and mean degree (right) of the R software network

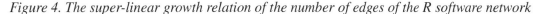

4.3. The Derivative Speed of the Software Package

The increase in the relationship between the software packages is derived from 2 factors: first, the integration and innovation between the old packages, and second, the direct derivation and innovation of single software packages. The occurrence of the former includes multiple derivative relations and the latter contains a relationship.

Figure 4 shows the growth trend of the R software network variables. If $M(T)$ and $N(T)$ are the number of edges and nodes that change with time, respectively, it is known from the relation formula of the density that when N goes to infinity, the network density p tends to a constant, that is, M and N^2 are in the same order, so the network is dense. If the density tends to 0 when N goes to infinity, M is lower than N^2, so it is sparse (Wang et al., 2012). The relation between fitting M (T) and N (T) in Figure 4 was found to be ln $M(T)$= -0.03+l.14ln$N(T)$, i.e., $M(t)\sim N(t)^{1.14}$. Obviously, this relation also explains the increase of the average degree and decrease of the density in Figure 3. Due to the logarithmic growth of the number of nodes and the number of edges, the slope of the relation is also called the dense power law index.

Figure 4. The super-linear growth relation of the number of edges of the R software network

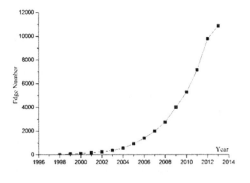
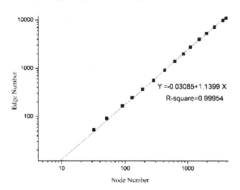

4.4. Connected Modules

The number of connected modules is used to measure the connectivity of a network. The more connected the modules are, the worse the connectivity of the networks is. The larger the scale of the largest connected module is, the better the connectivity of the network is. The scale of the largest connected module takes into account the connectivity of the network in a relative sense, and the size of the network connects the connectivity of the network in an absolute sense. For the R software network, the connectivity represents the continuity of the R software development. Other software packages that provide an interface to R software may not rely on the R software package, but they will still be dependent on the newly developed R packages, resulting in the fragmentation and dis-connectivity of the whole network. Because of the characteristics of the R tree growth, there is no strong connected structure similar to the Internet. For this reason, we studied the connectivity of R from the perspectives of the weakly-connected graphs, number of connected graphs, number of software packages, and ratio of the maximum connectivity graph in Figure 5.

Figure 5. The evolution of connectivity: The number of connected modules (left) and the maximum number of nodes connected to each other (right)

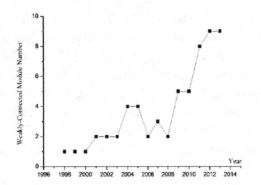 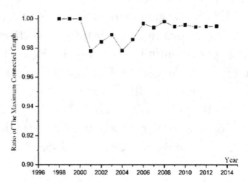

The number of weakly-connected modules increased from 1 to 9. The scale of the largest connected module was above 97%. The above phenomenon also indicated that the R package network had a good connectivity. Further research showed that the connectivity of the R software network increased between 1998 and 2013 and shows a very stable trend. Figure 6 shows that R software is different from other types of open source software due to its stable and unbranching development of the main body. Its method of development results from the fact that the largest connected giant is constantly absorbing and gathering free small connected segments. Among them, the largest connectivity occurs in the main body of the R development, so the total package number was basically stable at the 99.5% level. In addition, the increase in the other connected modules meant that the compatibility and integration of other software packages for R is increasing. In reality, commercial statistics, data mining, and large data software actively integrate R, which makes the connectivity of the peripheral R more likely to increase.

4.5. The Evolution Order of the Agglomerate

Based on the extension of knowledge structure of R software, the cohesion between R packages is measured by the average path length and network diameter indexes.

R is a purely statistical early programming language. It does not include graphical interfaces or its own KDE tools and is not friendly to new users. General statistical data processing was often unable to satisfy all the subjects' applications, so the application groups gradually expanded. The parties with needs extended the new algorithm and new model on the basis of the general packet. Subsequent developers can choose to join the original package author team to add their new achievements or extend the original packages to form new packages. From the length of the extension of the software package chain, a growth mode of R software may eliminate the distance between packages. However, newly generated packages can also continue to depend on the basic general statistical methods. From the point of view of the network model, there is a long-range edge that causes the average path length to be shorter. The growth mode of a software package reduces the growth rate of the global average path length, even though the absolute average path length is increasing. Due to the addition of a dependency packet on the longest geodesic line, it is possible to increase the diameter by 1. Beginning in 2009, the diameter of the R software network was stable at a level 5.

Figure 6. The evolution of the average path length (left) and diameter (right) of the R software network

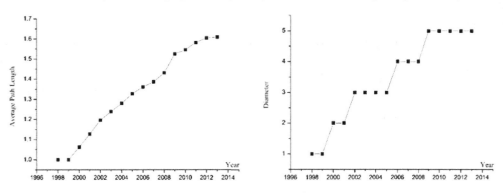

4.6. The Evolution Order of Heterogeneity

Network heterogeneity refers to the heterogeneity of the nodes, which occurs due to the uneven distribution of the degree values. The heterogeneity of the degree distribution is one of the most important discoveries in complex networks since 2009 (Barabási, 2009). The R software network is a spontaneous growth network. Its heterogeneity is related to whether there is a spindle in the software's growth, which may lead to bifurcation. The relatively high heterogeneity in the R software network corresponds to the relative concentration of derived relationships, which means that the development content is relatively stable and focused. Through fitting the degree sequence of the R software network over the years, we obtained the index evolution result shown in Figure 7. The power exponent distribution of the R software network was between (1.5, 2.1), which is a typical II type heterogeneity. Therefore, the development of R software is focused on some nodes, and the main axis is distinct. According to the process of the R software network node scale expansion, the scale of R software is still expanding rapidly, but the power exponent is basically stable at about 2, maintaining the characteristics of the type II heterogeneity.

Figure 7. The evolution of the power exponent and power exponent of R software with scale

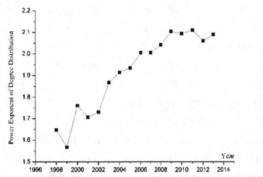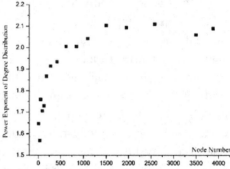

5. CONCLUSION

Mass production has attracted much attention as a new approach to knowledge production. Open source software, a typical application of mass production, is a very successful large-scale collaborative practice of the mass production mode in software on the Internet. The success of open source projects not only includes new software development methods but also changes the pattern of the software industry. The Internet-based knowledge production model has subverted the traditional business model. The unique extension structure of R software provides a rich research foundation for the propagation of knowledge. Therefore, in this study, we examined the dynamic evolution characteristics of a knowledge production structure by virtue of the specific structure system of the R software package and the dependence of the relationship between its software packages. Our results show that the network size increases with time, reflecting the tendency of R software to accelerate the accumulation of knowledge. The network density decreases with the increase of scale, and the network cohesion decreases with the increase of scale, indicating that the knowledge structure of R software presents a trend of expansion. The network connectivity is good. The proportion of the largest connected giant pass was more than 97%. The development mode of R software shows that the main body of the largest connected giant is continuously absorbing and gathering free, small connected segments. Finally, the network has a small number of nodes, which reveals that the main axis of the knowledge structure of R software is not bifurcated.

As we known, the division of labor and collaboration are the nature of market economy. The increase of economy scale is characterized by deepening of division of labor and expansion of collaboration. As Hayek pointed out, the essence of division of labor is division of knowledge. In this point of view, the booming of internet tremendously promotes the deepening of division of labor, which further promotes the economy growth. Nowadays, many information technology firms, such as IBM, Google, Facebook, Huawei and Xiaomi, deeply participate in online collaborative production activities under the open-source setting. Therefore, it has practical significance to investigate the division of labor and collaboration in online knowledge production. This paper studied the knowledge structure of the R software system's online production, and revealed evolution characteristics of this knowledge structure from several aspects. The results may help firms improve the efficiency of online software developments and of online open innovation.

ACKNOWLEDGMENT

This research was supported by the National Natural Science Foundation of China (71301054), the fundamental research funds for the central universities (2015QNXM13, 2017X2D14) and Provincial Nature Science Foundation of Guangdong (2015A030310271, 2015A030313679, 2015A030313681) and Zhongshan City Science and Technology Bureau Project (No. 2017B1015) and 2018 Zhongshan Innovation and Development Research Center and Guangdong Academy of Education Project (GDJY-2015-C-b010).

REFERENCES

Barabási, A.-L. (2009). Scale-free networks: A decade and beyond. *Science*, *325*(5939), 412–413. doi:10.1126cience.1173299 PMID:19628854

Barcellini, F., Détienne, F., & Burkhardt, J. M. (2009). Participation in online interaction spaces: Design-use mediation in an open source software community. *International Journal of Industrial Ergonomics*, *39*(3), 533–540. doi:10.1016/j.ergon.2008.10.013

Benkler, Y. (2006). *The Wealth of Networks: How Social Production Transforms Markets and Freedom*. Yale University Press.

Benkler, Y., & Nissenbaum, H. (2006). Commons-based peer production and virtue. *Journal of Political Philosophy*, *14*(4), 394–419. doi:10.1111/j.1467-9760.2006.00235.x

Cohendet, P., Creplet, F., Dupouët, O. (2001). Organisational Innovation, Communities of Practice and Epistemic Communities: the Case of Linux. *Economics with Heterogeneous Interacting Agents*, (51), 303-326.

Crowston, K., & Howison, J. (2005). The social structure of free and open source software development. *First Monday*, *10*(2), 405–411. doi:10.5210/fm.v10i2.1207

Crowston, K., & Howison, J. (2006). Hierarchy and centralization in free and open source software team communications. *Knowledge, Technology & Policy*, *18*(4), 65–85. doi:10.100712130-006-1004-8

Fox, J. (2009). Aspects of the social organization and trajectory of the r project. *The R Journal*, *1*(2), 5–13.

Gao, Y., Freeh, V., & Madey, G. (2003). Analysis and modeling of open source software community. *Naacsos*, *1*(1), 1–12.

Ghosh, R. A. (1998). Interviews with linus torvalds: What motivates software developers. *First Monday*, *3*(2), 1–12. doi:10.5210/fm.v3i2.583

Hann, I. H., Roberts, J. A., & Slaughter, S. (2004). Why Developers Participate in Open Source Software Projects: An Empirical Investigation. In *International Conference on Information Systems ICIS* 2004, Washington DC, December 12-15 (pp. 821-830). DBLP.

Hann, I. H., Roberts, J. A., Slaughter, S., & Fielding, R. (2002). Economic Incentives for Participating in Open Source Software Projects. In *International Conference on Information Systems ICIS 2002*, Barcelona, Spain (p. 33). DBLP.

Hars, A., & Ou, S. (2001). Working for free? Motivations of participating in open source projects. In *Hawaii International Conference on System Sciences*. IEEE.

Henkel, J. (2006). Selective revealing in open innovation processes: The case of embedded Linux. *Research Policy*, *35*(7), 953–969. doi:10.1016/j.respol.2006.04.010

Hunt, F., & Johnson, P. (2002). On the pareto distribution of sourceforge projects. In *Open Source Software Development Workshop*.

Koch, S. (2005). *Free/Open Source Software Development*.

Lakhani, K. R., & Von Hippel, E. (2003). How open source software works: "free" user-to-user assistance. *Research Policy*, *32*(6), 923–943. doi:10.1016/S0048-7333(02)00095-1

Lerner, J., & Tirole, J. (2002). Some simple economics of open source. *The Journal of Industrial Economics*, *50*(2), 197–234. doi:10.1111/1467-6451.00174

Madey, G., Freeh, V., & Tynan, R. (2002). The Open source software development phenomenon: An analysis based on social network theory.

Mockus, A., Fielding, R. T., & Herbsleb, J. (2000). A Case Study of Open Source Software Development: *The Apache Server. In International Conference on Software Engineering* (Vol. 11, pp. 263-272). IEEE. 10.1145/337180.337209

Orman, W. H. (2008). Giving it away for free? the nature of job-market signaling by open-source software developers. *The B.E. Journal of Economic Analysis & Policy*, *8*(1), 1875–1875.

Shah, S. K. (2006). Motivation, governance, and the viability of hybrid forms in open source software development. *Management Science*, *52*(7), 1000–1014. doi:10.1287/mnsc.1060.0553

Stol, K. J., & Babar, M. A. (2009). *Reporting Empirical Research in Open Source Software: The State of Practice. Open Source Ecosystems: Diverse Communities Interacting*. Springer Berlin Heidelberg.

Subramanyam, R., & Xia, M. (2008). Free/libre open source software development in developing and developed countries: A conceptual framework with an exploratory study. *Decision Support Systems*, *46*(1), 173–186. doi:10.1016/j.dss.2008.06.006

Wang, J., Hu, M. Y., & Shanker, M. (2012). Human agency, social networks, and foss project success. *Journal of Business Research*, *65*(7), 977–984. doi:10.1016/j.jbusres.2011.04.014

Wellman, B. (1997). *An electronic group is virtually a social network*. Kiesler S Culture of the Internet.

Wu, C. G., Gerlach, J. H., & Young, C. E. (2007). An empirical analysis of open source software developers' motivations and continuance intentions. *Information & Management, 44*(3), 253–262. doi:10.1016/j.im.2006.12.006

Xu, B., Jones, D. R., & Shao, B. (2009). *Volunteers' involvement in online community based software development.* Elsevier Science Publishers B. V. doi:10.1016/j.im.2008.12.005

Xu, J. (2007). *Mining and modeling the open source software community.*

Ye, Y., & Kishida, K. (2003). Toward an understanding of the motivation Open Source Software developers. In *International Conference on Software Engineering* 2003 *Proceedings* (pp.419-429). IEEE.

This research was previously published in the Journal of Information Technology Research (JITR), 12(4); pages 171-182, copyright year 2019 by IGI Publishing (an imprint of IGI Global).

Chapter 31
An Early Multi-Criteria Risk Assessment Model:
Requirement Engineering Perspective

Priyanka Chandani

Department of Computer Science and Information Technology, Jaypee Institute of Information Technology, Noida, India

Chetna Gupta

Department of Computer Science and Information Technology, Jaypee Institute of Information Technology, Noida, India

ABSTRACT

Accurate time and budget is an essential estimate for planning software projects correctly. Quite often, the software projects fall into unrealistic estimates and the core reason generally owes to problems with the requirement analysis. For investigating such problems, risk has to identified and assessed at the requirement engineering phase only so that defects do not seep down to other software development phases. This article proposes a multi-criteria risk assessment model to compute risk at a requirement level by computing cumulative risk score based on a weighted score assigned to each criterion. The result of comparison with other approaches and experimentation shows that using this model it is possible to predict the risk at the early phase of software development life cycle with high accuracy.

INTRODUCTION

In the field of software engineering, requirements engineering (RE) is the most crucial phase of software development life cycle (Denger & Olsson, 2005). It is a systematic approach which deals with understanding, documenting, evaluating and implementing customer's needs (Nuseibeh & Easterbrook, 2000). Any failures during RE phase have adverse impact on the overall development process (Hall, Beecham & Rainer, 2002) as it acts as a roadmap for calculating schedule and cost of the project. This implies that software project development is not only risky but challenging as well. The challenges are

DOI: 10.4018/978-1-6684-3702-5.ch031

due to constant evolution of stakeholder need, time to deliver project on time and within budget, meeting constant challenging market demands etc. Studies have shown that if requirement errors are surfaced out in the later stages of the project lifecycle, fixes take more time and have a huge cost involved as much as 200 times as compared to analyzing and checking defects at the initiation stage (Niazi & Shastry, 2003). Therefore, managing risk at the early stages of project is essential otherwise it will result in an exponential increase in the cost of the project. Risk assessment and management is an organized way of identifying, analyzing and assessing the impacts of risks and mitigating them when they arise. According to (Hamill & Katerina, 2009) most common types of defects in software development are requirement defects which are among the major sources of failure constituting 32.65% and these defects have high severity problem which affect software maintainability (Chen & Huang, 2009). It is one of the overlooked aspects in requirements engineering (Stern & Arias, 2011) and is generally considered as a potential problem that can affect the projects in a negative way. According to (McConnell, 1997) risk management only requires 5% of the total project budget in order to obtain a 50–70% chance of avoiding time overrun.

Literature in the past concludes that researchers have proposed considerable amount of risk identification, analysis and management models for better supervision of threats. As per studies conducted in (Ansar, 2006; Kontio, 2001; Ropponen & Lyytinen, 2000) risk management needs to be included as early as possible particularly, during the requirements engineering phase as inappropriate and misleading requirement gathering are most expensive and one of the main causes of project failure (Glass, 1998). This aspect of applying risk assessment in RE has not been sufficiently addressed in the past (Ropponen & Lyytinen, 2000; Pfleeger, 2000). Most research on software project risk analysis focuses on the discovery of correlations between risk factors and project outcomes (Procaccino et al., 2002; Jiang & Klein, 2000; Wallace & Keil, 2004).

This paper proposes a multi criteria risk assessment model, which analyzes requirements and estimates cumulative risk score value of implementing a particular requirement. The primary objective is to identify prime criteria's that will help in analyzing risk associated with requirement implementation in terms of project outcome, inter relationships, importance to stakeholder and market value. The foremost challenge here is to define the most appropriate target criterion for ranking individual requirements in terms of risk. If a single criterion is taken into consideration then it becomes easier to decide whether the requirement is risky or not but if there are more than one criteria's, then the decision becomes far more difficult, because a wrong decision can result in extra cost to the organization and the impact of same can be manifolds. The chosen criteria's will govern operation in risk assessment model holistically checking trends of impact and their usage in context flow for the user as well as in-depth while grading the benefit, penalty and relative defect ratio they provide. Hence to address this issue of multiple parameters – a multi criteria decision making risk assessment model is presented in this paper. The model is simple, practical, and easy to understand in order to make the risk assessment process effective and sustainable.

RELATED WORK

It can be observed from the literature that large numbers of software projects have failed to deliver on time & within budget and approximately 66% of projects fail to meet their business objective (Islam, 2009; Kotonya & Sommerville, 1998). According to The Standish Group's CHAOS survey (Boehm & Valerdi, 2008), of over 350 organizations and 8000 projects, only 16% of the projects are delivered within budget and schedule, 31% are cancelled before completion, 53% overrun in budget or schedule. As per data of (Pohl & Rupp, 2010) 60% of project failures fall into the requirements engineering phase and mostly aren't discovered until late during the project or when the system has already gone live (Boehm, 1981). The same facts are supported by (Lindquist, 2005) which concludes that "poor requirements management can be attributed to 71% of software projects that fail; greater than bad technology, missed deadlines, and change management issues" Hence organizations which apply risk management methods and techniques have more control on the pattern in projects (Sarigiannidis & Chatzoglou, 2011).

Risks in software projects can occur in any of phase of software development life cycle (SDLC) and should be handled there and then using strategies planned for individual phases of SDLC. For performing a full scan or wholesome analysis it is essential to identify cause and effect of associated risks. Traditional risk analysis defines risk as a function of likelihood and impact which are important measures, but they lack in estimating risks that are largely hidden in requirements. Most of the proposed methods are static in nature which performs qualitative and quantitative analysis on basis risk processes like risk identification, risk analysis, risk planning etc. to assess and control the risks (Guiling & Xiaojuan, 2011; Kumar et al., 2010). These models can fit diverse projects in small/large organizations, used for different domains or using suitable tools.

It has been noted in the past that when problems are surfaced out in the later stages of the project lifecycle, the fixes take more time and have a huge cost involved as compared to analyzing and checking defects at the initiation stage (Pohl & Rupp, 2010). Hence performing risk assessment at early stages of SDLC namely, requirement engineering can help in minimization of delays and reduction in cost and time. Since missing or incomplete requirements cause projects to fail, it is important to find solutions for improving the quality of requirements. However, in the current state scenario only a few models exist that considers risks associated with requirements phase and a summary of all those techniques are presented in Table 1. A part of these models other models such as SRAEP (Sadiq et al., 2010), PRO-RISK (Suebkhuna & Ramingwong, 2011), PRM (Westfall, 2011), RMM (Hillson, 1997) and SoftRisk (Keshlaf & Hashim, 2000) are also used in requirements phase for risk assessment.

Risk assessment at early stage helps in minimizing the impact of risk propagation and maintenance overhead and this is the main objective of this research.

PROPOSED MULTI-CRITERIA RISK ASSESSMENT MODEL

The proposed multi-criteria risk assessment model estimates the risk at requirements engineering phase by considering following criteria's applicable to each requirement: benefit, penalty, type of defect, interrelationship between requirements and trending factors. The whole idea is presented in Figure 1.

The following section discusses the whole process of risk estimation and detail of all these criteria used in computing cumulative risk score.

Criteria 1: Requirement Value

This criterion uses benefit and penalty as its sub-criteria to compute its final value. Benefit governs the value to software ecosystem, which requirement shall obtain when included in the software project. It estimates relative benefit the requirement shall provide to the customer on a scale of 0 to 5. Value 5 indicates that the requirement is most aligned with product's business strategy. Penalty is the cost a software ecosystem has to burn when a particular requirement shall not be included. The proposed model estimates relative penalty for each requirement shall provide to the customer on a scale of 0 to 5, with 5 being high penalty on a reducing scale to 0. Benefit is provided by stakeholders and corresponding penalty is computed by developers. For example, failing to comply with security policy of Amazon Web Services (AWS) for a project deployment can have a low benefit to the customer but high penalty. On the contrary, requirements that have low benefit/penalty could add unnecessary cost of implementation on the software project.

The final requirement value is calculated as the sum of the benefit and penalty. This value helps in estimating how important a particular requirement is from stakeholder's perspective and if not handled or implemented accurately what penalty a single requirement will have on overall system. In this study benefit and penalty are weighted equally to compute final requirement value. The developers can customize their weights as per requirement of specific project and demand.

Table 1. Risk models

Model	Purpose	SDLC Phase	Advantages	Disadvantages
BOEHM (Boehm,1991)	Risk Identification, analysis, Prioritization and control	Requirement analysis and planning	This model is relatively simpler and can cover over all of phases of software development	It doesn't handle generic risk implicitly
SRAM (Foo & Muruganatham, 2000)	Risk assessment, prioritization	Requirement analysis	This model considers the nine critical risk elements: software complexity, project staff, targeted reliability, product requirement, method of estimation, method of monitoring, development process, usability of software and tools. This model is questionnaire and provide quantitative assessment of risk.	It does not include the sources of uncertain estimation like measurement error, assumption errors and model error
RISKIT (Kontio & Basili, 1997)	Risk identification, analysis, monitoring and prioritization	Requirement phase, application and maintenance phase	This model is flexible, it was originally developed for software development projects, but it can be applied in many other domains. It models different stakeholder's perspective.	It fails to cover small and medium size organization. It is also difficult to predict the potential risk reliably as it does not bridge the gap between risk estimation and risk metrics
SEI-SRE (Carr et al., 1993)	Risk Evaluation:- Detection, specification, assessment, consolidation, mitigation	Requirement phase, coding phase, testing phase, maintenance phase	This method is not purely theoretical, can be used in any IT projects. Risk identification is more detailed in this method making it very efficient.	In this method everything is defined as a template so no scope of human intelligence to be applied here.
SERUM (Greer, 1997)	Implicit and explicit risk management	Requirement analysis and planning phase	SERUM is a method of risk management that looks at both explicit and implicit risk making the risk management easier and handling them more adequately. It is used in software released in versions.	SERUM doesn't take into account the feedback of similar kind of projects. Cost-benefit analysis is difficult.
SERIM (Roy, 2014)	Risk assessment and risk ranking	Requirement analysis and planning phase	This model follows "Just in Time" strategy. Basic statistics is used to assess the risks in the complex development environment and can be used to monitor risks at any point in the development cycle.	The major drawback of the SERIM method is the lack of explicit guidelines on how to use the actions plans based on various perspectives and how to identify the major risks.

Figure 1. Multi-criteria risk assessment model

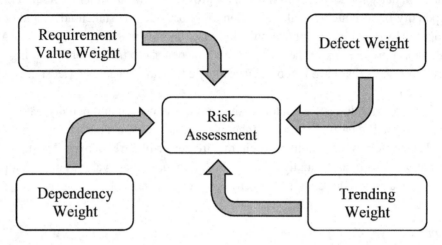

Criteria 2: Defect Weight

Poorly specified, incorrect or missing requirements lead to defects in system (Blackburn, Busser & Nauman, 2001) and the project ends up with crude design followed by wrong or unwanted focus in product development, directly affecting product and customers (Firesmith, 2007). There are several classifications or taxonomies available for classifying requirements defects which help in creating more accurate and efficient defect prevention and detection techniques (Alshazly et al., 2014; Beizer, 1990; Chillarege et al., 1992; Walia & Carver, 2009; Hayes, 2003). Historically, there has been lot of research on validating requirements using various techniques and some through defect taxonomies (Ackerman, Buchwald & Lewski,1989; Sommerville, 2004; Felderer & Beer, 2013, 2015). In practice, most defect taxonomies are used in the later stages of software development life cycle but the use of these taxonomies to validate requirements have not been fully exploited (Felderer & Beer, 2013, 2015) and only little has been done in the direction of linking and validating requirements with defect taxonomy. This study considers defect classification given by (Hayes, 2003) as one of its criteria to estimate risk shown in Table 2.

Each requirement is validated and analyzed according to the presence of defect. Defect weights are computed using formulae given in Equation (1):

$$\text{Defect weight} = \frac{\text{no. of defects in a requirement}}{\text{total number of requirements}} * 100 \tag{1}$$

Criteria 3: Inter-Relationship Among Requirements Analysis

Connections or associations among requirements can be used to analyze inter - relationships among requirements. These inter-relationships form the basis for analyzing change propagation analysis and are called dependencies among requirements. One way to find the dependency among requirements is context flow diagrams. The cumulative number inclusion of requirements in context flows also governs the importance of a requirement. The use of requirement in context flow shows that the implementation of the requirement is important for a context flow to stay valid and useful. From this context flow graph, a dependency graph can be obtained to identify the dependency among requirements. Consider an example scenario given in Figure 2 derived from some context flow. The corresponding dependency table is given in Table 3.

It can be concluded from Table 3 that requirement A has no dependency, requirement B is dependent on A hence dependent count of requirement B is 1 similarly requirement count of C is 1 whereas requirement D is directly dependent on B and B is dependent of A hence D is also dependent of A indirectly. Hence dependency count of D is 2. This dependency count is considered as weight count of each requirement.

Table 2. Defect types (Hayes, 2003)

Type of Defect	Remarks
Incomplete	Failure to fully describe all the requirements of a function
Missing	Failure to specify lower levels of abstraction of a higher level specified or specification of missing value or variable in a requirement
In-Correct	Failure to fully describe system input or output or specification of incorrect value or variable in a requirement or under or over stating the resources
Ambiguous	Difficult to understand or lack of clarity or improper translation
Infeasible	Requirement which is infeasible or impossible to achieve given other system factors e.g. process speed, memory
Inconsistent	Requirements which are pair –wise incompatible having external or internal conflicts
Over Specification	Requirements which are excessive for operational need leading to additional system cost
Non-Traceable	Requirements which cannot be traced to subsequent or previous phases
Unachievable	Requirements that are specified but very difficult to achieve, not possible in the lifetime of the product
Non-verifiable	Failure to verify the requirements by any reasonable testing method
Misplaced	Information which is marked in different section of requirements document
Intentional Deviation	Requirement which is specified at the higher level but intentionally deviated at the lower level from specifications
Redundant	Requirement which was already specified elsewhere in the specification

Figure 2. Example scenario

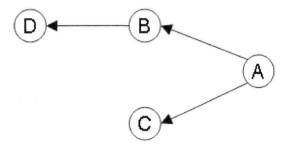

Table 3. Example dependency table

Requirement	Dependency
A	--
B	A
C	A
D	B and A

Criteria 4: Trending Weight

There are various factors which can contribute towards raising the risk in requirements which are often not functional in nature and have an external impact, they are called trending factors. The trending factors identified are explained in Table 4.

Table 4. Trending factors

Factor	Description
Volatility	The check on the concreteness of the requirement or whether it is volatile to change
Stakeholder	Stakeholder is a type of check when the project team is not agreed and aligned with the purpose of the requirement in the project
Time to market	The time of market is a timeline check on the completion of the software project with respect inclusion of the requirement
Integration	Integration check would mean to integrate the application with another application, which is outside its boundary.
Constraint	Constraint check is a type, which can be a bottleneck on the software system being proposed.
Dependency	Dependency check is a type when the inclusion of requirement would pose an issue with a dependency of operation
Cost	Cost check is a type which happens when the project does not complete on the agreed budget
Infrastructure	Environment risk is a type of risk when the environment required for a requirement is not available
Delight	Delight check is a type of risk in which the output to the system after including the requirement is a big delighter for the stakeholder.
Competition	Competition check is a type which happens when other players in the market have similar product lines

All the requirements are analyzed for above mentioned trending factors to assess any contribution towards risk. After mapping trending factors with requirements, each trending factor is assigned a weight on a scale of 0 to 10 according to following rules:

- All trending weights in this study have equal weightage i.e. 10% and all weights should sum up to 100%. As per the domain and requirement of a project these weights can be adjusted accordingly;
- The final trending weight of each requirement will be equal to summation of number of trending factors it has. For example, if a requirement has 3 trending factors then its total weight will be equal to 30% which is 3 on a scale of 1 to 10.

Calculation of Cumulative Risk Score

The cumulative risk is calculated after pollinating the results of the various weights that have been analyzed. For this study requirement value, defect weight and visit weight are given weightage equals to 30% whereas trending weight is given weightage equal to 10% and summation of all factors is equal to 100%. The ratios of weights to the criterions have been decided based on the importance/value of criterion with regards to requirement analysis/assessment process. The final score is computed using following formulae given in Equation (2):

Cumulative Risk Score = 0.3 * requirement value weight + 0.3 * defect weight + 0.3 * *dependency weight + 0.1 * trending weight*   (2)

TOOL SUPPORT AND RESULT OBSERVATION

For the ease of execution and legitimacy of calculation, a tool has been developed based on this model to estimate the cumulative risk for all the requirements. The multi-criterion risk assessment is a Microsoft excel spreadsheet-based tool. Each requirement is rated on four aspects: requirement value, defect, dependency (inter relationship) and trends. The developers can customize the weights of these criteria's in the beginning of risk assessment process as per the requirement of a particular project to compute final cumulative risk score. This score will be computed only when all the values for all criteria are entered for each requirement. This score can then be used to provide ranking to different requirements based on risk severity in them. Higher the score depicts high risk in particular requirement. Figure 3 presents the snapshot the proposed tool.

Figure 3. Multi-criteria risk assessment model worksheet (example scenario)

Requirements	Requirement Value		Defect Types	Inter Relationship (Depedency) Count	Trending Factor	Requirement Value Weight	Defect Weight	Dependency Weight	Trending Weight	Cumulative Risk Score	Risk Rank
	Benefit	Penalty				30%	30%	30%	10%	100%	
R1	5	5	Incomplete	1	Volatility	10	17	1	1	8.7	1
R2	5	4	Missing	2	Time to Market	9	8	2	1	5.9	2
R3	5	4	Ambigious	2	Integration	9	8	2	1	5.9	2

A benefit of using this tool is that it provides a discrete, measurable way to determine cumulative risk simply by entering values against identified criteria's. Using this tool, one can help improve the risk assessment process and help in developing a clear picture on the state of the requirements. The tool shall be an input in the requirement engineering process in which the requirements shall be viewed in a 360-degree purview and a level of certainty, which shall give an informal review of risk for a purpose of improvement and confidence.

ILLUSTRATION OF PROPOSED RISK ASSESSMENT APPROACH

To illustrate and validate proposed approach for applicability in software industry, a case study in the form of a small project was carried out. The project assists in digital parking company to manage their CMS (Content Management System) and automatically publish rates to their web/mobile applications. A total of 12 high level requirements are gathered for this study. The context flow diagram and dependency table for example project are shown in Figure 4 and Table 5. Figure 5 presents the snapshot of risk analysis conducted by proposed tool.

Figure 4. Context flow diagram of sample project

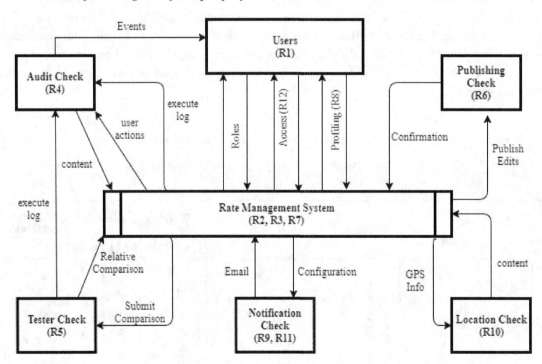

The result of analysis concludes that requirements R1, R10, R6, R8, R7 and R11 with cumulative risk score of 8.7, 8.5, 8, 7.8, 6.7 and 6.7 respectively are the riskiest requirements for implementation. The result is purely based on inputs received for various criteria's.

Table 5. Dependency table

Requirement	Dependency
R1	R10
R2	R1, R10
R3	R1, R10
R4	R2, R3, R1, R10
R5	R2, R3, R1, R10
R6	R2, R3, R1, R10
R7	R1, R10
R8	R1, R10
R9	--
R10	--
R11	--
R12	--

Table 6. Comparison table

Feature/Model	BOEHM (Boehm,1991)	RISKIT (Kontio & Basili, 1997)	SEI-SRE (Carr et al., 1993)	SRAM ((Foo & Muruganatham, 2000))	SERUM (Greer, 1997)	SERIM (Roy,2014)	Proposed Risk Assessment Model
Multi-criteria Approach						✓	✓
Tool support		✓	✓			✓	✓
Dependency (Inter relationships)							✓
Use of Trending Factors							✓
Generic Risks		✓			✓		✓
Risk Ranking						✓	✓
Requirement Phase	✓	✓	✓	✓	✓	✓	✓
Risk Identification	✓	✓	✓		✓	✓	
Risk Assessment	✓	✓	✓	✓	✓	✓	✓
Multiple Stakeholder Perspective		✓					✓
Self-Learning					✓		
Flexibility		✓					✓
Simplicity	✓						✓
Software Release versions					✓		
Risk Mitigation	✓		✓			✓	✓

Figure 5. Cumulative risk of sample project

No. of Requirements						12				Select	
	Criterions					Weight Computation				Risk Score and Ranking	
						30%	30%	30%	10%	100%	
Requirements	Requirement Value		Defect Types	Inter Relationship (Depedency) Count	Trending Factor	Requirement Value Weight	Defect Weight	Dependency Weight	Trending Weight	Cummulative Risk Score	Risk Rank
	Benefit	Penalty									
R1	5	5	Incomplete, ambiguous	1	volatility, constraint, stakeholder	10	17	1	3	8.7	1
R2	5	4	over-spec	2	dependency, time to market	9	8	2	2	5.9	7
R3	5	4	over-spec	2	dependency, time to market	9	8	2	2	5.9	7
R4	4	4	Incomplete, ambiguous	4	cost, time to market	8	8	4	2	6.2	6
R5	3	2	Missing	4	cost, constraint	5	8	4	2	5.3	8
R6	3	2	Missing, Notraceable	4	integration, infrastructure	5	17	4	2	8	3
R7	2	1	Incomplete, ambiguous	2	time to market	3	17	2	1	6.7	5
R8	2	2	Incorrect, Infeasible	2	NA	4	17	2	0	7.8	4
R9	2	2	Missing	0	NA	4	8	0	0	3.9	9
R10	5	4	Missing, Incorrect	0	cost, integration, time to market, infrastructure	9	17	0	4	8.5	2
R11	2	2	Incorrect, Inconsistent	0	stakeholder	4	17	0	1	6.7	5
R12	1	1	Incorrect	0	stakeholder, volatility	2	8	0	2	3.2	10

RISK MITIGATION

Risk mitigation is the process in which specific measures are used to minimize or eliminate unacceptable risks. These measures directly help in reducing the severity of risk consequences associated with implementation. As a part of risk mitigation strategy, the developers can roll back to the origin of these risks by analyzing specific criteria for a particular risky requirement. These specific steps can be taken to rectify specific problems.

COMPARISON WITH OTHER APPROACHES

Table 6 shows the comparison of the proposed model with some of the well-known models. The comparison was done based on the features each model exhibits and depth of criterion. The ability of tweaking the tool based on different needs was also put into consideration. The results showed that the proposed model is better when requirement analysis is in consideration.

CONCLUSION

This paper presents a multi criteria risk assessment model which computes risk of implementing requirements at the very first stage of software development life cycle. The model uses four criterions namely, a requirement scale to mark benefits/penalties, requirement defect scale to measure fault in requirements, dependency scale to mark inter relationships among requirements and trend scale to mark software ecosystem factors affecting requirements. Through the case study, we have shown the joined outlook showcased by the four criterions in risk assessment. The assessment caters to many unknowns fathomed. The assessment team can on one hand be prepared to address all the unknowns and keep the stakeholders informed and on the other work on the requirements to resolve the hitches.

REFERENCES

Ackerman, A. F., Buchwald, L. S., & Lewski, F. H. (1989). Software Inspections: An Effective Verification Process. *IEEE Software*, 6(3), 31–36. doi:10.1109/52.28121

Alshazly, A. A., Elfatatry, A. M., & Abougabal, M. S. (2014). Detecting defects in software requirements specification. *Alexandria Engineering Journal*, 53(3), 513–527. doi:10.1016/j.aej.2014.06.001

Ansar, Y., & Georgina, P. (2006). Modeling Risk and Identifying Countermeasure in Organizations. In *Proceedings of the first International Workshop on Critical Information Infrastructures Security*. Samos, Greece, Springer.

Beizer, B. (1990). *Software testing techniques* (2nd ed.). New York, NY: Van Nostrand Reinhold.

Blackburn, M. R., Busser, R., & Nauman, A. (2001). Removing Requirement Defects and Automating Test. In STAREAST- Software Testing Conference.

Boehm, B. (1981). *Software Engineering Economics*. Englewood Cliffs, NJ: Prentice Hall.

Boehm, B. W. (1991). Software Risk Management: Principles and Practices. *IEEE Software*, 8(1), 32–41. doi:10.1109/52.62930

Boehm, B. W., & Valerdi, R. (2008). Achievements and Challenges in Software Resource Estimation. *IEEE Software*, 25(5), 74–83. doi:10.1109/MS.2008.133

Carr, M., Konda, S., Monarch, T., Walker, C. F., & Ulrich, F. C. (1993). Taxonomy-Based Risk Identification (Report No. CMU/SEI- 93-TR-6). Pittsburgh, PA: Software Engineering Institute.

Chen, J. C., & Huang, S. J. (2009). An empirical analysis of the impact of software development problem factors on software maintainability. *Journal of Systems and Software, 82*(6), 981–992. doi:10.1016/j.jss.2008.12.036

Chillarege, R., Bhandari, I. S., Chaar, J. K., Halliday, M. J., Moebus, D. S., Ray, B. K., & Wong, M. Y. (1992). Orthogonal Defect Classification-A Concept for In-Process Measurements. *IEEE Transactions on Software Engineering, 18*(11), 943–956. doi:10.1109/32.177364

Denger, C., & Olsson, T. (2005). Quality assurance in requirements engineering. In A. Aurum & C. Wohlin (Eds.), *Engineering and managing software requirements* (pp. 163–185). Berlin, Germany: Springer. doi:10.1007/3-540-28244-0_8

Felderer, M., & Beer, A. (2013). Using Defect Taxonomies for Requirements Validation in Industrial Projects. In *Proceedings of the 21st IEEE International Requirements Engineering conference(RE)*, Rio de Janeiro, Brazil. IEEE. 10.1109/RE.2013.6636733

Felderer, M., & Beer, A. (2015). Using Defect Taxonomies for Testing Requirements. *IEEE Software, 32*(3), 94–101. doi:10.1109/MS.2014.56

Firesmith, D. (2007). Common requirements problems. their negative consequences and the industry best practices to help solve them. *Journal of Object Technology, 6*(1), 17–33. doi:10.5381/jot.2007.6.1.c2

Foo, S., & Muruganatham, A. (2000). Software Risk Assessment Model. In *International Conference on Management of Innovation and Technology,* Singapore. IEEE.

Glass, R. L. (1998). *Software Runaways: Monumental Software Disasters.* Upper Saddle River, NJ: Prentice-Hall, Inc.

Greer, D. (1997). SERUM - Software Engineering Risk: Understanding and Management. *Journal of Project and Business Risk Management, 1*(4), 373–388.

Guiling, L., & Xiaojuan, Z. (2011). Research on the risk management of IT project. In *Proceedings of International conf. on E-Business and E -Government (ICEE)* (pp. 1-4).

Hall, T., Beecham, S., & Rainer, A. (2002). Requirements problems in twelve software companies: An empirical analysis. *IEEE Software, 149*(5), 153–160. doi:10.1049/ip-sen:20020694

Hamill, M., & Katerina, G. P. (2009). Common Trends in Software Fault and Failure Data. *IEEE Transactions on Software Engineering, 35*(4), 484–496. doi:10.1109/TSE.2009.3

Hayes, J. H. (2003). Building a Requirement Fault Taxonomy: Experiences from a NASA Verification and Validation Research Project. In *Proceedings of the 14thInternational Symposium on Software Reliability Engineering (ISSRE'03),* Denver, CO. IEEE Computer Society.

Hillson, D. A. (1997). Towards Risk Maturity Model. *International Journal of Project and Business Risk Management, 1*(1), 35–45.

Islam, S. (2009). Software Development Risk Management Model – A Goal Driven Approach. In *ESEC/FSE'09 Joint 12th European Software Engineering Conference (ESEC) and 17th ACM SIGSOFT Symposium on the Foundations of Software Engineering (FSE-17).* Amsterdam, The Netherlands: ACM.

Jiang, J., & Klein, G. (2000). Software development risks to project effectiveness. *Journal of Systems and Software*, *52*(1), 3–10. doi:10.1016/S0164-1212(99)00128-4

Keshlaf, A. A., & Hashim, K. (2000). A Model and Prototype Tool to Manage Software Risks. In *Proceedings of the 1st Asia-Pacific Conference on Quality Software (APAQS'00)*. Washington, DC. 10.1109/APAQ.2000.883803

Kontio, J. (2001). *Software Engineering Risk Management: A Method, Improvement Framework, and Empirical Evaluation* [Doctoral dissertation]. Helsinki University of Technology.

Kontio, J., & Basili, V. R. (1997). Empirical evaluation of a risk management method. In *Software Engineering Institute Conference on Risk Management*, Atlantic City, NJ.

Kotonya, G., & Sommerville, I. (1998). *Requirement Engineering Process and Techniques*. Wiley.

Kumar, N. S., Vinay Sagar, A., & Sudheer, Y. (2010). Software risk management- an integrated approach. *Global Journal of Computer Science and Technology*, *10*(15), 53–57.

Lindquist, C. (2005). Required: Fixing the requirements mess; The requirements process, literally, deciding what should be included in software, is destroying projects in ways that aren't evident until its too late. Some CIOs are stepping in to rewrite the rules. *CIO*, *19*(4), 53–60.

McConnell, S. (1997). *Software Project Survival Guide: How to Be Sure Your First Important Project Isn't Your Last*. Redmond, WA: Microsoft Press.

Niazi, M., & Shastry, S. (2003). Role of requirements engineering in software development process: An empirical study. In *Proceedings of the 7th Intl. Multi Topic Conf. (INMIC2003)*, Islamabad, Pakistan. IEEE. 10.1109/INMIC.2003.1416759

Nuseibeh, B. A., & Easterbrook, S. M. (2000). Requirements engineering: A roadmap. In *Proceedings of the 22nd International Conference on Software Engineering (ICSE '00)*, Limerick, Ireland. IEEE.

Pfleeger, S. L. (2000). Risky business: What we have yet to learn about risk management. *Journal of Systems and Software*, *53*(3), 265–273. doi:10.1016/S0164-1212(00)00017-0

Pohl, K., & Rupp, C. (2010). *Basiswissen Requirements Engineering* (2nd ed.). Heidelberg: Dpunkt Verlag. doi:10.1007/978-3-642-12578-2

Procaccino, J. D., Verner, J., Overmyer, S., & Darter, M. (2002). Case study: Factors for early prediction of software development success. *Information and Software Technology*, *44*(1), 53–62. doi:10.1016/S0950-5849(01)00217-8

Ropponen, J., & Lyytinen, K. (2000). Component of Software Development Risk: How to address them? A project manager survey. *IEEE Transactions on Software Engineering*, *26*(2), 98–112. doi:10.1109/32.841112

Roy, G. G. (2014). A Risk Management Framework for Software Engineering Practice. In *Proceedings of the Australian Software Engineering Conference (AAWEC '04)*, Melbourne, Australia. IEEE.

Sadiq, M., Rahmani, M. K. I., Ahmad, M. W., & Jung, S. (2010). Software risk assessment and evaluation process (SRAEP) using model based approach. In *International conference on Networking and Information Technology(ICNIT)*, Manila, Philippines. IEEE. 10.1109/ICNIT.2010.5508535

Sarigiannidis, L., & Chatzoglou, P. (2011). Software Development Project Risk Management: A New Conceptual Framework. *Journal of Software Engineering and Applications*, *4*(5), 293–305. doi:10.4236/jsea.2011.45032

Sommerville, I. (2004). *Software Engineering (7ᵗʰ ed.)*. Pearson Addison Wesley.

Stern, R., & Arias, J. C. (2011). Review of Risk Management Methods. *Business Intelligence Journal*, *4*(1), 59–78.

Suebkhuna, B., & Ramingwong, S. (2011). Towards a complete project oriented risk management model: A refinement of PRORISK. In *Eighth International Joint Conference on Computer Science and software Engineering(JCSSE)*, Nakhon Pathom, Thailand. IEEE. 10.1109/JCSSE.2011.5930146

Walia, G. S., & Carver, J. C. (2009). A systematic literature review to identify and classify software requirement errors. *Information and Software Technology*, *51*(7), 1087–1109. doi:10.1016/j.infsof.2009.01.004

Wallace, L., & Keil, M. (2004). Software project risks and their effect on outcomes. *Communications of the ACM*, *47*(4), 68–73. doi:10.1145/975817.975819

Westfall, L. (2011). Software Risk Management. In *International Conference on Software Quality*. San Diego, CA.

This research was previously published in the Journal of Cases on Information Technology (JCIT), 21(2); pages 51-64, copyright year 2019 by IGI Publishing (an imprint of IGI Global).

Chapter 32
Building an Ambidextrous Software Security Initiative

Daniela Soares Cruzes
SINTEF Digital, Norway

Espen Agnalt Johansen
VISMA, Norway

ABSTRACT

Improving software security in software development teams is an enduring challenge for software companies. In this chapter, the authors present one strategy for addressing this pursuit of improvement. The approach is ambidextrous in the sense that it focuses on approaching software security activities both from a top-down and a bottom-up perspective, combining elements usually found separately in software security initiatives. The approach combines (1) top-down formal regulatory mechanisms deterring breaches of protocol and enacting penalties where they occur and (2) bottom-up capacity building and persuasive encouragement of adherence to guidance by professional self-determination, implementation, and improvement support (e.g., training, stimulating, interventions). The ambidextrous governance framework illustrates distinct, yet complementary, global and local roles: (1) ensuring the adoption and implementation of software security practices, (2) enabling and (3) empowering software development teams to adapt and add to overall mandates, and (4) embedding cultures of improvement.

INTRODUCTION

Today, nearly all sectors of society depend on software systems to operate efficiently. As the dependency on software has grown, so have the threats towards these systems and the potential consequences of incidents (Tøndel, Jaatun, Cruzes, & Moe, 2017). Though network security measures (such as firewalls and anti-virus software) can improve the security of the software systems, these only address the symptoms of the real problem: software that is crippled with vulnerabilities (McGraw, 2006).

DOI: 10.4018/978-1-6684-3702-5.ch032

Building security into the software through adopting software security activities and measures in the development process is a direct and effective way of dealing with cyber threats towards software systems (Tøndel, Jaatun, Cruzes, & Moe, 2017). This, however, adds to the development time and cost, and this addition needs to be well implemented to be effective. In many ways, security can be considered to be in conflict with the current trend of "continuous development" (Fitzgerald & Stol, 2017), reducing efficiency by delaying delivery of new features (at least in the shorter term, though costs may be saved through having to provide fewer fixes later).

Many researchers affirm that it may be more difficult to establish a working process for software security activities in agile development compared to waterfall-based development, where you could more easily have mandatory or recommended security activities for the different software development phases (Ben Othmane, Angin, Weffers, & Bhargava, 2014) (Ambler, 2008) (Microsoft, 2019). (Oyetoyan, Jaatun, & Cruzes, 2017) provide a brief overview of secure SDLs (Secure Development Lifecycle) and conclude that traditional approaches to software security do not necessarily work well with agile development processes. Additionally, security, as a non-functional requirement (NFR), is largely a systemic property, and with agile development it can be more of a challenge to have a complete view of the final system (Ben Othmane, Angin, Weffers, & Bhargava, 2014).

Non-functional requirements (NFRs) focus on aspects that typically involve or crosscut several functional requirements (Ambler, 2008). Although considered important and crucial to project success, it is common to see non-functional requirements losing attention in comparison to functional requirements. (Crispin & Gregory, 2009) argue that with that business partners might assume that the development team will take care of non-functional requirements such as performance, reliability, and security. But in reality, due to the agile philosophy that stimulates delivering user value early and often, the prioritization of quality attributes can be hard in early deliverable increments, resulting in hard-to-modify, unreliable, slow, or insecure systems (Baca, Boldt, Carlsson, & Jacobsson, 2015) (Bellomo, Gorton, & Kazman, 2015) (Wäyrynen, Bodén, & Boström, 2004). It is not rare to observe in software organizations that security practices are not prioritized, either because the practitioners are not able to see the relevance and importance of the activities to the improvement of the security in the project (Camacho, Marczak, & Cruzes, 2016) or because non-functional or cross-functional issues are perceived as a low risk for many systems (Jaatun, Cruzes, Bernsmed, Tøndel, & Røstad, 2015). Another issue is that agile development teams are generally composed of a small number of developers, and many times are composed of generalists. However, the proper handling of software security requires specialized tools and might need specialized knowledge. Given this need for specialized knowledge, a team member with specialized security skills might be required to avoid issues in production (Gregory & Crispin, 2014). As it is nowadays, there are usually not designated roles for security in the software development teams.

At the same time, agile development may come with some opportunities regarding security, e.g., to adapt to new security threats and to maintain the interaction with customers about security. (Tøndel, Jaatun, Cruzes, & Moe, 2017) propose a risk-centric approach to security. The authors found that the observed software security practices in software organizations were not based on an assessment of software security risks, but rather driven by compliance. Additionally, their practices could in many cases be characterized as arbitrary, late, and error driven, with limited follow up on any security issues throughout their software development projects. Based on the results of the study, the authors identified the need for improvements in three main areas: responsibilities and stakeholder cooperation, risk perception and competence, and practical ways of doing risk analysis in agile projects.

Still, to be effective, the software security initiative needs a good governance. In the agile software development world, a security engineering process is unacceptable if it is perceived to run counter to the agile values, and agile teams have thus approached software security activities in their own way. To improve security within agile settings requires that management understands the current practices of software security activities within their agile teams and to appropriately influence the adoption of these practices. Many roles in an organization can have major influences on a development project's approach to security and can have important parts to play when it comes to identifying and understanding risk, making risk-based decisions in the projects, and having a proper security focus (Tøndel, Jaatun, Cruzes, & Moe, 2017). In this chapter, the focus is on another angle of the establishment of a software security program: the top-down and bottom-up approach, an ambidextrous approach to build and maintain a software security initiative, which is very much related to the way developers address security in projects.

This chapter is based on results from the ongoing project named SoS-Agile, which investigates how to meaningfully integrate software security into agile software development activities (Cruzes, Jaatun, & Oyetoyan, 2018) (SoS-Agile Project (2015-2020), u.d.). The method of choice for the project is Canonical Action Research (Greenwood & Levin, 2006) which is one of the many forms of action research (Davison, Martinsons, & Kock, 2004) (Davison, Martinsons, & Ou, 2012); it is iterative, rigorous, and collaborative, involving focus on both organizational development and the generation of knowledge. The combination of scientific and practical objectives aligns with the basic tenet of action research, which is to merge theory and practice in a way such that real-world problems are solved by theoretically informed actions in collaboration between researchers and practitioners (Greenwood & Levin, 2006).

SOFTWARE SECURITY AND AGILE

Software security or security engineering is the idea of engineering a software system so that it keeps working correctly even under malicious attack (McGraw, Software Security, 2004). The (ISO/IEC 25010, 2011) defines security as a capability of the software to protect information and functionalities while allowing authorized users to access information and functionality to which they have permission. (Firesmith, 2003) from the Software Engineering Institute (SEI) published a technical note where he presents information models providing a standard terminology and set of concepts that explain the similarities between the asset-based, risk-driven methods for identifying and analysing safety, security, and survivability requirements as well as a rationale for the similarity in architectural mechanisms that are commonly used to fulfil these requirements. Firesmith's definition of security is, *"the degree to which malicious harm to a valuable asset is prevented, detected, and reacted to. Security is the quality factor that signifies the degree to which valuable assets are protected from significant threats posed by malicious attackers."* (Firesmith, 2003) decomposes security into many different quality subfactors:

- **Access control** is the degree to which the system limits access to its resources only to its authorized externals (e.g., human users, programs, processes, devices, or other systems). The following are quality subfactors of the access-control quality subfactor:
- **Identification** is the degree to which the system identifies (i.e., recognizes) its externals before interacting with them.

- **Authentication** is the degree to which the system verifies the claimed identities of its externals before interacting with them. Thus, authentication verifies that the claimed identity is legitimate and belongs to the claimant.
- **Authorization** is the degree to which access and usage privileges of authenticated externals are properly granted and enforced.
- **Attack/harm detection** is the degree to which attempted or successful attacks (or their resulting harm) are detected, recorded, and notified.
- **Availability protection** is the degree to which various types of Denial of Service (DoS) attacks are prevented from decreasing the operational availability of the system. This is quite different from the traditional availability quality factor, which deals with the operational availability of the system when it is not under attack.
- **Integrity** is the degree to which components are protected from intentional and unauthorized corruption. Integrity includes data, hardware, personnel and software integrity.
- **Nonrepudiation** is the degree to which a party to an interaction (e.g., message, transaction, or transmission of data) is prevented from successfully repudiating (i.e., denying) any aspect of the interaction.
- **Physical protection** is the degree to which the system protects itself and its components from physical attack.
- **Privacy** is the degree to which unauthorized parties are prevented from obtaining sensitive information. Privacy includes confidentiality, defined as the degree to which sensitive information is not disclosed to unauthorized parties (e.g., individuals, programs, processes, devices, or other systems).
- **Prosecution** is the degree to which the system supports the prosecution of attackers.
- **Recovery** is the degree to which the system recovers after a successful attack.
- **Security auditing** is the degree to which security personnel are enabled to audit the status and use of security mechanisms by analyzing security-related events.
- **System adaptation** is the degree to which the system learns from attacks in order to adapt its security countermeasures to protect itself from similar attacks in the future.

Once that all these factors shall be addressed during the software development lifecycle, security cannot be treated as an add-on functionality or isolated product feature (McGraw, 2006), and it is thus important that security is a "built-in" in the process and the product. However, a traditional security engineering process is often associated with additional development efforts and is likely to invoke resentment among agile development teams (Ben Othmane, Angin, Weffers, & Bhargava, 2014). A software security approach tailored to the agile mind-set thus seems necessary.

Some approaches have been proposed to integrate security activities into agile development, e.g., the Microsoft SDL for Agile (Microsoft, 2019). The Building Security in Maturity Model (BSIMM) (McGraw, 2006) has been used to measure security practices in different organizations and to give advice on which practices are more commonly adopted by organizations. BSIMM is useful for measuring the software security maturity of an organization and helping them formulate an overall security strategy. Recently, the OWASP organization also released a new version of their Software Assurance Maturity Model (SAMM 2.0) (Deleersnyder, 2019), which provides an effective and measurable way for organizations to analyse and improve their software security posture. While these activities could be argued to be beneficial and cost-effective to integrate, there are still gaps between what is "preached" and what is "practiced" in software organizations. These approaches have been criticized for looking similar to the traditional versions in terms of workload (e.g., performing a long list of security verification and validation tasks) (Ben Othmane, Angin, Weffers, & Bhargava, 2014). As a result, "agile" organizations have approached software security in a way that fits their processes and practices.

Thus, regardless of whether agile is perceived to be incompatible with any particular secure software development lifecycle, the major discussion we should have is how to improve security within the agile context (Bartsch, 2011). Previous studies (Ayalew, Kidane, & Carlsson, 2013) (Baca & Carlsson, 2011) have investigated which security activities are practiced in different organizations, and which are compatible with agile practices from cost and benefit perspectives. A set of challenges of developing secure software using the agile development approach and methods are reported in the literature (Oueslati H., Rahman, ben Othmane, & Ghani, 2016). (Oueslati, Rahman, & Othmane, 2015) performed a systematic review in which they identified 20 challenges for developing secure software using the agile approach, classified into 5 categories. A summary of the challenges is provided in Table 1.

Table 1. Classification of the security challenges by (Oueslati, Rahman, & Othmane, 2015)

Challenge
Software development life-cycle challenges
Security requirements elicitation activity is not included in the agile development methods
Risks assessment activity is not included in the agile development methods
Security related activities need to be applied for each development iteration
Iteration time is limited and may not fit time-consuming security activities
Incremental development challenges
Refactoring practice breaks security constraints
Changes of requirements and design breaks system security requirements
Continuous code changes hinder assurance activities
Requirement changes makes the trace of the requirements to security objectives difficult
Security assurance challenges
Security assessment favours detailed documentation
Tests are, in general, insufficient to ensure the implementation of security requirements
Tests do no cover in general, all vulnerability cases
Security tests are in general difficult to automate
Continuous changing of the development processes (to support lesson learned) conflicts with audit needs of uniform stable processes
Awareness and collaboration challenges
Security requirements are often neglected
Developers lack experience on secure software
Customers lack security awareness
Developer role must be separate from security reviewer role to have objective results
Security management challenges
Security activities increases the cost of the software
There is no incentive for organizations to develop security features in early increments
Organizations compromise security activities to accommodate accelerated releasing schedule

AN AMBIDEXTROUS SECURITY INITIATIVE

Research on ambidexterity represents a major effort to address the management of paradoxical tensions, contrasting efficiency, control, and incremental improvement on one hand, and flexibility, autonomy, and experimentation on the other (Xiao, Witschey, & Murphy-Hil, 2014). Ambidexterity as a capability for resolving organizational tensions has been studied in a variety of forms. Some forms focus on the alignment of disparate organizational processes in relatively static operating conditions, while other forms focus on dynamic re-alignments that adapt to changing demands (Xiao, Witschey, & Murphy-Hil, 2014).

Creative Industry Organizations' (CIOs') achieve ambidexterity in different ways. (Wu & Wu, 2016) performed a systematic review on how CIOs achieve alignment ambidexterity and adaptability ambidexterity. The authors found there is a dominance of contextual approaches and the prevalence of external engagements specific to CIO ambidexterity. It also reveals different solutions adopted for alignment ambidexterity and adaptability ambidexterity. Contextual approaches involve top-down system arrangements that coordinate individuals' actions and interactions to achieve organizational goals that would otherwise be conflicting on a daily and continuous basis. Creative production requires a close alignment of all goals for one product (alignment ambidexterity) and a constant pursuit of new creativity over time (adaptability ambidexterity).

(McDermott, Hamel, Steel, Flood, & Mkee, 2015), motivated by the need to improving healthcare governance, studied two national healthcare regulators who were adopting novel "hybrid" regulatory control strategies in pursuit of improvement, which combines: (1) top-down formal regulatory mechanisms deterring breaches of protocol and enacting penalties where they occur (e.g. standard-setting, monitoring, and accountability); and (2) bottom-up capacity building and persuasive encouragement of adherence to guidance by professional self-determination, implementation, and improvement support (e.g. training, stimulating interventions). (McDermott, Hamel, Steel, Flood, & Mkee, 2015) identify socio-historical contextual factors constraining and enabling regulatory hybridity, whether and how it can be re-created, and circumstances when the approaches might be delivered separately. They developed a goal-oriented governance framework illustrating distinct, yet complementary, national and local organizational roles: (1) ensuring the adoption and implementation of best practice, (2) enabling and (3) empowering staff to adapt and add to national mandates, and (4) embedding cultures of improvement.

This model, although designed in relation to healthcare governance, resonated very well to the context of governance for a software security initiative for agile software development teams. Adapted from the model from (McDermott, Hamel, Steel, Flood, & Mkee, 2015), Figure 1 details distinct, yet complementary, roles in the security program. It provides a framework for identifying potential company-improvement supporting roles to deliver together in pursuit of an ambidextrous program (e.g. combining top-down and bottom-up supporting roles). It also identifies supporting local roles in the development team. The approach assumes that the teams are self-managed agile teams that need leadership on security but must retain the continuity and self-management of their software development: (1) ensuring the adoption and implementation of software security practices, (2) enabling and (3) empowering software development teams to adapt and add to overall mandates, and (4) embedding cultures of improvement. The following subsections explain how the model from Figure 1 was instantiated in the Visma software security initiative.

Figure 1. Ambidextrous governance model
Source: Adapted from (McDermott, Hamel, Steel, Flood, & Mkee, 2015)

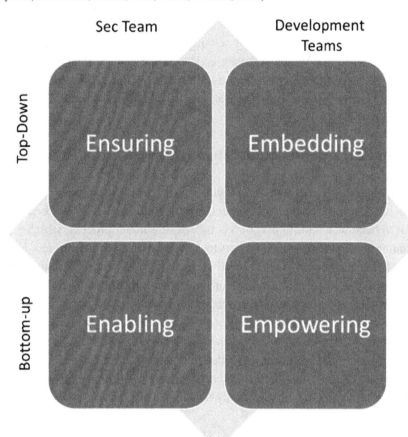

About Visma

Visma is a software company headquartered in Norway that delivers software that simplifies and digitizes core business processes in the private and public sector. Visma believes in empowering people through technology. Since Visma was founded in 1997, it has grown to become a family of more than 11000 employees. Today Visma has a local presence in more than 16 countries and over 200 offices. By taking advantage of opportunities in a fast-moving market characterized by rapid development in technology, Visma has turned into an international leader in cloud software delivery.

Visma is not a monolithically hierarchical organization; Visma is easier to understand if viewed as a federation of around 100 independent-minded companies, but with a shared infrastructure and services. Acquisitions are essential to Visma's strategy; Visma invests in local market leaders and specialists, making sure that local expertise is intact as it expands its operations globally. At the same time, Visma has the international reach to be at the forefront of development and support for both small businesses and large private and public organizations, with software tailored to their needs. It is important in this model that the company moves fast, has short decision processes, and empowers its employees with responsibilities.

Most teams in Visma are the direct result of acquisitions. The teams are maintained as individual companies and are not under centralized, strong governance, apart from financial governance. The teams are responsible for the entire lifecycle of their service, while the rest of the overhead is there to support them. That means the software teams should stay self-managed, but they still have to produce software that is secure and does not expose Visma software and customers to security risks. As every country has its own laws and regulations that impact the way a business is run, the software development also needs to be done in such a way that the software is always up to date and compliant with both local and global requirements.

Ensuring the Adoption and Implementation of the Security Practices

Visma has established processes, methods, and technologies, and has embraced proven standards to ensure security and accessibility for their customers. As the nature of threats is constantly changing, security focus needs to become a natural part of Visma's development process, which is constantly improving. From planning to deployment of new services or features. Visma products follow the Visma Secure Development Lifecycle (Figure 2 and Figure 3), meaning that security requirements are embedded and measured during the service's lifetime. For the definition of the Visma Secure Development Lifecycle, the security team, in a top-down approach, made an analysis of which activities to include in the lifecycle, agreeing on what needed to be done at the time, starting with some simple risk analysis. The program was inspired by activities described in BSIMM and OWASP SAMM. The main decision at that time was to figure out what was most important and what the security team was able to innovate and implement as soon as possible. The security team chose to start with the adoption of SAST (Static Analysis Tools) and extend from there. The security team was then composed by the security manager and four security team members.

The security manager's main task in this phase was to build a financial platform and a support system both inside and outside of Visma to ensure the program would succeed. A secondary task of security management was to embed the security program into the already-existing quality management systems (QMSs) to ensure the existing command line executes on the guidance from security management. This was chosen to avoid building a separate governance structure from the rest of the company and to enable the line managers to take an active part in security management. The rest of the security team focused on the services. Clearly the investment required in compiling and sharing best practice evidence, as well as engaging in scrutiny to ensure its adoption, makes it appropriate for a top-down organization to lead this role. After two years, the lifecycle evolved to what is shown in Figure 3.

Some of the software security activities that are executed in Visma are:

- **Security Self-Assessment:** A document/checklist that describes the high level of cyber security of a product. By answering the self-assessment, the teams are able start to document the security decisions and status of their product/services. And, threat modelling is integrated into the security self-assessment;
- **Security audits and penetration testing using both internal and external experts**. These include:
  - Security testing of source code (Static Application Security Testing - SAST);
  - Security testing of compiled code (Dynamic Application Security Testing - DAST);
  - Manual Application Vulnerability Testing (externally known as Penetration Tests);

- ○ Automated Third-Party Vulnerability Testing Service (ATVS) testing the security of the third party components in the finished products;
- **Cyber Threat Intelligence Service (CTI)**, an intelligence service that detects, analyses, and reports in a team context about external threats against their products;
- **Bug Bounty Program:** A service offered by websites, organizations and software developers by which individuals can receive recognition and compensation for reporting bugs, especially those pertaining to security exploits and vulnerabilities;
- **Responsible Disclosure Program:** A vulnerability disclosure model in which a vulnerability is disclosed only after a period of time that allows for the vulnerability to be patched or mended;
- **Red Teaming Service**, a service the teams may use to get a Red Team exercise delivered to their service;
- **Trust Centre:** A publicly available website with explanations about the Security Program.
- Documentation of compliance against the Security Program is maintained and is part of the Key Performance Indicators (KPIs) for the management of Visma.

Figure 2. First instantiation of the Visma secure software development lifecycle (2015-2018)

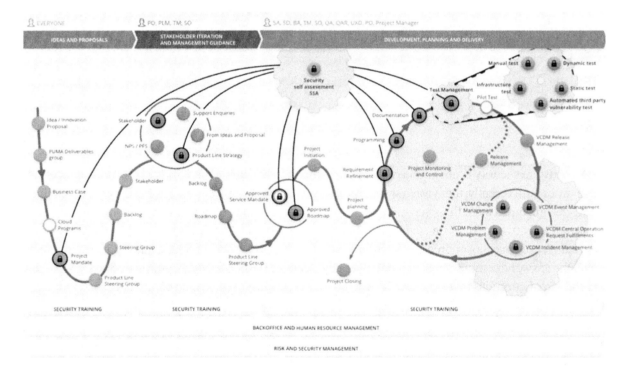

Enabling the Adoption and Implementation of the Security Practices

This quadrant identifies a persuasion-oriented, capacity-building role for an organization, to enable employees to engage in bottom-up improvement activities, including adapting organizational agendas. The focus is on education and training that enables action on the basis of performance information. The assumption is that the teams are unable to make qualified decisions if they are deprived of information that gives them direction. Although potentially counterintuitive for a bottom-up approach, the need to spread improvement capacity across the system means that the centralized provision of change resources and training—as well as networks to spread learning—is appropriate.

Figure 3. Second instantiation of the Visma secure software development lifecycle

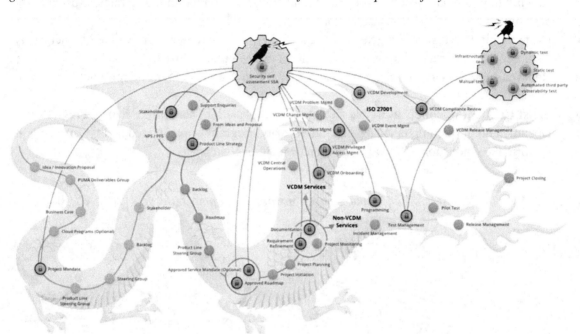

As software security is not a subject that was common in the curricula of many software engineering universities until recently, there was a strong need to build capacity in security. The basic concepts include secure design, threat modelling, secure coding, security testing, and privacy. But, for self-managed teams, it was not effective to focus on standard and generic classroom trainings. Visma's strategical thinking was to then use coaching approaches such as a security self-assessment (SSA), a questionnaire in which the teams answer questions about and document the security of their services/products. See Figure 4 for an example of questions that the teams have to answer on the use of up to date components and libraries. The purpose/background of the SSA is described in Visma as to:

- Provide teams with a documented way to assess the security of their service/product according to a common checklist;
- Identify improvements regarding the security of the service and decide how to prioritize them;
- Have a common approach on how to work with proactive security measures;
- Educate and increase awareness of security topics for team members;
- Place responsibility of security inside the teams;

Figure 4. Example of question from the self-assessment questionnaire

Another strategy to enable the teams was the provision of the whole infrastructure and licensing of the static analysis tools (SAST). Visma has decided to have one official SAST and configure it as a centralized resource that the software development teams could use. This enabled the teams to start as soon as possible with the use of the tools. The purpose/background defined in the security initiative was to:

- Prevent security problems due to implementation defects in source code;
- Support automation so it can be done more often and by more teams;
- Give teams visibility into the potential implementation defects and a way to manage them;
- Provide a capability to identify potential security defects early in the development cycle;
- Provide support for the majority of languages and compilers used in Visma; and
- Provide in-context remediation advice to developers to help them fix defects and learn.

In addition, as seen in Figure 2 and 3, all additional security activities are placed inline and the main effort is to control the leadership and enable the teams to make decisions themselves by reducing control elements to be rational and descriptive for the process they use.

Empowering the Teams

Quadrant 3 notes the important persuasive organizational role in empowering employees to utilize their bottom-up improvement capacity in their own teams—adding to organizational efforts via trial and error and innovative problem-solving and sharing findings from local evaluation efforts. Creating such a supportive climate for service improvement requires attention to sharing best-practice information and developing local leadership in security. In agile self-managed teams, the judgments and interactions of individual team members are not driven directly by managerial policies or intervention but occur as real-time responses in relation to the flexibility of each team member.

The security team in Visma is structured as shown in Figure 5. The Product Security Group supports Visma to deliver secure services to the customers; they are coaches and enablers for the development teams during the entire product development lifecycle. The product security group builds, maintains, and supports services such as the ones mentioned in Figures 2 and 3: the security self-assessment, manual application vulnerability assessment, SAST, responsible disclosure, bug bounty, etc. It was also decided to have one security engineer per team who was assigned to "champion" the security program in their teams. The security engineers are also seen as ambassadors and advocates for the program.

With the security engineer role, the teams were able to decide how to divide responsibilities on the different tasks that Visma has decided to include in the Secure Software Development Lifecycle. The security engineer can also delegate tasks to different team members and have even other security engineers in the team. The security engineers are given a task, but they decide the problem-solving strategy. For example, with the self-assessment questionnaire, the security engineer role is more of a facilitator to gather the information needed to answer all the questions and then go through the evaluation and approval process with the product security group. Having the security engineer role in the team increases the chances that the team will try activities and fail locally and also ask for help when they do not find ways to solve their problems with security locally. The security engineer has communication channels that were established with the product security group; through these communication channels, the security engineers can share information about the teams, hear about other teams' approaches, get informed about diverse threats and incident cases, and ask for help. To summarize, the security engineers are defined to have the following purpose/background:

- Spread and increase security awareness/culture;
- Share knowledge on the security program and how to use it;
- Scale security work in an efficient and tested way; and
- Be a point of contact to the security team—for example, for upcoming changes in the Security Program or sharing information, best practices, or questions among teams.

Additionally, empowering can be fostered by giving flexibility to the teams to adapt the way they adopt the practices/tools/techniques that are ensured by the top-down management. For example, for the SAST (Static Analysis Tools), the teams are given flexibility to decide how to implement the tools in their pipelines and how to follow up with the vulnerabilities that are disclosed by the tools. The teams also have the power to decide and reason the use of other tools in addition to the one that Visma has chosen to adopt company wide. In this way, the teams can foster local improvements to the use of the SAST by adding extra checks in their code and improving confidence in the security of their code. Many teams have done that. Many teams have also innovated in the way they have followed up with the compliance to use the SAST; in cases where the SAST chosen by Visma was too slow for their code base (sometimes up to a week), they have, for example, decided to conduct an incremental analysis of the code base using another tool and then running the Visma's SAST on a monthly basis. The teams report that the Visma's SAST takes longer but goes more thoroughly into the code and uncovers issues that other free tools do not.

Figure 5. Security team configuration in Visma

Annually, the Product Security group holds feedback sessions to get feedback from the teams on the security program and also to foster improvement actions on the program. These feedback sessions are called Security Chartering and provide a good channel to empower the security engineers giving them voice to raise their concerns, success cases, and experiences with the program. In addition, the Security Chartering meetings created an arena for them to talk with each other and share experiences. We have noticed that these meetings have triggered motivation to start some activities that they have not started. The sessions are run in 1,5 hours, and the structure consists of asking the security engineers to talk freely about the security program. As an example of one of these sessions was structured as follows:

- Around the table, getting to know each other (10 min);
- Rating the confidence of the team in software security (from 1-10) (10min);
- List the tasks that makes us great on security (30 min) (Things the team does already, Things that the team does but not part of the program, Things that the team wishes to have focus in Visma, Thing that the team are doing for security and it is meaningful, painful but meaningful, doing only because the team has to, not meaningful);
- Describing the motivation for performing security work - we used the technique of "Thumbs-up-thumbs-down-new-ideas-and-recognition" (30 min);
- Feedback for Security team (10 min) – giving written feedback to the security team on the security program.

Embedding the Security Activities

Lastly, Quadrant 4 (Figure 1) notes the importance of organizations engaging in top-down efforts to embed cultures of improvement, innovation, and learning—via board policies and priorities, governance, local improvement support units, and celebrating success. Quadrant 4's focus may arise via voluntarism, and also in response to the accountability mechanisms (performance and process standards). While deep-rooted change to values and mindsets may be difficult to achieve, behavioral compliance is more generally feasible, and may be captured via performance-monitoring mechanisms.

The Visma Security Maturity Index (SMI) was created in 2018. The purpose of this index is mainly to create a security gamification and KPI dashboard, as shown in Figure 6, by collecting and gathering data from multiple systems for an easy overview. The services are placed in tiers depending on their strategic importance, and they perform according to their measurements. The results from SMI are transparent and shared across the company to foster these two fundamental values that are critical for Agile/DevOps teams to work. The index is based on penalty points, depending on how serious the lack of compliance is. The initial priority for was to create a performance-monitoring mechanism based on the initial services of the Visma Secure software development lifecycle, such as the self-assessment, SAST, dependency checking, manual security testing, and triaging of the issues and how much this shows maturity in self-managing of the security issues. For example, security group in Visma recommends that each team will perform the self-assessment of their service/product once a year, and when the validity of the self-assessment expires, there is a penalty of 3,000 points. The same rule applies for the manual security testing, but the penalty is 1,000 points. The strategy in Visma was to initially only have in the SMI items that were easy to automate and to follow up on, and later on adding other, more qualitative, items. The gamification happens when internally the teams try to work their way up to the required tier and to keep their status, as well as across teams when the different service owners compare their services to others and work/prioritize work that will lead them to the required tier in the maturity index.

Figure 6a. Security maturity index Visma

Figure 6b. Security maturity index Visma

Transparency is very important for the SMI to work, first because it fosters the visibility of the internal working practices of the teams, and second because if there is manipulation of the data that are plotted by the SMI, the whole system loses credibility and effect. It was communicated to the development teams that the goals of the SMI are to have a tool for fostering and tracking improvement, and it is very important that this goal is shared in all levels of the organization, so the SMI is used as it should be and not misused for other reasons than it was originally intended for. It happens sometimes that the teams do not improve over time, and they do not advance in tiers, and then the motivation of the team goes down. The reasons for non-improvement can be various, but one recurrent reason is the lack of prioritization of the activities that will make an effect on the numbers and ultimately on the tier upgrade. When teams change tiers (e.g., from Silver to Gold), the teams can celebrate improvements, and this has been a good motivator for people to keep focusing on security over time. The teams that have leaders that base their motivational schemes on stimulating good behavior seem to be more focused on celebrations, while the individual leaders that base their motivation on fear seem to focus on "deviation from norm". From our observations it seem like the reinforcement of positive behavior trough celebrations and similar gives the most lasting results.

In the Trust Centre, the customer is provided an explanation on how the security program works and what to expect from their chosen product with regards to security. This effort is top down but designed in such a way that it only reflects externally what is possible to support with evidence for clients by the development teams. The teams are given an expectation to perform direct, one-on-one meetings with their clients and, in these, share details of how they have chosen to solve the security issues in their context. The meetings are called "Level 3 meetings" and require the team to share all outputs from the security program with their clients in a confidential setting. A requirement for the client is to ensure they have individuals in the meetings with sufficient technical competency to be a peer to the Visma representative.

PITFALLS WITH AN AMBIDEXTROUS SECURITY PROGRAM

Management Support for Security is Crucial

Security development activities are frequently prioritized lower than functional development activities owing to the customer's value-driven perspective. As there is a lack of an established risk-to-value calculation for security activities, prioritization becomes difficult, and often the most technical person is chosen to handle that calculation even though they are not equipped to do so. To build security into an organization's DNA, a company must create a security culture across the organization. If the organization does not invest in the people, tools and processes, then the innovation will not happen. It is therefore crucial to stablish a financial model that will support the pace of the program.

One Size Does Not Fit All

Implicit in the framework is a suggestion of a variety of contextually responsive ways of achieving the company's goal of continuous, proactive improvement. Therefore, an "one size fits all" approach does not work, and to achieve a uniform level of success overall with the teams, there is a need for customization of the approach to the different software development teams. Some teams are open for innovation in their way of working; others are not so open to changes. In addition, the teams have different levels of maturity in software development or with previous experiences with security incidents, also impacting their level of receptiveness for top-down demands. For some teams, the approach to security will have to be adopted first from the bottom-up and then top-down.

We have also faced differences in cultures in the different countries, which also deserves appropriate measures to balance the top-down or bottom-up approach. Cultural differences in leadership styles often create unexpected misunderstandings and, many times, conflicts and barriers against top-down decisions. Approaches to authority and decision making are not the only ways in which cultures differ, but they are quite important in the leadership context. When impacting the practices of the development teams on a daily basis, it is very important that the security group leaders are aware of these differences and address them appropriately.

In the case of Visma, the cultural bias was clearly identified by management. To create effective management of these units, the chosen approach was to use different people to relate to the various teams. Some teams seem to respond better to coaching from top management, while others seem to respond better to coaching from individuals seen more as peers to them. To achieve this, a very flat organizational structure, with a focus on self-management, was chosen by security management. Current evidence shows that this works if the trust is established and frequent communication is available to sort out differences in opinion.

The second part of this was to establish the client as the most powerful entity in the organizational chart. This change gives more power to the teams, allowing them to establish direct relations to the client and enabling to harvest, among other things, security requirements, directly from the client (as opposed to getting them from a rather large policy collection).

A Security Engineer/Champion is Not Always Easy to Find

An innovation can be any idea, product, process, or object that is perceived as new to an individual or group (Rogers, 1995). In the case of the software security initiative, it is any new software security task that the software development team will start performing. But the innovation needs a champion to survive. Traditionally, "champion" has not been part of anybody's job description; rather, this is a role that some people in the right place of the organization have taken informally upon themselves. The agile software development teams are not usually composed with one security expert or a security leader. (Howell, 2005) studied 72 innovations in 38 companies, and discovered there are personal characteristics and behaviors that differentiate effective champions from ineffective ones. This observation was also true in the security program in Visma. In order to function effectively, a champion must have access to the required resources (including intra-organizational networking skills), as well as past experience with the innovation process (Weidman, Young-Corbett, Fiori, Koebel, & Montague, 2015). He also needs to have other characteristics as also stated by (Howell, 2005):

- Convey confidence and enthusiasm about the innovation;
- Enlist the support and involvement of key stakeholders;
- Persist in the face of adversity;
- Scout widely for new ideas and information and rely on personal networks;
- Have wide general knowledge, breadth of experience, and diverse interests;
- View the role broadly, are well informed about issues that affect the organization;
- Frame ideas as opportunities and tie ideas to positive organizational outcomes such as profitability, enhanced reputation, or strategic advantage;
- Use both formal and informal selling channels; and
- Are high self-monitors: They analyze potential reactions of influence targets and tailor their selling strategies to be maximally persuasive.

It is not every software development team that will have a team member with all these characteristics. Sometimes the security engineer/champion will be appointed to the role without much predisposition to the role or pursuing the characteristics that it takes to perform a good job in championing the security program in the team. In those cases, these security champions/engineers need to be coached closely and supported in the role.

It is Easy to Forget to be Bottom Up

The model shown in this chapter involves top-down system arrangements that coordinate individuals' actions and interactions to achieve organizational goals that would otherwise be conflicting on a daily and continuous basis. There is a dynamic shifting between the poles of top-down and bottom-up. And sometimes it is hard to remember to do this shift. There is a tendency to focus only on one over the other because of leadership styles. Our observation leads us to conclude that forcing the teams, produces small, short-term achievements, but by creating interest and making it easy to use the security activities in context, it becomes a part of the everyday lives of the security leaders, but it also demands more time and new ways of thinking.

Teams' Motivation Towards Security Can Vary

Motivating the team is a prerequisite for a successful result. Ensuring application security is not a trivial task, especially for developers who are often mistaken as security experts. We have observed many different occasions when the developer's motivation to keep up with the work in software security went down. But also, other stakeholders have their motivators and demotivators for software security. (Assal & Chiasson, 2018) conducted an interview study with software developers to explore factors influencing their motivation towards security, and they identified both intrinsic and extrinsic motivations, as well as different factors that led participants to lack motivation towards software security. Intrinsic motivation is when an activity is voluntarily performed for the pleasure and enjoyment it causes. Intrinsic motivations are driven by humans' "inherent tendency to seek out novelty and challenges, to extend and exercise one's capacities, to explore, and to learn". In contrast, extrinsic motivation is when a person is engaged in an activity for outcomes separate from those innate to the activity itself. They have found that when the motivation stems from the developer, rather than external factors, their participants exhibited better attitudes towards software security.

FUTURE DIRECTIONS

Ambidexterity is seldom observed in organizations the same way. The framework described in this chapter depicts parts of the strategies used in Visma. It might be that it will be difficult to replicate the results from this context to other contexts. But with so many software development teams involved in Visma's initiative, we are confident that the results can be generalized but further studies could help to understand more of the confound effects of the context variables. Further research is needed to investigate further the model used in this chapter in more contexts. Other pitfalls can also emerge from other contexts as well as other strategies to deal with security in the context of self-managed teams. There is also a need for further research on how to measure the effectiveness and efficacy of this framework over a long period of time, and what needs to be focused on from a long-term perspective.

CONCLUSION

In this chapter, we have instantiated an ambidextrous approach for a software security initiative for self-managed software development teams. The approach is ambidextrous in the sense that it focuses on approaching software security activities both from a top-down and a bottom-up perspective, combining elements usually found separately in software security initiatives. This chapter illustrates distinct, yet complementary, global and local roles for a software security initiative: (1) ensuring the adoption and implementation of software security practices, (2) enabling and (3) empowering software development teams to adapt and add to overall mandates, and (4) embedding cultures of improvement.

ACKNOWLEDGMENT

This work was supported by the SoS-Agile project: Science of Security in Agile Software Development, funded by the Research Council of Norway (grant number 247678).

REFERENCES

Ambler, S. W. (2008). Beyond functional requirements on agile projects. *Dr. Dobb's Journal, 33*(10).

Assal, H., & Chiasson, S. (2018). Security in the software development lifecycle. In *SOUPS @ USENIX Security Symposium* (pp. 281-296). Springer.

Ayalew, T., Kidane, T., & Carlsson, B. (2013). Identification and Evaluation of Security Activities in Agile Projects. *NordSec, 2013*, 139–153.

Baca, D., Boldt, M., Carlsson, B., & Jacobsson, A. (2015). A Novel Security-Enhanced Agile Software Development Process Applied in an Industrial Setting. *ARES, 2015*, 11–19.

Baca, D., & Carlsson, B. (2011). Agile development with security engineering activities. *ICSSP, 2011*, 149–158.

Bartsch, S. (2011). Practitioners' Perspectives on Security in Agile Development. *ARES, 2011*, 479–484.

Bellomo, S., Gorton, I., & Kazman, R. (2015). Toward Agile Architecture: Insights from 15 Years of ATAM Data. *IEEE Software, 32*(5), 38–45. doi:10.1109/MS.2015.35

Ben Othmane, L., Angin, P., Weffers, H., & Bhargava, B. K. (2014). Extending the Agile Development Process to Develop Acceptably Secure Software. *IEEE Transactions on Dependable and Secure Computing, 11*(6), 497–509. doi:10.1109/TDSC.2014.2298011

Camacho, C. R., Marczak, S., & Cruzes, D. S. (2016). Agile Team Members Perceptions on Non-functional Testing: Influencing Factors from an Empirical Study. *ARES, 2016*, 582–589.

Crispin, L., & Gregory, J. (2009). Agile Testing: A Practical Guide for Testers and Agile Teams. Addison-Wesley Professional.

Cruzes, D. S., Jaatun, M. G., Bernsmed, K., & Tøndel, I. (2018). Challenges and Experiences with Applying Microsoft Threat Modeling in Agile Development Projects. *ASWEC, 2018*, 111–120.

Cruzes, D. S., Jaatun, M. G., & Oyetoyan, T. D. (2018). Challenges and approaches of performing canonical action research in software security: research paper. *HotSoS 2018*, 8:1-8:11.

Davison, R. M., Martinsons, M. G., & Kock, N. (2004). Principles of canonical action research. *Information Systems Journal, 14*(1), 65–86. doi:10.1111/j.1365-2575.2004.00162.x

Davison, R. M., Martinsons, M. G., & Ou, C. X. (2012). The roles of theory in canonical action research. *MIS Q, 36*(3), 763-786.

Deleersnyder, S. W. (2019). *Software Assurance Maturity Model - How To Guide - A Guide to Building Security Into Software Development.* Retrieved from https://owaspsamm.org/

Dingsøyr, T., Moe, N. B., Fægri, T., & Seim, E. A. (2018). Exploring software development at the very large-scale: A revelatory case study and research agenda for agile method adaptation. *Empirical Software Engineering Journal, 23*(1), 490–520. doi:10.100710664-017-9524-2

Eclipse. (2016). *Eclipse Process Framework (EPF).* Retrieved from http://www.eclipse.org/epf/

Fenz, S., & Ekelhart, A. (2011). Verification, Validation, and Evaluation in Information Security Risk Management. *IEEE Security and Privacy, 9*(2), 58–65. doi:10.1109/MSP.2010.117

Firesmith, D. (2003). *Common Concepts Underlying Safety Security and Survivability Engineering. No. CMU/SEI-2003-TN-033.* Carnegie-Mellon UNIV Pittsburgh Pa Software Engineering Inst. doi:10.21236/ADA421683

Fitzgerald, B., & Stol, K.-J. (2017). Continuous software engineering: A roadmap and agenda. *Journal of Systems and Software, 123*, 176–189. doi:10.1016/j.jss.2015.06.063

Greenwood, D. J., & Levin, M. (2006). *Introduction to Action Research: Social Research for Social Change.* Sage Publications, Inc.

Gregory, J., & Crispin, L. (2014). *More Agile Testing: Learning Journeys for the Whole Team* (1st ed.). Addison-Wesley Professional.

Howell, J. M. (2005). The right stuff: Identifying and developing effective champions of innovation. *The Academy of Management Perspectives, 19*(2), 108–119. doi:10.5465/ame.2005.16965104

ISO/IEC. (2011). *ISO/IEC 27005: 2011 Information technology–Security techniques–Information security risk management.*

ISO/IEC 25010. (2011). *Systems and software Quality Requirements and Evaluation (SQuaRE) — System and software quality models. Iso/Iec Fdis 25010:2011, 2010, 1-34.*

Jaatun, M. G., Cruzes, D. S., Bernsmed, K., Tøndel, I., & Røstad, L. (2015). Software Security Maturity in Public Organisations. *ISC, 2015*, 120–138.

Jaatun, M. G., & Tøndel, I. (2008). Covering Your Assets in Software Engineering. *ARES, 2008*, 1172–1179.

McDermott, A. M., Hamel, L. M., Steel, D., Flood, P. C., & Mkee, L. (2015). Hybrid health care governance for improvement? Combining top-down and bottom-up approaches to public sector regulation. *Public Administration, 93*(2), 324–344. doi:10.1111/padm.12118

McGraw, G. (2004). Software Security. *IEEE Security and Privacy, 2*(2), 80–83. doi:10.1109/MSECP.2004.1281254

McGraw, G. (2006). Software Security: Building Security. *ISSRE 2006.* http://bsimm.com

Microsoft. (2019). *Security development lifecycle for agile development.* Retrieved from http://www.microsoft.com/en-us/SDL/Discover/sdlagile.aspx

Oueslati, H., Rahman, M. M., & ben Othmane, L. (2015). Literature Review of the Challenges of Developing Secure Software Using the Agile Approach. *10th International Conference on Availability, Reliability and Security*, 540-547. 10.1109/ARES.2015.69

Oueslati, H., Rahman, M. M., ben Othmane, L., Ghani, I., & Arbain, A. F. B. (2016). Evaluation of the Challenges of Developing Secure Software Using the Agile Approach. *International Journal of Secure Software Engineering*, 7(1), 17–37. doi:10.4018/IJSSE.2016010102

Oyetoyan, T., Jaatun, M. G., & Cruzes, D. S. (2017). A Lightweight Measurement of Software Security Skills, Usage and Training Needs in Agile Teams. *International Journal of Secure Software Engineering*, 8(1), 1–27. doi:10.4018/IJSSE.2017010101

Poller, A., Kocksch, L., Türpe, S., Epp, F. A., & Kinder-Kurlanda, K. (2017). Can Security Become a Routine?: A Study of Organizational Change in an Agile Software Development Group. *CSCW, 2017*, 2489–2503.

Rogers, E. M. (1995). *Diffusion of innovations* (4th ed.). Free Press.

Shostack, A. (2014). *Threat Modeling: Designing for Security.* Wiley.

Smite, D., Moe, N. B., & Torkar, R. (2008). Pitfalls in Remote Team Coordination: Lessons Learned from a Case Study. *PROFES, 2008*, 345–359.

SoS-Agile Project (2015-2020). (n.d.). Retrieved from Science of Security for Agile Software Development research project, 2015-2020, funded by the Research Council of Norway: http://www.sintef.no/sos-agile

Tøndel, I., Jaatun, M. G., Cruzes, D. S., & Moe, N. B. (2017). Risk Centric Activities in Secure Software Development in Public Organisations. *International Journal of Secure Software Engineering*, 8(4), 1–30. doi:10.4018/IJSSE.2017100101

Tøndel, I., Line, M. B., & Johansen, G. (2015). Assessing Information Security Risks of AMI - What Makes it so Difficult? *ICISSP, 2015*, 56–63.

Tuma, K., Çalikli, G., & Scandariato, R. (2018). Threat analysis of software systems: A systematic literature review. *Journal of Systems and Software*, 144, 275–294. doi:10.1016/j.jss.2018.06.073

Wäyrynen, J., Bodén, M., & Boström, G. (2004). *Security Engineering and eXtreme Programming: An Impossible Marriage?* XP/Agile Universe.

Weidman, J., Young-Corbett, D., Fiori, C., Koebel, T., & Montague, E. (2015). Prevention through Design Adoption Readiness Model (PtD ARM): An integrated conceptual model. *Work.*

Wu, Y., & Wu, S. (2016). Managing ambidexterity in creative industries: A survey. *Journal of Business Research*, 69(7), 2388–2396. doi:10.1016/j.jbusres.2015.10.008

Xiao, S., Witschey, J., & Murphy-Hil, E. (2014). Social influences on secure development tool adoption: why security tools spread. In *Proceedings of the 17th ACM conference on Computer supported cooperative work & social computing (CSCW '14)* (pp. 1095-1106). New York, NY: ACM. 10.1145/2531602.2531722

KEY TERMS AND DEFINITIONS

Ambidextrous: Having the ability to use the right and left hands equally well; while few of us are naturally ambidextrous, there is a possibility to train the brain to become more ambidextrous.

Bug Bounty: A deal offered by many websites, organizations, and software developers by which individuals can receive recognition and compensation for reporting bugs, especially those pertaining to exploits and vulnerabilities.

DAST (Dynamic Application Security Testing): A process of testing an application or software product in an operating state.

Penetration Testing: A penetration test, colloquially known as a pen test, or ethical hacking, is an authorized simulated cyberattack on a computer system, performed to evaluate the security of the system.

Responsible Disclosure: A vulnerability disclosure model in which a vulnerability or an issue is disclosed only after a period of time that allows for the vulnerability or issue to be patched or mended. This period distinguishes the model from full disclosure.

SAST (Static Analysis Tools): Static program analysis is the analysis of computer software that is performed without actually executing programs.

Threat Modelling: A process by which potential threats, such as structural vulnerabilities or the absence of appropriate safeguards, can be identified and enumerated, and mitigations can be prioritized.

This research was previously published in Balancing Agile and Disciplined Engineering and Management Approaches for IT Services and Software Products; pages 167-188, copyright year 2021 by Engineering Science Reference (an imprint of IGI Global).

Chapter 33

Traditional or Agile Contracting for Software Development:
Decisions, Decisions

Dinah Payne
University of New Orleans, USA

ABSTRACT

As the use of software is present in so many activities today, it is important for business in particular to be aware of challenges that may seem different today than before the prevalence of software in our lives. Agile project management is one example: this more recent and nimble approach to software development presents its own challenges. Fortunately, the guiding legal principles related to traditional contract formation and execution are based in principles of fairness and equity, making the customization of legal principles to Agile contracting a reasonable endeavor. This chapter presents basic contract law and such law as it more specifically relates to contracts dealing with Agile software development.

INTRODUCTION: WHY DOES THE CONTRACT MATTER?

According to the Legal Executive Institute, United States (U. S.) companies spend approximately 40% of their revenues on legal services (2017). This is an astonishing number and considerably more than companies in other venues. Miller (2015) reports that CEOs and CFOs spend a great deal of their time on legal matters, from educating outside counsel about the business and the issues it confronts, to seeking to find information requested as a result of legal action, and to preparing for and complying with requests for discovery (depositions, interrogators and requests for documents). These managers must help prepare expert witnesses acting on behalf of the firm and attend hearings or go to trials. Litigation, then, is very expensive and time consuming. "Litigation …will reach deep into the business and the company needs to prepare for and accept that a number of different and valuable people will be taken away from big parts of their day jobs to assist with the (legal) effort (Miller, 2015)." One way to reduce the amount of time and energy wasted on legal disputes is to obviate their occurrence and one way to do this is to

DOI: 10.4018/978-1-6684-3702-5.ch033

fashion carefully researched and crafted contracts. This is no less true for Agile contracting than it is for any other business contracting. While Agile contracting may involve a higher degree of collaboration than tradition contracts, the need for trust and the need for as much specificity as possible, even in light of the existence of known uncertainties, is critically important. Software developers and owners must accept that there will be disputes arising out of their contracts: the best way to reduce the negative effects of these disputes is to anticipate as much as possible of what might be points of contention.

There is not yet a great deal of litigation involving project management using the Agile approach, so the development of this material is based on general contract law, which we will see is based on legal principle that works for traditional or Agile contracting. However, in 2019, there was an instance of a dispute that resulted in a split decision by a Texas court (Raysman and Brown, 2019). In *Polar Pro Filters Inc v. Frogslayer, LLC* (2019), the dispute arose from a software development agreement that ran significantly over the original cost estimate and over the revised cost estimate. Further, fraud was claimed as a result of the non-delivery of the software in a viable form. The developer did not receive what he considered to be his full payment and the owner did not receive a viable product. The claims in the case were all based on traditional contract law even though the subject matter was a contract for software development wherein iterations were to be used. The point is that, although traditional contract and Agile contract may focus on, for example, different kinds of payment schedules or different visions of what should be delivered at what times, what installments or iterations are due/owing, the law used to generate a fair and equitable resolution to the dispute is well-established contract law. As Agile contracts become more frequently used and as more litigation develops, it is certainly possible that specific rules will be developed for Agile contract attributes that warrant different treatment. At this time, however, as evidenced by the *Polar Pro* case, traditional notions of contract essentials like fraud and breach of contract have served Agile contracting as well as traditional contracting.

In every successful business relationship, the parties must have agreed as to the purpose of the relationship. Each party must have a reasonably definite concept of what his obligations are under any contract he enters into: this is axiomatic in business and in business law. In traditional contracts, there is certainly enough litigation to make the retention of an attorney a good idea to give the parties a path to redress alleged transgressions, as well as to assure pro-active work to prevent any legal conflict via a well-written contract.

In Agile contracts, the pro-active nature of the work is even more important, as the relationship between the owner of the project and the software developer is far more collaborative than unilaterally providing goods between the buyer and seller. "The unprecedented rate of change in business and technology has made it increasingly difficult for software teams to determine user requirements and respond to their changes…Agile development approaches differ from the traditional, plan-driven, structured approaches as the former put more emphasis on lean processes and dynamic adaptation than on detailed front-end plans and heavy documentation (Lee and Xia, 2010: 88)." This description of Agile project management itself is a description of the root of the difference in contract law between traditional contracts and Agile contracts: as the word denotes, agile means to move quickly and easily (Dictionary.com, n.d.).

The Agile form of project management, designed to be rapid and easily coordinated, is represented by a framework for organizing and managing work in iterative stages. This differentiates Agile contracts from others in a number of ways, not the least of which is that, by their nature, the structure and stability generally found in contracts alerting the contracting parties as to their obligations is not possible: since the work is done on an "as we go" basis, iteratively, concepts of performance, for example, are different between traditional contract law and the contract law associated with Agile. We present here basic elements of contract law and provide insights as to how to contract for Agile projects. In this process, it is important to note that the attorneys with whom the client and project owner is working are advocates for negotiating the best terms for their clients: thus, an important element of Agile contracting means having a lawyer who understands how Agile project management works. As Bhoola and Mallik (2014: 96) summarily describe the point of Agile project management and, by derivation, Agile contracts: "the highest priority (in Agile) is to satisfy the customer through early and continuous delivery of valuable software." As the whole point of Agile project management is to satisfy the customer, so should the contract to provide Agile project management work to identify and pro-actively manage points of contention, to avoid time and energy wasted in disputes that might easily have been avoided with careful contracting, so satisfying all customers.

FACILITATOR OR ADVERSARY: ATTORNEYS INVOLVED IN AGILE CONTRACTING

While courts are interested first and foremost with the ultimate fairness in contract dispute resolution, the roles of the parties' attorneys, however, is not to be "fair" to the opposing party, but to be adversarial if there is a contract dispute. Attorneys are charged with protecting their client's interests competently and zealously (American Bar Association, 2020). Arbogast, Larman and Bode (2010) express concern that attorneys dealing with Agile contracts are too concerned with protecting the client at all costs and that they should rather protect the project success. They describe the Agile attorney as in need of a crash course in uncertainty, inherent in Agile contracting, as differentiated from traditional contracts. In fact, everyone's attorney should be fully capable of grasping the issue of uncertainty in the nature of iterative projects; no attorney should accept any case the subject of which he does not or is not capable of understanding, whether it is a traditional contract or an Agile contract. Additionally, the attorneys for Agile project management should be able to make connections between principles of fairness and equity regardless of the contract being a traditional one or an Agile contract.

In their article comparing legal project management to Agile contracting, Hassett and Burke (2017) interestingly make the case that lawyers themselves, with their firms, can utilize principles of Agile contracting. They describe waterfall contracting, a more traditional approach to project management. This involves the "analysis, design, implementation, testing and evaluation (Hassett and Burke, 2017: 8-9)" of a legal (any) project. They suggest that Agile contract considerations associated with planning, documentation, expectation consistency, etc. are different from traditional waterfall contracts. For example, upfront planning, documentation and project manager control is lower for Agile contracting than traditional contracting, while consistency of expectations, response time to changes in requirements, reassessment of tasks, client involvement and team member autonomy is higher for Agile contracting. Friess (2019: 131) describes a waterfall approach as "each sequential aspect of a project was to be fully competed by specialists, such as designers or developers, before being handed off to the next specialist in line." She also notes that "upfront planning and control" was required, allowing little room for the project to develop organically. Many elements to contracting traditionally or for Agile projects have similar underpinning principles, like planning, but areas to be aware of are also highlighted regarding the differences of approaches (Siddique and Hussein, 2016). Table 1is a simple presentation of major contract issues that both more traditional and Agile contracts must adhere to and with which attorneys for all parties should be familiar with. This material will be presented with greater detail as this chapter proceeds.

Table 1. Waterfall vs. Agile Contracting: The Names Have Changed, but the Principles Remain the Same

Formation of a Valid Contract Requires/May Require:	Waterfall (Traditional) Contracts	Agile Contracts
Agreement	More certain/well defined responsibilities/ outcomes	More fluid responsibilities as iterations take shape
Consideration	Fixed price with installment payments or at contract conclusion Time and material basis	Iteration payments at end of each iteration Target cost: fixed price and time and material cost pricing
Capacity	One must understand the terms of the contract	One must understand the terms of the contract
Legality	Contract terms and performance must be legal	Contract terms and performance must be legal
A Writing	Depending on the time for performance, the contract must be in writing to be enforceable	If iterations are discrete contracts, a writing is less likely to be required

The attorneys for both the software developer and the owner must be cognizant of the issues prevalent in Agile project management, hall marks of which are trust and collaboration among the parties. Since "fault is a pervasive element in contract law (Eisenberg, 2009: 1414)," the mindset of attorneys tends towards trying to determine fault. Since Agile's iterative processes may be more or less productive per iteration, determining fault is not as important as moving forward to completion of the entire project. Eisenberg notes that litigation is very expensive; it would be better to achieve "performance of contracts through the internalization of the moral norm of promise keeping, which is very inexpensive (p. 1430)." This notion of promise keeping is the essence of contract, regardless of whether it is an Agile project or not. Further, it is the essence of Agile contracting: reliance on the trust and good faith of collaborators in software development is a central characteristic of Agile project management.

WHAT IS A CONTRACT?

Choice of Law

Contract law has developed over millennia across many cultures and with regard to many types of performance. The source of commercial, or contract, law in the U. S. is three-fold: common law contract, the Uniform Commercial Code and Louisiana's conventional obligations law. Common law contract, in effect in 49 states in the U. S., is derived from case law rather than legislative mandate. Courts have developed legal positions that have been followed or reversed in a cycle of continuous development, review and redevelopment of principles of law deemed to be most equitable by society as a whole. Common law contract covers anything not covered by the Uniform Commercial Code (UCC), i.e., sales of services, real estate, etc.: the Restatement of the Law of contracts (American Law Institute, 2020), devised by the American Law Institute, is a complete reference work used by courts to form and support legal opinions.

The Uniform Commercial Code (UCC; Legal Information Institute, 2002) is the second source of commercial law in the U. S. It has little relevance for Agile contracts as the nature of UCC contracts is sales and leases of goods, rather than services. Software developers provide the services of development, but no movable and tangible goods are generated in such development. While the UCC is perhaps less relevant to Agile contracting, it might also be worth a look from the standpoint of a contract template. It contains many provisions that parties might consider in forming an Agile contract; for example, reference may be made to industry standards, which the UCC allows to be used in the resolution of contract disputes. Again, however, the overall use of the UCC will be less helpful than common law contract.

Finally, civil law in Louisiana was developed as a result of Hammurabi's Code via the Napoleonic Code: Hammurabi's Code was "the world's first known set of laws (Marriott, 2016: 16)." The State of Louisiana is the only state in the U. S. to have adopted the Civil Code (Louisiana Civil Code, n.d.), which is based in articles of law deemed to be the set standard. Contract law in Louisiana is based on the Civil Code and is called the Law of Conventional Obligations and Contracts. While common law and civil law use a different vocabulary for many concepts, the principles remain the same or are similar, as are the basic rules of sales and leases law: courts are interested in the ultimate fairness of contracting regardless of the law invoked. This is also true for traditional or Agile contracts: while the contents of the Agile contract may be different from traditional contracts, the equitable principles are the same. In developing the contract for the software development, the parties should educate themselves as to which of these laws they would find most appropriate: the choice of law to be used in a dispute can then be included in the contract.

The Environmental Context of Agile Contracting

The nature of what a traditional contract is is not hugely different from an Agile contract in many principles. A contract is basically an agreement between two or more parties that a court will enforce. Contracts provide stability and structure within which business can be conducted more efficiently; the private law of contract protects promises that have been made between the parties. A contract is a legally binding promise or a set of promises for the breach of which the law gives a remedy, or the performance of which the law in some way recognizes as a duty. These parties can agree to perform some act now and/or refrain from performing some act now and/or perform some act in the future and/or refrain from performing some act in the future. A fundamental truth about contract law, either traditional or Agile, is that the parties are entitled to contract with regard to whatever they want to contract with regard to, as long as the subject matter of the contract is legal, the parties have legal capacity and each party knowingly and willingly enters into the contract.

In Agile contracts, the idea of performing some act in the future is key: each successive iteration is envisioned at the time of contract, but iteration scope, specificity and number can be unknown. Since each iteration of the process could be considered its own contract and each of these "contracts" foresees a cumulative end at the completion of the project, Agile contracting fits within these constraints of contractual performance obligations. Larusdottir, Cajander and Gulliksen (2014: 1118) note that the idea of iterative software development grew out of an acknowledgement that "it is difficult to fully specify systems beforehand." Thus, contracts regarding future software development with Agile terms/conditions satisfies the need to "address the perceived limitations of (the) more established, plan-driven processes" of traditional contracting. Exhibit 1 provides a list of major legal and managerial concerns surrounding Agile projects and contracts. To offset sources of conflicts like those listed, Siddique and Hussein (2016) make several suggestions; see Exhibit 2.

Exhibit 1: Contracting Process Management Environmental Conditions (Siddique and Hussein, 2016)
- Environmental context: knowledge and experience of Agile projects and contracting.
- Identification of causes of contract disputes.

- ○ Formal documentation of what is due, expected dates of completion, etc.
- ○ Unequal sharing of risk, i.e., the developer not getting paid if the owner is dissatisfied.
- ○ Waterfall contract approach or Agile contract approach.
- ○ Fixed scope vs. fixed objectives.
- ○ Inadequate owner/developer collaboration: the blame game.
- ○ Unsatisfied customers.
- ○ Conflicts regarding roles and responsibilities of owners and developers.
- ○ Unpaid efforts resulting from owner dissatisfaction.
- ○ Early termination of projects.
- ○ Delays and increased costs.

Exhibit 2: Contracting Process Management Strategies (Siddique and Hussein, 2016; Friess, 2019)

- ○ Clarity in obligations.
- ○ Capacity.
- ○ Planning.
- ○ Kick-off.
- ○ Trust.
- ○ Choosing the right contract format.
- ○ Maintenance.
- ○ Having a frequent-delivery option.
- ○ The use of gainsharing rather than risk-sharing.
- ○ Focusing on functionality above budget.
- ○ Flow management.
- ○ Customer involvement.
- ○ Iteration execution.
- ○ Forecasting.
- ○ Consciously proactively seeking conflict resolution strategies.

Generally, in contract, an offer is a promise that can be met with acceptance: "a definite undertaking or proposal made by one person to another indicating a willingness to enter into a contract (Mann and Roberts, 2013: 195)." Again, Agile contracting can follow the basic contract model, but with the caveat that the definite nature of the undertaking also includes a significant understanding that uncertainty is a hallmark of Agile project management. This does not mean that such offers cannot be met with acceptance; it means that the parties to the contract understand and incorporate the uncertainties into the contract. As one of the first, most fundamental elements of contract is that the parties exercise good faith, the notion that Agile projects should be completed in collaboration between the owner of the project and the software developer presumes and requires good faith performance. Arbogast, Larman and Bode (2010) and Ward (2019), for example, both suggest that a collaborative effort between the owner of the project and the software developer is a defining characteristic of Agile. Such collaboration would necessarily entail the use of good faith in the performance of the contract: again, traditional notions of contract law are suitable concepts for application to Agile project contracting. Bhool and Mallik (2014: 96) note that "Moving from a traditional software methodology to the agile is very challenging due to the nature of software projects which are adapting to the changing environments, business dynamics, and continuous process improvement." One could replace software methodology with contracting process and have a good idea of the environment in which Agile contracts must be crafted and concluded. Exhibit

3 represents a list of contractual issues that should be considered when drafting an Agile contract. It is very clear that critically thoughtful care should be given to the drafting of the contract: while it might be more time-consuming to think about all these things ahead of time, knowing only that trust and collaboration are the chief characteristics of the nature of the contract, in the final analysis, such planning might actually be the solution to possible legal disputes.

Exhibit 3: Upfront Planning Elements for Agile Contracting (Lukasiewicz and Miller, 2012)
- Configuration management.
- Measurement and analysis.
- Project monitoring and control.
- Process and product quality assurance.
- Managerial requirements.
- Decision analysis and resolution.
- Integrated project management.
- Product integration.
- Requirements development.
- Risk management.
- Technical solution.
- Validation.
- Verification.

Parties to An Agile Contract

Perhaps the most onerous burden in developing the contractual provisions is on the offeror: the offeror is the person who makes the offer/proposal or undertaking to the offeree. It is immaterial as to whether the owner/customer or the developer is the offeror or offeree. The offeror is the "master of the offer," who can include or not in the offer whatever terms, provisions, deadlines, payment provisions, etc. are legally allowable and desirable. Offerors and offerees also take on roles of obligors, those obligated to perform the contract, and obligees, those to whom obligations to perform contractual provisions are owed. Each party is both an obligor and an obligee: the owner, the obligor, is obligated to pay for what the developer, the obligee, provides, while the developer is the obligor who owes the performance of software development to his obligee, the owner. Regardless of who the offeror is in Agile contracting, the owner or the software developer, the offeror is in control and must guide the negotiations in the collaborative endeavor.

Bhool and Mallik (2014) offer definitions of the parties to the contract. Product owners represent all stakeholder interests in the project and the finished system, as well as maintaining the backlog (the prioritized list of desired requirements and capabilities coupled with an estimated timeline for completion (Rubin, 2013)). The team (software developer) is described as a cross-functional, self-managing and –organizing group and is responsible for achieving the desired requirements: they are accountable for getting the job done successfully in terms of product and timeliness. Other parties to the contract are numerous in terms of executing the contract. Exhibit 4 offers a list of possible parties. See also Table 2 for a review of parties and their primary roles. When considering the parties and their responsibilities, keep in mind that Agility is defined as "a software team's ability to efficiently and effectively respond to user requirement changes (Lee and Xia, 2010: 88)."

Exhibit 4: The Parties (adapted from Larusdottir, et al., 2014: 1123; Friess, 2019)

- Product Owner
- The Scrum Manager: responsible for identifying and prioritizing the needs of the owner.
- Team Members: responsible for delivering the iteration by designing, developing and testing the software; it can include an IT engineer, architect, ...
- Usability Specialists: providing requirements analysis, interaction design and evaluation, etc.
- Business Specialists: providing analysis of software requirements during pre-studies.
- Security Engineer
- Technical Writer

Good Faith

Contracts are presumed to be entered into in good faith, without being unconscionable (so unfair to one of the parties that the contractual unfairness "shocks the conscience"). Again, these concepts are not far off of what is necessary in Agile contracts: each party understands that each iteration of the project brings significant uncertainty, i.e., a client will discover that they did not even realize that they needed some other software development to be included in the project until the first, second, third, etc. iterations are complete. Since the best way to approach Agile software development is collaborative, the requirement of good faith is imminently reasonable, as is the prohibition against very unfair contractual provisions. Further, each party to the contract must seriously intend to be bound by the contractual provisions. In the Agile context, presumably each party would understand what the vision of the project would be (Moore, 1991) and, in good faith, anticipate that he can fulfil his contractual obligations satisfactorily in good faith.

For a comparison between traditional contracts and Agile contracts of relevant law, the attorney's role in the Agile contracting process, and several other basic elements to contracting, see Table 2.

CONTRACT CLASSIFICATION

Fully legally enforceable contracts are called valid contracts. A valid contract has four parts: agreement (the manifestation of the parties' intent regarding the substance of the contract, including offer constraints and acceptance), consideration, capacity, and legality. An agreement consisting of offer and acceptance must exist and be supported by legally sufficient consideration. The parties to the contract must have legal capacity to enter into the contract and the contract must be made for a legal purpose or object. These parameters for traditional contracts are likely to be the same in form and function as Agile contracts: the parties in Agile must have entered into an agreement, even if the agreement contains uncertainty, i.e., how many iterations will there be. Much has been written about payment for Agile software development; we will address this shortly. The issues of capacity and legality, too, are fairly straightforward for Agile contracting. For example, entering into an Agile contract with a minor is highly unlikely; again, we will address this element more subsequently. It is equally unlikely that either owner/customers or software developers would both agree to engage in contract performance that was actually illegal.

Table 2. The Preliminaries (Derived from Arbogast, Larman, Mallik, 2012; Baham, 2019; Edwards, Bickerstaff and Bartsch, n.d.; Bhool and Mallik, 2015; Lee and Xia, 2010; Berstein, 2015)

Element	Traditional Sales and Services Contracts	Agile Contracts
Attorney's role and perception of contractual process	Adversarial if necessary. Potential silo mentality with focus only on one's own client/needs.	Mediator encouraging trust and collaboration. Systems/holistic approach focusing on the project's completion rather than individual parties' needs.
Parties and their responsibilities	Offerors and offerees, like buyers and sellers of goods. Obligors and obligees. Responsibilities are more certain: contract performance is specified and the parties are responsible for fulfilling their promises. Focus is on project management (Bhoola and Mallik, 2015), highlighting the accountable person.	Offerors and offerees, like owners/customers and suppliers. Obligors and obligees. Responsibilities can be less certain as each iteration could change in direction from the last iteration, the owner could decide to terminate the project if his needs are satisfied, etc.: owners/customers will need to continuously assess and reassess what they want out of each iteration, the whole project, when to end the project, etc. (Bernstein, 2015). Focus is on team dynamics, possibly diffusing point of responsibility contact; this is prevented by identification of the product owner, who is "responsible for maximizing the value of the product and the work of the Development Team (Baham, 2019: 142)." The development team should be identified and the owner should be given the right to decline membership of team proposals (Edwards, Bickerstaff and Bartsch, n.d.).
Offer	More specific obligations are known: structure and stability are assured.	Inherently uncertain, but initially expected obligations are known within the scope of the project.
Acceptance	More specific obligations are known: structure and stability are assured.	Inherently uncertain, but known within the scope of the project.
Party knowledge of contract subject matter Bernstein	Both parties need to know enough about the nature of the thing they are contracting relative to, i.e., when one wants a mare to breed, one can trust the seller to provide him with one capable of breeding without knowing the lineage of the horse or even much about breeding horses: the buyer is relying on the seller to sell him a horse suitable for breeding purposes (warranty for a particular purpose).	Owner should be educated in Agile principles, i.e., that the process is iterative, that each iteration can have an impact on each other iteration and the course of the project, that the owner's and suppliers must develop a relationship of trust and collaboration: the "we are in this together" approach. The owner's and developer's attorneys should be sufficiently knowledgeable about the Agile process itself to be able to anticipate where disputes might arise and how best to prevent those disputes.
Good faith	Each party needs to feel trust in the other party's good faith promise of performance.	Each party must feel trust in the other party's good faith performance, but also fully engage in a collaborative relationship.
Unconscionability	Extreme unfairness.	Relative ignorance of one contracting party granting an unfair advantage to the other party.

Voidable and Voidable Contracts

Voidable contracts are valid contracts that reflect the lack of a minor element of contract; a prime example of such a contract would be when an adult enters into a contract with a minor. In this instance, the contract would be voidable at the option of the party who lacked capacity, an unlikely event in Agile contracting, but nevertheless worth confirming each party's capacity. A void contract is equally unlikely in relation to Agile contracting. Void "contracts" are not even really contracts, as there is a major element of contract missing, rendering the "contract" completely invalid and unenforceable by either party. A good example of this would be when one party defrauds another party. Recall that a fundamental tenant of contract law is that each party must knowingly and willingly enter into the contract; when fraud is perpetrated, one of the parties intentionally deceives the other party as to some major element of the contract. While this would certainly be possible in Agile contracting, it would seem unlikely that this would be significantly different from fraud as instigated by any other contracting party. Presumably, too, since iterations are concluded rapidly, fraud would be "found out" quickly and the partnership accordingly resolved or dissolved.

Executed or Executory Contracts

One classification of contract that may have extra meaning for Agile contracting is the classification of whether the contract is executed or executory. An executed contract is one that has been fully performed by all parties, i.e., in a real estate contract, all promises of the seller and buyer have been fulfilled and the title to the land has changed. An executory contract, on the other hand, is one that has not been fully performed by all parties, i.e., a sale of real estate is only an executory contract until the title of the real estate changes from the seller to the buyer. Thus, from the time the contract to sell the real estate is entered into and the time of the closing, this is merely an executory contract. In Agile contracting, the question of substantial performance may come up: if the contract isn't fully and completely performed, the contract may be classified as either executed or executory, depending on circumstances. Such circumstances could be dictated by the "completion" of an iteration: if the iteration does not provide the owner with the desired deliverables, but it still works to some extent, the question could arise as to whether full payment should be made by the owner who is dissatisfied with the iteration's performance. If the contracting parties contracted in good faith and in a collaborative spirit, this problem is less likely to occur, but must be acknowledged as a possible problem.

Express, Implied and Quasi Contracts

Another contract classification that is debatably different for traditional and Agile contracting is the nature of a contract as an express or implied contract. Express contracts are simply those that are fully and explicitly stated, either in writing or orally, at the time the contract is entered into. The only issue here is whether words are actually used. Implied contracts (implied in fact) are contracts implied by the behaviors of the parties. The source of the potential issues here speaks to fundamental Agile contracting tenants: good faith trust and collaboration. Agile creates a double-edged sword: good faith, trusting and collaborative parties want a reasonable amount of uncertainly, so don't want to put everything into words, but leaving contractual provisions to be interpreted by the behaviors of the parties is equally problematic. Having to express all the contractual provisions in words does not acknowledge the effervescent, rapidly changing nature of Agile development. In fact, implied contracts are not valid contracts when the subject matter of the contract is of a unique or personal nature because there is no way to reference what the parties might have wanted in the event of a dispute: there is no standard, which could very easily be a hallmark of Agile development.

If the parties to an Agile (any) contract chose to employ an implied contract model, several requirements must be met for a dissatisfied party: first, the injured party must have provided some service (or property) to the other party. Second, the injured party expected to be paid for the service and the other party did know or should know that the injured party expected payment. And, finally, the alleged transgressor had a chance to reject the services, yet did not do so. In an Agile contracting situation, it is not inconceivable that a software developer would work on an iteration, present that finished product only to have the owner proceed with the project with another software developer. Again, trust, good faith and close collaboration should ameliorate or eliminate this kind of dispute, but only if the parties to the Agile contract know about this sort of dispute.

If there is a dispute and implied contract principles did not result in a fair outcome, *quasi* contract may provide an avenue for relief. In this type of "contract," which is not a real contract because some element of contract is missing, the courts crafted this equitable relief. *Quasi* contracts are fictional contracts created by courts, imposed on the parties in the interests of fairness and justice (implied at law); they are judicial remedies aimed at preventing unjust enrichment when no contract actually exists. For this claim to succeed, some element of contract is lacking, but not to impose a contract would be to treat one of the parties very unfairly or inequitably. The doctrine of unjust enrichment applies: no one should be allowed to profit/enrich themselves inequitably at others' expense. Regarding Agile contracts, the same logic applies to the use of this equitable remedy as to the remedy of an implied contract. One party, for instance the developer, expends time and materials generating software pursuant to a contract found by a court to be unreasonably indefinite, yet produces a product that the owner says does not meet his needs. The developer could assay the equitable remedy of *quasi* contract.

Another element of contract that could differ between traditional contracts and Agile contracts is the necessity for knowing exactly what the terms of the contract are: to what is each party obligating himself? The terms of offers must be reasonably definite to assure seriousness of intent as to the obligations of the parties, i.e., parties to the offer should be identified, the subject matter and/or quantity of the offer should be identified, the consideration due between the parties should be identified, and the time for performance should be identified. Under the Restatement of Contracts, the concept of "reasonably definite terms" was created, allowing for a bit more latitude: this is essential in Agile contracting. For example, the courts can supply a missing term if a reasonable one can be implied from the behaviors of the parties or the circumstances under which the contract is to be completed. Given the nature of the Agile contract as one of trust and collaboration, the court can look at all the circumstances of the contract negotiation, initiation and course of performance to make appropriate determinations at to equitable remedies.

TERMINATION OF THE OFFER BY THE PARTIES

Traditional contract offers can be terminated in three ways: rejection, counter-offer and revocation. This is not going to be the real problem-maker in Agile contracting. Rather than the offer being the source of the dispute, it is more foreseeable that the performance and termination of the contract itself as a whole is at issue. However, briefly, in rejection, the offeree says "no" to the offer in some way. Counter-offer is first and foremost a rejection of the original offer and the communication of a new offer by the original offeree, while revocation is the withdrawal of the offer by the offeror.

ACCEPTANCE OF THE OFFER

Acceptance is voluntary agreement by the offeree to be bound by the offer terms: an objective indication of present intent to be bound. Clear, unambiguous, unequivocal words or conduct must be used in signifying acceptance. Again, for Agile contracts, this is less likely to be a source of friction than the performance of the contract, but nevertheless could constitute a problem. The nature of the problem for Agile contracts is simply that the "clear, unambiguous words" may not exist as in the traditional contract sense. Since performance of the project and each iteration is by nature unknown to some extent, the parties will have to grapple with language that is as clear as can be under these circumstances. This is a perfect instance in which to rely on the concept of good faith: the parties, in good faith, believe that they know what each is offering and what each is agreeing to. As iterations can shift with desired features and requirements, so can words of acceptance be crafted to acknowledge and accept such uncertainties. See Table 3 for a review of issues associated with the agreement.

Table 3. The Agreement (Derived from Arbogast, Larman and Mallik, 2012; Bernstein, 2015; Scully, 2014; Edwards, Bickerstaff and Bartsch, n. d.; McGregor and Doshi, 2018; Siddique and Hussein, 2016; Legal Insight, 2014; Bhool and Mallik, 2014)

Agreement Issue	Traditional Sales and Services Contracts	Agile Contracts
Offer and acceptance, con't.	Contract obligations must be reasonably definite	Agile projects "rarely start from a fully defined specification (Bernstein, 2015: 21)."
Complexity	Relatively predictable (Arbogast, Larman and Vodde, 2012); except that multiyear, multi-layered contracts can be very complex	Contracts here are less predictable though not necessarily more complex in terms: the complexity is a result of the inherent increased uncertainty Edwards, Bickerstaff and Bartsch (n.d.: 6): "exiting templates and contracting approaches cannot be easily adapted to properly reflect and support the requirements and philosophy of the Agile model."
Scope of work/vision	Reasonably definite "Contracts are written to contain every detailed specification of the requirements before the contract is signed (Siddique and Hussein, 2016: 53)"	Reasonably indefinite, which can cause friction in defining services to be provided; insightful, careful planning/identification of desired outcomes can reduce this source of friction Working software over comprehensive documentation (Scully, 2014; McGregor and Doshi, 2018) "(R)equirements can change during the development process; therefore it is not possible to state the exact scope of the work at the start of the project (Siddique and Hussein, 2016: 53)."
Start-up time: forming, storming, norming, performing, adjourning	With more specific contract requirements already specified, less time is needed to develop working relationships, particularly of trust, leaving less room for "storming (process of agreement on details)" and "norming (process of establishing standards)"	With less obligation specificity, more time is needed to determine the scope of project, build trust, assure transparency and the creation of a collaborative environment, particularly regarding "storming" and "norming" "(P)rojects that work well are generally those where customer and supplier both have experience of working in an agile way – and ideally with each other (Bernstein, 2015: 23)." Responding to change over following a plan is a hallmark of Agile contracting (Scully, 2014; McGregor and Doshi, 2018)
Environmental time to market constraints	Waterfall contracts (Chand, 2016; Bernstein, 2015) don't recognize rapidly needed software or rapidly evolving software needs	Recognition should be developed that services are subject to rapid evolution, product definition may be uncertain early in the process, and the ability to test for success may be diminished by time constraints Accept the parts of the contract that are agile, that is, subject to flexibility and those that are not, i. e., how payment will be made (Legal Insight, 2014)
Contractual provision comprehensiveness	Include as many foreseeable conditions of performance as possible	It is not possible to provide a comprehensive list of contractual provisions, but provisions that are within the scope of the project vision should be provided The use of "iteration reviews/demos" practices can help manage change to satisfy owner requirements (Bhool and Mallik, 2014)
Use of boilerplate language (industry standard language)	Can be appropriate (UCC Sales and Lease contracts)	More "industry standard" language is recommended against: the uncertainties in what the parties want as iterations proceed is prohibitive of language that is too standardized

continues on following page

Table 3. Continued

Agreement Issue	Traditional Sales and Services Contracts	Agile Contracts
Negotiations	Shark: "I win, you lose" approach	Owl: "I win, you win" approach "Agile development values individuals and interactions over processes and tools, working software over comprehensive documentation, customer collaboration over contract negotiation, and responding to change over following a plan (Lee and Xia, 2010: 89)." Customer collaboration over contract negotiation (Scully, 2014; McGregor and Doshi, 2018)

CONSIDERATION

In binding contracts, each party must exchange something of legal value for the other party's promise: this is the principle behind the concept of consideration. Giving someone a birthday present is not a bargained-for exchange as the recipient did not bargain for the birthday present: the promisor therefore receives no consideration and the "contract" is not binding. Consideration is exchanged for each party's promise (whatever that promise is): the parties bargain about what the consideration is, with each party getting something valuable they bargained for. Consideration can be an act, not acting or even a promise to act or not to act if it is bargained for and there is some measurable value (by contracting parties' standards). This last element of the concept of consideration is key for Agile contracting. For example, the developer will expect to be paid a fair amount for fair work; he will also understand, by the nature of Agile contracting, that some original requirements specified in a contract may be altered or dispensed with. Thus, consideration for Agile contracting is very suitable in the sense of "not acting or…a promise not to act." Whether the contract is a traditional one or an Agile one, there must be a legal detriment to the promisee or legal benefit for the promisor. Legal detriment is one of two things: a promise to do something that one has no prior legal duty to do is consideration or refraining from doing something that one has a legal right to do. Legal benefit occurs when the promisor obtains something that he had no prior legal right to obtain from the promisee. The *Hamer v. Sidway* (1891) case, though obviously about a traditional contract (1891), is a landmark case related to the value of legal rights, but also contains language apropos to Agile contracting. "Courts 'will not ask whether the thing which forms consideration does in fact benefit the promisee…or is of any substantial value to any one.' It is enough that something is promised, done, forborne or suffered by the party to whom the promise is made as consideration…: Thus, it is clear that courts believe that adequacy of consideration is in "the eye of the beholder." It is up to the parties to say what they value at what amount if there is truly legal detriment or benefit. Courts don't like to second guess the parties to the contract regarding their estimation of what something is worth (unless an element of fraud, duress, undue influence… exists). Since Agile contracts are uncertain relative to the number of iterations, for example, or the alteration of desired features or requirements, courts will not want to question the parties' estimations of what the contract should be worth (unless, of course, there is some claim of unconscionability, fraud, duress, etc.). Specifically pertinent to Agile contracts, because a contract has a cancellation clause in it, however, does not mean that it is an illusory promise lacking consideration and therefore validity: if the contract's cancellation clause puts limits on the cancellation of the project, time constraints on the cancellation or notice requirements for cancellation, it is not an illusory promise, i.e., "I can cancel after performance has begun with 30 days' notice" is not illusory.

CAPACITY, LEGALITY AND GENUINENESS OF ASSENT

All parties contracting in valid contracts must have capacity, the ability to understand the nature of the obligations they are committing. Perhaps with Agile contracts, one of the players in the contractual design, the lawyer who drafts the contract, is the one we must make sure has "capacity," not only legal capacity, but also the capacity to understand the similarities and differences between traditional contracts and Agile contracts. Attorneys less familiar with Agile projects should access literature such as the Agile Primer (Arbogast, Larman and Vodde, 2012) and other sources, to ease concern that the lawyer is the only player in the game that doesn't understand the nature of Agile contracting or how to properly construct such a contract that relies heavily on trust and collaboration between the parties. He should be able to design a contract that is written to reduce possible legal friction, but that acknowledges that disputes arise: suitable solutions can then be discussed/anticipated.

Legality

An agreement is illegal and thus legally unenforceable if either its formation or its performance is criminal, tortious, or opposed to public policy: in these cases, the courts will "leave the parties as they found them" and grant no relief to either party. Contracts contrary to statutory law, such as price fixing, are illegal, as is usury, selling things on days which prohibit the sale, etc. Unconscionable contracts are also illegal, as noted previously and below. It is hard to conceive that businesses associated with Agile development, either owners and developers, would enter into any contract that would violate public policy or be illegal. However, one example is good to highlight the possible issue: if the project development has begun and, before it is concluded, the law of the venue changes to prohibit such project use, the nature of the contract would be illegal and so would the contract be. This just means that the parties to any contract should be aware of the business and political environment in which they do business.

Unconscionable contracts would be a more reasonable problem to find in Agile contracts than illegal ones. An unconscionable contract is so one-sided, with one party having great bargaining power over the other, who had no other choice but to contract, allowing the powerful party to dictate the terms of the contract, that it will not be enforced. This principle is designed to protect the party with the less favorable or advantaged bargaining position. It can be applied to the process by which the unconscionable contract was entered into (i.e., bullying a small software developer into providing a better deal than is reasonable in business: procedural unconscionability) or to the terms of the contract (i.e., the price to be paid for software development: substantive unconscionability). This last is more likely to be in dispute simply because of the uncertainty of the progression of the iterations and the possibility of changes in feature and requirement specifications. Courts finding unconscionability may not enforce the contract, not enforce the unconscionable element of the contract or limit the unconscionable element of the contract.

Genuineness of Assent

Genuineness of assent occurs when the parties have a meeting of the minds: that is to say, when each party understands what they are obligating themselves to. Everyone understands and voluntarily agrees to be bound to the terms of the agreement. Contracting requires parties to knowingly and willingly enter into contracts. Such "knowing and willing" acceptance of obligations can be interrupted in several ways: mistake (unilateral, bilateral and mutual), fraud, duress or undue influence. In Agile contracting, the two failures of genuineness of assent that are easiest to envision are mistake and fraud, both of which concerns should be reduced as a result of the trust and collaborative nature of the relationship between the owner and developer.

In one case of bilateral mistake in which both parties to the contract were mistaken, *Flo-Products Co. v. Valley Dairy Farms Co.*, Flo-Products gave a phone quote of fifteen thirty six to a farm for some machinery: the company meant $1,536 but the Farm thought it was for $15.36. There was no "meeting of the minds" since both parties were mistaken as to the real amount of the contract in the other parties' eyes. The contract was not enforced. Again, the possibility of this problem should be at a minimum given level of trust and collaboration required in Agile project development.

Fraud is a misrepresentation of a material fact or an omission of material fact by words or actions. A material fact is one that might have changed one's mind. Intent to deceive is also a necessary element to proving fraud. Intent to deceive, scienter, is guilty knowledge. In this case, a party knows a fact is not as stated, a party makes a statement that he believes is not true or makes a statement with reckless disregard for the truth or a party says or implies that a statement is made on some basis, such as personal knowledge or investigation, when it is not. Reliance by the other party on misrepresentation and injury are the two other elements to proving fraud. In Agile contracts, the likelihood of substantial damages as a result of fraud is unreasonable, again, because of the nature of the contract and relationships. The contracting parties will be able to find out very soon in the performance of the contract if either party is engaged in fraud: when the first iteration does not go as planned. Thus, the specter of fraud is reduced in Agile contracts in comparison to traditional contracts. Statements of opinion or future facts are not actionable as fraud: this, too, is as applicable to Agile contracts/disputes as to traditional contracts. For example, the developer believes in good faith that the iteration will be complete by a certain date but is wrong: this is not actionable as fraud since the parties did not intend to deceive. On the other hand, negligent misrepresentation is carelessness or using reckless disregard for the truth and is actionable as fraud in either traditional contracting or Agile contracting. If the developer continues to assure the owner that viable iterations will indeed be forthcoming, though in a longer time frame than originally anticipated, and the developer is lying to continue to receive payment for working on the iteration, this would result in actionable fraud: knowledge of falsity is key.

A WRITTEN CONTRACT?

Some contracts must be in writing to be enforceable. The contract more likely to be required to be in writing in Agile contracting is a contract that cannot, by its own terms, be complete within a year. This is far more likely to be an issue than contracts, for example, involving interests in real estate or the promises to pay the debt of another, but they are, by the iterative nature of Agile contracting, not reasonably likely to create an issue. That Agile contracting is founded on short-term deliveries, at the presentation of one delivery, if the parties are satisfied with the project, the project is extended. If the customer is not satisfied, the contract can be terminated. Thus, by the very nature of performance time, Agile contracts won't be subject to this writing requirement. However, if the parties do have a writing, which is recommended, they can include any provision they would like to, in a knowing and willing way, as to what would constitute a writing and how the parties will be bound to the contract. Generally speaking, the contract must be signed by the party against whom enforcement is sought (not the one suing). The writing must contain the essential elements of the contract, i.e., the scope of the project. Further, contracts in general will be interpreted as a whole, not in parts. With Agile contracts, the agreement can be seen as an installment contract, with each iteration an "installment," all of which would be considered in reviewing the entire contract.

PERFORMANCE

Installment Contracts

In fact, an example of a legal concept that exhibits reassuring similarities between traditional contracting and Agile contracting can be seen in installment contracts. Traditional contracts called installment contracts are in the nature of iterative contracts in that they are contracts for separate lots of goods to be delivered and accepted over the course of the contract performance: each month, for example, six loads of aggregate will be delivered to the purchaser, who uses up each delivery in making concrete to build the foundation of a structure. Like Agile contracts, installment contracts are specialized contracts wherein the iterative, installment element of the performance is a defining characteristic of the contract. Again, like Agile iterations (Sprints) which don't meet the scope of work as agreed upon by the parties, an installment contract can be repudiated if any installment substantially impairs the value of the entire contract. Installment contracts and Agile contracts do differ, however, in that it would not be possible for the impairment of the value of the entire contract to be evident only at the completion of the last iteration. Since each iteration in an Agile contract could be considered a separate contract, rather than as a part performance of the whole contract, impairment in the value of the "entire" contract would be evident much more quickly than in an installment contract among good faith parties.

Conclusion of Performance

The parties can perform the contract and thus discharge their obligations in a variety of ways. First, they can discharge by performance: do what one is supposed to do under the contract. Discharge by substantial performance (with minor deviations) requires the parties to do most of what one is supposed to do. Discharge by agreement happens when the parties agree that the contract has been completed and that the contractual relationship is ended. Accord and satisfaction reflects the idea that the obligation between the parties may change, but the parties themselves will continue to work on the contract, while in novations, the parties change, but the obligation remains the same: to complete the original contract. Covenants not to sue are merely contractual provisions that reflect that the parties have agreed that they will not sue one another over contract disputes. Finally, commercial impracticability is the acknowledgement that the contract should not proceed as performance would be too expensive for good faith parties.

Of all of these ways to discharge contracts, many of these ways would be most reasonable for the Agile contract to be terminated. For example, if the parties agree that there are no more iterations needed, they can stipulate that that contract has been performed or substantially performed. If the parties agree to go in a different direction with subsequent iterations, they can agree that the original obligations under the contract have changed, resulting in completion of the first part of the contract by accord and satisfaction. Again, as we have noted throughout, many of the principles guiding traditional contracting and Agile contracting are similar.

The parties should also consider the provision of warranties as to a variety of things. Warranties are a seller's express or implied promise that the goods meet certain standards. An express warranty is one wherein the seller affirms that the goods meet certain standards of quality, description, performance or condition by written/oral words or conduct. Although the warranty of merchantability was developed in the law on UCC sales of goods and clearly software is not a movable, tangible good, the principle again carries over. Goods should be fit for the ordinary purposes for which they were intended/designed. They should conform to any promise or affirmation the developer makes about the software's performance. Finally, at the very least, the developer should warrant that the code used to create the software was open-source code or that he was granted permission to use any proprietary/copyright protected software during the development process.

Breach of Contract

Breach of any contract is a result of failure of performance in some way. This fear is reduced given the relatively short time periods each iteration is expected to be provided. Such fear can also be reduced if the parties clearly understand the consequences of breach: the inclusion of liquidated damages in the agreement can aid in that understanding. Liquidated damages are those agreed-upon in the contract at the initiation of the contract: the parties agree as to what each party will pay, at what triggers/times, in the event of a perceived breach of contract. Since the parties agree ahead of time to what they will pay the aggrieved party, the uncertainty as to what can be assessed as damages is either reduced or eliminated.

Another pro-active approach the parties can take to reducing damages is the use of anticipatory breach: a party who fears that performance will not be timely alerts the other party/ies that breach is imminent. At the very least, this alerts the damaged party that the performance he expected at a certain time will not be forthcoming, possibly giving him time to find other solutions to provide the software he had anticipated receiving. Rescission, wherein the parties back out of the contract for some reason, is also possible: perhaps the software developer comes to the conclusion that he is not the best suited to develop the software; he can go ahead, then, and request rescission, to simply back out of the contract. Finally, specific performance is an equitable remedy wherein the parties are required to complete performance specifically as listed in the contract. This remedy is usually reserved for things that are unique, which the Agile contract could be considered, but the remedy is not a reasonable solution from the perspective that the specificity of the contract requirements is by nature uncertain/unknown. Table 4 provides a thumbnail review of issues associated with performance and breach.

Table 4. Issues Associated with Performance and Breach (Derived from Chand, 2016; Edwards, Bickerstaff and Bartsch, n.d.; Bernstein, 2015; Bhool and Mallik, 2014; Rubin, 2012; Brightwell, 2017)

Time of delivery	As contractually specified As determined by a reasonable time period (which can be dictated by the subject of the contract: fireworks should not arrive at the stand on July 5th)	Each iteration should have a set time for performance (Edwards, Bickerstaff and Bartsch, n. d.) Avoid timeboxes (deadlines) to "focus experimentation and avoid waste," but also provide clarity with regard to "how far an engineer should go before they check to see if the direction (they are taking) is still correct (McGregor and Doshi, 2018)"
Performance appraisal timeliness	Liability for contract breach on a re-active basis	Iterative: specter of massive failure (liability for contract breach) is reduced Each iteration could represent a full "contract"
Course corrections	Installment contracts	Iterative delivery Each team member should act with appropriate levels of care and skill, reliance upon which should be made in relation to length of time for performance, reasonableness of iteration success (Edwards, Bickerstaff and Bartsch, n.d.) The team's iterations should be "minimally viable experiments (McGregor and Doshi, 2018)"

continues on following page

Table 4. Continued

Change management	Less flexible	More flexible within ranges/limits Review meetings can re-evaluate priorities, features to be incorporated into further iterations, etc. "Developing the requirements just before each new iteration allows the project to evolve despite changing circumstances (Dutton, 2018: 35)."
Risk acceptance, assessment, and apportionment	Contract provisions will address more certainty of risk and apportionment among the parties	Nature of contract increases uncertainty with each new iteration "Find ways of managing and mitigating risk rather than resisting it or trying to push it where it doesn't belong (Bernstein, 2015: 22)."
Damages	Full breach Anticipatory breach	Lesser damages could be possible with smaller "contracts" of each iteration Establish what will happen if the project "goes wrong (Edwards, Bickerstaff and Bartsch (n.d.: 7)."
Mitigation of damages	Courts are in favor of plaintiff attempts to lessen their damages	Provision of customer right to terminate the contract on an iteration basis Provide incentives for performance Set communications standards to effect transparency in completion issues Keep track, in writing or orally (recorded), of what the parties agree to on a set schedule and/or at the end of an iteration
Liquidated awards or penalties	These clauses provide incentives to timely and correct contract conclusion	Recommended against: the uncertain and iterative nature of the project precludes against penalties particularly Recommended for: the contract can stipulate that late or poor iteration performance is grounds for stipulated penalties (Dataitlaw, 2019)
Payment model/cycles	At agreed-upon intervals (i.e., installment contracts) At performance completion Fixed price per iteration or unit of work (Siddique and Hussein, 2016; Arbogast, 2012): price, scope and time are included and risk is with the supplier Time and material basis (costs of time and materials to date) for a minimum viable product and risk is with the customer (Bernstein, 2015; Siddique and Hussein, 2016)	Innumerable: as agreed upon by contracting parties Payment due at iteration completion with set limits for cost associated with each iteration Pay-per-use of software (Arbogast, 2012) Target cost contracts is a combination of fixed price and time and materials contracts: both parties understand that "software project requirements are uncertain and that they must work collaboratively to attain the goals. If the price of the project exceeds the estimated price, the two parties will share it, and if there is profit in the project (by delivering it for less than the agreed cost), it will also be shared between the customer and supplier (Siddique and Hussein, 2016: 54)." Use of Function Points (Brightwell, 2017) which are units of measure to express the functionality of the iteration
Ease of termination	Can be contractually specific Breach could be a problem if the contract termination is not allowed or if the contract is wrongfully terminated	What possible consequences could accrue from termination? (Dataitlaw, 2019) Clearly state each parties' right to terminate Clearly state at which point in the iteration presentation a contract can be terminated
Time constraints of termination	Is performance complete?	Is iteration complete and is that point a good termination point for the project? Can each iteration trigger termination of the project? Each party should be given the right to terminate the project without liability with identified triggers (Edwards, Bickerstaff and Bartsch, n.d.)
Early termination	See liquidated damages	See liquidated damages
End product	More certain	Iteratively
"Definition of Done"	Performance completion	Iteratively; "Done criteria are a set of rules that are applicable to all user stories in a given (iteration). (Such criteria) include ...completed unit testing..., completion of quality assurance tests, completion of all documentation..., (assurance that) all issues are fixed, (and) successful demonstration to stakeholders/business representatives (Bhool and Mallik, 2014: 100)."
Warranties	Implied warranty of merchantability	Granted on each iteration Products should be free from defects, comply with their descriptions, have time limits for imposition, refer to use of open source software and relate to virus protection: warranties of merchantability
Focus on specificity in all terms	Yes	Designate the purpose of the project and how the project is to be established, rather than using rigid terms/performance criteria (Edwards, Bickerstaff and Bartsch (n.d.)
Successful contract	Winning a lawsuit	Providing a good project
Intellectual property rights	Shop right, works for hire (Bernstein, 2015)	Shop right, works for hire (Bernstein, 2015)
Dispute resolution	Litigation Alternative dispute resolution	Parties should be aware of litigation as a dispute resolution process, but also of alternative dispute resolution methods, such as arbitration, mediation and negotiation: these alternatives could be very useful in Agile contracting, given that those helping to resolve the dispute would have knowledge and understanding of pertinent law, but, more importantly, of Agile practices as they relate to contract law

OWNERSHIP RIGHTS TO THE SOFTWARE

A final question unrelated to the way a contract is formed, but closely related to the nature of Agile software development is about ownership of the software that is ultimately developed. One way to deal with this question of ownership is to define the software as "works for hire." Works for hire happen when one of two things occur: first, an employee is paid to create a copyrightable work, in which case the employer retains the ownership of the work. Second, an independent contractor is hired to create a copyrightable work, i.e., the software, in which case the independent contractor retains the ownership of the work as its author. After the parties determine who the owner of the software is, either the customer or the developer, other questions are prompted. If the developer is the owner, specification of the time/trigger for ownership to change hands should be noted in the contract. The rights of the developer relative to the use of the customers' data should also be reviewed (Dataitlaw, 2019).

CONCLUSION

While it is true that lawyers may present as adversarial in zealously representing his client, such adversarially zealous representation is not only mandated by the legal canons of professional responsibility, but also by clients when a contract fails for some reason. Arbogast, Larman and Mallik (2012) seem to suggest that the lawyers are the enemies in Agile contracting because they are basically ignorant of the uncertain nature of the project in terms of what the parties want, how success is defined, when the project will be finished, etc. The only time anyone wants a lawyer is when he needs a lawyer: to mitigate the harm caused by any contract dispute, both the lawyer and the client should have an understanding of the fundamental aspects of the contract, any contract, like the uncertainties inherent in Agile contracts. Such understanding will obviate the need of a lawyer in an adversarial role. "The job of a technology lawyer is to protect clients from undue risk arising from relationships they form in the course of their business, or at least to flag that risk so they can make informed decisions (Sinclair, 2015: 15)." If all the parties to the contract are aware of these fundamentals, including the lawyers, there should be no more contractual contests on Agile contracts than on any other contract. In the final analysis, Kanth (2009: 20) sums up both the best and most challenging aspects of Agile software development that make it worth the efforts: "quality is never an accident, it is always the result of high intention, sincere effort, intelligent direction and skillful execution: it represents the wise choice of many alternatives." In fact, this is not just a description of Agile development principles, but also a description of how to craft an Agile contract. "A well drafted software development agreement benefits both parties and should define success, failure, remedies and an expedited resolution path (Costa, 2020)."

REFERENCES

American Law Institute. (2020). *Restatement of law, second, contracts.* Retrieved February 11, 2020, from https://www.ali.org/publications/show/contracts/

Arbogast, T., Larman, C., & Mallik, B. (2012). Agile contracts primer. *Practices for Scaling Lean & Agile Development: Large, Multisite, & Offshore Product Development with Large-Scale Scrum.* Retrieved February 5, 2020, from https://agilecontracts.org/agile contracts primer.pdf

Baham, C. (2019). Teaching tip: Implementing Scrum wholesales in the classroom. *Journal of Information Systems Education, 30*(3), 141–159.

Bernstein, A. (2015, Aug. 25). How to write supplier contracts for agile software development. *Computer Weekly*, 21-24.

Bhoola, V., & Mallik, D. (2014). Determinants of agile practices: A Gini index approach. *Vilakshan, XIMB. Journal of Management, 11*(2), 95–114.

Brightwell, I. (2017). *Is a 'fixed price' agile contract possible?* Retrieved February 5, 2020, from http:// web.b.ebscohost.com/ehost/detail/detail?vid=7&sid+afafbb04-744b-4f89-a249-1523bfdd2f41%sessio nmgr102&bdata=JnNpdGU9ZWhvc3QtbG12ZSZzY29wZT1zaXR1#AN=124565087&db=bth

Chand, K. (2016). *What is Agile contracting methodology?* Retrieved February 5, 2020, from https:// www.lexology.com/library/detail.aspx?g=b96675c0-6e23-47cb-be8b-e3cc0966250e

Costa, C. (2020). *Software development agreements: Polar Pro Filters Inc. v. Frogslayer LLC*. Retrieved August 17, 2020, from http://ccosta.com/index.php/2020/05/03/software-development-agreements-polar-pro-filters-inc-v-frogslayer-llc-2/

Dataitlaw. (2019). *5 basic legal issues of agile software development*. Retrieved February 4, 2020, from https://www.dataitlaw.com/5-basic-legal-issues-of-agile-software-development/

Definition of Agile. (n.d.). Retrieved February 11, 2020, from https://www.dictionary.com/browse/agile?s=t

Dutton, G. (2018). Choosing the right agile strategy. *Training (New York, N.Y.)*, 34–36. Retrieved February 10, 2020, from http://pubs.royle.com/publication/?i=482831&p=36#{%22page%22:%2236%22,%22 2issue_id%22:482831,%22publication_id%22:%2220617%22}

Edwards, I., Bickerstaff, R., & Bartsch, C. (n.d.). *Bird & Bird & contracting for agile software development projects*. Retrieved February 6, 2020, from https://www.twobirds.com/~/media/pdfs/brochures/ contracting-for-agile-software-development-projects.pdf?la=en

Eisenberg, M. A. (2009). The role of fault in contract law: Unconscionability, unexpected circumstances, interpretation, mistake, and performance. *Michigan Law Review, 107*, 1413–1430.

Flo-Products Co. v. Valley Farms Dairy Co. 718 S.W. 2d 207 (Ct. Appl. MO.).

Friess, E. (2019). Scrum language use in a software engineering firm: An exploratory study. *IEEE Transactions on Professional Communication, 62*(2), 130–147. doi:10.1109/TPC.2019.2911461

Hamer v. Sidway 124 N.Y. 538, 27 N.E. 256 (Ct. App. N. Y.).

Hassett, J., & Burke, E. (2017). Why the agile approach is so important to law firms. *Of Council, 36*(10), 6-9.

Kanth, S. K. (2009). Agile methodology in product testing. *Journal of the Quality Assurance Institute, 23*(1), 18–23.

Laakkonen, K. (2014). *Contracts in agile software development*. Aalto University School of Science.

Larusdottir, M., Cajander, A., & Gulliksen, J. (2014). Informal feedback rather than performance measurements – User-centred evaluation. *Behaviour & Information Technology*, *33*(11), 1118–1135. doi:1 0.1080/0144929X.2013.857430

Lee, G., & Xia, W. (2010). Toward Agile: An integrated analysis of quantitative and qualitative field data on software development agility. *Management Information Systems Quarterly*, *34*(1), 87–114. doi:10.2307/20721416

Legal Executive Institute, & Reuters, T. (2017). *US companies vastly outspend rest of the world on legal services, Acritas study shows.* Retrieved August 11, 2020, from https://www.legalexecutiveinstitute.com/acritas-legal-services-spending-study/#:~:text=US%20companies%20spend%20a%20whopping,new%20study%20by%20Acritas%20Research

Legal Information Institute. (2002). *UCC article 2 – Sales.* Retrieved February 11, 2020, from https://www.law.cornell.edu/ucc/index.html

Louisiana Civil Code. (n.d.). *Title iv – Conventional obligations or contracts.* Retrieved February 11, 2020, from https://lcco.law.lsu.edu/?uid=73&ver=en

Lukasiewicz, K., & Miler, J. (2012). Improving agility and discipline of software development with the Scrum and CMMI. *Institute of Engineering and Technology*, *6*(5), 416–422.

Mann, R. A., & Roberts, B. S. (2014). *Business law and the regulation of business* (11th ed.). Southwestern, Cengage Learning.

Marriott, E. (2016). *The history of the world in bite-sized chunks.* London, UK: Michael O'Hara Books Limited.

McGregor, L., & Doshi, N. (2018). Why Agile goes awry – and how to fix it. *Harvard Business Review*. Retrieved February 10, 2020, from https://hbr.org/2018/10/why-agile-goes-awry-and-how-to-fix-it

Miller, S. (2015). *Ten things you need to know as in-house counsel.* Retrieved August 11, 2020, from https://sterlingmiller2014.wordpress.com/2015/07/07/ten-things-explaining-litigation-to-the-board-and-the-ceo/

Moore, G. (1991). *Crossing the chasm.* HarperCollins Publishers.

Polar Pro Filters Inc. v. Frogslayer, LLC No. H-19-1706, slip op. (S. D. Tex. Oct. 22, 2019).

Raysman, R., & Brown, P. (2019). Software development agreement dispute produces a split decision. *New York Law Journal Online*. Retrieved November 8, 2019, from https://www.law.com/newyorklaw-journal/2019/11/08/software-development-agreement-dispute-produces-a-split-decision/

Rubin, K. S. (2012). *Essential Scrum: A practical guide to the most popular agile process.* Addison-Wesley.

Scully, J. (2014, Jan.). Agile HR delivery. *Workforce Solutions*, 8-11.

Siddique, L., & Hussein, B. A. (2016). Grounded theory study of the contracting process in agile projects in Norway's software industry. *The Journal of Modern Project Management*, 53-63. Retrieved February 10, 2020, from https://www.researchgate.net/publication/303336244_Grounded_Theory_Study_of_the_Contracting_Process_in_Agile_Projects_in_Norway's_Software_Industry

Sinclair, C. (2012). How to guide your lawyers in brokering agile software contracts. *Computer Weekly*, 23-29. Retrieved February 5, 2020, from http://web.b.ebscohost.com/ehost/pdfviewer?vid=8&sid=afafbb04-744b-4f89-a249-1523bfdd241%40sessionmgr102

Ward, D. B. (2019). *8 do's and dont's of agile contracts*. Retrieved February 3, 2020, from https://telegraphhillsoftware.come/8-dos-donts-agile-contracts-v2/

This research was previously published in Agile Scrum Implementation and Its Long-Term Impact on Organizations; pages 147-167, copyright year 2021 by Engineering Science Reference (an imprint of IGI Global).

Chapter 34
Building Ant System for Multi-Faceted Test Case Prioritization:
An Empirical Study

Manoj Kumar Pachariya
MCNUJC, Bhopal, Madhya Pradesh, India

ABSTRACT

This article presents the empirical study of multi-criteria test case prioritization. In this article, a test case prioritization problem with time constraints is being solved by using the ant colony optimization (ACO) approach. The ACO is a meta-heuristic and nature-inspired approach that has been applied for the statement of a coverage-based test case prioritization problem. The proposed approach ranks test cases using statement coverage as a fitness criteria and the execution time as a constraint. The proposed approach is implemented in MatLab and validated on widely used benchmark dataset, freely available on the Software Infrastructure Repository (SIR). The results of experimental study show that the proposed ACO based approach provides near optimal solution to test case prioritization problem.

1. INTRODUCTION

Software testing is an investigation conducted to provide stakeholders with information about the quality of the product or service under test. Software testing demonstrates the business view and helps in identifying the risks generated during software development (Kumar et al., 2013; Kumar et al., 2014). The prominent objectives of software testing are to meet the requirements that guided its design and development, work as expected by client, and satisfy the needs of stakeholders. Testing is done to ensure code and data flow coverageability of the program. The code coverageability includes the statement, branch, loop, and path coverageability. Testing team has to ensure that all program elements are executed at least once (Kumar et al., 2014; Epitropakis et al., 2015; Li et al., 2007).

In regression testing, execution of the selected test cases on SUT (Software Under Test) enhances the confidence, reliability and quality of software product (Li et al., 2007). The regression testing process is

DOI: 10.4018/978-1-6684-3702-5.ch034

concerned to maintenance phase. In regression testing, there is a need of rerunning the already executed test suite on software under test (SUT) after modification carried out in original software. In regression testing, test case prioritization is required to expose the faults in SUT at the early hours. Re-executing the complete test suite is not practical and not cost effective. Software industry requires cost effective approach for testing the software product adequately due to lacking time and resource constraint. The test case prioritization approaches will meet the requirement of software industry (Islam et al., 2012; Sun et al., 2013).

For testing a program, a test case is an input value for determining the failure and pass of program. It is used to ensure the validation of product and verification of process. The test case optimization is process of identifying the minimal cardinality subset of test cases from the large pool of test cases. The test case optimization is commonly concern with test case minimization, selection, prioritization, filtration and classification. The test case optimization reduces the efforts; duration and cost of testing as it provides optimal subset of test cases for audit (Kumar et al., 2011a; Kumar et al., 2011b; Kumar et al., 2011c).

Test case minimization is the process of identifying and removing the redundant test cases from large pool according to the objectives of testing. This subset of test cases is used to audit the program. This subset attains the same value of objective as the entire pool does. The identification of minimal cardinality subset of test cases from the large pool of test case is called the test case selection. The test case minimization reduces the set permanently by removing redundant and obsolete test case in the set while test case selection temporarily chooses optimal or the best fit test cases from the large pool according the test fitness criterion (Kumar et al., 2012; Kumar 2015).

For attaining the optimal value of testing objectives as early as possible, the ranking/ ordering/ scheduling of test cases is known as test case prioritization. Test case filtration is to chunk out subset of closely related test cases to optimize the objectives of testing (Tyagi & Malhotra, 2014). Test case prioritization is a critical problem of software testing. Since several factors may be considered in order to find the best order for test cases, several search-based techniques have been applied to find solutions for test case prioritization problem (Li et al., 2007; He & Bai, 2015).

Genetic algorithms are used to reorder test cases in a test suite using execution time as a constraint had shown that prioritization technique is appropriate for manual regression testing environment and explains how the baseline approach can be extended to operate in additional time constrained testing circumstances. Most of the researchers had explored genetic algorithm, ant colony optimization, linear programming etc. based approaches to find out the subset of test cases from a large pool of test cases but multi-faceted test case prioritization has not been explored and evaluated thoroughly (Sabharwal et al., 2011).

Literature study is the evidence that most of the researchers have explored and applied the greedy algorithms for test case prioritization. These algorithms provide the suboptimal solutions by identifying the local optimal solution in search space. For identification of the global optimal solution of test case optimization problem, nature inspired, and evolutionary algorithms are most suitable and helpful (Li et al., 2007; Kumar et al., 2011; Walcott et al., 2006). Some of these works apply ant colony-based algorithm, but the Statement Coverage along with time constraint was not considered. On the basis of fault detecting capability many interesting results have been received but the test case prioritization based on statement coverage with time constraint using Ant Colony Optimization technique has not been explored. So, there is still space for the researchers to experiment and validate the ant colony optimization-based approach to find out the order of test cases on the basis of statement coverageability (Singh et al., 2010;

Suri & Singhal 2011). In this study, multi-objective test case prioritization is explored by applying Ant Colony Optimization approach to meet industry demand.

Ant colony optimization (ACO) is nature-inspired and search space driven approach. It is best suitable for finding solutions of Combinatorial Optimization Problems (COP's). It also provides optimal solutions of several NP hard problems. Several real-life problems such as vehicle routing, quadratic assignment, scheduling, sequential ordering, routing in internet and other combinatorial problems are solved efficiently by employing artificial ants' systems (Dorigo et al., 1996; Colorni et al., 1991; Dorigo & Socha 2007).

In this article, ACO, a meta-heuristic and nature inspired approach has been applied for statement coverage-based test case prioritization problem. The proposed approach ranks test cases using statement coverage as fitness criteria and execution time as constraint. In this study, multi-objective test case prioritization problem is solved. This paper presents the empirically study of multi-faceted test case prioritization. The proposed approach is evaluated on multiple versions of widely used software. The results of experimental study show that the proposed approach provides near optimal solution test case prioritization problem in optimal time and cost.

This paper is organized as follows: Section 2 describes the basics of ACO techniques. Section 3 discusses the related work in area of test case prioritization. Section 4 discusses the proposed framework for multi-faceted test case prioritization. Section 5 insight into the experimental study and discussion of results. Final conclusion, which can be drawn from this study, is presented in Section 6. The possible future directions and guidelines to the researchers and academicians are presented in Section 7.

2. ANT COLONY OPTIMIZATION APPROACH

The ACO approach is a nature-inspired algorithm derived from the food searching behavior of the ant. The ANT SYSTEM is proposed by Dorigo et al. (1996) and Colorni et al. (1991). Despite being blind and small in size, they find the shortest route from source to food destination by using pheromones trails and intelligent communication system. They make the use of chemical substances, secreted by them known as pheromones and antennas to communicate with each other. ACO approach provides local optimal solutions because it maintains array of previous information and knowledge gathered by the ants in previous cycle.

In ACO approach, there are two key activities pheromone deposition and evaporation. Initially pheromone deposition is taken arbitrarily, and pheromone evaporation is done as per equation (3). Pheromone deposition refers to accumulation of pheromone traces on the trails while evaporation refers to decrement of amount pheromone traces on the trails due to legs of ants. As time passes the evaporation of pheromone occurs. When the ant completes the search of food, the updation of pheromone trail is carried out (Dorigo et al., 1996; Colorni et al., 1991; Dorigo & Socha 2007).

The path of each ant is constructed by selecting highest probability node as next node from current node of the ant as per equation (1) Artificial ants have now been successfully applied for test case prioritization problem.

$$P_{ij}(t) = \begin{cases} \dfrac{[\tau_{ij}(t)]^{\alpha} \cdot [\eta_{ij}]^{\beta}}{\sum_{\mu \in N_k(j)} [\tau_{ij}(t)]^{\alpha} \cdot [\eta_{ij}]^{\beta}}, & if\ j \in N_k(j) \\ 0. & Otherwise \end{cases} \tag{1}$$

where,

τ_{ij}^{α} is the amount of pheromone level on the path *(i, j)* of the graph

η_{ij}^{β} is the heuristic function

ζ is the array list (memory of ant) containing all the trails that ant has already passed and must not be chosen again .Heuristic function η_{ij}^{β} is used to search for the optimal path with the help of useful information, and the array list ζ stores the previous paths visited in the memory. Heuristic information h_{ij} can be calculated using equation (2).

$$h_{ij} = \frac{1}{\eta_{ij}^{\beta}} \tag{2}$$

Updating the trail is performed when ants complete their search of food source. The updated pheromone value can be computed by using equation (3).

$$\tau_{ij}(t+1) = (1 - \rho)\tau_{ij}(t) + \rho \tag{3}$$

Where ρ is pheromone trail evaporation that lies in the interval [0,1) and $\sum_{k=1}^{g} \Delta\tau_{ij}$ are pheromone deposited in the trail (i,j) followed by g ants after completing a tour. In case of equal or no pheromone on adjacent paths, ants randomly choose the path. The pheromone trail on a path increases the probability of the path being followed. The ant then reaches the next node and again does the path selection process as described above. This process continues till the optimal path is achieved. These final tours give the solution for shortest or best path which can be analyzed for optimality.

Thus, ants are able to find shortest path on the basis of:

- The pheromone lay down on ground by other ants of same colony which represents the experience of the colony.
- Memory and heuristic information which represents useful knowledge about the particular problem the ants are solving.

3. RELATED WORK

Test case prioritization is a crucial problem of the software testing and requires devising the intelligent techniques to solve it. The several fitness criteria and testing objectives are considered to identify the best ordered subset of test cases. The several search-based techniques and the greedy approaches have been applied to find solutions for test case prioritization but these approaches produce suboptimal (local optimum) results. The details of some of them are as follows:

Rothermal et al. (2001) has addressed the issues related to prioritization for large software development environments. He made an empirical study for analyzing the impact of size reduction test suite on fault detecting capability of test case. In this study, Siemens suite and space programs are used for experimentation purpose. Li et al. (2007) applied various meta-heuristics for test case prioritization, hill climbing algorithm, a genetic algorithm, a greedy algorithm, the additional greedy algorithm and a two-optimal greedy algorithm. The several search-based techniques are explored and exploited for test case prioritization, but ant colony optimization technique is not explored for time constraint and statement coverage-based test case prioritization. For reducing the cost of testing, Kim et al. (2002) used the history of execution or execution profile of test cases for ranking the test cases. In regression testing, if size of reduced test suite or execution cost is very high, then the test cases in test suite are further ranked or prioritized for execution. Under certain conditions, some can even guarantee that the selected test cases perform no worse than the original test suite. They prioritized the test cases and exercised only that fit within existing constraints. They pointed out that the existing prioritization techniques are memory less, implicitly, local choices.

Walcott et al. (2006) applied the genetic algorithms for test case prioritization. In this study, Walcott et al. (2006) measured the fitness of test cases on the basis of code coverage and also employed execution time as constraint for fitness function. They measured the fitness of test cases by estimating average percentage of statement, condition and path coverage. They concluded that genetic algorithm is better than others for small programs and additional greedy, two-optimal algorithm are good for large programs.

Singh et al. (2010) explored the ant colony optimization approach for fault detection-based test case prioritization. Singh et al. (2010) ordered the test cases on basis of their fault exposing ability. In this study, multi faults software subjects are considered. In graphical representation of test case prioritization problem, the number of nodes in graph is equal to number of test cases in pool. From the results of experimental study, Singh et al. (2010) concluded that proposed approach is better than random and reverse order approach.

Suri et al. (2011) also proposed evolutionary computing-based approach inspired from food searching behavior of real ants to order or rank the test cases. They have not validated their proposal. Moreover, Singh et al. (2011) and Suri et al. (2011) both approaches had not considered primacy of test cases. The precedence among test cases is highly required to be considered. The computing performance of proposed approach is low due to consideration of ants equal to huge number of test cases in pool because each ant communicates and share the information with other ants. Huge memory and high dimensional search space and computing time are required to get the local optimal solution.

Ahmed et al. (2012) applied Genetic Algorithms for test case prioritization using statement coverage information. They draw the flow graph and compared it with their previous work. They found that the results are close to that of their previous studies. Joseph and Radhamani (2014) proposed the hybrid intelligent approach for test case prioritization. They used the amalgam of Particle Swarm Optimization, Artificial Bee Colony and Fuzzy C-means approaches to optimization of test case. They considered maximum fault coverage as criteria to prioritize the test cases. Tyagi and Malhotra (2014) proposed three stage approach for test case optimization. In stage-one, they identified and removed the redundant and duplicate test cases on the basis of fault coverage. In Stage two, they passed the outcome of stage –one to particle swarm optimization approach. In stage-three, they used ratio fault coverage and execution time to prioritize the test case. The Coverage of original code and change code based Genetic

Algorithm based approach is proposed by Epitropakis et al. (2015). In experimental study, they used NSGA-II for prioritizing the test cases. They have also introduced a coverage compaction algorithm that reduces coverage data size, and execution time of all the algorithms used. Marchetto et al. (2016) have explored and applied Non-dominated Sorting Genetic Algorithm Version-II (NSGA-II) for prioritizing the test cases using fault coverage. They found that NSGA-II outperforms several techniques. Gupta et. al. (2019) carried out systematic review study and critical analysis of test case optimization approaches and identified several criteria and gapes in existing test case optimization techniques.

4. PROPOSED ACO BASED APPROACH FOR MULTI-FACETED TEST CASE PRIORITIZATION

Ant Colony Optimization (ACO) is a metaheuristic, stochastic, artificial intelligence-based search optimization, nature inspired algorithms. ACO is used to construct the probabilistic solution of combinatorial and search optimization problems such as test case prioritization, selection and classification using graph traversal (Kumar et al., 2011; Kumar et al., 2015; Singh et al., 2010). ACO algorithms are inspired by the behavior of the real ants of finding the shortest path between the nest and the food. They evolve the solutions identified in local search by communicating the local solutions to another ant through intelligent communication system. In the ACO, a set of artificial ants are used in cooperative nature to find the optimal solution of a problem through exchanging information via pheromone deposited on the edges of graph of the problem and heuristic information (Kumar et al., 2015; Dorigo et al., 1996; Colorni et al., 1991). In fact, solution components are iteratively added to a partial solution taking into account the heuristic information (prior knowledge) and also the pheromone trails. During the search, the pheromone trails are dynamically updated based on the ants searching experience.

It increases the probability of constructing high quality test suite eventually. The pheromone updating deals with pheromone deposition and evaporation and is performed when ants either complete their search or get the optimum test suite. The pheromone deposition is the process of adding the pheromone by ants on all paths they follow. Pheromone trail evaporation means decreasing the amount of pheromone deposited on every path with respect to time. Ref. 3, 7 and 12 has motivated the author to explore ACO for multi-faceted test cases prioritization.

In search-based software testing, the graph and search space may be used to represent the test case prioritization problem. So, the test cases prioritization is the problem of searching and identifying optimal path into fitness search space. In this proposal, statement coverage and execution time of the test case are considered as the dimensions of fitness search. It is very difficult to identify global rank of the test cases in multi-dimensional fitness search space. Ideally, tester would like to order/rank the test cases using fitness value in such manner that none of the decisions for test case selection will never be wrong (Kumar et al., 2014). Ref. 12 and 17 leads us to build the ant colonies for statement coverage-based test case prioritization with time constraint. In this paper, ant colony optimization-based time restricted framework is proposed for statement coverage-based test case prioritization to maximize the objective of software testing cost effectively. The proposed ACO based framework is implemented in Matlab and validated on widely used software artifacts. Details of proposed framework are as follows in figure 1:

Figure 1. Process diagram of proposed ACO_TEST_PRIORITIZE System

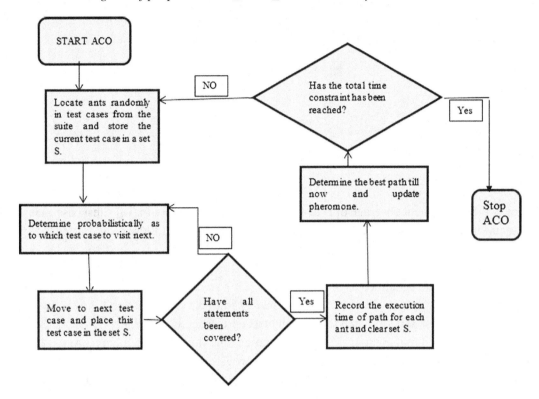

4.1 Statement of the Problem

Let P_0 be a modified version of P and let T be a test suite containing n test cases and $T' = \{t_1, t_2, t_3, \ldots t_n\}$ be a sequence on T. Let F be a function for test case set for some criteria on which total ordering relation $\geq$ is imposed. T' is a test case prioritization of T with respect to F if and only if for all i, $1 \leq i \leq n\text{-}1$ such that $F(t_i) \geq F(t_{i+1})$, that is F is monotonic over T.

4.2 Problem Formulation

A selective regression testing technique chooses a subset of test suite that was used to test the software before modifications were made and then uses this subset to test the modified software. Prioritization is the process of ranking or ordering the test cases to attain optimum value of objective as early as possible.

In search-based software testing, test case prioritization is the process of arranging or dividing the regions of high dimensional fitness search space. Test case prioritization is the process of arranging or ranking the test cases as per their fitness values. The fitness search space is arranged in such manner that decision regarding test case prioritization, and selection will never be wrong. Test cases in test suite are ranked on the basis of their maximum statement coverage and execution time. The total execution time of finally prioritized test suite will never exceed total execution time available for testing.

A test suite T is defined as an *n-tuple* of test case t_i, where $i = 1$ to n and $T = \{t_1, t_2, t_3, \ldots, t_n\}$. The prioritization of T is denoted as T'. In the problem formulation, the maximum time within which a prioritize test suite must execute is the maximum capacity of test suite, execution time of each test case is its weight and its value is percentage of statement coverage. The output of algorithm is prioritized list that fits the required time limit. Formally test case prioritization is defined as equation (4).

$$Maxmize\, Z = \sum_{i}^{n} S_i * X_i \qquad (4)$$

$$\text{Subject to} \sum_{i}^{n} Et_i * X_i \leq TET_{max} \; ; X_i = 0 \text{ or } 1$$

Where, S_i is the statement coverage of ith test case, Et_i is the execution time of ith test case t_i and TET_{max} is total execution time available for testing software. In this proposal, the following assumptions are made:

- Original test suite is taken as $T = \{t_1, t_2, t_3, ..., t_n\}$
- Set of all statements is defined as $St = \{s_1, s_2, s_3, ..., s_x\}$
- Each test case t_i, where $i = 1$ to n in the original test suite covers some or all the statements.
- Number of artificial ants to search through the test case space is n (number of test cases).
- For each ant j, a list that contains selected test cases (and thus the statements covered on the current path) is represented as $S_j = \{s_1, s_2, s_3, ..., s_m\}$ where, $m \leq n$.
- w_i is the weight of each edge i, which is assumed to be the amount of pheromone deposited on the edge.
- Assume pheromone deposition rate to be +1 or 100% for each ant that has crossed the edge on a best path.
- Assume pheromone evaporation rate to be $k\%$ of w_i (current weight of ith edge) to be reduced for each edge after each iteration of the loop.

4.2.1 Graphical Representation of Test Case Prioritization Problem (Figure 2)

The test case prioritization problem can be represented in the form of a directed graph $G(V,E)$, where V is the set of vertices (Test Cases) and E is the set of edges in the graph. In this representation, number of nodes in graph is equals to number of test cases in pool i.e. $V \equiv T$. Each edge in the graph represents the pheromone trail associated with the edge $e_{ij} \in E$, which reflects the amount of statement coverage the chosen path within time constraint, TC.

5. EMPIRICAL STUDY

In this study, multiple versions of Print_tokens and Print_tokens2 programs are used to validate the proposed approach. The details of software subject used in this study are presented in Sections 5.1 and section 5.2 describes the experimental setup used in this empirical study. The results and discussion of this experimental study is presented in Section 5.3.

Figure 2. Problem representation

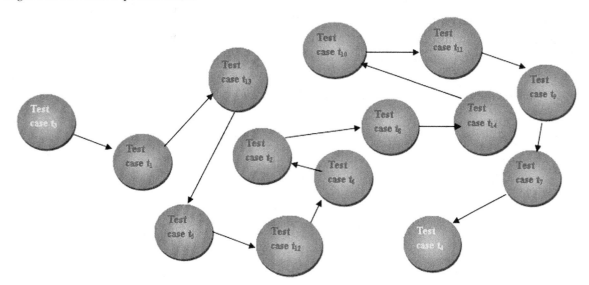

5.1 Experimental Subjects

For validation of the proposal, Print_tokens and Print_tokens2 programs of the Siemens suite are considered and details are given in Table 1. These programs are used for validation of the proposal because they have been widely used in the testing literature and represent an almost standard benchmark. In addition, most importantly, they are freely available together with extensive test suites and multiple versions at web address of the Software-artifact Infrastructure Repository (http://www.sir.unl.edu). Print_tokens and Print_tokens2 programs are lexical analyzer, written in C programming language. Size of Print_tokens and Print_tokens2 programs are 402 and 483 LOC. Non-comment lines are considered as size of programs. In this study, the seven versions of Print_tokens and ten versions of Print_tokens2 programs are used to carry out the experimentation. The number of test cases available at SIR for the programs Print_tokens and Print_tokens2 are 4130 and 4115.

Table 1. Programs used in experimental study

Program Used	Description	Size in LOC	Number of Test Cases	Number of Versions
Print_tokens	Lexical Analyzer	402	4130	7
Print_tokens2	Lexical Analyzer	483	4115	10

5.2 Experimental Setup

Data sets used for experimentation is taken from a Software Infrastructure Repository (SIR). The implementation of the proposed ACO based framework is done in MATLAB™- software in version7.02 on Windows 7 Home Basic, service pack1 with Intel Core i3-2310M CPU @2.10 GHz Pentium, 4 GB

RAM,64 bit operating system. The input information to ACO_TEST_PRIORITIZE is gathered by collecting measures while running each version of each subject programs against its complete test case. The *gcov* utility of Ubuntu 11 on same hardware configuration is used to know the statement coverage. It requires pre-compiled source programs with GCC GNU compiler. The time utility of Ubuntu 11 on same hardware platform is to find out execution time of test cases on subject source programs using scripts. The several scripts are written and executed for finding out the input information.

Figure 3. Block diagram of ACO_TEST_PRIORITIZE

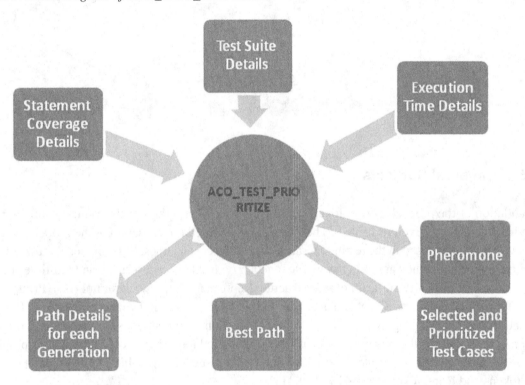

The proposed ACO based framework is implemented in MatLab using execution time restriction. ACO_TEST_PRIORITIZE requires the statement coverage, execution time, and other information of the regression testing as an input and produces the best order of test cases to be audited, finally prioritized test cases, and path details of each generation (figure 3).

The ACO_TEST_PRIORITIZATION System has main program and five modules namely ants_information(), ants_primaryplacing(), ants_cycle(), ants_cost(), ants_traceupdating. The module ants_information() did the initialization of the variables of proposed system. Subsequently, the module ants_primary_placing() initially places ants (test cases of the test suite) randomly in graph and the it calls the module ants_cost() that is used to selects edges of graph on the basis of attractiveness, which depends upon the density of pheromones and statement coverage. Then ants_traceupdating() module is used to update the pheromone trails.

5.2.1 Criteria and Policy used for Test Case Prioritization

The absolute criterions considered in this study are Statement Coverage and Execution Time which corresponds to Criterion #1 and Criterion #2. Test cases in the test suite should be prioritized in such manner that it should achieve maximum statement coverage of the test suite. The execution time of test suite should be minimum subject to constraint of total time available for testing [8,9,28,29]. In this study, < total/sum of the execution time of all the test cases (constraint)> is considered as test case prioritization stopping condition. In this experimental study, <number of iterations> is used as optimization stopping criteria. In this study, the fixed number of iterations (10000) or difference in total statement coverageability of suite is less than or equal to $\epsilon 0$ (a small amount such as 0.0025). The parameters and constant used in our experiment are given in table 2. These parameters are considered on the basis of preliminary experiment and experience for achieving good result. The proposed framework is tested on parameters values mentioned in table 2.

Table 2. Parameters used in ACO

Population (P)	No. of Iteration (I)	Error	Total Testing Time Available	Initial Pheromone (Iph)	Alpha (α)	Beta (β)	Roh (ρ)
350	10000	0.00000001	148	0.0001	1	5	0.01

5.3 Results and Discussion

Test prioritization schemes typically create reordering of the test cases in the test suite that can be executed after many subsequent changes to the program under test.

Table 3. Sample Test cases and statements executed in the program under test

Test Case	t_1	t_2	t_3	t_4	t_5	t_6	t_7	t_8	t_9	t_{10}	t_{11}	t_{12}	t_{13}	t_{14}
#Statements Covered	124	143	122	114	132	139	114	132	119	124	123	135	127	130
Execution time	4	3	5	4	3	3	3	3	3	9	8	5	12	18
Rate of Statement Covered	31	47.67	24.4	28.5	44	46.33	38	44	39.67	13.78	15.38	27	10.58	7.22

Limiting the length of the paper, here a test suite with 14 test cases of program under test (Print_tokens2) is considered to explain the process and details are given in Table 3. Regression test suite contains fourteen test cases with the initial ordering $\{t_1, t_2, t_3, t_4, t_4, t_5, t_6, t_7, t_8, t_9, t_{10}, t_{11}, t_{12}, t_{13}, t_{14}\}$. Following Table 3 illustrates the number of statements covered by each test case and the execution time.

Table 4. Order of test cases in first and last iteration

Iteration	Order of Test Cases in Test Suite													
First	t_6	t_2	t_{12}	t_{14}	t_3	t_{11}	t_{10}	t_4	t_9	t_7	t_1	t_{13}	t_5	t_8
Last	t_3	t_1	t_{13}	t_5	t_{12}	t_6	t_2	t_8	t_{14}	t_{10}	t_{11}	t_9	t_7	t_4

Figure 6 clearly shows that statement coverageability analysis of the proposed test cases. It can be said that the test cases having the high rate of statements coverage are executed and audited first and test cases having the low rate of statement coverage are executed in later sequence.

Finally, the proposed ACO_TEST_PRIORITIZATION System provides the rank of test cases of test suite to be executed and audited on SUT. The orderings of the test cases of the test suite for first and last iteration are given in Table 4 and the pictorial representation of the results of above-mentioned problem is decorated in Figure 4 - 6.

Figure 4. Test case prioritization for first iteration

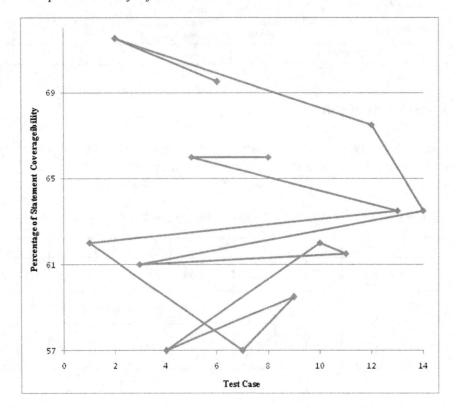

Figure 5. Test case prioritization for last iteration

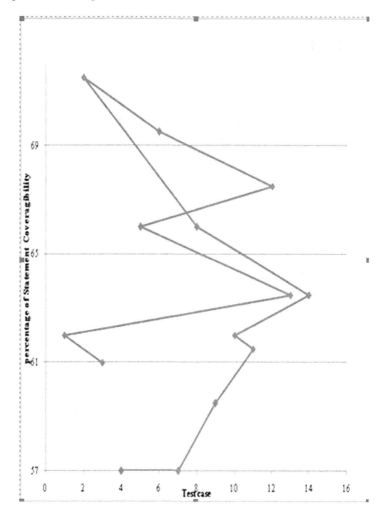

6. CONCLUSION AND FUTURE SCOPE

Test case prioritization is beneficial in several terms, when software testing team is being forced to terminate or stop testing process before the all the test cases of the pool have been executed and audited. The premature termination of testing process is the imperative requirement of software industry due to time constraint, budget constraint and fixed release date. Test case prioritization is an efficient way to improve the quality of software testing otherwise industry will have to prematurely terminate the testing process.

There are several criteria to prioritize the test cases such as fault revealing capability, mutation score, code coverage, execution time and cost, fault localization, faults severity, change code coverage, past faults coverage, suspicious code coverage etc. but existing techniques of the test case prioritization are single criterion /objective. The existing single objective prioritization techniques are not fulfilling the requirements of software industry. The author's previous works also pointed out that the test case optimization is a multi-faceted, NP-Complete, search space driven problem and require an intelligent and nature inspired techniques to solve them efficiently.

Figure 6. Statement coverageability analysis

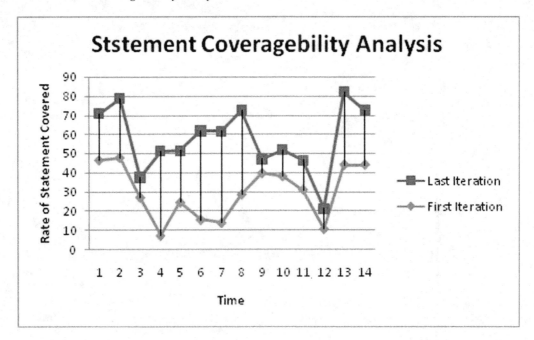

This paper presents the noble approach for the multi-faceted test case prioritization. In this paper, test case prioritization problem with time constraint is being solved by using Ant Colony Optimization (ACO) approach. Ant Colony Optimization is a meta-heuristic, nature inspired approach that has been applied for statement coverage-based test case prioritization problem. The proposed approach measures the fitness of test cases in terms of statement coverage and ranks test cases of pool using fitness value of test cases. This approach identifies the best set of ordered test cases using statement coverage and execution time as a constraint. The proposed approach is implemented in Mathlab and validated on widely used benchmark dataset of software, freely available on Software Infrastructure Repository (SIR). The results of experimental study show that the proposed approach provides near optimal solution to test case prioritization problem and also provides encouraging results. ACO is strong and robust as it involves positive feedback and parallel computations and hence, it can lead to better solution to multi-faceted test case prioritization problem in optimum time.

Though, the proposed framework is a nature driven intelligent approach and provides optimal solution to the multi-faceted test cases prioritization problem. In future, Pareto-ACO and Max-Min Multi-Objective ACO may be explored for improving the performance of the proposed approach. In the present study, the author has validated his proposal on two real industrial programs. For generalization and confidence, more experimentation is required on real live projects and will be carried out in future research work. Multi-faceted test case prioritization using nature inspired techniques such as Bat Algorithms, Firefly Algorithms, Flower Polarization, Grey Wolf Optimization, Intelligent Water Droplet Algorithms and Vulture Optimization, etc., will be explored in future.

7. REFERENCES

Ahmed, A. A., Shaheen, M., & Kosba, E. (2012). Software testing suite prioritization using multi-criteria fitness function. *Proceedings of the 23rd IEEE International Conference on Computer Theory and Applications (ICCTA)*. IEEE Press. 10.1109/ICCTA.2012.6523563

Colorni, A., Dorigo, M., & Maniezzo, V. (1991). Distributed Optimization by Ant Colonies. *Proceedings of European Conference on Artificial Life (ECAL 91)*. Elsevier.

Dorigo, M., Maniezzo, V., & Colorni, A. (1996). The Ant System: Optimization by a Colony of Cooperating Agents. *IEEE Transactions on Systems, Man, and Cybernetics. Part B, Cybernetics*, 26(1), 29–41. doi:10.1109/3477.484436 PMID:18263004

Dorigo, M., & Socha, K. (2007). An Introduction to Ant Colony Optimization. CRC Press.

Epitropakis, M. G., Yoo, S., Harman, M., & Burke, E. K. (2015). Empirical evaluation of pareto efficient multi-objective regression test case prioritization. *Proceedings of the 2015 International Symposium on Software Testing and Analysis* (pp. 234-245). ACM. 10.1145/2771783.2771788

Gupta, N., Sharma, A., & Pachariya, M. K. (2019). An insight into test case optimization: ideas and trends with future perspectives. *IEEE Access*, 7, 22310–22327. doi:10.1109/ACCESS.2019.2899471

He, Z.-W., & Bai, C.-G. (2015). GUI test case prioritization by state-coverage criterion. *Proceedings of the 10th International Workshop on Automation of Software Test*, Florence, Italy, May 16-24. IEEE Press. 10.1109/AST.2015.11

Islam, M. M., Marchetto, A., Susi, A., & Scanniello, G. (2012, March). A multi-objective technique to prioritize test cases based on latent semantic indexing. *Proceedings of the 2012 16th European Conference on Software Maintenance and Reengineering* (pp. 21-30). IEEE. 10.1109/CSMR.2012.13

Joseph, K. A., & Radhamani, G. (2014). Fuzzy C Means (FCM) clustering based hybrid swarm intelligence algorithm for test case optimization. *Research Journal of Applied Sciences, Engineering and Technology*, 8(1), 76–82. doi:10.19026/rjaset.8.943

Kim, J. M., & Porter, A. (2002). A history based test prioritization technique for regression testing in resource constrained environments. *Proceedings of the 24th International Conference on Software Engineering* (pp. 119-129). ACM. 10.1145/581339.581357

Kumar, M., Sharma, A., & Kumar, R. (2011). Optimization of test cases using soft computing techniques: a critical review. *WSEAS Transactions on information science and applications, 8*(11), 440-452.

Kumar, M., Sharma, A., & Kumar, R. (2011). Towards multi-faceted test cases optimization. *Journal of Software Engineering and Applications*, 4(9), 550.

Kumar, M., Sharma, A., & Kumar, R. (2011). Soft computing-based software test cases optimization: A survey. *International Review on Computers and Software*, 6(4), 512–526.

Kumar, M., Sharma, A., & Kumar, R. (2012). Multi faceted measurement framework for test case classification and fitness evaluation using fuzzy logic based approach. *Warasan Khana Witthayasat Maha Witthayalai Chiang Mai*, 39(3).

Kumar, M., Sharma, A., & Kumar, R. (2013). Test Case Classification and Selection: W-Shaped Metaphor. *Proceedings of International Conference On Computing Sciences WILKES100 - ICCS-2013* (pp. 298-304). Elsevier.

Kumar, M., Sharma, A., & Kumar, R. (2014). Fuzzy Entropy based Framework for Multi-Faceted Test Case Classification and Selection: An Empirical Study. *IET Software, 8*(3), 103–112.

Kumar, M., Sharma, A., & Kumar, R. (2015). An empirical evaluation of a three-tier conduit framework for multifaceted test case classification and selection using fuzzy-ant colony optimisation approach. *Software, Practice & Experience, 45*(7), 949–971.

Li, Z., Harman, M., & Hierons, R. M. (2007). Search algorithms for regression test case prioritization. *IEEE Transactions on Software Engineering, 33*(Apr), 225–237. doi:10.1109/TSE.2007.38

Marchetto, A., Islam, M. M., Asghar, W., Susi, A., & Scanniello, G. (2016). A multi-objective technique to prioritize test cases. *IEEE Transactions on Software Engineering, 42*(10), 918–940. doi:10.1109/TSE.2015.2510633

Rothermal, G., Untch, R. H., Chu, C., & Harold, M. (2001, October). Test case prioritization. *IEEE Transactions on Software Engineering, 27*(10), 928–948.

Sabharwal, S., Sibal, R., & Sharma, C. (2011). A genetic algorithm based approach For prioritization of test case scenarios in static testing. *Proceedings of the 2nd International Conference on computer and Communication Technology*, Allahabad (pp. 304-309). IEEE Press. 10.1109/ICCCT.2011.6075160

Singh, Y., Kaur, A., & Suri, B. (2010, July). Test case prioritization using ant colony optimization. *Software Engineering Notes, 35*(:4), 1–7.

Sun, W., Gao, Z., Yang, W., Fang, C., & Chen, Z. (2013). Multi-objective test case prioritization for GUI applications. *Proceedings of the 28th Annual ACM Symposium on Applied Computing SAC '13* (pp. 1074-1079). ACM. 10.1145/2480362.2480566

Suri, B., & Singhal, S. (2011). Implementing Ant Colony Optimization for Test Case Selection and Prioritization. *International Journal on Computer Science and Engineering, 3*(5), 1924–1932.

Tyagi, M., & Malhotra, S. (2014). Test case prioritization using multi objective particle swarm optimizer. *Proceedings of the International Conference on Signal Propagation and Computer Technology (ICSPCT)* (pp. 390-395). IEEE. 10.1109/ICSPCT.2014.6884931

Walcott, K. R., Soffa, M. L., Kapfhammer, G. M., & Roos, R. S. (2006). Time-Aware Test suite Prioritization. *Proceedings of the International Symposium on Software Testing and Analysis* (pp. 1-12). ACM.

Zhu, H. (1995). Axiomatic assessment of control flow-based software test adequacy criteria". *Software Engineering Journal, 10*(5), 194–204. doi:10.1049ej.1995.0025

This research was previously published in the International Journal of Software Innovation (IJSI), 8(2); pages 23-37, copyright year 2020 by IGI Publishing (an imprint of IGI Global).

Chapter 35
Application of Design Thinking Methodology to the Various Phases of the Software Development Life Cycle

Sahana Prabhu Shankar
https://orcid.org/0000-0001-8977-9898
Ramaiah University of Applied Sciences, India

Supriya M. S.
https://orcid.org/0000-0003-3465-6879
Ramaiah University of Applied Sciences, India

Naresh E.
https://orcid.org/0000-0002-8368-836X
M. S. Ramaiah Institute of Technology, India

ABSTRACT

Design thinking is often thought of as a creative way of problem solving. People are told to believe what they are told and what they read, and with that is the downfall of creativity. Designers need to see the world through the eyes of a 5-year-old. People needs to give themselves permission to be creative. It takes intelligence to answer a question, but it also takes creativity to answer the question. People have to imagine the world as it never existed before. Design thinking can be termed as "consumer-centric", "end-user centric" or simply "human-centric" thinking. It works from the perspective of the user in general with user satisfaction being the primary goal. The methodology that I adopted is thinking from the user's perspective and working towards user's satisfaction as the goal. Design thinking is a problem-solving technique evolved in different fields like architecture, engineering, and business. The key element to the success of designing a software system lies in user participation. Therefore, it was basically developed to derive a solution by understanding the user's need.

DOI: 10.4018/978-1-6684-3702-5.ch035

INTRODUCTION

Design thinking is often thought as a creative way of problem solving. We are told to believe what we are told and what we read, and with that is the down coming of creativity. Designers need to see the world through the eyes of a 5-year-old. We need to give ourselves permission to be creative. It takes intelligence to answer a question, but it takes creativity to answer the question. We have to imagine the world as to it never existed before. Design thinking can be termed as "consumer-centric", "end-user centric" or simply "human-centric" thinking. It works from the perspective of the user in general with user satisfaction being the primary goal. The methodology that I adopted is thinking from the user's perspective and working towards user's satisfaction as the goal.

Agile and Scrum methodologies are widely practiced almost amongst all the organizations. The design thinking methodology and agile methodology have many aspects in common, like aiming to get faster delivery while at the same time achieving highest customer satisfaction. The core of design thinking is iterative prototyping whereas agile focuses on what is the next step to be taken.

Figure 1. User-Centric Design Thinking Methodology

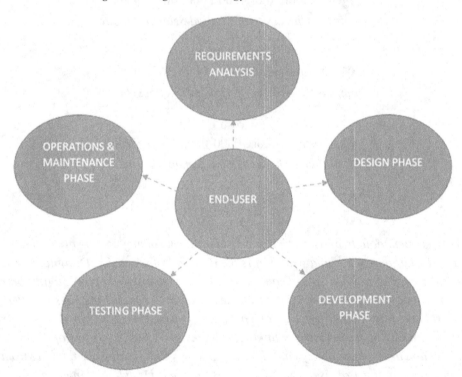

The Figure 1, depicts the influence of the end-user in all the phases of software development life cycle. It shows that the design thinking technique is mainly influenced and driven by the end users. The end user has a say in all the phases, and these phases are driven by thinking from end user's perspective.

BACKGROUND WORK

Design thinking is a problem-solving technique evolved in different fields like architecture, engineering and business. The key element to the success of designing a software system lies in user participation. Therefore, it was basically developed to derive a solution by understanding the user's need. Design thinking can be defined as "an approach that uses creative designers' sensibility and methods to understand the problems that people and society are dealing with" (Newman et al. 2015). The powerful methodology for innovation is design thinking. Design thinking distinguishes between innovative and existing real time activities, but not between artistic creation and engineering (Johansson-Skoldberg et al. 2013). The problem forming, solving and design can be accomplished by integrating human, business and technological factors with its use. Inventively, it is possible to deal with the ambiguity in wicked problems by applying design thinking. In this way, for non-deterministic nature of wicked problems, it is imperative for the architect to ground any plan within the setting in which it is conveyed (Plattner et al. 2013).

The core concepts involved in thinking is to understand, explore, porotype and evaluate. While exploring the problem, design thinking knowledge by understanding that can be done by observing the user scenarios. The evolved ideas in problem exploration are transformed into tangible representatives by sketching and prototyping techniques, thus opening an opportunity for exploring the solution space. After these problem and solution exploration phases, the built ideas and concepts can be communicated not only with the design team, but also with all the stakeholders involved in the entire process of designing the system. Thereby leading to innovative and suitable solutions for the social system. Converting design thinking into an action come with its own hurdles and obstruction and hence it is fundamental to educate and convey well-trained individuals, superior strategies as well as organizational back (Plattner et al. n.d.).

Design thinking is applicable to software engineering too and fits well in the agile methodology. Unlike the traditional way of software development life cycle, where the product is developed according to the requirements elicited from the customers, in design thinking the software is developed keeping in mind the end user's mindset while designing each requirement. This methodology encourages to radically empathize with the customer. Catering to the needs of customer is more important than just merely meeting the requirements. This design thinking consists of the following five steps namely Empathize, Define, Ideate, Iterate and Test.

The main advantage of this approach is design thinking from user's perspective can lead to the birth of new ideas. Such innovations can lead to filing of patents, white papers which in turn gives the organization a competitive edge in the market. These innovations act as very important intellectual assets for the company. A company that is in the industry just doing the job without innovation cannot survive for long or make a difference to the society. Design thinking need to not be restricted only to the software professionals but all the stake holders involved in the process of software development.

Testing team has also an important role to play in the quality assurance phase. One way of incorporating this methodology is to involve the quality team during the software architecture and design phase itself. The reason being the testing team is the one who will be simulating and working on the actual end user's environment and can get the same experience as that of a real user while using the product. In the entire process of software development, the tester is the one will be able to empathize better with the end user. This empathizing with the end user is a very important step and the very first step in design thinking.

Figure 2. Comparison between Traditional Thinking and Design thinking methodologies

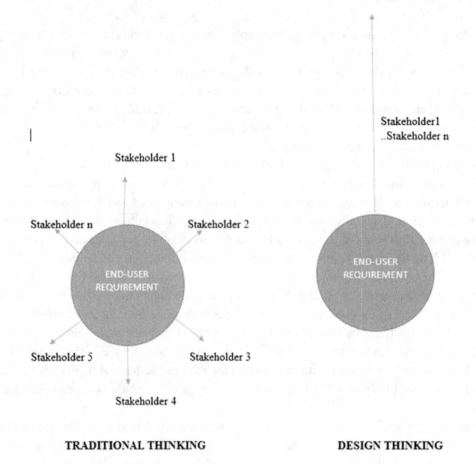

The figure 2 shows the difference in the perspectives of traditional thinking and traditional thinking methodologies. In case of traditional thinking, when we consider a user requirement for discussion during the stakeholders meeting, every stakeholder involved starts visualizing the same idea from his perspective on his mind, they only express their views verbally to others, which might be perceived in their perspective. Where in case of design thinking methodology, all the stakeholders think on similar lines when considering a requirement for discussion. This unison in thinking can be achieved by using various techniques as mentioned in the Table 1.

DIFFERENT PHASES INVOLVED IN THE DESIGN THINKING PROCESS

- **Perceive:**

Understanding the problem under consideration is a challenge in itself. It requires considerable amount of effort and patience. The problem formulation in the beginning gives just the skeleton, it needs to be fleshed out as the problem refines going further. The main aim is to do some research on the relevant data, identify the methodology, actors, and facts and then decide on the design using the above factors. (Carell et al. 2018)

- **Empathizing With End User:**

In this phase, we try to answer the questions such as, who are these end users and what is their level of knowledge with regards to using a software, their familiarity with the computers, their expectations from the software, possible shortcomings they might face. The tester's knowledge and experience will help to think ahead of the possible end user shortcomings.

- **Defining the End User Needs:**

By making use of the finding from the first phase, requirement engineer will be able to rephrase the user requirements to be able to give a better user experience to the end user while using the product. Then the design engineer can think of different ways of addressing this problem. From this first step, the test engineers would have already given an insight as to where to possible problems might arise, by making use of the same knowledge the design and development engineers can plan the remaining activities better in the software development life cycle.

- **Recreate:**

In this phase, instead of reusing the solution, like always. It is advised to think if the problem can be tackled in an innovative way that helps to address the problem in a more cost effective way or in general resource effective way and at the same time not compromising on the performance or rather aiming for better performance. A collaborative brainstorming approach is advised where all the stakeholders meet and do a mind mapping of different possible solutions. Innovative ideas are the result of this phase.

- **Repeat:**

Here the innovative ideas formulated during the recreate phase are combined and iterations are carried out with these combinations of best ideas until a good solution is arrived at. This removes the traditional mindset where testers are just thought of as bug reporters and these bugs result only in rework. The rework of design in response to a bug reported take considerable amount of effort. This can be avoided by adopting design thinking methodology.

- **Test:**

The recreation of the scenario with an interface to the prototype is made available to the users, this helps in better understanding of the problems. In this phase, if we face any hiccups instead of looking for a workaround to convince the end user, the design methodology encourages us to question ourselves as to why the user is feeling whatever he is feeling. The end user feedback is to be considered as a serious input for next iteration and not be neglected.

Thus design thinking, no longer sees that each iteration is a rework because of the bugs encountered as in the case of traditional software engineering life cycle approach.

Figure 3. Different phases in Design Thinking process

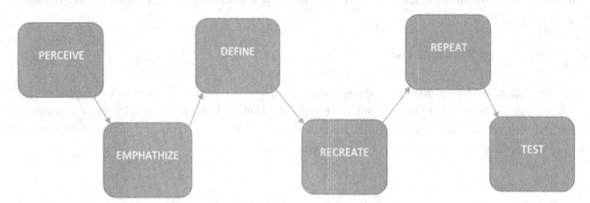

MOTIVATION FOR DESIGN THINKING IN REQUIREMENTS ENGINEERING PHASE

The requirements engineering phase is the very first and basic step in software development life cycle. The requirements engineering has to be carried out very carefully to make sure that correct requirements are elicited from the customers. This is that step where are the stakeholders interact with one another and freeze the requirements. This is the very first step where the client is involved. An end-user may/may-not be included as well because not always a client is also an end-user. In cases where the client is also an end-user he will be able to better empathize with the all the possible end-users who might use the software. The requirements engineering is the phase where maximum diversity and communication is involved when compared to all the other phases of software development life cycle. The projects these days demand human-centric agile approaches in order to fulfill the fuzzy needs of all the stakeholders especially the customers. Design thinking is the right way to address such a situation. It provides a chance to combine the innovative solutions of design thinking with the traditional ways of requirements engineering to provide human-centric solutions. It is also one of the longest phases and involves various sub phases such as:-

- **Requirements Elicitation:**

In this phase, various methods such as brain storming and interviews are used to communicate with the various stake holders. A representative of a software engineer from all the phases are present along with the requirements engineer whose main role is to elicit the requirements. While the requirements engineer directly interacts and questions the client, other stakeholders present during the elicitation phase may express their concern or suggestions if any for the requirements given by the customer. The other stakeholders generally record the minutes of the meeting and then later carry the same report for further analysis and discussion with their individual team.

- **Requirements Analysis:**

The individual team concerns may be different issues from technical to financial or unavailability required resources or skillset. These concerns are in turn discussed within the teams. The possible concern a design team might have is not having enough resources in terms of person or software to implement a certain type of architecture required to build the system. Development team might have concerns where the required skill set might not be available, for ex, knowledge of a certain tool or programming knowledge to implement the requirements. In that case they need not reject the requirements straightaway, instead they can negotiate and ask if management is ready to provide the required training to existing employees or hire a professional on contact basis to do that job. The test team might have concerns where some requirements are impossible to test due to same reasons as that of development team. The operations or maintenance team considering the complexity of the project might demand for more human resource to provide the required support.

- **Requirements Specification:**

The requirements elicited during the elicitation phase will be in plain simple English depending on the knowledge of the client regarding the technology or existing software in the same field.

Here the requirement analyst reconstructs the informal requirements into the formal requirements specification using technical jargons. This is the language which is understood by the software engineers down the life cycle. The requirements are here documented in a requirements document.

- **Requirement Validation:**

After the requirements are written formally, the next job is to cross verify if they are actually what the customers had told or if the meaning has changed during the requirements specification phase. If any clarifications are needed here, again the customers are contacted. Also not all the requirements elicited might be included in the project life cycle, so requirements may be dropped because of feasibility reasons while others might be modified for better performance and some suggestions might be provided to add new requirements. The functional and non-functional requirements are separately documented. The output of the entire requirements engineering phase is the SRS document.

LIMITATIONS IN TRADITIONAL REQUIREMENTS ENGINEERING PHASE

The most common problem during requirements elicitation phase is the customers won't be able to exactly tell what they actually mean, this might be because they won't be able to find exact words to express their feelings or the look and feel of the product. Quite often after the requirements analysis when the individual teams find that some requirements can be achieved by reusing some previously done solutions with the company with lower cost and effort, he might influence the customer to go back and modify the requirements. The requirements can sometimes not be correct because of misunderstanding the customer requirements. A few requirements might be contradicting each other, in such cases having to think from their viewpoint and coming up with an innovative solution that can possibly include both the contradicting requirements, rather than asking them to choose just one the conventional way. The requirements need not be complete always, in such cases it is either because the end user thought it wasn't needed or because of lack of knowledge. The engineer has to apply design thinking skills here to guess the possible missing requirement and encourage the end user to complete the requirement by providing appropriate hints. He should not just ask the end user to complete the requirements, instead he should think from his perspective to complete the requirements. The requirements sometimes might not be feasible to implement due to hardware or software limitations. After eliciting the requirements during the analysis phase, the engineers will be able to figure out what are the unfeasible requirements. Such requirements should be communicated clearly to customers. Other common hurdles include deciding if the requirements are testable and traceable.

DESIGN THINKING SOLUTION TO OVERCOME THE LIMITATIONS IN REQUIREMTS ENGINEERING

There are various methods that think on the similar lines of design thinking such as liberating structures, design sprint and contextual design. Design thinking is sometime referred to as 'attitude' more than a 'methodology'. Developing a user-centric innovative attitude for the requirement engineer is very important to empathize with the end user. In fact empathy is much needed during the initial stages of inception of a software project. Stepping into the shoes of the end user and thinking is what is more important. Design thinking especially unlike other creative methodologies has been created bearing in mind the IT context.

End-User Centric Requirements Engineering

The design thinking approach goes much beyond the regular human-centric thinking approach, as it involves deeper understanding of future user needs or requirements. Identifying those requirements that the end-users will not be able to articulate is an important aspect. The requirement engineer is not expected to just ask and write down the requirements directly from the end-user, instead he has to systematically evaluate the requirements and provide alternative options for every requirement assessed.

Focused Requirements Engineering of a Niche Group

Design thinking approach does not encourage the idea of replying on the results of big qualitative surveys because the results of these do not give ideas that are common to most users. The design thinking encourages out of the box thinking to develop innovative, astonishing, added-value solutions which will fetch greater returns to the company. The requirement engineers are required to talk to people from 'extreme groups'. Extreme groups can be either a group that does something extremely positive often or a group that always denies to everything. This is mainly because these people exhibit traits that are also there in other end-user groups which are in a much weaker form and difficult to assess.

Multifaceted Requirements Engineering Team

A good team is responsible for a successful design thinking project. It should consist of a mixed group of individuals from new joiners to experienced who will be able to appreciate and accept other's viewpoints and be open to criticism. Another good group is a representative from each of the teams i.e. design, development, testing, operations and maintenance who are capable of playing dual roles, both as an analyst as well as respective engineers in their teams.

Divergence to Convergence Requirements Engineering

The divergence implies seeing and tackling the problem from various innovative and creative perspectives and convergence implies trying to achieve unison among all the creative solutions identified. Every requirement engineer might come up with their innovative and unique way of addressing the problem. A conscience has to be reached at the end of the discussion to freeze on one solution or a combination of various solutions. This need not happen in a strict linear manner, but in various iterations and loops that include feedbacks from all the stakeholders. (Carell et al. 2018)

Challenges in Design Thinking for Requirements Engineering

- The requirements that are directly elicited from the customers are collected in an unstructured manner to speed the process of team collaborations i.e. design, development, and maintenance and to gear up the process. Design thinking has traceability issues.
- Another challenge faced by design thinking is availability of customers, however this problem is addressed to some extent due to good process-orientation that helps the interviews to be scheduled in advance.
- Design thinking fails to do justice in addressing the non-functional requirements such as security and performance. However, the non-functional requirement usability is addressed with utmost care, with it being the central topic.
- Time crunch in the planning phase in design thinking methodology, might lead to wrong architectural designs. However, the risk mitigation that is carried out by evaluating the various approaches, might help to achieve the trade-offs.
- Design thinking methodology believes in a team-based approach for requirements engineering. Taking too many viewpoints from different stakeholders might create some confusion during this phase.
- It might be difficult to do accurate effort estimates with design thinking methodology.
- Design thinking methodology struggles in prioritizing the requirements, no solution exist in design thinking methodology to address this challenge. (Hehn and Uebernickel, 2018)

MOTIVATION FOR DESIGN THINKING FOR SOFTWARE ARCHITECTURE AND DESIGN PHASE

The output of the requirements engineering phase acts as the primary input to the design phase. The SRS document provides all the details needed to carry out the design. The design phase mainly consists of software architecture, software design patterns and UML diagrams. The software architecture gives the overall skeleton; it is more like a blue print of the entire software to be built. The flesh would be filled in with the UML diagrams which provides a detailed low level design. The design patterns will help the designer to decide how the different elements of UML need to interconnected by using various relationships.

Software Architecture

Software Architecture is like the blue print of the software that needs to be developed. Just like how a building has an architectural plan designed by the software architect based on which it will be erected by the civil engineers. On the similar lines, software also has a plan laid out by the software architect and is constructed by software developers. There are many architectural standard template available such as the blackboard, model-view-controller, pipes and filters to name a few. Depending on what the intent is, these various patterns can be selected. Sometimes in case of complex systems, more than one architecture or a combination of architectures can be included.

Software Design Patterns

The software design patterns are repeatable solutions to commonly occurring problems. One of the main use of the design patterns is reusability. It is more like a software toolkit from which the software design engineers can choose as to which pattern to apply depending on the UML modelling elements such as number of classes present and the type of relationships between them. Various other factors such as coupling and cohesion also play a vital role in determining which pattern to use when. These software design patterns can be broadly classified into behavioral patterns, structural patterns and creational patterns. The creational patterns as the name suggests are used in situations when we have to create new objects or instantiate a class. One of the famous examples for creational patterns is singleton, which states that only one instance of a class can be created. Structural patterns tell us as to how the various elements i.e. the classes and the relationships are interconnected. One of the examples is proxy design pattern, which provides one object that represents the real object, so that the client can talk to the proxy instead of the actual original. The behavioral design patterns deal with communication among the various objects.

Software Design Using UML Modelling

The Unified Modelling Language is used for modelling the various elements and their relationships. They can be broadly classified into two categories such as structural diagram and behavioral diagram. The structural diagram as the name suggest represents the static aspects of the software and their interconnection. The behavioral diagram shows how the various elements interact with one another. The class diagram and entity relationship diagrams are examples of the class diagram. The other UML diagrams such as use-case, sequence, data flow, state chart, activity fall under the category of behavioral diagrams. Some of these diagrams are extremely important as most of the design software directly generates the skeletal code from them. This implies having a wrong design in place that could lead things going wrong down the lane.

LIMITATIONS IN THE TRADITIONAL DESIGN PHASE

Sometimes whenever a software fails, they are traced back to the requirements via the software design. If the fault lies in the design phase, then consideration is taken to modify the design. However, the designer that identified the failures cannot make or suggest changes without really understanding the original design. In this context design thinking can play an important role, where we apply this design thinking methodology to empathize with the earlier designer who had come up with this design to check all the relevant factors and do an estimation of the modifications i.e. both cost estimation and effort estimation.

Reusability is well encouraged in the software industry especially in software practices such as agile that has shorter development and delivery periods and stringent time frames. This is achieved by using the software design patterns in the design phase. However design thinking methodology tackles the application of design patterns from a different angle. Instead of blindly applying the same pattern when encountered with a similar situation from past, the design engineers are required to brainstorm and come up with a possible alternate innovative solution. The design engineers or design architects can take the feedback from customer from the previous release versions and analyze what design pattern had been used then. If they had expressed some hiccups in usage of the software earlier, they can recheck if some modifications can be brought into the design, to rectify the same.

The software designers should come up with a more formal method to formalize the design phase by applying the method of design thinking by taking into consideration the designer's intents and the design decision making.

The concept of design intent is applied for design thinking to the design phase. It explains 'what?' the software designers do during the design phase when encountered with a particular situation. The reason behind selecting particular way of doing the design i.e. 'why?' is given by design decision making. The justification part consists of the 'design rules' and the 'design criteria'. Design rules are accepted instructions that the designers follow to achieve the design intents by generating the design options. Design criteria are the standards for comparison of the various design options to determine the solution. (Sun and Liu, 2008)

DESIGN THINKING SOLUTIONS TO THE COMMON PROBLEMS ENCOUNTERED IN THE DESIGN PHASE

Design thinking helps to improve the co-ordination among the team members of the design phase. The most common problem with the traditional way of software development in the design phase is most of the software architecture that is laid out is decided by the primary software architect from his perspective alone. So, there can be a bias quite often in his thinking based his experience or otherwise.

Design thinking overcomes this problem by decentralizing the design of the application from a single person. It makes the process of design phase more interactive and dynamic. Design thinking makes sure that everybody in the team contributes towards the design of the application. This encourages everyone to improve existing designs and at the same time to suggest new features. One of the major setback of applying design thinking methodology to the design phase is achieving consensus in the given time framework. This might sometimes lead to extending the deadline a little longer, thereby affecting other phases that follow. The other problem is connecting with the different members in the team, because of a hierarchical barrier. Even though a junior member in the team might have a good innovative suggestion, he might be hesitant to open up regarding the same in front of the design architect.

In order to overcome this hurdle, persona technique was employed. Here, all the members in the design team impersonate some user and provide comments regarding a suggestion or change that is proposed. This way it encourages other to provide inputs that the designer might not have thought of like certain features. This can stimulate healthy discussion among the team members, hence enhancing the completeness of the application. Brain storming is one the techniques that encourages innovative thinking and can be adopted as a part of design thinking. This promotes thinking of design ideas that are out of box and away from the standards. Some members might still feel hindrance in accepting ideas offbeat and discussing openly with the other members of the design team. (Valentim et al. 2017)

A story board or sketching might be adopted in the design phase to put the design down in ink for everyone to discuss. This encourages everyone in the team to collaborate and contribute actively towards delivering an active healthy functional prototype. The design teams adopt a strategy known as 'Class Responsibility Collaborator' for identifying the user requirements that need to be modelled into a design. In order to create the class responsibility collaborator cards, the design team members sketch a scenario that identifies major classes i.e. the actors along with their responsibilities i.e. their functions. Adopting this practice in design thinking helps to convert the abstractions at the higher level to a low-level design which can be easily translated into a code in the next phase. (Corral & Fronza, 2018)

MOTIVATION FOR DESIGN THINKING IN SOFTWARE DEVELOPMENT PHASE

The software design document which is the output of the design phase acts as an input to the development phase. The development team consisting of software developers start working on individual modules of implementation based on the design document. There would be a number of development teams that would be working on individual modules that are interconnected to each other. First that individual team's work independently towards achieving their individual modules or components, later integration of these modules is taken care of.

One of the most common problems encountered during the implementation phase is most of the projects are maintenance projects and hence the team members generally do not get much scope to apply any thinking and are just doing the job of bug fixing. Reusability is one of the common practices in agile to achieve the shorter delivery time of the finished software product. This sometimes becomes a hindrance for creative and innovative thinking. Since the user is expected to achieve more in shorter time frames, he tends to blindly reuse the solutions that have worked really well in the past.

DESIGN THINKING SOLUTIONS TO THE COMMON PROBLEMS ENCOUNTERED IN THE DEVELOPMENT PHASE

The application of design thinking to software development can be broadly classified into three stages, they are as follows:

Problem Space Exploration

Before trying to address the problem the software developers try to understand the problem again from the user's perspective, thus empathizing with the end-user. They also look at the problem from a broader context. Then all the individual software developers discuss what the collaborative understanding of the situation is. The user instead of directly concluding on the problem under consideration, he must try to make a study on similar issues from the past, also observe if there has been a pattern in occurrence of the problem. The developer must try to study and understand the root cause of this problem from the end-user's perspective rather than finding a quick fix for the solution. The main ideology of design thinking is to pause and think before coding.

Solution Space Exploration

Rather than reusing one of the same previously used solution, it is better to think of an alternative creative solution. This could be either trying to code using a different new language that has been introduced in the market and is expected to perform better in relatively lesser execution time. However, this has to be brought up upfront during the stakeholders meeting in the early stages. Also when it comes to certain non-functional requirements such as security, the developer can think of adopting an alternative security protocol or algorithm, which might perform better. In most of the cases, they are maintenance projects and these are legacy softwares that are there from over a decade. So the developers generally hesitate to think out of the box in case of such projects. However, design thinking methodology on the contrary encourages to think out of the box and thus the innovative coding solutions. Another important area where design thinking can be applied by developers is, in the user-friendly feature i.e. the look and feel of the software. The developer must think from user's perspective if he can customize the front end of the software in a better way, than what the user has asked him to in order to achieve customer satisfaction. This way he might design a better attractive product that might as well increase the sales for the customer, thereby increasing customer satisfaction, which is ultimate goal of design thinking.

Aligning Both Spaces Iteratively

The above two stages need to occur in an iterative fashion. Once we identify an element in the problem space, we need to come to the solution space and explore for the possible solutions from the end-user perspective. Only after a number of iterations, a good solution for the problem can be obtained. It is observed that the number of iterations is greater in case of design thinking methodology as when compared to the agile methodology. This is because, in case of design thinking we consider many divergent options and then try to achieve consensus. This automatically encourages a number of iterations considering the number of ideas each individual developer comes up with in the ideate phase of design thinking.

A good working prototype is expected at the end of this phase, which can be passed onto the next testing phase for quality checks. The concept behind the design thinking prototype is that all the software developers must have a clear understanding about the underlying concepts. On the contrary, the software engineering prototypes generated in the traditional manner have the final software product of the same material. The same in case of agile, is iterated to the final product.

PROTOTYPE AND TEST IN DESIGN THINKING

Design Thinking applies an innovative solutions to the problems to be solved using the steps such as: Empathise, Define, Ideate, Prototype, and Test. Quality process performs the tasks of identifying the problem, analysing root cause, immediate containment, corrective and preventive actions. The corrective and preventive actions includes critical components such as ideation, prototyping and testing. User's feedback helps in building the better software there by providing possible iteration into the software. The end user feedback is to be considered as a serious input for next iteration and cannot be neglected. Thus

Design Thinking, no longer sees that each iteration is a rework on account of the bugs experienced as on account of conventional programming designing life cycle approach. With each new defect that is found, Design Thinking empowers this as a chance to concoct an inventive innovative solution to the problems.

Design Thinking not only tone development but also the testing process through regular observations and feedback during the early design in order to build the better prototype, based on which the testing is emphasized. The organizations like Apple, Airbnb, Nest, Square, and Tesla are working towards the customer needs and feedback throughout the development process to gain attention in the chosen markets. When quality team adopts Design Thinking processes, the successful products gets developed by referring to the past lessons learnt, test documentation helps in tracing the same. Documentation holds: feedback, collaboration and ideation. The documentation can be made available to the entire team working on the product that allows them to refer it over a long run.

PROTOTYPE PHASE

Prototyping is tied in with hypothetical thoughts and investigating their certifiable effect before the actual execution. Very often, structure groups touch base at thoughts without enough research or approval and facilitate them to conclusive execution before there is any sureness about their reasonability or conceivable impact on the objective gathering, thus, prototyping provides the physical representations of the solutions. A prototype is a chance to have another, coordinated discussion with a client. To bomb rapidly and economically. Submitting as a couple of assets as conceivable to every thought method less time and cash contributed in advance. It also helps in testing the potential outcomes. Remaining low-res enables us to seek after a wide range of thoughts without focusing on a heading too soon on. To deal with building a prototype, recognize a variable that additionally helps to separate a huge issue into littler, testable pieces.

Prototypes fulfills the following purposes:

- **Investigate and Experiment:** Prototypes are used to explore issues, ideas, and opportunities at intervals a particular space of focus and take a look at out the impact of progressive changes.
- **Learn and Understand:** The dynamics of the system, product or software can be understood better, by knowing whether different parts of the system are working fine or not.
- **Engage, Test and Experience**: Prototype can be used to have interaction with stakeholders, in ways in which reveal deeper insight and a lot of valuable experiences that helps to move forward.
- **Inspire and Motivate:** Use models to sell new thoughts, propel purchase in from inner or outside partners, or rouse markets towards radical better approaches for speculation, which in turn gets better marketing for the product or system to be launched.

Thus, building prototypes enhances potential solutions, by collecting user's feedback to determine the best possible solution for the problem undertaken. But, before putting it out into the market, full-scale testing has to be performed. The production can only be accomplished if the end users are satisfied. Entire process has to be repeated while incorporating gathered feedback to reframe the problems, if the customer is not satisfied.

MOTIVATION FOR DESIGN THINKING IN SOFTWARE TESTING PHASE

Testing makes the team realize the correctness about the chosen solution for the framed problem. When leading testing, it is better to get into the real-time environment where the client will eventually utilize the model. This is the clients' regular making where they are mostly feel relaxed and it's as near genuine as could reasonably be expected. In this setting their criticism will probably be open and unconstrained. In the event that it is beyond the realm of imagination to expect to perform direct testing in this sort of environments, urge the clients to pretend, showing how they would utilize the actual model from the developed prototype, all things considered. When planning a test scenario, provide options for users to compare. To attain the same, one must create a number of distinct prototypes. Therefore, it makes things easier as users has an option to say what they like or what they don't.

Test mode is when the organization solicits feedback, about the prototypes that are created. The intended focus is to interact with the users either in prototype or testing phase. If it is a physical object, them it can be issued to the users to use it in their normal routine that helps in working with different scenarios in realistic. If prototypes has to be tested, the situation would be entirely different. The best way to handle the situation is like one must build the prototype with an assumption of them being in right in development, but has to test it as if one was wrong in the development of prototypes, this makes solution refinement much better.

Testing advises the following emphases regarding models. Once in a while this implies returning to the planning phase. To get familiar with your client. Testing is another chance to construct sympathy through perception and commitment, it regularly yields unforeseen experiences. Some of the time testing uncovers that not exclusively did one not get the arrangement right, yet in addition that one neglected to outline the issue effectively. One more effective way to test in Design Thinking process is to handle the prototype to clients. Let users explore the prototype without any prior information on how to handle it and all. Make prototypes and test them with the end goal that feels like an experience that the customer is reacting to, rather than an explanation that the customer is evaluating. Solicitation that customers break down. Conveying various models to the field to test gives customers an explanation behind assessment, and relationships much of the time reveal inert needs.

Test Prototype and Test are modes that one considers couple more than progress between. What and how the prototype has to be tested is the angle that one must have thought about before building a prototype. Inspecting these two modes related raises the layers of testing a prototype. In spite of the fact that prototyping and testing are now and again completely entwined, it is regularly the situation that arranging and executing a fruitful testing situation is an extensive extra advance subsequent to making a prototype.

The fundamental of the good design is to make an iteration between the two very regularly. Emphasize both by going through the procedure on various occasions, and furthermore by repeating inside a stage, for instance by making different prototypes or attempting varieties of a conceptualizing themes with numerous gatherings. The scope narrows as one tries to iterate through multiple cycles without worsening the development.

In Design Thinking, the testing stage is the place the arrangement gets tried by clients in their genuine setting. During testing a definitive client encounters the prototype without express direction. For the plan mastermind it is an opportunity to see how clients respond to an item, and tune in to their criticism on various perspectives. On the off chance that the client is happy with the prototype, at that point the Design Thinking procedure finishes here. In the event that the client isn't yet fulfilled one must begin the entire procedure again thinking about their input.

Figure 4. Design thinking for prototype and test phase

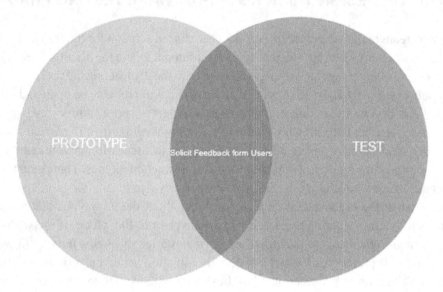

The crucial phase in Design Thinking includes gathering feedback form the stakeholder, that takes place in both prototype and testing phases as shown in Figure 4.

To maximize the benefits in these phases, the following guidelines can be referred:

WAYS TO DEAL WITH SOLICIT FEEDBACK

The organization team's request for criticism from clients depends entirely on the type of prototype that is manufactured. For example, if your model were a pretending session, the experience of showcasing the jobs would be a significant wellspring of perceptions and input in itself. Then again, paper interfaces and physical prototype may require extra meetings with clients to get them to discuss their reasoning procedure while utilizing the prototype.

In the first place, you can think about testing out a few forms of your model on clients to accumulate criticism. This requests basic input on the grounds that individuals will in general keep down on unmistakably scrutinizing porotypes. When presented to clients with choices, it enables them to look at the different porotypes and reveal to what they preferred and disdained about every rendition, thus it will help the team to get input that is increasingly legit.

To Test the Developed Prototype on the Right People

The usefulness and relevance of the client's feedback is taken for account only when the developed prototype gets tested by the right people. If the prototype is on the early stage, then the rough and simple feedback can be known by the team-mates. Otherwise, if 90% of the requirements are built into prototype to attain final product, the best way to get helpful feedback is to test the prototype on multiple users. To test the prototype, considering outrageous over regular users benefit it.

Testing your models on outrageous clients will frequently enables to reveal a few issues and significant issues that influence standard clients, on the grounds that the extraordinary clients will in general be increasingly vocal about their affection or aversion of doing things identified with the prototype. If the product that gets manufactured is international, then the developed prototype must be tested across several regions and countries. Therefore, when people with different customs and culture from the other countries tries to explore the product, there is a possibility of identifying more defects due to random exploration of the prototype.

Towards the last phases of the product development, it is likewise to put the prototype for testing by considering not only clients but also stakeholders. Inward partners in organization, makers, retailers and merchants will each have their very own criteria for structure, making or dispatching an item or administration, and can affect the accomplishment of team's thought. Social occasion criticism from these partners will hence keep team from accepting a terrible stun when it is understood that the team won't most likely execute the item or administration that has been creating as plausibly as team had accepted.

Ask the Right Questions

Every prototype that is about to get tested should cover all the central enquiries for which the clients reply is necessary. Therefore, one must know what they are testing for.

The prototype that is assembled to accumulate the input should equip testing session towards coaxing out how usable the prototype is to the client. In this manner, in a post-testing meeting session with client, it is possible to concentrate on discovering the positive and negative input identifying with convenience. The receptive outlook has to be maintained while testing the porotypes despite of concentrating on the center inquiries, while uncovering key focuses on the issues that is unintended for the group.

One Must Be Neutral While Presenting Ideas

For the given problem, one must uplift both the positive and negative aspects of the solution while presenting it to the users. Furthermore, abstain from attempting to sell team's thought. One must keep in mind that prototyping and testing is tied in with discovering approaches to improve ideas, and excessively selling team's thought can be inconvenient to that objective.

At the point when clients voice negative criticism about prototype, avoid attempting to shield it. Rather, test them further to discover what precisely isn't right with our proposed arrangement, so it always give a way to return and improve one's thoughts. Abstain from ending up excessively connected to one's thought, and consistently be prepared to disassemble, change, or even forsake it when the need emerges.

Adapt While Testing

To adopt flexible mindset is necessary while testing the prototype, when several components vary from the main/core functionalities of the prototype the team must realize to remove them to focus on the key element. The other point is to re-plan the testing session that are planned in prior if there is any confusion about it working well with users' feedback. So, there is always a way for improvising it.

Let the User Contribute Ideas

While testing is carried out, it is advisable to accept the ideas from the users on how the product can be improved according to them, for instance. This would encourage them to give the beneficial critiques in turn in improving the solution for the problem defined.

One can likewise turn a few inquiries that clients pose during the tests around, and ask the clients what they think. Regardless of whether you don't receive their thoughts, their input would almost certainly give you bits of knowledge about the key zones of worry that your clients have while utilizing the product.

MOTIVATION FOR DESIGN THINKING IN OPERATION AND MAINTENANCE PHASE

The maintenance phase is the final stage in software development life cycle. It occurs when the developed product is deployed in the real-time environment of the users and is in full operation. Maintenance phase works in accordance with the customers, if the customers wants to remove or add some features in order to upgrade the product, repairing and fixing the bug that arise during the business and may more. Software always needs an upgradation or integration with the new systems. It happens so to fix the existing defects or errors or new ones of the software such that the customers' business can never incur loss. Thus, monitoring the performance of the software is a great challenge.

Objectives of Maintenance Phase

After product development, it regularly requires maintenance. By and large, product stays operational for an all-inclusive timeframe after starting execution and requires ordinary upkeep to guarantee that the product works consistently in all the time. During the support period of the product life cycle, programming developers consistently issue programming patches to address changes in the requirements of an association, to address issues identifying with bugs in the product or to determine potential security issues. All through the support stage, designers address issues that are found to anticipate any obstruction to the normal execution of the product or to add expanded usefulness to the product.

Monitoring Performance in Maintenance Phase

The designers who worked on the software are the one who maintains that software to address several issues that gets into picture after the product deployment at customers place. When the defects are found, it is the job of software developers to address these issues and forward the modified part of the called patch to the system operators. System operators have to install these patches that are released after addressing the issue.

Most financially accessible software products are consistently refreshed utilizing downloads accessible through the online help webpage from the development team. System operators will download refreshes as they are discharged and introduce these to guarantee proceeded with execution of the product as per the first structure parameters. As software development moves toward becoming cost-restrictive to keep up and nears the finish of the product life cycle, developers start the way toward growing new components of the software to supplant the current ones. In most of the cases, the new programs that developers work on will actually overlap, before the commercial availability of the current software version.

Application of Design Thinking to Operation and Maintenance Phase

At present, product's success depends on the user experience and user-centric business is gaining a lot of attention and markets. As design thinking is the user-centric process to develop the software, each step taken ahead in operation and maintenance should be beneficial to the users. Towards this process; the following procedures can be followed:

- Identify the organization responsible for maintainability
- Criteria must be established to select the team members to operate in the maintenance phase
- Orient these team members to maintain the software in a better way
- Make them to maintain the document of the procedures this be followed during this phase
- Resources can be made available for maintainability process

Once the team members are selected, several sessions can be held to orient them towards maintainability. The sessions may include formal training sessions, internal and external networking, progress reviews, and access to company and industry experts. Each projects in the organization needs various resources and it should be made available anytime needed. To create a sense of responsibility and ownership, along with the team members the end-users can also be involved in this particular phase. Lessen support cost percent of substitution resource esteem; plan for ideal upkeep conditions ought to diminish yearly upkeep cost. Thus, reducing the maintenance cost a bit to help the users. Reduce the mean time repair, whenever there is a rise in defect in the software, the team must be ready to fix it in stipulated amount of time frame thereby, gaining the end users trust and avoiding the business loss.

Condition monitoring or the predictive maintenance helps in predicting the failures and identifying the corrective measures for the same that would save both time and money. Proactive maintenance steps can be taken by considering the information gained by predictive techniques to identify the problem and to solve the problem from the root causes. Maintenance strategy can be planned by following the below steps:

1. According to present situation, assessing the business goals
2. Relating these business goals to core functionalities of the project undertaken
3. Identify the resources needed and prioritize them
4. Identify maintainability capabilities by defining the key roles and responsibilities
5. Apply relevant maintenance design

The cost, schedule and safety plays the utmost vital role in the maintenance phase, In Design Thinking process, and one must consider to improve all those by inculcating best strategies for maintenance. It can be done by reducing the time taken to fix or repair the bug or equipment and also by minimizing the life cycle cost. Lessen support cost percent of substitution resource esteem; plan for ideal upkeep conditions ought to diminish yearly upkeep cost. Thus, reducing the maintenance cost a bit to help the users. Reduce the mean time repair, whenever there is a rise in defect in the software, the team must be ready to fix it in stipulated amount of time frame thereby, gaining the end users trust and avoiding the business loss.

Design Thinking Strategies for Maintenance Phase

- Regular meetings towards discussion on the procedures to be followed during maintenance process, any critical issues regarding the project can be addressed in these small meetings
- Designing the strategy to maintain a certain project, especially the maintenance cost that will be compatible with the end users with the available resources
- Selecting cost and time effective techniques to fix the defect during the maintenance phase
- Document the tasks done and the feedback in this view during entire process such that the same can be users to monitor and evaluate the future projects easily. Hence, data and informs collected during this phase can be used as a feedback to construct and maintain the future projects too
- The Design Thinking is user centric and therefore, on completion of the final project the software product gets deployed in the real-time environment. Thus, the organization should have a maintenance document that includes user manuals, operational manuals and warranties.
- The process may also allow the end user to get trained on project completion, about the usage of the software developed, thus, involving even them in the software maintenance

DESIGN THINKING TOOL KIT FOR DIFFERENT PHASES OF SOFTWARE DEVELOPMENT LIFE CYCLE

The ten tools mentioned in the Table 1 can be used across all the phases of software development life cycle (Liedtka et al. 2010).

CONCLUSION

The Design Thinking is the purely user centric and therefore, it can be applied to all the phases of software engineering. It gives good opportunity for the various teams across the software organization to communicate with the end users. Application of the design thinking strategy helps to elicit requirements, fix bugs, do better architectural design or any modifications to the existing software in a better way. The main motto is end user satisfaction.

Table 1. Tools for design thinking

SL.NO	DESIGN THINKING TOOL	DESCRIPTION	APPLICABLE PHASES
1.	Visualization	As the name suggests, it's visual thinking and deals with images. It encourages out of the box thinking and to visually represent the aspects of the system to the stakeholders which couldn't be expressed otherwise. As the saying goes, 'Action speaks loud than words' so do the pictures help in better understanding. Suppose the client makes a statement during stake holder's meeting such as "We need a new platform for growth", an IT engineer might visualize servers whereas a marketing executive might see advertising campaigns. In order to avoid this confusion, if we can visualize the same idea on a board, all can have the same understanding.	Requirement Analysis phase Design phase
2.	Experience mapping	Journey mapping is an ethnographic technique which is based on studying the service history of the way the clients have interacted with the company. This technique also pays careful attention to the emotions of the clients. This design thinking technique is used to identify those requirements that the customers often fail to convey. It is done by framing a hypothesis about a certain group of customer's journey, and then conducting interviews with the clients and recording the outcomes. Finally it does a comparison of the outcome with the actual to see the deviation in data (if any) and for what variables.	Requirement Analysis Testing Phase
3.	Value Chain Analysis	Examination of interaction of the company with its partner companies for production, marketing and distribution of new offerings. Perform analysis of the value chain to create awareness on their capabilities and shortcomings. This is like performing journey mapping but on the customer side. It works backwards from the end user side by creating value and then to add on the key supplier's bargaining power.	Requirement Analysis Operations and Maintenance
4.	Mind Mapping	Mind Mapping is a technique that is used to link several different ideas to a central idea. It is used in generation, visualization and classification of ideas to identify patterns. This encourages people to be a good team member. It involves creation of poster to capture data trends, invite a group of people to give a tour of this visual data and form new ideas and then clustering into new themes.	Requirement Analysis
5.	Rapid Concept Development	It involves generation of hypothesis regarding new business opportunities. This involves two stages, in the first stage we take the ideas generated from all of the above techniques and use this to generate new ideas. In the next stage, these ideas are boiled down to a fewer number of concepts. In the last stage, we elaborate business design of the previous stage. We need to create new ideas out of the above phase and show it to customer as soon as possible to gain confidence.	Requirement Analysis Development Phase
6.	Assumption Testing	It involves identifying assumptions considered for a hypothesis and using research data to check if they will turn out to be true. They are tested for later using experiments. First we identify the information needed and then figure out how to get. Classify the data into the following three categories: what we already have knowledge of, what we do not have knowledge of and cannot possess, what we do not have knowledge of but can learn.	Testing Phase
7.	Rapid Prototyping	The ideas developed as a part of rapid concept development are converted to a demonstrable prototype for the clients. They include storytelling, user scenarios, storyboards which involve stakeholder's involvement to provide valuable feedback. Prototyping here focuses on minimizing the cost of investment in the return of investment. The cost of a two dimensional prototype can be very low. The key is to experiment with different prototypes and receive feedback from others, not from those who created it.	Design Phase Development Phase
8.	Customer Co-Creation	This involves having a customer involved during the process of novel idea generation. This approach has the lowest amount of risk involved in terms of rejection. The fear of receiving negative comments from the clients or customers stops us from showing an unfinished product to them, the sooner we gather the courage to face the reality, better solutions arises. Purposely leaving out on one or two features in the prototype is done to draw the customer attention at this stage.	Development Phase
9.	Learning Launches	This technique is evaluating the current situation of the market for the product release. The potential customers are those who make promises telling they will just buy the software, what we are interested in those who are willing to pay be hard cash.	Requirements Analysis Operations Phase
10.	Storytelling	Following a story is much easier for anyone and it remains on our minds for a longer period similar to that of visualization. They give access to the human emotions and enhance user experience. They add flavors to the context and sell both the solution and the associated problem. It is advised to identify the audience first and then create a storyboard by paying careful attention to the logical flow. The climax must be able to provide the solution to the problem.	Requirements Analysis

REFERENCES

Carell, A., Lauenroth, K., & Platz, D. (2018). Using design thinking for requirements engineering in the context of digitalization and digital transformation: a motivation and an experience report. In *The Essence of Software Engineering* (pp. 107–120). Cham, Switzerland: Springer. doi:10.1007/978-3-319-73897-0_7

Corral, L., & Fronza, I. (2018, September). Design Thinking and Agile Practices for Software Engineering: An Opportunity for Innovation. *Proceedings of the 19th Annual SIG Conference on Information Technology Education* (pp. 26-31). International World Wide Web Conferences Steering Committee. 10.1145/3241815.3241864

Hehn, J., & Uebernickel, F. (2018, August). The Use of Design Thinking for Requirements Engineering: An Ongoing Case Study in the Field of Innovative Software-Intensive Systems. *Proceedings 2018 IEEE 26th International Requirements Engineering Conference (RE)* (pp. 400-405). IEEE.

Johansson-Sköldberg, U., Woodilla, J., & Çetinkaya, M. (2013). Design Thinking: Past, Present, and Possible Futures. *Creativity and Innovation Management, 22*(2), 121–146. doi:10.1111/caim.12023

Liedtka, J. M., & Ogilvie, T. (2010, December). Ten Tools for Design Thinking. Technical Note BP-0550, 27 pages.

Newman, P., Ferrario, M. A., Simm, W., Forshaw, S., Friday, A., & Whittle, J. (2015, May). The role of design thinking and physical prototyping in social software engineering. *Proceedings 2015 IEEE/ACM 37th IEEE International Conference on Software Engineering* (Vol. 2, pp. 487-496). IEEE. 10.1109/ICSE.2015.181

Plattner, H., Meinel, C., & Leifer, L. (2013). *Design Thinking*. Berlin, Germany: Springer Berlin.

Plattner, H., Meinel, C., & Leifer, L. (n.d.). Design thinking research.

Sun, Z., & Liu, J. (2008, October). A design thinking process model for capturing and formalizing design intents. *Proceedings 2008 International Symposium on Computational Intelligence and Design* (Vol. 2, pp. 330-333). IEEE. 10.1109/ISCID.2008.192

Valentim, N. M. C., Silva, W., & Conte, T. (2017, May). The students' perspectives on applying design thinking for the design of mobile applications. *Proceedings of the 39th International Conference on Software Engineering: Software Engineering and Education Track* (pp. 77-86). IEEE Press. 10.1109/ICSE-SEET.2017.10

This research was previously published in the Handbook of Research on Engineering Innovations and Technology Management in Organizations; pages 395-416, copyright year 2020 by Engineering Science Reference (an imprint of IGI Global).

Chapter 36
Adapting a Requirements Engineering Process by Key Factors Estimation

Graciela Dora Susana Hadad

iD https://orcid.org/0000-0003-4909-9702

Universidad Nacional del Oeste, Argentina & Universidad de Belgrano, Argentina

Jorge Horacio Doorn

Universidad Nacional de La Matanza, Argentina & Universidad Nacional de Tres de Febrero, Argentina

Viviana Alejandra Ledesma

Universidad Nacional de La Matanza, Argentina

ABSTRACT

Literature mainly focuses the adaptation of any requirements engineering process on the possible variations of elicitation techniques, mainly due to information sources characteristics. However, these particularities, usually called situational factors, are seldom considered in other activities of the requirements process. Most situational factors, when considered in software projects, have a high influence on the requirements process. Therefore, the different situations that may attempt against or may favor a successful requirements process should be identified at the beginning of the project. Additionally, some of such factors may evolve along software development life cycle; this should motivate a reengineering of the requirements process at some strategic milestones. In this chapter, a process for constructing and dynamically adapting a requirements process is proposed, focusing on the evolving factors. The process follows rules based on different combinations of situational factors at specific control points and manages a repository of process blocks to perform the tailoring.

DOI: 10.4018/978-1-6684-3702-5.ch036

INTRODUCTION

The monolithic application of any process, disregarding the context conditions, may lead to unnecessary lack of effectiveness. By the contrary, the adaptation of any process to a particular situation is considered a good practice in many fields. Literature shows that this practice is quite common in Software Engineering processes, such as the methodologies Rational Method Composer (Haumer, 2005) and OPEN Process Framework (Firesmith &Henderson-Sellers, 2002). However, Requirements Engineering (RE) approaches are seldom tailored to context or project situations (Potts, 1995; Leite, Hadad, Doorn, & Kaplan, 2000; Leffingwell & Widrig, 2003; Seyff et al., 2009). Nevertheless, sometimes the elicitation activity, as part of an RE process, is performed taking into account some environmental characteristics, usually called situational factors, such as number of information sources, users geographical distribution, users time availability, users experience, among others (Maiden & Rugg, 1996; Hickey & Davis, 2003; Coulin, 2007; Carrizo, Dieste, & Juristo, 2008). Recently, some proposals have appeared to design an RE process for a specific project by selecting existent RE techniques (Lauesen, 2002; Lobo & Arthur, 2005; Alexander & Beus-Dukic, 2009).

There are activities of most of the requirements processes that are invariant regardless of situational factors, while others should be modified, removed or replaced. Not only activities may be adapted, models created in the process may be also suited for the situation (Galster, Weyns, Tofan, Michalik & Avgeriou, 2014). This means that these processes may be assembled like a flexible puzzle using interchangeable pieces depending on the situational factors identified.

Situational Method Engineering (SME) is advocated to build methods tailored to specific situations for the development of systems (Kumar & Welke, 1992). Following its principles, the adaptation of any software development process is based on indicators describing the situation (Khan, bin Mahrin & bt Chuprat, 2014). Part of the task is to compose such indicators based on observable factors, like degree of business processes reengineering, context complexity, developer expertise in the application domain, and project size, among others. Ideally, these situational factors should be considered before beginning the software process. However, there are factors not accurately known when initiating a software project, while other factors may change during the project. Hence, a dynamic view of the adaptation of a software development process achieves a better performance of the process itself. Considering that defining requirements is the starting point of a software development, it should be necessary to pay more attention to factors influencing the RE process.

A frequent question of practitioners is related with the need of performing all the process steps to develop the software requirements. *Is it possible to shorten the road or to follow a different one?* Under some circumstances, there is an opportunity to reduce the RE process by deleting or simplifying activities; and sometimes different paths may be followed by choosing other techniques or even extending some activities. Project managers should make decisions depending mainly on the reality he or she is facing.

Therefore, the rational and some practice on the tailoring of an RE process according to a particular set of situational factors is presented in this chapter. Recommendations about the estimation of these factors are exposed as an enhanced solution. Additionally, some lessons learned, and future works are reported.

BACKGROUND

To follow a process guiding the development of an engineering project or system is valuable enough since it means that performing a predictable set of activities using techniques helps to get the outcome within a controllable quality.

Hence, the way the work is performed does not depend on individual criteria, allowing repeatability of costs, times and quality, and promoting the accumulation of knowledge about the process. The first activity of a process to develop a product consists in defining, as precisely as desirable, the expected outcome. When the product is a software system, this initial activity is an RE process, whose outcome is a consistent set of requirements. The RE process is particularly different from other activities of the software development process since it is the one that most interacts with people and their environment, while other activities are mainly carried out within the development team (Carrizo, 2009). Besides, project decisions impose constraints, tools and methods to carry out those activities. Therefore, if the requirements process takes into account the particularities surrounding the application context and the project itself, then it will probably result both in a better set of requirments and in a more efficient process.

Furthermore, a requirements process needs appropriate and continuous communication to gain as much customers and users compromise as possible. A better communication is achieved when all stakeholders use the same language. In RE, a proven way to accomplish this is by using the vocabulary of the application context (Leite, Doorn, Kaplan, Hadad, & Ridao, 2004). Communication occurs when stakeholders orally interact, also when reports, documents and models are exhibited to customers. In this sense, natural language (NL) models, such as glossaries, use cases and scenarios, stimulate stakeholders' communication (Leite et al., 2004), and they are the most frequently used in RE (Kaindl, 2000; Leffingwell & Widrig, 2003; Seyff et al., 2009; Jacobson, Spence, & Bittner, 2011; Antonelli, Rossi, Leite, & Oliveros, 2012).

Software development processes put into practice in real projects are often forced to be adjusted due to contingent circumstances, sometimes in a poorly controlled fashion while the projects are ongoing. Hence, the situations within their application context and projects should be observed as the processes go forward for better tailoring to such evolution. Possible adjustments to the processes can be known in advance based on certain characteristics, though they may change dynamically, i.e., settings are pre-planned but only implemented when an aspect of the situation changes (Rolland, 2008). In this regard, the process may be defined as a set of blocks, having process blocks common to all situations and variant process blocks according to situational factors. Thus, the process is made up by assembling blocks for the particular situation (Henderson-Sellers & Ralyté, 2010). Method Engineering has emerged to tackle this case, promoting the design, construction and adaptation of methods, techniques and tools in order to develop information systems (Brinkkemper, 1996). This discipline considers not only the creation of process blocks but also product blocks, and even blocks that assemble both process and product (Rolland, 2008; Henderson-Sellers & Ralyté, 2010; Ralyté, 2013). Rolland (2008) not only has pointed out that the software development should begin with a definition phase of the method to be used, but also she proposes that the process must be re-adjusted throughout its life cycle, an aspect not treated by Method Engineering. SME, as a sub-area of Method Engineering, focuses on building methods for software development, tailored to specific situations (Kumar & Welke, 1992). Thus, SME studies the factors affecting the software project and the application context (Bucher, Klesse, Kurpjuweit, & Winter, 2007). Its principles have been applied in RE to define requirements processes that are adaptable to particular circumstances by using existent modular components (Firesmith, 2004; Jafarinezhad & Ramsin, 2012; Bakhat, Sarwar, Motla, & Akhtar, 2015). These works can be grouped as follows:

Group A: Works oriented to define an RE process using frameworks. A knowledge base on RE activities and techniques is made available, serving as a guide to obtain an RE process according to the project' needs (Olsson, Doerr, Koenig & Ehresmann, 2005; Zowghi, Firesmith, & Henderson-Sellers, 2005; Jiang & Eberlein, 2008).

Group B: Approaches to select elicitation techniques that best suit to the situational context. These works only focus on the elicitation activity in the RE process (Hickey & Davis, 2004; Carrizo, Dieste, & Juristo, 2008; Al-Zawahreh & Almakadmeh, 2015).

Group C: Models that allow the RE process to be adapted when it is applied to a specific class of project. These are proposals of situational adaptation for projects of a certain nature or scope, such as global software development or agile methods (Bakhat, Sarwar, Motla, & Akhta, 2015; Abdullah & Khan, 2015; Kabaale & Mayoka Kituyi, 2015; Khan, bin Mahrin, & Mali, 2016).

Group D: Guides that facilitate the creation of an RE process adapted to the context. These works provide mechanisms for the creation of an RE process adjusted to the situational characteristics of the environment, within projects of any nature (Lobo & Arthur, 2005; Alexander & Beus-Dukic, 2009; Coulin, Zowghi, & Sahraoui, 2006; Jafarinezhad, & Ramsin, 2012), in contrast to works of Group C.

These works use notions of SME in different degrees of adherence to its principles, and they propose some factors to be evaluated in order to define the situation. Particularly, approaches in Groups A and D use process components to conform the new RE process. However, only proposals in Group D combine the concepts of SME with some principles of process variability.

The work presented by Hickey & Davis (2004), within Group B, poses a partially dynamic approach, an aspect that in general terms is not taken into account in other proposals. The authors emphasize that knowledge about the problem domain and the project domain is acquired as the RE process progresses, and thus, more appropriate elicitation techniques can be selected in each iteration. In addition, they mention that the situational characteristics of the problem context are usually static, while those related to the project may change, although they do not present evidence on the matter. In this sense, reminding what Rolland (2008) points out, contingent factors change during project life cycle, leading to a dynamic adaptation of the process.

Most of the studies related to the SME do not address two essential aspects: the incorrect adaptation of the process, and the probability of evolution or incorrect estimation of the factors that guide the adaptation. The first issue can occur under three variants: i) the inappropriate omission of doing an activity that could be necessary, ii) the incorrect replacement of an activity by another, or iii) the unnecessary insertion of an activity. It is clear that the process adaptation is strongly dependent on the factors estimation, so a study of the evolution and estimation of situational factors can reveal issues not so easily visible, which can lead to an unsuccessful adaptation.

The work presented in this chapter is part of Group D. It aims to establish clear mechanisms to adapt an RE process according to particular characteristics of the application context and the project context, and to context evolution, considering that evolution may come not only from a real change of the situation but also from a better understanding of that situation.

Some of the adaptation factors are related to development time constraints. Naturally, they lead to faster ways of developing software; these are steps toward agile methods (Pinheiro, 2002). A quality factor may depend on a time factor, or the other way around. However, a balance equation for both factors may be frequently achieved (Kohler & Paech, 2002; Pinheiro, 2002). This trade-off is more likely to be better faced by an RE process with the necessary tailoring (Kohler & Paech, 2002). Extremely, when time factor is a major concern, agile methods could be the best way. Though, agile practices are frequently assumed as opposite to RE practices (Cockburn, 2002; Beck, 2004), Kovitz (2002) remarks that both, a phased development and an agile one, do RE but in different styles, since requirements are always present. This vision is also shared by (Sillitti & Succi, 2005; Kohler & Paech, 2002). In this sense, an agile approach dealing with requirements may be also seen as a sort of dynamic adaptation of an RE process. As Cockburn (2002) said, making the decision on the right level of agility is the best way to succeed on a project. RE practices do not deny agility, considering that this property must be combined with quality and attending volatility without constant software fix (Pinheiro, 2002).

AN ADAPTABLE REQUIREMENTS ENGINEERING PROCESS

Tailoring a Requirements Base Process

RE process based on NL models strongly contributes to stakeholders' commitment to the project. As a standard or base process, it involves the following stages:

- **Identifying the general software goal and scope**.
- **Understanding the vocabulary used in the application context**, supported by the Language Extended Lexicon model (Hadad, Doorn, & Kaplan, 2009).
- **Understanding the application context**, supported by a set of current scenarios that represent the situations observed in the application context (Leite et al., 2000).
- **Refining the general software goal**, by decomposing it into sub-goals.
- **Defining the software context,** by producing a set of future scenarios that represent situations envisioned in a future application context where the software system will operate (Leite et al., 2004).
- **Defining the vocabulary used in software descriptions**, by producing a Language Extended Lexicon of the System (LEL-S) created from the previous one, adding terms used in the descriptions of future scenarios.
- **Making explicit the requirements,** by producing consistent requirement specs, after extracting requirements from future scenarios. Eventually, a Software Requirements Specification (SRS) document may be produced.

This RE process has been initially developed, tested and used in a monolithic fashion, as depicted in Figure 1(a), ignoring all special circumstances. Actually, this implies a somehow poorly defined standard context. It should be noticed that the base process in Figure 1(a) is decomposed in sub-processes, where most of them are composed of another level of processes, as shown in Figure 1(b). Recycles in the two diagrams of Figure 1 were removed to emphasize the variation points, which are introduced here only for the proposed adaptation solution. These recycles imply correcting or updating models because of a better understanding of the problem and of the evolution of the application context.

Figure 1. Requirements Engineering Base Process, expanding one main sub-process

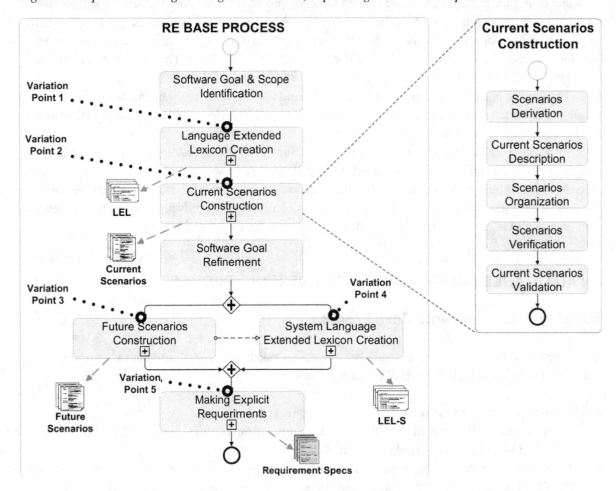

Though Figure 1(a) shows a monolithic process as part of a waterfall model, the strategy can be adapted to be used within different software process models, being this a project factor by itself (see Table 1). For instance, when following an iterative or incremental process model, all sub-processes (except the first one) are done in iterations along with a requirements change management activity throughout the software development life cycle. In case of developing an incremental RE process, the increments may involve the enhancement of previous functionalities and properties, or the addition of new ones; this is treated by a specific factor, which may take different values in each cycle. Regarding agile practices, additionally to time constraints, another leading factor is volatility (Cockburn, 2002), which may be well coped with a change management activity. However, it may not be the best manner when volatility is a core characteristic of the context. Therefore, an agile method might be a better proposal to satisfy customers.

This RE base process may be adapted at the variation points shown in Figure 1(a), depending on a combination of situational factors. Project managers should do the adaptation to improve the RE process and, thereby, the requirements product. Situational factors impacting on RE (see Table 1) have been selected based on experience in RE practice and literature proposals (Maiden & Rugg, 1996; Hickey & Davis, 2003; Carrizo et al., 2008; Ebling, Audy, & Prikladnicki, 2009; Jafarinezhad & Ramsin, 2012; Mighetti & Hadad, 2016). These factors can be characterized by the following attributes:

- **Value:** Admissible values depend on each factor
- **Confidence on the value:** Sure, Reasonably Sure or Doubtful
- **Origin:** Application Context or Project
- **Evolution type:** Invariant or Contingent
- **Variation points:** Where the factor impacts on

Table 1. Situational Factors impacting on RE process. Range Very High to Very Low includes five possible values

Context Factors	Acceptable Values	Type of Evolution
Context Complexity	Very High to Very Low	Invariant
Target Customer	Taylor-made, Market-driven	Invariant
Novelty of the Context	Yes, No	Invariant
Business Process Reengineering	Very High to Very Low	Contingent
Context Volatility	Very High to Very Low	Invariant
Volatility of Users Needs	Very High to Very Low	Invariant
Inconsistencies in the Context	Very High to Very Low	Invariant
Conflict among Users Interests	Very High to Very Low	Contingent
Users Rotation	Very High to Very Low	Invariant
Users Location	Co-located, Distributed	Invariant
Project Factors	**Acceptable Values**	**Type of Evolution**
Familiarity with the Domain	Very High to Very Low	Invariant
Project Size	Very High to Very Low	Contingent
Developers Rotation	Very High to Very Low	Invariant
Software Reliability	Very High to Very Low	Invariant
Reuse of Existing Requirements Artifacts	LEL, Current Scenarios, Future Scenarios, LEL-S, Requirements, No	Invariant
Demand to Create Requirements Artifacts for Reuse	LEL, Current Scenarios, LEL-S, Requirements, No	Contingent
Demand of Requirements Pre-Traceability	Total, Partial, No	Invariant
Demand of Requirements Post-Traceability	Yes, No	Invariant
Granularity of Requirements Traceability	Individual, Group	Invariant
Demand to Produce an SRS	Yes, No	Invariant
Project Time and Resources Constraints	Very High to Very Low	Contingent
Software Process Model	Waterfall, Incremental, Iterative, Formal Transformation, Other	Invariant
Type of Software Increment	New Functionality, Enhanced Functionality	Contingent
Experience in RE Process	Very High to Very Low	Invariant
Cultural and Language Barriers	Very High to Very Low	Invariant
Time Differences among Stakeholders	Very High to Very Low	Invariant

In order to adapt the RE process, project managers (or method engineers) assign values to factors, qualifying them with their degree of confidence on such values. It usually happens that at the very beginning some factors may be not precisely known, and right values are known after gaining a better understanding of the situation. Factors are classified according to their origin into those related to the specific application context, and those related to the specific software project. From an evolution dimension, factors are classified into: *Invariant*, being those that do not change during the RE process; and *Contingent*, being those that may naturally evolve due to changes in the application context and/or in the project context.

Interaction among factors should be taking into account when tailoring the RE process. *Neutral interaction* implies that two factors are fully independent, having no influence between them. *Overriding interaction* indicates that a factor is discarded when another factor takes a specific value. *Limiting interaction* points out that a factor may reduce the range of acceptable values of another factor. *Incompatible interaction* implies that the values of two or more factors cannot be accepted simultaneously at the same project; thereby, the value of at least one factor has to be changed through stakeholders' negotiation to solve the inconsistency. Examples of these interactions are:

- **Overriding interaction:** The factor Business Process Reengineering is not taken into account if the factor Novelty of the Context takes the value *Yes*.
- **Limiting interaction:** The factor Software Process Model cannot take the value *Waterfall* if factor Context Volatility is *Very High*.
- **Incompatible interaction:** The factor Software Reliability is *Very High* while the factor Project Time and Resources Constraints is *Very Low*.

Each sub-process is defined by a sequence of process blocks, some of which include product models. At each variation point, a base process block may: i) stay as it is; ii) be deleted; iii) be replaced by another process block; or iv) be replaced by a process block with a partial internal variation based on parameters. Figure 2, exploiting sub-process of Figure 1(b), shows how the instance of a process should be constructed according to specific situational factors, using a repository containing all possible atomic blocks. This Figure exemplifies one process block (*Deriving Current Scenarios*) that may be replaced by one of three different atomic processes and, by the way, all process blocks are parameterized.

There are common elements among the various parts of the RE process. For example, Figure 2 shows three process blocks *Scenarios Derivation*, *Scenarios Organization* and *Scenarios Verification* which are shared with another main sub-process *Future Scenarios Construction*. There are four types of atomic process blocks. An *own block* is that not shared by any other main sub-process and is independent of situational factors. A *shared block* is common to different sub-processes of the RE process and may depend on factors. A *variant block* belongs to a specific sub-process and depends on situational factors. A *null block* is an auxiliary block used when an entire sub-process or an atomic process must be deleted or skipped from the basic RE process. Table 2 shows operations that may be applied to each type of process block.

Some process blocks include product models, which contain minor variations of the NL models produced by the RE process. For example, if the lexicon model is not created, then the scenario model does not include hyperlinks to lexicon symbols.

Figure 2. Defining the Current Scenarios Construction Sub-Process

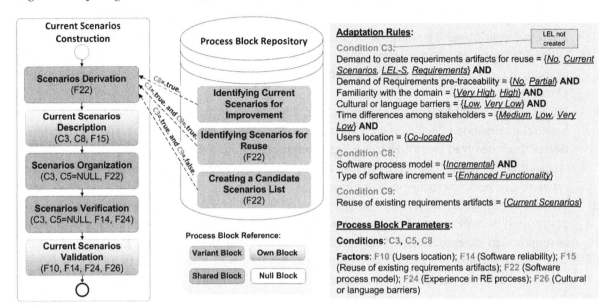

Table 2. Valid Operations on Basic Process Blocks

BLOCK TYPE	OPERATION			
	Stay	Delete	Replace	Parameterize
Own	✓	✓		✓
Shared	✓	✓		✓
Variant		✓	✓	

Meta-Process for a Dynamic Adaptation of a Requirements Process

The adaptation of the RE base process involves a mechanism of operations on process blocks at every variation point, using a specific combination of situational factors, following SME principles. The variation points are milestones used to review the RE process and to indicate possible re-designs of remaining RE activities. The way of constructing the RE process for a specific situation includes the following activities (see Figure 3):

1. **Factors Set-up:** The situational factors are evaluated, assigning a degree of confidence to each value, taking into account the interaction among factors. A simple form is used to collect the factors value. This form eases its filling with valid values by means of rules for factors interaction.
2. **Factors Analysis:** The factors setting is analyzed considering mainly interactions and factors with low confidence. Project managers should take a position on every factor with low confidence: optimistic, conservative or balanced position. Under an optimistic position, factors are assigned an extreme value of its valid range depending on the meaning of the factor, while under a conservative position factors take the opposite extreme value. A balanced position involves choosing intermedi-

ate values. This re-allocation of values is done to allow assembling the process, since the original values are preserved. When incompatible interactions are observed, a negotiation must take place.

3. **Factors Negotiation:** The purpose of this activity is to reach an agreement among stakeholders by modifying the causes that bring out the incompatibility. Then a re-assignment of values to one or more of the involved factors is done. After negotiation, a partial analysis of these factores takes place.

4. **RE Process Assembly:** The RE process is assembled departing from the base process, considering a subset of situational factors at each variation point. A set of rules based on a specific combination of those involved factors defines which operation is applied over each base process block (see an example at Figure 2, right part). Thus, this assembly activity consists in maintaining, deleting, replacing, or parameterizing process blocks.

5. **Factors Re-Evaluation:** At every variation point, those factors involved in remaining variation points must be re-evaluated. Low-confidence factors must be watched, since its level of confidence is supposed to increase due to a better perception of the situation. Contingent factors must be also watched to establish if a change in the situation has occurred. After this activity, a new factors analysis is needed in order to ensure the absence of inconsistencies among dependent factors.

Figure 3. Process for Dynamically Tailoring an RE Process, based on situational factors

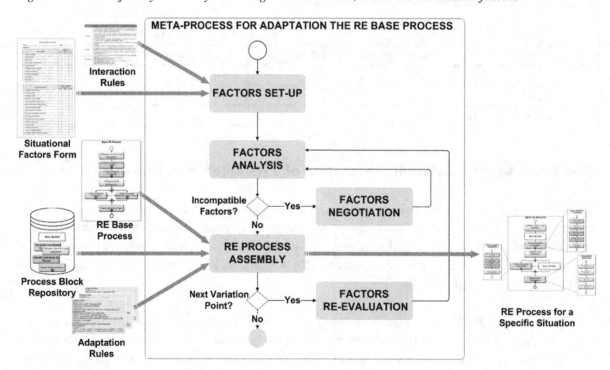

Issues on Situational Factors Evaluation

The evolution of 21 situational factors has been studied during the developing of the RE Process in 35 industry projects. This study has allowed corroborating the evolution of the situations and, additionally, to identify factors to which more attention must be paid for a suitable dynamic adaptation of the requirements process.

This study had confirmed some underlined initial hypothesis, such as:

- The confidence increased along the Requirements Engineering process: the initial percentage of doubtful factors was 12.8 and near to the ending, this figure was 4.7.
- The confidence on the context factors is higher than the confidence on the project factors: the initial percentages of doubtful factors were 7.2 and 17.0 respectively, while near o the ending they were 3.0 and 5.9.
- High level of variation along the project occurred in some presumed contingent factors. Most relevant variations were on factors: Business Process Reengineering with 54% of changes and Project Size with a variation of 46%.

However, some unexpected observations also occurred:

- There are still doubts on the value of some factors when the RE process was almost finishing, with a notorious 12% of Demand of Requirements Post-Traceability, 10% on Volatility of Users Needs and 9% on Project Size.
- The overall percentage of factors with relevant change was of 33.2, which is higher than expected; 86,5% of them were obtained with high degree of confidence. These does not discard estimation errors.
- High level of variation along the project occurred in some presumed invariant factors. Most relevant were Software Reliability with 53% of changes with an 87% of no doubtful estimation, and Demand of Requirments Pre-Traceability with 44% of changes in a context of 20% of doubts in the estimation.

SOLUTIONS AND RECOMMENDATIONS

Since selecting the appropriate RE process for a specific situation is crucial, project managers should define as precisely as possible the situational factors in order to construct a suitable RE process. However, they should be aware of the potential evolution of the situation and, thereby, review factors and adjust the RE process at pre-defined milestones.

Evolution of the situation is a key matter that must not be underestimated. Factors may naturally change due to context evolution, or some may require an update due to unprecise prior estimations. Therefore, the quality of estimating situational factors is critical for a satisfactory RE process adaptation.

The analysis of the results of the factors evaluation study lead to recognize that a good quality estimation may be not so easy to do at early stages

Factors estimation requires new evaluations while performing the RE process adaptation. This activity must be mainly focus on those most unpredictable factors (contingent factors), and on those whose values are more difficult to perceive. Furthermore, when reevaluation takes place, it should to be taken into consideration that changes in some factors may impact changes over others, and these changes should not be incompatible with the part of the RE process done before.

The factors evolution study has revealed that uncertain or incorrect factors estimations are mainly due to lack of or poor guides for developing the RE activities and, somehow, due to a poor factors definition.

FUTURE RESEARCH DIRECTIONS

Feasible variants of the process were identified due to the experience achieved after putting into practice the RE base process in many software projects in industry along more than two decades.

Situational factors were exhaustively studied in literature, although this set is likely to be extended. A first extension was made since the previous work published in (Hadad, Doorn & Ledesma, 2018). Factors affecting subsequent phases of the software development process will be studied to determine if they may influence backward on the RE process.

The decomposition of the RE process in base process blocks, along with the set of situational factors, has allowed identifying process commonality and process variability, and hence defining the different types of process blocks needed. It is planned to evaluate the convenience of using mixed blocks, or separated process blocks from model blocks. It is also considered that more cases should be done to confirm the different branches of the adaptable RE process.

New studies focusing on the weakness already detected on factors estimation will be carried out.

CONCLUSION

The proposal presented in this chapter deals with variability in an RE process, driven by a dynamic adaptation based on prevailing situational factors.

Most problems have distinctive features that must be taken into account to carry out a successful requirements process. Project managers should tailor the requirements process by choosing the techniques that are most suitable for specific situations. When guidelines on how to adapt the requirements process are provided, managers are more willingly to do it.

The meta-process for constructing an RE process involves a set of factors that typifies situations considering both the application context and the software project context. This adaptation process establishes when the RE process should be reviewed and re-tailored based on rules and operations at each variation point. Since it is frequently observed the natural and contingent evolution of situations, it is important to have the possibility of redefining the remaining activities of the RE process once the project is in course. Focus should be put on the possibility of an incorrect evaluation of certain factors, being aware of the necessity of re-adaptations to avoid a bias towards an unsuccessful process.

The adaptation of the requirements process for several real cases has contributed to its acceptance in host organizations. It is considered that the dynamic adaptation process could be implemented with minor adjustments in other RE strategies.

REFERENCES

Abdullah, A., & Khan, H. (2015). FreGsd: A Framework for Global Software Requirement Engineering. *JSW*, *10*(10), 1189–1198. doi:10.17706/jsw.10.10.1189-1198

Al-Zawahreh, H., & Almakadmeh, K. (2015). Procedural Model of Requirements Elicitation Techniques. In *Proceedings of the International Conference on Intelligent Information Processing, Security and Advanced Communication* (article 65). ACM. doi:10.1145/2816839.2816902

Alexander, I. F., & Beus-Dukic, L. (2009). *Discovering Requirements: How to Specify Products and Services*. John Wiley & Sons.

Antonelli, L., Rossi, G., Leite, J. C. S. P., & Oliveros, A. (2012). Deriving requirements specifications from the application domain language captured by Language Extended Lexicon. In *Proceedings of XV Workshop on Requirements Engineering*. Buenos Aires, Argentina: Universidad Nacional de La Matanza.

Bakhat, K. A., Sarwar, A. A., Motla, Y. H. B., & Akhtar, M. C. (2015). A Situational Requirement Engineering Model for an Agile Process. *Bahria University Journal of Information & Communication Technology*, 8(1), 21–26.

Beck, K. (2004). *Extreme Programming Explained: Embrace Change*. Addison-Wesley Professional.

Brinkkemper, S. (1996). Method Engineering: Engineering of Information Systems Development Methods and Tools. *Information and Software Technology*, 38(4), 275–280. doi:10.1016/0950-5849(95)01059-9

Bucher, T., Klesse, M., Kurpjuweit, S., & Winter, R. (2007). Situational Method Engineering. In Situational method engineering: fundamentals and experiences (pp. 33-48). Springer US. doi:10.1007/978-0-387-73947-2_5

Carrizo, D. (2009). *Marco para la selección de técnicas para educción de requisitos* (Doctoral Thesis). Universidad Politécnica de Madrid, Madrid, Spain.

Carrizo, D., Dieste, O., & Juristo, N. (2008). Study of elicitation techniques adequacy. In *Proceedings XI Workshop on Requirements Engineering* (pp. 104-114). Barcelona, Spain: Universitat Politecnica de Cataluya.

Cockburn, A. (2002). *Agile Software Development*. Addison-Wesley.

Coulin, C., Zowghi, D., & Sahraoui, A. (2006). A Situational Method Engineering Approach to Requirements Elicitation Workshops in the Software Development Process. *Software Process Improvement and Practice*, 11(5), 451–464. doi:10.1002pip.288

Coulin, C. R. (2007). *A Situational Approach and Intelligent Tool for Collaborative Requirements Elicitation* (Doctoral Thesis). University of Technology, Sydney, Australia.

Ebling, T., Audy, J. L. N., & Prikladnicki, R. (2009). Towards a Requirements Reuse Method Using Product Line in Distributed Environments. In *Proceedings of 12th Workshop on Requirements Engineering* (pp. 91-102). Valparaíso, Chile: Universidad Técnica Federico Santa María.

Firesmith, D. (2004). Creating a project-specific requirements engineering process. *Journal of Object Technology*, 3(5), 31–44. doi:10.5381/jot.2004.3.5.c4

Firesmith, D. G., & Henderson, B. (2002). *The OPEN Process Framework: An Introduction*. Addison-Wesley.

Galster, M., Weyns, D., Tofan, D., Michalik, B., & Avgeriou, P. (2014). Variability in Software Systems - A Systematic Literature Review. *IEEE Transactions on Software Engineering*, *40*(3), 282–306. doi:10.1109/TSE.2013.56

Hadad, G. D. S., Doorn, J. H., & Kaplan, G. N. (2009). Creating Software System Context Glossaries. In M. Khosrow-Pour (Ed.), *Encyclopedia of Information Science and Technology* (2nd ed., pp. 789–794). IGI Global. doi:10.4018/978-1-60566-026-4.ch128

Hadad, G. D. S., Doorn, J. H., & Ledesma, V. A. (2018). Dynamic Situational Adaptation of a Requirements Engineering Process. In M. Khosrow-Pour (Ed.), *Encyclopedia of Information Science and Technology* (4th ed., pp. 7422–7434). IGI Global, Information Science Reference. doi:10.4018/978-1-5225-2255-3.ch646

Haumer, P. (2005). *IBM Rational Method Composer: Part 1: Key concepts.* Retrieved June 28, 2019, from https://www.ibm.com/developerworks/rational/library/dec05/haumer/haumer-pdf.pdf

Henderson-Sellers, B., & Ralyté, J. (2010). Situational Method Engineering: State-of-the-Art Review. *J. UCS*, *16*(3), 424–478.

Hickey, A. & Davis, A. (2004). A Unified Model of Requirements Elicitation. *Journal of Management Information Systems*, *20*(4), 65-84. doi:10.1080/07421222.2004.11045786

Hickey, A. M., & Davis, A. M. (2003, September). Elicitation technique selection: how do experts do it? In *Proceedings of 11th IEEE International Requirements Engineering Conference* (pp. 169-178). IEEE. 10.1109/ICRE.2003.1232748

Jacobson, I., Spence, I., & Bittner, K. (2011). USE-CASE 2.0: The Guide to Succeeding with Use Cases. *Ivar Jacobson International.* Retrieved June 28, 2019, from https://www.ivarjacobson.com/sites/default/files/field_iji_file/article/use-case_2_0_jan11.pdf

Jafarinezhad, O., & Ramsin, R. (2012, March). Towards a process factory for developing situational requirements engineering processes. In *Proceedings of the 27th Annual ACM Symposium on Applied Computing* (pp. 1089-1090). ACM. 10.1145/2245276.2231946

Jiang, L., & Eberlein, A. (2008). A Framework for Requirements Engineering Process Development (FRERE). In *Proceedings of 19th Australian Conference on Software Engineering* (pp. 507-516). Perth, Australia. 10.1109/ASWEC.2008.4483240

Kabaale, E., & Mayoka Kituyi, G. (2015). A Theoretical Framework for Requirements Engineering and Process Improvement in Small and Medium Software Companies. *Business Process Management Journal*, *21*(1), 80–99. doi:10.1108/BPMJ-01-2014-0002

Kaindl, H. (2000). A design process based on a model combining scenarios with goals and functions. *IEEE Transactions on Systems, Man, and Cybernetics. Part A, Systems and Humans*, *30*(5), 537–551. doi:10.1109/3468.867861

Khan, H., bin Mahrin, M., & Mali, M. (2016). Situational Requirement Engineering Framework for Global Software Development: Formulation and Design. *Bahria University Journal of Information & Communication Technologies*, *9*(1), 74-84. doi:10.1109/I4CT.2014.6914179

Khan, H.H., bin Mahrin, M.N., & bt Chuprat, S. (2014). Factors for Tailoring Requirements Engineering Process: A Review. *International Journal of Software Engineering and Technology*, *1*(1), 7–18.

Kohler, K., & Paech, B. (2002). Requirement Documents that Win the Race: Not Overweight or Emaciated but Powerful and in Shape. *International Workshop on Time-Constrained Requirements Engineering (TCRE'02)*.

Kovitz, B. L. (2002). Hidden Skills that Support Phased and Agile Requirements Engineering. *International Workshop on Time-Constrained Requirements Engineering (TCRE'02)*.

Kumar, K., & Welke, R. J. (1992). Methodology Engineering: a proposal for situation-specific methodology construction. In W. W. Cotterman & J. A. Senn (Eds.), *Challenges and strategies for research in systems development* (pp. 257–269). John Wiley & Sons.

Lauesen, S. (2002). *Software Requirements: Styles and Techniques*. Addison-Wesley.

Leffingwell, D., & Widrig, D. (2003). *Managing Software Requirements: a unified approach*. Addison-Wesley Professional.

Leite, J. C. S. P., Doorn, J. H., Kaplan, G. N., Hadad, G. D., & Ridao, M. N. (2004). Defining System Context using Scenarios. In J. C. S. P. Leite & J. H. Doorn (Eds.), *Perspectives on Software Requirements* (pp. 169–199). Springer. doi:10.1007/978-1-4615-0465-8_8

Leite, J. C. S. P., Hadad, G. D., Doorn, J. H., & Kaplan, G. N. (2000). A scenario construction process. *Requirements Engineering*, *5*(1), 38–61. doi:10.1007/PL00010342

Lobo, L. O., & Arthur, J. D. (2005, April). An objectives-driven process for selecting methods to support requirements engineering activities. In *Proceedings of 29th Annual IEEE/NASA Software Engineering Workshop* (pp. 118-130). IEEE. 10.1109/SEW.2005.18

Maiden, N. A. M., & Rugg, G. (1996). ACRE: Selecting methods for requirements acquisition. *Software Engineering Journal*, *11*(3), 183–192. doi:10.1049ej.1996.0024

Mighetti, J. P., & Hadad, G. D. S. (2016). A Requirements Engineering Process Adapted to Global Software Development. *CLEI Electronic Journal*, *19*(3), paper 7. doi:10.19153/cleiej.19.3.7

Olsson, T., Doerr, J., Koenig, T., & Ehresmann, M. (2005). A Flexible and Pragmatic Requirements Engineering Framework for SME. In *Proceedings of 1st International Workshop on Situational Requirements Engineering Processes (SREP'05)* (pp. 1-12). Paris, France: Academic Press.

Pinheiro, F. (2002). Requirements Honesty. *International Workshop on Time-Constrained Requirements Engineering (TCRE'02)*.

Potts, C. (1995, August). Using schematic scenarios to understand user needs. In *Proceedings of the 1st conference on Designing interactive systems: processes, practices, methods, & techniques* (pp. 247-256). ACM. 10.1145/225434.225462

Ralyté, J. (2013). Situational Method Engineering in Practice: A Case Study in a Small Enterprise. *Proceedings of CAiSE'13 Forum at the 25th International Conference on Advanced Information Systems Engineering*, 17-24.

Rolland, C. (2008). Method engineering: towards methods as services. In *Making Globally Distributed Software Development a Success Story* (pp. 10–11). Springer Berlin Heidelberg. doi:10.1007/978-3-540-79588-9_2

Seyff, N., Maiden, N., Karlsen, K., Lockerbie, J., Grünbacher, P., Graf, F., & Ncube, C. (2009). Exploring how to use scenarios to discover requirements. *Requirements Engineering, 14*(2), 91–111. doi:10.100700766-009-0077-9

Sillitti, A., & Succi, G. (2005). Requirements Engineering for Agile Methods. In A. Aurum & C. Wohlin (Eds.), *Engineering and Managing Software Requirements* (pp. 309–326). Springer-Verlag. doi:10.1007/3-540-28244-0_14

Zowghi, D., Firesmith, D., & Henderson-Sellers, B. (2005). Using the OPEN Process Framework to Produce a Situation-Specific Requirements Engineering Method. In *Proceedings of 1st International Workshop on Situational Requirements Engineering Processes* (pp.59-74). Paris, France: Academic Press.

ADDITIONAL READING

Browne, G. J., & Ramesh, V. (2002). Improving information requirements determination: A cognitive perspective. *Information & Management, 39*(8), 625–645. doi:10.1016/S0378-7206(02)00014-9

Henderson-Sellers, B., Ralyté, J., Ågerfalk, P., & Rossi, M. (2014). *Situational Method Engineering*. Springer-Verlag Berlin Heidelberg., doi:10.1007/978-3-642-41467-1

Kotonya, G., & Sommerville, I. (1998). *Requirements Engineering: Process and Techniques*. John Wiley & Sons.

Lloyd, W., Rosson, M., & Arthur, J. (2002). Effectiveness of elicitation techniques in distributed requirements engineering. In *10th IEEE Joint International Conference on Requirements Engineering* (pp. 311-318). 10.1109/ICRE.2002.1048544

Ralyté, J., Deneckère, R., & Rolland, C. (2003, January). Towards a generic model for situational method engineering. In J. Eder & M. Missikoff (Eds.), *Advanced Information Systems Engineering* (pp. 95–110). Springer-Verlag Berlin Heidelberg., doi:10.1007/3-540-45017-3_9

Schnieders, A., & Puhlmann, F. (2007). Variability modeling and product derivation in e-business process families. In *Technologies for business information systems* (pp. 63–74). Springer Netherlands., doi:10.1007/1-4020-5634-6_6

Virtanen, P., Pekkola, S., & Paivarinta, T. (2013, January). Why SPI Initiative Failed: Contextual Factors and Changing Software Development Environment. In *46th Hawaii International Conference on System Sciences (HICSS)*, (pp. 4606-4615). IEEE. 10.1109/HICSS.2013.609

Vlaanderen, K., Valverde, F., & Pastor, O. (2008). Improvement of a web engineering method applying situational method engineering. In *10th International Conference on Enterprise Information Systems*, (pp.147–154). Barcelona, Spain.

KEY TERMS AND DEFINITIONS

Natural Language Model: A model built using a minimun set of structural components and completed with slightly restricted natural language text.

Process Block: A well-defined unit of process that can be reused as part of any process.

Process Commonality: The common elements of a process that facilitate the definition of a family of processes through reuse.

Process Variability: The variant elements of a process, identified at variation points, which produce deviation from the standard process.

Requirements Engineering Process: A process to construct software requirements by means of methods, techniques and tools during elicitation, modeling, analyzing and evolution of requirements.

Scenario: A representation of an observed or envisioned situation in the application context.

Situational Factor: A characteristic of the project or the application context that may be taken into account when defining an RE process.

Situational Method Engineering: A discipline that promotes the construction of methods for developing systems according to a pre-defined set of situational factors.

Variation Point: Specific location at a process where situational factors are evaluated and changes to the standard process are applied.

This research was previously published in the Encyclopedia of Information Science and Technology, Fifth Edition; pages 1165-1180, copyright year 2021 by Engineering Science Reference (an imprint of IGI Global).

Chapter 37
Fuzzy Ontology for Requirements Determination and Documentation During Software Development

Priti Srinivas Sajja
https://orcid.org/0000-0002-9676-0885
Sardar Patel University, India

Rajendra A. Akerkar
Western Norway Research Institute, Norway

ABSTRACT

Every business has an underlying information system. Quality and creditability of a system depend mainly on provided requirements. Good quality requirements of a system increase the degree of quality of the system. Hence, requirements determinations is of prime importance. Inadequate and misunderstood requirements are major problems in requirements determination. Major stakeholders of the requirements are non-computer professional users, who may provide imprecise, vague, and ambiguous requirements. Further, the system development process may be partly automated and based on platform such as web or Semantic Web. In this case, a proper ontology to represent requirements is needed. The chapter proposes a fuzzy RDF/XML-based ontology to document various requirements. A generic architecture of requirements management system is also provided. To demonstrate the presented approach, a case of student monitoring and learning is presented with sample software requirements specifications and interfaces to collect requirements. The chapter concludes with advantages, applications, and future enhancements.

DOI: 10.4018/978-1-6684-3702-5.ch037

INTRODUCTION

The quality of any software depends on the requirements considered during the development of the software. Requirements generally provide a basic skeleton of the software. The document containing well-formed requirements serve the basis for all phases of the software development activity. The inclusion of good quality requirements in the software requirement specifications leads towards good quality software. After proper analysis phase, once requirements are collected, analyzed and documented; a Software Requirements Specification (SRS) will be prepared. The SRS will be useful at the beginning of the design phase as well as at the end of the design phase to test whether the specified requirements are accommodated in the proposed design or not. Coding, testing and evaluation of the software are also done according to the requirements.

The requirements often contain imprecision and vagueness within them. Further, the importance of each requirement is different and affected by various parameters such as requirement initiator's (who has initiated the requirement) mindset, cost of adding the requirements, loss due to missing of the requirements, the priority of the requirements, etc. Such important but vague criteria can be added as a fuzzy tag to each requirement while documenting the requirements with the help of fuzzy logic. Fuzzy logic, with the virtue of fuzzy membership function, can efficiently handle such vagueness and impression in computer systems. In this scenario, there is a need for a documentation ontology that documents requirements on the Web platform and manages the fuzziness associated with it. In contrast to traditional knowledge-based approaches, e.g. formal specification languages, ontologies seem to be well suited for an evolutionary approach to the specification of requirements and domain knowledge (Wouters, Deridder, & Van Paesschen, 2000). Moreover, ontologies can be used to support requirements management and traceability.

Besides, varying requirements and evolving solutions are important challenges during the software development process. Agile software development is the way to tackle these challenges by adopting methods based on iterative and incremental development. The challenges are similar in the area of ontology engineering. Several situations ontology development is a continuous and collaborative task.

The proposed chapter introduces the current scenario and sets the necessary technical background of ontology, knowledge engineering and fuzzy logic in section 1 and section 2. After that, the chapter documents related work in the area of ontology, fuzzy logic, and use of ontology in software development activities with general observations and limitations. The related work is documented in section 3 of the chapter. The section also summarizes the survey on work done by presenting the observations and characteristics. Section 4 of the chapter proposes a fuzzy ontology for requirements determination. The section introduces various components of requirements with the necessary description along with the graphical representation of the components to highlight the relationship between them. An RDF/XML structure is proposed for the requirements documentation in section 4. A generic architecture to manage the fuzzy ontology repository along with a knowledge base and other components are also illustrated here. Section 5 discusses a case of a student's learning and monitoring system and presents sample software requirements specification with the requirements documented in the RDF/XML format and an interface screen for the acquisition of requirements. Section 5 also presents the fuzzy membership functions used for the experimental system. Section 6 presents advantages, applications and future directions based on the proposed approach.

FUNDAMENTALS

Software Engineering, Knowledge Engineering and Ontology

Ontology deals with the study of various objects, attributes and relationships that exist in the domain of interests. Ontology can be considered as the representation and explicit conceptualization of vocabularies such as entities, sub-entities, relations and properties in a domain of interest. With the help of such a formal definition, it is possible to represent a situation in an efficient manner. Proper designing of ontology in a given domain does not help only in the conceptualization of the domain entities but also provides a framework/structure to store knowledge about the domain. Ontology is a great tool not only for describing the domain but also for managing the domain knowledge. The ontology can be considered as a formal set of vocabularies, symbols and/or a model/schema in a predefined framework with linked data. Both computer science and philosophy domain identify ontology as *"the nature of being"*. In 1995, computer scientist Tom Gruber (1995) used the term ontology and introduced it as a means of specification of conceptualization. A formal definition of ontology as given by Mike Uschold and Michael Gruninger (1996) is quoted below:

Ontology is the term used to refer to the shared understanding of some domain of interest which may be used as a unifying framework to solve the above problems in the above-described manner.

For ontology representation in a machine-interpretable way, different languages exist. Ontology languages are typically declarative languages based on either first-order logic or on description logic. Ontology languages based on first-order logic have high expressive power, but computational properties such as decidability are not always achieved due to the complexity of reasoning. The most popular language based on description logic is OWL DL, which has attractive and well-understood computational properties (Akerkar R., 2009). Another relevant language in Ontological Engineering is the Resource Description Framework (RDF). RDF was originally meant to represent metadata about web resources, but it can also be used to link information stored in any information source with semantics defined in the ontology. The basic construction in RDF is an <Object, Attribute, Value> triplet: an object O has an attribute A with value V. A RDF-triplet corresponds to the relationship that could be written as <O, A, V>.

Importance of Ontology

Well defined vocabularies about entities, their types and their inter-relationships are always helpful in avoiding misunderstanding and communicating the basic objectives of the business. Ontology helps in enhancing communication between key-objects and key people of the organization. This is one of the major reasons to develop ontology. An ontology defines the requirements, situations and goals in a formal manner; which is easy to follow and communicate. Especially, requirements documented in proper ontology support and accelerate the system development process also. Further, the interoperability of the entities and concepts is also supported by ontology. Once an ontology is defined, tested and utilized, it can be reused in a similar situation for future decision making, problem-solving and learning. Various advantages of ontology are illustrated in Table 1.

Table 1. Various advantages of using ontology

Documentation and consistency	Ontology helps in modeling domain knowledge by modeling concepts, entities and their relationships.
Communication	An ontology may be formally defined and shared among the beneficiaries with clear understanding thus leaving a little scope of miscommunication. Meaning of objects, a possible relationship between the objects, and intended applications of the ontology are well defined at the time of ontology development; which leads to filling the gap of communication.
Inter-operability	Well documented ontology enables easy and smooth machine processing and helps in exchanging data without ambiguity.
Reusability and future use	Content once documented in a form of a suitable ontology, can be used for predefined applications and also can be extended or reused for similar applications without much change. It is advisable to go for modular and loosely coupled representation of content, so a component (or a module) can easily detach/attached as per need. Well documented concepts represented in the proper ontology can be reused many times in the future for learning, training, knowledge representation, and machine processing. Another key factor is the flexibility of ontologies. With information integration as a major use case, ontologies are well-suited to combine information from various sources and infer new facts based on this. The flexibility permits to widen existing ontologies very straight forward, thus fostering the reuse of existing work.
Ease of use and testing	An Ontology component undergoes thorough testing while its development phase and an integrated higher level ontology are built using such well-tested modules resulting in a good quality upper-level ontology. Concepts described via such ontology are comparatively error-free and have good quality.

Software Engineering and Knowledge Engineering

The field of software engineering provides guidelines for the development of software. There are many models and approaches suggested for the development of software systems as described in a review paper of Isabel M. del Aquila et al. (2014). In spite of the help offered by the established approaches and models, systems development is partly an art. Higher-level systems dealing with tacit knowledge such as expert systems and other intelligent systems face many problems related to the acquisition of domain knowledge, representing and inferring the knowledge for problem-solving. Many researchers have provided development models for such a knowledge-based system (Akerkar & Sajja, 2009). A new disciplined also has evolved namely knowledge engineering in the field of knowledge engineering which considers the application of various software development techniques as well as knowledge acquisition, knowledge representation and its use in co-operative form (Studer, Benjamins, & Fensela, 1998). The field considers the techniques, approaches, and models for software development for knowledge-based systems development. It can also consider the knowledge-oriented development of a typical (non-knowledge based) system. Figure 1 represents the relationship between the fields.

Software engineering as knowledge-based systems together can be applied in many ways. The broad categories for the same can be given as (i) use of software engineering guidelines to develop knowledge-based/intelligent systems; (ii) use of intelligent systems to invent new guidelines for software engineering; and (iii) a true hybrid manner, where intelligent systems are developed in an intelligent manner. It should be noted that both the fields have some similarities, which can help each other in evolving better for mutual advantages. Further, most of the systems use Web as a platform, where ontology can be considered as an effective tool for content representation. Considering these facts, in this chapter, we proposed the use of ontology as a knowledge representation tool, which will be helpful in systems development, specifically for the determination and management of the requirements related to the software system.

Figure 1. Knowledge engineering

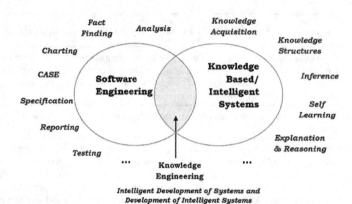

Fuzzy Logic

The term fuzzy logic was proposed by Lotfi Zadeh (1965). Fuzzy logic is a logic-based on fuzzy sets. Fuzzy sets are the special sets without a rigid boundary or sets without boundaries. Belongingness of an entity to a set is generally well defined and crisp in nature. That is, a given item belongs to a set is determined by the definition of the set; and there is no vagueness in it. An element, if belongs to a set, then it completely belongs to the set. Otherwise, it completely does not belong to the set. In any case, the belongingness is crisp and Boolean. That is the nature of a typical crisp set. However, the fuzzy sets talk about the partial or graded membership of an element to a set; hence incorporating multiple values between two extreme crisp values 0 and 1. To determine such partial membership, a specially designed function is utilized; which is known as fuzzy membership function.

An example of crisp and fuzzy membership functions for various fuzzy membership functions such as "Hot Temperature", "Cold Temperature", etc. is illustrated in Figure 2.

Figure 2 illustrates the crisp set of hot temperature which is by definition bivalent. That is, if the temperature is greater than or equal to 25 (in degree centigrade), then the temperature is 'Hot' otherwise not. That means temperature value 24.99-degree centigrade is not 'Hot', and similarly temperature value 13 degree centigrade is also not 'Hot'. The major difficulty with such typical bivalent logic is that, both the temperature values are considered in the same 'not hot' category and treated at par. The first value of temperature, 24.99-degree is nearly 25-degree and we normally considered that as a 'Hot'! Fuzzy logic helps to reduce such rigidness in belongingness of the candidate into a given set by considering set without boundary and suggest partial or graded membership to the set. As shown in the membership function illustrated in Figure 2, the 'Hot' temperature considers temperature values from 25-degree centigrade to 35-degree centigrade and provides multiple degrees of belongingness for various temperature values provided within the range.

Figure 2 also illustrates other fuzzy function for 'Cold', 'Cool', 'Warm', and 'Very Hot' temperature using triangular membership functions. Since all the functions are about the Temperature in a common domain and return values between 0 and 1, they can be presented as an integrated chart. Slight change in the triangular membership function for 'Hot' temperature, 'Slightly Hot' membership function can be generated. Similarly, many other variations of the previously defined membership functions can easily be generated.

Figure 2. Crisp and fuzzy membership functions for temperature

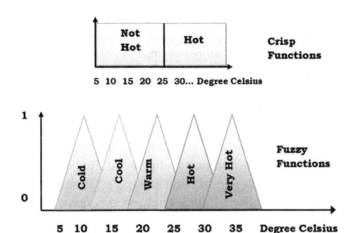

It is obvious that human beings are very comfortable with such linguistic representation of situations such as 'Hot temperature', 'High speed' and 'Tall man'; however, machines do not welcome such linguistic and native words. Machines are more comfortable with values. Because the membership functions are efficiently converting the linguistic parameters into its equivalent values, a human can use such native words in decision making. A linguistic variable can be defined as follows.

A **linguistic variable** *on a fuzzy set defined on universe U is characterized by a four-tuple (X,T,U,G,S) where X is the name of the* **variable***, T is the set of terms of X, U is the universe of discourse, G is a grammar to generate the name of the terms, and S is a semantic rule for assigning meaning to a term.*

Use of the linguistic words in logic opens up the possibility to interact with machines like human beings. This is possible with the help of fuzzy rules. Figure 3 illustrates some simple fuzzy rules associated with the fuzzy sets and membership functions illustrated in Figure 2. Figure 3 also shows a general form of fuzzy rule.

Figure 3. Sample fuzzy rules

```
If {Temperature is 'Hot'} then { Switch on AC_machine on 'High' mode}
If {Temperature is not 'Hot'} then { Switch on AC_machine on 'Fan'
mode}

The general form is
If { X is 'A'} then {Y is 'B'}
```

Such multiple rules are encoded and used as the major content of the knowledge base of the fuzzy logic-based system. Along with such knowledge base and meta-data for the fuzzy membership functions (for the meaning of linguistic variables used in fuzzy rules), the user interface, inference mechanism, reasoning and explanation facilities are also available with the fuzzy logic-based systems.

Exemplifying Fuzziness in Ontologies

Formalisms regarding fuzzy ontologies were introduced to represent semantic knowledge-based on vague concepts and relations (Straccia, 2006). A number of approaches have developed to implement those formalisms into OWL-based ontologies. Some approaches emphasize on building precise OWL ontologies formally defining the common elements of fuzzy set theory to be later populated with instances representing the fuzzy axioms and elements of specific domain ontology. Extending the OWL language to support fuzzy definitions is one strategy for building fuzzy ontologies. While some approaches (Stoilos, Stamou, & Pan, 2010) propose extending the standard building blocks of the OWL language, others use the OWL standard tools to represent such fuzzy information. However, the work on Fuzzy OWL2 (Bobillo & Straccia, 2011) is the most prominent effort in this area. It uses OWL2 annotation properties to encode fuzziness. The use of annotation properties makes fuzzy ontologies compatible with OWL2 management tools (editors, programmatic environments, etc.) and enables crisp OWL-based reasoners to compute inferences over this sort of ontologies discarding the fuzzy elements. Moreover, Fuzzy OWL2 also offers a general Java parser as a base for building specific parsers for translating from Fuzzy OWL2 syntax to the syntax of any fuzzy DL reasoner.

RELATED WORK

Requirements determination in software engineering plays a vital role. Well determined requirements are the skeleton of the systems being developed. The quality of the system directly depends on the quality of the requirements finalized for the system under devolvement. If the right requirements are considered for software, the purpose of the development will be served and users will get the required software. The requirements and other knowledge are acquired from multiple users and various sources in different forms/structures. Most of the software development projects suffer from the problem of communication and getting the right requirements from various categories of users. The following are the major common problems while the determination of requirements.

- Users are not aware of the requirements or users are not ready to provide the requirements- because of a lack of knowledge of advanced technology, lack of domain knowledge, and inability to foresee the change required in the business. Further, users may not know about their own requirements. They are habituated with exiting systems and technologies; so they do not want to change the working of the system.
- Users can not articulate their requirements correctly - users may want to share their requirements and expectations from the system; but cannot explain their needs effectively to the systems analyst.
- Requirements are not understood correctly- the requirements provided by the users may not be properly understood by the systems analyst in its intended manner. He may understand something else and communicate different requirements to the team of programmers. Programmers and other developers can also get the requirements in the wrong manner.

Above these, if the platform used for the development is Web or the semantic web, problems related to representation and documentation of the requirements also arise. Shared conceptualization of ideas (here requirements) can be helpful. This leads to the utilization of suitable ontology to document and communicate requirements. If software requirements are specified using a proper ontology, not only for experts and users but for machines also it would be easy to work with such requirements. Documentation, sharing, using and matching of requirements (with similar requirements of the other software project), etc. operations would become efficient and fruitful with the adaption of ontology in requirements engineering.

A lot of work is done in this area to resolve the above-mentioned issues and to use ontology as a requirements determination tool. Ontology for documentation of requirements is used by Jinxin Lin, et al., (1996) for the engineering domain. The authors have proposed ontology for engineering design with an objective to provide a common and generic ontology that can be used by many experts. A tool is also proposed by Michael Lang and Jim Duggan (2001) to manage requirements in a collaborative manner. In this work, the major importance is given to the communicability of the software requirements specification between various developers. An experiment on creating domain ontology in the area of public administration is proposed by Graciela Brusa, et al., (2008). The paper also discusses the problem of semantic heterogeneity while working in a large domain such as public administration.

A broad architecture of ontology-based engineering of requirements is also proposed by Katja Siegemund, et al., (2011). As per the claim of the authors, it is a meta-model capable of representing requirements into suitable ontology and checking for consistency. S. Murugesh and A. Jaya (2015) represented requirements in a suitable ontology and presents a mechanism to check the consistency of the requirements represented in the OWL DL form. The domain of interest considered for experimenting with the proposed research work is Automatic Teller Machine transactions. Hans-Jörg Happel and Stefan Seedorf (2006) have demonstrated the use of ontology during various phases of software engineering. The authors could prove that the use of ontology may be costly at the initial stage and also requires high efforts in the development of the ontology; however, later it is proved as cost-beneficial with its reusability.

To encode security-related requirements, many authors have used ontology. Their contributions can be seen in a survey paper by Amina Souag, et al., (2012). The paper articulates the work of more than 40 researchers in the field of ontologies for security requirements. The authors could classify the requirements into 8 different groups and discusses sample ontology for the groups. The work also presents a summary of various types of requirements ontologies with their comparative analysis.

The use of ontology for knowledge representation has started way back. Nicola Guarino and Pierdaniele Giaretta (**1995**) studied ontologies and large knowledge base together and explained the application of ontology in the domain of knowledge representation. The incorporation of fuzzy logic in ontology is experimented by Silvia Calegari and Davide Ciucci (**2006**). They have proposed a mechanism to generate a fuzzy value and assigning it to a suitable label used in the ontology by software. The authors have suggested the fuzzy modeling in two ways: linguistic and precise. Chang-Shing Lee, et. al., (**2005**) have used fuzzy ontology for news summarization. Jeff Pan, et al., presented the use of fuzzy logic in SWRL ontology. Verónica Castañeda, et al., (**2010**) have proposed the use of ontology in requirement engineering. However, fuzzy logic is not incorporated in their work. Priti Srinivas Sajja (**2014**) has also used fuzzy logic for XML based ontology to represent knowledge for a web-based expert system. A method for automatic extraction of attributes of concepts, leading to the automatic creation of ontologies was proposed by G. Cui, et. al., (**2009**). On the other hand, P. Alexopoulos, et al., (**2012**) proposed a method to convert a "crisp" ontology in a fuzzy one. Ismail Muhammad (**2016**) proposed a framework to create ontology in a semi-automatic manner and use it for requirements testing. This is a case of post-conversion of the available requirements documents into suitable ontology. Further, test case generation is also possible with the help of ontology as claimed by Tarasov et al. (**2016**). The ontology layer cake model is also proposed to deal with the specified ontology in natural language as mentioned by Abel Browarnik and Oded Maimon **(2015).**

Verification of requirements via pre-specified ontology is experimented by Dong, Q. et al. **(2012),** in which verification of the requirements is done from the acquired and documented requirements in a proper ontology. Work by Dzung, D. V., and Ohnishi, A **(2009)** extracts the key elements form the set of requirements and verifies them for their practical feasibility using natural language processing. The latest work in the ontology domain is done by Rizvi, S et al. **(2018),** which restricts itself to technical documents information to identify users' behavior using the virtue of ontology. However, the approach does not handle vagueness and imprecision. Work of Oriol X., Teniente E. **(2018)** describes a framework of the ontology-based discovery of various data services. This is purely related to data retrieval.

From the above mentioned related work and the discussion on underlying concepts, the observed advantages of using ontology for requirements determination are as follows:

- Documentation of requirements
- Communication of requirements
- Sharing of requirements
- Traceability of requirements
- Automatic use and matching of requirements
- Automatic testing the software product and cross-verification of requirements with developed source code
- Partial management of ambiguous requirements
- Dynamic requirements

These advantages are more strengthened with the use of fuzzy logic. As the field of software development is an art as well as science, it deals with more linguistic, uncertain and ambiguous knowledge related to the process of software development. The situation is manageable in comparison with the earlier scenarios, where software development was more art and less science. Currently, it has become a bit systematic and sophisticated because of available tools and technological advancements. Further, users have also become familiar with various systems/software in a given domain. Still, the major requirement providers are non-computer professionals. Though they may not aware of the automation and popular computing advancements, it is comparatively difficult for them to provide a clear requirement. Inadequate specification, changing requirements and requirements that are not completely defined (and may have chances to be interpreted in different ways) can be handled with the notion of a linguistic fuzzy variable. Section 4 proposes how fuzzy logic can be incorporated with ontology to determine requirements.

FUZZY ONTOLOGY FOR REQUIREMENTS DETERMINATION

Requirements determination typically involves requirements anticipation, requirements investigation through fact-finding techniques and requirements specification in suitable representation structure. Anticipated requirements are common and standard requirements that are ordinary and typical in nature. The anticipated requirements save time and effort, which is normally spent at the investigation phase. For requirements investigation time and effort must be given for the acquisition of requirements through fact-finding methods such as interviews, questionnaires, record reviews and observations. However, this effort will earn some extraordinary requirements. Whether anticipated or investigated, requirements once acquired need to be specified in various structures and ontology for its safekeeping, communication for further development and other future uses. To document requirements in ontology following components may be considered.

Requirements Statement: Description about the requirements in textual format. The text may use one or more fuzzy linguistic variables, which later on can be interpreted with the help of associated fuzzy membership functions.

Requirement Author: Name of the expert or user who has suggested the requirements.

Requirement Subject: Subject or the requirement suggested.

Requirement Section: The suggested requirements may be applicable to a particular section or a block of the organization/business. It may also be possible that more than one section can be benefited by the requirements or the requirement is truly generic in nature.

Requirement Identification Number: A unique identification number needs to be given to each specified requirement for ease of access and documentation. The identification number can be made by combining subfields/parts of the above-mentioned components such as requirement author, subject and sections.

Requirement Class Hierarchy: The suggested requirement may be part of or type of upper level/ generic requirements.

Requirement Type: The suggested requirement may be an anticipated requirement, quality requirement, a security requirement, network requirement, interface requirement, etc. Further, it can be generic, multi-disciplinary or hierarchical in nature.

Requirement Date of Last Used: The last used date of the requirement suggested. This will be helpful in auto-delete and back up procedures. Requirements that are no longer in use can be automatically shifted to the back up to create additional space to accommodate more latest requirements and temporary workspace, if required.

Frequency of Uses: This is a simple counter. Each time the requirement is utilized, the counter is incremented. The requirements with the maximum utilization (as per the value of the counter for each requirement) can be proactively presented to the users/developers for consideration.

Effect of the Requirement Use: This is really a fuzzy field. In many cases, it is difficult to describe the effect of the use of a requirement in values but description. Fuzzy linguistic variables can be used here for demonstrating the effect of using the requirements at an organizational level as well as the individual level.

Besides the above components, the requirements ontology may encompass sub-section names, product/service for which the requirement is meant, identification numbers of other similar requirements and some important comments on the requirements.

The above components are organized and represented in an RDF/XML structure to demonstrate the requirements ontology as shown in Figure 4.

The RDF is known as Resource Description Framework, which is used to represent information on the Web platform. The World Wide Web Consortium (W3C.org) has published a recommended set of syntax and specification for the use of RDF/XML[1]. We have added fuzzy tags within the RDF/XML schema as per the need and nature of the application. With such use of fuzzy RDF/XML, not only ontology-based advantages for knowledge engineering can be achieved, but advantages of the Web and semantic web platform can also be achieved. The graphical representation of the structure of the proposed requirement ontology is shown in Figure 5.

Figure 4. RDF/XML structure to demonstrate the requirements ontology

```
<?xml version="1.0"?>

<!-- RDF Schema Candidate Recommendation (27 March, 2000)
Section 2.3.2.1 -->

<rdf:RDF xml:lang="en"
        xmlns:rdf="http://www.w3.org/1999/02/22-rdf-syntax-ns#"
        xmlns:rdfs="http://www.w3.org/2000/01/rdf-schema#">
<rdf:Descriptionrdf:>
<dc:Title>Requirements Obntology</dc:Title>
<dc:Req_Id> Requirements Identification </dc:Req_Id>
<dc: Req_Author> Requirements  Author </dc:Req_Author>
<dc: Req_Subject> Requirements  Subject </dc:Req_Subject>
<dc: Req_Section> Requirements  Section</dc:Req_Section>
<dc: Req_Class> Requirements Class </dc:Req_Class>
<dc: Req_Type> Requirements  Type</dc:Req_Type>
<dc: Req_Date_Use> Requirements  Date _Used </dc:Req_Date_Use>
<dc: Req_Frequency> Requirements  Frequency </dc:Req_Frequency>
<dc: Req_Effect> Requirements  Effect </dc:Req_Effect>
<dc: Req_Path> Requirements  Path </dc:Req_Path>
<dc: Req_Alt_Path> Requirements  Alternative Path </dc:Req_Alt_Path>
<dc: Req_Trgg> Requirements  Trigger </dc:Req_Trgg>
<dc: Req_Pre> Requirements  Precondition </dc:Req_Pre>
<dc: Req_Exe> Requirements  Exceptions </dc:Req_Exe>
<dc: Req_Other> Requirements  Other  Information Path </dc:Req_Other>
.......
.......
</rdf:Description>
</rdf:RDF>
```

Figure 5. Graphical representation of the requirements ontology

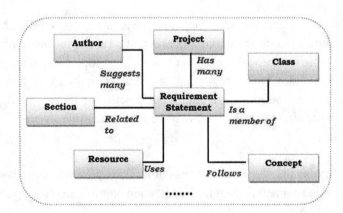

As per the structure shown in Figure 4, many requirements are documented with the required fuzzy variable embedded in it. All the requirements are placed at a common repository for centralized access on a need to multiple users. Along with the requirements repository, there is a need for a fuzzy rule base and fuzzy membership function definitions. Fuzzy membership definitions are used in conjunction with the fuzzy linguistic variables used within requirements. Fuzzy rules are needed to access and manage requirements within the centralized repository. The fuzzy inference mechanism is also required in conjunction with the fuzzy rules. Users such as manager, developer, programmer and testers can use the requirements for the typical development purposes such as documentation of requirements, cross-verification of requirements, reuse of requirements, testing the final product as per the requirements documented, etc. Optionally, an interface facility may be made available besides the major components mentioned here. The general architecture of the system is shown in Figure 6. Such an ontology management system keeps track of users, development procedures and resources associated with the development procedures besides the management of the requirements.

Figure 6. General architecture of the requirements ontology management system

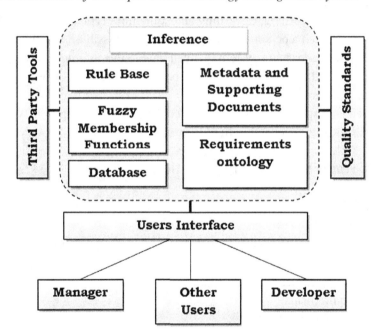

As shown in Figure 6, the two major components of the requirements ontology management are namely: (i) the repository of the requirements and (ii) fuzzy rule base. The requirements repository, as stated earlier, acts as a repository of the requirements in the ontology structure presented in the RDF/XML format proposed in this chapter. Independently, it is mere formal documentation of the requirements of the systems being developed. To efficiently access the requirements, to proactively suggest its possible uses and re-uses, and to automatically keep track of the development activities fuzzy rules can be designed. These fuzzy rules are application-specific and can be developed after considering the nature of the systems being developed and requirements are documented. Similarly, the fuzzy membership functions should be defined after documentation of the requirements is completed and the repository of the requirements is developed in a selected ontology. After that, the fuzzy linguistic variables used in the requirements can be defined formally and stored in fuzzy membership functions definition utility for automatic interpretation of fuzzy variables in requirements ontology as well as fuzzy rules. Necessary metadata, quality standards and other requirements of the organization also should be considered while finalizing requirements for the use. To clearly demonstrate the working of the proposed system, a case of students learning monitoring system is discussed in the next section.

DEVELOPMENT OF STUDENTS LEARNING AND MONITORING SYSTEM

In a classical teaching and learning system, students are manually monitored for their learning and understanding. An expert teacher always has an eye on students' ability to learning and applying the knowledge for day to day problem-solving. Teachers know about positive as well as weak points of the students and can provide personalized attention to the required students. To fast-learners, new challenges are also provided with the necessary guidance and to weak-students support during learning is also extended. In the case of distance learning, e-learning and sometimes typical classroom learning, where a number of students is high; such a personalized approach is not possible. A sample set of requirements is articulated for an effective e-learning system that can handle the automatic selection of content with the help of users' profiles and monitors the learning process of students. The general working of the system is as per the architecture shown in Figure 6.

The sample requirements specification with selected fields for the proposed system is given below along with the necessary fuzzy membership functions.

Sample Software Requirements Specification

Purpose of the system: The system documents various learning material as well as users and presents customized learning material as per the users' need and level.

1. **Users:** Administrator, instructor, learner, evaluator and guest (description of each with aliases can be made available here…)
2. **Glossary:** …..Glossary related to the system….
3. Basic functional requirements:
    a. **Management of course material**:
        i. Add course:
            Title Add Course
            Reference Reference if any
            Trigger Request from administrator to add a course with one or more material files
            Precondition The administrator login and no such course is existing
            Basic Path A new entry is made in database and path for the material is set
            Links between the material and the course are set
            Material is assigned categories such as 'High', 'Average' and 'Low'
            Access rights for edit and view are provided to the course
            Necessary validations are made
            Alternative Paths If the course already exists, then a direct path to the course is given
            Required validations are made
            Post-condition The Reviewer has been added to the database
            Exception Paths The operation may not be granted if the course has already existed
            The operation may be abandoned at any time

        Other Course code, title, prcrcquisites, author name and material types are added within the necessary database/files

  b.   Registrations of users

     i.   Add user: as per the format shown in add course, this requirement can be documented.

     ii. etc.

  c.   Report on masters

     i.   Reports on learners' strength with their details

     ii. Reports on authors who have added material

     iii. Topic wise list of material added between given dates

     iv. etc.

  d.   Reports on transactions

     i.   ….

  e.   Present a course material to a learner (as follows)

       Title Present Material

       Reference Reference if any

       Trigger Request from users to see material on an eligible topic

       Precondition The users have access to the requested material

       Basic Path The requested topic is searched from the database

       Users level is determined through a fuzzy membership functions

       If users level is low then the material with 'low' label is fetched and presented to the user

       Necessary validations are made.

       Alternative Paths Users log may be accessed for the last material category seen

       Post-condition Users feedback is taken on the material

       The material tag may be changed as per the users' feedback by the administrator. A call is raised for the same.

       Exception Paths The message is passed to the authors if no such material for the learner's(user's) category is available.

       Other --

  f.   Learner wise reports

  g. etc.

4. Quality requirements:

    ….

5. Database requirements:

    …..

6. Interface requirements

    …..

7. etc.

The XML/RDF representation of the above requirements is as follows:

```
< ? xml version = "1.0"? >
< !-- RDF Schema …. -->
< rdf:RDF xml:lang = "en"
xmlns:rdf="http://www.w3.org/1999/02/22-rdf-syntax-ns#"
xmlns:rdfs=http://www.w3.org/2000/01/rdf-schema# >
< rdf:Descriptionrdf: >
```

```
< dc:Title > Add Course </dc:Title >
< dc: Req_Id > Add_course_01 </dc: Req_Id >
< dc: Req_Author > Administrator </dc: Req_Autho r>
< dc: Req_Subjec t> Functional Add_Course </dc: Req_Subject >
< dc: Req_Section > Functional _General </dc: Req_Section >
< dc: Req_Class > Class_Master </dc: Req_Class >
< dc: Req_Type > Functional </dc: Req_Type >
< dc: Req_Date_Use > "27/07/2016" </dc: Req_Date_Use >
< dc: Req_Frequency >14 </dc: Req_Frequency >
< dc: Req_Effect > Good </dc: Req_Effec t>
< dc: Req_Path > Requirements Path </dc: Req_Path >
< dc: Req_Alt_Path > "path.txt" </dc: Req_Alt_Path >
< dc: Req_Trgg > "trigger_add_course01.txt" </dc: Req_Trgg >
< dc: Req_Pre > "Pre_trigger_add_course01.txt" </dc: Req_Pre >
< dc: Req_Exe > "Exe_trigger_add_course01.txt" </dc: Req_Exe >
< dc: Req_Other > "Other_ trigger_add_course01.txt" </dc: Req_Othe r>
.....
.....
< /rdf:Description >
< /rdf:RDF >
```

The fuzzy membership function used in the above-mentioned sample requirements is about the learner's level and material level. These functions are defined as follows.

Learners' level can be identified as "High", "Average" and "Low". The learners are presented with general questions from the domain for quick answers. Based on the number of correct answers given to the rapid questions in a given time, the speed correctness ratio is calculated. The initial set of questions fired to the users contains questions that are generic and above average level from the domain selected by the users. If the user cannot answers these questions to some efficiency, lower level questions can be selected otherwise higher-level questions are provided. From such exercise, the level of users can be calculated. See Figure 7.

Figure 7. Fuzzy membership functions for learner's level

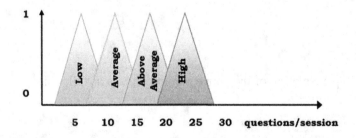

The above requirements with necessary definitions of fuzzy membership functions are well documented in the software requirements specification, which is used as a base to carry out further systems development process. The initial requirements acquisition interface is as shown in Figure 8.

Figure 8. Initial requirements acquisition interface

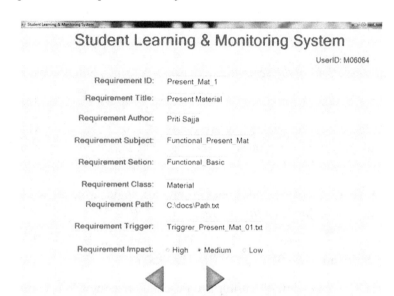

ADVANTAGES, APPLICATIONS AND FUTURE DIRECTIONS

The main stakeholders of the requirements determination about a system are the users of the system. The users, who have requested for system development and who are directly benefited by the system are generally domain experts and not the developers. Such non-computer professionals are key entities (major stack holders) in providing requirements about the system. Many times the requirements are fuzzy, incomplete and uncertain in nature. To correctly acquire requirements, to correctly specify them, to use them in throughout the development process, etc. needs an effective representation of the requirements. The use of fuzzy logic helps in documenting requirements in more native form as well as easy to understand them by non-computer professionals. This is the way to directly include the users in the determination of the requirements. Advantages related to the fuzzy logic such as covering a large number of requirements into a small, manageable set of requirements and simultaneously handing of the vagueness of the requirements can be achieved with the proposed approach. Further, if the platform of the semantic web is available, such requirements can be stored and accessed on the web platform automatically with the help of the metadata (semantic) associated with them. Once the requirements are in fuzzy ontology format, not only effective and machine-based assess of them is possible, but automatic searching, merging, interpretation and reuse of such requirements are also possible. Further, the documentation of the requirements specification is more native in nature and hence easy to handle.

In future the interface can be enhanced that interacts with the users, developers and other requirements providers and acquires useful requirements automatically. The system can also provide an auto-generated output of the software requirements specification (SRS) in standard formats such as IEEE. Various innovative algorithms can be developed for automatic matching of the requirements and control the software development procedures on the semantic web platform. It may lead to a general-purpose knowledge acquisition tool that acquires knowledge about a project under development and documents finding in the fuzzy ontology. One may propose a model for guiding software engineering using a fuzzy ontology.

REFERENCES

Akerkar, R. (2009). *Foundations of the semantic web*. London: Alpha Science International Ltd.

Akerkar, R. A., & Sajja, P. S. (2009). *Knowledge Based Systems*. Sudbury, MA: Jones & Bartlett Publishers.

Alexopoulos, P., Wallace, M., Kafentzisi, K., & Askounis, D. (2012). IKARUS-Onto: A methodology to develop fuzzy ontologies from crisp ones. *Knowledge and Information Systems*, *32*(3), 667–695. doi:10.100710115-011-0457-6

Aquila, I., Palma, J., & Tunez, J. (2014). Milestones in software engineering and knowledge engineering history: A comparative review. *The Scientific World Journal*, *2014*, 10. PMID:24624046

Berners-Lee, T., Hendler, J., & Lassila, O. (2001). The Semantic Web. *Scientific American*, *284*(5), 29–37. doi:10.1038cientificamerican0501-34 PMID:11234503

Bobillo, F., & Straccia, U. (2011). Fuzzy ontology representation using OWL 2. *International Journal of Approximate Reasoning*, *52*(7), 1073–1094. doi:10.1016/j.ijar.2011.05.003

Browarnik, A., & Maimon, O. (2015). Departing the ontology layer cake. In J. Zizka, & F. Darena (Eds.), Modern computational models of semantic discovery in natural language (pp. 167-203). IGI Global. doi:10.4018/978-1-4666-8690-8.ch007

Brusa, G., Caliusco, L., & Chiotti, O. (2008). Towards ontological engineering: A process for building a domain ontology from scratch in public administration. *Expert Systems: International Journal of Knowledge Engineering and Neural Networks*, *25*(5), 484–503. doi:10.1111/j.1468-0394.2008.00471.x

Calegari, S., & Ciucci, D. (2006). Integrating fuzzy logic in ontologies. *18th International Conference on Enterprise Information Systems: Databases and Information Systems Integration*, Paphos, Cyprus.

Castaneda, V., Ballejos, L., Caliusco, L., & Galli, R. (2010). The use of ontologies in requirements. *Global Journal of Researches in Engineering*, 2-8.

Chang-Shing, L., Zhi-Wei, J., & Lin-Kai, H. (2005). A fuzzy ontology and its application to news summarization. *IEEE Transactions on Systems, Man, and Cybernetics*, *35*(5), 859–880. doi:10.1109/TSMCB.2005.845032 PMID:16240764

Cui, G., Lu, Q., Li, W., & Chen, Y. (2009). Automatic acquisition of attributes for ontology construction. In L. Wenjie, & M.-A. Diego (Eds.), Computer Processing of Oriental Languages. Language Technology for the Knowledge-based Economy (pp. 248-259). Springer. doi:10.1007/978-3-642-00831-3_23

Dong, Q., Wang, Z., Zhu, W., & He, H. (2012). Capability requirements modeling and verification based on fuzzy ontology. *Journal of Systems Engineering and Electronics*, *23*(1), 78–87. doi:10.1109/JSEE.2012.00011

Dzung, D. V. (2009). Ontology-based reasoning in requirements elicitationon. In *Software Engineering and Formal Methods*, *2009 Seventh IEEE International Conference* (pp. 263–272). IEEE.

Gruber, T. (1995). Toward principles for the design of ontologies used for knowledge sharing. *International Journal of Human-Computer Studies*, *43*(5-6), 907–928. doi:10.1006/ijhc.1995.1081

Guarino, N., & Giaretta, P. (1995). Ontologies and knowledge bases: Towards a terminological clarification. In N. Mars (Ed.), Towards Very Large Knowledge Base: Knowledge Building and Knowledge Sharing (pp. 25-32). Amsterdam: IOS Press.

Happel, J., & Seedorf, S. (2006). Applications of ontologies in software engineering. *2nd International Workshop on Semantic Web Enabled Software Engineering*, Athens, USA.

Ismail, M. (2016). Ontology learning from software requirements specification. In *Knowledge engineering and knowledge management* (pp. 251–255). Springer.

Lang, M., & Duggan, J. (2001). A tool to support collaborative software requirements management. *Requirements Engineering*, *6*(3), 161–172. doi:10.1007007660170002

Lin, J., Fox, M., & Bilgic, T. (1996). *A requirement ontology for engineering design.* Toronto: Enterprise Integration Laboratory, University of Toronto.

Murugesh, S., & Jaya, A. (2015). Construction of ontology for software requirements elicitation. *Indian Journal of Science and Technology*, *8*(29). doi:10.17485/ijst/2015/v8i29/86271

Oriol, X. T. E. (2018). An Ontology-Based Framework for Describing Discoverable Data Services. In *Advanced Information Systems Engineering. CAiSE 2018.* Cham: Springer. doi:10.1007/978-3-319-91563-0_14

Pan, J., Stamou, G., Tzouvaras, V., & Horrocks, I. (2005). f-SWRL: A fuzzy extension of SWRL. *Notes in Computer Science*, 829-834.

Rizvi, S. M. (2018). Ontology-based Information Extraction from Technical Documents. In *Proceedings of the 10th International Conference on Agents and Artificial Intelligence (ICAART 2018)* (pp. 493-500). SCITEPRESS – Science and Technology Publications, Lda. 10.5220/0006596604930500

Sajja, P. S. (2014). Knowledge representation using fuzzy XML rules in web based expert system for medical diagnosis. In *Fuzzy Expert Systems for Disease Diagnosis* (pp. 138–167). Hershey, PA: IGI Global.

Siegemund, K., Thomas, E., Zhao, Y., Pan, J., & Assmann, U. (2011). Towards ontology-driven requirements engineering. *10th International Semantic Web Conference*, Bonn, Germany.

Souag, A., Salinesi, C., & Wattiau, I. (2012). Ontologies for security requirements: A literature survey and classification. In *24th International Conference on Advanced Information Systems Engineering*, (pp. 61-69). Gdansk, Poland: Academic Press. 10.1007/978-3-642-31069-0_5

Stoilos, G., Stamou, G., & Pan, J. (2010). Fuzzy extensions of OWL: Logical properties and reduction to fuzzy description logics. *International Journal of Approximate Reasoning, 51*(6), 656–679. doi:10.1016/j.ijar.2010.01.005

Straccia, U. (2006). A fuzzy description logic for the semantic web. *Capturing Intelligence, 1*, 73–90. doi:10.1016/S1574-9576(06)80006-7

Studer, R., Benjamins, V., & Fensela, D. (1998). Knowledge engineering: Principles and methods. *Data & Knowledge Engineering, 25*(1-2), 161–197. doi:10.1016/S0169-023X(97)00056-6

Tarasov, V., Tan, H., Ismail, M., Adlemo, A., & Johansson, M. (2016). Application of inference rules to a software requirements ontology to generate software test cases. In M. Dragoni, M. Poveda-Villalón, & E. Jimenez-Ruiz (Eds.), OWL: Experiences and directions – Reasoner evaluation (pp. 82-94). Springer.

Uschold, M., & Gruninger, M. (1996). Ontologies principles methods and applications. *The Knowledge Engineering Review, 11*(2), 93–136. doi:10.1017/S0269888900007797

Wouters, B., Deridder, D., & Van Paesschen, E. (2000). The use of ontologies as a backbone for use case management. *14th European Conference on Object-Oriented Programming*, Cannes, France.

Zadeh, L. (1965). Fuzzy sets. *Information and Control, 8*(3), 338–353. doi:10.1016/S0019-9958(65)90241-X

ADDITIONAL READING

Sure, Y., Staab, S., & Studer, R. (2003). On-To-Knowledge Methodology. In S. Staab & R. Studer (Eds.), *Handbook on Ontologies* (pp. 117–132). Berlin: Springer-Verlag.

KEY TERMS AND DEFINITIONS

Fuzzy Logic: It is a multi-valued logic based on sets without boundary and offers graded membership of an element to such set. Crisp logic always gives binary values say 0 or 1; however, the fuzzy logic provides many values between 0 and 1.

Fuzzy Membership Functions: Fuzzy membership function determines the graded membership of an element to the base fuzzy set.

Fuzzy Ontology: The ontology which uses fuzzy linguistic variables to demonstrate relationships between various objects and attributes.

Ontology: It is a study of various objects, attributes and their relationships that exist in the domain of interests. Ontology can be considered as the representation and explicit conceptualization of vocabularies such as entities, sub-entities, relations and properties in a domain of interest. With the help of such a formal definition, it is possible to represent a situation in an efficient manner.

Ontology Engineer: Ontology engineer is an expert, who is responsible for identifying, acquiring, conceptualizing and representing ontology. He also keeps track of the above-mentioned ontology cycle.

Ontology Life Cycle: Life cycle for typical phases of ontology development such as setting an objective, collection of knowledge, conceptualization, determination of suitable ontology model, knowledge representation into the ontology, evaluation of the ontology, documentation of ontology and sharing ontology.

Requirement Determination: It is the process of anticipating, investigating and specifying the necessary and important features about the system being developed in a predetermined format.

XML/RDF: The RDF is known as Resource Description Framework; XML is defined as eXtensible Markup Language. These tools are used to represent information on Web/Semantic Web platform. The World Wide Web Consortium (W3C.org) has published a recommended set of syntax and specification for the use of RDF/XML.

ENDNOTE

[1]   https://www.w3.org/TR/REC-rdf-syntax/

This research was previously published in Tools and Techniques for Software Development in Large Organizations; pages 21-44, copyright year 2020 by Engineering Science Reference (an imprint of IGI Global).

Chapter 38

Impact Analysis of Intelligent Agents in Automatic Fault–Prone Components Prediction and Testing:
Impact Analysis of Intelligent Agents in Test Automation

Jeya Mala Dharmalingam
https://orcid.org/0000-0002-2100-8218
Thiagarajar College of Engineering, India

ABSTRACT

Software quality is imperative for industrial strength software. This quality will be often determined by a few components present in the software which decides the entire functionality. If any of these components are not rigorously tested, the quality will be highly affected. Without knowing which of these components are really critical, it will not be possible to perform high level testing. Hence, to predict such fault-prone or critical components from the software prior to testing and prioritizing them during the testing process, an agent-based approach is proposed in this chapter. The framework developed as part of this work will certainly reduce the field failures and thus will improve the software quality. Further, this approach has also utilized important metrics to predict such components and also prioritized the components based on their critical value. Also, the work proposed in this research has also been compared with some of the existing approaches and the results reveal that, this work is a novel one and can both predict and test the components from the software.

DOI: 10.4018/978-1-6684-3702-5.ch038

INTRODUCTION

As per the study of National Institute of Standards and Technology, the cost for an inadequate infrastructure for software testing is estimated to be from $22.2 to $59.5 billion (Tassey, 2002). As exhaustive testing (testing 100%) is not feasible (David C., Jinlin Yang, Sarfraz Khurshid, Wei Le and Kevin Sullivan, 2005; Myers,1979), the industries are forced to stop the testing process at one point of time and deliver the software to the customers. This leads them to compromise the quality of the software due to customers' need for quick delivery of quality software, reduced software development lifecycle, changing markets with global competition and rapid development of new processes and technologies.

The surveys have indicated that, many of the complex systems' failures are due to insufficient testing of software before they are deployed to the customer side (Bernardi, 2011; Schneidewind, 1978). After the analysis, it has been identified that, the highly critical components are not being properly tested or simply ignored without knowing their critical level due to time and cost compromises.

The identification of such critical components from the software prior to testing is still a research area, since the automated testing tools available in the market doesn't address the said problem. Based on our field surveys conducted in several organizations during the past months, it has been identified that, most of the defects reported by the customers after delivery are present in these higher critical components. This gives us the insight on the importance of critical components identification and their verification prior to the delivery of the software. But, the identification of the criticality level of a component involves the evaluation of various metrics and measures associated with them.

Hence, an automated software testing framework that can identify and prioritize the critical components based on the various metrics and measures associated with each of the components and can also provide an optimized critical paths list which can reduce the time and cost needed in the testing process without compromising the testing of these critical components is the need of the hour.

From the literature survey, it has been identified that only a very few works have been conducted in the said research area, and that too have been limited by the type and number of metrics used by them. If the software under test is small and simple then the identification can be done manually. As the real time complex systems have huge functionalities, there is a need for an approach that embeds both intelligence and automation as a tool.

Since software testing is NP-hard (Non-Polynomial hard) (Nagappan, 2006), and as manual testing is costly and error prone, several existing research works on structural testing have employed computationally intelligent techniques, such as artificial intelligence and evolutionary computation methods, to achieve optimization in the testing process (Alok Singh, 2009; Basturk & Karaboga, 2006; Baykasolu A, Lale Özbakır & Pınar Tapkan, 2009; Dorigo M., Maniezzo, V., Colorni, A., 1996, Teodorović & Dell, 2006; Fathian M, Babak Amiri & Ali Maroosi., 2007; Karaboga, 2008, 2009; Pham D.T., Ghanbarzadeh A., Koc E., Otri S., Rahim S., & Zaidi M., 2006; R. Srinivasa Rao, S.V.L. Narasimham, M. Ramalingaraju., 2008; Wong Li-Pei, Chi Yung Puan, Malcolm Yoke Hean Low, Chin Soon Chong., 2008).

As several existing knowledge based approaches are population based approaches with sequential execution behavior, from the literature survey it has been identified that, agents based approach gives promising results when compared to the other solutions. However, this research work applied the multi agents based approach in which each agent is responsible for doing its activities in a parallel manner.

Hence, this research work proposed, an automated critical components identification and verification framework using multi-agents based approach to identify the critical components and to generate and optimize the number of critical paths needed for their verification.

PROBLEM FORMULATION

The proposed research problem has its origin from various industrial surveys taken during the recent years. Even though achieving zero-defect quality software is the ambition, it is not possible in reality (Pressman, 2007). Software testing can be very costly and it typically consumes at least 50% of the total cost involved in software development (Bernardi S, Javier Campos, & José Merseguer., 2011; Li and Lam, 2004). There should be some stopping criterion to be followed to stop testing at one point of time and release the software to the customer side. Generally, the industries have different stopping points based on cost, time, resource utilization or some acceptable level of quality.

Due to customers' need for quick delivery of quality software; reduced software development lifecycle; changing markets with global competition and rapid development of new processes and technologies, lead the industries to skip off some of the components during testing. If these skipped components are highly critical, then their impact on the quality of the software will be huge. Hence, an approach is the need of the hour to prioritize the testing of critical components and perform the testing process in an optimized way without compromising quality.

This insight is the motivation behind this research work to propose a novel framework to identify critical components early in the life cycle and generate the critical paths that will cover all the critical components in minimum number of test executions. This will in turn help to reduce the cost involved in testing and also the huge amount of loss incurred in terms time, resources, human life etc. because of the lack of testing of critical components.

This research work, proposed an multi-agents based framework, motivated by the intelligent behavior of the agents to act, react and work autonomously to automate the critical paths generation and optimization process. In the proposed approach, the SUT is converted into a graph based representation in which each node represents a component in the SUT. Each critical path is represented as a possible solution in the optimization problem and critical value - a heuristic introduced to each component corresponds to the quality or fitness of the associated component to be added to the critical path. The nodes are selected by means of an intelligent search through the Software under Test (SUT) based on the fitness value associated with each node which is calculated using the complexity and dependability metrics associated with each node in the SUT. The intelligent agents modify the search paths with time and the agent's aim is to discover the places of nodes with higher critical value and finally the one with the highest critical value.

The objective function is to maximize the critical value of each path by finding the sum of the critical values associated with each node along a test path based on constraint satisfaction. Now, a few efficient test paths that can cover all the critical components in the system model in less time are generated and stored in the optimal critical path repository.

Since the intelligent agents exhibit autonomy, social ability and interactivity with other agents (Russel & Norvig, 1995), they are well suited for applications that need intelligent decision making process. The performance of the agents in software test optimization was illustrated in a previous work (Mala & Mohan, 2009), for test sequence optimization. Based on the results of the previous work, the proposed approach implemented the agents to perform the critical path optimization activities seamlessly. In the proposed approach, since the local search methods and global search methods are managed by three types of agents, the proposed approach attains near global optimal solution.

The test adequacy criterion applied in this work ensures component coverage. This test adequacy criterion has been applied by researchers as a potential measure to evaluate the coverage during system testing (Horgan, J., London, S., & Lyu, M., 1994). Hence, in the proposed approach component coverage measure is applied as a way to optimize the test paths from the search space.

Further this paper is organized as follows: Section II discusses the related work in the proposed research area; Section III deals with the proposed work in which the proposed algorithm and the Critical Path Optimizer and Section IV gives the experimentation and result analysis.

RELATED WORK

Kaur (2015) has investigated various metrics that that have been used for fault prediction and have classified the existing metrics into three broad categories. Since no type of metric could accurately identify the fault prone modules, an integrated metric has been proposed to predict the fault prone modules.

Jin et.al. (2012), proposed a reduction dimensionality phase, which can be generally implemented in any software fault-prone prediction model. In this study, the authors presented applications of artificial neural network (ANN) and support vector machine in software fault-prone prediction using metrics. A new evaluation function for computing the contribution of each metric is also proposed in order to adapt to the characteristics of software data. The vital characteristic of this approach is the automatic determination of ANN architecture during metrics selection.

Bernardi et al.(2011) applied UML, model driven transformation and formal techniques for assessing the risk of timing failure by evaluating the software design.

Shin et al. (2011) showed that the metrics available from development history are stronger indicators of vulnerabilities than code complexity metrics. In their study they investigated three categories of metrics such as complexity, code churn, and developer activity metrics to identify vulnerable files.

According to Zimmerman et al. (2011), factors such as complexity measures, computed metrics, churns are related to field failures and dependencies. They observed that metrics such as size, churn metrics and code metrics like fan in, fan out, and cyclomatic complexity are related to field failures. Their study showed that depending on a component that has failures does not have an effect on failures of the dependent component.

Mizuno and Hata (2010), have applied two apporaches namely a text feature metrics based approach using naive Bayes classifier and a complexity metrics based approach using logistic regression to identify the fault-prone components from the given software. Their approach is an integrated one in which the text feature based approach's high recall, and complexity metrics based approach's high precision were applied.

Surl and Kumar (2010) designed a simulator to identify critical components. In their study they have used Component Execution Graph (CEG) for developing simulator. They have used only the reusability metric of the component to find the criticality index of each component.

Gegick et.al. (2009) have created a predictive model that identifies the software components that pose the highest security risk in order to prioritize security fortification efforts. The input variables to their model are available early in the software life cycle and included security-related static analysis tool warnings, code churn and size, and faults identified by manual inspections. These metrics have been validated against vulnerabilities reported by testing and those found in the field. But all these are dynamic metrics and can be obtained only after field test.

Andrea et al (2008) focused on the difficulties involved in testing the container classes with nature inspired algorithms. They applied input space reductions and a novel testability transformation to aid the search algorithms.

Xiao (2007) analyzed the evaluation of optimization algorithms when used in goal oriented automated test data generation. They identified that goal-oriented approach is a promising approach to devise automated test data generators to cover the software.

Li and Sun (2007) proposed an algorithm based on reversed binary tree for automated test data generation. They claimed that their algorithm can automatically find out all of the feasible paths in the program from the source node to the base node and can automatically generate test data for each founded feasible path thus covers all the components in the software.

Ramon and Jose (2006) described two approaches which employ Estimation of Distribution Algorithm as a Meta-Heuristic technique for test data generation. The approach first extracts a region in the initial search space that incorporates static information from the SUT. If this method is not enough, then a grid search method is applied.

Wes (2007) empirically evaluated several test case filtering techniques based on coverage and profile distribution based techniques. Also, they compared the performance of random sampling against filtering techniques in exercising various program elements or components. The observations indicated that, distribution based filtering techniques did not perform well when compared to coverage based filtering techniques.

Dennis et al (2006) described an approach for checking the methods of a class against a full specification. It shares with traditional model checking - the idea of exhausting the entire space of executions within some finite bounds.

Zhou and Leung (2006) in their study showed that design metrics are statistically related to fault-proneness of classes across fault severity and the prediction capabilities of the investigated metrics greatly depend on the severity of faults.

Nagappan et al. (2006) built a regression model to predict the likelihood of post-release defects on code metrics. According to their study metrics such as number of classes in a module, inheritance depth, class coupling measures have significant influence on post-release defects.

David et al (2005) have provided a bounded exhaustive testing technique for software quality assurance.

The research works (Basili,1996; Subramanyam & Krishnan, 2003; Zhou & Leung, 2006) have applied CK suite of OO design metrics for the analysis of design complexity. They have applied metrics such as Depth of Inheritance Tree, Response for a class, and Number of children, lines of code etc., to find out design complexity. The design metrics used in all their research works addressed only the static aspect of OO design complexity.

Martina and Antonia (2003) exploited entity subsumption and spanning trees to determine the reduced set of coverage entities or components such that coverage of reduced set implies the coverage of unreduced set.

Beydeda and Gruhn (2003) proposed a binary search based test case generation approach. The primary use of the BINTEST algorithm is in testing the methods of a class or component. In their paper, the proposed binary search algorithm which is used to determine the test cases, requires certain assumptions but allows efficient test case generation.

Katerina Goseva et al (2003) and McGregor (1997) have proposed risk analysis technique for critical component identification. Kemmerer (1985) demonstrated the need for testing formal specifications during design phase. The formal specification language that is used in this paper is a variant of Ina Jo®, which is a nonprocedural assertion language that is an extension of first-order predicate calculus. The language assumes that the system is modeled as a state machine. The key elements of the language are types, constants, variables, definitions, initial conditions, criteria, and transforms.

Kim and Boldyreff (2006) suggested four categories of metrics such as class, message, use case and methods applicable to UML model. They proposed a tool called UML metrics producer which is used to calculate complexity metrics value for each class in a program.

Ebert (2006) evaluated classification techniques such as pareto classification, classification trees, factor-based discriminate analysis, fuzzy classification, neural networks for identifying critical components. Their study showed that the fuzzy classification is the best technique among five techniques for complexity-based criticality prediction.

Genero et al. (2000) classified metrics based on the elements of UML class diagram such as packages, classes, attributes and operations of each class and their relationships such as association, aggregation, generalization and dependencies.

Agrawal (1994) used the notion of dominators and super blocks to derive coverage implications among the basic blocks with the goal of reducing coverage requirements for testing a program.

Schneidewind (1979) represented a matrix form of directed graph to identify structural complexity and error properties. According to them the matrix forms of the directed graph identify program properties which are useful for software program development and testing.

PROPOSED MULTI-AGENTS BASED FRAME WORK

Intelligent Agents: An Introduction

Intelligent Agents are pieces of software that are designed to make computing and other tasks easier by assisting and acting on behalf of the user. The user can interact with the agent through the user interface while the agent can sense and act according to the condition of the external environment. The agent performs its tasks by taking information from the environment in which it is working (Russel & Norvig, 1995).

Agents can be constructed with a wide range of capabilities. In agent-based approach a complex processing function can be broken into several smaller and simpler ones. An autonomous agent is a system situated within and a part of an environment that senses that environment and acts on it, over time, in pursuit of its own agenda and so as to effect, what it senses in the future (Russel & Norvig, 1995).

As in the earlier work on the application of Intelligent Agents in Software Testing (Dhavachelvan & Uma, 2003), agents can be implemented with sophisticated intellectual capabilities such as the ability to reason, learn, or plan. In addition, intelligent software agents can utilize extensive amounts of knowledge about their problem domain.

Among many type of Intelligent Agents, this approach has focused on the design of Task-Specific Software Agents to perform software testing task. Since testing activity consists of a number of uncertainties, the test agent which is used in this research work checks up all the conditions in the SUT in generating optimal test sequences.

In the proposed framework, the functionalities are extended to three agents namely Selector Agent, Exploration Agent and Random Selection Agent to generate the critical paths with priority being given for the coverage of critical components from the number of components in the SUT.

The three agents work independently as per their assigned task and communicate with other agents whenever they have to exchange information. Because of the parallel behavior of these agents, the solution generation becomes faster and makes the approach an efficient one.

Since the basic test adequacy criteria used is coverage based; the quality of the software is improved by not missing any of the critical components as the fitness function to cover the components is based on their critical value.

SOLUTION METHODOLOGY IN THE PROPOSED APPROACH

The proposed frame work shown in Figure 1 has the following modules:

- The SUT is given as input to the critical path optimizer module which consist of two sub modules namely
  - Critical component identification module and,
  - Execution of test cases along Critical test paths module.
- In critical component identification module, the critical components are identified by the modules such as component extraction, criticality calculation and criticality analysis. As a result, the critical component list will be prepared and will be given as input to the critical path identification module.
- In critical test path execution module, the critical test paths are identified and tested using this module.

Figure 1. Critical Path Optimizer Framework

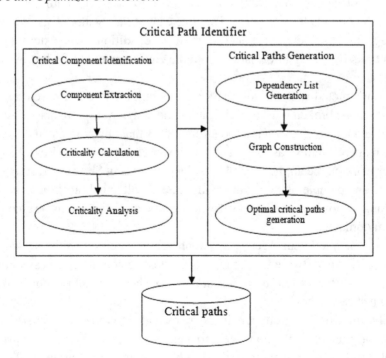

MATHEMATICAL MODEL FOR THE PROPOSED APPROACH

The proposed solution methodology is given by means of a mathematical model with multi-objective functions as given below:

Min.

$$Count\ (Cpath) \tag{1}$$

$$TTime\ (SUT) \tag{2}$$

Where, CPath – Critical paths;
Ttime(SUT) – Testing time required for testing SUT

Max.

$$CCover\ (CComp_i) \tag{3}$$

Where, CComp_i – Critical Component I;CCover (CComp_i) - Component Coverage of Critical Component i.

Sub. to

$$Cover\ (CComp_i) = \begin{cases} false & if\ CComp_i\ is\ uncovered \\ true & otherwise \end{cases} \tag{4}$$

$$Status\ (CComp_i) = \begin{cases} 1 & if\ Critical\_Value = MAX\ and\ Cover\ (CComp_i) = false \\ 0 & if\ Critical\_Value = 0 \\ -1 & if\ Dep\_Metric\_Value = 0 (Individual\ Component) \end{cases} \tag{5}$$

$$Critical\ Value\ (CComp_i) = \sum_k (C_k(CComp_i)) \tag{6}$$

Where, Ck = complexity and dependability metric values associated with node CComp_i

$$CPath_j = \begin{cases} CPath_j + CComp_i & if\ Status(CComp_i) = 1 \\ CPath_j & otherwise \end{cases} \tag{7}$$

$$Continue\text{-}execute\text{-}flag\ (SUT) = \begin{cases} 1 & if\ Cover(x) = false \\ 0 & otherwise \end{cases} \tag{8}$$

The objective function in Equation 1 is to minimize the number of critical paths. The next objective function in Equation 2 is to minimize the total testing time required to complete the testing activity. The objective function in Equation 3 is to maximize the coverage of critical components. Constraint in Equation 4 indicates the continuation of generation of critical paths till no more frontier nodes to explore. Constraint in Equation 5 shows the value of status flag associated with each node that guides the proposed search algorithm about the presence / absence of critical components. Its value is set as 1 if the component is associated with MAX value; it is set as 0 if the component is not the node with highest critical value; it is set as -1 if the component is an independent component or an empty or a dummy component that does not have any associated metrics. Constraint in Equation 6 indicates the C_k metric value associated with *CComp_i*. Constraint in Equation 7 is used to construct the critical path based on the Status flag associated with each node. Constraint in Equation 8 indicates whether the exploration has to be continued or not based on the result of constraint in Equation 4.

PROPOSED ALGORITHM

Phase I: Critical Components Identification and Critical Test Paths Execution using Multi-Agents

- **Step 1:** Read the SUT as input.
- **Step 2:** Convert it into a Component Relationship Graph.
- **Step 3:** Identify the critical components by the following steps from 3.1 to 3.4 using Selector Agent.
  - **Step 3.1:** Extract the components from the SUT.
  - **Step 3.2:** Calculate the criticality value for all the components based on the following dependability and complexity metrics.
    Fan-In: Fan-In is the number of other functions calling a given function in a module.
    Fan-Out: Fan-Out is the number of other functions being called from a given function in a module.
    Number of Children: Number of classes inherited from a given class.
    Inheritance Depth: Inheritance depth is the maximum depth of inheritance for a given class.
    Coupling: This metric signifies coupling to other classes through:
    a. Class member variables;
    b. Function parameters;
    c.   Classes defined locally in class member function bodies;
    d. Immediate base classes; and
    e. Return type.
    Number of Methods: Number of methods in a class including public, private and protected methods
    Number of Classes: This is the count of the number of classes in the component
    Number of Interfaces: This is the count of the number of interfaces in the component
    Number of Parameters: This is the count of the total number of parameters in the component
    Number of Fields: This is the count of the total number of fields in the component
    Number of Static Methods and Fields: This is the count of the total number of static methods and static fields in the component. The two metrics were counted separately
    Cyclomatic Complexity: This metric is used to show the complexity of a given component by counting the number of independent paths in the given component.
  - **Step 3.3:** Analyze the criticality of each component based on the critical value and generate a priority list.
- **Step 4:** Initialize the components list with extracted components with their critical values calculated in Phase I. Set j=0. Cycle = 1;
- **Step 5:** Apply **Selector Agent** to do the following:
  - **Step 5.1:** If this is the initial run/cycle, then search through the CRG using the components list to find the node with the highest critical value. Set *CPath[j] = node (max($\sum_k h(C_k(X_i))$)) for all i=1 to m and k=1 to p.*
  - **Step 5.2:** If the node is selected by the Random Selection Agent, then set *CPath[j] = X_i where X_i is the node selected by the Random Selection Agent.*

- ○ **Step 5.3:** For both the cases, mark the node as covered after executing the test cases for it and place it in the components list and color the node in the graph for visualization.
- ○ **Step 5.4:** Then, explore the frontier nodes from the current node to indicate a test sequence (A test sequence is composed of a sequence of executable components/nodes).
- ○ **Step 5.5:** Communicate the selection information to the Exploration Agent.
- **Step 6:** Apply **Exploration Agent** to perform the following tasks:
  - ○ **Step 6.1:** Evaluate the Critical value of each uncovered frontier node based on the information given by the Selector Agent.
  - ○ **Step 6.2:** If a node with next higher critical value is found, then remember the node by appending this with the previously selected node to indicate a part of the critical path.
  - ○ **Step 6.3:** Update *CPath[j] = CPath[j] + node (max ($\sum_k h(C_k(X_r)$))) where r = 1 to no. of currently explored nodes.* Mark the node as covered after executing the test cases for it.
  - ○ **Step 6.4:** Abandon the remaining nodes in the current exploration and store them in Temporary Node list. The temporary node list indicates the uncovered node information associated with the previous explored node list and is used to ensure the coverage of all nodes and is refreshed during every cycle.
  - ○ **Step 6.5:** Then, explore the frontier nodes from the currently selected node using Steps 5.4 and 5.5.
  - ○ **Step 6.6:** If no node is found with expected level of critical value, store the current test sequence as a critical path and store it in the Critical Path Repository for further exploration in the subsequent stages.
  - ○ **Step 6.7:** Send the nodes inefficiency information to Random Selection Agent.
- **Step 7:** Apply **Random Selection Agent** to perform the following tasks:
  - ○ **Step 4.1:** The Random Selection Agent identifies a new node from the search space with higher critical value among all the uncovered nodes in the search space, on its own.
  - ○ **Step 4.2:** Set j=j+1 to indicate a new exploration.
  - ○ **Step 4.3:** Communicate the new selection to the Selection Agent for further exploration process.
- **Step 5:** Set Cycle=Cycle+1;
- **Step 6:** The steps from 2 to 5 are repeated until all the components are covered at least once or the number of cycles reached the Maximum Number of Cycles (MCN).

EXPERIMENTATION AND EVALUATION

Tested Programs

A range of case studies is taken to find the efficiency of the proposed approach against the approaches based on Random Testing and Sequential search. The tested programs are listed in Table 1 and the experimental setup is done as in the Table 2. The tested problems are classified as industrial and academic.

The industrial problems are taken from various industrial surveys and through the online project libraries, from some software industries and also some of them are given by the industries such as IBM and Microsoft to compete in the National Project Competition such as 'The Great Mind Challenge' contest and 'Student Research Project' respectively. The specifications and technology are given by the industries and the code is sent to them for their evaluation. After the evaluations, the software is observed by the industries. Hence, these problems are also taken for testing the proposed approach.

Table 1. Tested Software

Case Study #	Object Oriented Systems – in Java		
	Case Study	Type	#Classes
1.	Patient Monitoring System	Industrial	22
2.	Banking Management System	Industrial	19
3.	Library Management System	Industrial	20
4.	Shopping Cart	Industrial	12
5.	Hospital Management System	Industrial	28
6.	Network Monitor	Industrial	23
7.	Workflow Management system	Industrial	35
8.	Dealership Management System	Industrial	17
9.	Insurance Management System	Industrial	27
10.	Stock Management System	Industrial	14
11.	Credit Card Validation	Industrial	22
12.	Vendor Management System	Industrial	16
13.	Anti Money Laundering System	Industrial	56
14.	Microfinance Management System	Industrial	12
15.	Online Bus Reservation Management System	Industrial	15

The experimental setup for each of the approach is shown in the table 2.

EXPERIMENTATION: CASE STUDIES

Case Study: Analysis of Banking Management System

The specification document has been delivered by constructing a rigorous analysis of several real time applications related to Banking Management System (BMS). It consists of 19 components.

From the Table 3, it has been identified that 'Admin' component has the highest critical value. The calculation of the criticality values and the critical path generation are done using the tool developed in this research work.

Once, the components criticality value is identified, a parallel selection, exploration and random selection processes are employed using multi-agents. The selection of components based on their critical values and the construction of critical paths based on their order of exploration and selection is shown in Table 4.

Table 2. Experimental Setup – Sequential, Proposed Parallel, ACO and Random Search

Parameter Setup	Proposed Multi-Agent Based Parallel Search	Linear Search	Ant Colony Optimization (ACO)	Random Search
Type of Algorithm	Parallel Search Based	Sequential Search Based	Sequential Search Based	Random Search Based
Fitness Function	Critical value based on Component Coverage	Critical value based on Component Coverage	Pheromone Level/ Critical value of each Component	Component Coverage
No. of Cycles	MCN (Prescribed by the tester) - Maximum Cycle Number	MCN (Prescribed by the tester) - Maximum Cycle Number	No. of Cycles	No. of Iterations
Termination Criteria	Max. no. of cycles / Acceptable Component coverage measure	Max. no. of cycles / Acceptable Component coverage measure	Max. no. of cycles / Acceptable Component coverage measure	Max. no. of Iterations
Pheromone / Non – Pheromone Based	Non-Pheromone Based	Non-Pheromone Based	Pheromone Based	Non-Pheromone Based
Communication About Selection	Status flag	Status flag	Pheromone Trace/ Status Flag	Status flag
Working Nature	Parallel	Sequential	Sequential	Random
Hardware Used for Experimentation	CPU Speed: 3GHZ Processor: Core i3 RAM: 2 GB Temporary Storage: 320GB	CPU Speed: 3GHZ Processor: Core i3 RAM: 2 GB Temporary Storage: 320GB	CPU Speed: 3GHZ Processor: Core i3 RAM: 2 GB Temporary Storage: 320GB	CPU Speed: 3GHZ Processor: Core i3 RAM: 2 GB Temporary Storage:320GB

In Table 4, each 'Cpath' represents a critical path that has higher priority on the execution of critical components. The components selection is done by analyzing the order of exploration from the currently selected component. If none of the explored components are having higher critical value than some other component which is not yet covered, then, that component will be selected by means of random selection by the Random Selection Agent. Hence, the component selection, exploration and random selection are done using the proposed approach within less time because of the parallel execution of the agents.

From the generated critical paths, the optimization is applied by identifying repeated components coverage. This is showed in Table 5 with information on the components that needs to be executed and the components that have been already covered.

From Table 5, the optimized list of critical paths are generated using the proposed framework and the final list of paths required to cover all the components at least once with priority being given for higher critical components is less. The final list of optimal number of critical paths is shown in Table 6.

From Table 7, it has also been inferred that, the critical components are executed with highest priority by creating execution sequences. Each execution sequence is a path that guides the testing process to do continuous execution using the test suit meant for that path. Some paths have single components, indicating that their connected components have been already tested and these components can be individually tested which thus reduce the total time spent if all the components in that path are executed again.

Table 3. Complexity Metrics Calculation using the proposed tool for BMS

Class_ID	Class_Name	fin	Fout	Child	Methods	Inhdep	Coupling	cc	Interfaces	par	Fields	Class	Staticmf	Total
C1	Account	4	0	4	1	0	0	11	0	2	4	0	0	26
C2	**Admin**	**0**	**0**	**0**	**4**	**1**	**0**	**35**	**0**	**16**	**14**	**0**	**0**	**70**
C3	CheckBalance	2	0	0	2	0	2	26	0	5	8	0	0	45
C4	ChequeBook	0	1	0	3	1	1	28	0	6	9	0	0	49
C5	CurrentAcc	1	1	0	1	1	0	5	0	2	5	0	0	16
C6	Customer	0	0	0	3	1	0	19	0	5	5	0	0	33
C7	Deposit	2	2	0	2	1	4	30	0	7	12	0	0	60
C8	FixedAcc	1	1	0	1	1	2	5	0	2	4	0	0	17
C9	FundTransfer	0	2	0	1	1	2	5	0	5	10	0	0	26
C10	Month	1	1	0	1	1	2	1	1	2	2	0	0	11
C11	OnlineServices	2	0	2	1	0	2	11	0	2	4	0	0	24
C12	ProfileUpdation	2	1	0	2	1	3	4	0	7	6	0	0	26
C13	RecurringAcc	1	1	0	1	1	2	5	0	2	4	0	0	17
C14	SavingAcc	1	1	0	1	1	2	5	0	2	4	0	0	17
C15	Statements	1	0	1	1	0	1	13	0	2	4	0	0	23
C16	Transaction	0	1	0	1	0	0	1	0	2	3	0	0	8
C17	User	0	0	0	2	0	0	7	0	4	4	0	0	17
C18	Withdraw	1	0	0	2	1	0	31	0	7	12	0	0	54
C19	Year	1	1	0	0	0	0	0	0	0	0	0	0	2

Table 4. Critical Paths Generation based on Critical Value of the Components

C.No.	Cpath1	Cpath2	Cpath3	Cpath4	Cpath5	Cpath6	Cpath7	Cpath8	Cpath9
C1					(*)	(*)	(*)	(*)	
C2	(*) (*)								
C3		(*)		(*) (*)					
C4			(*) (*)						
C5					(*)	(*)	(*)	(*)	
C6	(*)								
C7		(*) (*)							
C8								(*)	
C9		(*)		(*)					
C10									(*)
C11			(*)						
C12			(*)						
C13							(*)		
C14						(*)			
C15									(*) (*)
C16		(*)		(*)					
C17	(*)								
C18		(*)(*) (*)							
C19									(*)

Table 5. Critical Paths with Coverage Information

S.No.	Critical Paths With Coverage Identification	Components Executed
1.	C02-C17-C06-C02(Covered)	C02,C17,C06
2.	C18-C07-C03-C09-C07(Covered) -C16-C18(Covered)	C18,C07,C03,C09,C16
3.	C04-C12-C11-C04 (Covered)	C04,C12,C11
4.	C03 (Covered) -C09(Covered)-C16(Covered)-C03 (Covered)	For this path all the components are already covered
5.	C01-C15	C01,C15
6.	C01 (Covered) -C14-C05	C14,C05
7.	C01 (Covered) -C13-C05(Covered)	C13
8.	C01(Covered) -C08-C05 (Covered)	C08
9.	C15-C19-C10-C15(Covered)	C15,C19,C10

Table 6. Optimized List of Critical Paths

S.No.	Optimal No.of Critical Paths
1	C2-C17-C06
2	C18-C07-C03-C09-C16
3	C04-C12-11
4	C01-C05
5	C15-C19-C10
6	C13-C08
7	C14 (individual component)

Table 7. Total No. of Test runs taken by different approaches for Sample Case Studies

S.No.	Search Technique	Components Coverage %		Critical Components Coverage %		Number of Test Runs Required		Time Taken for Paths Generation (Nano Sec.)	
		PMS	BMS	PMS	BMS	PMS	BMS	PMS	BMS
1.	Random Search	62%	65%	30%	45%	>350	>350	840528866182	820423835201
2.	Linear Search	92%	94%	85%	82%	300	286	810725386562	634267763328
3.	ACO	100%	100%	100%	100%	125	78	77689005172	36455823855
4.	Proposed Multi-Agents Based Parallel Search	100%	100%	100%	100%	31	19	23388843385	23202043568

Testing of the Critical Components

Unit Testing

In this work, unit testing is done by generating test cases using Genetic Algorithm based approach based on our previous work (Jeya Mala et.al. 2013). To ensure the test effectiveness, branch coverage based test adequacy is used. This has been done by means of the automated testing tool developed as part of this research work. The screenshot is shown in the figure 2.

Integration Testing

The integration testing is done by means of pair-wise testing of components based on their connectivity. The identification of connected components is done by means of fan-in and fan-out measures calculated. The screenshot of the integration testing being done using the developed tool is shown in Figure 3.

Figure 2. Unit testing of each identified component

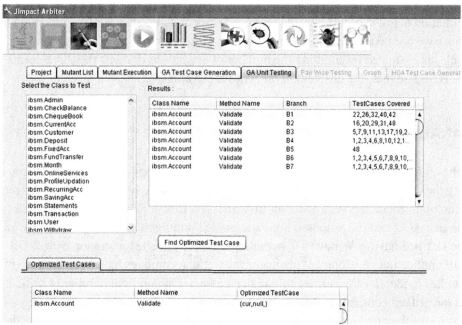

Figure 3. Integration Testing of Components

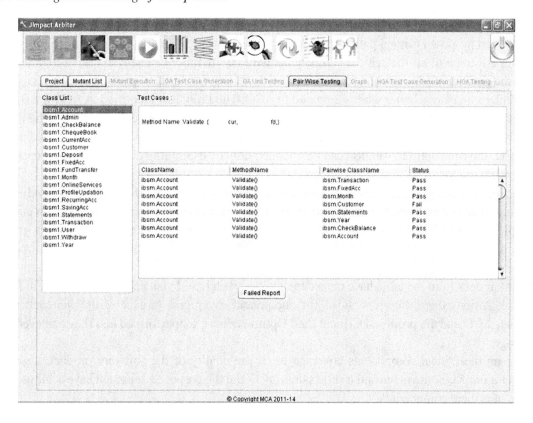

METHOD OF ESTIMATION

To do the estimation of test runs taken by the proposed work and the other existing searching techniques, the algorithms have been coded in Java. The time taken is estimated in nano seconds and the number of execution cycles is estimated by counting the number of executions done by the three agents to achieve optimization. Based on that, the different approaches are evaluated.

RESULT ANALYSIS

To conduct the comparative analysis in covering all the critical components within less amount of time and increasing the coverage of all the components, the existing graph searching approaches ranging from traditional searching techniques such as Random Search and Linear Search to intelligence based searching technique like ACO and the proposed heuristic guided intelligent searching technique are applied.

Under the test bed having Windows 7 operating system, Core I3 processor with 2 GB RAM and NetBeans IDE application development environment all the techniques have been executed for the two given case studies to identify the best technique that can generate optimal number of critical paths that can cover all the critical components within less time.

Table 7 provides the number of test runs required by existing search approaches and the proposed search approach to cover all the critical components. The maximum number of test runs is initialized as 350. For random and linear search techniques the number of test runs exceeds 300, but has not provided the optimal solution. It simply generated the paths without consideration on optimality.

When the results of ACO and multi-agents based approach are analyzed, it has been identified that both ACO and proposed critical path optimizer approach have provided the optimal number of critical paths with coverage of all the critical components with less number of test runs. But still when compared to the number of test runs and total time taken to generate the critical paths, the proposed 'critical path optimizer' performs better when compared to ACO. The Problems Identified in ACO are (i) as the tracking of nodes is based on the pheromone values at each node, the values of them must be updated frequently to keep its current level. This process presents substantial overhead in the optimization process; (ii) In ACO, the final optimal solution can be obtained only by examining all of the solution candidates created by ant exploration.

Since, the process is a sequential one in which the solution selection is done only at the end, it leads to computational overhead and memory limitation problems and (iii) Suppose a group of ten ants have been deployed for the optimal solution generation, and if this group of ants fails, then a new group of ten other ants have to be deployed. The time spent for the initial process will be a mere waste and leads to substantial time overhead.

The inferences from the table have been depicted by graph based visualizations as shown in Figures 4, 5 and 6. Among them, Figure 4 shows the component coverage% of each of the approaches. This shows that, ACO and the proposed Critical Path Optimizer have outperformed and they achieved 100% of coverage.

Based on the critical components coverage to ensure quality of the software product, a graph as shown in Figure 5 is constructed and it shows that, ACO and the proposed approach have achieved 100% coverage of critical components.

Figure 4. Components Coverage% Vs. Search Approaches

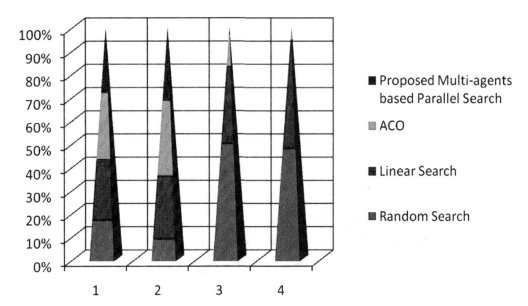

Figure 5. Critical Components Coverage% Vs. Search Approaches

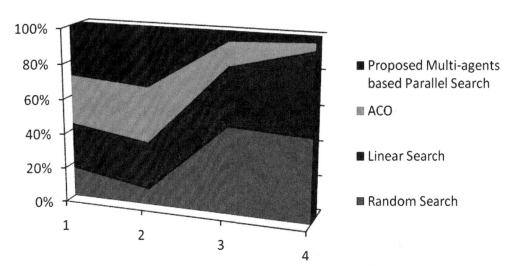

Eventhough, ACO and proposed approach provided 100% coverage in terms of components and critical components, the test runs required to identify the critical components and the critical paths which can ensure the coverage of critical components during testing shows that the proposed approach outperforms all the other approaches. This has been depicted in Figure 6.

Based on the sample case studies, the time required to generate the critical paths in order to cover all the critical components is analyzed and is depicted in Figure 7. It has been inferred that, the total time needed for critical paths generation and optimization is reduced using the proposed novel critical path optimization approach based on multi-agents based approach. Hence, it has been concluded that the proposed tool is a suitable one for the identification and verification of critical components within less amount of time without compromising quality.

From Table 8, one can infer that, the number of false positives in the proposed approach is 1 among the total of 19 components. The false negative, true negative are identified accurately using the proposed approach.

Figure 6. Test runs required to cover all the critical components by different approaches

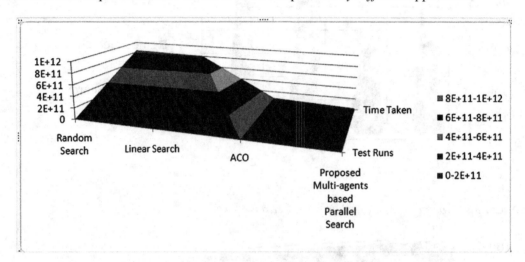

Figure 7. Time taken by various apporaches in (Nano Seconds)

Search Approaches Vs. Execution Time

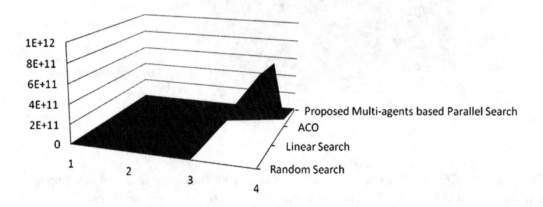

Existing Work Based Qualitative Analysis

The comparison of the performance of the proposed approach with existing research works in critical components identification based on various parameters is given in Table 9.

Table 8. Predicted vs. Actual fault prone components

Actual	Predicted	
	No fault Components (True)	Fault Components (False)
No Fault Components (Positive)	15 (True Positive)	1 (False Positive)
Fault Components (Negative)	3 (True Negative)	0 (False Negative)

Table 9. Comparison of Existing and Proposed Research works based on their working

S.No.	Research Work	Inference Based on	Metrics Used for Critical Components Identification	Traditional / Intelligence Applied	Components Verification / Critical Test Paths Generation and Tool Development
1.	Ruchika et.al.	Source Code Analysis	WMC, NPM, LOC, DAM, MOA, AMC, RFC, CBO, EC, IC,CBM, LCOM,CAM,CC	Traditional	No
2.	Janes et.al.	Source Code Analysis	RFC	Traditional	No
3.	Shin et al. (2011)	Development history	Complexity, Code Churn, And Developer Activity Metrics	Traditional	No
4.	Zimmerman et al. (2011)	Source Code Analysis	Size, Churn Metrics And Code Metrics Like Fan In, Fan Out, And Cyclomatic Complexity	Traditional	No
5.	Suri and Kumar(2010)	Simulator	Reusability Metric	Traditional	No
6.	Zhou and Leung (2006)	Design Documents	Design Metrics	Traditional	No
7.	Nagappan et al. (2006)	Source Code Analysis	Number Of Classes In A Module, Inheritance Depth, Class Coupling Measures	Traditional	No
8.	TiborGyimo´thy et.al (2005), Subramanyam and Krishnan (2003), and Basili et.al (1996)	Analysis of design documents	CK Suite Of OO Design Metrics Such As Depth Of Inheritance Tree, Response For A Class, And Number Of Children, Lines Of Code	Traditional	No
9	Proposed Multi Agents based Approach	Analysis of UML based design documents, OCL based formal specification documents, Source Code Analysis and Java Byte Code Analysis	Complexity and Dependability Metrics	Intelligence Based	Yes – Tool Name: Critical test path Optimizer

Other Observations

When compared to the other existing approaches on critical components identification and dynamic verification, the proposed approach provides an intelligent search process to do the testing of the components rigorously.

Also, the other observations related to the proposed approach:

- As per 'No Free Lunch' procedure, the proposed approach too has some tradeoffs. If the number of components in the given software is less, then time taken for completing the process is higher when compared to linear or random search processes because of the switching time between the agents.
- Also, prior to applying ABC, the algorithm itself takes some amount of time to complete its critical value calculation prior to testing. The time taken to complete the Phase – I of identification of critical components by calculating complexity, severity and Phase – II of risk exposure calculation, it requires some more time when compared to the design metrics alone based approach.

But, when considering the criticality and quality level of the problem concerned, the time it requires for the proposed approach is very less and is acceptable.

IMPACT ANALYSIS OF PROPOSED APPROACH USING STATISTICAL ANALYSIS

A correlation analysis is conducted to find the relationship between the number of classes in an application against the time taken and test runs required to complete the fault-prone components identification is conducted. For all the cases, the critical components coverage is 100%.

To identify the impact of the proposed multi agents approach in terms of total time taken to identify the fault-prone components and the number of test runs required to test them is statistically analyzed. Even though the proposed approach has taken only less time when compared to the existing approaches, it has been observed that, the total number of classes or class components present in an application will heavily impact on the time taken and test runs requirement. These analytical results are provided here for further research in this field.

```
Initial Set-up:
z for 95% CI= 1.96
Invalid: 0
Cases-N: 15
r (#classes.Timetaken)= 0.9691
p= 0
r (#classes.TestRuns)= 0.9813
p= 0
r (Timetaken.TestRuns)= 0.9242
p= 0
```

Table 10. Fault Prone Components Identification and Testing Results Analysis

Case Study #	Application	No.of Classes	Time Taken (NanoSec)	Time Taken (Sec)	Test Runs
1.	Patient Monitoring System	22	2.34E+10	23.3888434	31
2.	Banking Management System	19	2.32E+10	23.2020436	19
3.	Library Management System	20	2.32E+10	23.2150553	28
4.	Shopping Cart	12	2.17E+10	21.7154112	12
5.	Hospital Management System	28	3.2E+10	32.0147525	38
6.	Network Monitor	23	2.35E+10	23.5123874	31
7.	Workflow Management system	35	4.15E+10	41.520478	46
8.	Dealership Management System	17	2.22E+10	22.1542797	17
9.	Insurance Management System	27	3.15E+10	31.4715427	32
10.	Stock Management System	14	2.15E+10	21.4789875	11
11.	Credit Card Validation	22	2.32E+10	23.2478875	31
12.	Vendor Management System	16	2.19E+10	21.9471548	14
13.	Anti Money Laundering System	56	5.91E+10	59.1248643	72
14.	Microfinance Management System	12	2.17E+10	21.7154112	12
15.	Online Bus Reservation Management System	15	2.11E+10	21.1247885	16

The correlation coefficient (r) can range in value from −1 to +1. The larger the absolute value of the coefficient, the stronger the relationship between the variables. For the Pearson correlation, an absolute value of 1 indicates a perfect linear relationship. A correlation close to 0 indicates no linear relationship between the variables.

From our experimental results, the Pearson correlation values (r), r (#classes.Timetaken), r (#classes. TestRuns) and r (Timetaken.TestRuns) are highly correlated. They have exhibited a large positive relationship as the values are nearer to 1.

In the regression table shown in Table 11, corresponds to E(Time Taken) the s.e value which represents the standard error value shows the average distance that the observed values fall from the regression line. Conveniently, it tells how wrong the regression model is on average using the units of the response variable. Smaller values are better because it indicates that the observations are closer to the fitted line. From the regression table of E(Time Taken), the s.e value is 0.063 which is <=2.5 which produces a sufficiently narrow 95% prediction interval.

Table 11. Regression Table for E(Timetaken) against #classes

Regression Table for E(Timetaken)				
	B	s.e.	t	p
#classes	0.899	**0.063**	14.168	0
Intercept	7.127			

Now, the scatter plot is drawn between #classes and Time Taken and the relationship curve indicates that it is linear which means that, they are highly correlated. The points fall close to the line, which indicates that there is a strong linear relationship between the variables. The relationship is positive because as one variable increases, the other variable also increases.

Figure 8. Scatter plot for correlation analysis between mean differences of classes and time taken

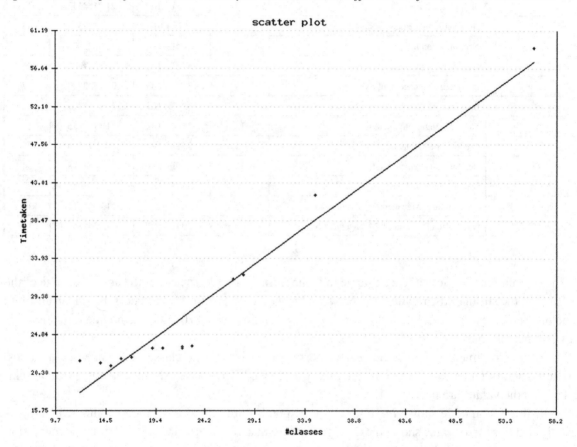

By using the box plot as shown in Figure 9, one can infer that, the relationship between #classes and Time taken are highly correlated and shows positive correlation.

From the regression Table 12, the s.e value is 0.078 which is <=2.5 which produces a sufficiently narrow 95% prediction interval.

Also, a scatter plot is drawn between #classes and Tesr Runs as shown in Figure 10. It has been observed that, the plot is a linear regression which means that, they are highly correlated and are providing a positive correlation.

From the regression Table 13, the s.e value is 0.166 which is <=2.5 which produces a sufficiently narrow 95% prediction interval. A scatter plot between Time Taken and Test Runs as shown in Figure 11, indicates that the two series of values show a positive correlation and shows a linear regression line.

Figure 9. Box Plot for correlation analysis between #classes and Time Taken

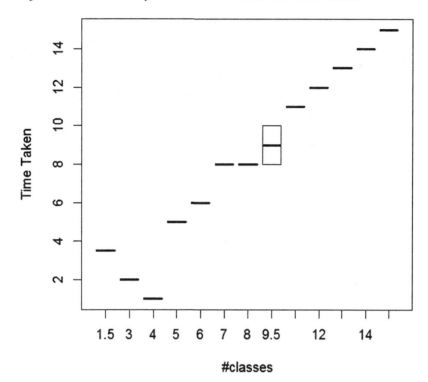

Table 12. Regression Table for E(TestRuns) against #classes

Regression Table for E(TestRuns)
B s.e. t p
#classes 1.426 **0.078** 18.374 0
Intercept -4.808

Variance Analysis Using ANOVA and the F-Test

ANOVA is used to compare differences of means among more than 2 groups. It does this by looking at variation in the data and where that variation is found. Specifically, ANOVA compares the amount of variation between groups with the amount of variation within groups. It can be used for both observational and experimental studies. Mathematically, ANOVA can be written as:

$$x_{ij} = \mu_I + \varepsilon_{ij} \tag{1}$$

where x are the individual data points (I and j denote the group and the individual observation), ε is the unexplained variation and the parameters of the model (μ) are the population means of each group. Thus, each data point (x_{ij}) is its group mean plus error. To use the F-test to determine whether group means are equal, it's just a matter of including the correct variances in the ratio. In one-way ANOVA, the F-statistic is this ratio:

F = variation between sample means / variation within the samples (2)

In general, an F-statistic is a ratio of two quantities that are expected to be roughly equal under the null hypothesis, which produces an F-statistic of approximately 1. The low F-value shows a case where the group means are close together (low variability) relative to the variability within each group. The high F-value shows a case where the variability of group means is large relative to the within group variability. In order to reject the null hypothesis that the group means are equal, we need a high F-value.

In the ANOVA table shown in Figure 12, one can conclude that, the F-Value is 0.7 which indicates that the group has low variability. That is the group means are close together relative to the variability within each group.

Figure 10. Scatter plot for correlation analysis between mean differences of classes and time taken

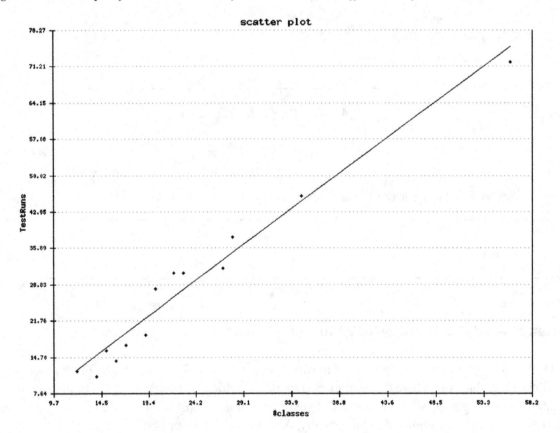

Table 13. Regression Table for E(TestRuns) against Time Taken

Regression Table for E(TestRuns)				
	B	s.e.	t	p
Timetaken	1.448	**0.166**	8.7237	0
Intercept	-12.321			

Figure 11. Scatter plot for correlation analysis between time taken and Test Runs

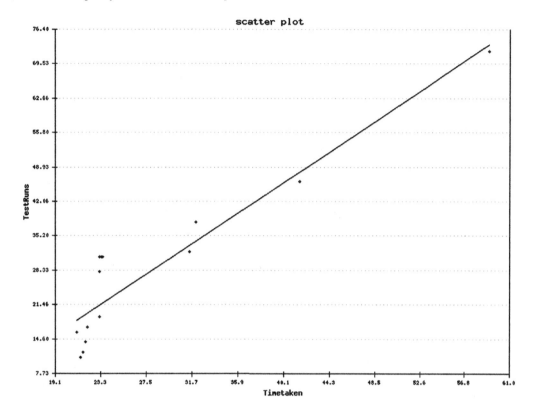

CONCLUSION

The intelligent agents based fault-prone components identification and testing framework was successfully implemented as a tool using Java. Also, the proposed framework has been compared with the existing approaches and found to be the better candidate to identify the fault-prone components within less time and cost. The merits of this research work include: (1) Critical Components Identification during early development process; (2) a multi-agent based Critical Components Coverage; (3) Critical Paths execution without redundancy of covering the same components to reduce total time and cost involved in the testing process without compromising quality.

Moreover, the proposed work has also statistically evaluated the significance of the proposed approach in identifying the fault-prone components from a given software. The correlation analysis results indicate that, the total number of classes/class components in the software has positive correlation with the total time taken and the number of test runs needed by the proposed approach. This means that, the traditional approaches which are not having the parallel behavior and the automation in terms of intelligent decision making will be heavily affected if the complexity of the software increases.

Hence, the proposed work has higher level of impact on the identification of fault-prone components in spite of the complexity of the software. As a future work, the components which are identified as fault-prone are going to be prioritized based on their test execution sequence so that, the total test runs needed to complete the testing task will be optimized.

Figure 12. Anova Table based on regression analysis

Data Summary

	Samples					
	1	2	3	4	5	Total
N	15	15	15			45
ΣX	338	410.8339	410			1158.8339
Mean	22.5333	27.3889	27.3333			25.7519
ΣX^2	9386	12775.921	14946			37107.921
Variance	126.4095	108.8302	267.0952			165.1316
Std.Dev.	11.2432	10.4322	16.343			12.8504
Std.Err.	2.903	2.6936	4.2198			1.9156

standard weighted-means analysis

ANOVA Summary   1

Source	SS	df	MS	F	P
Treatment [between groups]	233.0993	2	116.5497	0.7	0.502286
Error	7032.6896	42	167.445		
Ss/Bl					
Total	7265.7889	44			

Ss/Bl = Subjects or Blocks depending on the design.
Applicable only to correlated-samples ANOVA.

REFERENCES

Agrawal, H. (1994). Dominators, Super Blocks, and Program Coverage. *Proceedings of the 21st ACM SIGPLAN-SIGACT Symposium on Principles of Programming Languages*, 25-34. 10.1145/174675.175935

Andrea, A., & Xin, Y. (2008). A Novel Co-Evolutionary Approach to Automatic Software Bug Fixing. In *IEEE World Congress on Computational Intelligence*. IEEE Press.

Basili V. R., Briand L. C., & Melo W. L. (1996). A validation of object-oriented design metrics as quality indicators. *IEEE Transaction on Software Engineering, 22*(10), 751–761.

Basturk & Karaboga. (2006). An Artificial Bee Colony (ABC) Algorithm for Numeric function Optimization. *IEEE Swarm Intelligence Symposium*.

Baykasolu, Özbakır, & Tapkan. (2009). *Artificial Bee Colony Algorithm and Its Application to Generalized Assignment Problem*. Academic Press.

Bernardi, S., Campos, J., & Merseguer, J. (2011, February). Timing-Failure Risk Assessment of UML Design Using Time Petri Net Bound Techniques. *IEEE Transactions on Industrial Informatics*, *7*(1), 90–104. doi:10.1109/TII.2010.2098415

Beydeda, S., & Gruhn, V. (2003). Test Case Generation According To The Binary Search Strategy. *Lecture Notes in Computer Science*, *2869*, 1000–1007. doi:10.1007/978-3-540-39737-3_124

David, C., & Yang, J. (2005). Software Assurance by Bounded Exhaustive Testing. *IEEE Transactions on Software Engineering*, *31*(4), 328–339. doi:10.1109/TSE.2005.52

Dennis, F. S., & Chang, D. J. (2006). Modular Verification of Code with Sat. *ISSTA-2006*, 1-11.

Dhavachelvan, P., & Uma, G. V. (2003). Multi-agent based integrated framework for intra-class testing of object-oriented software. *LNCS, 2869*.

Dorigo, M., Maniezzo, V., & Colorni, A. (1996). The Ant System: Optimization by a Colony of Cooperating Agents. *IEEE Transactions on Systems, Man, and Cybernetics. Part B, Cybernetics*, *26*(1), 29–41. doi:10.1109/3477.484436 PMID:18263004

Ebert, C. (2001). Metrics for identifying critical components in software projects. In *Handbook of Software Engineering and Knowledge Engineering* (Vol. 1). World Scientific Publishers. doi:10.1142/9789812389718_0017

Fathian, M., Amiri, B., & Maroosi, A. (2007). Babak Amiri and Ali Maroosi, "Application of honey-bee mating optimization algorithm on clustering. *Applied Mathematics and Computation*, *190*(2), 1502–1513. doi:10.1016/j.amc.2007.02.029

Gegick, M., Rotella, P., & Williams, L. (2009). Predicting Attack-prone Components. *2009 International Conference on Software Testing Verification and Validation*, 181-190. 10.1109/ICST.2009.36

Genero, L. M., Piattini, M., & Calero, C. (2000). Early measures for UML class diagrams. *L'Objet*, *6*, 2000.

Gyimothy, T., Ferenc, R., & Siket, I. (2005, October). TiborGyimo´thy, Rudolf Ferenc, and Istva'nSiket (2005), "Empirical Validation of Object-Oriented Metrics on Open Source Software for Fault Prediction. *IEEE Transactions on Software Engineering*, *31*(10), 897–910. doi:10.1109/TSE.2005.112

Horgan, J., London, S., & Lyu, M. (1994). Achieving Software Quality with Testing Coverage Measures. *IEEE Computer*, *27*(9), 60–69. doi:10.1109/2.312032

Jeya Mala, D., & Iswarya, R. (2014). Multi Agents Based Approach for Critical Components Identification and Verification. *International Journal of Systems and Service-Oriented Engineering*, *5*(1), 21–39. doi:10.4018/ijssoe.2014010102

Jeya Mala, D., Kamalapriya, S., & Mohan, V. (2010). Automated Software Test Optimization Framework – an Artificial Bee Colony Optimization based Approach. *IET Software*, *4*(5), 334–348. doi:10.1049/iet-sen.2009.0079

Jeya Mala, D., & Mohan, V. (2009). On the Use of Intelligent Agents in Test Sequence Selection and Optimization. *International Journal of Computational Intelligence and Applications, 8*(2), 155–179. doi:10.1142/S1469026809002515

Jin, C., Jin, S.-W., & Ye, J.-M. (2012). Artificial neural network-based metric selection for software fault-prone prediction model. *IET Software, Vol, 6*(6), 479–487. doi:10.1049/iet-sen.2011.0138

Karaboga, D., & Basturk, B. (2008). On The Performance Of Artificial Bee Colony (ABC) Algorithm. Applied Soft Computing, 8(1), 687-697.

Karaboga, N. (2009). A new design method based on artificial bee colony algorithm for digital IIR filters. *Journal of the Franklin Institute, 346*(4), 328–348. doi:10.1016/j.jfranklin.2008.11.003

KaterinaGoseva, P. (2003, October). Architectural-Level Risk Analysis Using UML. *IEEE Transactions on Software Engineering, 29*(10), 946–959.

Kaur, I. (2015). A Compound Metric for Identification of Fault Prone Modules. *IOSR Journal of Computer Engineering, 17*(6), 31-35.

Kemmerer, R. A. (1985, January). Testing Formal Specifications to Detect Design Errors. *IEEE Transactions on Software Engineering, 1*(1), 32–44.

Kim, H., & Boldyreff, C. (2002). Developing Software Metrics Applicable to UML Models. *ECOOP Workshop on Quantitative Approaches in Object-Oriented Software Engineering (QAOOSE).*

Li, H., & Peng Lam, C. (2004). Software Test Data Generation using Ant Colony Optimization. *Transactions on Engineering, Computing and Technology.*

Li, J., & Sun, J. (2007). Automated Test Data Generation Algorithm Based on Reversed Binary Tree. *SNPD, 3*, 1124–1128.

Li-Pei, W., Puan, C. Y., Malcolm, Y. H. L., & Chong, C. S. (2008). Bee colony optimization algorithm with big valley landscape exploitation for job shop scheduling problems. *Applied Soft Computing, 8*(1), 687–697.

Martina, M., & Antonia, B. (2003). Using Spanning Sets for Coverage Testing. *IEEE Transactions on Software Engineering, 29*(11), 974–984. doi:10.1109/TSE.2003.1245299

McGregor, J. D. (1997). Component Testing. *Journal of Object-Oriented Programming, 10*(1), 6–9.

Mizuno, O., & Hata, H. (2010). An integrated approach to detect fault-prone modules using complexity and text feature metrics. *Proceedings of the 2010 international conference on Advances in computer science and information technology*, 457-468. 10.1007/978-3-642-13577-4_41

Myers. (1979). The Art of Software Testing. John Wiley & Sons, Inc.

Nagappan, N., Ball, T., & Zeller, A. (2006). Mining Metrics to Predict Component Failures. *28th International Conference on Software Engineering (ICSE).*

Pham, D. T., Ghanbarzadeh, A., Koc, E., Otri, S., Rahim, S., & Zaidi, M. (2006). The Bees Algorithm, (2006), "A Novel Tool for Complex Optimization Problems. In *Proc 2nd International Virtual Conf on Intelligent Production Machines and Systems (IPROMS 2006)*. Oxford, UK: Elsevier.

Pressman, R. S. (2007). *Software Engineering – A Practitioners Approach*. McGraw Hill Publishers.

Ramon, S., & Jose, A. L. (2006). Scatter Search in Software Testing, Comparison and Collaboration with Estimation of Distribution Algorithms. *European Journal of Operational Research, 169*(2), 392–412. doi:10.1016/j.ejor.2004.08.006

Russel, S., & Norvig, P. (1995). *Artificial Intelligence: A modern approach*. Prentice-Hall Inc.

Schneidewind, N. F. (1979, August). Application of Program Graphs and Complexity Analysis to Software Development and Testing. *IEEE Transactions on Reliability, R-28*(3), 192–198. doi:10.1109/TR.1979.5220563

Shin, Y., Meneely, A., & Williams, L. (2011). Evaluating Complexity, Code Churn, and Developer Activity Metrics as Indicators of Software Vulnerabilities. *IEEE Transactions on Software Engineering, 37*(99), 1–16.

Singh, A. (2009). An artificial bee colony algorithm for the leaf-constrained minimum spanning tree problem. *Applied Soft Computing, 9*(2), 625–631. doi:10.1016/j.asoc.2008.09.001

Srinivasa Rao, R., Narasimham, S. V. L., & Ramalingaraju, M. (2008). Optimization of Distribution Network Configuration for Loss Reduction Using Artificial Bee Colony Algorithm. *Proceedings Of World Academy Of Science, Engineering And Technology, 35*, 709–715.

Subramanyam, R., & Krishnan, M. S. (2003, April). Empirical Analysis of CK Metrics for Object-Oriented Design Complexity: Implications for Software Defects. *IEEE Transactions on Software Engineering, 29*(4), 297–310. doi:10.1109/TSE.2003.1191795

Surl, P. K., & Kumar, S. (2010, June). Simulator for Identifying Critical Components for Testing in a Component Based Software System. *IJCSNS International Journal of Computer Science and Network Security, VOL., 10*(6), 250–257.

Tassey, G. (2002). *The Economic Impacts of Inadequate Infrastructure for Software Testing. Final Report*. National Institute of Standards And Technology.

Teodorović, D., & Dell, M. (2006). *Bee Colony Optimization – A Cooperative Learning Approach To Complex Transportation Problems*. Advanced OR and AI Methods in Transportation.

Wes, M., Andy, P., & David, L. (2007). An Empirical Study of Test Case Filtering Techniques Based on Exercising Information Flows. *IEEE Transactions on Software Engineering, 33*(7), 454–477. doi:10.1109/TSE.2007.1020

Xiao, M., Mohamed, E. A., Marek, R., & James, M. (2007). Empirical Evaluation Of Optimization Algorithms When Used in Goal-Oriented Automated Test Data Generation Techniques. *Empirical Software Engineering, 12*(2), 183–239. doi:10.100710664-006-9026-0

Zhou, Y., & Leung, H. (2006, October). Empirical Analysis of Object-Oriented Design Metrics for Predicting High and Low Severity Faults. *IEEE Transactions on Software Engineering, 32*(10), 771–789. doi:10.1109/TSE.2006.102

Zimmerman, T., Nagappan, N., Herzig, K., Premraj, R., & Williams, L. R. (2011). An Empirical Study on the Relation between Dependency Neighborhoods and Failures. *IEEE fourth international conference on Software Testing (ICST)*, 347-356.

Chapter 39
Adapting Agile Practices During the Evolution of a Healthcare Software Product

Danilo F. S. Santos
Embedded Lab, Federal University of Campina Grande, Brazil

André Felipe A. Rodrigues
Embedded Lab, Federal University of Campina Grande, Brazil

Walter O. Guerra Filho
Embedded Lab, Federal University of Campina Grande, Brazil

Marcos Fábio Pereira
Embedded Lab, Federal University of Campina Grande, Brazil

ABSTRACT

Agile Software Development (ASD) can be considered the mainstream development method of choice worldwide. ASD are used due to features such as easy management and embrace of changes, where change in requirements should be taken as a positive feature. However, some domain verticals, such as medical-healthcare, are classified as critical-safety system, which usually requires traditional methods. This chapter presents a practical use case describing the evolution of a software product that was conceived as a wellness software for end-users in mobile platforms to a medical-healthcare product restricted to regulatory standard recommendations. It presents the challenges and how the ASD is compatible to standards such as ISO/IEC 82304-1.

INTRODUCTION

Agile methods can be considered one of the most adopted methodologies for software development nowadays. When considering the development of consumer-based services and applications, which are mostly focused for end-users in mobile and cloud platforms, Agile Software Development (ASD) is the

DOI: 10.4018/978-1-6684-3702-5.ch039

de-facto methodology. ASD are used due features such easily management and embrace of changes, where change in requirements should be taken as a positive feature. However, some domain verticals, such as medical-healthcare, are classified as critical-safety system, which usually requires traditional methods where requirements are well stablished before development, and validation and verification are usually executed in the end of development.

When considering new paradigms such as the Internet of Things (IoT) and Industry 4.0 revolution, new conflicts appears between market needs and safety regulations. In this new world, the need for fast development for market fit purposes is a reality, and that´s where ASD fits (Kumari, 2018) (Laukkarinen, 2018). These challenges appear in almost all domains, such as healthcare (Gupta, 2019) (Laukkarinen, 2017).

In this context, we present a practical use case describing how was the evolution of a software product that was conceived as a wellness software for end-users in mobile platforms. The product evolved to be a medical-healthcare product, restricted to regulatory standard recommendations, where agile software practices were adopted to fulfill such guidelines.

As most Minimum Viable Products (MVP), the presented target software was firstly developed using a standard agile process. As the product requirements changed due to integration with medical devices, its regulatory requirements also increased, including the need to be complaint to standards such as ISO 82304-1 (ISO/IEC 82304, 2012) and ISO 62304-1 (ISO/IEC 62304, 2006). Therefore, the previously adopted agile methodology was adapted to fulfill these new requirements, balancing recommendations required by regulatory standards, such as requirement traceability, with agile features such as the embrace of changes.

In this chapter we show that it is possible to use standard agile methodologies in the first stages of development, when creating an MVP, and then, reuse already developed artifacts and adapt the process to be complaint with regulatory rules for safety-critical systems in the healthcare domain. The chapter shows how Scrum artifacts were adapted to enhance traceability, as also, as automated management tools were customized and integrated, and finally, how new requirements for validation and verification were introduced into the agile process due regulatory standards.

The remainder of this chapter is organized as follows: In *Background* section we present a review of agile Software Development (ASD) main features, a literature review about the main challenges in ASD for health care, and the main standards used in our work. The next section presents the adopted software development process, highlighting the main challenges and decisions made during the process adaptation. In the *Future Research Directions* section, we discuss how intelligent tools could help in software engineering process as whole. Finally, in the *Conclusion*, an overall discussion and current challenges are presented.

Background

Traditional plan-based software development processes, or disciplined processes, are based on a sequence-based linear approach, where each phase is exhaustive executed before the next one. Disciplined methodologies, such as Waterfall or V-Process (Sommerville, 2011), are usually used in the development of systems that need extensive quality assurance processes, where verification and validation activities are one of the main drivers of the product release. Although they are well suited for healthcare product development, as they usually deal with the validation of critical requirements, nowadays new market needs in healthcare demand new innovations and fast time-to-market releases. Based on this new scenario, disciplined processes present challenges for embrace of changes, especially when facing the need for new products and features.

Talking about Agile Software Development (ASD), nowadays it can be considered the "the main-stream development method of choice worldwide" (Hoda, 2018). ASD arose from dissatisfaction with the overloads of development methods in the 1980s and 1990s. The main features of ASD can be listed as, (i) focus on code instead of project documentation, and (ii) interactive approach to development, where planning is carried iteratively, and project scope is continuously refined and prioritized (Ramesh, 2010).

Therefore, the main goal of ASD is to deliver software quickly, and deal with volatile requirements (Hoda, 2017). The goal is to reduce development process overloads, and to be able to respond quickly to requirements changing without excessive rework. One of the main features of ASD is that specification, design and implementation phases are interspersed. The system is developed in a series of versions or increments with business stakeholders involved in (almost) all phases. To achieve this, frequent delivery of new versions is executed, and extensible use of support tools are encouraged, such as automated test-ing, continuous integration, and management tools, etc.

When dealing with safety regulations, as the ones applied to software for healthcare, new challenges appears. Well stablished standards define how medical device software should follow, namely ISO/IEC 62304 (ISO/IEC 62304, 2006) and ISO/IEC 82304 (ISO/IEC 82304, 2012) family of standards. They are international standards that "provides a lifecycle with activities and tasks necessary for the safe design and maintenance of software for medical devices". Although it is not itself a regulation, it is recognized by many regulatory agencies as good standards for medical device software development. Therefore, companies and regulatory agencies are continuously discussing how to concretely meet the requirements from those standards.

ISO/IEC 62304 family of standards describes and provides guidance on development processes to be applied according to each classification. All these documents recommend that the risk associated with a software product be assessed to establish a development process with the appropriate level of rigor and robustness.

In general, they recommend manufacturers to show traceability between system requirements, soft-ware requirements, and tests, and to verify and document traceable software requirements to system requirements and other sources (Martins, 2018). Traceability is the degree to which a relationship can be established between two or more products of the development process. Several approaches exist that focus on establishing traces among different types of artifacts, such as requirements traceability, requirements-to-architecture, requirements-to-code, and others (Bianchini, 2019). Some works presented approaches about how to map requirements and enhance traceability in healthcare software development (Barbosa, 2018), however, they do not detail a practical case for the industry, mostly focusing on academic trials.

Mostly of these challenges are common in disciplined methodologies and ASD. However, when deal-ing with ASD, new challenges appears when managing requirements for traceability (Barbosa, 2018). For example, in (Heager, 2018), it is performed a systematic literature review about agile Requirements Engineering. The authors expose evidences about how agile practices respond to the traditional challenges from the Requirements Engineering and how to manage development teams in this context.

To easily the adoption of agile in these scenarios, initiatives were created to help the adaptation of ASD for safety critical systems development. For example, the SafeScrum approach (Hanssen, 2018) split the software development from the process of design, develop, deploy and maintain safety-related systems, as defined in the IEC 61508 standard. That way, the software development uses Scrum, and the decision making for safety are done in a separated process. Another initiative was presented by

(AAMI, 2012), defining practice guidelines for medical device software development using ASD. The adaptation of an ASD process for healthcare software development presented in this chapter, although share similar points, was defined and executed independently of those initiatives, and our experience is presented in the following sections.

Healthcare Software Product Development

The first developed MVP, namely Personal HealthCare System (PHC), was focused on monitoring newborns babies through mobile platforms and personal health devices. The goal was the consumer market in a B2C (Business to Consumer) chain. The system was composed by a cloud-hosted service and a mobile frontend application used to input vital signals such as temperature, weight and height. In this sense, a simple agile approach, strongly based on Scrum, was used for development. The product backlog was defined through standard User Stories, focusing only on user requirements, as illustrated in the following Table 1.

Table 1. Example of Simple User Stories for the MVP

User Story	Points
As a parent, I want to store height information using a web page	5
As a parent, I want to store height information using my Android phone	5
As a parent, I want to follow the evolution of my baby's height over the months through a line graph	13
As a system administrator, I want to register and unregister users from the system	3
As a physician, I want to access data from my patients and register comments	5

Short sprints were defined (two weeks), where about 80% of tasks were focused on feature development, and the remaining 20% on testing and validation activities for Quality Assurance (QA). Backlog was maintained through online management tools, and tasks were daily controlled through a wallboard and post-its. As a result, the MVP was developed into 6 months with the first product market fit release.

Some highlights are important to mention:

- Requirements were stored in a separated document, most as business requirements from stakeholders.
- QA activities were managed separated from the Backlog and Requirements, such as Bug management, test plans, and simple continuous integration systems.

Evolution to HealthCare Platform

As the product business requirements changed, new challenges appeared due a new goal of the system:

- Integration with personal and clinical health devices, such as thermometers, blood pressure devices, weight scales, etc.

The need for interoperability was an additional feature besides this integration. Therefore, as a new requirement, the need to be compliant with Continua Health Alliance Guidelines (Wartena, 2010), as also, Bluetooth SIG specifications (Bluetooth SIG, 2020) for wireless connectivity.

As a result, the HealthCare platform was conceived (Santos, 2016). The platform offers services for remote monitoring and management of patient health data. It allows the user to receive data from Personal Health Devices independently and automatically, and securely synchronize this data with Cloud services. The Cloud platform therefore shares this information as healthcare professionals or family members and offers value-added services such as a threshold alert system, appointment scheduling, user classification by health status, among others. In addition to offering personal patient monitoring solutions in their homes, the HealthCare platform enables continuous patient monitoring through its connection to multi-parameter monitors, enabling healthcare professionals to remotely monitor patient progress 24/7 and in real time.

The HealthCare Platform is divided into 3 main modules:

- Service Platform.
- Application Portals.
- Health Data Aggregators (HDA).

The Service Platform offers web services and stores data. In conjunction with Application Portals, which provide the application vision for the customer domain, the Service Platform provides a 24/7 online infrastructure for patients, healthcare professionals and system administrators.

Health Data Aggregators (HDA) can be considered as the modules where information flow is initiated, thus a health data collector. An HDA can work on a mobile device, such as a tablet or smartphone, or on a dedicated device, a health hub. HDA collects data from Personal Health Devices (DPS) or Medical Devices through communication interfaces such as Bluetooth, Bluetooth Smart, Wi-Fi, or Ethernet. An HDA can communicate with Personal Health Devices such as oximeters, blood pressure meters, glucometers, and more, or communicate with Medical Devices for continuous monitoring, such as a Multi-parameter Monitor. HealthCare Platform can be described using the diagram of Figure 1.

Adopted Agile Software Development

Adopting an ASD process, as expected, added a list of benefits for the product development, such as fast requirement review and update due to earlier releases; better interaction with stakeholders and users; fast adaptation of product specification due new market demands. However, as dealing with a healthcare product submitted for conformance rules, it was necessary to review all quality assurance processes to be compliant with international standards.

In order to achieved better conformance and QA metrics, the development process was reviewed. As before, the new software product development procedure adopted follows an agile approach. In this procedure, all phases required for project development are fulfilled, where records and artifacts are generated for each phase.

In general, project development goes through four phases: (i) Proposal, (ii) Planning, (iii) Execution and (iv) Closure. In the development process the following actors participate:

- **Product Owner:** Is the customer representative for the software product. Its responsibilities include defining features / requirements, maintaining Product Backlog, prioritizing, risk analysis, and accepting / validating results.
- **Development Team:** A team of engineers, architects and software developers responsible for product development, testing, verification.
- **Scrum Master:** Responsible for keeping the development process in compliance with its rules and following the development team.

Figure 1. Diagram of HealthCare System.

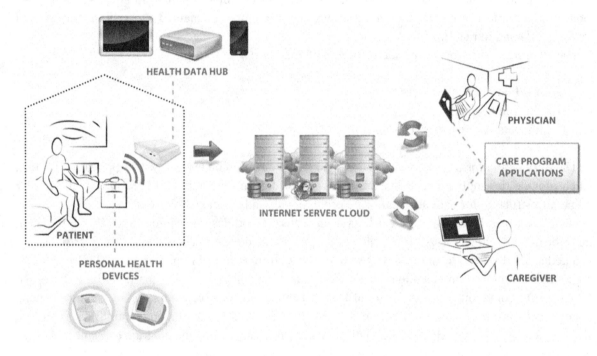

The following Figure 2 illustrates this process, and the artifacts delivered in each phase.

In particular, during implementation, the Scrum agile development approach is used. In the Scrum approach, you define a list of features that will be validated according to the provided specifications (requirements). The list describes a user story that forms what is called a product backlog. This list is developed in the Planning phase and continuously updated during Execution. Each story contains a description of the requirements and use cases that must be met by the product (validation).

During the Execution phase the stories, which reveal features / requirements, are implemented according to priorities and at equal time intervals ranging from 2 to 4 weeks. These time intervals are called Sprints. During a Sprint cycle 4 phases are performed:

- Sprint Planning, where the Product Backlog features to be developed are chosen.
- Development of features / requirements. In this phase verification and validation tests are performed continuously.
- Sprint Review, where features are reviewed and validated by the Product Owner.

- Sprint Retrospective, where a critical analysis of Sprint's development and results is performed. These results serve to improve the development process and the software product.

Figure 2. Adopted agile procedure

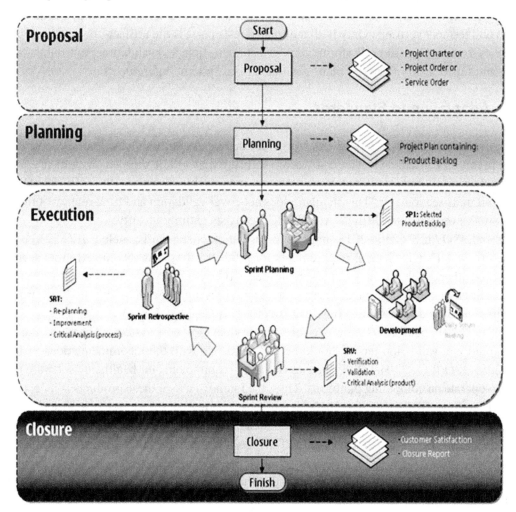

In the last phase, the Closure phase, the Customer (Product Owner) certifies that all functionality has been validated and that the final product is ready for its intended use. To perform this attestation, the Product Owner makes use of the acceptance results of the validation tests used during the development phase. At the end, the Product Owner signs a closure and acceptance report, validating and certifying that the software product is ready for its intended use.

In the new process, verification and validation procedure is continually integrated into the development process. In this context, it is listed 4 main large entities:

1. **Developers:** Develop all system modules. This group includes system architects, who define the requirements to be developed. The development process for the HealthCare platform is detailed

    in another document. It is important to note that all developed artifact is reviewed by another professional.

2. **Repository with Versioning:** Central system that maintains version control of artifacts (code, documents, etc.) generated by developers.

3. **Continuous and Automated Integration Tool:** Automated tool that builds and launches the modules of the HealthCare platform. This tool performs all automated tests developed by the development team and testers / verifiers. Only if all automated tests pass, is the artifact released.

4. **Quality Testers / Verifiers:** Performs all verification, testing, and validation procedures for system data and functionality from test plans generated from system requirements.

Process Adaptation to Standards

As introduced before, ISO/IEC 62304: 2015 provides details about the life cycle of a Medical Device Software. In this case, Medical Device Software is software that will be shipped on medical equipment, either in part or in full. Especially regarding software and system validation, ISO / IEC 62304: 2015 is clear in detail in its section 1.2: "This standard does not cover validation and final release of the MEDICAL DEVICE, even when the MEDICAL DEVICE consists entirely of software."

To this end, ISO / IEC 62304-2015 suggests the use of other standards, such as IEC 82304-1: 2015, "Health Software - Part 1: General requirements for product safety", as mentioned in its section 1.2: Validation and other development activities are needed at the system level before the software and medical device can be placed into service. These system activities are not covered by this standard but can be found in related product standards (e.g., IEC 60601-1. IEC 82304-1, etc.).

As the HealthCare platform is entirely a software product (software system). Therefore, the requirements required in a validation report should be in accordance with the recommendations of ISO/IEC 82304-1:2015. ISO/IEC 82304-1:2015 focuses on safety requirements for healthcare software products designed to operate on computing platforms. Thus, the intended use of these products is independent of hardware. Therefore, ISO/IEC 82304: 2015 covers the software product life cycle with respect to design, development, VALIDATION, installation and maintenance.

ISO / IEC 82304-1: 2015 defines VALIDATION as a process that aims to show that a healthcare software product meets the functionalities (or requirements) defined in the project for its intended use.

The VALIDATION report provides evidence that the process has been performed and that the product meets its requirements for its intended use. To this end, ISO / IEC 82304-1: 2015 defines that the following information should be presented in a validation report:

1. The "manufacturer" shall identify the individuals responsible for validation.
2. The validation report shall provide evidence that the health software product meets its requirements and intended use.
3. The validation report shall include a summary of the results of the validation process.
4. The validation report shall provide evidence that the validation results are traceable to the health software product requirements.

Practical Activities

As introduced before, as the product evolved to medical/healthcare domain, the development process was adapted to meet requirements of international standards. In addition, it was necessary to integrate new tools and create new testing, verification and validation processes.

The Product Backlog has been modified for each story to include references to the requirements to be met. These references were intended to increase the traceability of Sprint requirements. Risk analysis and mitigation activities were also considered in the Done definition of all Product Backlog stories.

To operationalize this process, a new project lifecycle management tool was used. Initially, all requirements and stories were registered in the tool. Sprints were recorded as they were executed with their respective user stories, description and effort estimation (points), as shown in Table 2.

Table 2. Example of simple user stories for the MVP

User Story	Description	Points
As a doctor, I want to see the main bed information in the main screen.	Short Description: Create the "reduced bed widget" which must be placed in the main screen. This "reduced bed widget" is dynamic, and must adapt to the number of lines available. Evaluate how to support horizontal scroll It is desirable, must not mandatory, to support the expansion of lines. Reference Use Cases: US011, US012 Acceptance Requirements: REQ-1002, REQ-1003, REQ-1004	8
As a doctor, I want to see vital signal information in the main screen	Short Description: Create integrated/connected monitor widget. The widget can have a "fixed" design for the alpha. Reference Use Cases: US101, US103 Acceptance Requirements: REQ1102, REQ1103, REQ1104	5

Throughout the Sprint, artifacts resulting from risk analysis of the executed stories were stored also in the tool. At the end of the project, it was possible to track exactly which Sprint a given requirement was met, including the risk analyzes performed for it.

A new Continuous Integration process has been incorporated to ensure quality deliveries. Daily, the latest project code was compiled to generate a new version. Automatic tests were performed to check for potential problems with each generation. In addition, source code anomalies were always checked using static analysis tools across generations. This way, problems were detected and fixed before the version was released.

The automation tool was used to deploy the Continuous Integration process. A task was set up to compile the latest version of the project at the end of each day with static analysis checks and automated test runs. In this tool, static analysis problems found in each project module were stored and presented as shown in Figure 3.

The testing process was rigorously modified to ensure that the released requirements were as expected. Tests are now planned for each release requirement. The test plan was always fully executed before releasing the production version. Some tests were performed manually and others automatically. The person responsible for applying the test plan recorded the result (success or failure) and date of execution.

Figure 3. Example of static problems found.

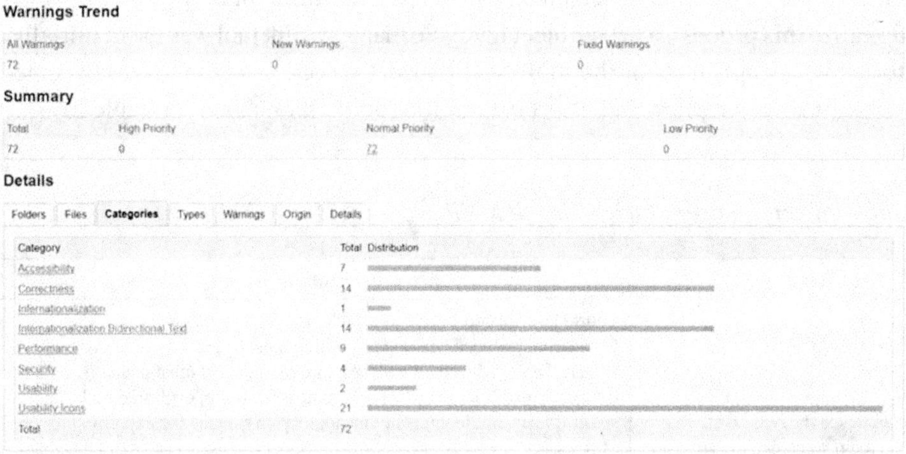

Warnings Trend

All Warnings	New Warnings	Fixed Warnings
72	0	0

Summary

Total	High Priority	Normal Priority	Low Priority
72	0	72	0

Details

Folders | Files | **Categories** | Types | Warnings | Origin | Details

Category	Total	Distribution
Accessibility	7	
Correctness	14	
Internationalization	1	
Internationalization Bidirectional Text	14	
Performance	9	
Security	4	
Usability	2	
Usability Icons	21	
Total	72	

The Testlink tool was used to perform test management. Initially, all project requirements were registered in the tool as exemplified in Figure 4. It is important to notice that all requirements have a test coverage for validation.

And, each the test case is described in detail, including its definition of criticality, preconditions, planned execution steps as shown in Figure 5.

Prior to each release, the test plan was fully executed in the candidate version. If the success percentage was less than 90% or a critical test case failed, the release was canceled. Finally, in order to speed up the execution of the test plan, tools were used to automate test cases whenever possible, such as automatic robot scripts to test external medical devices.

Compliance Validation Documentation

For software product validation, the following procedures and artifacts are used:

- During Sprint Review features are accepted by the Product Owner. These functionalities (requirements) presented in Product Backlog are mapped to test cases, which are executed, logged, and their results reviewed by the Product Owner for validation.
- At the end of software product development, the Product Owner makes a general acceptance of the product, thereby making a statement that the product meets the requirements for its intended use.

Figure 4. Example of requirements registration

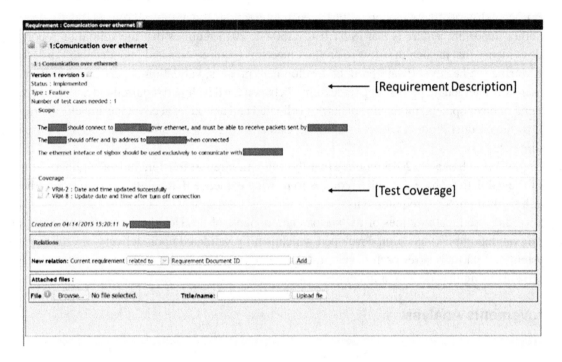

Figure 5. Example of test case traced to requirement

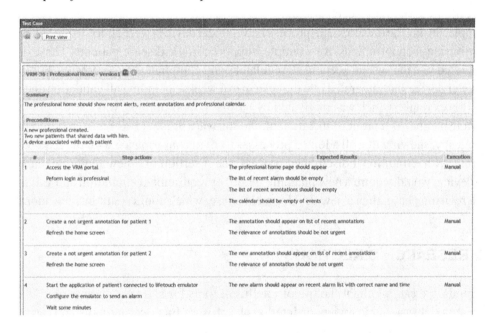

For example, ISO / IEC 82304-1: 2015 requires the "manufacturer" to identify the individuals responsible for validation. The tests performed within the previously presented software development process are performed by the testing team and developers, which are always identified in the documentation.

Acceptance and validation of requirements (functionalities) are performed by the project Product Owner upon delivery of new functionalities at each interaction, and at the end of each released version.

Another important feature is that ISO / IEC 82304-1: 2015 requires that the validation report must provide evidence that the health software product meets its requirements and intended use. As described before, during the health software product development process, validation is performed continuously with each new interaction, performing traceability between the developed requirement and its validation. At the end of development, all requirements are validated and a product acceptance and closure report is signed by the product Product Owner as evidence and attesting that the product meets the requirements for its intended use.

Also, ISO/IEC 82304-1: 2015 requires that the validation report must include a summary of the results of the validation process, as also requires to provide evidence that validation results are traceable to health software product requirements.

To validate the functionalities of the various components of the HealthCare platform, a test specification (validation plan) has been developed which is fully validated upon delivery of each version of the system and partially after each development interaction. This test specification traces all tests to requirements using the adopted online tool.

Improvements Analysis

After the adoption of this balanced approach, where ASD processes where adapted for healthcare software products, some improvements in terms of development and business opportunities could be highlighted. The observed main improvement was the fast and easily requirement changes due to new business opportunities and market changes.

For example, during the development process new clinical devices were added to the supported device list due new business opportunities, for example, support chronic disease patients. These devices were rapidly integrated into the system keeping all regulatory and compliance requirements. For instance, one new glucometer device was integrated into the system in 6 weeks, including all validation and verification processes. This example, which was motivated by business opportunities, was rapidly embraced by the development team and, as a proof of its efficient, the software product was registered into the Brazilian regulatory agency, showing that all adopted processes were in conformance with the required standards.

Comparing with a traditional disciplined process, the insertion of a new requirement, such as support a new device, would require a new planning phase for requirement elicitation and validation, a new architecture revision phase, then a new development phase, which could result in a few months of work.

FUTURE RESEARCH DIRECTIONS

As future trends, we can highlight the use of intelligent tools for software engineering. In (Perkusich, 2019) is presented a systematic review of Intelligent Software Engineering tools and methods applied to ASD. In this context, we can foresee the use of intelligent tools and artificial intelligence to map requirements for medical device software in the specification phase. This mapping would reduce the need of rework due missing specifications. Also, artificial intelligence tools would help in the mapping of requirements and implemented features, easing the traceability task.

CONCLUSION

For the last few years, we developed a process to adapt ASD to regulations requirements into the health-care domain. Our experience proved that it is possible to use agile methodologies in different domains, especially considering the fast-growing business opportunities that are appearing in the last few years. As result of our experience, it was proved that regulation requirements can meet agile development, keeping the software products updated and safety, and still fit the market time windows for business opportunities.

Although the development is fast, still, all the processes for registration with regulation agencies are necessary for every main update, making the ASD process even more important. As one of the main results of this adaptation process, we can highlight the fast release of new increments that were registered into regulatory agencies, attesting that all adopted procedures are in conformance with regulatory standards and recommendations.

REFERENCES

AAMI. (2012). TIR45:2012 - Guidance on the use of agile practices in the development of medical device software. Association for the Advancement of Medical Instrumentation, 21, 22-78.

Barbosa, P., Leite, F., Santos, D., Figueiredo, A., & Galdino, K. (2018, June). Introducing Traceability Information Models in Connected Health Projects. In *2018 IEEE 31st International Symposium on Computer-Based Medical Systems (CBMS)* (pp. 18-23). IEEE. 10.1109/CBMS.2018.00011

Barbosa, P., Queiroz, J., Santos, D., Figueiredo, A., Leite, F., & Galdino, K. (2018, June). RE4CH: Requirements Engineering for Connected Health. In *2018 IEEE 31st International Symposium on Computer-Based Medical Systems (CBMS)* (pp. 292-297). IEEE.

Bianchini, E., Francesconi, M., Testa, M., Tanase, M., & Gemignani, V. (2019). Unique device identification and traceability for medical software: A major challenge for manufacturers in an ever-evolving market-place. *Journal of Biomedical Informatics*, *93*, 103150. doi:10.1016/j.jbi.2019.103150 PMID:30878617

Bluetooth, S. I. G. (2020). *Bluetooth SIG specifications*. Retrieved February 20, 2020, from https://www.bluetooth.com/specifications/

Gupta, R. K., Venkatachalapathy, M., & Jeberla, F. K. (2019, May). Challenges in adopting continuous delivery and DevOps in a globally distributed product team: a case study of a healthcare organization. In *Proceedings of the 14th International Conference on Global Software Engineering* (pp. 30-34). IEEE Press. 10.1109/ICGSE.2019.00020

Hanssen, G. K., Stålhane, T., & Myklebust, T. (2018). *SafeScrum®-Agile Development of Safety-Critical Software*. Springer International Publishing. doi:10.1007/978-3-319-99334-8

Heeager, L. T., & Nielsen, P. A. (2018). A conceptual model of agile software development in a safety-critical context: A systematic literature review. *Information and Software Technology*, *103*, 22–39. doi:10.1016/j.infsof.2018.06.004

Hoda, R., Salleh, N., & Grundy, J. (2018). The rise and evolution of agile software development. *IEEE Software*, *35*(5), 58–63. doi:10.1109/MS.2018.290111318

Hoda, R., Salleh, N., Grundy, J., & Tee, H. M. (2017). Systematic literature reviews in agile software development: A tertiary study. *Information and Software Technology*, *85*, 60–70. doi:10.1016/j.infsof.2017.01.007

ISO/IEC 62304. (2006). 62304:2006 Medical Device Software—Software Life Cycle, Assoc. Advancement Medical Instrumentation, 2006.

ISO/IEC 82304. (2012). IEC 82304-1: Health Software–Part 1: General Requirements for Product Safety.

Kumari, A., Tanwar, S., Tyagi, S., & Kumar, N. (2018). Fog computing for Healthcare 4.0 environment: Opportunities and challenges. *Computers & Electrical Engineering*, *72*, 1–13. doi:10.1016/j.compeleceng.2018.08.015

Laukkarinen, T., Kuusinen, K., & Mikkonen, T. (2017, May). DevOps in regulated software development: case medical devices. In *Proceedings of the 39th International Conference on Software Engineering: New Ideas and Emerging Results Track* (pp. 15-18). IEEE Press. 10.1109/ICSE-NIER.2017.20

Laukkarinen, T., Kuusinen, K., & Mikkonen, T. (2018). Regulated software meets DevOps. *Information and Software Technology*, *97*, 176–178. doi:10.1016/j.infsof.2018.01.011

Martins, L. E. G., & Gorschek, T. (2017). Requirements engineering for safety-critical systems: Overview and challenges. *IEEE Software*, *34*(4), 49–57. doi:10.1109/MS.2017.94

Perkusich, M., Silva, L. C., Costa, A., Ramos, F., Saraiva, R., Freire, A., ... Almeida, H. (2019). Intelligent Software Engineering in the Context of Agile Software Development: A Systematic Literature Review. *Information and Software Technology*.

Santos, D. F., Rodrigues, A. F. A., Pereira, M. F., Almeida, H. O., & Perkusich, A. (2016). An interoperable and standard-based end-to-end remote patient monitoring system. In *Encyclopedia of E-Health and Telemedicine* (pp. 260–272). IGI Global. doi:10.4018/978-1-4666-9978-6.ch022

Sommerville, I. (2011). Software engineering (9th ed.). Academic Press.

Wartena, F., Muskens, J., Schmitt, L., & Petkovic, M. (2010, July). Continua: The reference architecture of a personal telehealth ecosystem. In *The 12th IEEE International Conference on e-Health Networking, Applications and Services* (pp. 1-6). IEEE.

KEY TERMS AND DEFINITIONS

Agile Software Development: Discipline that studies a set of behaviors, processes, practices, and tools used to create products and their subsequent availability to end users.

Connected Health: It is a new way for delivery of healthcare services using mobile and internet technologies.

Medical Device Software: Software intended to be part of a hardware medical device.

Medical Informatics: Also called Health Information Systems, Health Care Informatics, Healthcare Informatics, Medical Informatics, Nursing Informatics, Clinical Informatics, or Biomedical Informatics, is a discipline at the intersection of information science, computer science, social science, behavioral science, and healthcare.

Personal Health Device: It is a health device that is maintained by the patient.

Personal Health Record: It is a health record where health data and information related to the care of a patient is maintained by the patient.

Software Engineering: Is an area of computing focused on the specification, development, mainte-nance, and creation of software, with the application of technologies and project management practices and other disciplines, aiming at organization, productivity and quality.

This research was previously published in Balancing Agile and Disciplined Engineering and Management Approaches for IT Services and Software Products; pages 115-129, copyright year 2021 by Engineering Science Reference (an imprint of IGI Global).

Chapter 40
A Model Based on Data Envelopment Analysis for the Measurement of Productivity in the Software Factory

Pedro Castañeda

iD https://orcid.org/0000-0003-1865-1293

Universidad Peruana de Ciencias Aplicadas, Universidad Nacional Mayor de San Marcos, Peru

David Mauricio

iD https://orcid.org/0000-0001-9262-626X

Universidad Nacional Mayor de San Marcos, Peru

ABSTRACT

Productivity in software factories is very important because it allows organizations to achieve greater efficiency and effectiveness in their activities. One of the pillars of competitiveness is productivity, and it is related to the effort required to accomplish the assigned tasks. However, there is no standard way to measure it, making it difficult to establish policies and strategies to improve the factory. In this work, a model based on data envelopment analysis is presented to evaluate the relative efficiency of the software factories and their projects, to measure the productivity in the software production component of the software factory through the activities that are carried out in their different work units. The proposed model consists of two phases in which the productivity of the software factory is evaluated and the productivity of the projects it conducts is assessed. Numerical tests on 6 software factories with 160 projects implemented show that the proposed model allows one to assess the software factories and the most efficient projects.

DOI: 10.4018/978-1-6684-3702-5.ch040

INTRODUCTION

Software factories offer great advantages, such as the ability to decrease production costs per product by up to 60%; time savings of up to 98% for putting a product on the market; labor requirements reduced by up to 60%; a tenfold improvement in productivity; and better quality of each product with 10 times fewer errors. These advantages increase the company's portfolio of products and services as well as its chances of winning new markets (Clements & Northrop, 2001).

The importance of measuring productivity in a software factory is very important because of the close relationship between production-unit operations and profitability. In addition, once the company has quantified productivity, it has a solid foundation for strategic planning. Tracking historical productivity can reveal problem areas in the production units and promote improvements and efficient use of available resources. In turn, this outcome supports establishing specific dimensions for comparing the unit with its counterparts, since increased efficiency enables increased competitiveness (Castañeda & Mauricio, in press). Although a software factory's functional components are typically organized around Project Management and Software Production and Support, and each component is composed of work units (as shown in Figure 1), 90% of the factory's effort occurs in the Software Production component, and Analysis & Design, Programming, and Testing consume 85% of this component's efforts (Jacobson, Booch, & Rumbaugh, 2000; Castañeda & Mauricio, in press).

Figure 1. Structure of software factories (Castañeda & Mauricio, 2018)

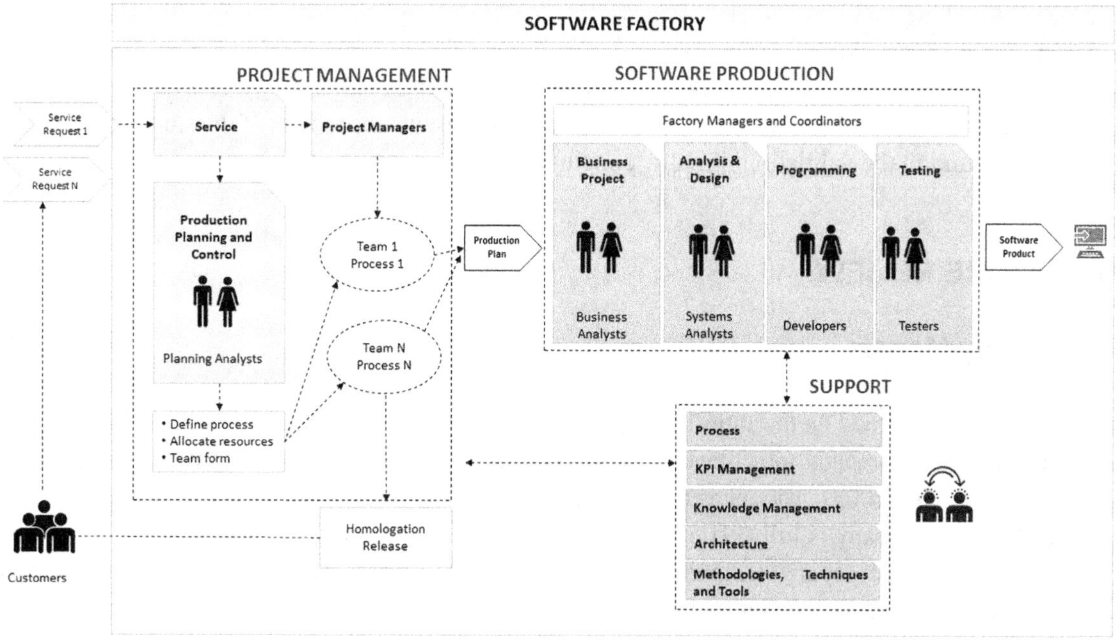

The software industry[1] is enthusiastically adopting the concept of a software factory[2], and one reason is the indicators that enable measuring its productivity and comparing them in the market. Measurement helps the business to consider actions that increase overall efficiency, using all resources effectively and efficiently to obtain the best possible results. The company must know how the organization is performing in relation to both its own previous periods and its competitors. This raises several questions, such as whether performance (i.e., productivity) of the factory is increasing, decreasing, advancing, or receding; the magnitude of this progress or setback; and the effectiveness of implemented strategies. However, measuring productivity is a complex activity because there is no consensus on what to measure (Scacchi, 1995; Asmild, Paradi, & Kulkarni, 2006, Moreira, Carneiro, Pires, & Bessa, 2010; Yilmaz & O'Connor, 2011; Cheikhi, Al-Qutaish, & Idri, 2012; Machek, Hnilica, & Hejda, 2012; Khan, Ahmed, & Faisal, 2014). Various publications on software productivity reviewed in recent years show that literature about measuring productivity in software factories is very scarce (Castañeda & Mauricio, 2018). Models for measuring productivity (Asmild et al., 2006; Nwelih & Amadin, 2008; Moreira et al., 2010; Yilmaz & O'Connor, 2011; Cheikhi et al., 2012; Machek et al., 2012) have considered only the unit of programming work, leading to a bias in measurement and the lack of measurement indicators that facilitate decision making in the organization.

As noted, the Software Production component accounts for 90% of the software factory's effort (Jacobson et al., 2000). However, related studies have measured the productivity of its Programming unit, implicitly considering other units relevant. Likewise, the measurement models use different units of measurement and compare all the projects using the same rubric, without taking into account the particularities of each project. As defined by the Project Management Body of Knowledge (PMBOK), a project is a temporary effort undertaken to create a unique product, service or result (Project Management Institute, 2017). Thus, Data Envelopment Analysis (DEA) should be considered as a model that allows establishment of efficient projects that, through the application of best practices, become benchmarks for projects that have similar characteristics.

This paper is organized in five sections. Section 2 presents a review of the literature about software factories, productivity, and existing models. Section 3 details the methodology in which the proposed conceptual model and its elements are explained. Section 4 presents the results of the study and discusses the findings found in the validation. Finally, conclusions are presented in Section 5.

LITERATURE REVIEW

Productivity Models

Productivity is understood as the ratio of outputs to inputs, while efficiency (technical) is understood as the capacity of a company to achieve maximum production from its set of inputs (Coelli, Estache, Perelman, & Trujillo, 2003). The measure of technical efficiency varies between 0 and 1. A value of 1 indicates that the company is fully efficient and operates on the production frontier, while a value less than 1 reflects that the company operates below that border. The difference between 1 and the observed value measures technical inefficiency (Coelli et al., 2003).

There is no standard definition of productivity. However, the authors consider that productivity to be the ratio of the product obtained as a result of the efforts expended. Nevertheless, studies carried out on the productivity of a software factory are oriented toward measuring the productivity in the software programming unit, represented as the inputs and outputs evaluated (source lines of code–SLOC; function points–FP; person hours–PH by the developer; and person months–PM by the developer). This has led to the development of many performance measurement models that have become inaccurate. However, studies have not comprehensively reviewed the software factory, ignoring other important work units such as Analysis & Design and Testing (Asmild et al., 2006; Nwelih & Amadin, 2008; Moreira et al., 2010; Yilmaz & O'Connor, 2011; Cheikhi et al., 2012; Machek et al., 2012; Castañeda & Mauricio, 2018)

In this context, productivity of the software factories is defined as "an indicator of the efficiency of the used resources over different units of work of a software factory for the achievement of the final product" (Castañeda & Mauricio, 2018, P.62). This definition considers all the work units that participate in software development and allows for the evaluation of the different factors that influence the entire software-production cycle.

Cardoso, Bert, and Podestá (2010) state that a model is a simplified representation of reality, defined through the different components and processes that are part of the system under study. Thirteen models have been identified that measure the productivity of software development and are based on different approaches. Table 1 summarizes these models based on the following approaches: Data Envelopment Analysis (DEA), Capability Maturity Model Integration (CMMI) & Six Sigma, Software Reuse, Structural Equation Modeling (SEM), Total Factor Productivity (TFP), Institute of Electrical and Electronics Engineers (IEEE) Std. 1045 & ISO 9216-4 (Castañeda and Mauricio, 2018).

Table 1. Software productivity measurement models

Id	Model	Approach	Reference
M1	Productivity = e1.95 FP 0.7 (*) Where: Productivity: The productivity is measured by Work Effort FP: Function Points	DEA	Asmild et al., 2006
M2	Physical Productivity = Number of LOC / man hours or days or months Functional Productivity = Number of FP / Man hours or days or months Economic Productivity = Value / Cost Where Value = f(Price, Time, Quality, Functionality)	Simple Model of Productivity	Card, 2006
M3	log (PDR) = 2.8400+0.3659 x log (Team Size)-0.6872 x I(3GL) - 1.2962 x I(4GL) – 1.3225 x I(ApG) – 0.1627 x I(MR) – 0.4189 x I(Multi) – 0.3201 x I (PC) – 0.4280 x I(OO) – 0.2812 x I (Event) + 0.7513 x I(OO:Event) – 0.2588 x I(Business) – 0.0805 x I(Regression) + 1.0506 x I(Business:Regression) Normalized PDR = (Normalized Work Effort) / (Adjusted FP)	Normalized Productivity Delivery Rate (PDR)	Jiang, Naudé, & Comstock, 2007
M4	$$\text{Productivity} = \sum_{i=1}^{n}(r_i + f_i + l_i + c_i) / \sum I$$ Where: r_i = Reuse f_i = Functionality l_i = Length c_i = Complexity $\sum I$ = Effort	Software Reuse	Nwelih & Amadin, 2008
M5	Productivity = 10.3 + 0.31701* N&C N&C: New and Changed code. It is considered as the physical lines of code (LOC). N&C is composed of added and modified code.	Fuzzy Logic	López, Kalichanin, Meda, & Chavoya, 2010

continues on following page

Table 1. Continued

Id	Model	Approach	Reference
M6	Productivity = 32.087 - 3.637 DDST + 11.71 LRU - 9.451 LCIU - 0.8187 LEX DENV Where: DDST: Defect Density in Systemic Tests DDST = 1.8955 – 0.5087 PDTR – 1.6020 UTC LRU: Level of the Requirements' Unstableness LCIU: Level of Continuous Integration Utilization LEX: Level of Experience DENV: Development Environment PDTR: Percentage of Defects in Technical Revisions UTC: Unit Test Coverage	CMMI & Six Sigma	Moreira et al., 2010;
M7	Productivity = f (Motivation, Process, Complexity, Reuse, Team Size, Social Productivity, Social Capital) Social Productivity= f (Team Leadership, Collective Outcomes, Information Awareness) Social Capital= f (Communication Transparency, Social Relations, Regular Meetings)	SEM	Yilmaz & O'Connor, 2011
M8	Productivity = f(n (OT), n (RT), n (PT), PO (MT, o), PXO (MT), PR (MT, e), PXR (MT), RO (MT, o), RO(MT))/ (labor hour variable) n (OT): Count of object types per technique n (RT): Count of relationship types per technique n (PT): Count of property types per technique PO (MT, o): Count of number of properties for a given object type PXO (MT): Average number of properties for a given object type PR (MT, e): Number of properties of a relationship type and its accompanying role types PXR (MT): Average number of properties per relationship type RO (MT, o): Number of relationship types that can be connected to a certain object type RO(MT): Average number of relationship types that can be connected to a certain object type	DEA VRS	Cao, Ching Gu, & Thompson, 2012
M9	Consolidated productivity model Productivity = f (Efficiency, Completeness, Accuracy) Where: Efficiency = f (Task time, Task costs, Frequency of Error, User efficiency, User efficiency compared to an expert, Task efficiency (time), Task Efficiency (cost), Proportion of the time the user is productive) Completeness = f (Percentage of tasks Accomplished, Percentage of users who were successful in completing the task, Percentage goal achievement for every unit of time) Accuracy = f (Percentage of tasks Achieved correctly, Percentage of users who achieve the task correctly, How often does the user encounter inaccurate results when accomplishing the task? How often does the user achieve the task with inadequate precision?)	ISO 9126-4 IEEE Std. 1045	Cheikhi et al., 2012
M10	Output definitions (y) Input definitions (x) Output and Input Prices' Determination (p, w) Total Factor Productivity Calculations (Fisher or Törnqvist productivity indexes)	TFP	Machek et al., 2012
M11	Productivity = f (Technology, Working Culture, Interest in Individual Job, Complexity, Team Size, Human Productivity) Human Productivity= f (Manager Skills, Team Unity, Social Life, Meeting Frequency)	SEM	Khan et al., 2014
M12	Productivity = FP, Quality/ Total Effort (Development Effort + EoC + EoNC) Conformance effort (EoC) = (Appraisal + Prevention) Costs. Example: review effort Non-conformance effort (EoNC) (Internal + External) Failure Costs. Example: The rework effort, including failure effort Quality = f (Defects)	DEA VRS	Pai, Subramanian, & Pendharkar, 2015
M13	$$\text{Productivity} = \left(\sum_{i=1}^{n} \left(\text{Quality}_i * \text{Quantity}_i \right) \Big/ \text{Net Task Hours}_i \right) * \text{Weighted Methods}$$ Quality = 1- ((10 * total # of Serious Defects + 3 * total # of Medium Defects + total # of Trivial Defects)/LOC) Quantity = LOC Weighted Methods = (3 * (total# of constructors + total# of destructors) + 5 * total # of selectors + 9 * total # of iterators + 15 * total # of modifiers) * (1/N) where N is the total number of methods for an individual programmer	Statistical technique	Unluturk & Kurtel, 2015

Source: (Castañeda & Mauricio, 2018, P.59)

Models have only been designed to measure internal productivity, but they are incomplete since they have been mostly oriented toward the programming work unit (Asmild et al., 2006; Nwelih & Amadin, 2008; Moreira et al., 2010; Yilmaz & O'Connor, 2011; Cheikhi et al., 2012; Machek et al., 2012) and very few have been oriented for testing and analysis & design units (Moreira et al., 2010; Cao et al., 2012; Pai et al., 2015; Unluturk & Kurtel, 2015). This situation generates a measurement bias, since it would not allow for assessment of productivity in other components of the software factory. No models have been found that measure productivity throughout the software factory, nor do the existing models measure external productivity. That is, they do not perform a comparative evaluation of productivity. This could have negative consequences for the organization, since a purely internal evaluation would produce biased information that would compromise any evaluation of how the market is behaving. Additionally, models propose a qualitative evaluation (Yilmaz & O'Connor, 2011; Cheikhi et al., 2012; Machek et al., 2012); although the precision of the model could be considered, such a model could not be generalized because it lacks a practical application or has not been applied in case studies.

Table 1 shows that the models consider different elements that often cannot be compared, which makes the measurement process difficult, particularly without a homogeneous unit of measurement.

DEA Productivity Models

DEA is a widely used mathematical programming technique originally developed by Charnes, Cooper, and Rhodes (1978) and extended by Banker, Charnes, and Cooper (1984) to include variable returns to scale. DEA generalizes the Farrell (1957) single-input single-output technical efficiency measure to the multiple-input multiple-output case, to evaluate the relative efficiency of peer units with respect to multiple performance measures (Charnes, Cooper, Lewin, & Seiford, 1994; Cooper, Seiford, & Tone, 2006). The units under evaluation in DEA are called decision-making units (DMUs). A DMU is considered efficient when no other DMU can produce more outputs using an equal or smaller number of inputs. DEA is a technique for measuring efficiency based on obtaining an efficiency frontier from the set of observations under consideration without estimating any production function (Charnes et al., 1994). Unlike parametric methods that require detailed knowledge of the process, DEA is not parametric and does not require an explicit functional form related to inputs and outputs (Cooper et al., 2006; Cook & Seiford, 2009)

Since its introduction, research in DEA has evolved both in theory and in practice, and has been applied in various areas (e.g., measuring the performance of educational institutions, benchmarking logistics processes, comparisons of branches of regional offices of banks, the regulation of public services, the measurement of research productivity and teaching in academic departments). It has also been applied in the software industry, as seen in the summary in Table 2 illustrating the literature review prepared by Pai et al. (2015).

Table 2 shows that most of the evaluations of productivity in software-development projects that use DEA consider the Variable Returns to Scale (VRS) model and only consider the work of the Programming unit. These considerations bias the measurement of productivity, since the development of software involves other very important work units such as Analysis & Design and Testing. This chapter considers the DEA methodology for the following reasons:

- It develops an optimization process for each individual observation, with the objective of calculating a discrete boundary determined by the efficient DMUs.

- It does not require any assumption about the functional form of the frontier.
- Inefficient DMUs are projected onto the frontier by a convex combination of the closest efficient DMUs.
- It allows one to identify the sources and the level of inefficiency of the inputs and outputs.

Table 2. Studies of software projects applying DEA

Id	Input	Output	Model	Work Unit	Reference
1	Effort	FP	DEA CRS	Programming	Banker & Kemerer, 1989
2	Effort	FP Quality	Stochastic DEA	Programming	Banker, Datar, & Kemerer, 1991
3	Effort	FP	DEA-based F-tests	Programming	Banker, Chang, & Kemerer, 1994
4	Effort	Comment Change, Code Change, Routines Change	Additive DEA CRS	Programming	Mahmood, Pettingell, & Shaskevich, 1996
5	Project Cost	Size (FP), Quality (Defects), Duration (Time to Market in days)		Programming	Paradi, Reese & Rosen, 1997
6	Effort	Users, EDI, Conversions	DEA VRS	Support	Myrtveit & Stensrud, 1999
7	Effort	FP, Locations, Business Units, Concurrent Users	DEA VRS	Support	Flitman, 2003
8	Effort	Users, EDI, Conversions	DEA VRS	Support	Stensrud & Myrtveit, 2003
9	Effort, Vendor Costs, Duration	SLOC		Programming	Yang & Paradi, 2004
10	Effort	FP		Programming	Asmild et al., 2006
11	Effort	FP, SLOC	DEA & Regression Analysis	Support	Parthasarathy & Anbazhagan, 2008
12	Developers, Bugs	Kilobytes per Download, Downloads, Project Rank Effort, Function Points as a Contextual Variable		Support	Wray & Mathieu, 2008
13	Effort, Team Size	Size (FP)	DEA VRS	Programming	Pendharkar & Rodger, 2009
14	Labor Hour Variable	UML Complexity Metrics	DEA VRS	Support	Cao et al., 2012
15	Development Effort (DE), Review and Testing Effort (EoC), and Rework Effort (EoNC)	FP, Quality (f(Defects)	DEA VRS	Programming	Pai et al., 2015
16	Team Size, Project Effort per Team,	Daily productivity, Requirements Completion Ratio per Team (%), Daily Maximum Work Hours per Team Member	DEA & Simpson's Diversity Index.	Support	Altiner & Ayhan, 2018

Source: (Pai et al., 2015)

METHODOLOGY

The purpose of DEA is to construct a non-parametric piecewise frontier over the data set in such a way that all observed points lie either on or below the production frontier as it enables to calculate the relative efficiencies of all DMUs with respect to the frontier. Each DMU, not positioned on the frontier, is scaled down against a convex combination of DMUs on the frontier facet closest to it (Charnes et al., 1978; Sahoo, 2016). The different aspects that have been taken into account for the definition of the DEA model and the data to be considered for its evaluation further discussed in the sub-section below.

Choice of DEA Model

The following paragraphs describe the considerations in defining the DEA model.

Isotonicity

A fundamental rule for DEA parameters is that an increase in one input variable must improve each of the outputs (Chung, Lee, Kang, & Lai, 2008). This rule reflects the isotonicity property of DEA parameters. Correlation analysis should be performed to ensure positive relationships between inputs and outputs. In the case of negative correlations, transformational techniques can be applied. However, several problems related to transformation of variables to satisfy the property of isotonicity have been described in Liu, Meng, Li, & Zhang (2010). Therefore, instead of leading to the transformation of parameters, negative correlations may be an indication that one or more parameters must be excluded from the model. The present case study considers two input variables (Effort and Project Cost) and one output variable (Function Points) that have already been used in previous studies (Banker & Kemerer, 1989; Banker et al., 1991; Banker et al., 1994; Mahmood et al., 1996; Paradi et al., 1997; Myrtveit & Stensrud, 1999; Flitman, 2003; Stensrud & Myrtveit, 2003; Yang & Paradi, 2004; Asmild et al., 2006; Parthasarathy & Anbazhagan, 2008; Pendharkar & Rodger, 2009; Pai et al., 2015). Therefore, it is not necessary to establish the isotonicity of the parameters.

Orientation of DEA Model

DEA provides two basic orientations of the model: maximization of the output and minimization of the input. A model oriented to maximizing the output determines the maximum proportional increase of the outputs in relation to the input values, adequate to establish a set of target output values. A model aimed at minimizing the input determines the amount by which the input values can be decreased while the same outputs continue to be produced (Zhu, 2014). This research adopts an input-oriented model to determine efficiency, based on the use of input parameters to produce the resulting quality and productivity values.

Selection of DEA Model

Now, through DEA, we will try to determine if we can create an ideal (virtual) software factory that is better than one or more real software factories. Any factory that is less productive than the virtual factory will be deemed an inefficient factory.

This study adopts the DEA Variable Return Scale (VRS) model, since some software factories of different sizes than efficient ones may not be able to achieve the same productivity. Thus, the study will be conducted using technical efficiency, since that stipulates that each DMU must take as a reference the highest productivity among those of its size (Yannick, Hongzhong & Thierry, 2016).

Because contracts established with software factories involve the delivery of defined products at the beginning of the service, the Input Orientation has been considered because the software factories must reach the productivity of the reference unit at cost to reduce the hours of effort and the cost of the real project. Additionally, input variables can be controlled.

DEA Model

Figure 2 shows parameters that constitute the DEA model: DMU, Input, Model, Output, and Phases (Banker et al., 1991; Zhu, 2014; Yannick, Hongzhong & Thierry, 2016). The factory will be evaluated in two phases. Phase 1 aims to determine the productivity of the software factories to establish the one that is the most efficient. This determination will allow for the discovery of the existing gap and best practices that have been applied in such a way that they are replicated in other software factories, leading to improvement in their efficiency. Phase 2 will determine productivity of the software-factory projects, to identify best practices and lessons learned from the most efficient projects, which will become models other projects in their category can follow and achieve the same efficiency.

Figure 2. Parameters for DEA model

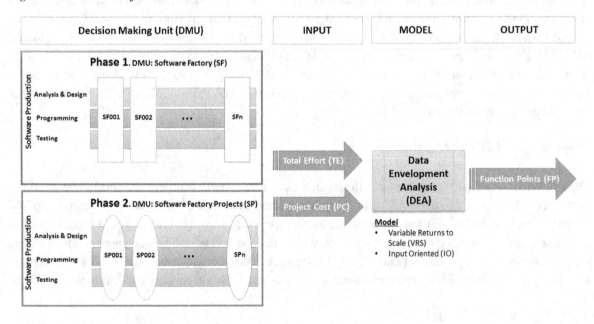

The parameters of the DEA model are described below.

Decision Making Unit (DMU). The DMU is any organization that generates products and/or services by consuming certain resources, with the ability to modify both consumed resources (inputs) and product created (outputs). For the case raised, evaluation has been considered in two phases.

- Phase 1: DMU–Software Factory. Considers the information related to the different organizations that have been working on the Software Factory model.
- Phase 2: DMU–Software Factory Projects. Consider the information related to the projects developed within each Software Factory.

For the two phases, information on the activities executed within the Software Production component has been collected, and only work in the Analysis & Design, Programming, and Testing units has been considered.

Input. The input variable will be evaluated by the DEA model. In the case considered, two variables have been considered for the two phases, and they have been widely studied to evaluate the efficiency of software-development projects. They are:

- *Total Effort (TE).* Measured in hours (hrs.), TE is the work effort used in the software factories and their respective projects. It considers the effort of the Analysis & Design, Programming, and Testing work units. This variable has been widely used in several studies (Banker & Kemerer, 1989; Banker et al., 1991; Banker et al., 1994; Mahmood et al., 1996; Myrtveit & Stensrud, 1999; Flitman, 2003, Stensrud & Myrtveit, 2003; Yang & Paradi, 2004; Asmild et al., 2006; Parthasarathy & Anbazhagan, 2008; Pendharkar & Rodger, 2009; Pai et al., 2015; Altiner & Ayhan, 2018).
- *Project Cost (PC).* PC is the cost of the project expressed in American dollars (US $), including costs incurred in the software factories and their projects through the Software Production work units. This variable has been analyzed and used in Paradi et al. (1997)

Output. The Output variable that will be evaluated by the DEA model. In the case considered, the variable Function Points (FP) represents the size of the software and is the unit of measurement used in the different software factories and for their projects, obtained through the estimation process and responsible for the accounting FPs at the end of the project. The development process specifies that the FPs are estimated at the beginning and end of the project to show the changes through the project. This variable has been widely used in the studies of Banker & Kemerer, 1989; Banker et al., 1991; Banker et al., 1994; Flitman, 2003; Asmild et al., 2006; Parthasarathy & Anbazhagan, 2008; Pendharkar & Rodger, 2009; Pai et al., 2015.

Model. The study, Input Oriented DEA Variable Returns to Scale model (DEA VRS-I) (Banker et al., 1984), because its goal is to minimize the Total Effort and Project Cost inputs and maintain the current outputs (number of Function Points) of the software factories and their respective projects.

Phases identify efficiencies in two phases: Phase 1 is the Software Factory and Phase 2 is the Software Factory Projects.

- *Phase 1.* This phase will identify the most efficient software factories through the minimization of the Total Effort and Project Costs consumed in a period determined by the factories. However, the number of Function Points must be maintained, so DEA VRS-I is used because the inputs are minimized, and the outputs remain at their current level. This model assumes two inputs, one output, and n DMUs:

Minimize θ (1)

s.t.

$$\sum_{j=1}^{6} \lambda_j \cdot x_{ij} \le \theta x_{io} \quad i=1,2 \tag{2}$$

$$\sum_{j=1}^{6} \lambda_j \cdot y_j \ge y_o \tag{3}$$

$$\sum_{j=1}^{6} \lambda_j = 1 \tag{4}$$

$$\lambda_j \ge 0 \quad j=1,2,\ldots,n \tag{5}$$

where θ represents the measure of productivity or efficiency of the software factory; x_{ij} is the ith input (x_{1j} is the Total Effort and x_{2j} is the Project Cost) of the factory j (DMU$_j$); y_j and λ_j are the output (Function Points) and the assigned coefficient or weight of factory j, respectively; and x_{io} and y_0 are respectively the ith input and the output of the factory under evaluation (DMU$_0$).

The model will determine the efficiency of the Software Factory through the minimization of the *Total Effort* and *Project Cost* (1) in the virtual DMU. Therefore, if $\theta = 1$ the virtual DMU requires as much input as does the real DMU under evaluation, so there is no evidence of inefficiency. If $\theta < 1$, the virtual DMU requires less inputs to obtain the output level achieved by the real DMU under evaluation, and thus the real DMU is inefficient. Restrictions are considered that will find the combination of inputs and weights (λ) that determine the most efficient software factory (2) and in which outputs are greater or remain constant (3). Likewise, the total weights that affect the inputs and outputs should be equal to 1 (4), and each weight must have a positive value (5). Table 3 shows the information to describe an example.

Table 3. Information about software factories

DMU	Sector	TE	PC	FP
SF001	Banking	54,788.36	2,161,797.26	1,700
SF002	Banking	17,268.00	663,962.77	594
SF003	Government	79,646.99	3,187,837.24	2,736
SF004	Government	62,700.98	1,779,787.46	1,500
SF005	Government	63,595.12	2,588,293.33	2,183
SF006	Government	109,362.63	4,232,423.03	3,760
Total		387,362.08	14,614,101.08	12,473

The DEA model of this example for the DMU *SF001* is as follows:

Minimize θ

$\lambda_1(54,788.36) + \lambda_2(17,268.00)\ldots + \lambda_6(109,362.36) \leq \theta(54,788.36)$

$\lambda_1(2,161,797.26) + \lambda_2(663,962.77)\ldots + \lambda_6(4,232,423.03) \leq \theta(2,161,797.26)$

$\lambda_1(1,700) + \lambda_2(594)\ldots + \lambda_6(3,790) \leq \theta(1,700)$

$\lambda_1 + \lambda_2 \ldots + \lambda_6 = 1$

$\lambda_1, \lambda_2, \ldots, \lambda_6, \theta \geq 0$

- Phase 2. This phase aims to identify the most efficient software factory projects through the minimization of the Total Effort and Project Cost consumed in a period determined by the projects, while maintaining the number of Function Points. This model assumes 2 inputs, 1 output, and *m* DMUs:

Minimize θ (6)

s.t.

$$\sum_{j=1}^{160} \lambda_j \cdot x_{ij} \leq \theta x_{io} \quad i=1,2 \tag{7}$$

$$\sum_{j=1}^{160} \lambda_j \cdot y_j \geq y_o \tag{8}$$

$$\sum_{j=1}^{160} \lambda_j = 1 \tag{9}$$

$$\lambda_j \geq 0 \quad j=1,2,\ldots,m \tag{10}$$

where θ represents the measure of productivity or efficiency of the software factory projects; x_{ij} is the ith input (x_{1j} is the Total Effort and x_{2j} is the Project Cost) of the project j (DMU$_j$); y_j and λ_j are the output (Function Points) and the assigned coefficient or weight of the project j, respectively; and x_{i0} and y_0 are respectively the ith input and the output of the project under evaluation (DMU$_0$).

Data Sources

Data Collection

The information for the present study was obtained from the different projects of the Software Factory of Palo Alto II (ex GMD SA), a Business Process Outsourcing, Information Technology (IT) and Digital Transformation company with great reliability and 33 years of experience in Peru. A staff of 3,000 professionals and adequate infrastructure make it the largest software factory in the country. It also has quality certifications such as ISO 9001, ISO 27001, OHSAS 18001, ISO 20000, ISO 22301, and NTP 392-030, and the methodologies CMMI-5, ITIL, and PMI (GMD, 2018). According to the international consultancy IDC (2017), it is the leading outsourcing company in Peru.

This company focuses on developing software solutions for the public and private sectors, under the software-factory model. It implements this model locally on each client's premises and uses its own staff, but it follows the guidelines of the parent software factory. Only 6 of the 18 existing software factories were selected for the present study, because they meet the criteria for conducting the activities of the Software Production component. Likewise, 160 projects distributed among the six software factories became part of the sample. They were developed between November 2015 and October 2017, and lasted approximately five to seven months. Initially, information on 200 projects was collected. However, due to inconsistencies in the data, a data depuration was conducted, resulting in 160 projects used for the respective analyses. The information obtained from the projects is related to the size of the project, the type of sector, the effort, and the costs of the project.

Descriptive Analysis of the Sample

The following paragraphs describe the information that has been considered for each phases of application of the model.

Phase 1

Information from software factories serving the Banking and Government (Table 4) is available at the following website: https://tinyurl.com/ycfyp5po

Table 4. Software factories considered in the sample

DMU	Sector	N° Projects	TE	PC	FP
SF001	Banking	23	54,788.36	2,161,797.26	1,885
SF002	Banking	7	17,268.00	663,962.77	594
SF003	Government	33	79,646.99	3,187,837.24	2,736
SF004	Government	22	62,700.98	2,424,477.46	2,153
SF005	Government	21	63,595.12	2,588,293.33	2,183
SF006	Government	54	109,362.63	4,232,423.03	3,760
Total		160	387,362.08	15,258,791.08	13,311

Table 5 shows the descriptive statistics for inputs and outputs of the software factories.

Table 5. Descriptive statistics for software factories' input and output variables

DMU	TE	PC	FP
Mean	64,560.35	$ 2,435,683.51	2,078.83
Median	63,148.05	$ 2,375,045.29	1,941.50
Std Dev	30,236.73	$ 1,221,597.77	1,091.09
Minimum	17,268.00	$ 663,962.77	594.00
Maximum	109,362.63	$ 4,232,423.03	3,760.00

Based on the information from the software factories, Figure 3 shows that only considering the amount of FPs produced, SF006 and SF003 have the highest productivity. However, factories SF004 and SF005 also present similar efforts and have lower costs, thus making it difficult to determine from the analysis whether these projects have been implemented efficiently. Thus, an analysis of productivity that considers only FPs is insufficient.

Figure 3. Software factories considered in the sample

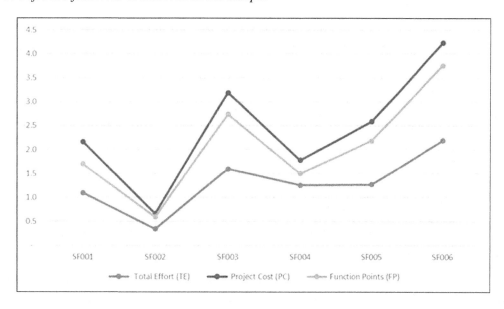

Additionally, Figure 4 shows that using the statistical technique of linear regression focused on averages indicates that factory SF004 is the most productive, since it is on the trend line, and the others (SF001, SF002, SF003, SF005, and SF006) should improve their productivity which is below average. Therefore, an analysis of productivity that considers only the averages of productivity is insufficient.

Figure 4. Statistical regression line for software factories

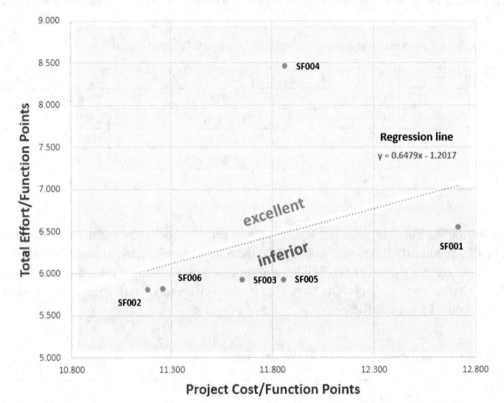

Phase 2

This phase considers 160 projects developed by the 6 factories selected from Phase 1. Table 6 shows 10 of the 160 software-factory projects used in the analysis. The information is available at https://tinyurl.com/ycfyp5po

Table 6. Software factories projects considered in the sample

DMU	TE	PC	FP
SP001	1,427.84	$ 45,267.01	49.00
SP002	1,279.90	$ 41,195.87	28.00
SP003	1,063.74	$ 41,162.56	25.00
SP004	1,043.02	$ 40,567.90	25.00
SP005	1,358.80	$ 52,708.51	36.00
SP006	1,385.02	$ 52,679.84	10.00
SP007	1,991.80	$ 77,004.22	69.00
SP008	3,888.00	$ 178,606.37	120.00
SP009	1,530.50	$ 69,905.58	50.00
SP010	2,304.00	$ 81,217.63	62.00

EMPIRICAL RESULTS AND INTERPRETATIONS

The DEA VRS-I model was used to evaluate the relative efficiency of the software factories and their respective projects with multiple inputs (Total Effort and Project Cost) and an output (Function Points). The results were computed with the DEAP v2.1 software (Centre for Efficiency and Productivity Analysis, 2018). Table 8 shows a list of abbreviations used in the interpretation of the results.

Table 7. Descriptive statistics for software factories projects' input and output variables

DMU	TE	PC	FP
Mean	2,421.01	$ 91,338.13	77.96
Median	1,781.07	$ 73,292.85	61.00
Std Dev	1,672.68	$ 54,284.23	47.47
Minimum	1,012.00	$ 34,196.03	10.00
Maximum	13,524.05	$ 328,033.66	282.00

Table 8. Table of abbreviations

Acronym	Full name
DEA	Data Envelopment Analysis
CRS	Constant Returns to Scale
VRS	Variable Returns to Scale
TE	Technical Efficiency
CRSTE	Constant Returns to Scale Technical Efficiency
VRSTE	Variable Returns to Scale Technical Efficiency
SE	Scale Efficiency
IRS	Increasing Returns to Scale
DRS	Decreasing Returns to Scale
VRS_{EFF}	VRS efficient projects

The results obtained for the two phases under evaluation are described below.

Phase 1

Of the six software factories analyzed, two efficient DMUs (VRSTE = 1) satisfy the one-third rule. This outcome indicates that the size of the sample is acceptable if the number of efficient DMUs is not more than one-third of the total number of DMUs in the sample (Cooper, Seiford, & Zhu, 2004). Therefore, the sample size is acceptable. Table 9 shows the efficiency (VRSTE) of the software factories for the DEA VRS-I model.

Table 9. DEA VRS-I efficiency – software factory

DMU	SF001	SF002	SF003	SF004	SF005	SF006
VRSTE	0.893	1.000	0.977	0.937	0.996	1.000

Figure 5 shows a summary of the efficiencies.

Figure 5. Efficiency summary

```
EFFICIENCY SUMMARY:

 firm  crste  vrste  scale

 SF001  0.893  0.893  1.000  -
 SF002  1.000  1.000  1.000  -
 SF003  0.977  0.977  1.000  -
 SF004  0.933  0.937  0.995 drs
 SF005  0.996  0.996  1.000  -
 SF006  1.000  1.000  1.000  -

 mean  0.966  0.967  0.999

Note: crste = technical efficiency from CRS DEA
      vrste = technical efficiency from VRS DEA
      scale = scale efficiency = crste/vrste

Note also that all subsequent tables refer to VRS results
```

According to Figure 5, on average, the efficiency scores of the software factories are as follows.

- 96.6% for CRSTE. In general, software factories could reduce their inputs by 3.4% to obtain the same number of FPs.
- 96.7% for VRSTE. A better software factory could reduce the consumption of inputs by 3.3%.
- 99.9% for SE. By adjusting the scale, software factories could reduce their inputs by 0.1%.

Results of the SF004 are analyzed below:

Figure 6 shows that SF004 has a "pure" efficiency score of 93.7% and a scale efficiency score of 99.5%, with a tendency toward decreasing returns to scale (DRS). By improving the operation of the software factory, the use of inputs could be reduced by 6.3% (100 - 93.7). By adjusting the software factory to its optimum size, the use of inputs could be reduced by 0.5% (100 - 99.5).

Figure 6. Results for SF004

```
Results for SF004:
Technical efficiency = 0.937
Scale efficiency    = 0.995   (drs)
 PROJECTION SUMMARY:
  variable              original      radial       slack     projected
                           value     movement    movement        value
  output  Points          1.500        0.000       0.000        1.500
  input   Effort         62.700       -3.959     -15.538       43.203
  input   Cost         1780.000     -112.388       0.000     1667.612
 LISTING OF PEERS:
  peer    lambda weight
  SF006      0.281
  SF002      0.719
```

Column "original value" contains the original values of the study variables of the software factory. SF004 produces 1.5 FPs with 62.7 hours of effort and with a total cost of $1,780. However, SF004 could produce the same number of FPs with fewer inputs, with 43.20 hours instead of 62.7, and $ 1667.612 instead of $1,780 (see column "projected value"). The reduction in TE and PC inputs is 6.31% of the original values: ((- 3.959 / 62.7) x 100) for the TE input and ((- 112.388 / 1780) x 100) for the PC input. However, in the case of the TE input, in order to become efficient, not only must it be reduced by 6.31% (minus 3.959 from the "radial movement" column), but it must also be reduced by an additional 15.538 (column "slack movement"). That is, for the TE input to become efficient, it must be reduced by 31.1%. To improve its efficiency, SF004 must analyze the practices of SF006 and SF002, which are identified as peers. To be a pair (or benchmark), a software factory must have a "pure" efficiency score of 100%. The lambda weight associated with each pair corresponds to its relative importance among the peer group. Ideally, SF004 should analyze the best practices from a software factory composed of 28.1% of SF006 and 71.9% of SF002. Since a "virtual" software factory does not exist, SF004 should concentrate on analyzing the best practices of the pair associated with the higher lambda value. Therefore, it should be compared with SF002.

Table 10 shows VRSTE reference software factories for each software factory considered in the sample. A reference software factory is always selected from a set of factories established at the efficient frontier. In the case of the VRSTE model, a reference factory will always be an efficient factory of similar size to the factories that consider it as a reference (Stensrud & Myrtveit, 2003)

Table 10. DEA VRS-I efficiency – software factory

DMU	Input-Oriented VRSTE	Benchmark (Optimal Lambda)	
		SF006	SF002
SF001	0.893	0.344	0.656
SF002	1.000		1.000
SF003	0.977	0.656	0.344
SF004	0.937	0.281	0.719
SF005	0.996	0.500	0.500
SF006	1.000	1.000	

Table 10 shows the list of all the factories in first column, their efficiencies in the second column, and weights associated with reference factories SF006 and SF002 in the third and fourth columns, respectively. For example, factory SF004 can improve its efficiency by approaching the efficient frontier, and the closest Pareto solution is given by the weighted combination (weights) of SF002 and SF006 (Virtual Software Factory A). Additionally, SF002 is more suitable as a reference factory because it allows for the generation of greater productivity with less effort and lower costs than SF006 (71.9% vs. 28.1%), as seen in Figure 7, where Factories SF002 and SF006 are located at the VRS efficiency frontier.

Figure 7. VRS reference set for the software factory

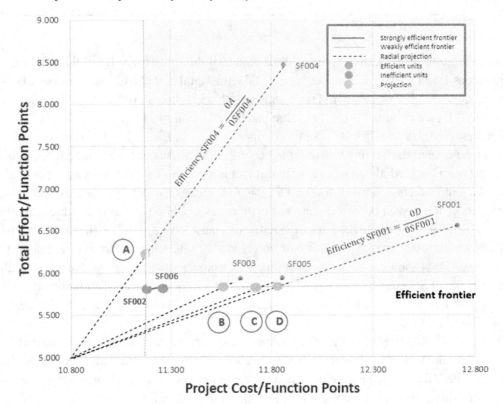

Phase 2

Ten efficient projects of 160 evaluated projects were identified (See Table 11).

Figure 8 shows efficient projects. Those projects that apply best practices and reflect greater productivity are SP036 (SF004) and SP030 (SF002). Note that the most efficient project is not within the most efficient software factory. If the efficient software factory projects were to replicate the best practices or strategies from project SP036, they would increase their productivity. Additionally, software factories with the most efficient projects are SF005 and SF004.

Table 12 shows descriptive statistics for the model.

Table 11. DEA VRS-I efficiency—software factory projects

DMU	VRSTE	Software Factory (SF)	Frequency
SP023	1	SF004	0
SP030	1	SF002	68
SP036	1	SF004	131
SP046	1	SF004	4
SP065	1	SF006	5
SP079	1	SF005	52
SP095	1	SF005	7
SP122	1	SF005	41
SP136	1	SF003	49
SP146	1	SF001	40

Figure 8. Times each project is a peer for another

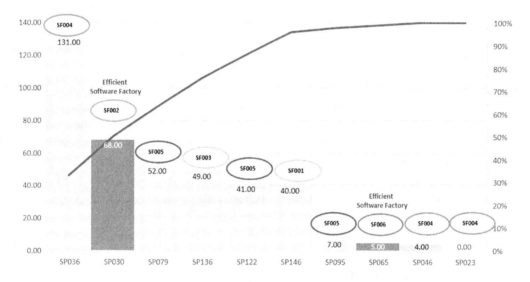

Table 12. DEA VRS average efficiency

	N	CRSTE	VRSTE	SE	VRS$_{EFF}$
Projects Software Factory	160	0.906	0.940	0.963	10

According to Table 12, the average efficiency scores of the software factories are:

- 90.6% for CRSTE. In general, software factory projects could reduce their inputs by 9.4% to obtain the same number of FPs.
- 94.0% for VRSTE. A better software factory project could reduce the consumption of inputs by 6%.

- 96.3% for SE. When adjusting the scale, software factory projects could reduce their inputs by 3.7%

Of the 160 projects analyzed, 10 are efficient DMUs (VRTSE = 1), approximately 6.3% of the DMUs. In addition, the one-third rule indicates that the sample size is acceptable if the number of efficient DMUs is not more than one-third of the total number of DMUs in the sample (Cooper et al., 2004). Since the number of DMUs is 160 and the number of efficient projects is 10, then the rule is satisfied (Banker & Kemerer, 1989). A DMU with efficiency less than 1 is relatively inefficient with respect to its benchmarks. In the Appendix, Table 13 shows the VRS reference projects for each software factory project considered in the sample. A reference project is always selected from a set of projects established in the efficient frontier. In the case of the DEA VRS model, a reference project will always be an efficient project of similar size to the projects that consider it as a reference (Stensrud & Myrtveit, 2003). The table shows the list of all the projects in the first column, and the reference projects with their respective Lambda in the second. For example, project SP001 has three projects in its reference set: projects SP030, SP036, and SP079. Additionally, project SP079 is a more important reference than projects SP036 and SP030 (84.8% vs. 12.3% and 2.9%, respectively).

CONCLUSION

This paper presents a model for the measurement of productivity based on DEA, which takes into account information from software factories and was implemented and executed in Peru. The study used the Input Oriented DEA Variable Returns to Scale model (DEA VRS-I) to achieve the goal of minimizing inputs (Total Effort and Project Cost) and maintaining the current output (Function Points) of the software factories and their respective projects. Accordingly, the analysis occurs in two phases. Phase 1 considers the evaluation of the software factories by considering the Total Effort and Project Cost as inputs and the Function Points as output. Phase 2 evaluates the productivity of the projects conducted by the software factory.

Results show that after analyzing 6 software factories and 160 projects variously implemented among them, the model identifies the most efficient software factory. The same factory serves as the model for factories of the same size and/or complexity. This facilitates the task of managing projects, since the orientation toward benchmarking operations will be to determine what efficient practices does this factory implement that make it the model to follow.

The model also identifies the most efficient projects in Phase 2, which shows that measurement is necessary at both the software factory level and the level of its projects. As the results show, a model software factory does not necessarily have the most efficient projects. Conducting a two-phase analysis illustrates factors of these projects that could be implemented and lead to improving efficiency. As verified with the results, the most efficient software factories could improve their productivity if they take into account the best practices that are implemented in the projects. This model enables elimination of the bias of measuring productivity in comparison with other statistical techniques, as seen in the linear regression analysis, where efficient projects are often considered unnecessarily.

Study Limitations

Tests conducted were limited to software factories in Peru and their respective projects, and have only been oriented to Analysis and Design, Programming, and Testing work units, which belong to the Software Production component.

Future Works

Future studies could consider the DEA variant (DEA Network) to measure the efficiency of the work units of the Software Production component in a way that enables performance of a comprehensive study of the software factory. Such a study may be able to establish improved opportunities for generating better results at the software factory level.

Additionally, future studies should consider the analysis of the software factory variants of DEA so as to be able to assess productivity by taking into account either the maximization of the outputs or the minimization of the inputs. Likewise, the design of strategies that allow software factories and / or projects to achieve better productivity should be considered, taking the factories and / or projects in the efficient frontier as their basis. An entity may not necessarily be efficient and homogeneous with the evaluation. However, it must have its roots in reality since the efficient entity is not real, but a linear combination of other existing entities (Virtual Software Factory).

ACKNOWLEDGMENT

Authors thank the reviewers for their suggestions that have helped improve this work. This research was partially supported by the Universidad Peruana de Ciencias Aplicadas and the Universidad Nacional Mayor de San Marcos.

REFERENCES

Altiner, S., & Ayhan, M. B. (2018). An approach for the determination and correlation of diversity and efficiency of software development teams. *South African Journal of Science*, *114*(3-4), 1–9. doi:10.17159ajs.2018/20170331

Asmild, M., Paradi, J. C., & Kulkarni, J. C. (2006). Using data envelopment analysis in software development productivity measurement. *Software Process Improvement and Practice*, *11*(6), 561–572. doi:10.1002pip.298

Banker, R. D., Chang, H., & Kemerer, C. F. (1994). Evidence on economies of scale in software development. *Information and Software Technology*, *36*(5), 275–282. doi:10.1016/0950-5849(94)90083-3

Banker, R. D., Charnes, A., & Cooper, W. W. (1984). Some models for estimating technical and scale inefficiency in data envelopment analysis. *Management Science*, *30*(9), 1078–1092. doi:10.1287/mnsc.30.9.1078

Banker, R. D., Datar, S. M., & Kemerer, C. F. (1991). A model to evaluate variables impacting the productivity of software maintenance projects. *Management Science, 37*(1), 1–18. doi:10.1287/mnsc.37.1.1

Banker, R. D., & Kemerer, C. F. (1989). Scale economies in new software development. *IEEE Transactions on Software Engineering, 15*(10), 1199–1205. doi:10.1109/TSE.1989.559768

Cao, Q., Ching Gu, V., & Thompson, M. A. (2012). Using complexity measures to evaluate software development projects: A nonparametric approach. *The Engineering Economist: A Journal Devoted to the Problems of Capital Investment, 57*(4), 274-283.

Card, D. N. (2006). The challenge of productivity measurement. In *Proceedings of Pacific Northwest Software Quality Conference*, Portland, OR. Academic Press.

Cardoso, C., Bert, F., & Podestá, G. (2010). Modelos Basados en Agentes (MBA): definición, alcances y limitaciones. *Landuse, biofuels and rural development in the La Plata Basin.*

Castañeda, P., & Mauricio, D. (2018). A review of literature about models and factors of productivity in the software factory. *International Journal of Information Technologies and Systems Approach, 11*(1), 48–71. doi:10.4018/IJITSA.2018010103

Castañeda, P., & Mauricio, D. (in press). New factors affecting productivity of the software factory. *International Journal of Information Technologies and Systems Approach.*

Centre for Efficiency and Productivity Analysis. (2018). *DEAP: A Data Envelopment Analysis (Computer) Program* V2.1. Retrieved from https://economics.uq.edu.au/cepa/software

Charnes, A., Cooper, W. W., Lewin, A. Y., & Seiford, L. M. (1994). Data envelopment analysis: theory, methodology, and applications'. New York: Springer Science + Business Media.

Charnes, A., Cooper, W. W., & Rhodes, E. (1978). Measuring the efficiency of decision making units. *European Journal of Operational Research, 2*(6), 429–444. doi:10.1016/0377-2217(78)90138-8

Cheikhi, L., Al-Qutaish, R. E., & Idri, A. (2012). Software productivity: Harmonization in ISO/IEEE software engineering standards. *Journal of Software, 7*(2), 462–470. doi:10.4304/jsw.7.2.462-470

Chung, S. H., Lee, A. H. I., Kang, H. Y., & Lai, C. W. (2008). A DEA window analysis on the product family mix selection for a semiconductor fabricator. *Expert Systems with Applications, 35*(1-2), 379–388. doi:10.1016/j.eswa.2007.07.011

Clements, P. C., & Northrop, L. M. (2001). *Software product lines: Practices and patterns.* Boston: Addison-Wesley Longman Publishing.

Coelli, T., Estache, A., Perelman, S., & Trujillo, L. (2003). *Una introducción a las medidas de eficiencia para reguladores de servicios públicos y de transporte.* Bogotá: Banco Mundial /Alfaomega.

Cook, W. D., & Seiford, L. M. (2009). Data envelopment analysis (DEA)–Thirty years on. *European Journal of Operational Research, 192*(1), 1–17. doi:10.1016/j.ejor.2008.01.032

Cooper, W. W., Seiford, L. M., & Tone, K. (2006). *Introduction to data envelopment analysis and its uses with DEA solver software and references.* New York: Springer Science and Business Media.

Cooper, W. W., Seiford, L. M., & Zhu, J. (2004). *Handbook on data envelopment analysis*. New York: Springer. doi:10.1007/b105307

Cusumano, M. A. (1989). The software factory: A historical interpretation. *IEEE Software*, 6(2), 23–30. doi:10.1109/MS.1989.1430446

Farrell, M. J. (1957). The measurement of productive efficiency. *Journal of the Royal Statistical Society. Series A (General)*, 120(3), 253–290. doi:10.2307/2343100

Flitman, A. (2003). Towards meaningful benchmarking of software development team productivity. *Benchmarking: An International Journal*, 10(4), 382–399. doi:10.1108/146357703104484999

GMD. (2018). GMD. Lima, Perú. Retrieved from http://www.gmd.com.pe/

IDC. (2017). *Latin America Semiannual IT Services Tracker*. Retrieved from http://www.gmd.com.pe/novedades/noticias/news-15

Jacobson, I., Booch, G., & Rumbaugh, J. (2000). *El proceso unificado de desarrollo de software* (pp. 321–322). Madrid: Pearson Educación S.A.

Jiang, Z., Naudé, P., & Comstock, C. (2007). An investigation on the variation of software development productivity. *International Journal of Computer and Information Science and Engineering*, 1(2), 72–81.

Khan, R., Ahmed, I., & Faisal, M. (2014). An industrial investigation of human factors effect on software productivity: Analyzed by SEM model. *International Journal of Computer Science and Mobile Computing*, 3(5), 16–24.

Liu, W., Meng, W., Li, X., & Zhang, D. (2010). DEA models with undesirable inputs and outputs. *Annals of Operations Research*, 173(1), 177–194. doi:10.100710479-009-0587-3

López, C., Kalichanin, I., Meda, M. E., & Chavoya, A. (2010). Software development productivity prediction of small programs using fuzzy logic. *Proceedings of the Seventh International Conference on Information Technology*, Las Vegas, NV, April 12-14. Academic Press.

Machek, O., Hnilica, J., & Hejda, J. (2012). Estimating productivity of software development using the total factor productivity approach. *International Journal of Engineering Business Management*, 4, 4–34.

Mahmood, M. A., Pettingell, K. J., & Shaskevich, A. I. (1996). Measuring productivity of software projects: A data envelopment analysis approach. *Decision Sciences*, 27(1), 57–80. doi:10.1111/j.1540-5915.1996.tb00843.x

Moreira, C. I., Carneiro, C., Pires, C. S., & Bessa, A. (2010). A practical application of performance models to predict the productivity of projects. In T. Sobh (Ed.), *Innovations and advances in computer sciences and engineering* (pp. 273–277). Dordrecht, Netherlands: Springer.

Myrtveit, I., & Stensrud, E. (1999). Benchmarking COTS projects using data envelopment analysis. *Proceedings of METRICS'99*, Washington, D.C. (pp. 269-278). Academic Press. 10.1109/METRIC.1999.809748

Nwelih, E., & Amadin, I. F. (2008). Modeling software reuse in traditional productivity model. *Asian Journal of Information Technology*, 7(8), 484–488. Retrieved from http://medwelljournals.com/abstract/?doi=ajit.2008.484.488

Pai, D. R., Subramanian, G. H., & Pendharkar, P. C. (2015). Benchmarking software development productivity of CMMI level 5 projects. *Information Technology Management, 16*(3), 235–251. doi:10.100710799-015-0234-4

Paradi, J. C., Reese, D. N., & Rosen, D. (1997). Applications of DEA to measure the efficiency of software production at two large Canadian banks. *Annals of Operations Research, 73,* 91–115. doi:10.1023/A:1018953900977

Parthasarathy, S., & Anbazhagan, N. (2008). Evaluating ERP projects using DEA and regression analysis. *International Journal of Business Information Systems, 3*(2), 140–157. doi:10.1504/IJBIS.2008.016583

Pendharkar, P. C., & Rodger, J. (2009). The relationship between software development team size and software development cost. *Communications of the ACM, 52*(1), 141–144. doi:10.1145/1435417.1435449

Project Management Institute. (2017). *A guide to the project management body of knowledge (PMBOK guide).* Newtown Square, PA: Project Management Institute.

Sahoo, B. K. (2016). Ownership, size, and efficiency: Evidence from software companies in India. *Benchmarking: An International Journal, 23*(2), 313–328. doi:10.1108/BIJ-02-2013-0024

Scacchi, W. (1995). Understanding software productivity. In D. Hurley (Ed.), *Software engineering and knowledge engineering: Trends for the next decade* (pp. 37–70). Los Angeles: World Scientific Press. doi:10.1142/9789812798022_0010

Slaughter, S. A. (Ed.). (2014). *A profile of the software industry: Emergence, ascendance, risks, and rewards.* Business Expert Press.

Stensrud, E., & Myrtveit, I. (2003). Identifying high performance ERP projects. *IEEE Transactions on Software Engineering, 29*(5), 398–416. doi:10.1109/TSE.2003.1199070

Unluturk, M. S., & Kurtel, K. (2015). Quantifying productivity of individual software programmers: Practical approach. *Computer Information, 34*(4), 959–972.

Wray, B., & Mathieu, R. (2008). Evaluating the performance of open source software projects using data envelopment analysis. *Information Management & Computer Security, 16*(5), 449–462. doi:10.1108/09685220810920530

Yang, Z., & Paradi, J. C. (2004). DEA evaluation of a Y2K software retrofit program. *IEEE Transactions on Engineering Management, 51*(3), 279–287. doi:10.1109/TEM.2004.830843

Yannick, G. Z. S., Hongzhong, Z., & Thierry, B. (2016). Technical efficiency assessment using data envelopment analysis: An application to the banking sector of Côte D'Ivoire. *Procedia: Social and Behavioral Sciences, 235,* 198–207. doi:10.1016/j.sbspro.2016.11.015

Yilmaz, M., & O'Connor, R. V. (2011). An empirical investigation into social productivity of a software process: An approach by using the structural equation modeling. *Proceedings of the European Conference on Software Process Improvement 2011* (pp. 155-166). Academic Press. 10.1007/978-3-642-22206-1_14

Zhu, J. (2014). *Quantitative models for performance evaluation and benchmarking: Data envelopment analysis with spreadsheets.* Switzerland: Springer International Publishing.

ENDNOTES

[1]   Software industry consists of companies engaged in developing and marketing system and application software (Slaughter, 2014).

[2]   Cusumano defines it in terms of "mass-produced products including large-scale centralized operations, standardized and deskilled job tasks, standardized controls, specialized but low-skill workers, divisions of labor, mechanization and automation, and interchangeable parts. The development about factory implies the best practices of Software Engineering are applied systematically" (Cusumano, 1989, P.23).

This research was previously published in the International Journal of Information Technologies and Systems Approach (IJITSA), 13(2); pages 1-26, copyright year 2020 by IGI Publishing (an imprint of IGI Global).

APPENDIX

Table 13. VRS reference set for the software factory projects

DMU	Input-Oriented VRSTE	Benchmark (Optimal Lambda)									
		SP023	SP030	SP036	SP046	SP065	SP079	SP095	SP122	SP136	SP146
SP001	0.98687		0.029	0.123			0.848				
SP002	0.98617						0.274				0.726
SP003	0.99381					0.396		0.604			
SP004	0.98791					0.473		0.527			
SP005	0.99168									0.545	0.455
SP006	0.99404					0.139		0.861			
SP007	0.99997		0.050	0.743			0.207				
SP008	0.99455			0.757					0.243		
SP009	0.9952			0.438						0.563	
SP010	0.99207		0.066	0.389			0.545				
...											
...											
SP151	0.97853									1.000	
SP152	0.99198			0.879					0.121		
SP153	0.99173			0.771					0.229		
SP154	0.99791			0.219						0.103	0.678
SP155	0.99504		0.142	0.757			0.101				
SP156	0.9899		0.005	0.562			0.433				
SP157	0.99979		0.003	0.389			0.608				
SP158	0.99489		0.025	0.485			0.490				
SP159	0.98488									0.220	0.780
SP160	0.99771		0.532	0.212					0.256		

Chapter 41
A Simulation Model for Application Development in Data Warehouses

Nayem Rahman

Portland State University, Portland, OR, USA

ABSTRACT

Software development projects have been blamed for being behind schedule, cost overruns, and the delivery of poor quality product. This paper presents a simulation model of a data warehouse to evaluate the feasibility of different software development controls and measures to better manage a software development lifecycle, and improve the performance of the launched software. This paper attempts to address the practical issue of code defects in each stage of data warehouse application development. The author has compared the defect removal rate of their previous project to the newly proposed enhanced project development life cycle that uses code inspection and code scorecard along with other phases of software development life cycle. Simulation results show that the code inspection and code score-carding have achieved a significant code defect reduction. This has also significantly improved the software development process and allowed for a flawless production execution. The author proposes this simulation model to a data warehouse application development process to enable developers to improve their current process.

1. INTRODUCTION

Software development is laborious, expensive and unreliable. Hence, software development projects quite often encounter schedule slippage, cost overruns, and poor-quality software in both commercial and government sectors (Raffo & Wernick, 2001). To address this potential issue, we propose changes to the software development process. Smith and Rahman (2017) observe that "without efficient processes through which Information Technology (IT) builds and supports the technology, the full business-value potential will remain unrealized." Bringing the software project lifecycle under the radar of simulation

DOI: 10.4018/978-1-6684-3702-5.ch041

models could be good effort (Kellner et al., 2001). For the last four decades systems dynamics modeling and simulation techniques were applied in diverse disciplines of scientific, engineering and manufacturing processes (Richardson, 2013; Rashidi, 2016). According to the Merriam-Webster Online Dictionary, "simulation is the imitative representation of the functioning of one system or process by means of the functioning of another." Simulations run in simulation time, an abstraction of real-time (Imagine That Inc., 2014).

Simulation models are used to solve problems that arise in manufacturing (Barra Montevechi, 2016), business process design (Liu & Iijima, 2015), inventory management system (Cobb, 2017) and health care decision-making (Chick, 2006; Chen & Zhao, 2014). Martinez-Moyano and Richardson (2013) and others (Morrison, 2012; Mould & Bowers, 2013) listed 41 best practices of systems dynamics modeling and categorized them in terms of problem identification and definition, system conceptualization, and model formulation. Hughes and Perera (2009) argue that simulation could be integrated as a daily tool to solve problems. They present an easy-to-follow framework – consisting of five key stages, such as foundation, introduction, infrastructure, deployment and embedding - for enabling companies to embed simulation technologies into their business processes (Hughes & Perera, 2009). The work of Eatock et al. (2001) indicates that describing the dynamic behavior of IT could be very helpful for business process modelers in predicting the impact on organizational processes (Eatock et al., 2001). Software process simulation is suggested to be helpful to achieve higher Capability Maturity Model (CMM) levels in software development (Raffo et al., 1999).

In software engineering, simulation modelling has attracted considerable interest during the last decade (Ahmed et al., 2008). Software process simulation is used mainly to address the challenges of strategic management of software development and to support process improvements (Raffo & Kellner, 2000). In this work, we are making an attempt to leverage simulation modeling in a data warehouse application development. We developed a simulation model based on defined processes for the application development of a data warehouse reporting environment called Next Generation Capital Reporting (NGCR). In our recent project, we developed and implemented a Financial Reporting System (FRS) in the Enterprise Data Warehouse (EDW) environment. A data warehouse is used a central repository of data of medium and large business organizations. A data warehouse is considered as one of the key infrastructures of IT. And the capability of IT has a strong correlation between the agility and performance of an organization (Rahman, 2016a).

Industry and academic research suggest that when an EDW becomes successful at an initial stage more and more application development and reporting projects start to land each year. Research suggest that there is a correlation between the increase of the size of the data warehouse and increase of the value it brings to an organization (Rahman, 2016b). Engineering projects are complex (Rahman et al., 2016). From the standpoint of EDW projects complexity arise from multiple factors including different stakeholders' buy-in, software development effort, frequent changes of relevant tools and technologies, query performance issue, data validation, data quality, and production release timeliness. Therefore, it is quite challenging to maintain a stable data warehouse environment given it is an enterprise platform as well as a shared environment. Hence, some degree of discipline is needed in code development, code changes, testing, code performance optimization, system resource usage and configuration of integration specification (Rahman, 2016b). An EDW-specific simulation model can help in bringing discipline in data warehousing applications development and in improving overall quality of application development and reporting environment.

Our new EDW application development and reporting project was as big as the previous project (FRS). We made an attempt to simulate the software development process for the new project based on available data from recently completed project. Using this data, we developed different if-then scenarios and simulate a process of software development for the new project to better manage, control and measure the success of it. Through this model, we simulated requirement analysis, design process, construction and unit testing, code score-carding, integration, function testing, system testing and deployment into production environment. The goal was to reduce defects in each stage of the application development.

Our recent project (FRS) life cycle had issues in development and testing phases which impacted system availability and performance in production system and took a while to stabilize. There were job failures in production after go-live. In the past project, we have noticed that requirements, designing decision, and coding have changed repeatedly in each of wave of development. This made the life-cycle unpredictable and often resulted in extensive overtime to meet the project deadlines. In past project, prior to unit test code inspections were not done. We tested and moved code to production without meeting performance measurement criteria and based on whatever code developers had written. We had to do code rework after production release as part of stabilization. The cost of fixing defective code in production is 100 to 200 times more than fixing them in early stage of software development (Boehm & Turner, 2003; Khramov, 2006).

In implementing technically challenging projects it is important to make sure technological product breakthroughs are achieved and emerging tools and technologies are adopted (Rahman et al., 2016). This helps in delivering a project successfully and on time. Our new project envisioned a new way of thinking to develop a state of the art reporting system. At the very beginning we tried to find answers to various questions. How can we track the actual effort to understand the inefficiencies? Can we drive down the rework by doing a better job upfront during explore and requirements analysis phase? Can we reduce the construction work by doing code inspection? Can we drive down the testing effort, reduce failure rates while in the testing phase by properly managing design and construction and also give an adequate time to the tasks? Can we reduce the defect rate, maintain a good coding standard, and improve performance of objects by doing code inspection? Can we drive down the change request for the product in production environment, where change requests originate due to defects in production?

So, in the current project we have added one new phase called "Inspect Code" to the application development life-cycle. In this phase developers' code in terms of database management systems (DBMS) objects (business views, stored procedures, and macros) will be peer-reviewed by all developers in a code review meeting. Once it is verified and confirmed by the developer team chaired by the Developer Lead the subsequent steps of the life cycle will be done. Based on past project experience we added one more phase called "Score-card Code" to the application development life cycle. Once coding and unit testing is done, a senior developer from the EDW will score-card the code using some SQL's suggested by the data warehouse DBMS (database management system) vendor to identify the performance issue. If the score-carding indicates that it would cause performance issue the code would be re-worked in order to make sure that the code does not cause performance issue in terms of virtual spool space usage, longer run time, use of huge CPU and IO on the production data warehouse server. This phase will be done after coding and unit testing and before integration process phase. These new steps were added to make sure we do not have to re-work code much once landed on production server. We modeled both previous project data and current project process improvements via two simulation models – ASIS (previous project's life cycle stages) versus new model (with code inspection and code score-card steps introduced to the development lifecycle).

2. RESEARCH METHODOLOGY

Research suggest that data availability and data quality are the most challenging issues in many simulation projects (Onggo & Hill, 2014). For our project, we collected data from our previous project implementations. Here we provide a brief description of data collection method and sources of data. We collected data regarding development and database objects from EDW source control repositories and Online Change Management (OCM) tools. The data consists of Extract-Transform-Load (ETL) code, defects in code, code-rework, and code-score-card. We looked at the history of code changes and reworks in each of the code units (stored procedures, macros, and business views) under previous project (FRS) and current project (NGCR system) and collected the statistics in terms of mean (average) values.

Based on source control repository we collected documentation relating to different phases of a past project. The repository was used to identify change requests and reworks in different phases. Gantt charts were used in the past project were utilized to get the data on resources used, amount of work and rework done in different releases of a past project. The OCM tool was used to track the list of items, implemented objects, failed objects, and error logs of different releases of the past project. The configuration management reports in terms of EDW source control and OCM tools have been used as the data source for each of the project phases. The EDW source control and OCM information against each code module and phases of the project life cycle were translated into effort / time used for each phase of project life. For simulation model purposes, they are compiled in a spreadsheet.

Simulation experimentation and analysis provided several opportunities (Taylor & Robinson, 2009): better integration of optimization, better visualization for experimentation, guidance on scenario selection, various options for exploring solution space, quick model development easy to understand analysis, real-time experimentation to assess likely effect of making different decisions, recommendations for number of replications, and wider experimentation support. Lorenzo and Diaz (2005) suggest a framework for process gap analysis and modelling of enterprise systems. They propose a four-step method which includes current situation analysis; business process improvements and requirements; gap analysis; and to-be processes based on which simulation is developed (Lorenzo & Diaz, 2005). Yang et al. (2015) propose adopting a simulation-based optimization algorithm in achieving performance and efficiency.

Figure 1 provides different stages of system to be tested in our model. First, we get business requirements from the business analysts (BA). We review the requirements with different stakeholders including customers, data analysts, developers and business intelligence (BI) analysts. Project BA's are contacted if more information is needed. After requirements are finalized data analysts (DA) are contacted to design the tables to create underlying tables for reporting environments. Data analysts will also provide design documents. The design documents are reviewed with ETL developers and handed over to the developers. The ETL developers will write code to perform ETL work. Their code will be reviewed by ETL architects. If changes are needed, code rework will be done and later unit test will be conducted. Before moving code from development environment to testing environment, ETL code will be score-carded using some pre-defined guidelines (Rahman, 2016c). This score-card involves selecting units of complex code and putting them in a SQL score-card tool and then running the code to identify if the program units were written with poor coding including longer runtime and database spool space, heavy utilization of computing resource such as IO and CPU. After identifying these issues, a senior developer will re-work code. This sometimes requires significant amount of code change as well as table structure change. After score-card is completed unit test of the code will be conducted again. If unit test does not pass, re-work of the code will be needed. The next step is to perform functional testing of the system. If the objects do not pass the testing then send for code rework. Once testing cycles go through successfully and user acceptance testing are completed the code will be deployed into production.

Figure 1. Behavioral diagram of ETL development

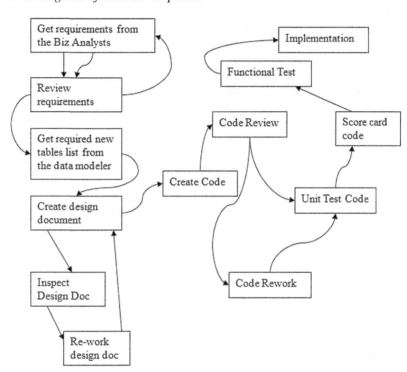

Lee et al. (2009) observe that development of enterprise software systems requires the collaboration of many stakeholders to allow them to perform what-if analyses before making their decisions (Lee et al. 2009). For data warehousing projects, we show stakeholders in the behavioral diagram consisting requirements gathering, analysis, design, development testing, score-carding, unit and functional testing and then implementing in production environment (Figure 1). "The utility and benefits of a well-defined requirements engineering process are cited in many articles describing software engineering research and similar industry studies" (Arthur & Nance, 2007). Ryan and Heavey (2006) present a process modelling technique and Simulation Activity Diagrams (SADs) which could be used to support the initial requirements gathering phases of a simulation project.

Figure 2 depicts the model process flow diagram used to build the simulation model. The purpose of building the simulation model is to (1) determine actual effort; (2) see how to reduce the re-work; (3) see how to reduce construction work by code inspection; (4) identify how to reduce testing effort and failure rates; (5) identify how to reduce defect rate; and (6) drive down job failure rate by code inspection.

Figure 2. Process flow diagram

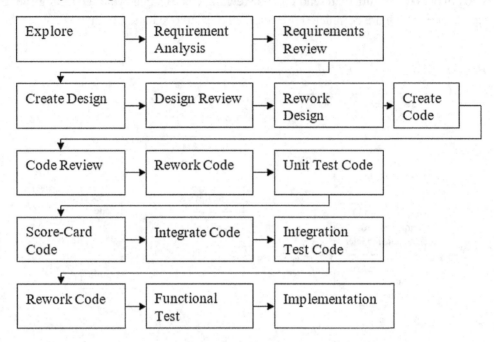

3. THE SIMULATION PROCESS MODEL

The simulation model was built based on certain timeframe, spatial boundaries, entities, attributes, and key assumptions. "A model is an abstracted and simplified representation of a system at one point in time" (Imagine That Inc., 2014). In this work, the simulation model was divided along the major life-cycle phases. As a result, there are separate model for requirement process, design process, code and unit test process, integration process, function testing process, and system testing process. These steps are incorporated into simulation and tested under different scenarios. Possible what-if analysis fills this gap by enabling users to "simulate and inspect the behavior of a complex system under some given hypotheses" (Golfarelli & Rizzi, 2009).

For this project, we used the ExtendSim® simulation software (Imagine That Inc., 2014) to build the model. In ExtendSim® blocks are used to model activities, resources, and the routing of jobs throughout the process. Additional blocks are used to collect data, calculate statistics, and display output graphically with frequency charts, histograms, and line plots (Imagine That Inc., 2014). The model predicts the number of person-months of efforts, calendar months of schedule and remaining defects shipped to the customer for about 1500 function point system. These 1500 function points flow through the model as a set of about 20 entities. Here we are using the same number of FP as used by Jones' baseline model (Jones, 2008). In his seminal book titled, Applied Software Measurement: Global Analysis of Productivity and Quality' Jones (2008) state that, "a function point is an abstract but workable surrogate for the goods that are produced by software projects. Function points are the weighted sums of five different factors that are of interest to users (inputs, outputs, logical files, inquiries, and interfaces)."

In our organization, we do not have any pre-defined function point (FP) system for software projects. So, we decided to use a FP of about 1500. We are calculating a total defect of 7500 to flow through the model. The defect per function point comes from requirements bug, design bugs, and source code bugs (Table 1). And defect per FP is calculated based on recent project data pulled from the EDW source code control, Visual Source Safe (VSS), OCM tool and log files.

Table 1. Defects per origin, per function point

Description	Data Source	Total Defects	Defects per FP
Requirements Bugs	Source Control and OCM - Calculated	1125	0.75
Design Bugs	Source Control and OCM - Calculated	2700	1.8
Soruce Code Bugs	Source Control and Production Logs	3675	2.45
Total		7,500	5

3.1. New Sub-Model - Score Card Process

Through score-carding (Rahman, 2016a) what we want to make sure is that the code we are introducing into data factory meets coding standards and performance criteria. At a high level, we were ensuring that tables referenced have the appropriate statistics on them, that we were not doing inefficient product joins with large tables, CPU and I/O are within reason for the system we are score-carding against, and that we were not introducing skewed processes on the system.

Figure 3. New component for score card

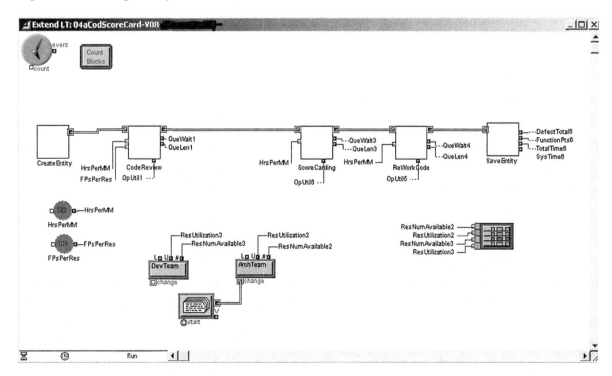

Figure 3 has the following underlying equations and calculations:

1. **Creates Entity:** Has inFile; Decision5: if (EntityNum >= 1) Path = Path1; else Path = Path2;
2. **CodeProcess:** Eqn to Calculate different values; defect rate=0.0;
3. **ScoreCarding:** Eqn to Calculate different values; defect removal rate= triangular;
4. **ReworkCode:** Eqn to Calculate different values;
5. **SaveEntity:** Has two out files:
    5. File-1:

EntityNum=Generated19

TotalTime=64105

FunctionPts= Generated -1565

DefectTotal=6265

DefectRem=563

    5. File-2:

TotOpr=37231

EntityNum=Generated19

Table 2 shows the triangular operation values per function point.

Table 2. Score carding, code re-work process

Activity	Data Source	Average Effort per FP/SM	Distribution/Comments
Import	Overall Model	0	None
Code Process		0.009 (Min = 0.0072; Max = 0.0108)	Triangle Operation - +/- 20%
Score Card Code		0.009 (Min = 0.0144; Max = 0.0216)	Triangle Operation - +/- 20%
Re-Work Code		0.002 (0.0016/0/0024) & 0.019 (0.0152/0.0228)	Operation - Number of Defects X Re/Def; Triangle Operation - +/- 20%
Export	Overall Model	0	None

Triangular provides a good first approximation of the true values consisting of three pieces of information (the minimum, the maximum, and the most likely values) which are known. (Imagine That Inc. 2014). A triangular distribution is flexible and it prevents extremes compared to uniform and normal distributions (Doane, 2004). We came up with parameter values based on previous data as well as current project's preliminary data. Parametric uncertainties in system dynamics models can cause undesirable behavior (Ng et al. 2012). We used Average Effort per FP/ SM and defects removal percent. And we used Triangular distribution with different values to handle uncertainty. The simulation software ExtendSim uses three parameters to sample from the triangular distribution.

3.2. Interpretation of the Results

Code inspection gives tremendous improvement. Table 3 shows that defect has reduced from 43% (AS-IS) to 86% (full model). Score-carding process has reduced defect rates and spool space, CPU/IO.

Table 3. Defect removal summary

Activity	Total Defects; Defect Remaining	New Model	AS-IS Model
Requirements	Defect Total = 1179; Defect Remaining = 353	70% Removed	70% Removed
Design	Defect Total = 3995; Defect Remaining = 1433	64% Removed	60% Removed
Code Unite Test	Defect Total = 6265; Defect Remaining = 879	86% Removed	43% Removed
Code Score Card	Defect Total = 6265; Defect Remaining = 563	91% Removed	Not used
Integration	Defect Total = 6265; Defect Remaining = 396	93% Removed	50% Removed
Functional Test	Defect Total = 6265; Defect Remaining = 274	95% Removed	65% Removed
System Test	Defect Total = 6265; Defect Remaining = 144	97% Removed	82% Removed

Table 4 shows that after introducing code inspection and score-carding the defect export to next phases of life-cycle has reduced significantly - AS-IS vs. Full model. Score-carding process had made it possible to send less defects in terms of spool space issue, CPU consumption and IO generations.

Table 4. Decreased defect export to the next phase

Activity	Total Defects; Defect Remaining	New Model	AS-IS Model
Requirements	Defect Total = 1179; Defect Remaining = 353	30% defect sent	30% defect sent
Design	Defect Total = 3995; Defect Remaining = 1433	36% defect sent	40% defect sent
Code Unite Test	Defect Total = 6265; Defect Remaining = 879	14% defect sent	57% defect sent
Code Score Card	Defect Total = 6265; Defect Remaining = 563	9% defect sent	Not used
Integration	Defect Total = 6265; Defect Remaining = 396	7% defect sent	50% defect sent
Functional Test	Defect Total = 6265; Defect Remaining = 274	5% defect sent	35% defect sent
System Test	Defect Total = 6265; Defect Remaining = 144	3% defect sent	18% defect sent to Prod

3.3. Questions Investigated and Results Obtained

We asked several questions in the simulation process:

1. Do source code inspections offer an improvement in process performance?
2. What would be the impact of reducing the error detection capability of source code inspection?
3. Would source code inspections still be worthwhile if the lowest reported error detection capability in the literature was achieved?
4. If there was only time to conduct either a source code inspection or a unit test, which method would be more effective?
5. Would source code inspections still be beneficial if the starting source code had more errors?
6. What is the cost currently being paid from conducting unit test incorrectly?

We reached the following conclusions:

1. Source code inspections significantly increase the quality of the resulting code;
2. The source code inspection process is an efficient error detection method if implemented correctly;
3. The process with source code inspections and unit test offers an overall improvement even if the inspection performance is poor;
4. If pressed for time, it is better to reduce unit testing rather than reduce inspections;
5. Inspections have a greater impact when the starting quality of the code is poor;
6. The process change offered significant reductions in remaining defects:
   a. Code inspection causes significant increases in error detection and do re-work;
   b. Score-carding makes sure code would perform efficiently in production;
   c. Doing code review would be a more effective process improvement than the creating unit test plans process change.

We decided not to relate the model with Return on Investment (ROI) and Net Present Value (NPV) due to the lack of specific data related to ETL development part of the project. We spoke with the business analysts to see if we could determine the ROI specifically for ETL part. They said ETL portion is not useful without the Front-End portion of the program/ system. The whole project has total ROI of several million dollars. Therefore, there was no need to value the simulation model's value in terms of ROI or NPV.

4. SIMULATION PROCESS STUDIED

"Discrete event simulation is a powerful tool that can address many problems that arise in manufacturing, business process design, health care decision-making, and a host of other areas" (Chick, 2006). This project was designed to simulate the ETL development process for the new project. In this model we simulated requirement analysis, design process, construction and unit testing, code score-carding, integration, function testing, and system testing before the deployment of an application development into production environment.

To see the difference between past and present project performance we made two versions of existing of the model. One contains only those life cycle phases that we had in previous project (FRS). In this simulation model, we have not used 'code inspection' phase. We call this model AS-IS. The other model, meant for new project, contains all phases of the simulation model provided by Jones (2008). In addition, we added one more sub-model/phase called "Score-card Code". This was introduced between sub-models Code-Unit-Test and Integration.

Figure 4. Overall simulation process model

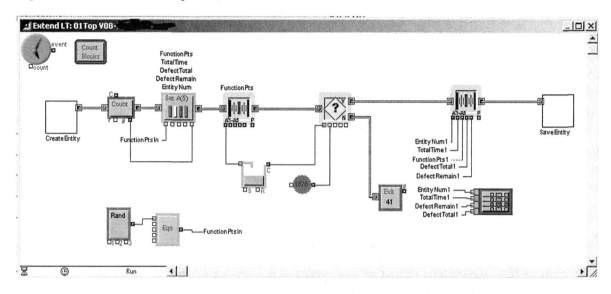

Figure 4 has the following underlying equations and calculations:

1. Creates Entity;
2. Random Input Number generates function points – triangular: min-25, max-150, mostlikely-75;
3. Constant value (limit function point): 1575;
4. Decision block:

if (TotalFpts < LimitFpts)

Path = YesPath;

else

Path = NoPath;

5. SaveEntity: Has outfile:

EntityNum=Generated19

TotalTime

FunctionPts= Generated -1565

DefectTotal=0

DefectRem=0

Based on new model and simulation we are able to improve the ETL development, testing, and production deployment significantly. We added one new phase, "Inspect Code", to the life-cycle. In this phase developers' code (business views, stored procedures, and macros) are reviewed by all developers in a code review meeting. Based on past project experience we added another phase named "Score-card Code" to the life cycle. Once coding and unit testing is done, a senior developer from the EDW does score-card the code using some SQL's suggested by the DBMS vendor to identify the performance issue (Rahman, 2016c). If the score-carding indicates that it might cause performance issue, the code would be re-worked in order to make sure that the code does not cause a lot of spool space, longer run time, use of lot CPU/IO on the production server. These new steps are added to make sure we do not have to re-work code much once deployed into production.

Table 5. New model defects reduction

Activity	Total Defects; Defect Remaining	New Model	AS-IS Model
Code Unit Test	Defect Total = 6265; Defect Remaining = 879	14% defect sent	57% defect sent
Code Score Card	Defect Total = 6265; Defect Remaining = 563	9% defect sent	Not used
System	Defect Total = 6265; Defect Remaining = 144	3% defect sent	18% defect sent to Prod

Table 5 shows that code inspection gives tremendous improvement – system defect has reduced from 82% (AS-IS) to 97% (full model). Score-carding has reduced defect rates, huge spool space generation, CPU consumption and IO generation.

5. MODEL VERIFICATION AND VALIDATION

Verification and validation are the critical aspects of a simulation model (Sargent, 2013). Model verification is the process of determining that a model operates as intended. Model verification is also meant for the "process of debugging a model to ensure that every portion operates as expected" (Imagine That Inc., 2014). With the help of verification process, we try to find and remove unintentional errors in the logic of the model. Using this process, we determine if we have to build the model right (i.e., if it matches our mental model). Verification compares implemented model to conceptual model. Model validation is the process of reaching an acceptable level of confidence that the inferences drawn from the model are correct and applicable to the real-world system being represented (Laguna & Markland, 2005).

We compared data with simulation results in terms of Average Effort per FP/ SM, add/ remove Defects Percent. We verified that measures are calculated in the same manner throughout the model in both as-is and to-be. We verified that simulation results accurately represented the data that was gathered. The model represents the assumptions (e.g., defects per FP, defect removal rate) that were made regarding how the system operates. Different phases of software life cycle correspond to the underlying structure of the model. We looked at data of the system and it confirms that the simulation model works as intended. The results of the simulation made sense to us. Simulation tests reveal that the flow of function points, defect accumulation, and defect removal worked properly through the model. Comparison of simulation results with historical data from the past projects and with some data from new project validated the results.

In testing phase, we did sensitivity analysis which allowed to vary a parameter incrementally, randomly, or in an ad hoc manner to determine how sensitivity model results look when a change is made to one variable. We used sensitivity set-up dialog and conducted sensitivity analysis on Average Effort per FP/ SM (Triangle Operation), Defects per FP, Defects Percent removal (Triangle Operation), and resource usage to see the total defects and defects remaining, etc.

6. CONCLUSION

We have developed two simulation models, one (AS-IS model) based on software life-cycle phases/ steps of previous project (FRS) and the other (NGCR Model) is based on current project (NGCR). The AS-IS model contains no Code Inspection and Score-carding steps as we did previous project without these steps. The NGCR model contains Code Inspection and Score-card phase/ step as we introduced these processes in new project.

After doing several runs of both AS-IS and new models we found that Code inspection gives tremendous improvement in driving down defects at the initial phase of PLC rather compared to the as-is model in which defects were exported to the last phases and even in production. The results show that the new model is able to remove 86% defects compared to 43% in as-is model. This indicates that 'code inspection' process worked well to achieve this defect removal rate. The results also showed that the new model was able to remove 91% defects at Score-card and rework phase. The results also showed that under new model, 97% defects are removed before it went to Production compared to 82% under the as-is model. The overall simulation result showed a pretty impressive overall defect removal rate at early stages compared to the as-is model.

The newly introduced Score-carding phase in the NGCR model also worked well to reduce defect rates and generate less spool space, CPU/IO. This phase has helped reduce by 5% defects after code unit testing and re-work phase and before integration phase. The source-code inspections and score-carding have significantly increased the quality of the resulting code. It has proved to be an efficient error detection method if implemented correctly. Even with poor inspection methodologies, the process with source code inspections and unit test still seemed to offer an overall improvement. Inspections made an even greater impact when the starting quality of the code is poor. Installing defective code in production causes job failure issue which in turn causes failure to meet service level agreement (SLA). We found it challenging to overcome this issue. The new steps under the NGCR simulation model shows that we performed well in production with regards to meeting the SLA.

This simulation modeling brings a lot of positive impact on the company: (1) it supports strategic process improvement goals of higher CMM levels (Sen et al. 2006); (2) the upcoming EDW ETL development projects will be benefited from the results of this simulation model; (3) it supports business case analysis of process changes; (4) it provides quantitative risk assessment prior to the introduction of process changes; and (5) it helps to obtain management buy-in for process change and collection of further metrics.

ACKNOWLEDGMENT

The author is grateful to anonymous reviewers whose comments have improved the quality of the article substantially. The author also thanks David Springer, a Supply Chain Product Manager, for doing an excellent editing job.

REFERENCES

Ahmed, R., Hall, T., Wernick, P., Robinson, S., & Shah, M. (2008). Software process simulation modelling: A survey of practice. *Journal of Simulation*, 2(2), 91–102. doi:10.1057/jos.2008.1

Arthur, J. D., & Nance, R. E. (2007). Investigating the use of software requirements engineering techniques in simulation modelling. *Journal of Simulation*, 1(3), 159–174. doi:10.1057/palgrave.jos.4250021

Barra Montevechi, J., da Silva Costa, R., de Pinho, A., & de Carvalho Miranda, R. (2016). A simulation-based approach to perform economic evaluation scenarios. *Journal of Simulation*, (February). doi:10.1057/jos.2016.2

Boehm, B., & Turner, R. (2003). Observations on balancing discipline and agility. In *Proceedings of the IEEE Agile Development Conference (AGILE'03)* (pp. 32-39).

Chen, C., & Zhao, S. X. (2014). Modeling and simulation analyses of healthcare delivery operations for inter-hospital patient transfers. *International Journal of Operations Research and Information Systems*, 5(1), 76–94. doi:10.4018/ijoris.2014010106

Chick, S. E. (2006). Six ways to improve a simulation analysis. *Journal of Simulation*, 1(1), 21–28. doi:10.1057/palgrave.jos.4250006

Cobb, B. R. (2017). Optimization models for the continuous review inventory system. *International Journal of Operations Research and Information Systems*, 8(1), 1–21. doi:10.4018/IJORIS.2017010101

Doane, D. P. (2004). Using simulation to teach distributions. *Journal of Statistics Education: An International Journal on the Teaching and Learning of Statistics*, 12(1).

Eatock, J., Paul, R. J., & Serranto, A. (2001). A study of the impact of information technology on business processes using discrete event simulation: A reprise. *International Journal of Simulation Systems, Science & Technology. Special Issue on Business Process Modelling*, 2(2), 30–40.

Golfarelli, M., & Rizzi, S. (2009). What-if simulation modeling in business intelligence. *International Journal of Data Warehousing and Mining*, 5(4), 1–20. doi:10.4018/jdwm.2009010101

Hughes, R. W. C., & Perera, T. (2009). Embedding simulation technologies into business processes: Challenges and solutions. *International Journal of Simulation and Process Modelling*, 5(3), 184–191. doi:10.1504/IJSPM.2009.031093

Imagine That Inc. (2014). ExtendSim user guide, ExtendSim. Retrieved from http://www.extendsim.com/

Jones, C. (2008). Applied software measurement: Global analysis of productivity and quality (3rd ed.). McGraw-Hill Osborne Media.

Kellner, M. I., Madachy, R. J., & Raffo, D. M. (1999). Software process simulation modeling: Why? What? How? *Journal of Systems and Software, 46*(2-3), 91–105. doi:10.1016/S0164-1212(99)00003-5

Khramov, Y. (2006). The cost of code quality. In *Proceedings of the IEEE Agile 2006 Conference (AGILE'06)* (pp. 119-125). 10.1109/AGILE.2006.52

Laguna, M., & Markland, J. (2005). *Business process modeling, simulation, and design.* Upper Saddle River, New Jersey, USA: Pearson Education, Inc.

Lee, S., Celik, N., & Son, Y.-J. (2009). An integrated simulation modelling framework for decision aids in enterprise software development process. *International Journal of Simulation and Process Modelling, 5*(1), 62–76. doi:10.1504/IJSPM.2009.025828

Liu, Y., & Iijima, J. (2015). Business process simulation in the context of enterprise engineering. *Journal of Simulation, 9*(3), 206–222. doi:10.1057/jos.2014.35

Lorenzo, O., & Diaz, A. (2005). Process gap analysis and modelling in enterprise systems. *International Journal of Simulation and Process Modelling, 3/4*(3/4), 114–124. doi:10.1504/IJSPM.2005.007642

Martinez-Moyano, I. J., & Richardson, G. P. (2013). Best practices in system dynamics modeling. *System Dynamics Review, 29*(2), 102–123. doi:10.1002dr.1495

Morrison, J. B. (2012). Process improvement dynamics under constrained resources: Managing the work harder versus work smarter balance. *System Dynamics Review, 28*(4), 329–350. doi:10.1002dr.1485

Mould, G., & Bowers, J. (2013). A comparison of process modelling methods for healthcare redesign. *International Journal of Simulation and Process Modelling, 8*(2/3), 168–176. doi:10.1504/IJSPM.2013.057539

Ng, T. S., Sy, C. L., & Lee, L. H. (2012). Robust parameter design for system dynamics models: A formal approach based on goal-seeking behavior. *System Dynamics Review, 28*(3), 230–254. doi:10.1002dr.1475

Onggo, B. S. S., & Hill, J. (2014). Data identification and data collection methods in simulation: A case study at ORH Ltd. *Journal of Simulation, 8*(3), 195–205. doi:10.1057/jos.2013.28

Raffo, D. M., & Kellner, M. I. (2000). Empirical analysis in software process simulation modeling. *Journal of Systems and Software, 53*(1), 31–41. doi:10.1016/S0164-1212(00)00006-6

Raffo, D. M., Vandeville, J. V., & Martin, R. H. (1999). Software process simulation to achieve higher CMM levels. *Journal of Systems and Software, 46*(2-3), 163–172. doi:10.1016/S0164-1212(99)00009-6

Raffo, D. M., & Wernick, P. (2001). Guest Editorial: Software Process Simulation Modelling. *Journal of Systems and Software, 59*(3), 223–225. doi:10.1016/S0164-1212(01)00063-2

Rahman, N. (2014). A system dynamics model for a sustainable fish population. *International Journal of Technology Diffusion, 5*(2), 39–53. doi:10.4018/ijtd.2014040104

Rahman, N. (2016a). *An empirical study of data warehouse implementation effectiveness. International Journal of Management Science and Engineering Management.* doi:10.1080/17509653.2015.1113394

Rahman, N. (2016b). Enterprise data warehouse governance best practices. *International Journal of Knowledge-Based Organizations*, 6(2), 21–37. doi:10.4018/IJKBO.2016040102

Rahman, N. (2016c). SQL scorecard for improved stability and performance of data warehouses. *International Journal of Software Innovation*, 4(3), 22–37. doi:10.4018/IJSI.2016070102

Rahman, N., Wittman, A., & Thabet, S. (2016). Managing an engineering project. *International Journal of Information Technology Project Management*, 7(1), 1–17. doi:10.4018/IJITPM.2016010101

Rashidi, H. (2016). Discrete simulation software: A survey on taxonomies. *Journal of Simulation*, (May). doi:10.1057/jos.2016.4

Richardson, J. (2013). The past is prologue: Reflections on forty-plus years of system dynamics modeling practice. *System Dynamics Review*, 29(3), 172–187. doi:10.1002dr.1503

Ryan, J., & Heavey, C. (2006). Requirements gathering for simulation. In *Proceedings of the 3rd Simulation Workshop*.

Sargent, R. G. (2013). Verification and validation of simulation models. *Journal of Simulation*, 7(1), 12–24. doi:10.1057/jos.2012.20

Sen, A., Sinha, A. P., & Ramamurthy, K. (2006). Data warehousing process maturity: An exploratory study of factors influencing user perceptions. *IEEE Transactions on Engineering Management*, 53(3), 440–455. doi:10.1109/TEM.2006.877460

Smith, A. W., & Rahman, N. (2017). Can agile, lean and ITIL coexist? *International Journal of Knowledge-Based Organizations*, 7(1), 78–88. doi:10.4018/IJKBO.2017010105

Sterman, J. D. (2000). *Business dynamics: Systems thinking and modeling for a complex world*. USA: McGraw-Hill Higher Education.

Taylor, S. J. E., & Robinson, S. (2009). Simulation software: Evolution or revolution? *Journal of Simulation*, 3(1), 1–2. doi:10.1057/jos.2008.25

Yang, N., Wang, S., & Schonfeld, P. (2015). Simulation-based scheduling of waterway projects using a parallel genetic algorithm. *International Journal of Operations Research and Information Systems*, 6(1), 49–63. doi:10.4018/ijoris.2015010104

This research was previously published in the International Journal of Operations Research and Information Systems (IJORIS), 9(1); pages 66-80, copyright year 2018 by IGI Publishing (an imprint of IGI Global).

Section 3
Tools and Technologies

Chapter 42

Use of Qualitative Research to Generate a Function for Finding the Unit Cost of Software Test Cases

Mark L. Gillenson
University of Memphis, Memphis, USA

Thomas F. Stafford
Louisiana Tech University, Ruston, USA

Xihui "Paul" Zhang
University of North Alabama, Florence, USA

Yao Shi
University of Memphis, Memphis, USA

ABSTRACT

In this article, we demonstrate a novel use of case research to generate an empirical function through qualitative generalization. This innovative technique applies interpretive case analysis to the problem of defining and generalizing an empirical cost function for test cases through qualitative interaction with an industry cohort of subject matter experts involved in software testing at leading technology companies. While the technique is fully generalizable, this article demonstrates this technique with an example taken from the important field of software testing. The huge amount of software development conducted in today's world makes taking its cost into account imperative. While software testing is a critical aspect of the software development process, little attention has been paid to the cost of testing code, and specifically to the cost of test cases, in comparison to the cost of developing code. Our research fills the gap by providing a function for estimating the cost of test cases.

DOI: 10.4018/978-1-6684-3702-5.ch042

INTRODUCTION

This is a demonstration of case research used to generate an empirical function, and it is an unusual contribution to the literature in that respect. Mathematical expressions of functionality are usually developed statistically, supported with survey or simulation data (Akhavein et al., 1997; Kurfman et al., 2003). It is rare for a case study to be quantitative, yet mathematical functions can (conceivably) be derived in this way since deductions involving mathematical propositions are a subset of formal logic and nothing in formal logic is tied to a specific methodology (Lee, 1989). The evidence that is considered in case studies can be qualitative, quantitative, or both (Eisenhardt, 1989), but the primary purpose of a case study is to generate theory (Yin, 2013) and a theoretical representation of cause and effect (as is typically found in a statement of mathematical logic, such as a response function) is not out of the question in case research, just rare (Lee, 1989). It is, practically speaking, more likely that response equations would lead to case studies (Hengl et al., 2007), since many statistical techniques benefit greatly from a qualitative interpolation process. In contrast to the conventional wisdom on case study uses and outcomes, however, we utilize an in-depth case study of industry experts to directly induce an empirical function through qualitative generalization (e.g., Yin, 2013).

Our methodology demonstrates the derivation of the variables and interrelated functionality of a candidate empirical expression. This methodology can be used in any situation in which there is a need to develop an empirical expression from case-based, qualitative research. While we will describe our innovative methodology in general terms, we believe that a detailed exposition of its actual use is essential to both understanding the process and to demonstrating its worth.

The actual example we have chosen is that of developing a function to estimate the cost of developing and executing a test case in the software testing process. The outcome of this process results in the description of the cost of generating and utilizing a functional test case for software testing purposes; this outcome of our case research is much in the way that Yin (2013) and Eisenhardt (1989) each suggests extracting theoretical meaning from case research. In that sense, the contribution of this study lies in generalizing from qualitative inquiry to a theoretical construction, as Yin and Eisenhardt would put it. For clarity, this will necessitate our providing some explanation of the elements of generating and executing software test cases, and of the software testing process, itself.

Case studies, concentrated as they are on a focused and bounded phenomenon embedded in a context, are particularly useful for identifying context-specific meaning (Eisenhardt, 1989; Miles et al., 2013). We consider that case study methods are typically intended to lead to theoretical developments as their own unique modality of generality (Yin, 2013), rather than the broad extension of generality to other contextual areas as is so typically the case with quantitative research. In that manner, we consider this in-depth investigation of software testing cost factors to be a revelatory approach (Sarker et al., 2012; Yin, 2013) meant for specific and detailed understanding of a unique context.

In addition, one of the most important potential theoretical contributions that could be made in the software development literature would be a functional model useful for determining the costs components of software testing, and this is an additional contribution of this study: the derivation of an empirical cost function as a generalization from an interpretive case study of software testing engineers brought together in a cohort as part of a certification program on software testing.

RESEARCH BACKGROUND

Importance of the Software Testing Problem

With the pervasiveness of software in most human activities, software defects may result in tremendous monetary and human loss. For example, in April 2015, a Bloomberg terminal in London crashed due to a technical issue in a third-party platform supplier. The shutdown forced the British Treasury to postpone 3 billion pounds (about USD $4.46 billion), in a short-term debt sale (Popper & Gough, 2015). Then in March 2018, a pedestrian was killed by an Uber's self-driving car in Tempe, Arizona. The self-driving software detected the pedestrian but incorrectly classified her as a "false positive" and decided the self-driving car did not need to stop (Lee, 2018). This fatal crash also resulted in Uber's self-driving program being stopped in North American where a large amount of money had been invested. There are numerous other cases resulting from software defects which ultimately could be attributed to insufficient software testing.

Software testing is a critical and an integral aspect of software development (Batra et al., 2016; Whitaker et al., 2012; Zhang et al., 2013), designed to find and correct the errors that arise in the software development process (Khan, 2010). However, the dilemma is that software cannot be tested exhaustively given testing resource constraints. Moreover, testing is increasingly costly, as a direct function of the increased complexity of software that is produced (Subramanian et al., 2017), yet there is little research that objectively demonstrates the way in which testing, costly as it is, contributes to the overall value of the development process (Balijepally et al., 2017; Talby et al., 2006). With the vagaries of development requirements, the complexity of designing and writing code, and the translation issues in moving from one stage of software development to the next, testing software to make sure that it accurately does what it was intended to do is an imperative part of the process. In fact, the artifacts produced in each development stage must be tested. In earlier stages of development, such as requirements and systems analysis stages, testing generally means conducting reviews and inspections of the development artifacts for comments by a knowledgeable team (Crowston & Scozzi, 2008; Whitaker et al., 2012). While the code itself can be (and often is) reviewed in this manner, historically most software testing effort has gone into executing the code with well-planned test cases (Mathur, 2014).

All types of testing represent a significant cost to the software development organization (Tassey, 2003). With the pressure that these organizations face to produce, maintain, and upgrade large numbers of applications, there is a natural tendency to invest their resources in code generation rather than in code testing. Some suggest that testing is more important in scenarios where internal software development is eschewed in favor of outside purchase of software (e.g., Subramanian et al., 2017). Others highlight the importance of a robust testing regime in coordination with internal software development processes (e.g., Talby et al., 2006). It is our view that the importance of testing should not be underestimated in either case, and that it is essential to manage testing effectively, across the board.

One key aspect of managing testing has to do with gauging its cost (Burnstein, 2006). Much is known of how to cost out the broader activity of software development (e.g., Boehm, 1981), but the art of putting a cost base to the software testing process rarely enters consideration in contrast to the larger question of overall development costs. It is important to understand software testing costs better, as they contribute in important but subtle ways to the overall quality – hence business value – of the software product that is developed (Haas, 2014; Jefferey et al., 2000; Koch & Neumann, 2008; Xu et al., 2011).

It is not an easy task to develop objective cost models for the key components of software testing, as there are several cost components to deal with and not much agreement on how to deal with them. Just as with the broader concept of development costs, understanding cost bases is typically approached as a constructive model (e.g., Boehm, 1981; Jefferey et al., 2000), and it stands to reason that aspects of testing costs will array in similar component-oriented models, as well. In this case, we consider the components of cost for software test cases, one of the critical aspects of software testing and a critical component of both testing costs and quality control performance.

These components of cost include a variety of costs associated with personnel, equipment, and time needed for testing. There is also the issue of testing effort as related to the cost of software development at a general level (Batra et al., 2011; Subramanian et al., 2017), and while empirical results of assessing the performance of leading software cost models generally indicated "poor" performance (Subramanian et al., 2017), this still does not decouple the specific testing cost issue for detailed consideration.

Of course, we understand that the costs specifically related to software testing are necessary since the costs associated with fixing an application with defects found later in production can be much higher (Haas, 2014), but it is hard to develop an objective understanding of software testing costs when they are embedded as part of an overall software development cost approach. As a discipline, our philosophical approach to software development and analysis is linked to the notion of functional decomposition and the separate and unique consideration of software testing costs serves a similarly useful goal when decoupled. That is the basis of our approach, in response to a clear gap in the literature that indicates very little work done in the way of specific consideration of aspects of the cost basis of testing outside its role as an embedded process in the larger context of software development.

The Gaps in Software Testing Cost Research

The existing literature pertaining to development and testing cost/effort estimates in software engineering indicates three logically related themes. One, accurate estimation of software development and testing effort is critical (Srinivasan & Fisher, 1995). Two, estimates obtained at a very early stage are more useful (Sharma & Kushwaha, 2012). Three, predicting the cost of software development and testing at an early stage is difficult (Srivastava, 2015). A comprehensive literature review on software cost research has led us to identify two issues: (1) the existing literature pertaining to development and testing cost/ effort estimates focuses more on development than on testing (e.g., Idri et al., 2015; Srinivasan & Fisher, 1995); (2) the existing literature pertaining to development and testing cost/effort estimates rely more on algorithmic models or techniques such as CoCoMo, fuzzy logic, and genetic algorithms (e.g., Idri et al., 2015; Srivastava, 2015).

This paper focuses on one aspect of the cost of testing: the unit cost associated with a test case used in functionality testing. By this we mean the costs incurred by creating and running a single particular test case. There are compelling reasons for an interest in this. There is a gap in research on software testing, and it resides largely in the lack of explanation of what is known about software development costs to the cost basis of software testing. Well-established software development cost models, such as the Constructive Cost Model (CoCoMo) (Boehm, 1981), are fulsome guides to the functional decompensation (i.e., work breakdown structure) of the testing process for costing purposes (e.g., Tausworth, 1979-1980), and yet the functional components of software testing do not receive much attention despite their critical nature in their contribution to the overall quality perceptions of developed software (Hass, 2014).

It is in recognition of this gap in the literature that we engaged in our effort to derive and quantify an empirical cost function through our interactions with a cohort of highly experienced software testing engineers. The richness of our emerging understanding of the details related to the costs of software testing led us to realize that targeted interaction with experienced software testers from industry would yield incredibly rich information about the testing process and its economic costs to the firm.

WORK BREAKDOWN STRUCTURE OF TEST CASE COSTING

The number of test cases used to test a piece of code can vary widely and in some ways is a function of the manner in which the test cases were developed (Dorofeeva et al., 2010). For that matter, the abilities of testers to generate effective test scenarios vary greatly between individuals (Talby et al., 2006), leading to further issues of cost-benefit outcomes in the testing regime. To this end, knowing the costs associated with the elements of the testing processes, to wit, the test case generation process, provides for a firmer understanding of the overall testing process and can lead to greater work efficiency and cost effectiveness, with attendant organizational benefits.

Test cases for functionality testing can be created in several ways with varying costs. They can be created manually as part of the requirements writing process. They can be created by any of several "black box" or "white box" heuristic techniques (Alijumaily et al., 2014). They can also be introduced from actual production inputs of an existing system that is being modified or completely rewritten.

To our knowledge, no one has attempted to develop a function that will guide the calculation of the cost of a functional test case and this was the goal of our research, in combination with the demonstration of the novelty of developing empirical cost functions from qualitative case analysis. This paper addresses a gap in the literature that concerns the value of testing as a contribution to the overall software development process (Talby et al., 2006) as expressed in the relative absence of a codified understanding of the specific costs associated with testing. It also generates a unique application of theoretical generality from case analysis in qualitative contexts related to the software development process.

In consideration of the value that testing contributes to the software development process, there is a story to be told about how testers view the costs of assembling, evaluating, and using test cases as part of the software development quality control regime, and we tell that story here with the aid of a group of experienced professional software developers and testers whom we interviewed in depth and from which we develop important perspectives of the costs associated with the testing approach.

To further our investigation, we engaged in interpretive research (e.g., Walsham, 1995; 2006), building a case study with a cohort of software testing engineers who were highly knowledgeable professionals in the software testing craft. A descriptive phenomenological approach was undertaken aimed at close examination of the cohort's experiences in order to elucidate the essence of the phenomena of focus in order to understand, distill, and explicate an emergent model of the costs associated with creating and running a test case for effective software testing purposes.

THE LITERATURE ON SOFTWARE TESTING COSTS

There is some scholarly literature on the nature of processes of software testing, but there is almost nothing for scholarly consideration about the costs of software testing. What exists is a more generalized literature on the costs of software development, which is not quite the same thing, but is tangentially useful to generalize from. Important books such as Boehm's (1981) work on software economics, Whittaker et al.'s (2012) insider view of how software is developed at Google, Wysopal et al.'s (2006) insights of software security testing, and Hass's (2014) guide to advanced software testing have been useful if not specifically on target for purposes of grounding the notion of testing costs for further examination.

On the Books – Popular Press Approaches

Boehm (1981) provides a complex and comprehensive overview of the entirety of software development costs from an almost econometric perspective. It is useful in that it provides the well-known and intuitive Constructive Cost Model (CoCoMo), which is the foundational basis for most work breakdown structure approaches to software development costing that follow in later writings by other authors. We readily adhere to the same notion in our derivation of an empirical cost function for software test cases: the problem is made manageable by detailed examination of its component elements. Hass' (2014) recent book on software testing does not provide a derived modeling approach as per Boehm, but rather emphasizes the quality control perspective of software costing: the predominant philosophy is that the tester contributes greatly to firm value by finding defects early rather than later, and the efficient and expedient identification and correction of defects contributes to the bottom line in the form of boosting perceptions of the business value of the delivered product.

Google's approach to software testing, as documented in the book from Whittaker et al. (2012), is concerned more with the tools that catalog and track testing processes than the costs entailed; the implicit point is that testing costs are best controlled through better test management and documentation. The Wysopal et al. (2006) book from Symantec on security testing simply espouses leading edge methods for threat modeling and, as such, represents yet another quality-control perspective to the testing process as opposed to illuminating any particular cost factors – such as the cost of functional test cases, which is our focus.

Lack of Testing Costs Literature

Owing to the demonstrable lack of specifically focused software test costs literature, we feel that there is a story to be told in a scholarly journal context and from a scientific viewpoint about the software testing process and its costs. This can benefit other researchers interested in this process. Investigating the software testing process in a context in which its nature can be examined in deep and descriptive ways for the benefit of other interested researchers is an essential first step in the development of scientific literature on the cost of software testing. A revelatory case study achieves this end, and this is why we chose it as our research approach.

There are some scholarly journal articles on the economic factors of software development from which generalizable ideas can be gathered. Boehm's published work in journals (as opposed to his similarly valuable books on the topic) is particularly useful since his primary view has been on the economic factors of software engineering (cf., Boehm et al., 1995; Boehm et al., 2000). There is also Ellims et al.'s (2006) perspective of unit testing economics, which comes very close to what we study here, as well as Jørgensen and Shepperd's (2007) review of software development cost studies. Authors such as Gray and MacDonell (1997), Jefferey et al. (2000), and Tausworthe (1979-1980) also provide detailed views of the costs of software development and cost estimation that can be considered for grounding purposes.

What is known from this small body of cost-based work related to the broader topic of the software development process is that researchers do not exactly agree on how to accurately estimate software costs under various contexts (Boehm et al., 2000), which implies the potential for a similar disagreement on testing costs. Tallying in the billions of dollars every year (Tassey, 2003), the cost of software is not an inconsiderable topic. To that end, one presumes that the cost of testing software is similarly impactful and important, since estimates are that as much as half of total software development expenditures are consumed in software testing (Ellims et al., 2006).

Generalizing From Expertise-Based Estimating Methods

In view of the lack of scholarly literature on the topic, the way forward appears to lie in tapping the expertise of industry professionals directly involved in the process of estimating costs related to software testing (e.g., Boehm, 1981). A prominent approach exists for tapping such expertise, familiar to most researchers: case analysis (e.g., Jeffery et al., 2000). In such analysis, the meaning necessary to understand emergent phenomena is developed and generalization is limited to theoretical development (Yin, 2013) of which the generation of a descriptive cost function for software test cases might be representative.

Case Studies for Understanding Software Testing

Learning-oriented techniques based on specific cases can be applied to estimate software engineering costs, and such case studies dealing with the underlying relationships between cause and effect can be used as critical reference points. Such approaches are supported by several knowledgeable authorities on the software development process (cf., Boehm, 1981; Briand et al., 1999; Jeffery et al., 2000), and the approaches are characterized variously as "analogy estimating techniques" or "estimation by analogy," referring to the approach of learning from historical projects. Gray and MacDonell (1997) considered that case-based reasoning may be favored because it can provide simpler, more effective, and more intuitively appealing methods of classification and estimation than other approaches. This is quite consistent with Yin's (2013) guidance on case-based theoretical generalizations.

Work Breakdown Structure in Case Analysis

The various approaches to understanding costs in software development, and by extension, the generalizations that may be made to costs of software testing, benefit greatly from specific identification of individual cost elements, and this is best identified by the work breakdown structure (WBS) method. WBS, as it is known in the practice, is an important planning tool which links objectives to resources and activities in a logical framework (Tausworthe, 1979-1980). This approach has been used in software engineering cost estimation (e.g., Boehm, 1981). It stands to reason that a piece-by-piece consideration for the cost structure of software testing would be similarly beneficial.

Considering the convergence of expert opinion in a case-based approach to understanding the costs of generating and running software test cases, in combination with the functional decomposition inherent in the WBS approach, provides a ready scenario for developing a rich and detailed rubric for the costs related to the development and the use of software test cases to support the testing process. Although some scholars, e.g., Malishevsky et al. (2006) and Huang et al. (2012), have attempted to take cost into account in their methods, their approaches neglect the testing context and the testing process. To that end, we leverage a case-based, expert-led methodology for developing an initial iteration of a test case cost model.

THE METHOD AND OUR SAMPLE APPLICATION: DEVELOPING COMPONENTS FOR A TEST CASE COST FUNCTION

We employ case research as the basis for this method. Specifically, we leverage a descriptive phenomenology approach (e.g., Walsh & Downe, 2005) wherein small samples of respondents are leveraged to gain great detail on the experiences of interest in order to discern the key theoretical aspects of the phenomenon of study (e.g., Yin, 2013).

The method begins with the selection of the problem to be solved. The nature of the problem for which this method is applicable is the development of a mathematical function that will produce a useful result apropos to the problem. The nature of the result depends on the nature of the problem and the expectation of the derived function. To wit, the result may be an exact value, an approximate value, or a set of relative, comparative values.

The first step in creating the function is the selection of a "key informant." The key informant is an industry expert in the subject field who can work with the study principals to develop an initial function. This melding of expertise serves two purposes. One is to create a broadly plausible initial function. The other is to protect against any hidden biases within the study principals. In addition to the initial function, another outcome of the first step is the development of a series of probing questions about the elements of the function that will be used in the forthcoming interviews of a cohort of industry experts who will provide further guidance about the function.

Next, the cohort of industry experts is identified. Specifically, a cohort of 25-30 industry practitioners is identified, preferably from among several companies or organizations. The cohort can be from one company, making it something of a single-company case study, but, aside from possible single-company bias, this may be no less valuable.

Then, over several weeks, each industry practitioner is interviewed by a study principal. The duration of the interview is determined by the complexity of the problem being studied and of the initial function. Obviously, the more complex the problem and the initial function, the longer the duration of the interview. During each interview, the study principal explains the goal of the function being developed, describes the initial function in detail, and asks the probing questions about the function that were developed for this purpose. Additional questions about the initial function that arise as a result of a given interview may be added to the question list for succeeding interviews. The industry practitioner is expected to respond to the questions and is also encouraged to make any other comments about the initial function that come to mind. The principal dutifully takes notes (or records) the practitioner's comments. Later, the principal organizes the notes or transcribes the recordings into a reasonably standard format for later analysis.

After the practitioner interviews are completed, the principals study the accumulated comments and summarize them as they deem appropriate. One strategy is to order the comments based on perceived importance, as indicated by the practitioners and/or by the principals. Another is to note how many times essentially the same comment was made by different practitioners. After this is completed, the principals use the accumulated knowledge to modify and improve the function. The modifications and improvements can take several forms. New factors can be added to the function, existing factors can be modified or deleted, or factors can be combined and calculated in any appropriate way.

The final step is to present the improved function to the industry key informant and to the industry practitioners for comment and possible further adjustments. This can be done in person or by email. If done by email, the improved function must be accompanied by a clear, written description of the nature and reasoning behind the modifications to the function. If done in person, these can be presented verbally.

The Development of the Cost-of-a-Test Case Function

In order to understand the basis of test case cost components and methods, we initially sought the viewpoints of a senior manager in software testing from a Fortune 100 transportation company with extensive software testing operations. This key informant was utilized to guide the formation of our inquiry, and to begin the process of initiating our case study analysis (e.g., Kumar et al., 1993; Marshall, 1996; Tremblay, 1957). We utilized our initial meetings with our informant to set the context and benchmark our perceptions for the larger study. This served the purpose of the establishment of a conceptual framework in order to guide early phases of our data collection, as recommended by Miles et al. (2013).

In an extended interview, our informant guided us in our development of a conceptualization of the software testing regime, and the costs involved with developing and running test cases for the process. From this interaction, we derived candidate elements for an initial test case cost function, which was used as the focal basis for qualitative interviews with a series of software testing professionals at several leading technology companies.

The Initial Software Test Cost Function

Our initial functional unit cost calculus was based on the premise that when considering the cost of a test case, one must take into account not only the cost of creating the test case, but also the cost of running it, the cost of determining its success or failure, and, when necessary, the cost of using it to fix a defect in the code that it discovered. In our initial function, based on key informant guidance, the unit cost of functional testing is based on the following factors:

- Cost to create the test case input values (CIV);
- Cost to determine the expected output of the test case (CEO);
- Cost to run the test case (CRT);
- Cost to record the test results (CRR);
- Cost to evaluate the test results (CER);
- Cost to fix a defect if found (CFD).

Combining these factors in functional form, where n is the number of times the test case is run until the defect is fixed, the initial cost function is:

$$\text{Unit Cost} = \text{CIV} + \text{CEO} + \sum_{1}^{n} (\text{CRT} + \text{CRR} + \text{CER} + \text{CFD}) \tag{1}$$

Indeed, some of these factors are already well-known to software testing professionals, but they have not heretofore been organized into this type of comprehensive cost function.

The basic concept underlying this function is the recognition that the cost to create the test case and to determine its expected output is a one-time event, while the cost to run it and work with its results is repetitive and recurs each time it is executed in testing. This cost function is presented graphically in Figure 1.

Figure 1. Initial test case costs model

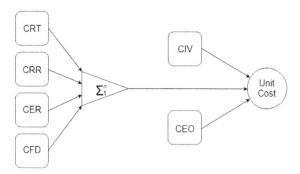

In detailing the elements of the initial cost function, the input values to the test cases can be created in several different ways. They can be created manually from text, which is the most expensive way. They can be created manually from pseudo-code, which is less expensive if requirements permitted. They can be created automatically using appropriate software, which is the least expensive way although set up costs would be incurred. They can also be created by any of several heuristic techniques. Finally, they can be adopted from actual inputs into production systems in the case where the current development effort either upgrades an existing system or completely replaces one. The associated cost of test case creation, CIV, varies among all of these various techniques. The cost to determine the expected output of the test case, CEO, is zero if the test case comes from a production system and has not been affected by requirements changes. Otherwise, the activity is a manual one with appropriate costs accruing to the lack of automation.

The cost to run a test case, CRT, varies depending on whether the test case is run manually or in an automated fashion. If automated, there is a cost to build the test scripts which should be amortized across all test runs. CRT also varies with the number of physical devices, operating systems, and combinations thereof, on which the software is to be tested. Additional costs associated with running a test case include the cost to record and report test results, CRR; also, the cost to evaluate the test results, CER, which varies depending on whether it is being done manually or in an automated fashion. Finally, there is CFD, the cost to fix a defect, arising from the cost of determining the source of the defect and the cost of actually fixing the code.

A functional test case can be designed to test a small module of code, an entire application, or any part of an application, such as the code that implements a particular feature of the application. What is necessary to the process is a well-defined set of input variables to the code and, for a given set of input variable values, an expected output based on the applicable business rules governing the application or part of the application being implemented by that code. Thus, a functional test case consists of a set of input variable values and an expected output value based on how the code is supposed to function.

Having developed an initial understanding of the breakdown structure of unit costs for a test case with key informant assistance, we determined to explore the meaning and potential expansion and modification of the model through a case-based consensus approach with a larger group of software testing professionals.

Qualitative Data Analysis

The preliminary cost function, as developed with our key informant, was used as the case-based focus for subsequent in-depth interviews with 28 industry expert software testing professionals recruited from a locally-sponsored software testing certification workshop (see Table 1 for participant characteristics).

Table 1. Characteristics of the case study cohort

Source	Business Sector	Interviewee Position / Role
Organization #1	Fortune 100 transportation company	Senior software testing engineer
		Senior software testing engineer and adjunct professor
		Software testing manager
		Senior software testing engineer and assistant to VP of software testing
		Software testing engineer
		Software testing engineer
		Senior software testing engineer
		Senior software testing engineer
		Software testing engineer
		Software developer and tester
		Senior software developer and tester
		Software testing engineer
		Software testing manager
		Software testing engineer
		Senior software testing engineer
		Software testing engineer
		Software testing engineer
		Software testing engineer
		Software testing engineer
Organization #2	Fortune 500 retailing company	Software testing engineer
Organization #3	Municipal utilities provider	Software developer and tester
		Software developer and tester
		Software developer and tester
Organization #4	IT consulting company	Software testing consultant
Organization #5	IT consulting company	Senior software testing consultant
Organization #6	University medical complex	Software developer and tester
Organization #7	US government department	Senior software testing engineer
		Senior software testing engineer

Most of the participants came from the Fortune 100 transportation company from which we originally recruited our key informant for study development. Other members of the cohort came from such diverse areas as the U.S. Military, a municipal utility company and city government, and a Fortune 500 retailer. As the topics of certification did not cross the issue of cost calculations, but were instead concentrated on testing methods and quality control, our interaction with them led to unique revelations that were not contextually related to the topics of the seminars they were engaged in.

In the interactive process of interviewing our case study respondent software testing professionals, the initial test cost function was explained to them and then their comments and feedback were solicited. Each of the interactive interviews with the software testing professionals was conducted either in person or by telephone and ranged in time from 45 to 90 minutes.

In the initial function, $\text{Unit Cost} = \text{CIV} + \text{CEO} + \sum_{1}^{n}(\text{CRT} + \text{CRR} + \text{CER} + \text{CFD})$, the first thing to take note of is the fact that in preparing for testing through the creation of test cases, there are certain costs that recur for each test case creation instance, while there are other costs that only occur once in the testing process.

One-Time Versus Recurring Costs in Testing

In the consideration of costs which may not recur and those which might, the cost to create input values (CIV) and the cost to determine the expected outcome of the testing process (CEO), are the one-time costs, while a summation of repeating critical cost factors – the cost to run the test case (CRT), the cost to record and report the results (CRR), the cost to evaluate the results (CER), and the cost to fix identified defects (CFD) – all summed together as a common area of cost – are the repeating costs. Hence, our investigation centered initially on the overarching costs, CIV and CEO. As we considered their impact on the test case costing process, one comment made by a testing manager was worth noting:

Over time, the cost to create the input values (CIV) and the cost to determine the expected output (CEO) become an increasingly smaller factor as the test case is repeatedly run, eventually disappearing in significance.

The case in point suggests the possibility that CIV and CEO might actually be situationally diminishing values, rather than established single-instance values as our initial equation suggests.

Cost of Input Values

In the specific case of the cost for creating input values, CIV, a respondent noted that:

The cost to create the test case input values varies with the complexity of the application. The number of input variables influences the amount of time it takes at each stage.

This was useful to understand, as it lent the notion of variability to the scale of the testing project. This suggests, in turn, that more complex testing regimes will have higher costs of CIV than more basic testing situations. But, also:

The cost to verify the requirement is part of CIV if the tester is expected to do it... [and] ...there is a cost of changes in the input values of a test case as it goes through the lifecycle of changing application features.

Another respondent also pointed out:

The cost of creating a test case can be based on first having to determine the desired output, then going backwards to create the test case input values, CIV...[and that]... a defect can be caused by bad input data, or, errors in the test case input values. Thus, a test case may be negative when it was not intended to be. In this case, the cost to fix the defect, CFD, should be charged to the testers.

This put a new perspective on the notion of the costliness of the input values, pointing attention back to the "variable" costs factors (specifically, CFD) that were summed across the number of test cases that were required to be created. More to the point, as noted by another coworker: "A defect can be caused by a mistake in the test case input values," placing emphasis on the critical nature of the cost of input values in the process. As further noted:

...there is a significant cost in understanding the data to be used in creating the test case input values, CIV.

But also:

...pairwise testing results in a smaller cost to create the test case input values, CIV, than the other methods.

Determining the Expected Outcome

In critical overview of the role that the "one-time" costs of input value creation and expected outcome determination played in the first version of the function, one manager put it quite succinctly:

In creating the test case input values, CIV, developing test cases from use cases is more expensive than developing test cases from pairwise analysis. Dealing with use cases is one of the biggest costs. In general, you can't break out the activity (and therefore the cost, CEO) of determining the expected output of a test case from the activity of creating the test case input values, CIV.

This was the point that reinforced our resolve to continue considering CIV and CEO as costs to be held separately from the constantly summated factors related to reiterative test case production: CRT, CRR, CER and CFD.

Variable Cost Factors

In considering factors related to the variable factors of cost in our initial equation, the first factor – CRT, or cost to run the test case – generated interesting discussion among the respondents. For instance, this point was cogent:

There is a set up cost for automating test cases, but it costs more to execute a manual test case than to execute an automated test case. This affects CRT, CRR, and CER.

In further consideration of factors that might impact the full range of variable costs, the same respondent added:

In addition to the cost of automating test execution, there is also a cost to validate the effects of running the test case, which affects CRT, CRR, and CER.

The sense is that running a test case entails costs that also implicate the cost structure for reporting, evaluating, and executing the test case. A factor limiting cost of the variable factors in the equation appears to be the choice to run manually versus automating test case execution:

The set-up cost for running the test cases for CRT, CRR, [and] CER is a one-time cost if its execution is automated.

Cost for Recording and Reporting

It was also considered that the defect management process involved its own cost structure contributory to the reporting process:

If a defect is found, there is a cost associated with managing the defect, including generating reports, through all of the steps involved in the fix.

Clearly, the cost for running a test implicates variability in the other cost factors. The question to consider will be whether this is the case with other variable cost factors or not. This is a point that may impact potential revision of the cost function.

In consideration of the recording and reporting costs for test cases, CRR, a point raised by one respondent is that there may be informal calculations of cost made by testers going into the testing regime that are later revised in the face of fuller information:

Sometimes the expected output is not determined before testing but the actual output is recorded when the test case is run and is studied later.

In considering reporting costs, a respondent pointed out that the recording and reporting process also involves a double-check to see if a given defect had been reported before. This amounts to a small but subtle hidden cost in the reporting process in this respondent's view:

The cost of recording results includes the cost of checking to see if a defect that has been found has previously been found and recorded in the defect management system and the cost of cleaning up such duplicates.

More to the point, the actual planning of the test process can impact the reporting cost, with the choice to take an easier path in use of heuristic generation as opposed to generating a case from user requirements impacting eventual reporting costs:

The cost of reporting a defect, part of the cost of recording results and perhaps the cost of fixing the defect can be greater if the test case that caused it was generated by a heuristic method rather than from requirements because it cannot be traced back to a requirement and may require more explanation.

But, another respondent – an employee of a major public utility – pointed out that, "The cost to record test results involves labor cost only if using open source software for the defect management system," which was an interesting observation, since it clearly delineated between the companies and their inclination to use popular commercial testing suites and more cost-effective open source tools. A further point was that:

The cost to record the test results can vary depending on whether the defect management system is home grown or is a standard product.

However, the sense that reporting costs varied with tools choice did not seem to be limited to commercial versus open source alternatives, as noted by a tester employed by a major automotive parts retailer: "The cost to record the result depends on the defect management system in use." Some systems were noted to have automated reporting capabilities, further impacting the cost reductions for the reporting factor.

Evaluation Costs

In thinking about the impact of the cost of evaluating results (CER), an important point noted by a respondent is that "…sometimes test scripts are run several or many times before results are evaluated." It seems that CER can have very high variability, potentially. One respondent, who worked in testing for the transportation company in the sample, continued the point…

The cost to evaluate results includes a decision, based on whether a defect was found, of whether to create more test cases based on an unexpected defect. This is more likely to happen as the complexity of the interacting systems increases and there is more opportunity for defects to appear.

There is also the notion that, "…the cost to evaluate the test results depends on the severity of the defect." Yet, "…the cost of recording the test results may be automated and therefore have little or no cost," and "…the cost to evaluate results, CER, can vary as it may be manual versus automated."

Costs to Fix What is Found

As part of our investigation, during interviews we noted that a number of respondents did not feel that the cost factor related to fixing identified defects belonged in the initial form of the equation, which was used as a focal point for encouraging discussion on cost elements. In considering the impact of the variable costs factors, one of the transportation company testers had a telling point: "The cost to fix a defect belongs to development."

This led us to consider whether or not CFD belonged in the mix of variable cost factors or not – a point bearing further discussion below.

Some were rather introspective on the point, carrying the conclusion to an ultimate economic end:

The cost to fix a defect is a benefit, not a cost, as it is applied to "internal technical debt."

Respondents' comments varied, and some, such as this one from a healthcare institution software tester, were rather detailed:

The cost to fix a defect is the most important part of the cost [of software testing], but the cost to fix a defect is variable and is in the hands of the developer.

Other respondents were more direct in their assessment of the propriety of CFD being a part of the summated cost equation we presented for their consideration:

Defect remediation should not be part of the equation because it is not part of testing.

or:

The cost to fix a defect is a development cost and should not be included in this function.

and, as is noted by a tester with a military organization:

...the cost to fix a defect is not directly associated with the cost of the test case. CFD cannot be predicted in advance.

A tester with a major software development company simply said, "The cost to fix a test case is a development cost," implying it should be dropped from the test case costs equation while testers from the transportation company were more diplomatic: "Possibly don't include [in the equation] the cost to fix a defect."

An emerging and related point in the face of these comments was that the limit "n" in the equation summation passage should not be the number of times the test case is run until the defect is fixed, because defects are discovered only some of the times that a test case is run. The ultimate logical conclusion of this point was that CFD, the cost to fix a test case, had to be removed from the summation for the same reason: the test case may be run many times even if there is no defect to fix.

To that end, we undertook a revision of the test case cost function equation based on the guidance of our respondents.

Interpretive Assessment of Initial Equation

One major area of comments in the interviews was that there are a number of preparatory activities that have to be included in the cost of a test case. These include the cost of creating a test plan, the cost of reviewing the test plan, the cost of reviewing and validating requirements, the cost of setting up the test environment, the cost of acquiring, developing, or upgrading test tools, the cost of collecting test data for a test database, the cost to write temporary code to facilitate testing before the application is completed, and the cost of reviewing the test cases. It seems important to explicitly affirm that all of these costs apply to an entire set of test cases as a group. If so, the costs should be amortized across all of the test cases in order to consider the cost attributed to a single test case for use in our unit cost function.

Another point was that the mathematical form of the variable costs factors summation should not be the number of times a test case is actually run. This might result in a cost element being repetitively counted over a number of similar test case iterations, and the pragmatic point is that defects are discovered only some of the times that a test case is run. In fact, a test case may be run many times as part of a regression test suite and subsequently produce a defect in only a small number of those runs. For this reason, we felt that the costs of running a test case and the costs of dealing with a possible code defect discovered by it should be allocated into two different summations.

The cost to run a test case would still include CRT, CRR, and CER, less CFD, as discussed. However, in removing the cost to fix a defect (CFD) from the initial function, it occurred to us in the process of interpreting the comments and advice provided by our respondents that a more complicated issue might be at hand than just the test case failures. A second summation associated with defects discovered by a test case should be created with an upper limit of "a" (the number of times the test case causes a code failure) rather than "n" as in the initial function (which represented the number of times the test case was run).

Based on what we learned in the interviews, we introduce CMD – the cost to manage a defect – which is a cost that will always be charged to the testers. This defect management activity includes tracking the failure through assigning it to the responsible party for correction, making sure the correction has been completed, and reintroducing the test case into the mix. The cost to determine the failure category, CFC, should also be borne by the testers. There are four major failure categories: a code error, an error in calculating the expected output of the test case, a hardware or software problem with the test environment, or an error in the intended input values (derived from requirements) leading to an unintended negative test case. The cost of resolving the test case failure, CRF, should be assigned to the party responsible for the error that caused the failure. A code error should certainly be charged to the developers. A problem with the test environment should be charged to the testers. Errors in calculating the test case input values or the expected output should be charged to whoever was responsible.

Revising the Test Case Cost Function

The revised function, based on these interview results where n is the number of times the test case is run and where a is the number of times the test case fails, is as follows:

$$\text{Unit Cost} = \text{Prep Costs} + \text{CIV} + \text{CEO} + \sum_{1}^{n}(\text{CRT}+\text{CRR}+\text{CER}+\text{CME}) + \sum_{0}^{a}(\text{CMD}+\text{CFC}+\text{CRF}) \quad (2)$$

Notice that the upper limit, "n," in the summation, now reflects the number of times the test case is run, independently of any issue of test case failures. The full set of factors is shown in Table 2, and the interrelationships of the factors are graphically represented in Figure 2. Also note that the lower limit of the second summation factor is 0 because some test cases may never produce a failure.

Again, while some of these individual factors are well-known, the contribution here is the way we have combined them into a comprehensive cost function.

There are a couple of other points to be made regarding the revised unit cost function. First, how do we factor in the costs associated with having to modify a test case in a regression suite later on, due to a change in a requirement that results in the test case having to be revised? It would be too complex to try to figure out the costs associated with such a situation into the cost of the original test case. As this would be very problematic, the solution is to simply consider the revised test case to be a new test case. Second, while our function is designed to determine the cost of a single test case, alternatively, the total cost of all functional test cases could be calculated. In this case, the preparation costs would not have to be amortized across all of the test cases but the costs for the individual test cases would have to be summed for inclusion in the total cost.

Figure 2. Revised test case costs model

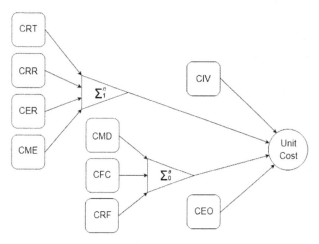

Table 2. Factors of the unit cost function

Factor	Category	Code	Items
1		CTP	Cost to create test plan
2		CPR	Cost to review test plan
3		CRV	Cost to review and validate requirements
4		CPC	Cost to set up test environment, including hardware and software, as necessary
5	Prep Costs	CTT	Cost to acquire, develop, or upgrade test tools
6		CAD	Cost to collect associated test data
7		CTS	Cost to write temporary code needed to test part of code before the rest of the code is ready
8		CTR	Cost to review test cases
9	Creation Costs	CIV	Cost to create the test case input values
10		CEO	Cost to determine the expected output of the test case
11		CRT	Cost to run the test case
12	Run Costs	CRR	Cost to record and report the test results
13		CER	Cost to evaluate the test results
14		CME	Cost to collect and record test metrics, if required
15		CMD	Cost to manage a defect
16	Failure Costs	CFC	Cost to determine failure category
17		CRF	Cost to resolve test case failure

Returning to the Respondents

The last step in our analysis and interpretation was to return to our case study cohort with our findings and solicit their feedback on the final product of the process. We provided our respondents with the original function, the revised function, and a brief explanation of how we arrived at the revised function based on the sum of the responses in the original interviews. Our engagement with the group began with a return visit to our Key Informant, who represented the starting point of our study. In considering our results, he said that the revised function "makes sense." He stressed the importance of our including the cost of the preparation work in the function, as we did. He emphasized that not every test case finds defects and so he agreed with our decision to split the summation function into two separate functional expressions. We pointed out that we were changing the lower limit of the second summation function from 1 to 0 (based on an interviewee's comment about the revised function since some test cases NEVER find a defect) and he concurred.

We then solicited feedback by email from the rest of the cohort. Of the 28 participants, 12 responded with substantive guidance, all of whom provided written responses which were in agreement that our revised function was a significant improvement over the original function and that the revised function "made more sense." Hence, the iterative case study approach of development of an initial function, and then consultative revision of it yielded a refined outcome in terms of the final theoretical generalization from the study.

A common theme of the respondents revolved around our choice of which of the factors to utilize for representation of certain costs. For example, one of the respondents wondered whether the Preparation Costs should be part of the cost to create input values (CIV). Another respondent thought that perhaps the cost to determine the failure category (CFC) could be part of the cost to manage a defect (CMD). We consider comments such as these to be options that do not materially affect the substance of the revised function.

In sum, our case study group considered the outcome of the process to be valid and representative of their views of the software testing process, in support of the veracity of our generalization from interpretive analysis to empirical cost function.

Uses and Advantages of the Function

There are a couple of reasons that we think this new cost function is an advance in cost estimation in contemporary software development.

First, there currently is no comprehensive function for cost estimation of test cases. To our knowledge, most testers currently still rely on their intuition and experience to evaluate test case costs, if they consider cost at all. Although several estimation models have been conceived to assess the entire software development cost, such as the well-known Boehm's Constructive Cost Model (COCOMO), they are not applicable to estimating the cost of the test cases. But cost is an important factor in selecting appropriate test cases. In other words, all else being equal, choosing the test cases with the lowest costs can help in optimizing software testing in a limited resource environment.

Another advantage of the new function is the ability to distinguish the relative cost difference among the test cases. Although the cost value derived from the cost function might be somewhat subjective, the function can be applied within an organization or group where testers can create their own standard of scoring the cost. So, the cost function can be applied in a consistent way that allows for differentiating the cost among the test cases.

Finally, we recognize that there is a potential issue in the cost of using the proposed method to the software organization. The cost of using the proposed method is in time and personnel resources. We believe that while this is difficult to quantify, the cost of using the proposed method will be offset by the benefits gained by the improved understanding of the true costs of testing to the organization.

Given the above arguments, we contend that the final cost function can play a critical role in optimizing software testing and would be a good complementary instrument in software engineering development.

DISCUSSION

Summary of Content

In this paper, we demonstrated a novel use of case research to generate an empirical function through qualitative generalization. Specifically with this innovative technique, we applied interpretive case analysis to define and generalize an empirical cost function for test cases through qualitative interaction with an industry cohort of subject matter experts involved in software testing at leading technology companies. Following the steps of our methodology, two rounds of in-depth interviews were conducted in our revelatory case study. In the first round interviews, we initiated the unit cost function of a test case as the basis for the second round interviews. Specifically, in the first round interviews, we had an extended interaction with a key informant who is a senior manager in the technology development division of a Fortune 100 transportation company. In the second round interviews, we revised and finalized the cost function based on the insights of 28 software testing professionals drawn from seven nationally prominent technology organizations. The final function uncovers the unit cost of a functional test case from four perspectives as follows: preparation costs, creation costs, run costs, and failure costs. Each of these costs is developed from several sub-costs. Particularly preparation costs and creation costs are one-time costs, while run costs and failure costs are repeating costs. Run costs accrue each time a test case is executed; failure costs accrue each time a test case fails.

The progression from determining the initial cost function to finalizing the cost function revealed some interesting insights about test case costs. One was the importance of preparation costs which, as we have pointed out, have to be amortized among all of the test cases involved. Another was noting the distinction between the costs involved in managing a defect and the cost to actually fix the defect. Further, we determined that the cost to fix a defect belongs in our cost model only if the defect was the fault to the testers. Finally, we found that the number of times a test case is executed and the number of times a test case fails are distinct and must be separated, thus the division of the summation function in the initial model into the two summation functions in the final model.

Theoretical and Practical Contributions

The key theoretical contribution of our study lies in the use of qualitative inquiry to support the development of an empirical function. Specifically, we have derived the empirical function from the theoretical generalization of a case study investigation, which is an unusual but highly useful approach. In particular, our novel use of expert practitioners to directly induce an empirical function through qualitative generalization is a novel, theoretical advance. As we said earlier, it is rare for a case study to be quantitative, yet mathematical functions can be derived in this way since deductions involving mathematical propositions are a subset of formal logic and nothing in formal logic is tied to a specific methodology (Lee, 1989).

As for the key practical contribution, we demonstrated our methodology with a qualitative study of the perceptions of software testers, in which we utilized their professional expertise and perceptions to "break down" the functionality and cost factors pertinent in developing and employing test cases. This breakdown served as the initial basis for inducing an empirical cost function to be used in further assessment of testing costs in research perspectives more broadly focused on the testing process in industry settings. As such, we consider it a unique application of our qualitative methodology for purposes of empirical generalization in the production of our empirical function and this procedure could potentially be applied to other contexts for validation, verification, and further testing. The importance of this practical contribution lies in the constant challenge of maximizing the use of the always limited resources available for software testing. Understanding the relative cost of test cases is a major step forward in the best utilization of these limited resources.

Additionally, the substantive contributions of this study beyond the generalized methodology are twofold in the software testing arena. First, from the theoretical perspective, we fill the gap that exists in that no one has attempted to develop a function that will guide the calculation of the cost of a functional test case. Prior studies either address the issue of software testing techniques or emphasize the impact of testing on software development, but no study focuses on the testing cost which can influence software development as a whole significantly. Second, from the practical perspective, putting aside the obvious value of an empirical cost function for guiding future research, we built a concise model for analyzing and assessing the cost of a functional test case. This method offers a good reference point for testers and managers to evaluate the cost of a functional test case. It also quantifies the amount of resource consumed during the test process.

CONCLUSION AND FUTURE RESEARCH

The advancement in theoretical generalization that this represents forms a useful new direction for researchers interested in a deep understanding of specific business models. In our example, it demonstrated a deep understanding of budgetary phenomena and cost factors inherent in software development and testing research. We believe that there are fruitful directions for future research in regard to both our theoretical contribution and our practical contribution. First, in terms of the theoretical contribution, work can be done to utilize text mining and other tools to automate the analysis of the interview responses to both speed up and sharpen the focus of the modifications to the original function. In terms of the practical contribution concerning the cost of test cases, work can be done to expand beyond the cost of test cases into the value of test cases in terms of risk and priority of the software modules and competing applications being tested.

REFERENCES

Akhavein, J. D., Swamy, P. A. V. B., Taubman, S. B., & Singamsetti, R. N. (1997). A general method of deriving the inefficiencies of banks from a profit function. *Journal of Productivity Analysis*, *8*(1), 71–93. doi:10.1023/A:1007776431663

Alijumaily, H., Cuadra, D., & Martinez, P. (2014). Applying black-box testing to UML/OCL database models. *Software Quality Journal*, *22*(2), 153–184. doi:10.100711219-012-9192-9

Balijepally, V., DeHondt, G., Sugumaran, V., & Nerur, S. (2017). Agility in software development and project value: An empirical investigation. *Journal of Database Management*, *28*(4), 40–59. doi:10.4018/JDM.2017100103

Batra, D., VanderMeer, D., & Dutta, K. (2011). Extending agile principles to larger, dynamic software projects: A theoretical assessment. *Journal of Database Management*, *22*(4), 73–92. doi:10.4018/jdm.2011100104

Batra, D., Xia, W., & Rathor, S. (2016). Agility facilitators for contemporary software development. *Journal of Database Management*, *27*(1), 1–28. doi:10.4018/JDM.2016010101

Boehm, B., Abts, C., & Chulani, S. (2000). Software development cost estimation approaches - A survey. *Annals of Software Engineering*, *10*(1-4), 177–205. doi:10.1023/A:1018991717352

Boehm, B., Clark, B., Horowitz, E., Westland, C., Madachy, R., & Selby, R. (1995). Cost models for future software life cycle processes: COCOMO 2.0. *Annals of Software Engineering*, *1*(1), 57–94. doi:10.1007/BF02249046

Boehm, B. W. (1981). *Software engineering economics*. Upper Saddle River, NJ: Prentice Hall.

Briand, L. C., Emam, K. E., Surmann, D., Wieczorek, I., & Maxwell, K. D. (1999). An assessment and comparison of common software cost estimation modeling techniques. *Proceedings of the 1999 International Conference on Software Engineering*, Los Angeles, CA (pp. 313-323). Academic Press. 10.1145/302405.302647

Burnstein, I. (2006). *Practical software testing: A process-oriented approach*. New York, NY, USA: Springer.

Crowston, K., & Scozzi, B. (2008). Bug fixing practices within free/libre open source software development teams. *Journal of Database Management*, *19*(2), 1–30. doi:10.4018/jdm.2008040101

Dorofeeva, R., El-Fakih, K., Maag, S., Cavalli, A. R., & Yevtushenko, N. (2010). FSM-based conformance testing methods: A survey annotated with experimental evaluation. *Information and Software Technology*, *52*(12), 1286–1297. doi:10.1016/j.infsof.2010.07.001

Eisenhardt, K. M. (1989). Building theories from case study research. *Academy of Management Review*, *14*(4), 532–550. doi:10.5465/amr.1989.4308385

Ellims, M., Bridges, J., & Ince, D. C. (2006). The economics of unit testing. *Empirical Software Engineering*, *11*(1), 5–31. doi:10.100710664-006-5964-9

Gray, A. R., & MacDonell, S. G. (1997). A comparison of techniques for developing predictive models of software metrics. *Information and Software Technology*, *39*(6), 425–437. doi:10.1016/S0950-5849(96)00006-7

Hass, A. M. (2014). *Guide to advanced software testing* (2nd ed.). Norwood, MA: Artech House.

Hengl, T., Heuvelink, G. B. M., & Rossiter, D. G. (2007). About regression-kriging: From equations to case studies. *Computers & Geosciences*, *33*(10), 1301–1315. doi:10.1016/j.cageo.2007.05.001

Huang, Y.-C., Peng, K.-L., & Huang, C.-Y. (2012). A history-based cost-cognizant test case prioritization technique in regression testing. *Journal of Systems and Software*, *85*(3), 626–637. doi:10.1016/j.jss.2011.09.063

Idri, A., Amazal, F. A., & Abran, A. (2015). Analogy-based software development effort estimation: A systematic mapping and review. *Information and Software Technology*, *58*, 206–230. doi:10.1016/j.infsof.2014.07.013

Jeffery, R., Ruhe, M., & Wieczorek, I. (2000). A comparative study of two software development cost modeling techniques using multi-organizational and company-specific data. *Information and Software Technology*, *42*(14), 1009–1016. doi:10.1016/S0950-5849(00)00153-1

Jørgensen, M., & Shepperd, M. (2007). A systematic review of software development cost estimation studies. *IEEE Transactions on Software Engineering*, *33*(1), 33–53. doi:10.1109/TSE.2007.256943

Khan, M. E. (2010). Different forms of software testing techniques for finding errors. *International Journal of Computer Science Issues*, *7*(3), 11–16.

Koch, S., & Neumann, C. (2008). Exploring the effects of process characteristics on products quality in open source software development. *Journal of Database Management*, *19*(2), 31–57. doi:10.4018/jdm.2008040102

Kumar, N., Stern, L. W., & Anderson, J. C. (1993). Conducting interorganizational research using key informants. *Academy of Management Journal*, *36*(6), 1633–1651.

Kurfman, M. A., Stock, M. E., Stone, R. B., Rajan, J., & Wood, K. L. (2003). Experimental studies assessing the repeatability of a functional modeling derivation method. *Journal of Mechanical Design*, *125*(4), 682–693. doi:10.1115/1.1625400

Lee, A. S. (1989). A scientific methodology for MIS case studies. *Management Information Systems Quarterly*, *13*(1), 33–50. doi:10.2307/248698

Lee, T. B. (2018, May 7). *Report: Software bug led to death in Uber's self-driving crash*. Ars Technica. Retrieved from https://arstechnica.com/tech-policy/2018/05/report-software-bug-led-to-death-in-ubers-self-driving-crash/

Malishevsky, A. G., Ruthruff, J. R., Rothermel, G., & Elbaum, S. (2006). *Cost-cognizant test case prioritization*. Lincoln, NB: Department of Computer Science and Engineering, University of Nebraska-Lincoln.

Marshall, M. N. (1996). The key informant technique. *Family Practice*, *13*(1), 92–97. doi:10.1093/fampra/13.1.92 PMID:8671109

Mathur, A. P. (2014). *Foundations of software testing* (2nd ed.). Boston, MA: Addison-Wesley Professional.

Miles, M. B., Huberman, A. M., & Saldaña, J. (2013). *Qualitative data analysis: A methods sourcebook* (3rd ed.). Thousand Oaks, CA: Sage Publications.

Popper, N., & Gough, N. (2015, April 17). *Bloomberg terminals suffer widespread failures*. NY Times. Retrieved from https://www.nytimes.com/2015/04/18/business/dealbook/bloomberg-terminals-outage. html

Sarker, S., Sarker, S., Sahaym, A., & Bjørn-Andersen, N. (2012). Exploring value cocreation in relationships between an ERP vendor and its partners: A revelatory case study. *Management Information Systems Quarterly*, *36*(1), 317–338. doi:10.2307/41410419

Sharma, A., & Kushwaha, D. S. (2012). Applying requirement based complexity for the estimation of software development and testing effort. *Software Engineering Notes*, *37*(1), 1–11. doi:10.1145/2088883.2088898

Srinivasan, K., & Fisher, D. (1995). Machine learning approaches to estimating software development effort. *IEEE Transactions on Software Engineering*, *21*(2), 126–137. doi:10.1109/32.345828

Srivastava, P. R. (2015). Estimation of software testing effort using fuzzy multiple linear regression. *International Journal of Software Engineering. Technology and Applications*, *1*(2-4), 145–154.

Subramanian, G. H., Pendharkar, P. C., & Pai, D. R. (2017). An examination of determinants of software testing and project management effort. *Journal of Computer Information Systems*, *57*(2), 123–129. doi :10.1080/08874417.2016.1183428

Talby, D., Keren, A., Hazzan, O., & Dubinsky, Y. (2006). Agile software testing in a large-scale project. *IEEE Software*, *23*(4), 30–37. doi:10.1109/MS.2006.93

Tassey, G. (2003). *The economic impacts of inadequate infrastructure for software testing: Final report*. Collingdale, PA: Diane Publishing.

Tausworthe, R. C. (1979-1980). The work breakdown structure in software project management. *Journal of Systems and Software*, *1*, 181–186. doi:10.1016/0164-1212(79)90018-9

Tremblay, M.-A. (1957). The key informant technique: A nonethnographic application. *American Anthropologist*, *59*(1), 688–701. doi:10.1525/aa.1957.59.4.02a00100

Walsh, D., & Downe, S. (2005). Meta-synthesis method for qualitative research: A literature review. *Journal of Advanced Nursing*, *50*(2), 204–211. doi:10.1111/j.1365-2648.2005.03380.x PMID:15788085

Walsham, G. (1995). Interpretive case studies in IS research: Nature and method. *European Journal of Information Systems*, *4*(2), 74–81. doi:10.1057/ejis.1995.9

Walsham, G. (2006). Doing interpretive research. *European Journal of Information Systems*, *15*(3), 320–330. doi:10.1057/palgrave.ejis.3000589

Whittaker, J. A., Arbon, J., & Carollo, J. (2012). *How Google tests software*. Boston, MA: Addison-Wesley Professional.

Wysopal, C., Nelson, L., Zovi, D. D., & Dustin, E. (2006). *The art of software security testing: Identifying software security flaws.* Boston, MA: Addison-Wesley Professional.

Xu, B., Lin, Z., & Xu, Y. (2011). A study of open source software development from control perspective. *Journal of Database Management, 22*(1), 26–42. doi:10.4018/jdm.2011010102

Yin, R. K. (2013). *Case study research: Design and methods (Applied social research methods)* (5th ed.). Thousand Oaks, CA: Sage Publications.

Zhang, X., Dhaliwal, J. S., Gillenson, M. L., & Stafford, T. F. (2013). The impact of conflict judgments between developers and testers in software development. *Journal of Database Management, 24*(4), 26–50. doi:10.4018/JDM.2013100102

This research was previously published in the Journal of Database Management (JDM), 31(2); pages 42-63, copyright year 2020 by IGI Publishing (an imprint of IGI Global).

Chapter 43
Using Epistemic Game Development to Teach Software Development Skills

Christos Gatzoulis
https://orcid.org/0000-0003-2959-9793
Bahrain Polytechnic, Bahrain

Andreas S. Andreou
Cyprus University of Technology, Cyprus

Panagiotis Zaharias
The UXProdigy, Greece

Yiorgos Chrysanthou
University of Cyprus, Cyprus

ABSTRACT

This paper presents a pilot study on the evaluation of instruments for data gathering for an epistemic game development competition for high school students. The initial results show that a significant percentage of the students who participated in the competition appear to exhibit a skillset of professional attitude, software-related knowledge, and employability traits, and this skillset may be attributed to the intervention. The data was validated through a two-method triangulation technique that utilized expert evaluation and participant interviews. The data analysis shows early indicators of the desired learning outcomes, although a more thorough methodology is needed to verify this. Furthermore, the competition acts as an awareness campaign that promotes computer science studies through a gamification process. It is proposed that competitions of this type are held and evaluated on an annual basis to maximize the benefits and to further prepare students to acquire early in their studies a skillset that will make them the innovators of the future society.

DOI: 10.4018/978-1-6684-3702-5.ch043

1. INTRODUCTION

The Computer Science industry faces two major challenges among others: First, due to the fact that computers became ubiquitous (new types of software and hardware are progressively used not only within work environments but also for personal purposes) the industry is expanding, and an increasing number of professionals are required to work in the field. Second, as the technology evolves, job descriptions and their person specifications demand increased specialisation and a larger amount of technical knowledge and skills from university graduates (World Economic Forum, 2018). This creates a demand for students who enter higher education to be familiar with basic computer science concepts so that universities can start delivering more advanced and dedicated courses in their curriculum to achieve the industry demands. A common method to increase the number of high school students that pursue computing studies at university level is to increase their knowledge in the general field and provide them with examples of stimulating job opportunities that may arise from the computing discipline. Game development is a topic that excites young students due to its playful nature and has been widely used to get students involved and familiar with fundamental computing development activities. It has been well-examined and proved that developing games increases student motivation (Robertson & Howells, 2008; Repenning & Ioannidou, 2008; Seif El-Nasr et al., 2007; Martins et al., 2019) and interest and knowledge in the computing field (Denner, Werner, & Ortiz, 2012; Hayes & Games, 2008; Basawapatna, Koh, & Repenning, 2010; Werner, Denner, Bliesner, & Rex, 2009; Barcelos, Soto & Silveira, 2015). More recent studies highlight the benefits of games development in computing curriculum in schools (Renton, 2016; Kafai & Burke, 2016; Topalli and Cagiltay, 2018; Liu, 2018; Martins & Oliveria, 2018; Petri et al, 2019). However, despite the large volume of research in the area, there is still more to be discovered on what type of specialised computing principles and soft skills can high students learn during game development courses.

This paper presents a pilot study of delivering an annual game development competition to provide high school students with an opportunity to acquire knowledge and skills required in the software industry. Students formed teams of four within their schools and delivered their games (and accompanying reports documenting the development process) within a six months period. The study aimed to identify whether the students who participated in the study acquired understanding of fundamental software development skills. More specifically, the skills that were assessed are software engineering methods (prototyping, testing, and maintenance), design methods (using diagrams, reusability, interface design, content design) and team management techniques (role-playing, brainstorming). The study also examined if the exercise of the above skills correlated with good practice on game design, which was measured by a set of playability heuristics. The heuristic evaluation was performed by a group of game development experts that spend time playing testing the game and reading the submitted reports. The pilot study proves that the instruments utilised manage to capture important aspects of the software development process, the achievement of game development guidelines and real-life practical skills and provide an initial approach toward detecting correlations between them. The pilot study yielded stimulating results and proved that further investigation with a more solid intervention methodology may have potential of a positive impact.

2. THEORETICAL FRAMEWORK

2.1. Constructivism

The major learning theory behind the described strategy is constructivism. In constructivism, learning takes place when people are actively engaged in making a meaningful product. In our case and for the game development competition, the meaningful product is a game with explicit theme, and aimed at a specific audience. Constructivism also proposes that learning environments should support multiple perspectives or interpretations of reality, knowledge construction, and context-rich, experience-based activities (Duffy & Jonassen, 1992). In the context of this study, multiple perspectives can be generated by members of the game development teams about the game theme and engagement and interaction among them. Knowledge construction is achieved as students make knowledge their own, identify with it and understand it rather than memorize it (Mayer, 2003). Finally, context-rich, experience-based activities involve different activities in the software development cycle.

2.2. Game-Based Learning

Game-Based Learning (GBL) is an emerging learning method that is becoming very popular at various levels of education. Playing games is one of the most important activities for children, as GBL provides significant benefits to them. Games' capacity to increase interest and engage users makes them powerful learning platforms. A major benefit of the utilization of games in teaching context is their effect on user's motivation. Games augment motivation during learning processes, by providing learning tasks in meaningful context, fully controlled by the user himself (Kirriemuir & McFarlane, 2004) through entertainment (Kim, Park, & Bayek, 2009). There are many studies that support that GBL improves user motivation, flow and immersion (Cordova & Lepper, 1996; Rosas et al., 2003; Lopez-Morteo & Lopez, 2007; Tuzun et al., 2008; Hamari et al. 2016). Tuzun compared the motivation of students who learned in a game-based learning environment to those who learned in a traditional school environment and found that students demonstrated statistically significant higher levels of intrinsic motivation in the game-based environment. The benefits of GBL apply to any form of games (such as traditional role-playing games, board games) rather than just computer games. Jabbar and Felicia (2015) provide a systematic review in engagement and achieved learning during game-based activities.

2.3. Epistemic Games

Computers are continuously transforming our world in terms of innovation and creativity. Today's premium job positions require more than knowledge of math and physics or any other kind of basic skill. Students need to learn the art of being innovative. They need to be able to solve complex problems that are important to our society. GBL is an example of a constructivist learning environment, also described as 'learning by doing', where students develop the skill to structure their thoughts and actions (Barron & Darling-Hammond, 2008). Shaffer (Shaffer, 2006) highlights that today's students need to learn about internet technology, graphic design, urban sprawl, global warming, political science, international relations, biomedical ethics and a host of other expertise that will provide them with the capacity to live and proffer to a global society that is far more complicated than 20 years ago. This can be achieved by providing the tools for our students to learn the epistemologies of creative innovation. A method to achieve this is through the design and application of epistemic games to education. Shaffer defines epistemic games as "games that are fundamentally about learning to think in innovative ways; a solution that uses technology to think about learning in new ways appropriate for a postindustrial, global economy and society". In his book (Shaffer, 2006) Shaffer describes a collection of epistemic games (either at pre-packaged or not forms) such as a debating game (students take on roles on a debate, acting as politicians or diplomats), and a list of computer games that help students build knowledge, skills and values. Other researchers have also investigated the capacities of epistemic games and have evaluated diverse examples of their utilization (Triantafyllakos, Palaigeorgiou, & Tsoukalas, 2011; Vos, Meijden, & Denessen, 2011; Hainey et al, 2011; Magnussen et al, 2014). Referring to game design as an epistemic game, Robertson and Howells (2008) argue that making a game is an authentic learning process in which students displayed motivation and enthusiasm for learning, determination to achieve and links to learning transfer. Robertson and Howells suggest making a game could indeed be a powerful learning environment in which students control their own learning and thinking processes. Kafai states that game construction puts children in control of their own learning and thinking and encourages them to plan and manage the complex process of creating their individual game (Kafai, 1995). Another study highlighted the importance of early education game competitions in the development of a game industry (Gatzoulis, Loizides & Zaphiris, 2016). Apart from academic projects, there are also commercially available epistemic games such as Sid Meier's Civilisation (Meier, 2010), which is based on a historically accurate model of advances in technology and art. Civilisation allows user to play historical experiments that indicate the importance of geographical location, ease of trade and access to raw materials in shaping structural conditions that shape historical developments (Squire, in press). A list of examples of such games includes Spore (Spore, 2009), SimCity (SimCity, 2010), Zoo Tycoon (Tycoon, 2017) and even more. Markauskaite and Goodyear (2016) offer a description and analysis of the variety of professional epistemic games.

2.4. Computer Games Development

The computer games industry is one of the largest industries at the world and the most emerging among all entertainment industries. The complexity of many of the commercial games calls for (a) multifaceted requirements specification and (b) development with state-of-the-art specialized tools that are constantly introduced to the games market. Fifteen years ago, for a graduate student to break into the industry, a typical person specification comprised programming skills with a specific procedural language (the C programming language), experience with one graphics library and some basic knowledge of fundamental mathematics, such as trigonometry, algebra, and calculus. Nowadays, in order to excel in the industry, graduates need to have the capacity to develop on multiple platforms using different programming interfaces and libraries and possess specific specialized knowledge on gaming technologies (such as programming for graphical processors, networking massively multiplayer online games, advanced animation techniques, novel artificial intelligence models, component-based development, usability measures etc.). Moreover, the technology emerges and changes continuously, which makes it important for professional to constantly continue learning. Further to this, other skills such as learning, collaboration, problem solving, planning and organising, communication and initiative are becoming important in career building. To support students in becoming competent in tomorrow's gaming job roles, we must provide them with specialization from the early stages in education and move the knowledge chain further down. By providing the fundamentals of gaming and scaffolding of employability skills in secondary education, students can start learning the more advanced topics earlier during higher education, resulting in a more complete professional profile accompanied by a more powerful portfolio.

2.5. Student Learning Outcomes During the Game Development Competition

In summary, the paper has identified and selected several competencies and knowledge items that are important for high school students who wish to pursue computer science studies and can lead to successful software development through best practices. These include: (a) software engineering methods such as testing, maintenance, reusability and prototyping (b) design methods such as brainstorming and application design (in our case, game design) and (c) collaboration and organisation skills. While there are more competencies that are important and have evolved with the 4.0 industrial evolution, the above were selected to be tested in the pilot study as they are fundamental and easy to comprehend by high school students, and remain important to the industry based on skills reported by stakeholders that seek ICT related skills (Bortz, 2020) and also generic skills for modern careers (O'Neil, 2015; Magen-Nagar et al., 2019). Further skills can be developed and tested in future alternative executions in areas such as data literacy, cybersecurity, artificial intelligence; however, this pilot study was focused on software development and game design.

The pilot study used a questionnaire that assesses the development of the above competencies and knowledge and used it during an open-ended interview with the participating students. The study also tested if the above correlate to successful game design measured using playability heuristics. This is an item with major significance and the success in teaching software development is not only linked to evidence of activities but also to the quality of the product.

3. METHODS

3.1. Participants

The students that participated in this study were volunteers in after-school work. There were a total of 29 teams that participated in the competition. Each team comprised two to four students as members. Each game took around six months to be developed. The age of the students ranged between 15 and 18 years old. All the participants are fluent in Greek and English. From the 29 teams that submitted a game, the 10 teams with highest scores were invited to present their game in a final stage and compete for the first three places that received awards. All 10 finalist teams were invited to participate in an interview after their presentations. Five of these teams exhibited availability and were interviewed on a set of open-ended questions investigating software engineering and game design practices (Appendix A, Table 5). Each of the interviewed teams comprised four members, totalling twenty participants (group team interviews). All students were from five different high schools in Cyprus. The development platform menus and interfaces are in English language, while the interviews took place in the Greek language.

3.2. Procedure

The methodology that was followed was empirical and was designed based on the concept of embedding constructivism within a role-playing epistemic game where students must develop a game that covers one of a given competition themes (see Section 3.4 for the themes). The development must cover fundamental software development requirements, game design requirements and students are asked to pitch their idea in the final judging day. Students must construct their own game idea, choose the game genre, gameplay challenges, game features/content in a project-based learning setting. They practice this in a simulated game development team, in which they must take on a role within the team and the associated responsibilities. They need to balance the technical requirements with the creative elements of the game. The fact that the target application is a game offers an additional level of gamification, as students enjoy making games more than other software types.

Students were asked to develop their games using either GameMaker (YoYo Games, 2020) or the XNA Framework (Microsoft, 2013). The reason was to allow the students adapt the difficulty level to their capacities, as GameMaker allows the developer to create the game using visual tools and scripting, while XNA requires extensive object-oriented programming using Microsoft's commercial language C#. A seminar was given at the early stages of the competition to introduce the students to the game development process and to explain the basic requirements for the competition. The marking criteria that set the competition requirements comprised game story writing, game content design, user-interface design, game balancing, difficulty levels, progressive score system, gameplay, and bug-free execution. No specific guidelines were given towards those goals, so students then had to determine appropriate development strategies on how to meet the competition requirements. It is noted that those requirements are mapped to the criteria - heuristics that evaluators used to grade the game (Appendix A, Table 2). Teams had to submit the game along with a detailed report on the development process. A pool of evaluators with academic or expertise in game design and development reviewed the report, along with the game demo and other supplementary material. During the day of the competition, students had to make a presentation to the expert game reviewers (open to the public), in which they had to demonstrate their game and its features, explaining how it meets the competition requirements. The following section describes in more detail the data collection process and analysis.

3.3. Data Collection and Analysis

The data from the evaluation reports was collected in a Likert scale scored from 1 to 5 which was attributed to a specific heuristic. The Likert scale was preferred over a dichotomous scale as it was used to measure feeling of agreement with the statements of the heuristics presented in the Tables 2, 3 and 4 in Appendix A. While there are no absolute recommendations on the number of point scales, there are studies who claim that 5-point scale offers better quality of data than 7 and 11-point scales (Revilla et al., 2013). The heuristics aim to capture belief of evidence of good software development practice in the context of game development (based on the published competition requirements) enriched with playability heuristics (Korhoren, 2016; Desurvire, Caplan & Toth, 2004; Ponnada and Kannan, 2012). The experts that participated in the evaluation are higher education academics that are active in research in the general area of game development. During this day the students were interviewed by the authors with open-ended questions that aimed to determine whether the students acquired understanding of important software development skills, such as software engineering procedures, design methods and team management/organisation techniques. More specifically, the questions were selected to see if students discovered and applied software engineering methods (testing, maintenance, reusability and prototyping), design methods (brainstorming, advanced game design) and collaboration techniques (team organisation). For details, see Table 5 in Appendix A. The study was exploratory rather than hypothesis-driven as many parameters were investigated. However, the overall goal was to detect correlation between evidence of formal execution of software development practices and game design principles with (a) the playability score and overall user experience, and (b) the evidence of acquired knowledge of professional practices in the field of software engineering and game design.

3.4. Heuristics for Software Development, Game Design and Playability

As stated above, the evaluators used a set of heuristics to evaluate the requirements described earlier and the playability. Those heuristics are given in detail in Appendix A. Table 2 includes the Software Development Lifecycle (SDLC) criteria in both general (analysis, design and testing) and game development specific (game design, usability and mechanics). Those were determined by the authors based on criteria taken from the University courses on software development and game development. Table 3 includes the playability heuristics that were extracted from previously tested lists of playability heuristics mentioned in the previous section and were also used to determine the final score of the games. For analysis purposes, they were separated in categories similar to the requirements heuristics (game design, usability, mechanics and quality). While there are well-defined usability questionnaires available to use, they are not the most relevant for the evaluation of the intended research, as games differ from utility software. The purpose in games is to have fun, face and overcome challenges, and face unexpected and varying situations. Therefore, applying standard usability heuristics would measure some interesting but not the most significant elements of the game (Federoff, 2002; Korhoren, 2016). Finally, Table 4 lists two important additional evaluation items, which assess the educational value and the learning outcome of the game. These items were also important as the game themes were centred on the United Nations Development Goals (UN, 2015), so that students had to develop a serious game that serves a chosen purpose. The main point under evaluation here is the educational/instructional quality of the game since this would be the starting objective of students' projects.

4. RESULTS AND DISCUSSION

This section analyses the collected data and presents the results.

4.1. Quantitative Data

As stated in 3.3 above, the project aims to detect correlations among the measured variables, therefore a correlation analysis approach was carried out. Prior to this, the mean values show that some heuristics scored significantly higher than other. One example is software quality heuristics (HS1 and HS2) that evaluate a bug free fully developed game. This shows that students understand the importance of completeness and have possibly performed some testing during their development. Another high scoring family of heuristics was those of usability (HU3, HU4 from Table 3) that report if the game is easy to learn and play. However, this can also be attributed to the simplicity of the developed games.

A set of Pearson correlation tests were conducted to evaluate the relation between (a) the formal execution of a software development cycle and game design practices (variable A in Table 1) with (b) the playability and user experience of the final product (variable B in Table 1). The total scores of all thirty games for the software development practice are compared with the total scores for the playability.

Also, the subcategories of usability, design and mechanics are compared separately and so is the software development practice with the game quality. To ensure that the above grouping to the categories A and B is valid, the internal consistency was tested using Cronbach's alpha. The variables for the categories A and B resulted in alpha values of 76% and 64% respectively. Considering the exploratory nature of the study and the conceptual heterogeneity of the playability heuristics, the above values are acceptable and validate the grouping as reliable.

The results of the Pearson correlation and the p-Values are shown in Table 2. As we can see from the values that are calculated, it appears to be a moderate-to-strong correlation between the total scores of the published competition requirements (regarding software and game design) and the playability scores of the games, $r(27)=.65$, $p<.01$. There seems to be low correlation of usability practice and results, as well as SDLC practice and game quality. A detailed analysis and explanation is given in the discussion section.

Table 1. Pearson's correlation coefficient results

Variable A (Scores on Heuristics for Software Development Cycle and Game Design Practices)	Pearson's r	T Statistic	P-Value (N=29, DF=27)	Variable B (Scores on Heuristics for Playability and User Experience of the Final Product)
Total score on software development and game design practices	.6459	4.40	1.5E-04	Total score on playability and user experience
Game Usability practice	.0864	0.45	.66	Game Usability result
Game Design practice	.7349	5.63	5.6E-06	Game Design result
Game Mechanics practice	.57	3.64	.0011	Game Mechanics result
Software Development Lifecycle practice	.19	1.06	.30	Game Quality

It is worth noting that 9 out of the 29 teams received a score of average and above (>50%) in the overall software development heuristics.

4.2. Qualitative Data

The data that was collected from the interviews was coded based on a framework derived from the categories of the interview questions. The number of categories was then reduced to a higher-level set that highlights the important areas of the current study. The final categories were agreed after two of the authors conducted individual analysis of the data and constructed their own initial coding frameworks. The two coding frameworks were then discussed in the group of authors to reach consent and construct the final coding framework. The later comprises the categories professional behaviour, software development skills and employability skills. The professional behaviour category reflects evidence of professional attitude on decisions and application. The software development skills category includes evidence on practice of testing, maintenance, reusability, prototyping and design. The employability skills category refers to planning and organising and teamwork.

4.2.1. Professional Behaviour

The interviews provided evidence that the students were able to exhibit professional judgment that was beyond the scope of the requirements completion. The statements that can be seen are epistemic and sophisticated. They provide evidence of informed decisions that take into consideration knowledge and theories that require research and only specialists in the field would reflect on. Team A commented as follows:

We didn't want a conventional 2D game, rather we believed that a 3D world would be more appropriate. However, as there are limited free 3D game content materials, we decided to go for an isometric game as it was easier to design and would make the game genre more appropriate to the topic.

The discussion for the game genre resulted in a strategy game as it's gameplay links well with the educational purpose and the game competition theme of 'productivity'. In the game story, it is vital to make appropriate resource management to optimise your productivity. At the same time, there is a reflection element of the game, because the questions that are being asked on the player provide a chance for self-learning.

We are not experts in psychology, but we tried to use appealing details in the game, for example we made extensive use of the green colour that represents ambition and wealth, so the player believes that he will be rich, and is attracted to play more to achieve this. We also used colour combinations that are appealing to the human eye, so that the player will remain active for hours.

Team A exhibits strong professional judgment traits. The explanation of the isometric and strategy game type decision is similar to standard game design principles taught in University degrees. The students take into consideration physical and virtual resources in game development to make judgement calls on how they design. They have a clear rationale on the game genre which is decided based on the game them of productivity, which is a conventional element of strategy games. The comment on colours and their associations with qualities like ambition and wealth was indicative of the fact that students went beyond the scope of achieving requirements and conducted research on special topics of game and software design that related to multidisciplinary theory decisions.

Team B who developed a game about healthy diet and living, made the following comment:

We added the option to select player gender and then the game operates upon this decision in order to calculate the Body Mass Index (BMI) and Basal Metabolic Rate (BMR) which are given by different formulas for each gender.

This is evidence of market analysis and acquisition of knowledge around the thematic area prior to designing the game. BMI and BMR are terms that may be familiar to players but provide the foundation for formal game feedback to the user based on the game theme. Feedback is a core element of games and this team ensured it is appropriate to the learning outcome of their game.

Team C developed a 3D strategy game and reported the following:

We added online high scores for a social element of competition. In order to compete higher, the use has to play more, and learn more. There is no single way to the win condition.

It was difficult to complete the game because it was 3D. We had to give extra effort to the content of the game, because a 3D game without appealing 3D models is not worth much.

To make the game more customised we built a separate level editor so players can build their own levels and play them, it makes a good impression.

We assigned construction of buildings on keyboard buttons based on the initial of the building name, we researched on other games and tried different setups.

The first comment highlights the identification of a major trend in games nowadays; the social element. Despite the single player mode, their online score allows competition among friends or groups. They also showed a clear understanding of the importance of the visual output in 3D and its effect in players. They made extensive research and tests in user interface which was beyond following guidelines and catered replay ability with the advanced feature of the level editor.

Team D made the following comments during the Game Design questions:

In game story design, we followed the recipe of a commercial successful game (name given) in which you commence with inventory and explore the map, aiming to acquire the box.

Team D showed that although they didn't have a novel approach to their game story, they followed a standard way of story writing that is based on elements from successful games. In game design, this may not be the most desired approach, but is one of the options taught in game design. Team E did not present any evidence of significant professional behaviour during the interview. The student seemed unsatisfied with the produced game and highlighted communication issues and that a team member dropped out which resulted in deprived team cohesion. The team scored low in the competition scores and during the interview, only one of the members attended. A more detailed discussion is given below on the evaluation of this team's interview.

4.2.2. Software Development

This section summarises the findings for the software related items of the interview.

4.2.2.1. Testing

Team A: "We would test every part we developed before we proceed. Then we would have both specific tests as well as user testing". "Finally, we would try to play the full game all the way to the end to see if it is ok".

Team B: "We asked our schoolmates to try to make the game fail. We didn't use scenarios but let them randomly act so we can detect bugs. We let them perform crazy things to spot unexpected issues. They would fill questionnaires as well". "We kept playing ourselves the game every week to see if there are bugs and we would list them".

Team C: "We tested each level separately. We tried weird scenarios of play by a member who knows the game well."

Team D: "Me and Andreas tested immediately every part we complete". "At the end we asked school-mates to play and tell us detected bugs. Then we played ourselves as well". "We stopped testing before we submit. If we had time we would continue".

Team E: "I did the testing once I finished all the coding". "It so happened it was me". "We played the game to see the bugs".

In the above comments, we can see evidence of different testing methodologies that are used in software (within the game development context). There is clear evidence of unit testing, level testing, "break the game" testing, as well as user alpha testing with questionnaires and feedback. Most game (and software) companies follow similar procedures while testing components, modules and early versions of their systems. Also, all teams reported that they kept testing till they submit, which indicates they all realised that there is no *perfect* version and that there are continuous opportunities for improvement. They all agreed they would like to test more if given more time. This is in line with professional software houses that test a product until they release it.

4.2.2.2. Maintenance and Reusability

Team A: "We used drawings first to decide where each button in the interface will be". "We used classes and graphs from early stages and we parameterised the size of objects to make it reusable and change-able". "We applied inheritance in order not to rewrite code and to be able to fix simultaneously".

Team B: "We provided user customisation for character selection and difficulty level". "We separate the game levels from the system operation. You can add or remove levels as desired; it is very flexible". "We reused the final room, but we parameterised it based on the user performance. So it is different each time".

Team C: "We had to change our idea and delete 50% of our work towards the end". "We made the level editor which makes it easy to reuse the game and create new levels". "We reused the artificial intelligence of the objects with minor modifications".

Team D: "We created objects and used them across levels. For example, a tree object, but sometimes we just had to resize it". "There is user configuration on the character and difficulty level". "We didn't plan for reusability, we realised along the way is needed and we worked on it."

Team E: "We used the same object but with different numbers". "We didn't configure parts of the game". "Some things I planned to reuse but I found more on the way".

There is evidence of emergent learning of higher education computer science fundamentals. The first team managed to give a simplified explanation to a significant object-oriented design principle: inheritance. This term is normally introduced in the 2nd year of university studies and not all students can apply this concept on their design. Most students appear to understand the importance of objects in game software design. There are multiple examples of parameterisation of object properties. What is important is that students came to realise the importance of reusability across the journey of this competition and that is a major learning outcome.

4.2.2.3. Design and Prototyping

Team A: "We prepared paper mockups to see how the interface will look like, we thought about the game story, we prepare graphical material and select the ones we liked more. We started coding immediately, but we always had an alternative way". "We initially added the mouse functionality, but it didn't work well while our friends played, so we changed it. We have keyboard functionality mostly". "At first we made the game progress fast, but we saw it doesn't work well all times, so we added difficulty levels".

Team B: "It was during analysis that we decided on the game and its levels". "We added a surprise bonus level at the end. This was decided at the very end of development". "We designed on paper first, then we used tablets". "We first used the mouse for input, but the accuracy was not good, so we changed to keyboard arrows".

Team C: "We made paper drawings and then discuss. After we would prepare the game". "We wanted the animation to be realistic. We used a specialised animation tool to design the movement of the character". "The game was too difficult initially, the earthquakes and aliens were coming too often, and we had to find the balance".

Team D: "We made some little sub-stories about the game while we were talking, I was designing". "We designed characters initially, but they changed on the way. We added something new, more novel".

Team E: "We didn't use any scenarios. We tried to prototyped but..". "We tried to combine our ideas with other elements, somehow with the story". "Colours and graphics are very important, but we cannot use the same for all players". "The help bar was added, but was not visible, something went wrong with the coding". "We had to change the difficulty to the right level".

Teams used a diverse set of methodologies in terms of building their games. We can see references to mockups and storyboarding, which is a very standard approach followed in games and software. Students somehow combined practices of the waterfall software development and prototyping. All teams make comments on how their games changed after their initial design, so this shows an iterative approach followed. Interface items, character and level design, were all considered at the initial design and were then refined. Students had to deal with specialised topic such as character animation and they used dedicated tools for that, so they had to research and learn to use this.

4.2.3. Employability Skills

The third skill set that this paper addresses has to do with non-technical employability skills. The questionnaire data reports on the following evidence.

4.2.3.1. Planning and Organising/Initiative

Team A: "Depending on our skills and interests, we divided the tasks". "We met 3 times or more. It helped a lot as we didn't know how to proceed".

Team B: "We went through the analysis phase to decide the topic and the game story. Then we distributed the roles". "We had more experience in coding, so we were responsible for this, [Name] handled the sound design while the other member took care of the graphics". "We first assigned roles".

Team C: "I was the programmer because I am better at it, [Name] took over documentation and technical, [Name] designed the 3D models".

Team D: "Based on what we are better, we separated the tasks. I took the video editing, [Name] did the coding, ...". "I was sending the briefing messages".

Team E: "To prepare the scenario we would gather at a member home. Discuss and keep notes. Then distribute the tasks and inform the teacher. We would then work from home individually". "I was under more pressure as I was graduating". "The teacher coordinated our activities weekly, as much as he could of course afford time".

From the above comments, it is apparent that teams practiced planning and organising. There was an analysis phase and development tasks that were planned and organised across the team members. The common pattern was that all interviewed teams followed a role-playing approach to separate tasks. It was rationalised based on their skills and interests to maximise their performance. Students acted as professionals taking responsibility and initiative on their tasks, and (in most teams) some student took the leader role to coordinate the development. The planning had an iterative approach, as the regular meetings provided the opportunity to reschedule their activities. All teams identified the importance of roles and how the made the selection of who takes which tasks.

4.2.3.2. Teamwork and Communication

Team A: "[Name] was responsible for the game testing, [Name] took care of the graphics, and I did the programming and also sound design". "We all synchronised our activities and we worked alongside to see how the game evolves".

Team B: "We had amazing brainstorming, especially in the early stage. It helped really a lot". "We kept meeting every day during class breaks to coordinate".

Team C: "We all together determined the idea". "I and [Name] took the lead as we were more experienced", "We kept having regular meetings, first twice a week, then almost every day". "Exchanging ideas helped change the game, make it better".

Team D: "We kept meeting at class breaks. Sometimes after school too, around 10 times total. This could last up to two hours". "At first, I designed the characters based on productivity topic, but we then got better ideas. But if we didn't meet and discuss we wouldn't be able to reach our final design. I could end up doing something else".

Team E: "Brainstorming helped a lot, to avoid arguments on ideas and proceed".

Students did not simply distribute tasks and worked autonomously. They performed regular meetings, shared ideas and gave each other constructive feedback. In earlier quotes, there is evidence of teamwork across tasks as well (such as testing and coding). Students appreciated the brainstorming sessions and the contribution of all in those. There is a solid sense of respect over each other contribution and reported positive communication outcomes on their output.

Further to the above skillsets, looking at the earlier technical skills we can see how students practiced analysing and problem-solving steps, learning new technology and applying it on the context. Even though there is no summative evaluation of the employability skills, there is enough qualitative self-reported data that can be used to formatively conclude that the competition may help students develop the soft skills required in the industry.

A simplified quantification of the above qualitative data of the 5 teams into frequency can allow making estimates of learning outcome success. For example, let us make the following mapping: for each team that shows evidence of practice and learning for any of the above professional behaviour, software and employability skills, a score of 1 (success) is given. For absence of evidence, a score of 0 (failure) is given. In most of the skills that are addressed above, a minimum of three out of five successful teams per categories are extracted. For example, in the testing skills, four out of the five teams exhibit real-life testing experience through their development. Four out of five is the most frequent percentage encountered above.

5. DISCUSSION

Initially, the limitations of the study need to be outlined. The study has a sampling bias for the qualitative data since it was not possible to interview all the participant teams of the competition due to time and availability constraints. However, the sampling bias does not apply to the quantitative data as all games were reviewed and scores across the heuristics were given. There is also a measurement bias due to the type of questions used in the interviews. However, the questions were given in an abstract setting and did not provide details that guided the answers of the participants. Also, as can be seen above, only detailed answers were included that provided evidence of an informed opinion by the participants. Plain affirmative answers were ignored to eliminate the measurement bias. Moreover, the group-style interviews provided a sufficient number of participants in this empirical pilot study, however in future iterations and to provide a concrete evaluation of the intervention, the sample size may need to be redesigned, alongside with the intervention type, such as the design and inclusion of a pre-test, or the introduction of comparison groups. Finally, as stated earlier, the final coding framework was the product of iterations and discussions among the researchers to reach consensus.

The presented research uses two different approaches to evaluate how well the students apply the software development techniques in their game development: (a) expert evaluation on their submitted games and reports, and (b) open-ended interviews collecting more detailed information about the process and the cultivated skills. The two methods triangulations allowed the exposure of different type of information from each resource. The first method used a formal heuristic-based score approach to rate students in a course-based assessment approach. The second method gave insight into the student experience and the dynamics of their team-based progress across the duration of the competition (more than six months total). The combination of the two approaches give added validity and trustworthiness of the evaluation of the software development practice as they address both formative and summative assessment of the research question.

From the quantitative analysis data, it is apparent that there is a direct correlation between the application of software development techniques and the end-result of the game based on playability heuristics. Considering that playability heuristics are an important indicator of the potential success of games, we can conclude that students who worked better on their software development practices have produced a more playable game and have a higher success to succeed in their theoretical strategic objective. There is evidence of correlation between game design and game mechanics practice and their corresponding results. This was expected, as those two comprise the core of the game development practice. The relation of software development practice with the game quality is smaller than expected, but this can be attributed to a small set of heuristics used for this correlation test (three for variable A and two for variable B). The same applies to the test on usability practice, although this can be attributed to the fact that even though students used some usability principles (as was seen in their submitted reports) they didn't complete a comprehensive test on their interfaces.

Looking at the overall scores of effectively completing software development (see last statement of Section 4.1) we can predict the success of the competition in the software development learning outcome: since 9 out of 29 teams passed the above average rate of 50%, we can expect based on the adjusted Wald method and with 95% confident that at least 17% of the teams will practice sufficiently the software development cycle. In that case the best estimate would be 32%, which presents a significant range of success of the competition considering that is it not related to credits or academic progression; it is a voluntary activity for the students. That means that given a competition with the requirements presented in this project, we can expect 17-49% of participating high school students to exhibit software development practical skills prior to their higher education studies. This is a significant capacity building, which can create room for more scaffolding in the university courses, leading to better equipped and ready to work graduates.

Regarding the outcome of the interviews, four out of the five teams interviewed showed evidence of specialised experience (see last paragraph before the discussion chapter). Considering that the sample was taken from the 10 teams in the final using the adjusted Wald method, we can conclude with 95% confidence that at least 35% of the teams that made in to the final will have experienced practical real-life experience. The average would be 71% with the range 35-97%. In the worst-case scenario when from the teams that did not make it to the final none exhibits of the desired evidence, we would have at least 12% of the teams successful with a 26% average. Overall, the success of the competition is noteworthy considering that the students who practice well can bring a wealth of practical experience to their future studies by applying their skills in Computer Science or transferring the skills to other fields of study.

Perhaps the above numbers can be further improved, but they are already of significant value to early computer science education.

6. CONCLUSION

The pilot study presented a way to teach software development to high school students using a long-term competition that requires students to satisfy a set of requirements. Students from various schools participated by forming groups and following the software development lifecycle throughout the competition duration. The teams were evaluated using a set of heuristics that relate to software development, game design practice, playability, and game value. The best scoring teams pitched their ideas to a group of experts and five of them were interviewed to determine additional information. The collected data from the heuristics and interviews provided the opportunity to determine noteworthy correlations between software development practices with playability outcomes and with acquisition of specialised real-life experience. The pilot study has several limitations because of the nature of the competition. The procedure was not designed to allow concrete causal conclusions as there is no control group, a pre-competition test or comparison groups to get more detailed and informative data. The latter would allow testing different approaches on the intervention, such as different requirement sets, different development methodologies, different mentoring opportunities, online learning support and so on. For example, by utilising the SCRUM development model, we can evaluate progress at intervals and capture scaffolding information. Moreover, even if one of the above methodologies were applied, considering also that students take school classes during the competition, there is uncertainty whether part of the achieved learning is solely a result of the competition. It would be nest for the competition to run during a summer school and fully engage the students over a few weeks. Finally, there are more sophisticated employability skills frameworks (PCRN, 2018) that extend communication and collaboration to more specific skills and qualities sought-after by employers in the IT industry. The study can be designed to focus on either a wider set or a more specialised. It would be interesting to engage industry partners in the design and evaluation of any employability skills as they can offer a different - and more valid - viewpoint. Finally, the playability heuristics data should be collected from game playing sessions with real users from the targeted audience or experienced game testers since the evaluation experts are not always game enthusiasts or even casual gamers. Nevertheless, despite the above limitations, the pilot study exposed potential in utilising epistemic game development in teaching software development skills. A more profound intervention that addresses the above limitations can offer more detailed insight into the topic.

REFERENCES

Barcelos, T. S., Soto, R. M., & Silveira, I. F. (2015). *Improving Novice Programmers' Skills through Playability and Pattern Discovery: A Descriptive Study of a Game Building Workshop. In Human Factors in Software Development and Design* (pp. 141–172). IGI Global.

Barron, B., & Darling-Hammond, L. (2008). Teaching for meaningful learning. In *Powerful learning: What we know about teaching for understanding*. Jossey-Bass.

Basawapatna, A., Koh, K. H., & Repenning, A. (2010). Using scalable game design to teach computer science from middle school to graduate school. In *Proceedings of the fifteenth annual conference on Innovation and technology in computer science education (ITiCSE '10)* (pp. 224–228). New York, NY: ACM. 10.1145/1822090.1822154

Bortz, D. (2020). Top skills for software engineers. *Monster.com Online Recruitment*. Available at: https://www.monster.com/career-advice/article/software-engineer-skills

Cordova, D., & Lepper, M. (1996). Intrinsic motivation and the process of learning: Beneficial effects of contextualizations, personalizations, and choice. *Journal of Educational Psychology*, *88*(4), 715–730. doi:10.1037/0022-0663.88.4.715

Denner, J., Werner, L., & Ortiz, E. (2012). Computer games created by middle school girls: Can they be used to measure understanding of computer science concepts? *Computers & Education*, *58*(1), 240–249. doi:10.1016/j.compedu.2011.08.006

Desurvire, H., Caplan, M., & Toth, J. A. (2004). Using Heuristics to Evaluate the Playability of Games. In *CHI '04 extended abstracts on Human factors in computing systems* (pp. 1509–1512). Vienna, Austria: ACM. doi:10.1145/985921.986102

Duffy, T. M., & Jonassen, D. H. (1992). *Constructivism and the Technology of Instruction: A Conversation*. Hillsdale, NJ: Lawrence Erlbaum Publishing.

Federoff, M. (2002). *Heuristics and Usability Guidelines for the Creation and Evaluation of FUN in Video Games* (Thesis). University Graduate School of Indiana University.

Gatzoulis, C., Loizides, F., & Zaphiris, P. (2016). Planning for Computer Games Research and Industry: A Structured Dialogue Design Approach. *The Computer Game Journal*, *5*(3-4), 95–114. doi:10.100740869-016-0019-y

Hainey, T., Connolly, T. M., Stansfield, M., & Boyle, E. A. (2011). Evaluation of a game to teach requirements collection and analysis in software engineering at tertiary education level. *Computers & Education*, *56*(1), 21–35. doi:10.1016/j.compedu.2010.09.008

Hamari, Shernoff, D. J., Rowe, E., Coller, B., Asbell-Clarke, J., & Edwards, T. (2016). Challenging games help students learn: An empirical study on engagement, flow and immersion in game-based learning. *Computers in Human Behavior*, *54*, 170–179. doi:10.1016/j.chb.2015.07.045

Hayes, E., & Games, A. (2008). Making computer games and design thinking: A review of current software and strategies. *Games and Culture*, *3*(3–4), 309–332. doi:10.1177/1555412008317312

Jabbar, A. I. A., & Felicia, P. (2015). Gameplay engagement and learning in game-based learning: A systematic review. *Review of Educational Research*, *85*(4), 740–779. doi:10.3102/0034654315577210

Kafai, Y. B. (1995). *Minds in play: Computer game design as a context for children's learning*. Mahwah, NJ: Lawrence Erlbaum.

Kafai, Y. B., & Burke, Q. (2016). Constructionist Gaming: Understanding the Benefits of Making Games for Learning. Educational Psychologist, 50(4).

Kim, B., Park, H., & Baek, Y. (2009). Not just fun, but serious strategies: Using meta-cognitive strategies in game-based learning. *Computers & Education, 52*(4), 800–810. doi:10.1016/j.compedu.2008.12.004

Kirriemuir, J., & McFarlane, C. A. (2004). Literature review in games and learning. *Futurelab*. Available at: https://www.nfer.ac.uk/publications/FUTL71/FUTL71.pdf

Korhonen, H. (2016). Evaluating Playability of Mobile Games with the Expert Review Method. Dissertations in Interactive Technology, 24.

Liu, C. (2018). Toward creator-based learning: Designs that help student makers learn. In J. Voogt, G. Knezek, R. Christensen, & K.-W. Lai (Eds.), *Second handbook of information technology in primary and secondary education* (pp. 921–933). New York: Springer. doi:10.1007/978-3-319-71054-9_61

Lopez-Morteo, G., & Lopez, G. (2007). Computer support for learning mathematics: A learning environment based on recreational learning objects. *Computers & Education, 48*(4), 618–641. doi:10.1016/j.compedu.2005.04.014

Magen-Nagar, N., Shachar, H., & Argaman, O. (2019). Changing the Learning Environment. Teachers and Students' Collaboration in Creating Digital Games. Journal of IT Education. [Informing Science Institute.]. *In Practice, 18*, 61–85.

Magnussen, R., Hansen, S. D., Planke, T., & Sherson, J. F. (2014). Games as a platform for student participation in authentic scientific research. *Electronic Journal of E-Learning, 12*(3), 259–270.

Markauskaite, L., & Goodyear, P. (2016). Professional Epistemic Games. *Professional and Practice-based Learning., 14*, 395–434. doi:10.1007/978-94-007-4369-4_14

Martins, A. R., & Oliveira, L. R. (2018). Students as creators of educational games: Learning to use simple frameworks and tools to empower students as educational game designers. In T. Bastiaens (Ed.), *Proceedings of EdMedia: World Conference on Educational Media and Technology* (pp. 1210-1215). Amsterdam: Association for the Advancement of Computing in Education (AACE).

Martins, V. F. (2019). *Using Game Development to Teach Programming. In Handbook of Research on Immersive Digital Games in Educational Environments* (pp. 450–485). IGI Global. doi:10.4018/978-1-5225-5790-6.ch016

Mayer, R. E. (2003). Theories of learning and their application to technology. In H. F. O'Neil & R. S. Perez (Eds.), *Technology applications in education: A learning view* (pp. 127–155). Mahwah, NJ: Lawrence Erlbaum Associates, Inc.

Meier, S. (2010). *Civilisation*. Take-Two Interactive Software.

Microsoft. (2013). *XNA Game Studio 4*. Available at: https://www.microsoft.com/en-us/download/details.aspx?id=23714

O'Neil, R. (2015). Why the future of work is about specialisation. *World Economic Forum*. Available at: https://www.weforum.org/agenda/2015/03/why-the-future-of-work-is-about-specialisation/

PCRN. (2018). *Employability skills framework Handout*. Available at: https://s3.amazonaws.com/PCRN/docs/Employability_Skills_Framework_OnePager_20180212.pdf

Petri, G. (2019). *Digital Games for Computing Education: What Are the Benefits? In Handbook of Research on Immersive Digital Games in Educational Environments* (pp. 35–62). IGI Global. doi:10.4018/978-1-5225-5790-6.ch002

Ponnada, A., & Kannan, A. (2012). Evaluation of mobile games using playability heuristics. In *Proceedings of the International Conference on Advances in Computing, Communications and Informatics (ICACCI '12)*. ACM. 10.1145/2345396.2345437

Renton, D. (2016). The Importance of Computer Games Development in the Computing Curriculum in Schools. *Computer Games Journal, 2016*(5), 1–5. doi:10.100740869-015-0016-6

Repenning, A., & Ioannidou, A. (2008). Broadening participation through scalable game design. In *ACM Special Interest Group on Computer Science Education Conference, (SIGCSE)*. ACM Press. 10.1145/1352135.1352242

Revilla, M. A., Saris, W. E., & Krosnick, J. (2013). Choosing the Number of Categories in Agree-Disagree Scales. *Sociological Methods & Research, 43*(1), 73–97. doi:10.1177/0049124113509605

Robertson, J., & Howells, C. (2008). Computer game design: Opportunities for successful learning. *Computers & Education, 50*(2), 559–578. doi:10.1016/j.compedu.2007.09.020

Rosas, R., Nussbaum, M., Cumsille, P., Marianov, V., Correa, M., Flores, P., ... Salinas, M. (2003). Beyond Nintendo: Design and assessment of educational video games for first and second grade students. *Computers & Education, 40*(1), 71–94. doi:10.1016/S0360-1315(02)00099-4

Seif El-Nasr, M., Yucel, I., Zupko, J., Tapia, A., & Smith, B. (2007). Middle-to-high school girls as game designers - what are the implications? In Academic Days. ACM.

Shaffer, D. W. (2006). *How Computer Games Help People Learn*. Palgrave MacMillan. doi:10.1057/9780230601994

SimCity Societies. (2010). *Electronic Arts*. https://www.ea.com/simcity-societies

SporeE. A. (2009). http://www.spore.com

Squire, K. (in press). Civilization III as a world history sandbox. In *Civilization and its discontents. Virtual history. Real fantasies*. Milan, Italy: Ludilogica Press.

Topalli, D., & Cagiltay, N. E. (2018). Improving programming skills in engineering education through problem-based game projects with Scratch. *Computers & Education, 120*, 64–74.

Triantafyllakos, G., Palaigeorgiou, G., & Tsoukalas, I. A. (2011). *Designing educational software with students through collaborative design games: The We!Design&Play framework*. Academic Press.

Tuzun, H., Yilmaz-Sollu, M., Karakus, T., Inal, Y., & Kizilkaya, G. (2008). The effects of computer games on primary school student's achievement and motivation in geography learning. *Computers & Education, 52*(1), 68–78. doi:10.1016/j.compedu.2008.06.008

TycoonZ.CoorpM. (2017). Available at: https://www.microsoft.com/en-us/p/zoo-tycoon-ultimate-animal-collection/9pj06tzx4nmh?activetab=pivot:overviewtab

UN. (2015). *United Nations Millenium Goals and Beyond.* Available at: https://www.un.org/millenniumgoals/reports.shtml

Vos, N., Meijden, H., & Denessen, E. (2011). *Effects of constructing versus playing an educational game on student motivation and deep learning strategy use.* Academic Press.

Werner, L., Denner, J., Bliesner, M., & Rex, P. (2009, April). Can middle-school students use Storytelling Alice to make games? Results of a pilot study. *Fourth International Conference on the Foundation of Digital Games.*

World Economic Forum. (2018). *The Future of Jobs Report, Insight Report, Centre for the New Economy and Society.* Available at: http://www3.weforum.org/docs/WEF_Future_of_Jobs_2018.pdf

YoYo Games. (2020). *GameMaker Studio 2.* Available at: https://www.yoyogames.com/gamemaker

This research was previously published in the International Journal of Game-Based Learning (IJGBL), 10(4); pages 1-21, copyright year 2020 by IGI Publishing (an imprint of IGI Global).

APPENDIX: EXPERIMENT HEURISTICS AND INTERVIEW QUESTIONS

Table 2. Software development life cycle and game design heuristics

ID	Software Development Life Cycle Heuristics
SDLC1	There is evidence that regular meetings were conducted that allowed initial analysis and strategic decisions in the development process
SDLC2	There are detailed software design diagrams available in the report
SDLC3	There is evidence of a formal testing procedure that occurs at some point before the submission of the game
ID	**Game Usability Design Practice**
GU1	There is evidence of methodological user interface design
GU2	There are user tutorials/hints in game or external that support the game player
ID	**Game Design Practice**
GD1	There are detailed game scripts or game concept/design sheets that capture the game story and characteristics
GD2	There are comprehensive storyboarding material in the story design section of the report
GD3	There is evidence of methodological character/object/game setting design
GD4	There is evidence of a graphics design process
GD5	There is evidence of a sound effects engineering/design process
GD6	The game follows a narrative style (i.e. Hero's Journey)
ID	**Game Mechanics Design Practice**
GP1	There is a description of the gameplay challenge design
GP2	There is a planned learning curve for the user
GP3	There is evidence of methodological game balancing in the gameplay
GP4	There is a justifiable AI system in place

Table 3. Playability heuristics

ID	Game Quality
HS1	Game is bugs free
HS2	Game appears to be complete in terms of development
ID	**Game Usability**
HU1	User Interface is challenging
HU2	There is feedback on player actions
HU3	Game is easy to play (in a positive way)
HU4	Game is easy to learn
ID	**Game Design**
HD1	The game creates an empathetic feeling for the player
HD2	There are funny elements in the game
HD3	Game is fun to play
HD4	Game is interesting
HD5	Game has some novel feature
ID	**Game Mechanics**
HM1	Reward System is meaningful
HM2	AI is unpredictable
HM3	There are multiple strategies of gameplay
HM4	The game is easy to start, challenging to conquer
HM5	Skills learned are useful for future gameplay

Table 4. Game value questions

ID	Game Value
GV1	Describe and rate the educational value of the game in the given theme
GV2	Describe and rate any learning that you believe you achieved regarding the competition theme while playing the game
GV3 -1	The game is compatible with the theme
GV4	Give details on any advise to improve the user experience of the game and add to its educational value

Table 5. Interview questions

ID	Testing
TS1	Who was in charge of testing? (Dedicated member of whoever was available?)
TS2	How did you perform testing? (Per unit or overall?)
TS3	Did you use scenarios in testing or did you just playtest the levels and report issues?
TS4	When did you decide that testing was sufficient and may be stopped?
	Team Organisation
TO1	How did you distribute the tasks?
TO1	Did you assign specific roles in the team? How was this decided?
TO1	Who was the leader of the team? Was it one member of did you all lead different parts?
	Maintenance
MN1	During the development phase, did you encounter cases were some game elements will have to be modified along the way?
MN2	How did you deal with those cases?
MN3	Did you design the game to be customisable by users/administrators?
	Reusability
RU1	Did you reuse any items you developed at different game parts? Either identical or with modifications?
RU2	Did you try to predict such items?
RU3	If the above answer in RU1 is yes, was it based on a plan or did it appear on the way?
	Prototyping
PT1	Did you use scenarios during development? If yes, how many and in what form?
PT2	Did you develop a prototype aimed for requirement verification?
	Brainstorming
BS1	Did you perform regular meetings, so you can generate ideas and discuss them before you start developing the game (or during)?
BS2	If answer in BS1 is yes, how many meetings did you have, and can you describe duration and process?
BS3	If answer in BS1 is yes, do you believe this process augmented your development (and how much?)
	Game Design
GD1	How did you come up with the specific style of game content? What do you believe you achieve with that?
GD2	Why did you choose the specific game genre over others?
GD3	Which is your game story's strongest element?
GD4	Did you try different UI items? How did you decide on the existing one?
GD5	Did you modify the game difficulty along the way?
GD6	Are there any motives for a player who started playing to continue playing?
GD7	Is there replay value? Why?

Chapter 44

Evolutionary Approaches to Test Data Generation for Object–Oriented Software:
Overview of Techniques and Tools

Ana Filipa Nogueira
Polytechnic Institute of Leiria, Portugal & University of Coimbra, Portugal

José Carlos Bregieiro Ribeiro
Polytechnic Institute of Leiria, Portugal

Francisco Fernández de Vega
University of Extremadura, Spain

Mário Alberto Zenha-Rela
University of Coimbra, Portugal

ABSTRACT

In object-oriented evolutionary testing, metaheuristics are employed to select or generate test data for object-oriented software. Techniques that analyse program structures are predominant among the panoply of studies available in current literature. For object-oriented evolutionary testing, the common objective is to reach some coverage criteria, usually in the form of statement or branch coverage. This chapter explores, reviews, and contextualizes relevant literature, tools, and techniques in this area, while identifying open problems and setting ground for future work.

DOI: 10.4018/978-1-6684-3702-5.ch044

INTRODUCTION

Search-Based Software Engineering (SBSE) seeks to reformulate Software Engineering (SE) problems as search-based optimisation problems. It has been applied to a wide variety of SE areas, including requirements engineering, project planning and cost estimation, automated maintenance, service-oriented software engineering, compiler optimisation and quality assessment (Harman, 2007). Most of the overall literature (an estimated 59%) in the SBSE area is, however, concerned with Software Testing (ST) related applications, with structural test data generation being the most studied sub-topic (Harman, Mansouri, & Zhang, 2009).

The application of Evolutionary Algorithms (EAs) to test data generation or selection is often referred to as *Evolutionary Testing (ET)* (Tonella, 2004b; Wappler & Wegener, 2006b) or *Search-Based Test Data Generation (SBTDG)* (McMinn, 2004). ET consists of exploring the space of test programs by using metaheuristic techniques that direct the search towards the potentially most promising areas of the input space (Bertolino, 2007); its foremost objective is usually that of searching for a set of test programs that satisfies a predefined test criterion.

EAs have already been applied, with significant success, to the search for test data; the first application of heuristic optimisation techniques to test data generation was presented in 1992 (Xanthakis, Ellis, Skourlas, Gall, & K. Karapoulios, 1992). However, research has been mainly geared towards generating test data for procedural software, and traditional methods – despite their effectiveness and efficiency – cannot be applied without adaptation to Object-Oriented (OO) systems.

The application of search-based strategies to unit testing of OO programs is, in fact, fairly recent – the first approach was presented in 2004 (Tonella, 2004b) – and is yet to be investigated comprehensively (Harman, Hassoun, Lakhotia, McMinn, & Wegener, 2007). Interesting review articles on the topic of SBSE, and Search-Based Software Testing (SBST) in particular, include: (McMinn, 2004; Mantere & Alander, 2005; Xiao, El-Attar, Reformat & Miller, 2007; Afzal, Torkar, & Feldt, 2009; Ali, Briand, Hemmati, & Panesar-Walawege, 2009; Harman et al., 2009; Harman & McMinn, 2010; Maragathavalli, 2011; McMinn, 2011; Harman, Mansouri, & Zhang, 2012; Varshney & Mehrotra, 2013; Anand *et al.*, 2013). McMinn surveys the use of metaheuristic search techniques for the automatic generation of test data (McMinn, 2004); because the work on SBST had, thus far (2004), been largely restricted to programs of a procedural nature, these are the main subject of this review. In (Mantere & Alander, 2005), a review of the application of Genetic Algorithm (GA)-based optimisation methods to ST is presented; the authors stress out that all the researchers in this area report good (or, at least, encouraging) results regarding their use. Xiao *et al.* reported the experimental results regarding the effectiveness of five different optimisation techniques over five different C/C++ programs (Xiao *et al.*, 2007). The results show that the GA-based approach outperformed the remaining techniques – e.g., Simulated Annealing (SA), Genetic Simulated Annealing (GSA), Simulated Annealing with Advanced Adaptive Neighborhood (SA/ANN) and Random Testing – achieving the best overall performance.

The work proposed in (Afzal *et al.*, 2009) builds on on McMinn's research (McMinn, 2004) and presented a review on how search-based techniques are used to test non-functional properties of the software, focusing on: the properties studied, the fitness functions implemented and the constraints and limitations found when testing each property. The set of non-functional properties identified include (listed in descending order of the number of papers that investigate it): execution time, security, usability, safety and quality of service. A systematic review on the way SBST techniques have been empirically assessed is presented in (Ali *et al.*, 2009). In (Harman et al., 2009, 2012) a thorough index and classification of SBSE-related literature is provided, supported by an online repository. Local search, SA, GAs and Genetic Programming (GP) are identified as the most widely used optimisation and search techniques. Harman and McMinn conducted a theoretical and empirical study on the SBST field with the purposes of predicting the scenarios in which ET should perform properly and of justifying the reasons why a specific technique suited a particular situation (Harman & McMinn, 2010). The predictions were supported by empirical studies which showed that sometimes a simpler solution can be more suitable than a more sophisticated one, and it was theoretically and empirically proved that an evolutionary approach is suitable for several scenarios.

Maragathavalli also performed an overview of the current SBST techniques, and pointed out that for programs in which the complexity of the input domain grows, the efficacy of GA is quite significant when compared to random testing (Maragathavalli, 2011). (Varshney & Mehrotra, 2013) overviews the SBST techniques employed to automatically generate structural test data. The authors point out that control-flow based coverage criteria are the most often used to assess the effectiveness of the SBST techniques. In particular, the branch coverage metric is the most used by the researchers. Possible future research directions are also present, and are in accordance with the open problems discussed in (McMinn, 2011). In (Anand *et al.*, 2013), an orchestrated survey on the most prominent techniques for automatic test case generation was conducted, in which SBST is included. The survey focuses on several SBST emerging areas including: (i) the combination of SBST with other techniques – e.g., dynamic symbolic execution; (ii) the oracle problem; (iii) the co-evolutionary computation paradigm; (iv) the use of hyper-heuristics to combine different SE activities; and (v) the optimisation and better understanding of failures. Nevertheless, none of these surveys is devoted to the specific topic of Object-Oriented Evolutionary Testing (OOET). This paper extends previous work by the authors (Nogueira, Ribeiro, Fernández de Vega, & Zenha-Rela, 2014) with the latest advances in the field; and its goal is precisely that of overviewing current literature in the area while providing a primer to newcomers to this field of study.

Relevant literature was retrieved from three main sources: (i) the *Repository of Publications on Search Based Software Engineering (Centre For Research on Evolution, Search And Testing (CREST), 2008)*, a page maintained by the CREST which provides a complete collection of the literature addressing SE problems using metaheuristic search techniques. Only those papers belonging to the "Testing and Debugging" category were considered; (ii) the Google Scholar (Google, 2004) search engine, which allowed us to retrieve other studies, including some *grey literature* that may otherwise be missing (the following search terms were used: *"search based software testing"*, *"search based test data generation"*, *"evolutionary testing"*, and *"search based software engineering"*); and (iii) the bibliography sections of previously analysed relevant literature and surveys.

This paper is organized as follows. The next Section starts by providing background information on Object-Oriented Evolutionary Testing; relevant literature and research is explored, reviewed and contextualized in the following Section; and finally, in the concluding Section, achievements and open problems in the area are summarized and discussed.

BACKGROUND

This Section provides background on the most relevant aspects related with the interdisciplinary area of OOET. The OO paradigm is overviewed in the following Subsection. Then, key ST concepts are reviewed, and Metaheuristics and EAs are explored in the subsequent Subsections. The final Subsection introduces the reader to the ET area.

Object-Orientation

The use of OO technology is not restricted to any particular language; rather, it applies to a wide spectrum of programming languages, such as C++, Java, C# and Visual Basic. A language is considered OO if it directly supports data abstraction and classes, and also encapsulation, inheritance, and polymorphism (Booch *et al.*, 2007).

An *Object* is a software bundle of related state and behaviour. This is the key difference between OO and procedural programming methodologies: in OO design, the state and behaviour are contained within a single object, whereas in procedural (or structured) design they are normally separated, with data being placed into totally distinct functions or procedures. With the procedural paradigm, procedures ideally become "black boxes", where inputs go in and outputs come out. Also, the data is occasionally global, so it is easy to modify data that is outside the scope of the code, this means that access to data is uncontrolled.

Hiding internal state and requiring all interaction to be performed through an object's methods is known as data *encapsulation* – a fundamental principle of OO programming. The most important reason underlying the usage of encapsulation is that of separating the interface from the implementation (Eckel, 2002); this allows establishing boundaries within a data type and hiding its internal mechanism, and prevents client programmers from accidentally treating the internals of an object as part of the interface that they should be using.

OO programming allows classes to inherit commonly used state and behaviour from other classes. *Inheritance* expresses this similarity between classes by using the concept of *base classes* and *derived classes*: a base class contains all of the characteristics and behaviours that are shared among the classes derived from it. Semantically, inheritance denotes an "is a" relationship; inheritance thus implies a generalization/specialization hierarchy, wherein a subclass specialises the more general structure or behaviour of its superclass.

Polymorphism means "different forms" and it represents a concept in type theory in which a single name (such as a variable declaration) may denote objects of many different classes that are related by a common superclass. Any object denoted by this name is therefore able to respond to some common set of operations; distinction is expressed through differences in behaviour of the methods that can be called through the base class.

Testing OO software is particularly challenging: in an OO system, the basic test unit is a class instead of a subprogram, and testing should hence focus on classes and objects. While a test program for procedural software typically consists of a sequence of input values to be passed to a procedure upon execution, test programs for class methods must also account for the state of the objects involved in the methods' calls. This *state problem* (McMinn & Holcombe, 2003) is, in fact, one of the main hindrances posed to search-based approaches to test data generation, and one of the main reasons why procedural testing techniques cannot be applied directly to OO programs.

Software Testing

Software Testing (ST) is the process of exercising an application to detect errors and to verify that it satisfies the specified requirements. The general aim of testing is to affirm the quality of software systems by systematically exercising the software in carefully controlled circumstances (Marciniak, 1994). Despite advances in formal methods and verification techniques, a program still needs to be tested before it is used; testing remains the truly effective means to assure the quality of a software system of non-trivial complexity.

"Test early, test often" is the mantra of experienced programmers; however, developing conformance testing code can be more time consuming and expensive than developing the standard or product that will be tested (Tassey, 2002). Automating the testing process is, thus, key to improve the quality of complex software systems that are becoming the norm of modern society (Bertolino, 2007).

Although testing is involved in every stage of the software life-cycle, the testing done at each level of software development differs in terms of its nature and objectives, and normally targets specific types of faults. It is, nevertheless, clear that most errors are introduced at the coding/unit stage, and that the cost of repairing these errors increases significantly if they are dealt with at later stages of software development (Marciniak, 1994; Tassey, 2002). *Unit testing* thus plays a major role in the total testing efforts: it can be defined as the process of testing the individual subprograms, subroutines, procedures or methods in a program (Beizer, 1990), and is typically performed by executing the unit – i.e., the smallest testable piece of software – in different scenarios, using a set of relevant and interesting test programs.

To gain sufficient confidence that most faults are detected, testing should ideally be exhaustive; since in practice this is not possible, testers resort to test models and adequacy/coverage criteria to define systematic and effective test strategies that are fault revealing. Distinct test strategies include: *functional (or black-box) testing*, which is concerned with showing the consistency between the implementation and its requirements or functional specification; and *structural (or white-box) testing*, in which test program design is performed with basis on the internal structure of the software entity under test, with the basic idea being to ensure that all of the control elements in a program are executed by a given *test set* providing evidence of the quality of the testing activity. As will be made clear in subsequent sections, most SBTDG approaches rely on structural testing – not only because a formal specification of the test object is seldom available but also, and most importantly, because it is problematic to guide the search towards the definition of pertinent test scenarios with basis on the specification alone.

Evolutionary Algorithms

Computing optimal solutions for many problems of industrial and scientific importance is often difficult and sometimes impossible; automating the *test data generation process* is a paradigmatic example. Unlike exact methods, metaheuristics allow solving hard and complex problem instances by delivering satisfactory solutions in a reasonable time.

Evolutionary Algorithms (EAs) are the most studied metaheuristics; they are stochastic algorithms, which use simulated evolution as a search strategy to iteratively evolve candidate solutions, using operators inspired by genetics and natural selection (Michalewicz, 1994). They draw their inspiration from the works of Mendel on heredity and from Darwin's studies on the evolution of species. *Genetic Algorithms (GAs)* are the most well-known form of EAs (Holland, 1962). The term "Genetic Algorithm" comes from the analogy between the encoding of candidate solutions as a sequence of simple components and the genetic structure of a chromosome. Like other EAs, GAs are based on the notion of competition: they maintain a population of solutions rather than just one current solution. In consequence, the search is afforded many starting points, and the chance to sample more of the search space than local searches. The population is iteratively recombined and mutated to evolve successive populations, known as *generations*. Various selection mechanisms can be used to decide which individuals should be used to create offspring for the next generation. Key to this is the concept of the *fitness* of individuals – the idea of selection is to favour the fitter individuals, in the hope of breeding better offspring.

Genetic Programming (GP) is a type of EA usually associated with the evolution of tree structures; it focuses on automatically creating computer programs by means of evolution (Koza, 1992). Fitness evaluation is typically performed by executing the individuals and assessing their behaviour; GP is generally interested in the space where there are many possible programs, but it is not clear which ones outperform the others and to what degree. In most GP approaches, the programs are represented using variable-sized tree genomes. The leaf nodes are called *terminals*, whereas the non-leaf nodes are called *non-terminals* or *functions*. The *function set* is the set of functions from which the GP system can choose when constructing trees; GP builds new trees by repeatedly selecting nodes from a function set and putting them together. The individuals in the initial population are typically randomly generated. The specification of the control parameters in a run is a mandatory preparatory step. There are several parameters, which some of the most important being: i) the population size; ii) the probabilities of performing the genetic operations; iii) the minimum and maximum tree sizes; and iv) the stopping criteria. It is impossible to define general guidelines for setting optimal parameter values, as these depend greatly on the details of the application. Nevertheless, GP is in practice robust, and it is likely that many different parameter values will work (Poli, Langdon, & Mcphee, 2008). When applied to testing, GP trees are representations of the test programs that exercise the software under test.

The nodes of a GP tree are usually not typed – i.e., all the functions are able to accept every conceivable argument. *Type consistency* (Koza, 1994) ensures that operators will always produce legal offspring – i.e., *crossover* is not able to attempt incompatible connections between nodes, and *mutation* does not produce illegal programs. An implicit assumption underlying *type consistency* is that all combinations of structures are equally likely to be useful; in many cases, however, it is known in advance that there are constraints on the structure of the potential solutions. What's more, the nonexistence of types may lead to the generation of syntactically incorrect parse trees; specifically, non-typed GP approaches are unsuitable for representing OO programs (Haynes, Schoenefeld, & Wainwright, 1996). *Strongly-Typed Genetic Programming (STGP)* (Montana, 1993) is arguably the most natural approach to incorporate types and their constraints into GP (Poli *et al.,* 2008), since constraints are often expressed using a type system. Variables, constants, arguments and returned values can be of any data type, with the provision that the data type for each such value is specified beforehand in the function set. The STGP search space is the set of all legal parse trees and is thus particularly suited for representing OO programs, as it enables the reduction of the search space to the set of *compilable*, i.e., formally *feasible* (Wappler, 2007), programs by allowing the definition of constraints that eliminate invalid combinations of operations. In addition, STGP has already been extended to support more complex type systems, including simple generics (Montana, 1995), inheritance (Haynes et al., 1996), and polymorphism (Olsson, 1994; Yu, 2001).

Object-Oriented Evolutionary Testing

Software Testing can benefit from OO technology, for instance, by capitalising on the fact that a super-class has already been tested, and by decreasing the effort to test derived classes, which reduces the cost of testing in comparison with a flat class structure. However, the myth that the enhanced modularity and reuse brought forward by the OO programming paradigm could prevent the need for testing has long been rejected (Bertolino, 2007). In fact, the OO paradigm poses several hindrances to testing due to some aspects of its very nature (Barbey & Strohmeier, 1994): (i) inheritance opens the issue of retesting (*should operations inherited from ancestor classes be retested in the context of the descendant class?*); (ii) polymorphism and dynamic binding call for new coverage models, and induce difficulties because they introduce *undecidability* in program-based testing. The hidden state, in particular, poses a serious barrier to the OO software testing. This issue – usually referred to as the *state problem* (McMinn & Holcombe, 2003) – is related with the fact that, due to the encapsulation principle of the OO paradigm, the state of an object is accessible only through an interface of public methods. As such:

- The only way to change the state of an object is through the execution of a series of method calls (i.e., it is not possible to directly manipulate the object's attributes);
- And the only way to observe the state of an object is through its operations, which hinders the task of accurately measuring the quality of a candidate test program.

The term *OOET* usually refers to the search-based unit test generation for OO software (Harman *et al.*, 2009), and involves the search for unit test programs that define interesting state scenarios for the objects involved in the call to the *Method Under Test (MUT)*. During test program execution, all participating objects must be created and put into particular states by calling several instance methods on these objects. The search space thus encompasses the set of all possible inputs – and their states – to the public methods of a particular *Class Under Test (CUT)*, including the implicit parameter (i.e., the *this* parameter) and all the explicit parameters.

A test program for OO software typically consists of a Method Call Sequence (MCS), which represents the test scenario. In general, a MCS is a sequence of method calls, constructor calls and value attributions, when assuming that no decision or repetition structures are present (Wappler, 2007). Given that each MCS usually focuses on the execution of one particular method (the MUT), at least one method call must refer to that method – in general, the last element of the sequence. Also, it is usually not possible to test a single class in isolation; other data types may be necessary for calling the CUT's public methods. The set of classes which are relevant for testing a particular class is called the *Test Cluster* (Wappler & Wegener, 2006a).

Let us consider the search method of the *Stack* class of Java Development Kit (JDK) 1.4 for illustration purposes. The *Stack* container class represents a *last-in-first-out* stack of objects; and the *search* method returns the 1-based position (i.e., the distance from the top) where an object is on the stack.

The behaviour of the *search* method differs depending on both the state of the stack on which the method call is issued (i.e., empty or containing elements) and on the properties of the *Object* instance passed to the method as an argument (i.e., the stack instance may either contain it or not). Modifying and "tuning" the state of the *Stack* and *Object* instances, however, is not trivial. The state of the *Stack* can only be modified by calling one of the 5 public methods made available by its public interface (*push*, *pop*, *empty*, *peek* and *search*), and these methods have method call dependencies themselves (e.g., an *Object* instance must be created and passed to the *push* method in order to issue a method call).

Table 1 depicts an example test program for OO software. The MUT is the *search* method of the *Stack* class. In this program, instructions 1, 3 and 5 instantiate new objects, whereas instructions 2 and 4 aim to change the state of the *stack1* instance variable that will be used, as the implicit parameter, in the call to the MUT at instruction 6.

Table 1. Example unit test program for Object-Oriented Java Software

```
1 Stack stack1 = new Stack();
2 stack1.peek();
3 Object object2 = new Object();
4 stack1.push(object2);
5 Object object3 = new Object();
6 stack1.search(object3);
```

Source: adapted from Ribeiro, 2010

It should be noted that syntactically correct and *compilable* test programs may still abort prematurely, if a *runtime* exception is thrown during execution (Wappler & Wegener, 2006a). In the example test program shown in Table 1, instruction 2 will throw a *runtime* exception (an *EmptyStackException*), rendering the test program *unfeasible*; when this happens, it is not possible to assess the quality of the test program because the final instruction (i.e., the call to the MUT) is not reached. Test programs can thus be separated in two classes: (i) *feasible* test programs that are effectively executed, and terminate with a call to the MUT; and (ii) *unfeasible* test programs which terminate prematurely because a *runtime* exception is thrown by an instruction of the MCS.

METHODOLOGIES AND TECHNIQUES FOR OBJECT-ORIENTED EVOLUTIONARY TESTING

In this Section, the existing literature on Object-Oriented Evolutionary Testing (OOET) is explored. Firstly, GA-based techniques are described; a discussion on methodologies which employ the GP technique follows; and finally, special attention is paid to approaches that employ other metaheuristic strategies.

Genetic Algorithms-Based Approaches

The first approach to the field of OOET was presented in (Tonella, 2004b), and proposes a technique for automatically generating input sequences for the structural unit testing of Java classes by means of GA. Possible solutions are represented as chromosomes, which consist of the input values to use in test program execution; the creation of objects is also accounted for. Because the GA performs on chromosomes with a specific organization, the standard evolutionary operators cannot be applied; special mutation operators (for replacing input values, changing constructors, and inserting/removing method invocations) and a one-point crossover operator are defined. A population of test programs is evolved in order to increase a measure of fitness accounting for their ability to satisfy a branch coverage criterion;

new test programs are generated as long as there are targets to be covered or a maximum execution time is reached. The *eToc* framework for the evolutionary testing of OO software was implemented and made available as a result of this research.

Experimental studies were performed on 6 Java classes; full branch coverage was not achieved in all of them, but the only branches remaining corresponded to non-traversable portions of code. Even though several ET-related problems were not addressed on this work (e.g., the usage of universal EAs, encapsulation, complex state problems, test program feasibility, search guidance, MCS minimisation), it was able to prove the applicability of EAs to test data generation. Several approaches built on Tonella's experiments with GAs in the following years.

Wappler and Lammermann defined a grammar-based encoding for test programs which enabled the application of any given universal EAs (e.g., Hill Climbing or SA) to OOET. Unlike Tonella's previous approach, this methodology allows an effortless change of the evolutionary strategy employed (Wappler & Lammermann, 2005). Objective functions based on the distance-oriented approach, which guide the evolutionary search in cases of conditions that are hard to meet by random, are also defined. However, the technique proposed permits the generation of individuals that cannot be decoded into test programs without errors; this hindrance is circumvented by the definition of a fitness function which penalises invalid sequences. Experiments were performed on a custom-made Java class; even though coverage metrics were not provided, relevant results included the observation that the number of inconvertible individuals visibly decreased constantly over the generations.

In (Cheon, Kim, & Perumandla, 2005), the authors combined the Java Modelling Language (JML) and GAs in order to automate test data generation for Java programs. JML is used both as a tool for describing test oracles and as a basis for generating test data; each class to be tested is assumed to be annotated with JML assertions. A proof-of-concept tool is briefly described with basis on a custom-made example. In (Cheon & Kim, 2006), a specification-based fitness function for evaluating *boolean* methods of OO programs was presented, with an example being provided for illustration and experimentation purposes. The evolutionary search's efficiency was reported to improve from 300% up to 800% as a result of application of the fitness function.

In (Inkumsah & Xie, 2007), a technique that merges *Concolic Testing* (a combination of concrete and symbolic testing techniques) and ET was introduced; this approach was implemented into the *Evacon* framework, which integrated Tonella's *eToc* ET tool and the *jCUTE* concolic testing tool (which tests Java classes using the dynamic symbolic execution technique). ET is used to search for desirable method sequences, while concolic testing is employed to generate desirable method arguments. The inclusion of concolic testing into the process was supported by the perception that typical ET tools do not use program structure or semantic knowledge to directly guide test generation, nor provide effective support for generating desirable primitive method arguments. Empirical studies were conducted on 6 Java classes, with the results showing that the tests generated using *Evacon* achieved higher branch coverage than ET or concolic testing alone.

The *Evacon* tool is described with further detail in (Inkumsah & Xie, 2008). Additionally, *Evacon* is empirically compared to *eToc*, *jCUTE*, *JUnit Factory* (an industrial test generation tool developed by *AgitarLabs*), and *Randoop* (a random testing tool). *Evacon* is reported to achieve higher branch coverage than any of the aforementioned tools for the 13 Java classes tested. The *Evacon* framework includes 4 components: evolutionary testing, symbolic execution, argument transformation (for bridging from ET to symbolic execution), and chromosome construction (for bridging from symbolic execution to ET). In a short position paper (Xie, Tillmann, Halleux, & Schulte, 2008), the authors briefly describe an additional tool for the generation of method sequences with a demand-driven mechanism and a heuristic-guided mechanism, which is incorporated into *Pex* (a test data generation framework for .NET).

In (Dharsana, Jennifer, Askarunisha, & Ramaraj, 2007), a GA-based tool for generating test cases for Java programs is briefly described. Experiments were performed on 3 JDK classes and 2 custom-made programs, but no details were provided on the setup or results.

The work described in (Ferrer, Chicano, & Alba, 2009) proposes dealing with the inheritance feature of OO programs by focusing on the Java *instanceof* operator. The main motivation is that of providing guidance for an automatic test case generator in the presence of conditions containing the aforementioned operator, and is supported by the fact that it appears in 2700 of the 13000 classes of the JDK 1.6 class hierarchy. Two *mutation* operators, which change the solutions based on a distance measure that computes the branch distance in the presence of the *instanceof* operator, were proposed. Experiments were performed on 9 custom-made test programs, each consisting of 1 method with 6 conditions; the mutation operators proposed were reported to behave well when used in place of a simpler mutation operator, and when compared to random search.

Genetic Programming-Based Approaches

GP emerges as a natural candidate to address OOET problems, for reasons which include: (i) the fact that GP is usually associated with the evolution of tree structures and is thus particularly suited for representing and evolving test programs; (ii) the existence of a number of typing mechanisms (most notably STGP) which facilitate the encoding of OO programs using GP; (iii) the possibility of having a tree vary in length throughout the run, thus allowing experimenting with different sized test programs; and (iv) the possibility of evolving active structures, enabling the solutions to be executed without post-processing. The first GP-based approaches to OOET were presented in 2006 in (Wappler & Wegener, 2006a, 2006b), and in (Seesing, 2006; Seesing & Gross, 2006).

The encoding of potential solutions using the STGP technique was first proposed in (Wappler & Wegener, 2006b). Test programs are represented as STGP trees, which are able to express the call dependencies of the methods that are relevant for a given test object. In contrast with previous approaches in this area, neither repair of individuals nor penalty mechanisms are required in order to achieve sequence validity; the usage of STGP preserves validity throughout the entire search process (i.e., only *compilable* test programs are generated by tree builders and genetic operators). To account for polymorphic relationships which exist due to inheritance relations, the STGP types used by the function set are specified in correspondence to the type hierarchy of the test cluster classes: the function set is derived from the signatures of the methods of the test cluster classes, and the type set is derived from the inheritance relations of the test cluster classes. *Runtime* exceptions are dealt with by means of a distance-based fitness function. Experiments were performed on 4 JDK classes, with full structural coverage being achieved in all cases.

Wappler and Wegener extended their previous work and focused on dealing with unfeasible test programs; unlike previous approaches, the search is guided in case of uncaught *runtime* exceptions (Wappler & Wegener, 2006a). They propose a minimising distance-based fitness function in order to assess and differentiate the test programs generated during the evolutionary search, which rates them according to their distance to the given test goal (i.e., the program element to be covered). The aim of each individual search is therefore to generate a test program that covers a particular branch of the CUT. This fitness function makes use of a distance metric that is based on the number of non-executed methods of a test program if a *runtime* exception occurs. The *EvoUnit* framework, which implements the concepts proposed in (Wappler & Wegener, 2006a, 2006b), is also described; unfortunately the tool is proprietary and is thus not openly available. Experiments were performed on a custom-made test cluster with full branch coverage being achieved.

An improvement to the aforementioned ET approach was suggested in (Wappler & Schieferdecker, 2007), which particularly addresses the test of non-public methods. The existing objective functions are extended by an additional component that accounts for encapsulation; candidate test programs are rewarded if they cover calls to specific non-public methods. Experiments performed on 6 Java classes yield better branch coverage for non-public methods in comparison with random search and with their previous approach.

In his Ph.D. Thesis, Wappler provides a thorough explanation of his approach to automatic test data generation for OO software, and compares it to other testing techniques, e.g., symbolic execution and constraint solving (Wappler, 2007). An empirical investigation also demonstrated the effectiveness of the methodology; it outperformed random testing and 2 commercial test sequence generators (*CodePro* and *Jtest*) when being allocated the same resources. Limitations on the current stage of development of the approach were also pinpointed: the efficiency level of the approach decreases as the test cluster (and, in consequence, the function set) increases in size; and the test sequences might include unnecessary method calls.

Ribeiro *et al.* also employed STGP for representing test programs, and presented a series of studies on defining strategies for addressing the challenges posed by the OO paradigm, which include methodologies for: (i) systematizing both the test object analysis (Ribeiro, Vega, & Zenha-Rela, 2007; Ribeiro, Zenha-Rela, & Vega, 2007) and the test data generation (Ribeiro et al., 2007; Ribeiro, 2008) processes; (ii) introducing an *input domain reduction* methodology, based on the concept of *purity analysis*, which allows the identification and removal of entries that are irrelevant to the search problem because they do not contribute to the definition of relevant test scenarios (Ribeiro, Zenha-Rela, & Vega, 2008; Ribeiro, Zenha-Rela, & Vega, 2009); (iii) proposing an adaptive strategy for promoting the introduction of relevant instructions into the generated test cases by means of *mutation*, which utilizes Adaptive EAs (Ribeiro, Zenha-Rela, & Vega, 2010a); and (iv) defining an *object reuse* methodology for GP-based approaches to ET, which allows one object instance can be passed to multiple methods as an argument (or multiple times to the same method as arguments) and enables the generation of test programs that exercise structures of the software under test that would not be reachable otherwise (Ribeiro, Zenha-Rela, & Vega, 2010b).

Ribeiro elaborates on these topics in his Ph.D. Thesis (Ribeiro, 2010) and provides a thorough description of the authors' technical approach, embodied by the *eCrash* OOET tool. Special attention is put on bridging and automating the static test object analysis and the iterative test data generation processes; the function set is computed automatically with basis on the test cluster, and the test programs are evolved iteratively solely with basis on function set information. Experiments were performed on JDK 1.4 container classes; the results demonstrated the pertinence of the approach and the applicability of STGP as a basis for developing an automated, general-purpose test data generation tool for OO software.

Seesing and Gross proposed a distinct typed GP mechanism for creating test data for OO systems; in (Seesing & Gross, 2006), the advantages of employing a tree-shaped data structure (which can be mapped instantly to the abstract syntax trees commonly used in computer languages) for representing test programs is discussed, and the proposed GP methodology is compared to previous GA-based approaches (Tonella, 2004b; Wappler & Lammermann, 2005). A custom-made encoding of OO test programs is presented, and mutation operators for method introduction, method removal, and variable introduction are described. Experiments were performed on 5 Java classes; the results demonstrated the advantage of GP over random search, with much higher structural coverage being achieved. In (Seesing, 2006), the author elaborates on the approach and describes the *EvoTest* test case generation and software analysis framework.

Arcuri and Yao employed STGP in a different scenario. (Arcuri & Yao, 2007a) introduces the idea of employing Co-Evolution (Hillis, 1990) for automatically generating OO programs from their specification; STGP is used to evolve these programs and, at the same time, the specifications are exploited in order to co-evolve a set of unit tests. More specifically, given a specification of a program, the goal is to evolve a program that satisfies it; at each step of the evolutionary process, each program is evaluated against a set of unit tests that also depends on the specification. The more unit tests a program is able to pass, the higher its fitness will be; similarly, unit tests are rewarded on how many programs they make fail. The experiments performed on 4 array-related problems achieved successful results. In (Arcuri, 2008; Arcuri & Yao, 2008a), the authors elaborate on the topic and provide further details on the approach, and in (Arcuri, White, Clark, & Yao, 2008) they present a related co-evolution approach to optimising software, which also involves Multi-Objective Optimisation; still, and even though it is argued that it possible to apply the methodology proposed to any problem that can be defined with a formal specification, its application to the OO software was not the subject of the latter study.

Cody-Kenny *et al.* (Cody-Kenny, Galván-López, & Barrett, 2015) presented a GP system for improving the performance of Java programs named *locoGP*. Program performance is measured by: counting the number of instructions taken to execute a program; and problem-specific functions for counting functionality errors. Experiments were performed on a number of sort algorithms; results showed improvements, encouraging further studies on larger programs.

Other Metaheuristics and Hybrid-Based Approaches

Even though the majority of the OO literature is devoted to the study of either GAs or GP, there are several studies that focus on distinct evolutionary techniques. In fact, as stated in (Arcuri & Yao, 2007c), other metaheuristic techniques have the potential to achieve promising results in this area.

An approach which employed a hybrid of Ant Colony Optimisation and Multi-Agent GAs was the subject of the work described in (Liu, Wang, & Liu, 2005). The focus was on the generation of the shortest MCS for a given test goal, under the constraint of state dependent behaviour and without violating encapsulation. This hybrid algorithm was reported to yield encouraging results on the experiments performed.

In (Sagarna, Arcuri, & Yao, 2007), the authors addressed the OOET problem using Estimation of Distribution Algorithms (EDAs). EDAs only differ from GAs in the procedure to generate new individuals; instead of using the typical breeding operators, EDAs perform this task by sampling a probability distribution previously built from the set of selected individuals. The focus was put on generating test data for Java container classes. Relevant conclusions include the observations that the positions at which methods are called in the test program are (considering the particular conditions of the approach) independent of each other, and that coverage grows as the length of the MCS increases.

In (Liaskos & Roper, 2008), the authors investigated whether the properties of the Clonal Selection (CS) algorithm (memory, combination of local and global search) could help tackling the hindrances posed by OOET. CS is one of the most popular population-based Artificial Immune Systems (AIS) algorithms (computational systems inspired by theoretical immunology and observed immune functions). Despite employing mutation to generate new populations, and unlike GAs, CS performs mutation on the selected solutions with a rate that is inversely proportionate to their fitness, and does not use crossover;

also, high quality solutions are stored for future use, leading to a faster immune response. The encoding of solutions is identical to the one used by the GAs (test programs are encoded as chromosomes), and the goal is to minimise the distance between "*receptors*" (i.e., the executed paths) and "*antigens*" (i.e., the test targets). Comparative experiments were performed on 6 Java classes to assess the behaviour of the hybridisation of a GA with both AIS and Local Search. The results suggested that hybridised approaches usually outperform the GA; however, there are scenarios for which the hybridisation with Local Search is more suited than the more sophisticated CS algorithm. This paper extended the authors' previous works (Liaskos & Roper, 2007; Liaskos, Roper, & Wood, 2007), which also addressed the problem of automated testing with data-flow as the adopted coverage criterion.

Arcuri *et al.* performed extensive research on the application of distinct search algorithms to the test data generation for container classes (i.e., classes designed to store any arbitrary type of data). This is precisely the topic of (Arcuri & Yao, 2007b). Hill Climbing, GAs and Memetic Algorithms were the evolutionary approaches used and compared (extending their previous work presented in (Arcuri & Yao, 2007d)). While GAs are global metaheuristics and Hill Climbing is a local search metaheuristic, Memetic Algorithms can approximately be described as a population-based metaheuristics in which, whenever an offspring is generated, a local search is applied to it until it reaches a local optimum. Case studies conducted on 5 Java container classes showed that the Memetic Algorithm outperforms the other algorithms; also, novel search operators and a search space reduction technique were able to increase its performance. In (Arcuri & Yao, 2008b), the authors elaborate on their previous studies, and focused on the difficulties of testing OO container classes with metaheuristic search algorithms. The performance of five search algorithms (Random Search, Hill Climbing, SA, GAs and Memetic Algorithms) was compared on 10 Java classes. The experimental studies revealed *TreeMap* (an implementation of Red-Black Tree) as the most difficult container to test, with Memetic Algorithms arising as the best technique for the problem. Also interestingly, Hill Climbing performed better than GAs (Local Search algorithms are generally supposed to behave worse in these situations (Wegener, Baresel, & Sthamer, 2001)), and Random Search behaved poorly especially on more complicated problems. In his Ph.D. Thesis (Arcuri, 2009), the author compiles and elaborates on his previous proposals. Relevant contributions to the SBSE area include: theoretical analyses of search algorithms applied to test data generation (and, in particular, to OOET); and the proposal of methodologies for (i) automatic refinement – i.e., automating implementation with basis on a formal specification, (ii) fault correction – i.e., automatically evolving the input program to make it able to pass a set of test cases, (iii) improving non-functional criteria – e.g., execution time and power consumption, and (iv) reverse engineering – i.e., automatically deriving source code from bytecode or assembly code. Test suites targeting branch coverage, for real Java classes, were generated by employing GA and Random techniques and compared in the empirical study conducted by Shamshiri et al. (Shamshiri, Rojas, Fraser, & McMinn, 2015); it included 1000 classes randomly selected from SF110 corpus of open projects (Fraser & Arcuri, 2014). In this study, for the majority of the classes, the behaviour observed was quite similar; most notably when optimisation techniques were applied (e.g., seeding). The authors argumented that one reason for the unexpected similarity between algorithms resides on the fact that there are a huge number of branches that don't provide any type of guidance (when compared with the ones that provide guidance that can be leveraged by GA algorithms); as a consequence, low coverage values for the GA algorithms were observed in large classes containing these type of branches (no guidance), and better results were observed by randomly generated test suites..

Miraz *et al.* proposed a holistic incremental approach to the generation of test data for OO software, as the internal states reached with previous test programs are used as starting points to subsequent individuals (Miraz, Lanzi, & Baresi, 2009; Baresi, Lanzi, & Miraz, 2010; Baresi & Miraz, 2010). Strategies for enhancing the efficiency of the approach include: (i) local search – integrating the global evolutionary search in order to form a hybrid approach; (ii) seeding – providing an initial population so as to speed up the start of the evolutionary process; and (iii) fitness inheritance – replacing the evaluation of the fitness function by replacing the fitness of some individuals with estimated fitness inherited from their parents. A multi-objective approach is used to combine coverage and length criteria. Test program quality is evaluated with a technique which merges black-box analysis (to evaluate the behaviours of tested classes and reward test programs accordingly) and white-box analysis (which utilises coverage criteria). These techniques were implemented in the *Testful* tool.

EvoSuite, which was presented in (Fraser & Arcuri, 2011a), is a tool that applies a hybrid approach – integrating hybrid search, dynamic symbolic execution and testability transformation – for generating and optimizing test suites, while suggesting possible oracles by adding assertions that concisely summarize the current behaviour. *EvoSuite* implements a "whole test suite" (Fraser & Arcuri, 2011c) approach towards evolving test data, meaning that optimisation is performed with respect to a coverage criterion, rather than individual coverage goals. The rationale for this methodology is related with the observation that coverage goals are not independent nor equally difficult, and are sometimes infeasible; test suites are thus evolved with the aim of covering all coverage goals at the same time, while keeping the total size as small as possible. In (Fraser & Arcuri, 2013), the authors evaluated the approach on open source libraries and an industrial case study for a total of 1,741 classes, showing that *EvoSuite* achieved up to 188 times the branch coverage of a traditional approach targeting single branches, with up to 62% smaller test suites.

The *EvoSuite* tool was extended and utilised as a platform for experimentation. Pavlov and Fraser presented a semi-automatic test generation approach based on *EvoSuite* in (Pavlov & Fraser, 2012); a human tester is included in the test generation process, with the tester being given the opportunity to improve the current solution (an editor window is presented to the user with a pre-processed version of the current best individual) if and when the search stagnates, under the assumption that where the search algorithm struggles, a human tester with domain knowledge can often produce solutions easily. Another prototype that extends *Evosuite* was presented in (Gross, Fraser, & Zeller, 2012): *EXSYST* is a test generator for interactive Java programs, which operates at system-level; it synthesizes input actions in order to test a program through its Graphical User Interface. The maximization of coverage is the main goal of the tool, and it uses *Evosuite* as the mechanism to incorporate search-based techniques that aim to reach the maximum of coverage possible. A major advantage of this approach is the fact that every reported failure is a real failure, as each one is a consequence of sequences of input events. (Gross et al., 2012) also reports the study conducted on five study subjects, for which *EXSYST* has revealed errors that were in fact real errors of the programs being tested.

In (Fraser, Arcuri, & McMinn, 2013), the authors addressed the issue of *primitive value* (e.g., numbers and strings) optimisation by extending the global search applied in *EvoSuite* with local search on the individual statements of method sequences: at regular intervals, the search inspects the primitive variables and tries to improve them. The Memetic Algorithm described achieved up to a 32% higher branch coverage than the standard GA; still, the authors identify the need for future work to make the local search adaptive, so as to make it less dependent of a specific parameter configuration. (Goffi, Gorla, Mattavelli, Pezzè, & Tonella, 2014) propose a search-based technique (the prototype implementation uses *EvoSuite*) to synthesize sequences of method invocations that are equivalent to a target method within a finite set of execution scenarios (e.g., the method *pop( )* of the *Stack* class is equivalent to the method sequence *remove(size()-1))*, with the goal of achieving a higher level of redundancy and thus increase code reusability. Experiments performed on 47 methods of 7 classes taken automatically synthesized 123 equivalent method sequences, which represent more than 87% of the 141 sequences manually identified.

Evosuite - MOSA (Panichella, Kifetew, & Tonella, 2015a) is an extension of *Evosuite* tool (search-based testing) which incorporates an additional technique referred as Many-Objective Sorting Algorithm (MOSA) -- a many-objective GA. Similarly to several search-based testing tools, its uses branch coverage as criteria; however, in MOSA, branch coverage is addressed as a many-objective problem, in which different branches pose as different optimization problems/goals. The MOSA considers a search population composed by test cases generated randomly; it uses the traditional operators in each generation (crossover and mutation), and for each generation, the selection of the fittest individuals takes into account the sort algorithm. This sort algorithm attributes higher survival probability to test cases that are closest to at least one of the uncovered branches (many-objective optimization problem). In a search-based testing tool competition (Panichella, Kifetew, & Tonella, 2015b) *Evosuite-MOSA* was able to reach better coverage results, for a set of 63 classes, when compared with its competitors; however, it was penalised by the execution time. Limitations of this tool include the ones belonging to *Evosuite* version used, for instance: issues with non-deterministic code and code that uses external/environmental dependencies.

(Boussaa, Barais, Sunye, & Baudry, 2015) introduced the Novelty Search (NS) algorithm to address the test data generation problem for Java programs, with focus on the statement-coverage criteria; this algorithm aims to explore the search space without an objective, i.e. a fitness-based function. Instead, the selection is done with basis on how different individuals are from the solutions evaluated until that moment. The authors presented the concept of *archive* which stores, as a memory, the set of test cases generated; the *archive* is then used as a means to measure an individual's novelty degree; and if a new level of novelty is reached (higher than a specified threshold *T*) then the test case is included in the *archive*. Typical EA operators (crossover and mutation) are then applied to the test cases with the purpose of generating offspring that will settle the next population. The aim of the authors was to promote the variety among the solutions found by the generation process; and measures of statement coverage are kept during the generation process so that at the end, the best test cases are selected. Finally, the generation process ends when a certain criteria is reached (e.g., number of iterations). The concept of novel search/behaviour as alternative to fitness functions was also addressed in a previous work from Lehman and Stanley (Lehman & Stanley, 2010).

An empirical study was conducted on 100 Java Classes by Rojas et al. (Rojas, Vivanti, Arcuri, & Fraser, 2016) with the purpose of comparing the whole test suite approach employed by *Evosuite*, which searches for tests that cover all goals at the same time, with approaches that target specific individual goals (branch coverage, for instance). The individual test goals addressed in this paper were: line coverage, branch coverage and weak mutation, and the authors concluded that traditional approaches can be best to cover a few and specific set of individual testing goals -- a very rare occurrence (if we compare those with the cases for which only *Evosuite* is able to cover the criteria goals). This work is an extended version of the research presented by Arcuri and Fraser (Arcuri & Fraser, 2014) and it includes an impact analysis focusing the usage of a test *archive*: by analysing the results, the average performance was improved but some negative side-effects were also observed due to the necessity of having specialized search operators that are able to handle the test *archive* concept.

SBES (Search-Based Equivalent Synthesis) is a Java prototype that utilises a search search-based technique to automatically synthesize and validate sequences functionally equivalent to sequences of method calls (Goffi et al., 2014). If we consider the method *put(<key>, <value>)* as an example which is available in collections' objects (and inserts the pair in a collection object), the technique proposed in SBES would be able to generate an "equivalent" set of instructions that would test the put method, example: *m=new Multimap(); m.putAll(key, new List().add(value))* (adapted from (Mattavelli, Goffi, & Gorla, 2015)). The equivalence notion proposed by the authors is based on the notion defined by De Nicola and Hennessy (De Nicola & Hennessy, 1984). The search-based engine used by SBES is a custom version of *Evosuite*; the exclusive goal to be covered is the "TRUE" branch of the MUT. In (Mattavelli et al., 2015) the authors reported an improvement of the tool by implementing means to handle a language feature that was not originally supported -- Java generics. (Mattavelli et al., 2015) reports an experiment using Google Guava library as the case study which, according to the authors, present a large search space mainly due to the high number of classes, methods and parameter values. Memetic algorithms were used to address the specificities of such search space. A total of 220 methods from 16 classes belonging to the Google Guava collections library were evaluated by SBES, and the new prototype that includes generics support and memetic algorithms is able to "find 86% more true functionally equivalent method sequences."

In (He, Zhao, & Zhu, 2015), the authors propose to integrate Reinforcement Learning into OO Evolutionary Testing; GP is used to evolve candidate method call sequences in ET, and Reinforcement Learning to steer search towards pertinent individuals -- namely, by replacing method calls with others that return subclasses of the original type, and public method with others that can call specific non-public methods. The aim is to tackle the hindrances posed by the inheritance and encapsulation properties of the OO paradigm. Empirical studies conducted on the proposed *EvoQ* prototype showed encouraging results in comparison with *eToc* and *Randoop*.

(Chawla, Chana, & Rana, 2015; He et al., 2015) presents a hybrid Particle Swarm Optimization and GA methodology for the automatic generation of test suites, with the objective of making use of the diversity of GA and fast convergence rate of Particle Swarm Optimization. Empirical studies yielded positive results for the container classes used as Test Objects, although it was stated that further experiments were required in order to extend the conclusions to generic OO software.

CONCLUSION

Test data generation by means of EAs requires the definition of a suitable representation of OO test programs. Even though it is still a relatively young field of study and no definitive conclusions have been reached on deciding the best search algorithm to apply for this purpose, existing OOET approaches have mainly used GAs and GP.

An analysis of the current literature on OOET allows making some observations: nearly all studies have been developed with basis on the program's structure, with the objective being that of attaining a coverage criterion (usually statement or branch coverage). Java is clearly the programming language of choice for the purposes of implementation and experimentation; and even though several test objects have considered for experimentation purposes, nearly all works (and, in particular, those that do not use custom-made classes) employ container classes (e.g., Stack, BitSet, Vector, TreeMap) as a basis for their studies, mostly due to the lack of a common benchmark which can be used by researchers to test and compare their techniques (Arcuri & Yao, 2007c).

Even though several OOET techniques have been proposed, the test data generation frameworks developed are seldom publicly available, with the only exceptions known to the authors being *eToc* (Tonella,

2004a), *Testful* (Miraz, Lanzi, & Baresi, 2011), *EvoSuite* (Fraser & Arcuri, 2011b), *EvoSuite-MOSA* (Panichella, Kifetew, & Tonella, 2015a) and *eCrash* (Ribeiro, Nogueira, Vega, & Zenha-Rela, 2013). This makes it difficult for researchers to experiment and compare their approaches; as such, comparisons are usually performed against Random Search, e.g., (Gupta & Rohil, 2008; Ribeiro et al., 2010b; Seesing & Gross, 2006; Wappler & Schieferdecker, 2007). A recent study (Nogueira, Ribeiro, Vega, & Zenha-Rela, 2013) compared the performance of three test data generation tools – the *Randoop* (Pacheco & Ernst, 2007) random testing tool, and the *EvoSuite* and *eCrash* ET tools – when applied to a complex software product – the Apache Ant project (The Apache Software Foundation, 2012) release 1.8.4. The results provided solid indicators of the effectiveness and efficiency of the ET tools, and allowed pinpointing some limitations and hindrances to be addressed in future work, including the difficulty of generating tests for some instance methods that enter infinite loops, for some static methods in classes that are not able to provide instances of that data type (namely, when public constructors are not defined), and for specific problematic methods (e.g., class loaders; input handlers; task and thread handlers; file and folder managers; compilers; audio and image processors; and encapsulators of Unix commands). The difficulty in testing classes related to certain system's features and functionalities had, in fact, already been reported in the literature (Fraser & Arcuri, 2012). In (Shamshiri, Just, et al., 2015) three generation tools for Java (*Randoop*, *EvoSuite*, and *Agitar*) were employed to empirically evaluate automatic unit test generation; the goal was that of investigating whether the resulting test suites could find faults. Results indicated that any individual tool on a given software project is far from providing confidence about finding faults, providing basis for concluding that code coverage remains a major problem and that improved techniques to achieve fault propagation and generation of assertions are still required.

It is, nevertheless, clear that significant success has been achieved by applying metaheuristics to automate the generation of test data for OO software. In fact, nature-inspired algorithms seem to perform better than "traditional" techniques (Arcuri & Yao, 2008b) (e.g., based on symbolic execution and state matching) as they seem able to solve more complex test problems in less time. Still, several open problems exist in the field of OOET, mostly arising from the challenges posed by the three cornerstones of OO programming: encapsulation, inheritance, and polymorphism. The *Search Space Sampling* issue is particularly pertinent; it deals with the inclusion of all the relevant variables to a given test object into the test data generation problem, so as to enable the coverage of the entire search space whenever possible and improve the effectiveness the approach. Because the test cluster cannot possibly include all the subclasses that may override the behaviours of the classes which are relevant for the test object, adequate strategies for search space sampling – which take the commonality among classes and their relationships with each other into account – are of paramount importance.

Future research should also involve addressing the *Oracle Generation* problem; although it is possible to generate inputs for certain classes of programs using search-based techniques, automatically determining whether the corresponding outputs are correct also remains a significant problem; one that is not limited to ET, but is orthogonal to the entire field of ST. This is because an *oracle* (i.e., a mechanism for checking that the output of a program is correct given some input), is seldom available. In (Davis & Weyuker, 1981), the authors proposed the use of a "pseudo-oracle" to alleviate this problem. A pseudo-oracle is a program that has been produced to perform the same task as its original counterpart. The two programs, the original and its pseudo-oracle, are run using the same input and their respective outputs compared; any discrepancy may represent a failure on the part of the original program or its pseudo-oracle. In (Tonella, 2004b), the oracle problem is handled by manually adding assertions; Tonella reported that the test suites produced by the ET method proposed were quite compact, and that augmenting them with assertions would thus be expected to require a minor effort. McMinn introduced testability transformations (i.e., techniques that change a program in order to make it more "testable") to automatically generate pseudo-oracles from certain classes of OO programs (McMinn, 2009). *EvoSuite* suggests possible oracles by adding assertions that concisely summarize the current behaviour, utilising a mutation testing approach; still, the authors state that they are investigating strategies to support the developer by automatically producing effective assertions (Fraser & Arcuri, 2011a) and by increasing the readability of the produced test cases (Fraser & Zeller, 2011).

REFERENCES

Afzal, W., Torkar, R., & Feldt, R. (2009). A systematic review of search-based testing for non-functional system properties. *Information and Software Technology, 51*(6), 957–976. doi:10.1016/j.infsof.2008.12.005

Ali, S., Briand, L. C., Hemmati, H., & Panesar-Walawege, R. K. (2009). A systematic review of the application and empirical investigation of search-based test-case generation. *IEEE Transactions on Software Engineering, 99*(1).

Anand, S., Burke, E. K., Chen, T. Y., Clark, J., Cohen, M. B., Grieskamp, W., ... Mcminn, P. (2013). An orchestrated survey of methodologies for automated software test case generation. *Journal of Systems and Software, 86*(8), 1978–2001. doi:10.1016/j.jss.2013.02.061

Arcuri, A. (2008). On the automation of fixing software bugs. In *ICSE companion '08: Companion of the 30th international conference on software engineering* (pp. 1003–1006). New York, NY: ACM. 10.1145/1370175.1370223

Arcuri, A. (2009). *Automatic software generation and improvement through search based techniques* (Doctoral dissertation). University of Birmingham.

Arcuri, A., & Fraser, G. (2014). On the Effectiveness of Whole Test Suite Generation. In Lecture Notes in Computer Science (pp. 1–15). Academic Press. doi:10.1007/978-3-319-09940-8_1

Arcuri, A., White, D. R., Clark, J., & Yao, X. (2008). Multi-objective improvement of software using co-evolution and smart seeding. In *Proceedings of the 7th international conference on simulated evolution and learning (seal '08)* (p. 61-70). Springer. 10.1007/978-3-540-89694-4_7

Arcuri, A., & Yao, X. (2007a). Coevolving programs and unit tests from their specification. In *ASE '07: Proceedings of the twenty-second IEEE/ACM international conference on automated software engineering* (pp. 397–400). New York, NY: ACM. 10.1145/1321631.1321693

Arcuri, A., & Yao, X. (2007b). A memetic algorithm for test data generation of object-oriented software. In *Proceedings of the 2007 ieee congress on evolutionary computation (CEC)* (p. 2048-2055). IEEE. 10.1109/CEC.2007.4424725

Arcuri, A., & Yao, X. (2007c). On test data generation of object-oriented software. In *Taicpart-mutation '07: Proceedings of the testing: Academic and industrial conference practice and research techniques - mutation* (pp. 72–76). Washington, DC: IEEE Computer Society. 10.1109/TAIC.PART.2007.11

Arcuri, A., & Yao, X. (2007d). *Search based testing of containers for object-oriented software* (Tech. Rep. No. CSR-07-3). University of Birmingham, School of Computer Science.

Arcuri, A., & Yao, X. (2008a). A novel co-evolutionary approach to automatic software bug fixing. In *Proceedings of the IEEE congress on evolutionary computation (CEC '08)* (p. 162-168). IEEE Computer Society. 10.1109/CEC.2008.4630793

Arcuri, A., & Yao, X. (2008b). Search based software testing of object-oriented containers. *Information Sciences, 178*(15), 3075–3095. doi:10.1016/j.ins.2007.11.024

Barbey, S., & Strohmeier, A. (1994). The problematics of testing object-oriented software. In M. Ross, C. A. Brebbia, G. Staples, & J. Stapleton (Eds.), *SQM'94 second conference on software quality management* (Vol. 2, pp. 411–426). Academic Press.

Baresi, L., Lanzi, P. L., & Miraz, M. (2010). Testful: An evolutionary test approach for java. In *Proceedings of the 2010 third international conference on software testing, verification and validation* (pp. 185–194). Washington, DC: IEEE Computer Society. 10.1109/ICST.2010.54

Baresi, L., & Miraz, M. (2010). Testful: automatic unit-test generation for java classes. In *Proceedings of the 32nd ACM/IEEE international conference on software engineering - volume 2* (pp. 281–284). New York, NY: ACM. 10.1145/1810295.1810353

Beizer, B. (1990). *Software testing techniques*. New York: John Wiley & Sons, Inc.

Bertolino, A. (2007). Software testing research: Achievements, challenges, dreams. In *Fose '07: 2007 future of software engineering* (pp. 85–103). Washington, DC: IEEE Computer Society.

Booch, G., Maksimchuk, R. A., Engel, M. W., Young, B. J., Conallen, J., & Houston, K. A. (2007). *Object-oriented analysis and design with applications* (3rd ed.). Addison-Wesley Professional.

Boussaa, M., Barais, O., Sunye, G., & Baudry, B. (2015). A Novelty Search Approach for Automatic Test Data Generation. *2015 IEEE/ACM 8th International Workshop on Search-Based Software Testing*. 10.1109/SBST.2015.17

Chawla, P., Chana, I., & Rana, A. (2015). A novel strategy for automatic test data generation using soft computing technique. *Frontiers of Computer Science, 9*(3), 346–363. doi:10.100711704-014-3496-9

Cheon, Y., & Kim, M. (2006). A specification-based fitness function for evolutionary testing of object-oriented programs. In *Gecco '06: Proceedings of the 8th annual conference on genetic and evolutionary computation* (pp. 1953–1954). New York: ACM. 10.1145/1143997.1144322

Cheon, Y., Kim, M., & Perumandla, A. (2005). A complete automation of unit testing for java programs. In H. R. Arabnia & H. Reza (Eds.), *Proceedings of the international conference on software engineering research and practice, SERP 2005* (vol. 1, pp. 290–295). CSREA Press.

Cody-Kenny, B., Galván-López, E., & Barrett, S. (2015). locoGP: Improving Performance by Genetic Programming Java Source Code. In *Proceedings of the Companion Publication of the 2015 on Genetic and Evolutionary Computation Conference - GECCO Companion '15* (pp. 811–818). New York: ACM Press.

Davis, M. D., & Weyuker, E. J. (1981). Pseudo-oracles for non-testable programs. In *ACM 81: Proceedings of the Acm '81 conference* (pp. 254–257). New York: ACM. 10.1145/800175.809889

De Nicola, R., & Hennessy, M. C. B. (1984). Testing equivalences for processes. *Theoretical Computer Science, 34*(1-2), 83–133. doi:10.1016/0304-3975(84)90113-0

Dharsana, C. S. S., Jennifer, D. N., Askarunisha, A., & Ramaraj, N. (2007). Java based test case generation and optimization using evolutionary testing. In *ICCIMA '07: Proceedings of the international conference on computational intelligence and multimedia applications (ICCIMA 2007)* (pp. 44–49). Washington, DC: IEEE Computer Society. 10.1109/ICCIMA.2007.445

Eckel, B. (2002). *Thinking in java*. Prentice Hall Professional Technical Reference.

Ferrer, J., Chicano, F., & Alba, E. (2009). Dealing with inheritance in oo evolutionary testing. In *Gecco '09: Proceedings of the 11th annual conference on genetic and evolutionary computation* (pp. 1665–1672). New York: ACM. 10.1145/1569901.1570124

Fraser, G., & Arcuri, A. (2011a). Evosuite: automatic test suite generation for object-oriented software. In *Proceedings of the 19th ACM SIGSOFT symposium and the 13th European conference on foundations of software engineering* (pp. 416–419). New York: ACM. 10.1145/2025113.2025179

Fraser, G., & Arcuri, A. (2011b). *Evosuite – automatic test suite generation for java*. Available from http://www.evosuite.org/

Fraser, G., & Arcuri, A. (2011c). Evolutionary generation of whole test suites. In *Proceedings of the 2011 11th international conference on quality software* (pp. 31–40). Washington, DC: IEEE Computer Society. 10.1109/QSIC.2011.19

Fraser, G., & Arcuri, A. (2012). Sound empirical evidence in software testing. In *34th international conference on software engineering, ICSE 2012* (pp. 178–188). IEEE. 10.1109/ICSE.2012.6227195

Fraser, G., & Arcuri, A. (2013). Whole test suite generation. *IEEE Transactions on Software Engineering, 39*(2), 276–291. doi:10.1109/TSE.2012.14

Fraser, G., & Arcuri, A. (2014). A Large-Scale Evaluation of Automated Unit Test Generation Using EvoSuite. *ACM Transactions on Software Engineering and Methodology, 24*(2), 1–42. doi:10.1145/2685612

Fraser, G., Arcuri, A., & McMinn, P. (2013). Test suite generation with memetic algorithms. In *Proceeding of the fifteenth annual conference on genetic and evolutionary computation conference* (pp. 1437–1444). New York: ACM. 10.1145/2463372.2463548

Fraser, G., & Zeller, A. (2011). Exploiting common object usage in test case generation. In *Proceedings of the 2011 fourth ieee international conference on software testing, verification and validation* (pp. 80–89). Washington, DC: IEEE Computer Society. 10.1109/ICST.2011.53

Goffi, A., Gorla, A., Mattavelli, A., Pezzè, M., & Tonella, P. (2014). Search-based synthesis of equivalent method sequences. *Proceedings of the 22nd ACM SIGSOFT International Symposium on Foundations of Software Engineering - FSE 2014.* 10.1145/2635868.2635888

Google. (2004). *Google scholar*. Available from http://scholar.google.com/

Gross, F., Fraser, G., & Zeller, A. (2012). Search-based system testing: high coverage, no false alarms. *Proceedings of the 2012 International Symposium on Software Testing and Analysis - ISSTA 2012.* 10.1145/2338965.2336762

Gupta, N. K., & Rohil, M. K. (2008). Using genetic algorithm for unit testing of object oriented software. In *ICETET '08: Proceedings of the 2008 first international conference on emerging trends in engineering and technology* (pp. 308–313). Washington, DC: IEEE Computer Society. 10.1109/ICETET.2008.137

Harman, M. (2007). The current state and future of search based software engineering. In *FOSE '07: 2007 future of software engineering* (pp. 342–357). Washington, DC: IEEE Computer Society. doi:10.1109/FOSE.2007.29

Harman, M., Hassoun, Y., Lakhotia, K., McMinn, P., & Wegener, J. (2007). The impact of input domain reduction on search-based test data generation. In *Esec-fse '07: Proceedings of the 6th joint meeting of the European software engineering conference and the ACM SIGSOFT symposium on the foundations of software engineering* (pp. 155–164). New York: ACM Press. 10.1145/1287624.1287647

Harman, M., Mansouri, S. A., & Zhang, Y. (2009). *Search based software engineering: A comprehensive analysis and review of trends techniques and applications* (Tech. Rep. No. TR-09-03). Academic Press.

Harman, M., Mansouri, S. A., & Zhang, Y. (2012). Search-based software engineering: Trends, techniques and applications. *ACM Comput. Surv., 45*(1), 11:1–11:61.

Harman, M., & McMinn, P. (2010). A theoretical and empirical study of search-based testing: Local, global, and hybrid search. *Software Engineering. IEEE Transactions on, 36*(2), 226–247.

Haynes, T. D., Schoenefeld, D. A., & Wainwright, R. L. (1996). Type inheritance in strongly typed genetic programming. In P. J. Angeline & K. E. Kinnear Jr., (Eds.), *Advances in genetic programming 2* (pp. 359–376). Cambridge, MA: MIT Press.

He, W., Zhao, R., & Zhu, Q. (2015). Integrating Evolutionary Testing with Reinforcement Learning for Automated Test Generation of Object-Oriented Software. *Liangzi Dianzi Xuebao. Liangzi Dianzi Xuebao, 24*(1), 38–45.

Hillis, W. D. (1990). Co-evolving parasites improve simulated evolution as an optimization procedure. *Physica D. Nonlinear Phenomena, 42*(1-3), 228–234. doi:10.1016/0167-2789(90)90076-2

Holland, J. H. (1962). Outline for a logical theory of adaptive systems. *Journal of the Association for Computing Machinery, 9*(3), 297–314. doi:10.1145/321127.321128

Inkumsah, K., & Xie, T. (2007). Evacon: A framework for integrating evolutionary and concolic testing for object-oriented programs. In *Proc. 22nd IEEE/ACM international conference on automated software engineering (ase 2007)* (pp. 425–428). IEEE. 10.1145/1321631.1321700

Inkumsah, K., & Xie, T. (2008). Improving structural testing of object-oriented programs via integrating evolutionary testing and symbolic execution. *Proc. 23rd ieee/acm international conference on automated software engineering (ASE 2008).* 10.1109/ASE.2008.40

Koza, J. R. (1992). *Genetic programming: On the programming of computers by means of natural selection (complex adaptive systems).* The MIT Press.

Koza, J. R. (1994). *Genetic programming II: Automatic discovery of reusable programs.* Cambridge, MA: The MIT Press.

Lehman, J., & Stanley, K. O. (2010). Efficiently evolving programs through the search for novelty. *Proceedings of the 12th annual conference on Genetic and evolutionary computation - GECCO '10.* 10.1145/1830483.1830638

Liaskos, K., & Roper, M. (2007, September). *Automatic test-data generation: An immunological approach.* IEEE Computer Society.

Liaskos, K., & Roper, M. (2008). Hybridizing evolutionary testing with artificial immune systems and local search. In *ICSTW '08: Proceedings of the 2008 IEEE international conference on software testing verification and validation workshop* (pp. 211–220). Washington, DC: IEEE Computer Society. 10.1109/ICSTW.2008.21

Liaskos, K., Roper, M., & Wood, M. (2007). Investigating data-flow coverage of classes using evolutionary algorithms. In *GECCO '07: Proceedings of the 9th annual conference on genetic and evolutionary computation* (pp. 1140–1140). New York: ACM. 10.1145/1276958.1277183

Liu, X., Wang, B., & Liu, H. (2005). Evolutionary search in the context of object-oriented programs. *Mic'05: Proceedings of the sixth metaheuristics international conference.*

Mantere, T., & Alander, J. T. (2005). Evolutionary software engineering, a review. *Applied Soft Computing, 5*(3), 315–331. doi:10.1016/j.asoc.2004.08.004

Maragathavalli, P. (2011). *Search-based software test data generation using evolutionary computation.* CoRR, abs/1103.0125

Marciniak, J. J. (Ed.). (1994). *Encyclopedia of software engineering.* New York: Wiley-Interscience.

Mattavelli, A., Goffi, A., & Gorla, A. (2015). Synthesis of Equivalent Method Calls in Guava. In Lecture Notes in Computer Science (pp. 248–254). Academic Press. doi:10.1007/978-3-319-22183-0_19

McMinn, P. (2004). Search-based software test data generation: A survey. *Software Testing, Verification & Reliability, 14*(2), 105–156. doi:10.1002tvr.294

McMinn, P. (2009). Search-based failure discovery using testability transformations to generate pseudo-oracles. In *GECCO '09: Proceedings of the 11th annual conference on genetic and evolutionary computation* (pp. 1689–1696). New York: ACM. 10.1145/1569901.1570127

McMinn, P. (2011). Search-based software testing: Past, present and future. In *Software testing, verification and validation workshops (ICSTW), 2011 IEEE fourth international conference on* (p. 153-163). IEEE.

McMinn, P., & Holcombe, M. (2003). *The state problem for evolutionary testing.* Available from citeseer.ist.psu.edu/mcminn03state.html

Michalewicz, Z. (1994). Genetic algorithms + data structures = evolution programs (2nd ed.). New York: Springer-Verlag New York, Inc.

Miraz, M., Lanzi, P. L., & Baresi, L. (2009). Testful: using a hybrid evolutionary algorithm for testing stateful systems. In *Proceedings of the 11th annual conference on genetic and evolutionary computation* (pp. 1947–1948). New York: ACM. 10.1145/1569901.1570252

Miraz, M., Lanzi, P. L., & Baresi, L. (2011). *Testful – an evolutionary testing framework for java*. Available from https://code.google.com/p/testful/

Montana, D. J. (1993). Strongly typed genetic programming (Tech. Rep. No. #7866). Academic Press.

Montana, D. J. (1995). Strongly typed genetic programming. *Evolutionary Computation*, *3*(2), 199–230. doi:10.1162/evco.1995.3.2.199

Myers, G. J., & Sandler, C. (2004). *The art of software testing*. John Wiley & Sons.

Nogueira, A. F., Ribeiro, J. C. B., de Vega, F. F., & Zenha-Rela, M. A. (2013). ecrash: An empirical study on the apache ant project. In *Proceedings of the 5th international symposium on search based software engineering (SSBSE '13)* (Vol. 8084). St. Petersburg, Russia: Springer. 10.1007/978-3-642-39742-4_25

Nogueira, A. F., Ribeiro, J. C. B., Fernández de Vega, F., & Zenha-Rela, M. A. (2014). Object-Oriented Evolutionary Testing: A Review of Evolutionary Approaches to the Generation of Test Data for Object-Oriented Software. *International Journal of Natural Computing Research*, *4*(4), 15–35. doi:10.4018/ijncr.2014100102

Olsson, J. R. (1994). *Inductive functional programming using incremental program transformation and execution of logic programs by iterative-deepening a* sld-tree search* (research report No. 189). University of Oslo.

Pacheco, C., & Ernst, M. D. (2007). Randoop: feedback-directed random testing for java. In *Oopsla '07: Companion to the 22nd ACM SIGPLAN conference on object-oriented programming systems and applications companion* (pp. 815–816). New York: ACM. 10.1145/1297846.1297902

Panichella, A., Kifetew, F. M., & Tonella, P. (2015a). Reformulating Branch Coverage as a Many-Objective Optimization Problem. In *2015 IEEE 8th International Conference on Software Testing, Verification and Validation (ICST)*. IEEE. 10.1109/ICST.2015.7102604

Panichella, A., Kifetew, F. M., & Tonella, P. (2015b). Results for EvoSuite -- MOSA at the Third Unit Testing Tool Competition. In *2015 IEEE/ACM 8th International Workshop on Search-Based Software Testing*. IEEE. 10.1109bst.2015.14

Pavlov, Y., & Fraser, G. (2012). Semi-automatic search-based test generation. In *Proceedings of the 2012 ieee fifth international conference on software testing, verification and validation* (pp. 777–784). Washington, DC: IEEE Computer Society. 10.1109/ICST.2012.176

Poli, R., Langdon, W. B., & Mcphee, N. F. (2008). *A field guide to genetic programming. Lulu Enterprises*. UK Ltd.

Ribeiro, J. C. B. (2008). Search-based test case generation for object-oriented java software using strongly-typed genetic programming. In *GECCO '08: Proceedings of the 2008 gecco conference companion on genetic and evolutionary computation* (pp. 1819–1822). New York: ACM. 10.1145/1388969.1388979

Ribeiro, J. C. B. (2010). *Contributions for improving genetic programming-based approaches to the evolutionary testing of object-oriented software* (Doctoral dissertation). Universidad de Extremadura, España.

Ribeiro, J. C. B., de Vega, F. F., & Zenha-Rela, M. (2007). Using dynamic analysis of java bytecode for evolutionary object-oriented unit testing. In *Sbrc wtf 2007: Proceedings of the 8th workshop on testing and fault tolerance at the 25th Brazilian symposium on computer networks and distributed systems* (pp. 143–156). Brazilian Computer Society (SBC).

Ribeiro, J. C. B., Nogueira, A. F., de Vega, F. F., & Zenha-Rela, M. A. (2013). *eCrash – evolutionary testing for object-oriented software.* Available from http://sourceforge.net/projects/ecrashtesting/

Ribeiro, J. C. B., Zenha-Rela, M., & de Vega, F. F. (2007). ecrash: a framework for performing evolutionary testing on third-party java components. In *Cedi jaem'07: Proceedings of the i jornadas sobre algoritmos evolutivos y metaheuristicas at the ii congreso español de informática* (pp. 137–144). Academic Press.

Ribeiro, J. C. B., Zenha-Rela, M. A., & de Vega, F. F. (2008). Strongly-typed genetic programming and purity analysis: input domain reduction for evolutionary testing problems. In *Gecco '08: Proceedings of the 10th annual conference on genetic and evolutionary computation* (pp. 1783–1784). New York: ACM. 10.1145/1389095.1389439

Ribeiro, J. C. B., Zenha-Rela, M. A., & de Vega, F. F. (2010a). Adaptive evolutionary testing: an adaptive approach to search-based test case generation for object-oriented software. In Nicso 2010 - international workshop on nature inspired cooperative strategies for optimization. Springer. doi:10.1007/978-3-642-12538-6_16

Ribeiro, J. C. B., Zenha-Rela, M. A., & de Vega, F. F. (2010b). Enabling object reuse on genetic programming-based approaches to object-oriented evolutionary testing. In *Eurogp 2010 - 13th european conference on genetic programming.* Springer. 10.1007/978-3-642-12148-7_19

Ribeiro, J. C. B., Zenha-Rela, M. A., & Vega, F. (2009). Test case evaluation and input domain reduction strategies for the evolutionary testing of object-oriented software. *Information and Software Technology*, *51*(11), 1534–1548. doi:10.1016/j.infsof.2009.06.009

Rojas, J. M., Vivanti, M., Arcuri, A., & Fraser, G. (2016). A detailed investigation of the effectiveness of whole test suite generation. *Empirical Software Engineering*, *22*(2), 852–893. doi:10.100710664-015-9424-2

Sagarna, R., Arcuri, A., & Yao, X. (2007). Estimation of distribution algorithms for testing object oriented software. In D. Srinivasan & L. Wang (Eds.), 2007 IEEE congress on evolutionary computation. Singapore: IEEE Press. doi:10.1109/CEC.2007.4424504

Seesing, A. (2006). *Evotest: Test case generation using genetic programming and software analysis* (Master's thesis). Delft University of Technology.

Seesing, A., & Gross, H.-G. (2006). A genetic programming approach to automated test generation for object-oriented software. *International Transactions on System Science and Applications*, *1*(2), 127–134.

Shamshiri, S., Just, R., Rojas, J. M., Fraser, G., McMinn, P., & Arcuri, A. (2015). Do Automatically Generated Unit Tests Find Real Faults? An Empirical Study of Effectiveness and Challenges (T). In *2015 30th IEEE/ACM International Conference on Automated Software Engineering (ASE)*. IEEE. 10.1109/ase.2015.86

Shamshiri, S., Rojas, J. M., Fraser, G., & McMinn, P. (2015). Random or Genetic Algorithm Search for Object-Oriented Test Suite Generation? *Proceedings of the 2015 on Genetic and Evolutionary Computation Conference - GECCO '15*. 10.1145/2739480.2754696

Tassey, G. (2002). *The economic impacts of inadequate infrastructure for software testing (Tech. Rep.)*. National Institute of Standards and Technology.

The Apache Software Foundation. (2012). *The apache ant project, release 1.8.4*. Available from http://ant.apache.org/

Tonella, P. (2004a). *eToc – evolutionary testing of classes*. Available from http://star.fbk.eu/etoc/

Tonella, P. (2004b). Evolutionary testing of classes. In *Issta '04: Proceedings of the 2004 acm sigsoft international symposium on software testing and analysis* (pp. 119–128). New York: ACM Press. 10.1145/1007512.1007528

Varshney, S., & Mehrotra, M. (2013). Search based software test data generation for structural testing: A perspective. *SIGSOFT Softw. Eng. Notes*, *38*(4), 1–6. doi:10.1145/2492248.2492277

Wappler, S. (2007). *Automatic generation of object-oriented unit tests using genetic programming* (Doctoral dissertation). Technischen Universitat Berlin.

Wappler, S., & Lammermann, F. (2005). Using evolutionary algorithms for the unit testing of object-oriented software. In *Gecco '05: Proceedings of the 2005 conference on genetic and evolutionary computation* (pp. 1053–1060). New York: ACM Press. 10.1145/1068009.1068187

Wappler, S., & Schieferdecker, I. (2007). Improving evolutionary class testing in the presence of non-public methods. In *Ase '07: Proceedings of the twenty-second ieee/acm international conference on automated software engineering* (pp. 381–384). New York: ACM. 10.1145/1321631.1321689

Wappler, S., & Wegener, J. (2006a). Evolutionary unit testing of object-oriented software using a hybrid evolutionary algorithm. In *Cec'06: Proceedings of the 2006 ieee congress on evolutionary computation* (pp. 851–858). IEEE. 10.1109/CEC.2006.1688400

Wappler, S., & Wegener, J. (2006b). Evolutionary unit testing of object-oriented software using strongly-typed genetic programming. In *Gecco '06: Proceedings of the 8th annual conference on genetic and evolutionary computation* (pp. 1925–1932). New York: ACM Press. 10.1145/1143997.1144317

Wegener, J., Baresel, A., & Sthamer, H. (2001). Evolutionary test environment for automatic structural testing. *Information and Software Technology, 43*(14), 841-854.

Xanthakis, S., Ellis, C., Skourlas, C., Gall, A. L., & Karapoulios, K. (1992). Application of genetic algorithms to software testing [application des algorithmes génétiques au test des logiciels]. In *Proceedings of the 5th international conference on software engineering* (pp. 625–636). Academic Press.

Xiao, M., El-Attar, M., Reformat, M., & Miller, J. (2007). Empirical evaluation of optimization algorithms when used in goal-oriented automated test data generation techniques. *Empirical Software Engineering, 12*(2), 183–239. doi:10.100710664-006-9026-0

Xie, T., Tillmann, N., de Halleux, J., & Schulte, W. (2008). Method-sequence exploration for automated unit testing of object-oriented programs. *Proc. workshop on state-space exploration for automated testing (sseat 2008).*

Yu, T. (2001). Hierachical processing for evolving recursive and modular programs using higher order functions and lambda abstractions. *Genetic Programming and Evolvable Machines, 2*(4), 345–380. doi:10.1023/A:1012926821302

This research was previously published in Incorporating Nature-Inspired Paradigms in Computational Applications; pages 162-194, copyright year 2018 by Engineering Science Reference (an imprint of IGI Global).

Chapter 45
Software Cost Estimation and Capability Maturity Model in Context of Global Software Engineering

Ayub Muhammad Latif

PAF Karachi Institute of Economics and Technology, Pakistan

Khalid Muhammad Khan

PAF Karachi Institute of Economics and Technology, Pakistan

Anh Nguyen Duc

(iD) https://orcid.org/0000-0002-7063-9200

University of South-Eastern Norway, Norway

ABSTRACT

Software cost estimation is the process of forecasting the effort needed to develop the software system. Global software engineering (GSE) highlights that software development knows no boundaries and majority of the software products and services are developed today by globally-distributed teams, projects, and companies. The problem of cost estimation gets more complex if the discussion is carried out in the context of GSE, which has its own issues. Temporal, cultural, and geographical distance creates communication and software process implementation issues. Traditional software process models such as capability maturity model (CMM) lacks the dynamism to accommodate the recent trends in GSE. The chapter introduces GSE and discusses various cost estimation techniques and different levels of CMM. A couple of GSE-based case studies having CMM-level projects from multiple organizations are studied to analyze the impacts of highly mature processes on effort, quality, and cycle time.

DOI: 10.4018/978-1-6684-3702-5.ch045

GLOBAL SOFTWARE ENGINEERING

The world has become a global village and software engineering industry has kept pace with the changing circumstances by establishing a new dimension known as Global Software Engineering (GSE) in which geographical location, culture and distance is no more a barrier and software engineers across the globe must collaborate and play their part in achieving the desired goal (Carmel, 1999; Prikladnicki et al, 2003). There are many technological factors that have made it possible but the most important is the advent of low cost international telecommunication infrastructure that facilitated the outreach of internet and email (O'Brien, 2002). Further, the political circumstances across the globe has also played its part as getting visa for the work force is no more simple and getting the people to fly to one location and providing them all the necessities is expensive as well. Letting the highly skilled software engineers work from low cost locations such as Eastern Europe, Latin America and Far East (Crow et al, 2003) is a better proposition. Another benefit of GSE is that the operations are established near emerging markets which has its own advantages. A variation of this model is just to shift the application development and maintenance by using out sourcing model to remote third party organizations. These remote organizations can even be subsidiaries of big companies established in low cost economies (Carmel et al, 2005; Toaff, 2005).

There can be several challenges in a typical GSE environment but the top most is team building and project management. The success of any GSE project depends upon the operations of virtual teams which forms the core building block of the virtual organization (Davidow et al, 1992; Jarvenpaa et al, 1994; Mohrman, 1999). Virtual teams are bit different from traditional teams hence they needed to be managed differently as well. A traditional team is a group of individuals who are gather to achieve a common objective. They undertake interdependent tasks, coordinate among each other and share responsibility of the outcomes (Powell et al, 2004).Though virtual teams also behave like traditional teams but with certain challenges involving different time zones and geographical location. There are no organizational boundaries as the environment is multicultural and multilingual. The most complex area of handling virtual teams is of communication as it is mostly dependent on electronic communication infrastructure. It is asynchronous with very few possibilities for synchronous contact. The virtual team may assemble / disassemble as per requirements which is true for traditional teams as well.

Project management become complex with virtual teams due to co-ordination, communication and cooperation (Nidiffer et al, 2005) challenges. The electronic and asynchronous means can never be equivalent to a good face to face discussion. Even the video calls cannot capture the emotions of all the participants or the positive / negative energy in the room. The distance is not just geographical; it's the temporal and cultural distance that creates new barriers and complexities in the project management activities (Herbsleb et al, 2003).

Temporal distance is a measure of the distance of time people participating in communication are experiencing (Agerfalk et al, 2005). It can be caused by time zone difference or different work timings. The difference in temporal distance effects communication (Sarker et al, 2004) and the response time increases when working hours at remote locations do not overlap. While developing virtual teams, one must take a note of the temporal overlap of the team members to facilitate better communication. The temporal overlap can be achieved by understanding time zone difference and by adjusting the time shifting work patterns.

The cultural distance of team members is the understanding of each other's values and cultural practices (Herbsleb et al, 2003). In (Kotlarsky et al, 2005), it is identified that culture can have a huge effect on how people would behave in certain situation. Cultural distance is dependent on many factors such as national culture, language, political understanding, individual motivations and work ethics. If there is a large cultural distance between team members in terms of national culture or language, it is difficult for them to adopt to same organizational culture. Cultural distance is not entirely based on geographical distance, low geographical distance does not automatically mean low cultural difference.

In the next section we discuss the process modeling and capability maturity model and introduce the reader with all the five levels of CMM.

Process Modeling and Capability Maturity Model

Software process can be defined as "a set of activities, methods, practices and transformations that people use to develop and maintain software and the associated products" (Curtiz et al, 1992). Software industry has come a long way which is depicted by huge number of improves software products available in the market. To develop better software products, software processes are required to be improved and many software process models have been proposed and utilized by the software practitioners. The most widely used process modelling technique is Capability Maturity Model Integration (CMMI).

The Capability Maturity Model (CMM) is a development model and the term "maturity" refers to formality and optimization (Paulk et al, 1993). The CMM deployment will take the organization from the ad hoc practices to formally defined steps that result into continuous improvement. The early adopter organizations have found it difficult to implement CMM due to integration issues with multiple models. To solve these issues, Capability Maturity Model Integration (CMMI) model was developed that defines five levels of maturity (Team, 2006). It is believed that organization's software processes would improve as the organization moves up the level. These levels are shown in Table 1.

Table 1. CMMI level description

CMMI Level No	CMMI Level Name	CMMI Level Description
1	Initial	Starting point for use of a new or undocumented repeat process
2	Repeatable	Process is documented sufficiently enough to attempt repeat
3	Defined	Process is defined/confirmed as a standard business process
4	Capable	Process is quantitatively managed in accordance with agreed-upon metrics
5	Efficient	Process management having deliberate process optimization/improvement

Each maturity levels have Key Process Areas and for each such area there are five factors: goals, commitment, ability, measurement, and verification. The CMMI model provides a range of theoretical boundaries so that the process maturity can be developed incrementally. Skipping levels is neither recommended nor allowed/feasible.

Level 1: Initial

Processes at this level are (typically) undocumented and prone to changes. They are driven in an *ad hoc* and uncontrolled manner. They are handled reactively in light of user suggestions or other events. Such chaotic or unstable environment results in no or low process improvement.

Level 2: Repeatable

Having repeatable processes in an environment is a sign of maturity and if the results are also consistent then it is even better. Ability to keep the processes in place in stressful circumstances depicts deep rooted process discipline. The key process areas of this level are:

- **CM**: Configuration Management
- **MA:** Measurement and Analysis
- **PMC:** Project Monitoring and Control
- **PP:** Project Planning
- **PPQA:** Process and Product Quality Assurance
- **REQMP:** Requirements Management
- **SAM:** Supplier Agreement Management

Level 3: Defined

At this level, processes are well defined and documented. Standard processes are established and get improved with the passage of time. The processes may not be used repeatedly but they are validated in multiple situations and are sufficient enough for the users to become competent. Implementation in wider range of conditions can take the process to next level of maturity. The key process areas of this level are:

- **DAR:** Decision Analysis and Resolution
- **IPM**: Integrated Project Management
- **OPD:** Organizational Process Definition
- **OPF:** Organizational Process Focus
- **OT:** Organizational Training
- **PI:** Product Integration
- **RD:** Requirements Development
- **RSKM:** Risk Management
- **TS:** Technical Solution
- **VAL** - Validation
- **VER**: Verification

Level 4: Capable

Process objectives can be achieved effectively in a range of operation conditions at this level by using process metrics. The processes are tested, refined and adapted in multiple environments. Process users also have developed competence on the processes in different conditions. Process maturity improves capability and enables adaptions to particular projects without much deviation from specifications. The key process areas of this level are:

- **OPP**: Organizational Process Performance
- **QPM:** Quantitative Project Management

Level 5: Optimizing (Efficient)

Processes at this level are continually improved through incremental and innovative technological changes. Statistical common causes of process variation are addressed to improve process performance. This would be done at the same time as maintaining the likelihood of achieving the established quantitative process-improvement objectives. The key process areas of this level are:

- **CAR:** Causal Analysis and Resolution
- **OPM:** Organizational Performance Management

Please refer (Chrissis et al, 2003), to clear the understanding on the key process areas of CMMI levels. The next section discusses the different costing and estimation techniques which can be used for making an estimate of effort and time of software that is undergoing development.

Software Costing and Estimation Techniques

The software development process comprises of numerous activities which needs to be performed separately. Cost estimation of software development project helps us in calculating the effort and time required for the development for a particular software system (Boehm et al, 2000). It can further help in even calculating the overall cost of the software that is being developed. The software costing and estimation helps in answering the following questions:

1. How much effort is required for a particular activity of the software process?
2. How much calendar time is needed to complete each activity?
3. What is the total cost of each activity?

Project cost estimation and project scheduling are two different activities which are usually carried out together and work breakdown structure which is a part of project scheduling also helps in estimating the different activities of the software. The costs of development are primarily the costs of the effort involved, so the effort computation is used in both the cost and the schedule estimate. The initial cost estimates may be used to establish a budget for the project and to set a price for the software for a customer. The total cost of a software development project is the sum of following costs:

1. Effort costs of paying software developers.
2. Ratio of the fixed expenditure for development house.
3. Hardware and software costs including maintenance.
4. Travel and training costs.

For most of the projects, the most significant cost is the effort cost. Effort costs are not just the salaries of the software engineers who are involved in the project. The following overhead costs can also be included in the effort cost:

1. Costs of support staff (accountants, administrators, system managers, cleaners, technicians etc.).
2. Capital Expenditure of networking and communications.
3. Capital Expenditure of the facilities for employees.
4. Costs spent on Employees' benefits.

Software Estimation Metrics

The software estimation metrics can be broadly divided in one of the two metrics which are given under (Trendowicz, 2013).

1. **Size-related software Metrics:** These metrics are related to the size of software. The most frequently used size-related metric is lines of delivered source code and it is also known as direct metric.
2. **Function-Related Software Metrics:** These are related to the overall functionality of the software. For example, function points and object points are metrics of this type and it falls under the category of indirect metric.

The reason to classify them as direct and indirect metric is that direct metric can be measured directly by using a single metric. A non software example of direct metric could be the weight of an individual which can be known in Kilograms. On the other hand indirect metrics initially use some direct measures and then give the result through some regression based formula. A non software example of indirect metric could be "that how a particular person is". This is more difficult to analyze as we need to look into many parameters of an individual to claim whether he/she is a good person, a bad person etc. Same goes for the indirect metrics of software.

The Productivity Metric and Lines of Code

Other then the stated metrics a metric known as the productivity metric is known by the source lines of code written by each developer in a month. It tells the general productivity of a developer in a given month (Trendowicz, 2013). Very important to note here is that if a software practitioner has a productivity of 1500 LOC per month, this simple doesn't mean that he/she will be writing 1500 Lines of code in any specific language. It will mean that the work he/she performs in his/her organization during a month is equivalent to writing 1500 lines of code. The case may be that the individual only writes 200 lines of code during the whole month is any development environment. It is also a known fact now that maximum effort in coding for particular software can never exceed 25% of the overall software development effort. This fact also helps in understanding that the total lines of code for the development of software does not mean the physical lines of code in the development environment.

The Function Point and Object Point Metric

In the function point metric the total number of function points in a program measures or estimates the following program features (Naik, 2018).

1. Number of external inputs
2. Number of external outputs
3. Number of user interactions/inquiries
4. Number of external interfaces,
5. Number of files used by the system.

These program features are also regarded as the information domain. To differentiate the complex feature with simple features the function point metric applies some weight to the listed information domains. The unadjusted function point count (UFC) is computed by multiplying the number of a given feature by its estimated weight for all features and finally summing products:

$$\text{UFC} = \sum(\text{number of a given feature}) \times (\text{weight for the given feature})$$

Object points are used as an alternate to function points. The number of object points is computed by the estimated weights of objects:

1. Separate screens that are displayed are counted as object points and a value of 1, 2 or 3 is assigned to them with respect to their complexity with 1 object point assigned as a value for a simple screen.
2. Reports that are produced are also counted as object points and value of 2, 5 or 8 are assigned to them with respect to their complexity with 2 object points as a value for a simple report.
3. All modules are also counted in object points that are developed to supplement the database programming code. Each of these modules are assigned a value of 10 object points.

The final code size is calculated by multiplying the number of function points and the estimated average number of lines of code (AVC) required for deploying a function point. Obviously organizations depends either on some historical data for assuming the LOC for each function point or by using the productivity metric of how many function points can be delivered by a staff member each month. The estimated code size is computed as follows:

$$\text{CODE SIZE} = \text{AVC} \times \text{UFC}$$

Software Cost Estimation Techniques

Estimation is never an easy task; therefore few techniques are listed in the table 2 below that can be used for the estimation of the project (Keim et al, 2014). The management is interested in getting an early estimate of the software that is under development.

Table 2. Software cost estimation techniques

Technique	Description
Algorithmic cost models	Relating some software metrics a mathematical model is developed to estimate the project cost
Expert judgment	Several experts on the proposed software development techniques and application domains are asked to estimate the project cost. The estimation process iterates until an agreed estimate is reached.
Estimation by previous projects	The cost of a new project is estimated by a completed project in the same application domain
Application of Parkinson's Law	Parkinson's Law states that work expands to fill the time available and the cost is determined by the resources used.
Pricing to win	The software cost is estimated by the price what the customer has available to spend on the project

Each listed technique has its own merits and demerits and it is a known principle that if the estimate is within the range of plus/minus 25% of the actual outcome and an estimator can predict such efficiency in 75% of his all estimations then that estimator and estimate is considered good. This definition of good estimate is discussed in (Jarvenpaa, 1994). Please note that there can be different classification of software costing techniques then compared to the table which is stated above. We have kept things simple for basic understanding of the famous techniques, for more detailed classification and the reader can refer to the software cost estimation book by Steve McConell (Jarvenpaa, 1994).

Some Details of Algorithmic Cost Models

Algorithmic cost modeling uses a mathematical expression to predict project costs based on estimates of the project size, the number of software engineers, and other process and product factors (Naik, 2018). An algorithmic cost model can be developed by analyzing the costs and attributes of completed projects and finding the closest fit mathematical expression to actual project. In general, an algorithmic cost estimate for software cost can be expressed as:

$$EFFORT = A * SIZE^B * M$$

In this equation A is a constant factor that depends on local organizational practices and the type of software that is developed. Variable SIZE may be either the code size or the functionality of software expressed in function or object points. M is a multiplier made by combining process, product and development attributes, such as the dependability requirements for the software and the experience of the development team. The value of M is also known as the effort/environment adjustment factor (EAF). The EAF either increases the effort of decreases it. The exponential component B associated with the size estimate expresses the non-linearity of costs with project size. As the size of the software increases, extra costs are emerged. The value of exponent B usually lies between 1 and 1.5.

Now we have a basic understating of the software costing and estimation techniques, please note here the main purpose of this chapter is not to discuss the software costing and estimation techniques but to see how costing and estimation is applied along with the effects of CMM and Global software engineering. The next section discussed the CMMI perspective of the software costing and estimation.

CMMI PERSPECTIVE OF SOFTWARE COSTING AND ESTIMATION

The main purpose of this section is to analyze the connection between CMMI and the techniques that are used for the estimation of software. In this section we have tried to classify the costing and estimation techniques with respect to process areas of CMMI for the different levels.

Estimation Techniques for Level 1 of CMMI

At maturity level 1, processes are usually ad hoc and chaotic because the organizations don't have a stable environment for development. We know that success for such organization depends on the individual effort of individuals who are the star performers of an organization. The process itself is not defined so the success is not because of the define processes. These organizations end up creating products but the problem is they mostly exceed the time and allocated budget.

The best way to estimate software on Initial Level is to use LOC method as basic LOC method is simple and it is direct metric and therefore also easier to use. We have already discussed that at the initial level the companies do often exceed their budget due to the absence of proper process. Therefore it is best to use the LOC metric at this level of CMMI.

Estimation Techniques for Level 2 of CMMI

At maturity level 2, an organization has achieved all the key process areas of CMM level 2. It will not be wrong to state that at this level the organization have ensured that requirements are managed and that processes are planned performed, measured, and controlled. The process discipline reflected by maturity level 2 helps to ensure that existing practices are retained during times of stress. When these practices are in place, projects are performed and managed according to their documented plans (Wagner et al, 2018).

The best way to estimate software at the level 2 which is the managed Level is to use FP method because it decomposes the software in well defined functions and estimates accordingly.

Estimation Techniques for Level 3 of CMMI

At maturity level 3, an organization has achieved all the specific and generic goals of the key process areas which are assigned to maturity levels 2 and 3. At maturity level 3, processes are well character-ized and understood, and are described in standards, procedures, tools, and methods (Vyas et al, 2018). A critical distinction between maturity level 2 and maturity level 3 is the scope of standards, process descriptions, and procedures, as at level three their scope is much wider than compared to the scope at level 2. At maturity level 2, the standards, process descriptions, and procedures may be quite different in each specific instance of the process (for example, on a particular project). At maturity level 3, the standards, process descriptions, and procedures for a project are tailored from the organization's set of standard processes to suit a particular project or organizational unit. A level three organization is much matured and generally specializes in the development of similar software systems that helps in much similar standardized procedures. COCOMO model with Function Point estimation is a good criterion to estimate cost at level 3 as at this stage companies can manage their input, output transaction and their transactions through proper documented procedures.

Estimation Techniques for Level 4 and 5 of CMMI

At maturity level 4 and 5, organizations collect project data for future use and it becomes historical data for upcoming projects that is why analogy based estimation is good for level 4 and level 5 as analogy based estimation is extensively used for very large projects. Estimation requires data and most accurate results can be acquired if project data that is the data of the current project is used for the estimation purpose. One limitation for using project data is that it can only be used in iterative development where the data of a previous iteration can be used for the estimation of later iterations. When the process models are less iterative then historical data can be used for the estimation of future projects. Historical data is the data of the previous projects. It is believed that estimation becomes easier at these maturity level as generally software development organizations specialize in similar type of software system development and generally because of similar types they are involved in similar sized software development which keeps away the problem of diseconomies of scale which comes into action when the project size increases then compared to previous estimations as simple ratio cannot work in such situations. This phenomenon is discussed in later sections of this chapter.

Table 3. Recommended estimation techniques with respect to different maturity levels

CMMI Level	Recommended Software Estimation Techniques
Level 1: Initial	Basic Lines of Code technique because of its simplicity
Level 2: Repeatable	Function Points techniques as some form of decomposition is applied in CMMI level 2
Level 3: Defined	The very famous Constructive Cost Model (COCOMO), can be used with functions points or even LOC
Level 4: Capable	Analogy based techniques, based of previous data of the software. Proxy based techniques can also be used here.
Level 5: Efficient	Improved and better analogy based techniques that rely on project data along with historical data.

Table 3 summarizes the concepts learned in this section and shows the recommended estimation techniques that can be used at the different maturity levels of an organization. The next section talks more about GSE and identifies the limitations of CMMI in context of GSE.

Global Software Engineering and Limitation of CMMI

As stated earlier, GSE is bit different from the traditional software engineering because the software is developed by different team members who are disbursed in different parts of the world. They have geographical, temporal and cultural distance; hence the traditional software process modelling techniques may not work. If we look at the software project management failures, the most common causes of the failure are identified as under (Dhir et al, 2019).

1. Insufficient end-user involvement
2. Poor communication among customers, developers, users and project managers
3. Poor Team Building Approaches
4. Unrealistic project goals

5. Inaccurate estimates of needed resources
6. Badly defined or incomplete system requirements and specifications
7. Poor reporting of the project's status
8. Poorly managed risks
9. Team competency
10. Inability to handle the project's complexity
11. Sloppy development practices
12. Stakeholder politics (e.g. absence of executive support, or politics between the customer and end-users)

A close look at the above mentioned points depicts that more than half of the causes are related to team building and management which is more complex in GSE hence it is logical to evaluate CMMI (the most widely used software modelling technique) in context of team handling in GSE. The use of planned processes to improve efficiency and productivity in software engineering has been appreciated for long (Leemans et al, 2018) but there have been arguments in favour of not implementing planned processes as well, suggesting that it decreases the efficiency of the software development process (Lacerda et al, 2018). We studied existing software process models to understand whether they can be helpful for GSE or not. We tried to analyse whether CMM in general and CMMI in particular would be able to accommodate the dynamism of GSE in the context of virtual teams.

CMM defines level of maturity along with key process areas and practices for process improvement but it does not provide any information regarding the effective implementation strategies and deployment of key practices. The CMM model does not discuss issues related to human nature, such as employee motivation etc. On the other hand, the structure of CMMI is based on the core components of CMM and talks about the integration of various process models. However, the CMMI model also does not provide detailed information about the implementation of key practices and team handling. It is observed that the support for the implementation of virtual teams is missing and therefore authors have proposed various ways to handle teams. By analyzing various team handling processes proposed for GSE, we describe here few general artefacts of team handling process for GSE with the assumption that team is comprised of members dispersed across the globe having geographical, temporal and cultural distances. Team management issues at individual locations can be handled with traditional process management techniques. The general artefacts for the team handling process in GSE are:

1. Organisational and team structure
2. Geographical distance allowed
3. Cultural distance allowed
4. Temporal distance allowed
5. Team members competencies
6. Communication strategy
7. Task allocation approach
8. Cooperation and coordination procedure
9. Reporting procedure
10. Risk management strategy

In the next section we have incorporated the CMMI levels and GSE to software costing and estimation case studies. We find some very interesting results about costing and estimation applied with GSE and CMMI.

APPLYING SOFTWARE COSTING AND ESTIMATION IN GLOBAL SOFTWARE ENGINEERING WITH CMMI PERSPECTIVE

There are certain known concepts which we have understood in this chapter. The core concepts are bulleted below so that you can refresh yourself:

- Global Software Engineering has numerous challenges and we have already discussed those challenges with respect to software project management, process modeling, team building and software costing and estimation.
- CMMI implements in improving the software development process and the greater maturity level we achieve the better predictability we have in our software process.
- Software costing and estimation is also a challenge for global software engineering and therefore we go through a case study for software costing and estimation using multiple techniques and see which technique helps us under which situation.

It is assumed that a software which is 10 times larger than some other software will require 10 times more effort than the smaller software or less than 10 times effort of the smaller software. In software development this is not the case as if the effort of the larger software would have been in proportion or lesser than the smaller software, this would have been the case of economies of scale which unfortunately does not apply to the software development. Here we have diseconomies of scale which means the effort of 10 tens larger software will be greater than 10 times effort of the smaller software. The reason we have diseconomies of scale in software development is because the communication path increases as squared functions with the increase in the number of team members for software. For example for a two member team there will only be one communication path but for a three member's team the communication paths will be three and for a four member team we will have six communication paths assuming that all team members will need to communicate with everyone else.

This phenomenon is also explained by Steve McConnell in his book (1999). The negativity of diseconomy of scale has also been discussed by (Mohrman et al, 1999) when the documentation of software increases.

Table 4 depicts the phenomenon of the diseconomies of scale.

Table 4. Relation in between project size and productivity of staff members per month

Project Size (in Lines of Code)	Productivity of staff members(staff-month)
1000	400-500
10000	250-300
100000	150-200

It is evident from the table 4 above that productivity of staff member decreases when the project size increases. There is good news about economies of scale and that is the mature organizations generally develop software which is of equal size and therefore the impact of diseconomies of scale is not evident on them. Unfortunately our study of two organizations reveled that irrespective of equal size of software the productivity decrease when the development organizations are geographically disbursed.

CASE STUDIES AND RESULTS

We studied two organizations that have a fairly matured software development organization and it is between CMM level 3 and 4 and is involved in the process of global software engineering and gets software made through its development offices at multiple locations. We present the case studies for two different organizations which we have studied. One of the two organizations operates at three locations which are in Asia and the countries are Pakistan, Bangladesh and Sri Lanka. The other organization is spread in multiple continents and has development offices in Pakistan, USA and UK.

A very interesting factor here to analyze is the diseconomies of scale which is applicable to software costing and estimation. However after analyzing the two organizations we believe that the diseconomies of scale work differently for global software engineering and also when the organizations is more disbursed with respect to more geographical distance and more number of location offices.

We demonstrate the usage of the discussed principle about the diseconomy of scale applied to the global software engineering methodology identified few interesting results. The results proved that GSE in different locations with more cultural differences has more impact of the diseconomies of scale. Both the organizations we studied were involved in global software engineering and local software engineering. In this section of the chapter first we discuss the productivity of similar sized projects which were developed locally and did not involve the factors of global software engineering. As they are near the CMM level 4, their preferred costing technique was analogy based techniques; this was also discussed in section 6 of this chapter.

In analogy based technique, the organization A depends on historical data of previous projects for the development of new projects. We went through a payroll system that was made for local industry and was to be deployed in a company in Pakistan.

Table 5. The main use cases and actors of the payroll system

Use Case	Actors
Time Management	Hourly/Salaried Employee
Purchase Order Management	Commissioned Employee
Maintain Employee Information	Payroll Administrator
Run Payroll	Payroll Administrator

Problem Statement of the Payroll System

The table 5 shows that the company employs three types of employee, monthly salaried employees, hourly based employees and employees that work on commission. The hourly and monthly salaried employees enter information in the time management module,

whereas the commissioned employees enter information in the purchase management system so that the sales made by them could be recorded. The payroll administrator performs two major tasks, first is to maintain the employee information and the other is to run the payroll. After the payroll is run a message is sent to the respective employee that their salary is dispatched. It's a web based system and is developed in ASP .Net technology.

Case of Applying Historical Data to the Payroll System Developed Locally

In the case study for the purpose of effort calculation the organization has used the standard components technique. The main category of standard components is proxy based techniques. The proxy technique is used when you use something as a dummy for the actual effort calculation of software (Jarvenpaa et al, 1994). The core idea behind standard components is that you develop many programs that are architecturally similar to each other; you can use the standard components approach to estimate size. For estimation purpose, we have chart of historical data as depicted in table 6 to apply estimation using the standard components technique

Table 6. Historical data for LOC per component

Standard Component	LOC per Component
Dynamic Web Pages	460
Static Web Pages	60
Database Tables	1350
Reports	450

The estimated components and total LOC for the payroll system are given in table 7

Table 7. Estimate of the Payroll system developed locally

Type of Component	No. of Components in Payroll System	LOC/component	Total LOC for specific component
Dynamic Web Pages	12	460	5520
Static Web Pages	5	60	300
Database Tables	10	1350	13500
Reports	9	450	4050
Business Rules	3	3000	9000
Total LOC for the payroll system			**32370**

There was no historical data available for the business rule, that's why a value of 3000 LOC per component of business rules is used which can be seen in table 7. The estimate of the project was 32 KLOC, and the actual completion of the project was approximately 30 KLOC.

When we discussed the productivity metric used for this particular we were informed that productivity on such projects which had size of about 30 KLOC and were mainly information systems were about 1500 LOC persons-months. This means that an individual if deployed on such type of a project will be able to deliver 1500 Lines of code in a calendar month. When we used this productivity on the given case study the effort turned out to be:

Effort=32370/1500 = 21.28 staff-months

The effort of 21.28 staff months means that if a single developer works on this project then the project will be completed in 21 months approximately. Obviously the organization might have a team of 5 people working on this project wish would help to finish this sized software in 21/5 which will help in completing the software in approximately 4 calendar months. Obviously depending upon the supported concurrent activity we will never reach a stage where deploying 21 staff members will help in finishing the software in a single month because not all activities can be performed concurrently.

Productivity Metric for Global Software Engineering Organization A

When inquired about the productivity metric in case of GSE based development for organization A which only operated in three countries of Asia, we were informed that the productivity for 30 KLOC information systems decline from 1500 LOC to 1100 LOC. This actually increases the effort by 38 percent because the productivity for a similar sized software system developed through GSE by a company operating three offices in three different countries in the same continent the effort for 30 KLOC is:

Effort=32370/1100 = 29.42 staff-months

Percentage of Increased Effort When Similar Sized Software Was Developed Globally

The change in effort can be calculated by using the formula given below:

Percentage change in Effort=Change in Effort/Initial Effort * 100

Change in Effort=New Effort-Old Effort

Change in Effort= 29.42-21.28= 8.14

Percentage change in Effort=8.14/21.28*100 = 38.25%

Productivity Metric for Global Software Engineering Organization B

Initially we have already discussed that organization B operates in three countries of three different continents which were Asia, America and Europe and the countries were Pakistan, USA and UK.

When inquired about local development confined to a single country the productivity was about 1500 LOC per staff-month. The interesting thing to notice here is that when GSE based development was studied for organization B which operates in three countries of three different continents we identified that productivity metric for 30 KLOC information system was about 850 LOC. Putting the case of our studied payroll system we find that:

Effort= 32370/850 = 38.08 staff-months

The effort increased further from 29 staff-months to 38 staff-months when GSE comprised of multiple continents. The percentage from the local development case of organization A for the payroll system is given as under:

Percentage change in Effort=Change in Effort/Initial Effort * 100

Change in Effort=New Effort-Old Effort

Change in Effort= 38.08-21.28= 16.8

Percentage change in Effort=16.8/21.28*100 = 78.94%

For the multiple continents case the effort increased by 78.94%. This was tremendous increase in effort from the local development case. We also calculated the percentage change in effort for the two global development cases.

Percentage change in Effort=Change in Effort/Initial Effort * 100

Change in Effort=New Effort-Old Effort

Change in Effort= 38.08-29.42= 8.66

Percentage change in Effort=8.66/29.42*100 = 29.43%

SUMMARIZING THE CASE STUDIES

We summarize the case studies discussed in this section in the table 8.

The table 8 says it all; it creates an interesting relation between efforts of GSE based development and productivity of the team members. There is an inverse relation among the two factors. The more factors of GSE is applied to the development process with respect to cultural and geographical differences the effort of the software under development will increase and the productivity of people will decrease.

Another interesting thing to notice here is that increase in effort does not always mean more development cost as monthly wages of staff members and operational cost of software development organizations varies in two to three times among developed and under developed countries.

Table 8. Summary of the case studies

Software Development Methodology	Developed Software	Software Size	Software Effort	Productivity	Percentage change in Effort from local development
Local development	Payroll System Developed Locally (Information System)	30 KLOC	21.28 staff-months	1500 LOC per person-month	Not Applicable
GSE based development in single continent comprising three countries	Information Systems developed in multiple countries of same continent	30 KLOC	29.42 staff-months	1100 LOC per person-month	38.25%
GSE based development comprising three countries of three different continents	Information Systems developed in multiple countries of different continents	30 KLOC	38.08 staff-months	850 LOC per person-month	78.94%

CONCLUSION

We conclude the learning outcomes of this chapter in the points given below:

- When the development methodology changes from local development (which is within a single country) to global software engineering the effort of the software increases.
- The increase in effort for GSE is similar to the concept of diseconomies of scale, but in the case of GSE diseconomies of scale is applied when number of development countries for single software (under development) increases.
- The more global you get in terms of number of countries or same number of countries but different cultures that is different continents the effort will always increase with respect to changing cultures.
- Increase in effort does not always mean more development cost as monthly wages fluctuates even three to four times between under developed countries and developed countries for people belonging to almost similar skill sets. The other reason is operational cost also vary two to three times among different countries.
- The more mature an organization is the better data they have at their disposal for achieving predictability in software process.
- Mature organizations use better practices for software costing and estimation and better techniques than compared to less matured organizations.

REFERENCES

Agerfalk, P. J., Fitzgerald, B., & Holmstrom Olsson, H. (2005). *A framework for considering opportunities and threats in distributed software development.* Academic Press.

Boehm, B. W., Madachy, R., & Steece, B. (2000). Software cost estimation with Cocomo II with Cdrom. Upper Saddle River, NJ: Prentice Hall PTR.

Carmel, E. (1999). *Global Software Teams: Collaboration Across Borders and Time Zones.* Saddle River, NJ: Prentice Hall.

Carmel, E., & Tjia, P. (2005). *Offshoring Information Technology: Sourcing and Outsourcing to a Global Workforce.* Cambridge, UK: Cambridge University Press. doi:10.1017/CBO9780511541193

Chrissis, M. B., Konrad, M., & Shrum, S. (2003). CMMI guidlines for process integration and product improvement. Boston, MA: Addison-Wesley Longman Publishing.

Crow, G., & Muthuswamy, B. (2003). International outsourcing in the information technology industry: Trends and implications. *Communications of the International Information Management Association, 3*(1), 25–34.

Curtis, B., Kellner, M. I., & Over, J. (1992). Process modeling. *Communications of the ACM, 35*(9), 75–90. doi:10.1145/130994.130998

Davidow, W. H., & Malone, M. S. (1992). *The Virtual Corporation.* New York, NY: Edward Brulingame Books/Harper Business.

Dhir, S., Kumar, D., & Singh, V. B. (2019). Success and Failure Factors that Impact on Project Implementation using Agile Software Development Methodology. In *Software Engineering* (pp. 647–654). Singapore: Springer. doi:10.1007/978-981-10-8848-3_62

Herbsleb, J. D., & Mockus, A. (2003). An empirical study of speed and communication in globally distributed software development. *IEEE Transactions on Software Engineering, 29*(6), 481–494. doi:10.1109/TSE.2003.1205177

Jarvenpaa, S. L., & Ives, B. (1994). The global network organization of the future: Information management opportunities and challenges. *Journal of Management Science and Information Systems, 10*(4), 25–57. doi:10.1080/07421222.1994.11518019

Keim, Y., Bhardwaj, M., Saroop, S., & Tandon, A. (2014). Software cost estimation models and techniques: A survey. *International Journal of Engineering, 3*(2).

Kotlarsky, J., & Oshri, I. (2005). Social ties, knowledge sharing and successful collaboration in globally distributed system development projects. *European Journal of Information Systems, 14*(1), 37–48. doi:10.1057/palgrave.ejis.3000520

Lacerda, T. C., & von Wangenheim, C. G. (2018). Systematic literature review of usability capability/maturity models. *Computer Standards & Interfaces, 55*, 95–105. doi:10.1016/j.csi.2017.06.001

Leemans, M., Van Der Aalst, W. M., Van Den Brand, M. G., & et al, . (2018, September). Software Process Analysis Methodology–A Methodology Based on Lessons Learned in Embracing Legacy Software. In *2018 IEEE International Conference on Software Maintenance and Evolution (ICSME)* (pp. 665-674). Piscataway, NJ: IEEE. 10.1109/ICSME.2018.00076

Mohrman, S. A. (1999). The context for geographically dispersed teams and networks. In C. L. Cooper & D. M. Rousseau (Eds.), *The Virtual Organization (Trends in Organizational Behaviour)* 6, (pp. 63–80). Chichester, UK: John Wiley & Sons.

Naik, P. (2018). *Insights on Algorithmic and Non-algorithmic Cost Estimation Approaches Used by Current Software Industries across India.* Academic Press.

Nidiffer, K. E., & Dolan, D. (2005). Evolving distributed project management. *IEEE Software*, *22*(5), 63–72. doi:10.1109/MS.2005.120

O'Brien, J. A. (2002). *Management Information Systems – Managing Information Technology in the Business Enterprise* (6th ed.). New York, NY: McGraw Hill Irwin.

Paulk, M. C., Curtis, B., Chrissis, M. B., & Weber, C. V. (1993). Capability maturity model, version 1.1. *IEEE Software*, *10*(4), 18–27. doi:10.1109/52.219617

Powell, A., Piccoli, G., & Ives, B. (2004). Virtual teams: A review of current literature and direction for future research. *The Data Base for Advances in Information Systems*, *35*(1), 6–36. doi:10.1145/968464.968467

Prikladnicki, R., Audy, J. L. N., & Evaristo, R. (2003). Global software development in practice, lessons learned. *Software Process Improvement and Practice*, *8*(4), 267–279. doi:10.1002pip.188

Sarker, S., & Sahay, S. (2004). Implications of space and time for distributed work: An interpretive study of US–Norwegian systems development teams. *European Journal of Information Systems*, *13*(1), 3–20. doi:10.1057/palgrave.ejis.3000485

Team, C. P. (2006). *CMMI for Development, version 1.2.* Academic Press.

Toaff, S. S. (2005). Don't play with "mouths of fire" and other lessons of global software development. *Cutter IT Journal*, *15*(11), 23–28.

Trendowicz, A. (2013). Software Cost Estimation, Benchmarking, and Risk Assessment: The Software Decision-Makers' Guide to Predictable Software Development. Berlin, Germany: Springer Science & Business Media. doi:10.1007/978-3-642-30764-5

Vyas, M., Bohra, A., Lamba, C. S., & Vyas, A. (2018). *A Review on Software Cost and Effort Estimation Techniques for Agile Development Process.* Academic Press.

Wagner, S., & Ruhe, M. (2018). *A systematic review of productivity factors in software development.* Academic Press.

This research was previously published in Human Factors in Global Software Engineering; pages 273-296, copyright year 2019 by Engineering Science Reference (an imprint of IGI Global).

Chapter 46
Security Assurance in Agile Software Development Methods:
An Analysis of Scrum, XP, and Kanban

Kalle Rindell
University of Turku, Finland

Sami Hyrynsalmi
 https://orcid.org/0000-0002-5073-3750
Tampere University of Technology, Finland

Ville Leppänen
University of Turku, Finland

ABSTRACT

Agile software development was introduced in the beginning of the 2000s to increase the visibility and efficiency software projects. Since then it has become as an industry standard. However, fitting sequential security engineering development models into iterative and incremental development practices in agile methods has caused difficulties in defining, implementing, and verifying the security properties of software. In addition, agile methods have also been criticized for decreased quality of documentation, resulting in decreased security assurance necessary for regulative purposes and security measurement. As a consequence, lack of security assurance can complicate security incident management, thus increasing the software's potential lifetime cost. This chapter clarifies the requirements for software security assurance by using an evaluation framework to analyze the compatibility of established agile security development methods: XP, Scrum, and Kanban. The results show that the agile methods are not inherently incompatible with security engineering requirements.

DOI: 10.4018/978-1-6684-3702-5.ch046

INTRODUCTION

During the last decade, agile software development methods have become an industry *de facto* standard. The aim of these methods has been to improve efficiency as well as transparency of software development (Abrahamsson et al., 2002). The methods promote iterative development and informal interaction, and put a lower or even negative value to strict processes. This is particularly stressed in cases where documentation is used as a means of communication, whether used to convey the customer requirements to the development team, or for communication within the team itself, e.g., in the form of specifications (Beznosov and Kruchten, 2004; Ko et al., 2007; LaToza et al., 2006).

Introducing strict security requirements to the software development process usually results in creation of excess security assurance, such as a formal security architecture, out of necessity to fulfill the strict external security criteria. Integrating the security requirements, such as reviews, security testing, processes and documentation into an agile method, the cost of the development effort is very likely to increase (Beznosov and Kruchten, 2004). The entire extra 'management overhead' is in direct contradiction with agile methods' core philosophy of leanness and informality (Beck et al., 2001). Thus, applying the security processes to the agile or lean development methods has the potential of rendering the methods, by definition, something that is neither agile nor lean.

On the other hand, the need for software security has been always one of the main drivers in software development. While quality assurance remains a key process to ensure software robustness, effectiveness and usability, security assurance provides the means to develop and deploy software components and systems that protect the system's data, their users' privacy and the system resources.

The operating environment of the software products and services has been evolving and changing due to extensive use of the Internet and public services as well as the ever-increasing pervasiveness and ubiquitous characteristic of software solutions. In addition, the software industry itself has gone through an unprecedented shift from sequential development methods (e.g. waterfall-type) towards iterative and incremental software development methods (e.g. agile and lean). In addition, due to the large scale adaptation of agile methods in the industry (Licorish et al. 2016, VersionOne 2018), the new agile development methods seem to be able to reclaim at least some of their claimed benefits.

Furthermore, the need for security has also been realized in the form of several commercial, international and national standards. To comply with these, several security frameworks and security-focused development methods have been presented. However, knitting together strict security engineering practices and adaptable agile software methods is not straightforward and may cause remarkable problems.

Furthermore, the selection of a software development method to be used in a development project has consequences into the software architecture and design. While the manifesto for agile software development states that the best architectures and design emerges from self-organized teams (Beck et al., 2001), this statement has been often criticized. For example, renowned software engineering researcher Philippe Kruchten (2010) has repeatedly questioned whether the concept of 'agile architecture' combines two incompatible approaches. In the context of security sensitive projects, this question is even more topical as it is a hard and arduous task to embed security into a product afterwards.

Therefore, the objective of this chapter is to study how well the selected agile methods are adaptable to security development practices. For the purposes of this study, we have selected three widely-used development methods, Scrum, XP and Kanban. We use Microsoft Secure Development Lifecycle (SDL) model as a benchmark for the evaluation – as the model is designed for high regulation environment and therefore its practices as well as the required frequency of occurrence should define the baseline required for this kind of activities in the industry.

These agile development methods are evaluated against a security requirement framework. The security requirement framework is created with adaption from the Finnish governmental security instructions, named *VAHTI* (VAHTI, 2016). The evaluation framework presented in this study consists of 22 different security requirements, selected from the instructions from software development. The compliance of the selected development methods is then evaluated against the requirements of VAHTI, and the applicability and adaptability of the 'security-enhanced' methods themselves are evaluated. In this analysis, SDL's activities and their properties are used to guide the analysis.

The remaining of this chapter is structured as follows. The next section discusses shortly on different software development methods as well as related work. It is followed by a presentation of the evaluation framework and VAHTI security regulation as defined by Finnish government. After that, the results of applying the presented evaluation framework into XP, Scrum and Kanban are presented. Finally, in the last three sections the findings are discussed, future research avenues presented, and the study summarized.

BACKGROUND

The security claims of a software product or a service need to be backed with evidence; it cannot be declared only by the developer. To verify the security claims stated by the software, evidence is gathered through several activities such as reviewing the software, documentation written during the development, and processes as well as through security testing, and security auditing.

Combined, these requirements create a need for the software developers to be able to choose a development methodology that supports not only the creation of software for the selected software domain, but also satisfies the security requirements (SAFECode 2012). Preferably, this is done in the most efficient way possible, taking into account the organization and the operational environment. In software development, efficiency is gained by close integration to the utilized development methodology.

In the following, we will first take a look on different agile software development methods later studied in this chapter. It is followed by a review of related studies done in examining security engineering in agile software development context.

Software Development Methods

A series of different kinds of software development methods have been presented (Abrahamsson et al., 2002). In our use, a 'software development method' defines how a software development process is divided into different phases, how the phases are arranged, and what kinds of artefacts are produced during the different phases. Instead of more traditional methods, as so-called 'waterfall' and spiral models, our focus turns on modern lightweight development methods labelled as *agile*.

For this study, we have chosen three agile software development methods: Ex*treme Programming* (XP), *Scrum*, and *Kanban*. These methods were selected as they are among the most popular and most used ones in the latest surveys (Licorish et al. 2016) as well as they have been the among the most popular ones during the last decade (cf. VersionOne 2013, 2018). That is, these methods can be interpreted to present the core of agile software development methods. All of these methods can be considered archetypes of agile software development methods, with strong use base in the industry. Thus, they are also eligible candidates for development work carried out in highly regulated environments.

In addition to the selected agile methods, we take a look on Microsoft's SDL model that acts as a reference point for the evaluation. As the SDL model is designed especially for highly regulated information security environments, it should lay the needed level of security engineering activities in software projects.

Extreme Programming. XP is one of the first and most widely used agile development models. The XP method principally consists of a collection of practices and values; that is, it does not define strictly how the actual development process should be carried out (Beck, 1999). In addition, XP promotes a number of techniques, such as 40-hours week, iteration planning game, test-first development and small releases.

However, the guidelines given by the method are quite practical, such as the use of pair programming or continuous integration. Popularity of the XP method, especially in the beginning of the first decade of the 21st century, has spun attempts to bring security elements into the method. Previous work of security enhancements into the XP method consist of security-related user stories and abuser stories in the planning phase (Boström et al., 2006; Ge et al., 2007).

Scrum. Scrum can be considered as the current mainstream of the software industry (see VersionOne, 2018). The method defines certain roles for the team members, their responsibilities as well as certain tools, activities and a loose framework for the development process. The development work is divided into sprints that usually last from two to four weeks. (Schwaber, 1995, 2004)

In the extant literature, earlier examples of security enhancement to Scrum consist of loosely SDL-based security features specifically aimed for regulated environments, such as in a case presented by Fitzgerald et al. (2013). These features and processes include 'hardening sprints', which consist entirely of security-related planning and documentation, and regulation-driven security and quality assurance reviews and checks. This methodology includes new roles that are not included in baseline Scrum. Scrum has been selected due to its overwhelming popularity in the current software development industry (VersionOne, 2013, 2018).

Kanban. Kanban, much like XP, can be understood simply as a set of development concepts, ideas and principles, rather than a tightly-defined set of processes, practices and roles. It therefore provides a rather flexible framework for development, focusing on the work flow: the work flow is visualized, the amount of work in progress is limited, and the development lead time is measured. This helps the developers to stay informed of the work backlog, aims to ensure that the team members do not get overloaded, and provides metrics to optimize the development time. Kanban is typically combined with more prescriptive methods, leading into creation of e.g. Scrumban (Nikitina et al., 2012) and other hybrid methods.

Security Development Lifecycle. Microsoft's effort to improve the security of their software has led them to develop their own security framework, the Security Development Lifecycle process. SDL is based on iterative spiral model borrowed from and adaptable to agile methodologies (Microsoft, 2012; Baca and Carlsson, 2011).

The approach selected in the SDL, when adapted without modification, is quite heavy on processes, documentation and organization – a contrast to the agile methods discussed above. This forms part of the motivation of this study, aiming to identify the minimal set of SDL elements required to fulfill the security requirements. SDL divides activities into three categories: *one-time* requirements, *bucket* requirements and *every-sprint* requirement. The naming of the categories appears to suggest that SDL for Agile is meant for Scrum or Scrum-like methods. SDL emphasizes the use source code static analysis tools as the principal security activity, followed by threat modeling and security testing.

Related Work

A starting point for the research was formal categorization of security aspects for software development, and conducting a feature analysis using DESMET (Kitchenham et al., 1997). DESMET framework was presented in the 1990s for evaluation of software development methods. The evaluation may be quantitative or qualitative, and based on experiments, case studies, screenings, effect analyses, feature analyses or surveys. The nature of this study suggested a screening feature analysis, with easily quantitative results: the requirement is either fulfilled or not, and each method and security process is analyzed as a simulated case study, based on expert opinions and without instantiation.

Beznosov and Kruchten (2004) earlier used a similar approach; however, they did not use established security criteria or framework, nor an external evaluation criteria. In addition, there exists a number of studies concerning secure software development concept in general, also covering the topic of security-focused testing (Fitzgerald and Stol, 2014). Furthermore, Abrahamsson et al. (2003) made an early contribution comparing agile software development methods by their suitability for different stages of development life cycle, and their support for project management — both important aspects from the security point of view. In their study, security engineering was not considered *per se*, as they focused more on general issues in different agile software development methods.

Regarding more specifically literature on security engineering in agile software development, a series of work has been presented (cf. Rindell et al., 2017b). A common nominator for the earlier literature seems to be an approach of documenting a proprietary corporate software development method, or even specify own development method (e.g., Baca and Carlsson, 2011; Boström et al., 2006; Rindell et al., 2015). For example, Baca and Carlsson (2011) also compare existing software methodologies, including SDL, with a proprietary method, and claim also a new proprietary method of their own. In addition, for instance Vuori (2011) discusses how IEC 61508 standard can be used to improve agile software development methods' suitability for a safety-critical development environment.

Furthermore, Wäyrynen et al. (2004) discusses whether security engineering approach can be implemented into XP development method at all. They also discussed certain activities – e.g., static code reviews, security policies –that might need to be included into XP to make it more security engineering friendly. Boström et al. (2006) continued this topic and proposed the use of abuser stories and security-related user stories as a part of XP to make it more suitable for security engineering.

Similar approach has been utilized by Köngsli et al. (2006), who notes the mismatch between requirements for security engineering projects and agile software development. Yet, the study does not specifically discuss on the claimed shortcomings. Nevertheless, the study reviews a bulk of literature and lists several different security activities that should be taken into account. Chivers et al. (2005) also note the mismatch between XP and security engineering. Their proposal is iterative security architecting to maintain a 'good enough' (from a security point-of-view) architecture during iterative and incremental development work. Also Ge et al. (2007) aim to improve security engineering in XP through security training and security architecture. Their security activities include, e.g., security stories.

Adelyar and Norta (2016) and Adelyar (2018) adopted a different approach and studied what kind of security challenges there are in agile methods. Their results show that there are certain developer and customer activities that might enable the presence of security flaws in the software product.

De Win et al. (2009) used an alternative approach and focused on three security engineering standard processes in the field: CLASP, SDL and Touchpoints. Their focus is on these practices and whereas they acknowledge, e.g., XP, it is not clear how well the studied cases are suitable for mainstream software security engineering projects with an agile approach. Ayalew et al. (2013) continue this work and focus on cost-benefit analysis. However, their work produces also a list of comparable agile security activities.

Sonia et al. (2014) assigns an agility value to different security engineering activities. In their analysis, all security activities studied are seem to be incompatible with at least one modern agile activity. Thus, their work further emphasizes the difference and incompatibility of security engineering and agile software development methods.

Othmane et al. (2014) propose their own secure agile development method for *continuous security*. Their approach is to adapt different security engineering activities in each development sprint in order to guarantee that the software produced in each iteration is secured.

In addition, empiric research has been conducted on the impact of agile methods on software security (Alnatheer et al., 2010). There also exists case studies in adapting Scrum-based methods in an environment with strict formal security regulations (Fitzgerald et al., 2013; Rindell et al., 2016, Oyetoyan et al., 2016).

The study by Fitzgerald et al. (2013) discusses security regulations and Scrum in considerable depth, yet only within the scope of a single company and a single development method. The case study by Rindell et al. (2016, 2017a) focuses also on a case using Scrum-based method but it is as well restricted by the scope of a single project. Oyetoyan et al. (2016) studied two organizations using Scrum in their development work. The focus of the study is on the skills, trainings and experience of the development teams. The study shows that security awareness improves the use of security activities in the development work.

To summarize the review of related work, it can be noted that there are a series of work devoted for improving different aspects of security engineering in agile software development methods. However, a common claim seems to be that agile methods are inherently insecure and inapplicable for security engineering (Rindell et al., 2017b). Yet, there is a lack of work addressing whether this can be considered to be true or just a myth.

This study takes an alternative approach and aims to evaluate the vanilla versions of different agile software development methods against a security engineering framework. To depart from the previous work, that have assumed the insecurity of these methods, we instead use an industry standard (i.e., VAHTI regulation) as a baseline for defining security activities needed.

EVALUATION FRAMEWORK

This chapter aims to assess how well agile software development methods are suitable for security engineering projects by using a nationwide criteria and new development methods, and the SDL security framework as a benchmark. In contrast to most of the previous approaches, security is in this chapter considered to be an *absolute* requirement for software. In the agile method terminology, security is considered an essential part of the customer satisfaction, which the agile methods aim to promote (Beznosov and Kruchten, 2004).

We concentrate on the challenges this brings into the development process and the quality assurance closely associated with security controls. This study also makes the security requirement more specific by using a well-established security criteria, VAHTI, and inspecting the applicability of the selected software methodologies to comply with this criteria. The term 'security assurance' is used to describe the drive to mitigate security vulnerabilities in a measurable and evidence-backed way, comparable to the term 'quality assurance', which aims to mitigate software discrepancies in general. In a regulatory context, security assurance conveys also the meaning of security proof, referring to written security documentation and e.g. logs.

The specific set of security requirements used in this chapter is based on VAHTI (literally translated *'Guard'*, a mnemonic acronym in Finnish for 'Government Information Security') security regulation. VAHTI is one of the earliest and most comprehensive sets of open and public information system security regulations. The instructions consist of 51 documents, published since 2001, aiming at covering the whole life cycle of the governmental information systems. The guideline covers also various aspects of information systems management, governance, use, and, ultimately aid implementing Finland's national information security strategy, published in 2009.

VAHTI instructions specify three security levels ('basic', 'increased' and 'high'). The instructions were originally targeted only for government's internal information systems work; due to public sector's integral part in the Finnish society, VAHTI is in the process of becoming a de facto security standard in any information system that interacts with a governmental system. VAHTI exists to harmonize the security requirements among the public institutions, a set of national standards has been developed, based on standards such as ISO/IEC 27002 (ISO/IEC, 2013), and derived from Systems Security Engineering – Capability Maturity Model (ISO/IEC standard 21827, 2008). These requirements aim to cover the life cycle and various use cases of the public information systems, and span over several dozen public documents.

VAHTI was selected due to two main reasons. First, the selection of a governmental regulation that is in active use in Finland allows us to focus on aspects and activities that are actively used in the industry. That is, instead of developing an own evaluation framework from the scratch, we depart from the previous work by using an existing and widely-used instruction set in our analysis. Second, VAHTI allows us to focus on a more comprehensive picture of a security engineering instead of a single standard. While this also forces us to select the suitable criteria for the evaluation of the software development methods, the evaluation framework based on this kind of an instruction set should be more general than one based on a more narrow standard.

For developing the evaluation framework for this study, we focused on all VAHTI criteria in different phases and regulation levels. VAHTI security criteria for application development comprises the whole life cycle of software. The complete list of security requirements in VAHTI includes 118 activities (FMoF, 2013). This list was analyzed through by the authors and relevant criteria for the software development methods were selected. The selection was made based on the relevance of the requirements to the software development method: the selected criteria are either requirements for the documentation, reviews or the development process itself.

We excluded requirements that did not directly relate to the software development method or approach used. For example, requirements for handling data storage as well as physical access to the server room are not relevant for the software development method's point-of-view. That is, those can be handled regardless of the development method used.

The only selected organizational requirement, the one for security training, was included due to the fact that SDL as well as previous work (e.g., Ge et al., 2007 and Oyetoyan et al., 2016) emphasizes this as a security-enhancing mechanism. Furthermore, it may affect the development roles in the software development method.

From the complete list of VAHTI's security requirements, 22 activities directly concerning the software development methods were selected. The selected security requirements are presented in Table 1. The table also links each requirement back to the respective VAHTI security level.

We evaluate each criteria through four dimensions: i) requirements *integrality* in a development method, ii) requirement's *frequency* of occurrence in the development work, iii) level of *automation* and iv) *cost* of performing or carrying out the requirement. Each of these dimensions are clarified more in the latter.

In the evaluation, we study whether each requirement is i) an integral part of the method; ii) the method can be adjusted to support the requirement; or iii) the method is incompatible with the requirement or there are needs for improvement in the method. This evaluation was done by the authors discussing and analyzing how well the requirement can be implemented in each of the selected software development methods. All authors are expert in software engineering and it was required that a mutual agreement needed to be reached before continuing.

The other assessment criteria of the frequency requirement for each technique is defined as it is by SDL. That is, the analysis of these requirements needed frequency is based on how often SDL requires them to be used. The frequency is encoded into three values: i) one-time requirements; ii) bucket requirements and iii) every-sprint requirements.

Each task is further ranked to either Automated, Semi-automated or Manual. Semi-automated means the bulk of the work is done by automated tools, which in turn may require a considerable amount of manual configuration. This analysis is based on the description in the VAHTI instruction set and it is subjectively evaluated by the authors. However, the authors mutually agreed on the level of the automation during the analysis.

Cost is calculated by multiplying the level of automation with the frequency of the task. The cost of security requirement's, that has to be carried out only one-time during the project and which can be easily automated, would be considered as a very low. Similarly, manual requirement that has to be carried out in each sprint would be considered as a very high in its cost. The remaining combinations are similarly categorized into the following scale: Very Low, Low, Medium, High, and Very High.

RESULTS

Table 2 summarizes the Scrum's, XP's and Kanban's compliance with each security requirement in the evaluation framework. In addition, Table 3 reports each criterion's level of automation and estimated cost as this was found an important factor. In the following, we will discuss on the central observations based on these analyses.

The three first criteria (*Application Risk Analysis*, *Test Plan Review* and *Threat Modeling*) of the framework can be considered as a basic requirement for all kinds of application development projects. That is, *Application Risk Analysis* is an essential security element and it has been or it can be well integrated into all methods. Yet, it can be done only manually as SDL requires it to be carried out in each iteration. Therefore, it is costly.

Test Plan Review is an internal security activity in which the personnel reviews the test plan. All of the studied development methods support this integrally while its cost is high. *Threat Modeling* consists of compiling the list of the threats and keeping that up to date during every sprint. This is a cornerstone activity of SDL and essential to any security related development project. The activity provides a baseline for risk analysis and guides architectural choices, among other things. The threat 'landscape' is dependent on the software's intended users and use environment. This is essential to all methods and easily integrated to them. This requirement was not mandatory even at VAHTI's highest level, which can be considered as a clear omission to the instruction set. A potential explanation to this could be the restrictions in the availability of threat modeling tools. Alternatively threat modeling can be performed as a manual task using e.g. Microsoft's STRIDE mnemonics for component analysis. In this approach, the system and its components are reviewed for security threats in the categories of Spoofing, Tampering, Repudiation, Information disclosure, Denial of Service, and Elevation of Privilege.

The following six criteria (i.e., the requirements from number 4 to 10 in Table 1) can be considered to be essential to all security engineering projects with increased information security alertness. With the notable exceptions of *Application Security Requirements* and *Application Security Settings Definition,* the cost of these requirements is estimated to be low in a development project.

The *Goal and Criticality* requirement means classification of the software and documentation of its purpose. Both XP and Scrum were found lacking in this respect while the Scrum-based methods are more readily adaptable to produce planning phase documentation. Kanban-based methods are also considered adaptable.

Business Impact Analysis is basically method independent requirement, and as such, considered adaptable to all methods. This document should be produced in the planning phase, and updated during the implementation when the application's incremental threat analyses implicate further threats to the business environment.

Table 1. The evaluation framework's criteria

No.	Criterion	VAHTI level
1	Application Risk Analysis	Basic
2	Test Plan Review	Basic
3	Threat Modeling	Basic
4	Goal and criticality	Increased
5	Business Impact Analysis	Increased
6	Documentation of Security Solutions	Increased
7	Application Security Requirements	Increased
8	Application Security Settings Definition	Increased
9	Security Testing	Increased
10	Security Auditing	Increased
11	Architecture guidelines	High
12	External Interface Review	High
13	Use of Secure Design Patterns	High
14	Attack Surface Reduction	High
15	Architectural Security Requirements	High
16	Internal Communication Security	High
17	Security Test Cases Definition	High
18	Test Phase Code Review	High
19	Use of Automated Testing Tools	High
20	Security Mechanism Review	High
21	Application Development-time Auditing	High
22	Security training	High

Table 2. Compliance of XP, Scrum and Kanban with different security requirements presented in the evaluation framework

No.	Requirement	XP	Scrum.	Kanban
1	Application Risk Analysis	Integral	Integral	Integral
2	Test Plan Review	Adaptable	Adaptable	Adaptable
3	Threat Modeling	Integral	Integral	Integral
4	Goal and Criticality	Adaptable	Adaptable	Adaptable
5	Business Impact Analysis	Adaptable	Adaptable	Adaptable
6	Documentation of Security Solutions	Adaptable	Adaptable	Adaptable
7	Application Security Requirements	Integral	Integral	Integral
8	Application Security Settings Definition	Adaptable	Adaptable	Adaptable
9	Security Testing	Integral	Integral	Integral
10	Security Auditing	Adaptable	Adaptable	Adaptable
11	Architecture guidelines	Adaptable	Adaptable	Adaptable
12	External Interface Review	Integral	Integral	Integral
13	Use of Secure Design Patterns	Integral	Integral	Integral
14	Attack Surface Reduction	Integral	Integral	Integral
15	Architectural Security Requirements	Integral	Integral	Integral
16	Internal Communication Security	Integral	Integral	Integral
17	Security Test Cases Definition	Adaptable	Adaptable	Adaptable
18	Test Phase Code Review	Integral	Integral	Integral
19	Use of Automated Testing Tools	Integral	Integral	Integral
20	Security Mechanism Review	Adaptable	Adaptable	Adaptable
21	Application Development-time Auditing	Incompatible	Incompatible	Incompatible
22	Security training	Adaptable	Adaptable	Adaptable

Documentation of Security Solutions is a direct requirement to communicate the security requirements to the developers through documentation. All agile methods are fundamentally against this approach, and will need improvement to be able to take into efficient use.

Document on *Application Security Requirements* is a high-level description, covering the criticality of the information handled by the software, threat analysis, and other functional security requirements. All security related development methods were deemed to support creation of this document in the planning phase. Similarly, *Application Security Settings Definition* is an extensive documentation step, where all the software settings, interfaces, administration steps, test data, encryption details etc. are listed and thoroughly documented. A suggested action would be a separate documentation sprint, to be added into the agile methods.

On one hand, *Security Testing* states that security testing should be incorporated into the standard testing procedure. This requirement is supported by all methods. On the other hand, *Security Auditing* is a requirement for Increased and High VAHTI levels. Furthermore, it requires an external auditor. This requirement was included due to its strain on the development process, mainly through architecture auditing. Also this requirement is supported by all selected methods.

Table 3. The level of automation, frequency of occurrence and relative cost of the evaluation framework's security requirements

No.	Requirement	Level of automation	Frequency	Cost
1	Application Risk Analysis	Manual	Every sprint	Very high
2	Test Plan Review	Manual	Bucket	High
3	Threat Modeling	Manual	Every sprint	High
4	Goal and Criticality	Manual	One-time	Low
5	Business Impact Analysis	Manual	Bucket	Low
6	Documentation of Security Solutions	Manual	Bucket	Low
7	Application Security Requirements	Manual	Bucket	High
8	Application Security Settings Definition	Manual	Bucket	High
9	Security Testing	Automated	Every sprint	Medium
10	Security Auditing	Manual	One-time	Low
11	Architecture guidelines	Manual	One-time	Low
12	External Interface Review	Manual	Bucket	High
13	Use of Secure Design Patterns	Manual	One-time	Low
14	Attack Surface Reduction	Manual	Every sprint	Very high
15	Architectural Security Requirements	Manual	One-time	Low
16	Internal Communication Security	Semi-automated	Every sprint	Medium
17	Security Test Cases Definition	Manual	Every sprint	Very high
18	Test Phase Code Review	Manual	Every sprint	Very high
19	Use of Automated Testing Tools	Automated	Every sprint	Very low
20	Security Mechanism Review	Manual	One-time	Low
21	Application Development-time Auditing	Manual	One-time	Low
22	Security training	Manual	Every sprint	Very high

The remaining twelve criteria can be considered to be essential for a software development project where information security requirements are extremely high. As the VAHTI instruction set is defined by a governmental agency, it is not a surprise that special emphasizes has been put on these requirements. Furthermore, on average these requirements are more costly to carry out than the ones belonging essentially in the increased security category.

Architecture guidelines define the principles guiding the application development, in this context especially from the security point of view. This requirement is adaptable to all development methods. *External Interface Review* is an analysis of the software's external interfaces and comparison to architectural and application level principles. All methods support the performance of this action. *Use of Secure Design Patterns* mandates classifying the software due to its architecture type, such as client-server, mobile, web or embedded application. The design pattern is then selected based on the architectural type. All of the studied methods support this requirement.

Attack Surface Reduction includes identifying and analyzing all software functionality where the participants cannot completely trust each other, such as open services, user or administrator actions or database connections. All methods support this step. *Architectural Security Requirements* mean analysis of the application's architecture against known or anticipated threats. All methods support this requirement. *Internal Communication Security* concerns especially applications utilizing multi-tier architecture and ties the deployment of the application into the development phase. Largely method independent planning-phase activity, but still supported by each method.

Security Test Cases Definition is an absolute requirement for almost all security-related development, and VAHTI gives here specific instructions how the test cases should be defined, such as use of empiric evidence, known issues and several sources. This requirement is adaptable to all methods. *Test Phase Code Review* is informally performed by the internal security personnel, and documented either separately or even straight into the source code. This requirement is also supported by all of the studied methods.

Use of Automated Testing Tools is more or less standard practice for all agile software development, regardless of the used methodology. On the security side, the tools include fuzz testing tools, vulnerability scanners, code analyzers and continuous integration tools. This requirement is quite naturally supported by all three included agile methods.

Security Mechanism Review is a code-level review of how security components are implemented. Basically it is method independent, but may be difficult to implement in iterative methods as after changes this review has to be done again. As such, this activity might require a specific hardening sprint, as a time-consuming activity like this may be difficult to fit into the work flow.

Application Development-time Auditing is a high-level security audition at various points of application development. Intrinsically a waterfall-type approach, causing difficulties with iterative methods. *Security training* means organizing purpose-oriented and role-based training for the personnel responsible for the application development, such as the product owner, developers and testers. This requirement is adaptable to all of the studied methods.

DISCUSSION

The three agile methods (Scrum, XP and Kanban) studied in this chapter were found to have certain issues with adaptability of security tasks. Repetitive (i.e., multi-sprint or every-sprint) documentation and review tasks were found specifically incompatible with these methods. While a theoretical examination cannot establish concrete benefits gained from the use of agile methods, it was deemed unjustifiable to claim that their use would have an adverse effect on security assurance. Instead, use of agile prompts including security items e.g. in the user stories and integrating them into the backlog as a part of regular conduct of an agile development project. All three methods were found inherently compatible with or adaptable to all planning and implementation phase activities. Incorporating security reviews and auditing into the iterative development processes proved to be a tougher issue. The SDL prompts these activities to be completed in "each and every sprint", or "the sprint is deemed incomplete". However, the wording of the SDL has since 2015 been altered, and the word *sprint* is no longer used as a synonym for *release*, which is the current term. It appears that Microsoft, too, has awoken to the reality in which not every agile sprint produces a released version of software.

When compared to the previous work in the field, this study is produces somewhat different results, explained by the different research approach. Whereas the previous work has been focused on defining more or less a 'perfect' method for agile security engineering and underlining all possible obstacles, we adapted a different route for our analysis. Instead of a rigid model, this study concentrated on the aspects that are needed to be changed in order to use a popular agile method in a development project that needs to fulfill governmental security development instructions. That is, we were looking for a 'good enough' solution and the result shows that mismatch between agile methods and security engineering might be too harshly reported. Especially the concerns of agile methods' compatibility with formal requirements can be quite readily dismissed based on a theoretical analysis only.

Nevertheless, the use of studied agile methods clearly requires quite heavy process customization, in order for them to be applicable to projects with formal security requirements. The key findings were that *continuous security planning*, in the form of iterative design and architecture activities, has the most potential to improve the security of the finalized product. On other hand, at the higher security levels, incorporating every-sprint security reviews make it difficult to retain the 'agility' of a method – and formal auditing requirements worsen this situation altogether. Incorporating the 'hardening sprints', suggested by e.g. Fitzgerald et al., (2013), or focusing on security only in the planning phase of the project (Boström et al., 2006; Ge et al., 2007), may simply lead to superficial fulfillment of the requirements, potentially leading to security issues afterwards. Methodology-based evaluation suggests that security assurance is best achieved through investing in both planning and implementation tasks.

Scrum is the only one of the methods that include any kind of role definitions. Security methodologies, on the other hand, tend to have specific role definitions and push for strict separation of duties. Table 4 presents a summary of key tasks and properties required from a security assured software development method. The table states whether the selected methods have the roles defined (Yes or No), or support the extension of existing roles to cover the more security-specific one. This comparison reveals a more worrying side of the secure agile methods, especially regarding role definition.

Table 4. Security task role definition

No	Task	XP	Scrum	Kanban
1	Security specialist roles defined	No	Yes	No
2	Documentation and guidelines produced	Yes	Yes	Yes
3	Support for development time security reviews	No	Yes	No
4	Support for delivery time security reviews	No	Yes	No
5	Compliant development process roles defined	No	No	No

SDL defines several security roles for the development team, such as reviewer/advisor, auditor, expert, and team champions. It also promotes strict and vigorous separation of duties, all while the agile methods typically define only a minimum set of roles or none at all. Scrum, in its basic form, defines only the roles of Product Owner, Developers and the Scrum Master. Of these, the Developer is the most appropriate one to assume the responsibilities of a security specialist. This, however, is a clear violation of the industry standard 'separation of duties' rule: the developers themselves are rarely the best persons to break their own code. This approach is anti-agile in two ways: teams not sharing information is a clear violation against the agile philosophy, and having separate teams working in parallel bogs down the development speed while increasing the cost. The same lack of defined security roles also characterizes XP and Kanban, all while giving organizations more freedom in choosing the development tools, mechanisms and processes.

In addition, the message in the studied literature is clear about certain benefit of employing agile methods to develop security-oriented software: developing the software in numerous iterations towards the finalized product may actually improve security assurance, as the product is kept potentially shippable after every sprint – an agile ideal, although rarely achievable. This greatly helps in tracking the changes in security development and detecting possible security threats. In addition, the promoted use of automated testing and other tools is an inherent part of security development, directly applicable also to fuzz testing.

FUTURE RESEARCH DIRECTIONS

This study opens new fruitful research avenues for future development in security regarding software architecture and design fields. While there are different adaptations defined and presented for secure agile software development, there is a lack of empirical evidence and test regarding these adaptations. Future work should be aimed to develop usable agile software development improvements that comply with the requirements of security engineering. Furthermore, this kind of a development work should incorporate the 'good enough' principle in order to keep the benefits achieved with agile methods. If the method aims for too good or too strict security process, it might be that transparency and efficiency of agile methodologies will be lost.

In addition, this chapter calls for a new kind of thinking into the security engineering. While security is and will be a main driver in many, if not in all, software development projects, also other aspects are important. These include, e.g., efficient and fast development. The current development in this field has been based purely on the security engineering perspective and much of the realism in the industry is bypassed. Therefore, especially in the agile security engineering field a new fresh start is needed for defining, e.g., cost-efficient solutions and integrating security engineering practices into other activities. While improving awareness has been showed to have good effect on security engineering, lightweight solutions could also work.

The limitation of this study is a lack of empiric evidence, and the logical next step would be to instantiate the methods and possibly include more of them. While security should be based on 'defined' rather than 'empiric' logic, practice will show not only the applicability of the methods themselves, but also the real cost of security mechanisms to the development process. Security cost is becoming increasingly necessary to pay, as Finland's public sector's software security regulations show. As the cost of development is much smaller than rewriting and refactoring an existing code base, integrating the security processes to the development method is crucial. The ultimate objective should be nothing less than finding a framework for the software developers to choose the correct set of roles, methods and processes for each situation and purpose.

CONCLUSION

This study used established and widely-used Finnish government's security criteria, VAHTI, as a basis for evaluation of three approaches to software development for a regulated environment. Selected security framework was Microsoft SDL and the methods XP, Scrum, and Kanban. Research objective of this study was to use lightweight DESMET evaluation criteria to analyze the adaptability of agile methods to security development, and to estimate the cost of security-related tasks. The study shows that in a theoretical framework the agile methodologies are readily adaptable to even the most strict security requirements. This result departs from the extant literature, which too often presents agile software development methods incompatible with security engineering practices. Therefore, this chapter suggests future activities in developing and using agile methods for the use of security work in software architecture and design.

REFERENCES

Abrahamsson, P., Salo, O., Ronkainen, J., & Warsta, J. (2002). *Agile software development methods.* VTT Publications.

Abrahamsson, P., Warsta, J., Siponen, M. T., & Ronkainen, J. (2003). New directions on agile methods: A comparative analysis. In *Proceedings of the 25th International Conference on Software Engineering* (pp. 244–254). Washington, DC: IEEE Computer Society.

Adelyar, S. H. (2018). *Secure Agile Agent-Oriented Software Development. Tallinna University of Technology, Dissertations in Natural Sciences No. 51.*

Adelyar, S. H., & Horta, A. (2016). Towards a Secure Agile Software Development Process. In *2016 10th International Conference on the Quality of Information and Communications Technology* (pp. 101-106). IEEE. 10.1109/QUATIC.2016.028

Alnatheer, A., Gravell, A., & Argles, D. (2010). Agile security issues: A research study. *Proceedings of the 5th International Doctoral Symposium on Empirical Software Engineering.*

Ayalew, T., Kidane, T., & Carlsson, B. (2013) Identification and Evaluation of Security Activities in Agile Projects. Springer. doi:10.1007/978-3-642-41488-6_10

Baca, D., & Carlsson, B. (2011). Agile development with security engineering activities. In *Proceedings of the 2011 International Conference on Software and Systems Process, ICSSP '11* (pp. 149–158). New York: ACM.

Beck, K. (1999). Embracing change with extreme programming. *IEEE Computer, 32.*

Beck, K., Beedle, M., Van Bennekum, A., Cockburn, A., Cunningham, W., Fowler, M., . . . Thomas, D. (2001). *Manifesto for agile software development.* Retrieved from http://agilemanifesto.org/

Beznosov, K., & Kruchten, P. (2004). Towards agile security assurance. *NSPW '04 Proceedings of the 2004 workshop on New security paradigms*, 47–54.

bin Othmane, L., Angin, P., Weffers, H., & Bhargava, B. (2014). Extending the Agile Development Process to Develop Acceptably Secure Software. *IEEE Transactions on Dependable and Secure Computing, 11*(6), 497-509.

Boström, G., Wäyrynen, J., Bodén, M., Beznosov, K., & Kruchten, P. (2006). Extending XP practices to support security requirements engineering. *Proceedings of the 2006 International Workshop on Software Engineering for Secure Systems, SESS '06.* 10.1145/1137627.1137631

Chivers, H., Paige, R. F., & Ge, X. (2005) Agile security using an incremental security architecture. *Proceedings of the 6th international conference on Extreme Programming and Agile Processes in Software Engineering.* 10.1007/11499053_7

De Win, B., Scandariato, R., Buyens, K., Grégoire, J., & Joosen, W. (2009). On the secure software development process: CLASP, SDL and Touchpoints compared. *Information and Software Technology, 51*(7), 1152–1171. doi:10.1016/j.infsof.2008.01.010

Fitzgerald, B., & Stol, K.-J. (2014). Continuous software engineering and beyond: Trends and challenges. In *Proceedings of the 1st International Workshop on Rapid Continuous Software Engineering* (pp. 1–9). New York: ACM. 10.1145/2593812.2593813

Fitzgerald, B., Stol, K.-J., O'Sullivan, R., & O'Brien, D. (2013). Scaling agile methods to regulated environments: An industry case study. *Proceedings of the 2013 International Conference on Software Engineering, ICSE '13*, 863–872. 10.1109/ICSE.2013.6606635

FMoF (2013). *Sovelluskehityksen tietoturvaohje.* FMoF.

Ge, X., Paige, R., Polack, F., & Brooke, P. (2007). Extreme programming security practices. In Agile Processes in Software Engineering and Extreme Programming, volume 4536 of Lecture Notes in Computer Science (pp. 226–230). Springer Berlin Heidelberg. doi:10.1007/978-3-540-73101-6_42

ISO/IEC (2013). Information technology - security techniques - code of practice for information security controls iso/IEC 27002:2013.

ISO/IEC standard 21827 (2008). Information Technology – Security Techniques – Systems Security Engineering – Capability Maturity Model (SSE-CMM). ISO/IEC.

Kitchenham, B., Linkman, S., & Law, D. (1997). Desmet: A methodology for evaluating software engineering methods and tools. *Computing & Control Engineering Journal, 8*(3), 120–126. doi:10.1049/cce:19970304

Ko, A. J., DeLine, R., & Venolia, G. (2007). Information needs in collocated software development teams. In *Proceedings of the 29th International Conference on Software Engineering, ICSE '07.* IEEE Computer Society. 10.1109/ICSE.2007.45

Kongsli, V. (2006). Towards agile security in web applications. In *Companion to the 21st ACM SIGPLAN symposium on Object-oriented programming systems, languages, and applications (OOPSLA'06)* (pp. 805-808). ACM.

Kruchten, P. (2010) Software Architecture and Agile Software Development – A Clash of Two Cultures? In *Proceedings of the International Conference on Software Engineering, ICSE'10* (pp. 497-498). ACM.

LaToza, T. D., Venolia, G., & DeLine, R. (2006). Maintaining mental models: A study of developer work habits. In *Proceedings of the 28th International Conference on Software Engineering, ICSE '06* (pp. 492–501). New York: ACM. 10.1145/1134285.1134355

Licorish, S. A., Holvitie, J., Hyrynsalmi, S., Leppänen, V., Spínola, R. O., Mendes, T. S., ... Buchan, J. (2016). Adoption and suitability of software development methods and practices. In *23rd Asia-Pacific Software Engineering Conference, APSEC 2016* (pp. 369–372). IEEE Computer Society. 10.1109/APSEC.2016.062

Microsoft. (2012). *Microsoft security development lifecycle (SDL) process guidance - version 5.2.* Microsoft.

Nikitina, N., Kajko-Mattsson, M., & Stråle, M. (2012). From Scrum to Scrumban: A case study of a process transition. In *Proceedings of the International Conference on Software and System Process, ICSSP '12* (pp. 140–149). IEEE Press. 10.1109/ICSSP.2012.6225959

Oyetoyan, T. D., Cruzes, D. S., & Jaatun, M. G. (2016). An Empirical Study on the Relationship between Software Security Skills, Usage and Training Needs in Agile Settings. In *2016 11th International Conference on Availability, Reliability and Security* (pp. 548—555). ACM.

Rindell, K., Hyrynsalmi, S., & Leppänen, V. (2015) Securing Scrum for VAHTI. In *Proceedings of 14th Symposium on Programming Languages and Software Tools (SPLST)* (pp. 236-250). University of Tampere.

Rindell, K., Hyrynsalmi, S., & Leppänen, V. (2016). Case study of security development in an agile environment: building identity management for a government agency. In *Proceedings of 2016 11th International Conference on Availability, Reliability and Security (ARES)* (pp. 556-593). IEEE. 10.1109/ARES.2016.45

Rindell, K., Hyrynsalmi, S., & Leppänen, V. (2017a). Case Study of Agile Security Engineering: Building Identity Management for a Government Agency. *International Journal of Secure Software Engineering*, *8*(1), 43–57. doi:10.4018/IJSSE.2017010103

Rindell, K., Hyrynsalmi, S., & Leppänen, V. (2017b). Busting a Myth: Review of Agile Security Engineering Methods. In *Proceedings of the 12th International Conference on Availability, Reliability and Security (ARES'17)* (pp. 74:1-74:10). ACM. 10.1145/3098954.3103170

SAFECode. (2012). *Practical security stories and security tasks for agile development environments.* Retrieved from http://www.safecode.org/publication/SAFECode_Agile_Dev_Security0712.pdf

Schwaber, K. (1995). Scrum development process. *Proceedings of the 10th Annual ACM Conference on Object Oriented Programming Systems, Languages, and Applications (OOPSLA)*, 117–134.

Schwaber, K. (2004). *Agile Project Management with Scrum.* Redmond, WA: Microsoft Press.

Sonia, S. A., & Banati, H. (2014). FISA-XP: An agile-based integration of security activities with extreme programming. *Software Engineering Notes*, *39*(3), 1–14. doi:10.1145/2597716.2597728

VAHTI. (2001-2016). *VAHTI instructions.* Retrieved from https://www.vahtiohje.fi/web/guest/home

VersionOne. (2013). *8th Annual State of Agile Survey.* Retrieved from http://www.versionone.com/pdf/2013-state-of-agile-survey.pdf

VersionOne, C. (2018). *12th Annual State of the Agile Survey*. Author.

Vuori, M. (2011). *Agile Development of Safety-Critical Software*. Tampere: Tampere University of Technology.

Wäyrynen, J., Bodén, M., & Boström, G. (2004). Security Engineering and eXtreme Programming: An Impossible Marriage? Springer Berlin Heidelberg.

Chapter 47
The Role of Neural Networks and Metaheuristics in Agile Software Development Effort Estimation

Anupama Kaushik

Maharaja Surajmal Institute of Technology, Delhi, India; Indira Gandhi Delhi Technical University for Women, Delhi, India

Devendra Kumar Tayal

Indira Gandhi Delhi Technical University for Women, Delhi, India

Kalpana Yadav

Indira Gandhi Delhi Technical University for Women, Delhi, India

ABSTRACT

In any software development, accurate estimation of resources is one of the crucial tasks that leads to a successful project development. A lot of work has been done in estimation of effort in traditional software development. But, work on estimation of effort for agile software development is very scant. This paper provides an effort estimation technique for agile software development using artificial neural networks (ANN) and a metaheuristic technique. The artificial neural networks used are radial basis function neural network (RBFN) and functional link artificial neural network (FLANN). The metaheuristic technique used is whale optimization algorithm (WOA), which is a nature-inspired metaheuristic technique. The proposed techniques FLANN-WOA and RBFN-WOA are evaluated on three agile datasets, and it is found that these neural network models performed extremely well with the metaheuristic technique used. This is further empirically validated using non-parametric statistical tests.

DOI: 10.4018/978-1-6684-3702-5.ch047

INTRODUCTION

In software development firms, two development approaches are present, the traditional software development approach and agile software development approach. In traditional software development approach requirements are well understood and there are predefined stages of development. This type of development is driven by process and tool. The requirements once decided is difficult to change and the customer's involvement is limited in this development. Here, the iterations are longer and the working software is not quickly available.

In agile software development approach customers can do modifications until late in project's life. They are people and collaboration driven. So, there is a continuous involvement of customers'. This development approach is more user friendly and follows incremental and iterative development. The iterations are shorter here and working software is available quickly. Now-a-days, software development firms are moving towards adopting agile methodologies (Dingsøyr, Nerur, Balijepally, & BredeMoe, 2012; Papadopoulos, 2015).

The success of a software project mainly depends upon the accuracy of estimation of its resources like effort, schedule etc. There are many effort estimation studies for traditional software development present in literature (Nguyen, Boehm &LiGuo, 2019; Venkataiah, Mohanty, Pahariya & Nagaratna, 2017; Kaushik, Verma, Singh & Chabbra, 2017; Kaushik, Tayal, Yadav & Kaur, 2016). These studies are based on algorithmic and non-algorithmic approach. The COCOMO model (Boehm, 1994) commonly used for effort estimation in traditional software development uses algorithmic approach. The non-algorithmic approach uses various soft computing techniques like fuzzy logic, neural network, genetic algorithms etc.

In agile software development approach, not much of work has been done in estimation of resources for the projects but a lot of work is going on for developing agile methodologies (Curiel, Jacobo, Alfaro, Zepeda & Delgado, 2018; Tolfo, Wazlawick, Ferreira & Forcellini, 2018; Perkusich, Gorgônio, Almeida, & Perkusich, 2017).This work is dedicated towards estimation of effort for agile projects using story point approach which finds the effort of a project in terms of story points. In the past, few researchers have applied various machine learning techniques for effort estimation using story point approach (Satapathy, Panda & Rath, 2014; Panda, Satapathy & Rath, 2015; Satapathy & Rath, 2017).

The current work integrates artificial neural networks (ANN) with a metaheuristic technique for effort estimation of projects following agile methodologies. The ANN used are RBFN and FLANN and, the metaheuristic technique used is whale optimization algorithm (WOA).

The ANN models incorporated have no relationship with each other and they are evaluated independently. These models are used as they have their own advantages. The major advantages of FLANN are: it has less computational complexity, faster convergence and handles the non-linear data (Mishra & Dehuri, 2007) ; and the major advantages of RBFN are: its easy design, good generalization, strong tolerance to input noise and has faster online learning ability (Yu, Xie, Paszczyñski & Wilamowski, 2011). These models are also chosen as no earlier study exists based on these models for agile environment.

Now-a-days metaheuristic techniques have come up. These are the optimization techniques which mimics the biological or physical phenomenon to solve various engineering problems. They can even find the solutions for the problems with very less and incomplete information. Many new metaheuristic algorithms are developed and many researchers (Kaushik, Tayal, Yadav, & Kaur, 2016; Kaushik, Verma, Singh, & Chhabra, 2017; Benala & Mall, 2018) have used these techniques in estimations for traditional software development environment, but according to the best of our knowledge these techniques have not been explored for resource estimations in agile software development. So the current work is an attempt to introduce metaheuristic techniques in effort estimation for agile software development environment. Here, whale optimization algorithm (WOA) is the metaheuristic approach used with ANN due to its striking features which are at par than other optimization methods (Mirjalili & Lewis, 2016). The study also examines the effort estimation accuracy of the selected ANN models by incorporating WOA.

The paper consists of literature review section which discusses the work done by the researchers concerning software effort estimation in agile environment, followed by the section on background concepts used in the current work. After that, innovation in the paper is discussed in research contribution section followed by simulation and results section. Finally, conclusion of the study is presented.

LITERATURE SURVEY

Few of the effort estimation studies related to agile software development are discussed below.

Lang, Conboy and Keaveney (2011) discussed four case studies to explain the cost estimation process, causes of inaccurate estimates and steps to improve the process in agile software development. They also discussed, how agile handles the classical problems which affects the cost estimation in comparison to traditional information system development. Their study recommended three points for agile projects and they are: estimation models are not necessarily required, documentation of past project data and experience, and fixed price budgets.

Coelho and Basu (2012) discussed effort estimation in agile software development in detail using story points and directed further scope of improvement. They also provided various size estimation techniques used traditionally, discussed user stories prioritization and delivery date estimations. They concluded that some hidden factors were also responsible for the delay in software project deployment.

Ziauddin, Tipu and Zia (2012) provided a software effort estimation model based upon user stories. This model included all the characteristics of agile software development. The model used various equations and demonstrated its effectiveness using data collected from 21 software projects. They provided guidelines to measure user story size and complexity in the scale of 1-5. They also discussed various factors affecting the projects velocity and provided a way to handle uncertainty in calculation of completion time.

Choudhari and Suman (2012) proposed an effort estimation model for software maintenance which was validated using various types of maintenance projects. This was based on story points to calculate the volume of maintenance and value adjustment factors. The model was developed in order to help the project managers to estimate the software maintenance for agile and extreme programming environment.

Hussain, Kosseim and Ormandjieva (2013) used COSMIC standard to approximate the functional size in early effort estimation in agile processes. Their methodology used supervised text mining approach where COSMIC function size is calculated from the textual requirements and it was also able to recognize the striking features of the functional processes in order to determine their size.

Popli and Chauhan (2014) provided an estimation method for projects using agile methodologies. The algorithm efficiently proposed effort, cost and duration for small and medium sized agile projects. They also discussed already existing methods of agile estimation along with their limitations. Their estimation model was based on story point approach and a case study was discussed with the proposed model.

Satapathy, Panda and Rath (2014) used Support Vector Regression (SVR) for effort estimation method using story point approach. They optimized the result of story point approach using SVR kernel methods for better prediction accuracy. The kernel methods used by them were linear, polynomial, Radial Basis

Function (RBF) and Sigmoid kernels. They concluded that RBF kernel based SVR was at par than the rest of the three kernel methods for effort estimation.

Panda, Satapathy and Rath (2015) used different types of Neural Networks to increase the accuracy estimation of agile projects using story point approach. The parameters used by them in estimation were story points, velocity and actual effort. They used dataset of 21 projects to validate their approach and used Mean Square Error (MSE), squared correlation coefficient (R^2), Mean Magnitude of Relative Error (MMRE) and Prediction Accuracy (PRED) as the evaluation criteria.

Garg and Gupta (2015) proposed a cost estimation method where they identified the key attributes that have maximum impact on development cost using principal component analysis. In order to satisfy the criteria imposed by agile manifesto they further used constraint solving approach. Their model also worked in absence of historical data and expert opinion. The model provided lower MMRE value in comparison to planning poker and mapped the agile manifesto.

Tanveer (2016) provided a hybrid methodology with tool support for effort estimation which handled change impact analysis, expert judgement and software visualization. They proposed that agile projects were usually estimated using expert judgement which was not accurate and reliable. So a new technique was proposed by them to improve the estimation process in agile environment.

Raslan, Darwish and Hefny (2015) proposed an effort estimation methodology using fuzzy logic. They used story point approach and trapezoidal membership functions to represent the input parameters which consisted of Story Points (SP), Implementation Level Factor (ILF), FRiction factors (FR), and Dynamic Forces (DF). They designed the proposed fuzzy inference system in MATLAB and calculated the effort.

Dragicevic, Celar and Turic (2017) proposed an effort prediction model for agile projects using bayesian network. They validated their technique on the agile project data of a single company. The model was further assessed using various statistical parameters. The model could be used with any agile methodology in the initial planning phase. It basically provided task effort estimation based on various parameters like working hours, requirements complexity, developer's skills etc.

Salmanoglu, Hacaloglu, and Demirors (2017) evaluated three case studies on agile projects to compare effort estimation using COSMIC and story points. They found that effort estimation models developed using COSMIC size performed better on all the three case studies. They also concluded that COSMIC provided better productivity for the data which was less dispersed than story points. They also shared their datasets for future research.

Satapathy and Rath (2017) improved the prediction accuracy of story point approach using various machine learning techniques and compared the proposed techniques with the existing techniques in the literature. The machine learning techniques used were decision tree (DT), stochastic gradient boosting (SGB) and Random forest (RF). They developed this estimation model considering scrum projects. The technique SGB gave the best results than the rest of the two techniques on the examined dataset.

Tanveer, Vollmer and Braun (2018) proposed an estimation technique for agile development teams. They designed a hybrid method where the impact of change is analysed and incorporated for effort estimation. They also proposed an estimation technique using boosted trees and discussed their methodology using a case study on a German software company. Their method was more effective and accurate than the expert based methods.

Usman, Britto, Damm and Borstler (2018) identified and analysed the effort estimation process in large scale distributed agile projects. They also identified various factors effecting the effort of such projects. They devised a two stage effort estimation and restimation process to improve the accuracy of estimation in such projects. They concluded that effort overruns in large scale distributed agile projects could be limited by considering various factors like requirements size, its priorities, maturity and team distribution of agile projects.

Martínez, Noriega, Ramírez, Licea and Jiménez (2018) proposed a Bayesian network model to handle the complexity and importance associated with the user stories used for estimation of scrum projects. Their model could replace the traditional planning poker used in estimations and could be used by an inexperienced or a new developer. They used estimations provided by students and professionals in order to validate the model. They found professionals' estimation more correlated to the proposed model than the students' estimation as the proposed model included various factors considered in real world application.

Mensah, Keung, Bosu, and Bennin (2018) designed a duplex output model for software effort estimation. The first output here was software effort and the second output was the classification of effort in order to identify the level of effort. The study was motivated by conclusion instability problem faced by effort estimation models. They did comparison of six different regression-based techniques which included the state-of-the-art baseline model (ATLM) and ElasticNet regression to solve conclusion instability. They found ElasticNet regression providing superior accuracy than the rest of the techniques.

Bilgayian, Das and Mishra (2019) solved effort estimation problem for agile projects by using back propagation neural networks and Elman neural networks. They validated the model on Zia dataset using standard evaluation criteria used in software effort estimation. They simulated their model using MATLAB and found feed forward back propagation neural networks performed better than Elman neural networks and cascade correlation network present in the literature.

Tanveer, Vollmer, Braun and Ali (2019) proposed a hybrid model based on gradient boosted trees (GBT) which estimates the effort including the impact of changes on the existing system. They evaluated their model in a German software company. The results showed that their model provided more accurate estimates than expert based and model based techniques.

The given literature review reveals that there are many effort estimation studies present but the studies using metaheuristic techniques are still unavailable. All the above studies have their strengths and weaknesses. As the plethora of new techniques are introduced every year, there is always a scope of improvement which exists.

BACKGROUND CONCEPTS USED

In this section the background concepts used are reviewed.

Story Point Approach

In agile environment story point is the most commonly used unit of measure followed for effort estimation. In story point approach the user story is the term for requirements (Cohn, 2005). The effort of a particular user story is determined by its size and complexity and based upon that a story point value is assigned (Ziauddin, Tipu, & Zia, 2012). The commonly used assignment criteria for story points are t-shirt sizing, Fibonacci sequence or simply small vs. needs-to-be-split. Story point is the amount of effort completed in a unit time. For agile projects the unit of Effort is Story Point (SP) (Ziauddin, Tipu, & Zia, 2012). Agile velocity is the amount of work done by a project team in a single sprint. It is calculated based upon the effort and sprint time. Sprint time is the time period during which a particular work is completed by the project team and the work is available for review.

In all the effort estimation studies based upon story point approach and using machine learning techniques and neural networks, the input parameters are story points and velocity, and the output is the effort of a project (Popli & Chauhan, 2014; Satapathy, Panda & Rath, 2014; Panda, Satapathy & Rath, 2015; Satapathy &Rath, 2017; Bilgayian, Das & Mishra, 2019).

Functional Link Artificial Neural Networks (FLANN)

FLANN consists of three layers i.e. first, middle and the last layer. As the name goes by, FLANN uses various functions like Power Series polynomials, Boubaker polynomials, Fibnocci polynomials, Chebyshev polynomials and Legendre polynomials etc. to expand the input pattern supplied to it. The input data is supplied to the first layer, which navigates it to middle layer where the polynomial function is applied which converts the n-dimensional input data to K dimensions where $n < K$. These data values are represented in the matrix form and are combined linearly after multiplying with the weight matrix. This provides a scalar quantity which forms the required output. The current work uses Chebyshev polynomial function which is defined as:

Chebyshev polynomials: $F_0(z) = 1$

$$F_1(z) = z$$

$$F_2(z) = 2z^2 - 1$$

$$F_3(z) = 4z^3 - 3z$$

$$F_4(z) = 8z^3 - 8z^2 + 1 \tag{1}$$

These polynomials are further generated as:

$$F_n\left(z\right) = 2zF_{n-1}\left(z\right) - F_{n-2}\left(z\right), n \geq 2 \tag{2}$$

Chebyshev polynomials were also used by early researchers in software cost estimations and are considered as a basis function in this field (Benala, Korada, Mall, & Dehuri, 2013).

Radial Basis Function Network (RBFN)

RBFN is a three layer neural network consisting of the first, middle and the last layer (Idri, Zahi, Mendes, & Zakrani, 2007; Kaushik, Soni, & Soni, 2013). The input supplied to the network is first clustered and its output is provided to the middle layer neurons where the Gaussian radial basis function as given by (3) is applied.

$$f\left(y\right) = e^{\left(-\frac{\|y - v_i\|^2}{\sigma_i^2}\right)} \tag{3}$$

Here, y is the input, v_i and σ_i are the center and the wideness of the ith neuron of the middle layer respectively. ‖.‖ denotes the Euclidean distance. Intutionistic Fuzzy C-Means (IFCM) clustering algorithm (Bezdek, 1981; Kaur, Soni, & Gossain, 2012; Chaira, 2011; Atanassov, 1983) is used to determine v_i and σ_i is calculated using p-nearest neighbour heuristic (Moody, & Darken, 1989).

In this study, the weights of ANNs are obtained using whale optimization algorithm and updated using delta rule. The delta rule is a learning rule for updating the weights of the neurons using gradient descent learning which minimizes the error between the target value and the estimated value.

Whale Optimization Algorithm (WOA)

Mirjalili and Lewis (2016) framed this algorithm on hump back whales for optimization which modelled the spiral bubble-net feeding behaviour of these whales. The basic phases are:

Encircling Prey

Hump back whales encircles their prey after recognizing them. Here, the prey which is targeted, is assumed as the current best candidate solution and a best explore agent is defined. This is shown by:

$$\vec{E} = \left| \overrightarrow{D.K_p}(l) - \vec{K}(l) \right| \tag{4}$$

$$\vec{K}(l+1) = \overrightarrow{K_p}(l) - \vec{B}.\vec{E}(l). \tag{5}$$

Where, $\vec{B}$ and $\vec{D}$ are the coefficient vectors, l is the current iteration, K_p is the position vector of the predator, $\vec{K}$ is the position vector of the whale. $\vec{B}$ and $\vec{D}$ are calculated as follows:

$$\vec{B} = 2\vec{b_1}.\vec{s_1}.\vec{b_1} \tag{6}$$

$$\vec{D} = 2.\vec{s_2} \tag{7}$$

Where, $\vec{b_1}$ is linearly reduced from 2 to 0 over the course of iterations and $\vec{s_1}, \vec{s_2}$ are the random vectors in [0, 1].

Bubble Net Attacking Method

In this method bubbles are formed by the whales to attack their prey either along a circle or 9 shaped path. It is mathematically modelled using two approaches:

Shrinking Encircling Mechanism

It is obtained by decreasing $\vec{b_1}$ in (6). It also affects the range of $\vec{B}$ which is in [-1, 1]. It finds the new location of an explore agent.

Spiral Updating Position

It finds the distance between the whale and prey and mimics the spiral motion of whales as shown in (8):

$$\overrightarrow{K}(l+1) = \overrightarrow{E'}.e^{ol}.\cos(2\pi l) + \overrightarrow{K_p}(l) \tag{8}$$

Where, $\overrightarrow{E'} = \left| \overrightarrow{K_p}(l) - \vec{K}(l) \right|$ and gives the distance of the ith whale to the predator, o is constant that represents the shape of the logarithmic spiral, l is a random number in [-1, 1].

Search for Prey

The $\vec{B}$ vector is varied between [-1, 1], to allow these hump back whales to randomly search for their predator according to position of each other. WOA performs global search as the location of the explore agent is upgraded according to randomly chosen explore agent which is given as:

$$\vec{E} = \left| \vec{D}.\overrightarrow{K_{rand}} - \vec{K} \right| \tag{9}$$

$$\overrightarrow{K}(t+1) = \overrightarrow{K_{rand}} - \vec{B}.\vec{E} \tag{10}$$

Where, $\overrightarrow{K_{rand}}$ is a random position vector (a random whale) which is chosen from the current population.

This algorithm was tested on 29 mathematical optimization functions by the authors Mirjalili and Lewis (2016) in order to test its efficiency and it gave the best results for all the problems. The function used in algorithm for the current work is given in (11) (Mirjalili & Lewis, 2016):

$$F5(y) = \sum_{i=1}^{n-1} \left[100\left(y_{i+1} - y_i^2\right)^2 + \left(y_i - 1\right)^2 \right] \tag{11}$$

This function is used as a cost function in WOA to create the optimized weights of range [0, 1]. There are various reasons for choosing WOA over other metaheuristic algorithms. WOA exhibits high exploration, exploitation, local optima avoidance and convergence speed. The whales randomly move around each other initially and their positions get updated. This represents the high exploration behaviour of WOA as given in (10).In later iterations they exhibit high exploitation and convergence. As these two phenomenon are separately performed by whales, this leads to high local optima avoidance (Mirjalili & Lewis, 2016).

RESEARCH CONTRIBUTION

Effort estimation is an important issue faced by the project managers. A good estimation model will always help the managers to estimate accurately which will lead the project to success. The work presented in this paper contributes to effort estimation of agile projects following the story point approach. The novelty here is the integration of a metaheuristic technique and neural networks. There are limited studies present in the literature for effort estimation of agile projects based on machine learning and neural networks (Popli & Chauhan, 2014; Satapathy, Panda & Rath, 2014; Panda, Satapathy & Rath, 2015; Satapathy &Rath, 2017; Bilgayian, Das & Mishra, 2019) and none of them have used FLANN and RBFN for agile effort estimation, also no study has incorporated any metaheuristic technique in their estimation model. The models proposed in the current work are FLANN-WOA and RBFN-WOA described subsequently.

FLANN-WOA

In this framework, first the input data to be trained is supplied as an input to the first layer of the neural network. The data is expanded by FLANN using Chebyshev polynomials as shown in (1) and (2). After applying Chebyshev expansion, the non-linear outputs become the nodes for the middle layer. The estimated effort is then calculated by multiplying these nodes with the weight vector calculated using WOA. The block diagram is represented in Figure 1.

Figure 1. FLANN-WOA block diagram

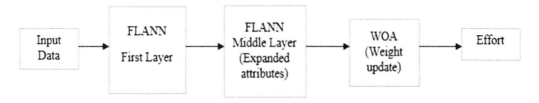

The procedure of FLANN-WOA is given in Figure 2:

RBFN-WOA

The input neurons of the first layer of RBFN receives the input data and, the gaussian radial basis function as given by (3) is applied to form the middle layer. The nodes of the middle layer is multiplied by the weight values obtained using WOA and the weighted sum is obtained to get the required output. This is demonstrated in Figure 3.

Figure 2. FLANN-WOA

```
FLANN-WOA
Step 1: Preprocess the input data.
Step 2: Split the input data into training and testing data.
Step 3: For all the training and testing data do
        {
              Expand the input data using Chebyshev polynomial expansion.
              While (the stopping condition not met)
              {
                  For each expanded input pattern
                  {
                      •  Call WOA () and assign the best position between the second layer and the last layer as
                         the weight.
                      •  Calculate the weighted sum and generate the estimated output at the last layer.
                      •  Generate the difference between the actual output and the calculated output.
                      •  Upgrade the weights between the second and the last layer.
                  }
              }
        }
```

Figure 3. RBFN-WOA block diagram

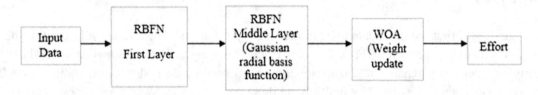

The procedure for RBFN –WOA is given below in Figure 4.

Figure 4. RBFN-WOA

```
RBFN-WOA
Step 1: Preprocess the input data.
Step 2: Split the input data into training and testing data.
Step 3: For all the training and testing data do
        {
          Feed the input data to the first layer.
            While(the stopping criteria not met)
            {
                  •  Generate the middle layer by injecting the Gaussian function on input neurons.
                  •  Call WOA () and assign the best position between the second layer and the last layer as the
                     weight.
                  •  Produce the estimated output at the last layer by calculating the weighted sum.
                  •  Generate the difference between the actual output and the calculated output.
                  •  Upgrade the weights between the second and the last layer.
            }
        }
```

Both the above models are described by taking examples from the datasets in the next section.

SIMULATION AND RESULTS

The proposed approaches FLANN-WOA and RBFN-WOA are evaluated on three datasets. The input datasets are Zia dataset, Company Dataset -1 (CD1) and Company Dataset-2 (CD2).The first dataset is taken from Zia (Ziauddin, Tipu, & Zia, 2012). This dataset was a collection of 21 agile software projects taken from 6 software houses. The features of the dataset used in the study is given in Table 1.

Table 1. Zia dataset

P.No	Effort	V	Actual Time (months)
1	156	2.7	63
2	202	2.5	92
3	173	3.3	56
4	331	3.8	86
5	124	4.2	32
6	339	3.6	91
7	97	3.4	35
8	257	3	93
9	84	2.4	36
10	211	3.2	62
11	131	3.2	45
12	112	2.9	37
13	101	2.9	32
14	74	2.9	30
15	62	2.9	21
16	289	2.8	112
17	113	2.8	39
18	141	2.8	52
19	213	2.8	80
20	137	2.7	56
21	91	2.7	35

Here, the first dimension is P.No showing the project number, the second is Effort in developing the project, the third one shows the velocity values for different projects and the fourth gives the actual time in completing a project.

As the agile studies lack in availability of public datasets, the second and third dataset as given in Table 2 and Table 3, is shared by a company in Delhi NCR on special request. The information provided by the datasets is on two different projects only. The Company Dataset -1 (CD1) consists of a project with 23 issues and the Company Dataset-2 (CD2) points to a project with 25 issues. Both the datasets are mapped according to the requirement of the existing study by calculating the estimated effort of various issues using the proposed methodologies.

Table 2. Company dataset-1

Issue No.	Effort	Time (*minutes*)	Story Point
1	5600	93600	9
2	4879	15000	8
3	7200	15000	7
4	7654	14000	9
5	5674	22200	6
6	8900	23400	8
7	57600	25800	8
8	8432	18000	7
9	28800	136800	8
10	7896	10800	8
11	9879	25200	5
12	3789	28800	8
13	9756	9000	9
14	8763	14400	8
15	3567	12600	12
16	9875	25200	8
17	8945	21600	8
18	5678	10800	8
19	5699	12780	9
20	4321	11900	8
21	8754	8600	8
22	7542	9300	7
23	9050	7800	8

Table 3. Company Dataset-2

Issue No.	Effort	Time (*minutes*)	Story Point
1	8700	99800	9
2	6487	76000	8
3	7872	25000	9
4	9876	19000	9
5	6675	56200	13
6	3489	23500	9
7	7876	15800	9
8	7832	28000	12
9	52880	128800	10
10	3487	20600	9
11	8987	15200	7
12	7785	12800	8
13	7785	5000	6
14	5769	24200	12
15	4356	22600	11
16	6879	15200	8
17	8843	25600	8
18	8671	20800	8
19	8856	12880	8
20	2352	12600	9
21	7651	6800	9
22	3542	6300	7
23	4550	8800	7
24	6879	4800	6
25	8543	6500	6

In Table 2 and 3, the first dimension is the Issue Number of various issues, the second gives the Effort values for these issues, the third and fourth dimension provides the time and story point values for these issues.

In order to test the validity of the proposed estimation models leave-one-out (LOO) sampling method, which is a type of K-fold Cross-Validation is used. Here K equals to N, the number of data points in the dataset. This sampling method is employed due to its advantages over N-Way sampling (Kocaguneli & Menzies, 2013).

Overfitting is another issue faced by the estimation models. It is important to recognize and manage this issue otherwise our models will not be able to generalize well and make predictions on the unseen data. An important technique to handle it is the resampling technique which is, LOO in our case.

Before running the procedures of FLANN-WOA and RBFN-WOA, the three datasets are pre-processed. The following three steps are used for data pre-processing:

Step 1: Check whether the data is normally distributed or not. It is found that for the given datasets, the data values were not normally distributed, so logarithmic transformation is done on the data values in order to make it normally distributed.

Step 2: Normalize the input data between [0 1] to discard the scaling effects on various dimensions.

Step 3: Partition the dataset into training and testing datasets.

Now, both the procedures, FLANN-WOA and RBFN-WOA are called individually on the pre-processed data as discussed in the previous section. The results are recorded and evaluated using the commonly used evaluation criteria used in software cost estimations (Foss, Stensrud, Kitchenham, & Myrtveit, 2003; Stensrud, Foss, Kitchenham, & Myrtveit, 2002) . They are Magnitude of Relative Error (MRE), Mean Magnitude of Relative Error (MMRE), Prediction (t) and Median Magnitude of Relative Error (MdMRE) which are given below:

$$MRE = \frac{\left|Actual\,Data - Estimated\,Data\right|}{Actual\,Data} \tag{12}$$

MMRE is the average of all the MRE values.

$$MMRE = \frac{1}{N}\sum_{X=1}^{N}MRE \tag{13}$$

$$MdMRE = Median(MRE) \tag{14}$$

$$Pred\left(t\right) = \frac{k'}{n'} \tag{15}$$

Where, n′ shows the total number of projects and k′ is the number of projects with MRE less than or equal to 0.25 (Rao et al., 2009).

All the above evaluation criteria are the accuracy measurers. They show how close a measurement is to an existing value that has already been known.

Table 4 lists the initialization of parameters done for WOA for both FLANN and RBFN.

Let us consider the dataset CD1 to explain FLANN-WOA. In this dataset for Issue No. 2, the normalized input values for story points and velocity are 0.4285 and 0.3252 respectively. This data is mapped to the input layer of FLANN which expands it using Chebyshev polynomial expansion given in (1). The WOA algorithm is then called with the parameters given in Table 4 which provided the best value as 0.3387 in this case. This value is now assigned as a weight between the hidden layer and the output layer. The weighted sum is now calculated using the weight and hidden layer values to produce the estimated output. It is then tuned by reducing the error as given in Step 3 of Figure 2 to calculate the final estimated output which is 0.02399, whereas the normalized actual effort is 0.02428. So, the estimated effort is very near to the actual effort.

In order to explain RBFN-WOA, let us consider the Zia dataset given in Table 1. In this dataset for P. No. 4, the normalized inputs provided to RBFN-WOA are 0.984 and 0.778. These values are provided as input to the first layer of RBFN. The Gaussian Radial Basis Function given in (3) is then applied to form the middle layer. Now the WOA algorithm is called which provided the best value as 0.2768. This value is used as a weight between the middle layer and the final layer. The estimated output is obtained by finding the weighted sum of middle layer inputs and the weight. This value is fine-tuned as given in Step 3 of Figure 4 to calculate the final estimated effort which is 0.950 and the normalized actual effort is 0.971. Here also, there is not much difference between the estimated and the actual output.

In this manner all the datasets are processed using FLANN-WOA and RBFN-WOA techniques to obtain the estimated effort. They are further assessed using evaluation criteria and the results are recorded in Table 5, 6 and 7.

Table 4. Initialization of parameters for WOA

Parameters Initialization
SearchAgents_no 30
Max_iteration 500
o 1
l [-1 1]
q [0 1]
$\vec{s_1}$ [0 1]
$\vec{s_2}$ [0 1]

The output after applying the proposed approaches are demonstrated in Table 5, 6 and 7 respectively. There is a comparison of FLANN to FLANN-WOA and RBFN to RBFN-WOA in order to judge whether the performance of FLANN and RBFN improves upon integration with WOA, as the current work discusses the role of neural networks and metaheuristics in agile software development effort estimation. From the results it is found that the performance of FLANN-WOA and RBFN-WOA are at par than FLANN and RBFN.

Table 5. Results on Zia Dataset

Approaches Used	MMRE		MdMRE		PRED(0.25)	
	Train Data	Test Data	Train Data	Test Data	Train Data	Test Data
FLANN	.619	.672	.49	.510	.33	.34
FLANN-WOA	.180	.193	.167	.179	.869	.859
RBFN	.548	.512	.243	.232	.571	.587
RBFN-WOA	.196	.201	.172	.174	.876	.882

Table 6. Results on Company Dataset 1

Approaches used	MMRE		MdMRE		PRED(0.25)	
	Train Data	Test Data	Train Data	Test Data	Train Data	Test Data
FLANN	.612	.623	.449	.412	.394	.412
FLANN-WOA	.183	.192	.109	.172	.890	.874
RBFN	.721	.730	.77	.78	.26	.29
RBFN-WOA	.153	.185	.128	.143	.869	.871

Table 7. Results on Company Dataset 2

Approaches used	MMRE		MdMRE		PRED(0.25)	
	Train Data	Test Data	Train Data	Test Data	Train Data	Test Data
FLANN	.425	.487	.2	.294	.642	.631
FLANN-WOA	.123	.138	.17	.185	.912	.893
RBFN	.283	.311	.224	.247	.566	.581
RBFN-WOA	.151	.160	.191	.182	.882	.870

In order to have more clarity and representation of facts the performance of FLANN, FLANN-WOA, RBFN and RBFN-WOA is depicted graphically in Figure 5, 6 and 7 for the three datasets respectively. Satapathy and Rath (2017) provided results on Zia dataset for effort estimation using story points on agile software development. The results are from the techniques Decision Tree (DT), Stochastic Gradient Boosting (SGB) and Random Forest (RF) which are compared with the results of the proposed techniques and depicted in Table 8.

Figure 5. Performance of FLANN, FLANN-WOA, RBFN and RBFN-WOA on ZIA dataset

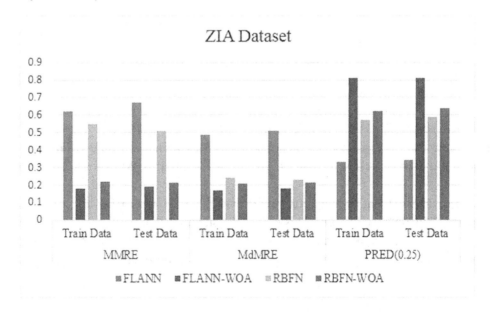

Figure 6. Performance of FLANN, FLANN-WOA, RBFN and RBFN-WOA on Company Dataset-1

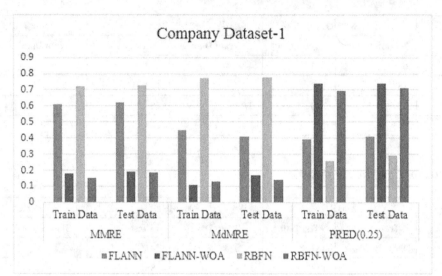

Figure 7. Performance of FLANN, FLANN-WOA, RBFN and RBFN-WOA on Company Dataset-2

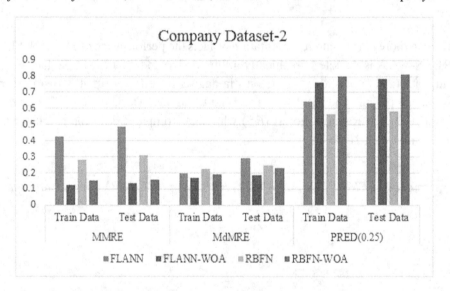

From, the given data in Table 8 it can be seen that FLANN-WOA and RBFN-WOA gave better results than the techniques used by researchers, except for Stochastic Gradient Boosting (SGB) technique. The SGB technique provided better results than FLANN-WOA and RBFN-WOA for MMRE and MdMRE criterias.

So, it can be concluded that by integrating WOA with FLANN and RBFN has definitely enhanced the performance of FLANN and RBFN. This is also statistically validated.

Statistical validation is required to confirm the validity of any proposed approach. The statistical tools allow researchers to know whether the results evaluated with the proposed approaches can be accepted with confidence or rejected. These tools allow one to trust the new developed method. Therefore, it is necessary and valuable to compare FLANN to FLANN-WOA and RBFN to RBFN-WOA using these tests.

Statistical inferential tests are categorized into three kinds: parametric, semi-parametric and non-parametric. The parametric statistical tests relies on prior information. They make an assumption about the population parameters and its probability distribution whereas the non-parametric tests doesn't assume anything about the population parameters and its distribution. The merits of both the parametric and non-parametric tests are present in semi-parametric tests.

The existing study uses IBM SPSS tool to statistically validate the models. The input to the tool is MRE values obtained after applying FLANN, FLANN-WOA, RBFN and RBFN-WOA on the datasets. Tests of normality is then performed on this data through SPSS and it is found that the data is not following a normal distribution. So, non-parametric tests are chosen to further validate the model. The first non-parametric test used is Friedman test. It is used for finding the differences between several related samples. Here, this test is used in order to initially compare whether the two techniques are different or not. The test statistics for Friedman test is defined as:

$$\chi_F^2 = \frac{12Q}{n(n+1)} \left[\sum_{j=1}^{n} R_j^2 - \frac{n(n+1)^2}{4} \right] \tag{16}$$

With, R_j, the average rank of algorithms $j=1,2,\ldots n$ over Q datasets.

Here, the null hypotheses and alternate hypotheses for both FLANN and RBFN are:

(a) *Null Hypotheses:* Performance of FLANN = FLANN-WOA
     Alternate Hypotheses: Performance of FLANN $\neq$ FLANN-WOA
(b) *Null Hypotheses:* Performance of RBFN = RBFN-WOA
     Alternate Hypotheses: Performance of RBFN $\neq$ RBFN-WOA

Table 9 provides the output of Friedman test on all the three datasets.

Table 8. Comparison with earlier approaches on ZIA dataset

Techniques	MMRE	MdMRE	PRED (25)	PRED (50)	PRED (75)	PRED (100)
DT	.382	.289	38.095	71.428	80.952	90.476
SGB	.163	.115	85.714	95.238	95.238	95.238
RF	.251	.203	66.666	80.952	90.476	95.238
FLANN-WOA	.186	.173	86.4	95.238	100	100
RBFN-WOA	.198	.173	87.9	95.238	100	100

Here, N is the total data in each dataset, Chi-Square is the value of test statistics calculated by the test, DF is the degree of freedom which is 1 as DF= n-1 . As there are two approaches to be tested on all the datasets, here n is 2 and DF is 2-1 = 1.The last row gives the Asymptotic Significant values calculated by the test. The $\chi 2$ (Chi-Square) value for DF= 1 and $\alpha = 0.05$ is 3.841. If $\chi 2$ (Chi-Square) in our test statistics is greater than 3.841 for asymptotic significant (p-value) less than 0.05 then the null hypothesis is rejected. From the Chi-Square and asymptotic significant values present in Table 9, the null hypotheses is rejected and alternate hypotheses is accepted.

To further confirm the performance of FLANN-WOA and RBFN-WOA, a second non-parametric test is applied which is Wilcoxon matched pair's test. It ranks the two models by calculating the positive and negative differences of ranks and is calculated as:

$$\min\left(\sum_{d_i>0} R(d_i) + \frac{1}{2}\sum_{d_i=0} R(d_i), \sum_{d_i<0} R(d_i) + \frac{1}{2}\sum_{d_i=0} R(d_i)\right) \tag{17}$$

Where, $R(d_i)$ is the difference of ranks of performance between two models, ignoring signs. The null hypotheses and alternate hypotheses are:

Null Hypotheses: Median difference between pairs of observations is zero i.e. there is no difference in performance of FLANN and RBFN with and without WOA.

Alternate Hypotheses: Median difference between pairs of observations is not zero i.e. there is difference in performance of FLANN and RBFN with and without WOA.

Table 10 gives the result of the test. Here, for all the instances the null hypothesis is not accepted as the asymptotic significant values are less than 0.05. It is also found that for all the cases the approach with WOA has lower mean rank than its counterpart.

Table 9. Test statistics of Friedman test on all the datasets

Test Statistics	ZIAFLANN & ZIAFLANN-WOA	ZIARBFN & ZIARBFN-WOA	CD1FLANN & CD1FLANN-WOA	CD1RBFN & CD1RBFN-WOA	CD2FLANN & CD2FLANN-WOA	CD2RBFN & CD2RBFN-WOA
N	21	21	23	23	25	25
Chi-Square	5.000	7.200	8.909	4.545	6.000	10.667
DF	1.0	1.0	1.0	1.0	1.0	1.0
Asy. Sig.	.025	.007	.003	.033	.014	.001

So after applying statistical tests it is observed that FLANN and RBFN performed differently with and without WOA and the performance of FLANN-WOA and RBFN-WOA is higher than FLANN and RBFN.

Table 10. Test statistics of Wilcoxon Matched Pairs test on all the datasets

	Mean Rank	Asymptotic Significance
ZIAFLANN ZIAFLANN-WOA	12.13 5.60	0.004
ZIARBFN & ZIARBFN-WOA	11.25 7.50	0.005
CD1FLANN CD1FLANN-WOA	11.83 10	0.005
CD1RBFN CD1RBFN-WOA	14.13 4.50	0.001
CD2FLANN CD2FLANN-WOA	13.72 8.83	0.006
CD2RBFN CD2RBFN-WOA	7.25 13.55	0.001

CONCLUSION

Effort estimation forms an integral part of any software development. A good estimation model is always the need of the hour. The paper has proposed effort estimation models for the projects using agile methodology. There are few studies existing in the literature based on neural networks for effort estimation of agile projects but none of the study has explored the fusion of ANN and a metaheuristic algorithm. The proposed study integrates ANN models, FLANN and RBFN with a metaheuristic algorithm, Whale Optimization Algorithm (WOA). Both FLANN-WOA and RBFN-WOA are evaluated on three agile datasets, one is Zia dataset and the rest two datasets are gathered through a firm in Delhi NCR incorporating agile software development. The details of these datasets are shared so that it can be used for future work. The study uses MMRE, MDMRE and PRED (0.25) as the evaluation parameters. The experimental results demonstrated that the ANN models provided excellent results by integrating with the metaheuristic technique used. This is further validated by using two statistical tests i.e. Friedman test and Wicoxon test. Though the techniques performed well but due to lack of availability of public datasets on agile software development methodology the proposed approaches are evaluated on limited datasets. So, the future work can include evaluating these techniques on more number of agile datasets.

REFERENCES

Atanassov, K. T. (1983). Intuitionistic fuzzy set. VII ITKR's Session, Sofia, 983. (Deposed in Central Science –Technology Library of Bulgaria Academy of Science, 1697/84)

Benala, T. R., Korada, C., Mall, R., & Dehuri, S. (2013). A particle swarm optimized functional link artificial neural networks (PSO-FLANN) in software cost estimation. In Proceedings of the International Conference on Frontiers of Intelligent Computing: Theory and Applications (FICTA) Advances in Intelligent Systems and Computing (vol. 199, pp. 59-66). Academic Press.

Benala, T. R., & Mall, R. (2018). DABE: Differential evolution in analogy-based software development effort estimation. *Swarm and Evolutionary Computation*, *38*, 158–172. doi:10.1016/j.swevo.2017.07.009

Bezdek, J. C. (1981). *Pattern Recognition with Fuzzy Objective Function Algorithm*. New York: Plenum. doi:10.1007/978-1-4757-0450-1

Bilgayian, S., Mishra, S., & Das, M. (2019). Effort estimation in agile software development using experimental validation of neural network models. *International Journal of Information Technology*, *11*(3), 569–573. doi:10.100741870-018-0131-2

Boehm, B. W. (1994). *Software Engineering Economics*. Englewood Cliffs, NJ: Prentice-Hall.

Chaira, T. (2011). A novel intuitionistic fuzzy C means clustering algorithm and its application to medical images. *Applied Soft Computing*, *11*(2), 1711–1717. doi:10.1016/j.asoc.2010.05.005

Choudhari, J., & Suman, U. (2012). Story Points Based Effort Estimation Model for Software Maintenance. *Procedia Technology*, *4*, 761–765. doi:10.1016/j.protcy.2012.05.124

Coelho, E., & Basu, A. (2012). Effort estimation in agile software development using story points. *International Journal of Applied Information System*, *3*(7), 7–10. doi:10.5120/ijais12-450574

Cohn, M. (2005). *Agile Estimating and Planning*. Addison-Wesley.

Curiel, I.E.E., Jacobo, J.R., Alfaro, E.V., Zepeda J.A.F., & Delgado D.F. (2018). Analysis of the changes in communication and social interactions during the transformation of a traditional team into an agile team. *The Journal of Software Evolution and Process*. doi:10.1002/smr.1946

Dingsøyr, T., Nerur, S., Balijepally, V., & Moe, N. B. (2012). A decade of agile methodologies: Towards explaining agile software development. *Journal of Systems and Software*, *85*(6), 1213–1221. doi:10.1016/j.jss.2012.02.033

Dragicevic, S., Celar, S., & Turic, M. (2017). Bayesian network model for task effort estimation in agile software development. *Journal of Systems and Software*, *127*, 109–119. doi:10.1016/j.jss.2017.01.027

Foss, T., Stensrud, E., Kitchenham, B., & Myrtveit, I. (2003). A simulation study of the model evaluation criterion MMRE. *IEEE Transactions on Software Engineering*, *29*(11), 985–995. doi:10.1109/TSE.2003.1245300

Garg, S., & Gupta, D. (2015). PCA based cost estimation model for agile software development projects. In *Proceedings of International Conference on Industrial Engineering and Operations Management* (pp. 1–7). 10.1109/IEOM.2015.7228109

Hussain, I., Kosseim, L., & Ormandjieva, O. (2013). Approximation of COSMIC functional size to support early effort estimation in Agile. *Data & Knowledge Engineering*, *85*, 2–14. doi:10.1016/j.datak.2012.06.005

Idri, A., Zahi, A., Mendes, E., & Zakrani, A. (2007). Software cost estimation models using radial basis function neural networks. In *Proceedings of International Conference on Software process and product measurements,* (vol. 4895, pp. 21–31). 10.1007/978-3-540-85553-8_2

Kaur, P., Soni, A. K., & Gossain, A. (2012). Novel intuitionistic fuzzy C means clustering for linearly and nonlinearly separable data. *WSEAS Transactions on Computers*, *11*(3), 65–76.

Kaushik, A., Soni, A. K., & Soni, R. (2013). Radial basis function network using intuitionistic fuzzy C means for software cost estimation. *International Journal of Computer Applications in Technology*, *47*(1), 86–95. doi:10.1504/IJCAT.2013.054305

Kaushik, A., Tayal, D. K., Yadav, K., & Kaur, A. (2016). Integrating firefly algorithm in artificial neural network models for accurate software cost predictions. *Journal of Software Evolution and Process*, *28*(8), 665–688. doi:10.1002mr.1792

Kaushik, A., Verma, S., Singh, H. J., & Chhabra, G. (2017). Software Cost Optimization Integrating Fuzzy System and COA-Cuckoo Optimization Algorithm. *International Journal of System Assurance Engineering and Management*, *8*(S2), 1461–1471. doi:10.100713198-017-0615-7

Kocaguneli, E., & Menzies, T. (2013). Software effort models should be assessed via leave-one-out validation. *Journal of Systems and Software*, *86*(7), 1879–1890. doi:10.1016/j.jss.2013.02.053

Lang, M., Conboy, K., & Keaveney, S. (2011). Cost Estimation in Agile Software Development Projects. In *Proceedings of International Conference on Information Systems Development* (pp. 1-12). Prato, Italy: Academic Press.

Martínez, J. L., Noriega, A. R., Ramírez, R. J., Licea, G., & Jiménez, S. (2018). User stories complexity estimation using bayesian networks for inexperienced developers. *Journal of Cluster Computing*, *21*(1), 715–728. doi:10.100710586-017-0996-z

Mensah, S., Keung, J., Bosu, M. F., & Bennin, K. E. (2018). Duplex output software effort estimation model with self-guided interpretation. *Information and Software Technology*, *94*, 1–13. doi:10.1016/j.infsof.2017.09.010

Menzies, T., Chen, Z., Hihn, J., & Lum, K. (2006). Selecting best practices for effort estimation. *IEEE Transactions on Software Engineering*, *32*(11), 883–895. doi:10.1109/TSE.2006.114

Mirjalili, S., & Lewis, A. (2016). The Whale Optimization Algorithm. *Advances in Engineering Software*, *95*, 51–67. doi:10.1016/j.advengsoft.2016.01.008

Mishra, B. B., & Dehuri, S. (2007). Functional Link Artificial Neural Network for classification task in Data Mining. *Journal of Computational Science*, *3*(12), 948–955. doi:10.3844/jcssp.2007.948.955

Moody, J., & Darken, C. J. (1989). Fast learning in networks of locally tuned processing units. *Neural Computation*, *1*(2), 281–294. doi:10.1162/neco.1989.1.2.281

Nguyen, V., Boehm, B., & Huang, L. G. (2019). Determining relevant training data for effort estimation using window based COCOMO calibration. *Journal of Systems and Software*, *147*, 124–146. doi:10.1016/j.jss.2018.10.019

Panda, A., Satapathy, S. M., & Rath, S. K. (2015). Empirical Validation of Neural Network Models for Agile Software Effort Estimation based on Story Points. In *Proceedings of 3rd International Conference on Recent Trends in Computing* (*vol. 57*, pp.772 – 781). Procedia Computer Science. 10.1016/j.procs.2015.07.474

Papadopoulos, G. (2015). Moving from Traditional to Agile Software Development Methodologies Also on Large, Distributed Projects. *Procedia: Social and Behavioral Sciences, 175*, 455–463. doi:10.1016/j.sbspro.2015.01.1223

Perkusich, M., Gorgônio, K. C., Almeida, H., & Perkusich, A. (2017). Assisting the continuous improvement of Scrum projects using metrics and Bayesian networks. *Journal of Software Evolution and Process, 29*(6), e1835. doi:10.1002mr.1835

Popli, R., & Chauhan, N. (2014). Cost and Effort estimation in agile software development. In *Proceedings of International conference on Reliability, Optimization and Information Technology* (pp. 57-61). Faridabad, India: Academic Press. 10.1109/ICROIT.2014.6798284

Rao, B. T., Dehuri, S., & Mall, R. (2012). Functional link artificial neural networks for software cost estimation. *International Journal of Applied Evolutionary Computation, 3*(2), 62–82. doi:10.4018/jaec.2012040104

Rao, B. T., Sameet, B., Swathi, G. K., Gupta, K. V., Ravi Teja, Ch., & Sumana, S. (2009). A novel neural network approach for software cost estimation using functional link artificial neural network (FLANN). *International Journal of Computer Science and Network Society, 9*(6), 126–131.

Raslan, A. T., Darwish, N. R., & Hefny, H. A. (2015). Towards a fuzzy based framework for effort estimation in agile software development. *International Journal of Computer Science and Information Security, 13*(1), 37–45.

Salmanoglu, M., Hacaloglu, T., & Demirors, O. (2017). Efort Estimation for Agile Sofware Development: Comparative Case Studies Using COSMIC Functional Size Measurement and Story Points. In Proceedings of IWSM /Mensura'17 (pp.42-50). Gothenberg, Sweden: Academic Press.

Satapathy, S. M., Panda, A., & Rath, S. K. (2014). Story point approach based agile software effort estimation using various SVR kernel. In *Proceedings of 26th International Conference on Software Engineering and Knowledge Engineering* (pp. 304–307). Vancouver: Academic Press.

Satapathy, S. M., & Rath, S. K. (2017). Empirical assessment of machine learning models for agile software development effort estimation using story points. *Innovations in Systems and Software Engineering, 13*(2-3), 191–200. doi:10.100711334-017-0288-z

Stensrud, E., Foss, T., Kitchenham, B. A., & Myrtveit, I. (2002). An empirical validation of the relationship between the magnitude of relative error and project size. In *Proceedings of the IEEE 8th metrics symposium* (pp. 3–12). Ontario: Academic Press. 10.1109/METRIC.2002.1011320

Tanveer, B. (2016). Hybrid Effort Estimation of Changes in Agile Software Development. *Lecture Notes in Business Information Processing, 251, 316-320.* doi:10.1007/978-3-319-33515-5_33

Tanveer, B., Vollmer, A. M., & Braun, S. (2018). A hybrid methodology for effort estimation in Agile development: An industrial evaluation. In *Proceedings of International Conference on Software and System Process* (pp. 21-30). 10.1145/3202710.3203152

Tanveer, B., Vollmer, A. M., Braun, S., & Ali, N. B. (2019). An evaluation of effort estimation supported by change impact analysis in agile software development. *Journal of Software Evolution and Process.* . doi:10.1002/smr.2165

Tolfo, C., Wazlawick, R.S., Ferreira, M.G.G., & Forcellini, F.A. (2018). Agile practices and the promotion of entrepreneurial skills in software development. *Journal of Software Evolution and Process.* . doi:10.1002/smr.1945

Usman, M., Britto, R., Damm, L. O., & Borstler, J. (2018). Effort estimation in large scale software development: An industrial case study. *Journal of Information and Software Technology.*, *99*, 21–40. doi:10.1016/j.infsof.2018.02.009

Venkataiah, V., Mohanty, R., Pahariya, J. S., & Nagaratna, M. (2017). Application of ant colony optimization techniques to predict software cost estimation. In Computer Communication, Networking and Internet Security. Springer. doi:10.1007/978-981-10-3226-4_32

Yu, H., Xie, T., Paszczyñski, S., & Wilamowski, B. (2011). Advantages of Radial Basis Function Networks for Dynamic System Design. *IEEE Transactions on Industrial Electronics*, *58*(12), 5438–5450. doi:10.1109/TIE.2011.2164773

Ziauddin, T. S. K., & Zia, S. (2012). An effort estimation model for agile software development. *Advances in Computer Science and Its Applications*, *2*(1), 314-324.

This research was previously published in the International Journal of Information Technology Project Management (IJITPM), 11(2); pages 50-71, copyright year 2020 by IGI Publishing (an imprint of IGI Global).

Chapter 48

Usability Cost–Benefit Analysis for Information Technology Applications and Decision Making

Mikko Rajanen
ⓘ https://orcid.org/0000-0002-3281-7029
University of Oulu, Finland

ABSTRACT

Usability is an important quality attribute for information technology (IT) applications. However, integrating usability design and evaluation as an integral part of the development processes in information technology development organizations is still a challenge. This chapter gives an overview on the usability cost-benefit analysis models and provides some example cases of the importance of usability. These models and cases can be used by usability professionals to motivate the organizational management to provide resources for usability work and to integrate usability work as part of the development process. The target audience for this chapter are professionals and researchers working in the field of IT, managers in IT development organizations, as well as managers in organizations acquiring and using IT.

INTRODUCTION

Today, we use Information Technology applications, software, information systems and online services more than ever before. These applications, systems and services play a crucial role in the everyday and working life of individuals, organizations and the society at large, and they impact the lives of all people. Therefore, it is more important than ever to ask why these systems are often so difficult to use. To quote the founder of Macintosh project at Apple, Jef Raskin (2001): "As far as the customer is concerned, the interface is the product." This means that as far as the real users are concerned, all the innovative and creative technical solutions and functionalities of the system created by the development organizations have been designed and developed in vain if the users cannot easily use them.

DOI: 10.4018/978-1-6684-3702-5.ch048

The mission of this chapter is to give a 1) comprehensive overview as well as 2) example cases of the importance of good usability and user experience (UX) for the development organizations, customer organizations and end users, as well as providing 3) practical tools for the management for making strategic business cases for better usability and UX, and introducing usability and UX activities into the development process. The target audience for this chapter are professionals and researchers working in the field of Information Technology, managers in IT development organizations, as well as managers in organizations acquiring and using IT. While the topic is important for the managers in development organizations and customer organizations, there are surprisingly few books or research articles on this topic, and even the newest practical guidebook, the "Cost-Justifying Usability" is now over 15 years old. The overview on usability and UX, as well as the example cases presented in these old books and articles are in great need of a complete update. In addition to providing a new and up to date overview on the importance of usability and UX, and giving modern example cases of usability benefits, this chapter will further expand the usability cost-benefit analysis into new contexts which are not currently presented in books or articles, namely games, gamification and open source software development. To achieve this mission, the author of the chapter will reflect on his own research on the topic from the last 15 years, as well as the experience and data that he has gathered during this research.

BACKGROUND

Usability is defined as one of the main quality attributes for Information Technology applications, software products, information systems and online services (Marghescu, 2009). There are many international standards and recognized definitions of usability and user-centered design, which all have different focuses (Marghescu, 2009) First international standard referring to the usability defined it as the capability of the product to be understood, learned, used by, and attractive to the user, when used under specified conditions (ISO 9126). The second international standard defining usability is the standard ISO 9241-11, where usability is defined as being the extent to which a product can be used by specified users to achieve specified goals with effectiveness, efficiency, and satisfaction in a specified context of use (ISO 9241). The third common usability definition is by Nielsen and Schneiderman, who define usability as consisting of five quality components: learnability, efficiency, memorability, errors, and satisfaction (Nielsen 1993, Schneiderman 1998). Usability can be achieved through a user-centered design process, usability activities (e.g., usability testing, paper prototyping, heuristic evaluation), and having an overall focus on usability issues through the entire development process (c.f. Rajanen et al. 2017, Rajanen & Rajanen 2017). Furthermore, since the turn of the millennia, the concept of user experience (UX) has been introduced to take into account the emotions and attitudes of user about using a particular product, system or service (ISO 13407, Marghescu 2009).

Usability design and evaluation as a field has struggled since its beginning for legitimacy (Rajanen & Iivari 2007). Furthermore, there is a wide diversity on the usability professionals' design and evaluation practices, as well as their conceptualization of usability and user experience (Rajanen et al. 2017). Fortunately, there has also been a lot of progress when it comes to making usability improvement activities an integral part of the development process. These days the development companies usually acknowledge the importance of usability and see it as important factor for their success. However, still too often the usability improvement activities are amongst the first to be sacrificed whenever the product needs to be on the market as soon as possible. Furthermore, there is still some traditional views amongst the development company management that see the usability improvement activities as just an additional and maybe even an optional task in software development projects. In the eyes of these managers, such an 'extra' task is always a potential risk for project deadlines and can be among the first to be cut from the project planning. Often these managers try to justify poor usability with the argument that the users can be trained and that sooner or later, these users will learn to overcome the usability problems in the system and adapt their workflow to the intricacies of the software. However, it is also possible that the users simply refuse to learn to use the system with poor usability, and that the functionality that has been implemented in the system with so much cost and effort is never used. Furthermore, poor usability, and hence a stressful work situation, is still a severe problem in computer-supported work, despite efforts to solve these issues. Stressful work situation due to poor usability of the Information Technology applications that need to be used in the day to day work has been identified as an important reason for high employee turnover. The most skilled and experienced employees can start searching for a better place for working, if they feel that their current work is hampered by these unsuitable and difficult to use information systems, tools and services. The less experienced employees may not be able to change their employer so easily, but their work satisfaction and efficiency decreases. Systems with bad usability cause errors and inefficiency.

Usability has many different forms of potential benefits also for the development organization. These benefits include increased productivity due to less user errors and less time spent on work tasks. An Information Technology application was introduced few years ago in hospitals in Finland for recording dictations by medical doctors as part of their routine practice after their appointment with a patient. However, the usability of this system was bad and for example saving one dictation required sixty (60) mouse clicks (National Audit Office of Finland 2012). So, if we assume that each selection took at least one second, just saving the dictation took one full minute extra time from the medical doctors that could had been used for patient appointments. One extra minute per patient may not sound like a too long time, but when we multiply this time with the target amount of patients per doctor in one day (12) we can see that each doctor was missing at least one patient meetings each day due to having to do unnecessary selections in a task that should had required only couple of clicks from the user interface. And if we want to calculate the worst-case scenario, when we multiply this wasted time with the total amount of medical doctors in Finland (21.000), we can do a rough estimation that cumulatively there may be as much as 525 working days (1 minute lost per patient * 12 patients per doctor per day * 21.000 doctors = 252.000 minutes or 4200 hours or 525 working days) potentially lost *every day* because of just one usability issue in just one task performed using just one Information Technology application.

In addition to the traditional software development context, the emergence of online commerce has shifted the emphasis from the advantages of better usability to the penalties of the online commerce site not having good usability. But even today there are quite few product development organizations reportedly having incorporated usability activities fully in their product development process (Rajanen et al. 2017). Bringing usability activities into the commercial development life cycle has been a challenge since the beginning of the usability activities over fifty years ago (Rajanen & Iivari 2007, Rajanen 2011). One reason for these difficulties is that the benefits of better usability are not easily identified or assessed. Usability activities have been competing for resources against other stakeholders in the SW development projects that do have objective and convincing cost-benefit data available for management decision making when the resources are allocated. Justifying the costs and identifying the benefits of the usability improvement activities have been seen as challenges for bringing usability activities into Information Technology Application development projects. Bringing usability into commercial software development is still a challenge. Furthermore, explicit introduction and justification of user centred design and usability work by managers is important in software development context, because software developers cling to status quo and seek to preserve it, by claiming that they follow the principles of user centred design and evaluation while in practice they do not, even if they desire to develop for high usability (Wale-Kolade & Nielsen 2016). Usability work will be integrated in the organization and software development context when a strategic decision is made by the decision makers to incorporate it into the business and development processes of the organization (Venturi et al. 2006). According to Venturi et al. (2006), the usability work is fully integrated in the organization when it is included in the product lifecycle, the usability experts have access to required skills and expertise, there is organizational usability infrastructure in place, management is fully committed to usability work, usability and user centred culture is disseminated inside and outside of the organization, and results from usability work inform and impact the design decisions.

In the early days of information technology, the SW developers were usually themselves the users of the SW they wrote and, therefore, knew their own needs and the context of use. Now IT solutions are used everywhere, and users can be of any age, from any culture, or from any context imaginable. The SW developers no longer have direct knowledge about the tasks, skills, and experience of the users, or information about the context within which the system is used. This can result in SW that does not answer to the functional needs of the user, but has plenty of extra unnecessary features, and does not sit well in the established work process of the user. SW developers need information about users and the context of use. User-centred design (UCD) has been developed to fulfill this role. According to international standard ISO 13407, user-centred design can be described as consisting of four principles and four iterative design activities. The four principles of user-centered design identified in ISO 13407 are:

- Active involvement of users in design activities
- Iterative design where design solutions are produced in iterative and incremental fashion
- Multi-disciplinary design where skills and views of people with various backgrounds are utilized in the design
- Allocation of tasks and functions to system and to user where appropriate

The four user-centered design activities need to start at the beginning of a development project in iterative fashion, and these activities identified in ISO 13407 are:

- Understanding and specifying the context of use
- Specifying the user, task, and organizational requirements
- Producing design solutions
- Evaluating designs against requirements

The iterative and incremental user-centered design process continues until the design solution is evaluated as fulfilling all the user and organizational requirements (ISO 13407).

The user-centered design process may include several usability actions to improve usability. In understanding and specifying the context of use and specifying the user and organizational requirements, these usability improvement actions can be, for example, creating personas, customer visits, and usability requirement workshops (c.f. Gulliksen et al. 2003). In producing design solutions and evaluating those against requirements, the usability improvement actions can be in the form of paper prototyping, expert evaluation, usability testing, and so on (Gulliksen et al. 2003).

One recent study has examined user-centeredness in the systems development context from the viewpoint of the four principles of user-centered design. This study found that there are considerable variations in how four allegedly user-centered systems design methods address the four principles of user-centeredness (Iivari & Iivari 2010).

Furthermore, a user centred design justification survey illustrated that 62% of the respondents felt that user centred design was justified through individual testimonials of practitioners, case studies, as well as demonstrated potential results, while 23% of the respondents were convinced by support from customers, management, and outside companies, and only 15% of the respondents of the survey identified usability cost-benefit analysis as a method for justifying user centred design (Harrison et al. 1994). However, more than half of the informants believed that usability cost-benefit analysis for user centred design justification would have been more convincing for them if more details were provided on how the usability cost-benefit analysis model worked and what kind of assumptions and data were provided (Aydin & Beruvides 2014; Harrison et al. 1994). Indeed, the usability cost-benefit analysis is one of the most important tools that is advocated in the literature by the researchers for justifying the costs of usability work, even though the usability researchers and practitioners do not have access or reference for reliable quantitative data for justifying usability work (Rajanen 2011). However, if quantitative approach for usability cost-benefit justification is used, it is extremely important to show to the decision makers that the data and the assumptions are reliable, or else there may be unforeseen consequences such as costs becoming more tangible than the benefits, and the focus shifting from the users to paying customers (Rajanen & Iivari 2007).

COST-BENEFIT ANALYSIS

Cost-benefit analysis is a method for making a judgement about project or related actions from the investment point of view (Karat 1994). The cost-benefit analysis method is based on making investment decisions based on the comparison between estimated costs and benefits of the planned project or actions. The comparison between costs and benefits is based on collected and analyzed quantitative and qualitative data regarding technology and finance. This comparison allows the management to focus the limited resources that are available to the planned activities that have potentially low costs and potentially high benefits, bringing the company net benefit. While there are numerous cost-benefit models for different contexts ranging from restricting carnivorous plants (Givnish et al. 1984), rural to urban migration (Speare 1971), and to electronic medical records (Wang et al. 2003), there are surprisingly few published models for analyzing the costs and benefits of usability in the software development context. There is still a need for studies where usability cost-benefit analysis models have been employed in empirical settings, or where the results of using usability cost-benefit analysis in a case study would have been contrasted with the literature on usability cost-justification or usability cost-benefit analysis.

According to Burrill & Ellsworth (1980) the general cost-benefit analysis method has three steps:

1. Identify the financial value of expected project cost and benefit variables.
2. Analyze the relationship between expected costs and benefits using simple or sophisticated selection techniques.

3.   Make the investment decision.

Cost means the estimated monetary or abstract expense of doing an action, such as performing usability evaluation, or starting a project. This cost can be either easily measurable and quantifiable, or it can be abstract and, therefore, difficult quantify in financial terms (Burrill & Ellsworth 1980). The objective of the cost-benefit analysis is to find more or less accurate financial estimates for each of the concrete and abstract. Sometimes it is not possible to estimate the financial impact of the abstract costs reliably. In that case, the best estimate or the range of various estimates should be used and the inaccuracy of the estimation should be taken into account.

In a software development project, the typical concrete and easily measurable costs are direct expenses (e.g., project personnel salaries and project office expenses), one-time purchases (e.g., equipment and software needed in development), one-time deployment costs (e.g., reduced individual and organizational productivity due to implementing new technology) and continuous overall expenses (e.g., training of the personnel). In addition to these easily measurable concrete costs, there many kinds of abstract costs. For example, the lack of knowledge transfer due to high staff turnover causes substantial indirect costs that are very difficult to estimate and quantify in monetary terms.

Benefit in cost-benefit analysis is a positive result of the planned action through either cost saving or estimated added value for the organization (Burrill & Ellsworth 1980). Just like costs, benefits can be divided into concrete and abstract benefits. Typical concrete benefits in projects can be divided as improved productivity (e.g., due to less expenses or when limited resources are used more efficiently), improved effectiveness (e.g., by optimizing the provided services) and indirect benefits (e.g., using the analysis for process improvement) (DIRKS 2003). Abstract benefits that are difficult to quantify might be, for example, increase in customer loyalty or better reputation of the company.

USABILITY COST-BENEFIT ANALYSIS

Different metrics have been used to justify the costs of usability activities, such as Return on Investment on Usability and Total Cost of Ownership (Aydin et al 2011). However, these metrics include many subjective estimations on costs and benefits of usability improvements, and even at best the accuracy of these estimations depend largely on the experience of the usability practitioner and the quality of the data that is available for them (Aydin et al 2011, Rajanen 2011, Rajanen 2006). And without good data and good estimations, the cost-benefit analysis can be unreliable. Usually, the costs of usability can be estimated quite reliably, while the benefits of usability are far more difficult to identify, estimate and quantify, which may lead to the management focusing on the costs of usability and unintended consequences (Rajanen & Iivari 2007, Rajanen 2011). Furthermore, there are few actual case studies reported in the literature that would show concrete data on the costs and benefits of usability improve-ments (Aydin et al 2011, Rajanen 2011), as the companies may be reluctant to reveal required financial and operational information to researchers. Furthermore, only one study addresses the comparison of the estimated and realized usability costs and benefits (Wilson & Rosenbaum 2005), while realized us-ability benefits are usually brought up in blogs, private conversations, and workshops. Therefore, while it would be very interesting to conduct and report a usability cost-benefit analysis based on empirical data from a company, in practice companies either do not want to reveal such information or they want researchers to keep such information confidential. For example, it would be interesting to conduct a longitudinal study with usability cost-benefit analysis, spanning for example 5 years, but there has not been any reported cases or available empirical data. However, the literature still identifies the usability cost-benefit analysis as one of the key methods for practitioners to justify the costs of usability work. However, the reliability of the existing usability cost-benefit analysis models may not be any more as good as it might have been over 15 years ago when these models were originally made. Information Technology applications have made great advancements in capabilities of technology and support of organizations and users. Furthermore, also the capabilities and the level of experience of the average users is much higher now than it was back then. At that time making an e-commerce web shop usability better might have given the company a substantial competitive advantage, whereas now the required level of usability is much higher in e-commerce and the companies cannot afford to launch web shops with poor usability. However, the usability experts in small, medium and large organizations still have the extremely important responsibility of convincing the organizational management and other decision makers to invest in usability work (Aydin & Beruvides 2014).

There are surprisingly few published models for analyzing the benefits of usability in development organizations. This chapter presents usability cost-benefit analysis models that are both seminal and modern. The seminal models have been presented in the book Cost-Justifying Usability (Bias & Mayhew 1994) are by Ehrlich and Rohn, Karat, and Mayhew and Mantei. The second edition of the book had a specific focus of applying usability cost-benefit considerations to web and intranet contexts, but it did not change the usability cost-benefit analysis models presented already in the first edition of the book (Bias & Mayhew 2005). This book includes studies by various researchers in the field on usability cost benefit analysis. These studies are seminal, and they still continue to influence researchers and practitioners (Aydin et al. 2011, Rajanen 2011, Rajanen & Rajanen 2017). In addition, the chapter explores usability cost-benefit analysis models by Bevan (2000) and Donahue (2001), as well as more modern models that relate to usability cost-benefit analysis in open source software development context (Rajanen 2011, Rajanen & Iivari 2010), in games and gamification (Rajanen & Rajanen 2017), and the most recent and radically different model (Aly & Sturm 2019). These models are very different in their categorization, view and approach of the usability cost and benefits. Next, the usability cost-benefit analysis models and usability cost-justification models are presented.

Potential Benefits Through Usability Work

Ehrlich and Rohn (1994, 2005) view the potential benefits of better usability through usability work and adoption of user-centred design from three points of view: vendor company, corporate customer and end user. According to them both the development company itself and the customers can gain benefits when usability activities are incorporated into software development project.

According to Ehrlich and Rohn the software development company can have three types of benefits:

1. Increased sales
2. Reduced support costs
3. Reduced development costs.

It may be difficult to estimate the impact of better usability and increased sales, but one way is to identify how important role does the usability has in buying decision (Rajanen 2006). One of the most prominent examples of the importance of usability to sales is by Spool (2008) in article "The $300 million button". This article presents a rare case of quantified usability benefit analysis. In this case e-commerce site that had a simple interface as part of their online purchasing form: two fields, two buttons, and one link (Spool 2008). However, it turned out this part of the purchasing process was preventing customers, to the tune of $300,000,000 a year. Furthermore, the designers of the site had no clue the web form had a problem that was costing the company huge amounts of money every year in lost sales.

The form itself was very simple, it had fields "Email Address" and "Password", buttons "Login" and "Register", and the link was "Forgot Password". The usability issue was not in the form elements or the layout itself, as much as it was the context where the form was presented to the users (Spool 2008). Users would be presented this form after they added products to their shopping cart and pressed the "Checkout" button. The problem was that the form came before the users could actually enter the information for payment and shipment for the product. The users were mentally prepared to finish the sale process and then the e-commerce site required them to either register or to remember login information from their past. As one shopper told the usability experts who were fixing the problem: "I'm not here to enter into a relationship. I just want to buy something" (Spool 2008). Other e-commerce sites offered a more streamlined shopping experience and good usability, and surprisingly large number of users abandoned their shopping process, the e-commerce company losing their sale. The usability issues were fixed, and the process was made streamlined. As a result of these usability improvements, the number of customers finalizing their purchases went up by 45%. These extra purchases resulted in an extra $15 million during the first month. For the first year, this e-commerce company saw increase of sales worth for an additional $300,000,000 (Spool 2008).

The cost of providing product support for the customer companies and end users can be surprisingly high if there are usability problems in important product features and the product has lots of users who contact the customer support. Usability improvements have direct impact to the amount of product support needed and therefore less need for support due to better usability can lead to great savings (Rajanen 2002, Rajanen 2003, Rajanen & Jokela 2004, Rajanen 2006). The customer organization can have potential benefits when a more usable product reduces time needed for the end user training. Furthermore, in addition of the official training, organizations have also hidden costs from unofficial peer-support. End users often seek advice from their colleagues, who spend their time helping rather than being productive. It is estimated that hidden support cost can be as high as $15.000 per PC every year if the users are not experienced PC users (Bulkeley 1992).

End users are the final beneficiaries of a more usable product. According to Ehrlich and Rohn (1994, 2005) the better usability can bring benefits for end users through higher productivity, reduced learning time and greater work satisfaction. The users can benefit from higher productivity when the most frequent tasks take less time, such as in the earlier mentioned case of system for recording dictations by doctors.

Benefits of Usability Work

Bevan (2000) categorizes the potential benefits of usability work, user-centered design and better usability to the organizations during development, sales, use and support. The development organization can gain benefits in development, sales and support. Customer organization can benefit in use and support. When system is developed to be used in-house by the development organization it can gain benefits in development, use and support. In each of these categories, there are numerous possible individual benefits where either savings or increased revenue can be gained. The total amount of potential benefits from better usability can be estimated by adding all identified individual benefits together. Bevan identifies usability benefits from increased sales, less need for training and increased productivity. Benefits from decreased development time are identified but not discussed in detail.

Quantifying Human Factors Work

Karat (1994, 2005) approaches the usability benefits through evaluating and quantifying the human factors work. This viewpoint differs from other usability benefit models in the literature. Karat identifies some examples of potential benefits in three categories:

1. Increased sales
2. Increased user productivity
3. Decreased personnel cost through smaller staff turnover

The development organization can expect benefits through better usability giving them a competitive edge and therefore increased market share and sales. Customer organization can gain benefits through increased end user productivity when task times are reduced and further indirectly when better usability increases staff satisfaction and reduces staff turnover. Karat has three phases in usability cost-benefit analysis. In the first phase all expected usability costs and benefits are identified and quantified. In the second phase the costs and benefits are categorized as being either tangible or intangible. The intangible costs and benefits are moved into separate list, as they are not easily estimated and quantified. The third phase is to determine financial value for all the tangible costs and benefits, but not to the intangible costs and benefits. Karat also highlights the importance of business cases in the usability cost-benefit analysis, as the business cases can provide an objective and debatable basis for making decisions on organizational investments such as usability work (Karat 1994).

Identifying Benefit Categories

Mayhew and Mantei (1994, 2005) view what the cost-benefit analysis of usability work is best made by focusing the attention of the audience, such as the managers, on the benefits that are of most interest to them. The benefit categories which are relevant for this particular target audience are then identified and the potential benefits are identified, estimated and calculated. Examples of relevant benefit categories are given for development company and developing in-house system for the development organization:

1. Increased sales
2. Decreased customer support
3. Making fewer changes in late design life cycle
4. Reduced cost of providing training.

The benefits for in-house development can be gained from increased user productivity due to better usability resulting less mistakes, decreased number of user errors, decreased training costs, having to make fewer changes in late design life cycle and the less need for user support. To estimate each of these possible benefits, a unit of measurement is chosen. Then an estimation is made concerning the magnitude of the benefit for each unit of measurement. The estimated benefits per unit are then multiplied by the number of units.

Cost-Justifying Usability Through Fear-setting

Aly and Sturm (2019) have a completely different approach to usability cost-benefit analysis and justi-fication of usability work. They argue that the usability, user experience and user-centered design pro-fessionals are in essence running negotiations with product owners about cost justification of usability activities, and that a different approach from traditional usability cost-justification or "goal-setting" is needed for convincing the managers and decision-makers to invest in usability work. They suggest a new approach, namely "fear-setting", which highlights the importance of avoiding losses resulted from bad usability and the related costs and losses in sales that originate from not taking any action related to usability improvement (Aly & Sturm 2019). The cost of inaction is defined as the opportunity cost which is associated with organizations not deploying the necessary technological or business improve-ments to match the complexity of their business (Hagan 2017). This radical change of approach from promising benefits to avoiding losses originates from the need that the usability experts must commu-nicate the value of usability across multiple levels in organization and that is why several "languages" are needed to communicate in different levels (Bloom et al. 1997). So instead of speaking about need for usability work in defensive mode and trying to argue that eventually the benefits will be greater than initial costs, the usability professionals should consider their audience and language appropriately, and in case of management the "fear-setting" language might be more effective, focusing on potential losses if no usability work is done, instead of focusing on cost-justification (Aly & Sturm 2019). They argue that presenting losses that might result from inaction, might have more influence on management deci-sion, than notions of potential profits gained from an action, as the fear of loss is the most undesirable feeling a business owner or manager can feel, and therefore addressing the missed opportunities due to bad usability, costs and losses resulted from indecision about investing to usability work can work as intimidating stimuli, and then there is no need to justify the usability costs any further (Aly & Sturm 2019). Their results give a first direction for future studies, for example taking into account the age of the audience: the younger and less experienced managers might consider potential profit and be better targets for traditional usability cost-benefit analysis, while the older and more experienced managers consider more losses and cost of inaction (Aly & Sturm 2019). However, this approach and its psycho-logical aspects have not been yet tested empirically.

Dangers of Traditional Usability Cost-benefit Analysis

Rajanen & Iivari (2007) examined in their case study the process of meanings negotiation related to usability and its cost-benefit analysis in Information Technology application development organization. Existing literature shows that very divergent meanings can be attached to usability in practice, as there are studies showing that usability as a concept has been used only as a slogan, or buzzword without any proper understanding of it (Rajanen & Iivari, 2007). In their case study Rajanen & Iivari (2007) identi-fied that the case organization used the potential usability benefit of increased sales as a tool in sales and marketing, as a tool for convincing the customer, resulting in marketing demos that sell themselves and conquer the world, while not actually conducting much usability work (Rajanen & Iivari 2007). In the eyes of the management, the reduced development costs through usability meant that the customers should be kept out of the development by any means. Furthermore, the costs of usability work, such as user interface design and development costs that would have been realized in any case even if no us-ability work was done, resulted the management condemning the usability activities as ineffective and time consuming. In the eyes of these managers, the benefits of better usability remained too distant and difficult to estimate (Rajanen & Iivari 2007).

It can be argued that as the result of the introduction of usability cost-benefit analysis as a concept, the costs of usability were made to appear very clearly, while the possible usability benefits remained too vague to really make an impact to the attitude of the managers (Rajanen & Iivari 2007). The benefits of better usability were not given any time to become visible, as the managers decided to halt the usability improvement efforts so quickly. The promises of future usability benefits were clearly not enough for the management to continue the usability activities. The traditional usability cost-benefit models assume that the usability benefits could and should be quantifiable and comparable. However, these assumptions are problematic because many of the usability benefits identified in the traditional usability cost-benefit analysis models are intangible and speculative by nature and trying to quantify them without any evidence only seems to raise suspicions (Rajanen & Iivari, 2007). Therefore, it can be argued that the usability benefits should only be quantified when there is both an empirically tested formula for calculating the usability benefits and also reliable data to be inputted into that formula (Rajanen & Iivari 2007).

In addition, some of the possible benefits of better usability that the traditional usability cost-benefit models identify were considered as insignificant by the managers. For example, having to print fewer pages for the product manual was raised as a possible benefit through better usability by many traditional usability cost-benefit analysis models, but the managers in the case organization even discussing this benefit just a waste of time. In their view the impact of this benefit was insignificant in first place, and furthermore the identified benefit did not take into account the transition from printed manuals to digital and online manuals. This example shows that the traditional usability cost-benefit analysis models are in great need of modernization and therefore they should be used only with great care (Rajanen & Iivari 2007, Rajanen 2011).

Usability Benefits in Games and Gamification

Computer games, online gaming and mobile gaming, as well as different forms of gamification have rapidly entered into our everyday life. Game development industry has boomed since the last decade. And since the last twenty years the game development has changed a lot in both scope and player requirements (Blow 2004). Game development covers a wide spectrum of developers ranging from an individual hobbyist creating a simple game to a large-scale AAA game development project costing hundreds of millions and having hundreds of development staff. The global sales of the game industry has already surpassed 100 billion US dollars (Newzoo 2016). The large gaming market has also become extremely competitive, and it has been estimated that just one out of five games reaching the markets make profit. Therefore, this one profitable game must pay not only its own development costs but also the development of the other less successful four games.

Because of competitiveness of the market and the increased demands of the gamers, bad game usability can cause monumental financial and reputation losses. Unlike many other forms of Information Technology applications, playing games is a voluntary activity and the players can freely choose which games they invest their money on (Rajanen & Marghescu 2006). Furthermore, the gamers, game critics and game communities are very vocal about all problems. Therefore, critical reviews and views of bad usability reach far and fast and can seriously impact the success of the game (Rajanen & Marghescu 2006).

One of the most prominent examples of the impact of bad usability was the original version of the Final Fantasy XIV, an online multiplayer MMORPG which had a catastrophic first launch in 2010.

Being part of very popular game series, the launch was eagerly anticipated by large number of players and the expectations were high. However, the released game had numerous very severe user interface and usability problems, starting from the convoluted process for opening an account to play the game. When entering the game, the players were not sure what to do and where to go, as the game map did not label any important locations, did not allow zooming out and players had to use non-standard keyboard controls to scroll it. Furthermore, the user interface of the game was very unintuitive, slow, cumbersome and convoluted for PC gameplay, because it was designed for a console version, which did not even exist at the time of the launch. Additionally, the user interface did not follow the established best practices and standards of the MMORPG genre. As one game reviewer put it bluntly: "These and countless other oddities make interacting with Final Fantasy XIV a chore" (GameSpot 2010). These kinds of negative professional and amateur reviews, forum posts and word-of-mouth were disastrous for the sales. Because of these usability problems and in response to heavy criticism and massive losses in the numbers of paying players, the publisher Square Enix abandoned the original version of the game and sacked its development team. Completely new version of the game was released in 2013, and in this version the usability problems were fixed.

Rajanen & Rajanen (2017) address the benefits of better usability in the development of games and gamification. Gamification is defined as using game-like elements in non-gaming context, usually for motivating and engaging the user to act in a certain way, such as to learn something or to change their behavior in some way (Deterding et al. 2011). Rajanen & Rajanen (2017) categorize the benefits of better usability in two categories: usability benefits in gamification development and usability benefits in gamification use.

In the context of developing a game or gamified system, better usability can contribute to 1) increased sales as the business objectives are well defined, understood and embedded in the game, 2) reduced development costs due to iterative design and development making sure that the critical issues of target behaviours, players profiles, activity loops for player engagement and motivation, fun of the game, and deployment solutions are well tested before implementation, thus resulting in less need for later costly changes, 3) reduced training and support costs as the game is tailored and adapted to the players and not vice versa, and by understanding, knowing and modelling the target players for the optimal effect, and 4) increased acceptance and reputation since the potential customers and end-users are adopting the game and provide positive feedback though different channels.

In the context of using a game or gamified system, better usability can contribute to 1) increased productivity as the game design is based on the business objectives and ensuring the usability, UX, flow and fun, as well as engagement and achieving the target behaviour, 2) reduced errors as the game is designed according to usability requirements for ease of use, effectiveness, and efficiency, as well as UX requirements of subjective experience with respect to the target behaviour and business objectives, 3) reduced training time and learning effort when the activity loops for progression and engagement are designed by continuously involving the users, and 4) increased customer and user satisfaction as the potential customers and end-users are adopting the game and provide positive feedback through different channels.

Usability Benefits in Open Source Software Development Context

Open source software development means development of software where the source code is made freely available for everyone to read and modify (Rajanen & Iivari 2010). The fundamental philosophy is to enable software to evolve by exploiting voluntary community participation (Rajanen 2011). Open source software development makes it possible also for the end-users to adapt the software they use to their personal needs and to fix defects. Since the last decade, also Information Technology companies have started to use open source software development in their business. Using open source software applications and development tools has been common for a long time, but also using the actual source code as part of software development has become popular. The availability of free, ready-made components updated by volunteer developers can reduce the development costs substantially. Additionally, software development companies have also started to participate in OSS communities and even to launch new open source projects. Therefore, introducing and incorporating usability work into open source software development context is important (Rajanen 2011). However, introduction of usability into open source software development has been a challenge for a long time (cf. Rajanen & Iivari 2010).

Rajanen & Iivari (2010) and Rajanen (2011) introduced usability cost-benefit analysis model for open source software development context. Their model categorizes the benefits of better usability into two categories: community open source software development context and company open source software development context.

In the traditional community open source software development context the better usability can 1) increase the popularity and distribution of that particular open source software, 2) attract an increased number of active and committed developer-users and non-developer –users, 3) increase the developer-user and non-developer-user satisfaction, 4) put less pressure for redesign through change requests in the forums, 5) having more systematic redesign, and 5) less need for peer support in the forums

In the company open source software development context, where a commercial software development company is involved in open source software development, better usability can benefits through 1) increased number of active and committed developer-users and non-developer –users, and some of them are also willing to become paying customers, 2) increased developer-user and non-developer-user satisfaction, 3) reduced development costs, 4) less pressure for changes presented in the forums, 4) more systematic redesign, 5) reduced training and support costs, and 6) if company provides training and support, less need for them

CONCLUSION

The aim of this chapter was to give a 1) comprehensive overview as well as 2) example cases of the importance of good usability and user experience (UX) for the development organizations, customer organizations and end users, as well as providing 3) practical tools for the management for making strategic business cases for better usability and UX, and introducing usability and UX activities into the development process.

Therefore, this chapter contributes to the usability cost-benefit analysis research in three ways. First, there is still a considerable lack of studies on different usability cost-benefit analysis models. This chapter identified the main strengths, weaknesses, commonalities and differences between usability cost-benefit analysis models. There are considerable differences between models in the usability cost-benefit analysis literature, in identifying and documenting the individual usability costs and benefits, and the necessary steps of the outlined cost-benefit analysis in general, as well as the theoretical soundness. These existing usability cost-benefit analysis models should be further updated to match the needs of the new era of ubiquitous and mobile Information Technology applications. These results are in line with the research which has pointed out a declining trend in primary theory development in usability cost-benefit analysis research and usability cost justification research (Aydin et al., 2011). Therefore, this chapter repeats this call for action for the researchers to do further primary theory development on this field and to test their theoretical frameworks empirically.

Second, this research contributed to the theoretical and practical usability cost-benefit analysis by highlighting the risks of applying the usability cost-benefit analysis or usability cost justification without great care, as there are risks that the intended purpose of using the usability cost-benefit analysis as motivation for usability work is jeopardized because the inherent costs of better usability become too apparent. This chapter identifies a reported empirical case where usability cost-benefit analysis raised new and unexpected issues. Therefore, this chapter can be useful for usability cost-benefit

Third, this chapter explored applying the usability costs and benefits into new contexts to fit them in important Information Technology development contexts: open source software development context and game and gamification development context. The results indicate that it is possible to fit the usability cost-benefit consideration into these new contexts, and that similar usability cost-benefit analysis models and usability cost-justification models should be created for similarly important Information Technology application development contexts, such as ubiquitous technologies, Virtual Reality, Augmented Reality, Mixed Reality, and the 5G and 6G networks, to name just a few potential areas for future studies.

Fourth, this chapter can help the usability practitioners in development organizations to find the best arguments for investing to usability work and better usability, and to convince the management that investing on better usability is not just economically smart, but that it can be also vital for the very survival of the organization.

Future research should be aimed for developing new and up-to-date cost-benefit analysis aspects, techniques and models with strong theoretical and empirical backgrounds, that are suitable for researchers and practitioners in private and public sectors.

REFERENCES

Aly, M., & Sturm, C. (2019). Hacks for Cost-Justifying Usability: Fear-Setting vs. Goal-Setting. In *Proceedings of the 21st International Conference on Human-Computer Interaction with Mobile Devices and Services* (p. 77). ACM. 10.1145/3338286.3347544

Aydin, B., Millet, B., & Beruvides, M. G. (2011). The State-Of-The-Art Matrix Analysis for Cost-Justification of Usability Research. *Proceedings of the American Society for Engineering Management: Winds of Change, Staking paths to explore new horizons*, 221-229.

Bloomer, S., Croft, R., & Kieboom, H. (1997). Strategic usability: introducing usability into organisations. In CHI'97 Extended Abstracts on Human Factors in Computing Systems (pp. 156-157). ACM. doi:10.1145/1120212.1120320

Blow, J. (2004). Game development: Harder than you think. *ACM, 1*(10), 28-37.

Deterding, S., Sicart, M., Nacke, L., O'Hara, K., & Dixon, D. (2011). Gamification: using game-design elements in non-gaming contexts. In *CHI'11 Extended Abstracts on Human Factors in Computing Systems (pp. 2425-2428)*. ACM. doi:10.1145/1979742.1979575

Hagan, J. (2017). *The Cost of Status Quo: When is it Time to Look at a Software Change? Managing Partner of One Motion Technologies Inc*. Retrieved from https://www.linkedin.com/pulse/cost-status-quo-when-time-look-software-change-josh-hagan

Harrison, M. C., Henneman, R. L., & Blatt, L. A. (1994). Design of a human factors cost-justification tool. In *Cost-justifying usability* (pp. 203–241). Academic Press, Inc.

Iivari, J., & Iivari, N. (2010). Varieties of user-centredness: An analysis of four systems development methods. *Information Systems Journal, 21*(2), 125–153. doi:10.1111/j.1365-2575.2010.00351.x

ISO 13407. (1999). ISO/IEC 13407, *Human-Centred Design Processes for Interactive Systems,* International Standard.

ISO 9126. (1991). *ISO/IEC 9126 Information technology-Software Product Evaluation-Quality characteristics and guidelines for their use*. International Standard.

ISO 9241-11. (1998). ISO/IEC. 9241-14 *Ergonomic requirements for office work with visual display terminals (VDT)s*, International Standard

Marghescu, D. (2009). Usability evaluation of information systems: A review of five international standards. In *Information Systems Development* (pp. 131–142). Springer. doi:10.1007/978-0-387-68772-8_11

National Audit Office of Finland. (2012). *Käyttäjäystävällisillä tietojärjestelmillä jopa 400 000 lääkärin vastaanottoaikaa lisää*. Retrieved from: https://www.vtv.fi/tiedotteet/kayttajaystavallisilla-tietojarjestelmilla-jopa-400-000-laakarin-vastaanottoaikaa-lisaa/

Newzoo. (2016). *Global Games Market Report*. Q2 2016 Update.

Nielsen, J. (1993). *Usability engineering*. Academic Press. doi:10.1016/B978-0-08-052029-2.50007-3

Rajanen, D., Clemmensen, T., Iivari, N., Inal, Y., Rızvanoğlu, K., Sivaji, A., & Roche, A. (2017). UX professionals' definitions of usability and UX–A comparison between Turkey, Finland, Denmark, France and Malaysia. In *IFIP Conference on Human-Computer Interaction* (pp. 218-239). Springer. 10.1007/978-3-319-68059-0_14

Rajanen, M. (2002). Assessing the Business Benefits of Usability in the Product Development Project - Analysing the Existing Models. *Proceedings of 25th Information Systems Research Seminar In Scandinavia (IRIS25)*.

Rajanen, M. (2003). Usability Cost-Benefit Models - Different Approaches to Usability Benefit Analysis. *Proceedings of 26th Information Systems Research Seminar In Scandinavia (IRIS26)*.

Rajanen, M. (2006). Different Approaches to Usability Cost-Benefit Analysis. *Proceedings of 13th European Conference on Information Technology Evaluation (ECITE 2006)*.

Rajanen, M. (2007). Usability Cost-Benefit Models - Different approaches to Usability Cost Analysis. *Proceedings of the 9th International Conference on Enterprise Information Systems (ICEIS 2007)*.

Rajanen, M. (2011). *Applying Usability Cost-Benefit Analysis - Explorations in Commercial and Open Source Software Development Contexts* (PhD Dissertation). Acta Universitatis Ouluensis Series A 587. University of Oulu.

Rajanen, M., & Iivari, N. (2007). Usability Cost-Benefit Analysis: How Usability Became a Curse Word? *Proceedings of the INTERACT 2007*. 10.1007/978-3-540-74800-7_47

Rajanen, M., & Iivari, N. (2010). Traditional Usability Costs and Benefits - Fitting them into Open Source Software Development. *proceedings of the 18th European Conference on Information Systems (ECIS 2010)*.

Rajanen, M., & Iivari, N. (2015). Examining usability work and culture in OSS. In *IFIP International Conference on Open Source Systems* (pp. 58-67). Springer. 10.1007/978-3-319-17837-0_6

Rajanen, M., & Jokela, T. (2004). Analysis of Usability Cost-Benefit Models. *Proceedings of the 12th European Conference on Information Systems (ECIS2004)*.

Rajanen, M., & Marghescu, D. (2006). The Impact of Game Usability to Player Attitude. *Proceedings of 29th Information Systems Research Seminar In Scandinavia (IRIS29)*.

Rajanen, M., & Rajanen, D. (2017). Usability Benefits in Gamification. *Proceedings of the 1st GamiFIN Conference*.

Raskin, J. (2001). *The humane interface: new directions for designing interactive systems*. Addison-Wesley Professional.

Schneiderman, B. (1998). *Designing the User Interface: Strategies for Effective Human-Computer Interaction* (3rd ed.). Addison-Wesley.

Spool, J. (2008). The $300 million button. In Web form design: filling in the blanks. Rosenfeld Media.

Venturi, G., Troost, J., & Jokela, T. (2006). People, organizations, and processes: An inquiry into the adoption of user-centred design in industry. *International Journal of Human-Computer Interaction*, *21*(2), 219–238. doi:10.120715327590ijhc2102_6

Wale-Kolade, A., & Nielsen, P. A. (2016). Apathy towards the integration of usability work: A case of system justification. *Interacting with Computers*, *28*(4), 437–450. doi:10.1093/iwc/iwv016

KEY TERMS AND DEFINITIONS

Cost-Benefit Analysis: Making an investment decision based on the estimated costs and benefits of the planned activity.

Usability: The extent to which an Information Technology application, product, software, system, or service can be used easily, can be used without errors and can be learned easily by the users.

Usability Cost Justification: Motivating investing to usability improvements by showing that benefits of better usability are greater than costs.

Usability Cost-Benefit Analysis: Comparing the costs and benefits of usability improvement activities in order to motivate investing to usability improvement.

Usability Improvement: Measurable improvement in usability of an Information Technology application, product, software, system, or service, when compared to previous version or to competitors.

Usability Work: Planning, design, and testing activity, which aims to improving usability of an Information Technology application, product, software, system, or service.

User Experience: Experience of an individual user in terms of ease and pleasantness of the use of an Information Technology application, system, or service.

User-Centered Design: Iterative and incremental process for designing and developing systems with good usability.

This research was previously published in the Handbook of Research on IT Applications for Strategic Competitive Advantage and Decision Making; pages 136-152, copyright year 2020 by Business Science Reference (an imprint of IGI Global).

Chapter 49
The Mythical Lines of Code Metric:
A Form of Moral Hazard

Charley Tichenor
Marymount University, USA

ABSTRACT

Using the lines of code (LOC) metric in software project management can be a financial moral hazard to an organization. This is especially true for upper management who handles an organizational budget and strategic plan. Software project managers have their own budgets. However, if they fail to meet the budget, the organization's cash flow, rather than the project manager's personal cash flow, will suffer. This chapter will discuss the practice of software project management, the field of software metrics, game theory, and the game theory issue of moral hazard. It will demonstrate why using LOC as a metric can present a moral hazard to senior management and an organization.

INTRODUCTION

Cost overruns are significant problems encountered by the software development industry. One example is the United States Federal Bureau of Investigation's (FBI) Sentinel software development project. As reported by the Cato Institute in Washington, DC (DeHaven, 2010):

Sentinel is currently 32% over-budget and two years behind schedule. Worse, an independent assessment of the project concluded that the project will need another $351 to $453 million and won't be finished for another 6 to 8 years. As the inspector general notes, "… the longer the full implementation of Sentinel takes, the more likely it is that already implemented hardware and software features will become obsolete.

In 2011, a report from the Office of the Under Secretary of Defense, Acquisition, Technology, and Logistics indicated that after studying nine ERP systems, "ERP schedule delays and cost overruns were common and sometimes large" (G. Bliss, personal memorandum, February 23, 2011).

DOI: 10.4018/978-1-6684-3702-5.ch049

Those working in the software development industry can identify others within their organization or similar organizations.

A major cause of cost overruns in software development is the use of unsound cost forecasting methods. Often, software cost estimations are poorly taught or overlooked in IT academic programs. Operations research/analytics programs rarely address the issue or will teach unsound methods. Probably less than 10 successful software cost estimation management consulting firms operate in the U.S.

An effective approach to forecasting software development costs is to look for a strong statistical regression correlation between a predictor variable (representing the amount of software developed) and the resulting cost to develop the software. While many predictor variables have appeared in practice, the LOC variable has a strong following in both government and industry. Written in a programming language, programmers generate LOC. According to the LOC metric approach, as software requirements increase, more LOC will be required. Work to write the LOC (as well as perform testing, deployment, and project management tasks) will increase as the number of LOC increase.

This chapter will detail the LOC metric and show how fundamentally in error its use can be.

BACKGROUND

The Force Multiplier

In the military, a force multiplier is "a capability that, when added to and employed by a combat force, significantly increases the combat potential of that force and thus enhances the probability of successful mission accomplishment" (Force multiplier, 2016). Many military examples discuss the employment of a force multiplier. For example, suppose that a modern army unit of 10 soldiers was to transport back in time to face 100 of Napoleon's soldiers. Who would have the competitive advantage? Napoleon's soldiers were equipped with single shot rifles; the modern army unit is equipped with automatic rifles with magazines. This advanced technology gives the modern army a competitive advantage over Napoleon's army. This is a force multiplier. The modern army unit has helmets and body armor. The modern army unit would enter the battle dug into foxholes. Napoleon's army would enter the battle without armor and firing from a standing position. The modern army unit would have better field rations, camouflaged uniforms, vaccinations, automatic deposits of their paychecks, and a military family support group program. These force multipliers give the modern army unit a competitive advantage over Napoleon's. The modern army unit 10 soldiers could probably defeat Napoleon's unit of 100. Although it is more expensive "per unit" to recruit, train, and equip modern army soldiers, a force of 10 would achieve a victory at a significant overall cost reduction in terms of resources and manpower.

The multiplier effect can also work in reverse. Suppose that the modern army unit of 10 had weapons that always misfired. In that scenario, Napoleon's army would easily defeat them with a complete loss of expensive resources and soldiers.

The multiplier effect is not limited to military combat. Business, government, and military organizations need administrative force multipliers to be more efficient and effective. Consider the organization of 2016 compared to its counterpart organization of 1966: replace letters and the desk in-box with e-mail; replace electric typewriters with word processors; and use computers to significantly reduce the manpower to perform payroll and other accounting calculations, supply chain accountability, inventory management, production forecasting, etc. Today's organizations are more effective and efficient per capita than their counterparts of 50 years ago.

The reverse multiplier effect can also occur in this situation. For example, the organization can experience tremendous reductions in efficiency and effectiveness if the office network is down, the network is hacked, or help-desks are unresponsive.

The Field of Analytics

When used properly, the analytics force multiplier results in significant increases in efficiency, effectiveness, and competitive advantage. According to the Institute for Operations Research and the Management Sciences analytics is defined as "the scientific process of transforming data into insight for making better decisions" (https://www.informs.org/About-INFORMS/What-is-Analytics).

Moneyball, a 2016 movie starring Brad Pitt, is a popular example on the use of analytics for competitive advantage (Rudin, Kimmel, Karsch, & Bakshi, 2016). According to the website, "the Oakland A's general manager Billy Beane (played by Brad Pitt) challenges the system and defies conventional wisdom when he is forced to rebuild his small-market team on a limited budget. Despite opposition from the old guard, the media, fans, and their own field manager, Beane—with the help of a young, number-crunching, Yale-educated economist—develops a roster of misfits ... and along the way, forever changes the way the game is played." By carefully collecting and analyzing player performance data, the team's needs are matched. The low-budget Oakland A's used this analytics information as a force multiplier to improve performance. In just one season, the team went from last to first place, baffling their competitors.

The U.S. federal government extensively uses analytics and has an analytics career field called "operations research." According to the Office of Personnel Management website, "The primary requirement of operations research work is competence in the rigorous methods of scientific inquiry and analysis rather than in the subject matter of the problem. Therefore, applicants should have sufficient knowledge of applied mathematics to understand and use the fundamental concepts and techniques of operations research methods of analysis. In addition, some positions may require knowledge of a specific subject area" (opm.gov, n.d., para. 2). Operations research/systems analysis (ORSA) is an analytics professional certification offered by the U.S. Army at a research school in Fort Lee, Virginia. A publication by ORSA Committee describes the career field (docplayer.net, n.d.).

ISSUES, CONTROVERSIES, AND PROBLEMS

Software Metrics as a Branch of Analytics

Software metrics are a branch of analytics. The Software Engineering Institute (SEI) of Carnegie Mellon University stated that the purpose of software metrics "... is to quantitatively measure or forecast certain aspects of software development (writing software). Effective management of any process requires quantification, measurement, and modeling. Metrics provide a quantitative basis for the development and validation of models of the software development process. Metrics can be used to improve software productivity and quality" (Mills, 1988).

Our culture ubiquitously uses metrics. Metrics measure the effectiveness of baseball players, including batting average, base percentage, and earned run average. Metrics are used by major organizations to measure their progress in achieving strategic plans and returns on investment. Human resource departments use metrics to evaluate employee performance. Metrics can also measure the effectiveness of software development. This chapter will focus on software metrics involved with forecasting software development costs.

For example, suppose that a driver wants to forecast the cost to fill his/her car's gas tank. The driver pulls into a highway gas station with the car's dashboard gas gauge near empty. How much will it cost to fill the tank? Two items are involved in this calculation: (1) the volume of the tank and (2) the price per gallon. If the tank holds 12 gallons of gas and the price per gallon is $2.50, then the forecast cost to fill the tank is 12 * $2.50 ($30.00).

number of gallons * cost/gallon $\approx$ final cost (1)

Equation 1 uses the approximately equal sign ($\approx$) to reflect that the exact number of gallons remaining in the tank at the time of filling is probably not known by the driver. Additional, the precise capacity of the tank is probably not known. The accuracy of the gas pump, while probably excellent, is not perfect. This chapter will continue to use the approximately equal sign in these contexts.

Many items are bought in this manner (i.e., by the "piece"). Examples include: milk sold in gallons; butter sold in pounds; electricity sold in kilowatt hours; and beer sold in cases. Knowing the number of pieces, cost per piece, and the ultimate cost is easy to either calculate or estimate.

What are the "pieces" of software? When using analytics, the early software cost estimating process begins with estimating the number of pieces of software that the final product will contain. A "price per piece" is estimated (or is already known). The final cost to develop and deliver the completed software is estimated by using a form of the following equation.

number of pieces * cost/piece $\approx$ final cost (2)

In early software development, software was written in a programming language containing LOC. Short and quickly-developed applications contained few LOC (less than 50). Home computers provided personal programming capability in the BASIC language. Owners of home computers may have written short programs to automate a variety of calculating tasks, including balancing a checkbook, comparing investments and interest rates, or calculating depreciation schedules. Today's applications can require millions of LOC. For example, the space shuttle's primary flight software contains approximately 400,000 LOC (NASA.gov, 2017). The Microsoft Windows operating system has roughly 50 million LOC (code. org, 2017). According to this LOC approach, forecasting the cost to develop software amounts to estimating the number of LOC in the final product, and multiplying by a cost per line.

number of LOC * cost/LOC $\approx$ final cost (3)

Many organizations use LOC counts to determine software financial value. One major U.S. organization requires its senior acquisitions managers to learn valuing software based on LOC as a requirement for advanced career certification. Another U.S. organization requires LOC as its fundamental software sizing metric for its software cost estimating and project cost auditing.

Is counting the number of LOC a good representation of the number of "pieces" of software? For example, during the first class of the new semester, a university professor directs students to develop an academic paper. The paper will be worth 33% of the students' grades. "How are you grading the paper?" asks one student. "Will it be based on the number of words, number of sentences, or number of pages?" The professor replies, "The paper will be graded on its content." The professor points to a grading rubric in the back of the syllabus.

Imagine, however, if the professor graded on the number of sentences. Should the grading criteria mirror the following system (adapted from Tichenor, 2016)?

900 sentences – A
800 sentences – B
700 sentences – C
600 sentences – D
< 600 sentences – F

Faculty and students know that the number of sentences in a paper has little relationship to the content value. This grading method encourages students to write sentences without focusing on value. What if a student downloaded 101 sentences from the internet? How would the grade be determined if the student self-generated 799 sentences and added the 101 downloaded sentences? Is the grade a C or an A? If the semester lasted 14 weeks and 450 sentences were completed by week 7, is the "A" paper already 50% completed?

To continue this analogy, suppose that a software development company and its client measure the amount of software delivered by LOC. Each LOC is a sentence of software in the programming language. The software development company has an economic incentive to increase the number of sentences in the software to deliver the same functionality to their client as with fewer sentences. Should a client conclude that 900 LOC provided more value than 800 LOC? Just as the college professor could not conclude that 900 sentences provided a more valued paper than an 800-sentence paper, the client should not conclude that 900 sentences of software provide a more valued software product than 800 sentences of software. The number of sentences of software is no more indicative of software value than the number of sentences in a student's paper.

In his *Scientific American* article, Jones (1998) called the use of LOC a "perplexing paradox." Jones, an internationally-recognized premier software metrics researcher, is a lifetime achievement award winner of the International Function Point Users Group (IFPUG). IFPUG, the world's largest software metrics trade association, maintains a function point metric and software non-functional assessment process (SNAP) metric, hosts professional certification programs, releases regular publications, and holds annual conferences (www.ifpug.org).

Many applications used today consist of more than one million discrete statements. Some applications have more than 10 million. The expense of writing such large software is determined by considerably more than just the cost of the actual coding process. In practice, companies spend a greater amount of money to produce paper documents (specifications and user manuals) and to test the program and correct the errors that invariably turn up. Furthermore, the cost of managing a large software project can itself be quite steep.

The fact that much of the work of building large applications is not directly related to coding leads to a surprising paradox ... Suppose that two companies decide to create programs that do exactly the same things. One firm uses assembly language, which requires many instructions to handle basic tasks, such as adding one number to another. With such a low-level language, the application requires, say, one million lines of code. The second company uses COBOL, a business-oriented language that takes fewer statements to perform the same functions. With this high-level language, the program contains perhaps just 400,000 statements. These line counts would superficially indicate that the former software is more than twice as "large" as the latter even though both programs are, in effect, identical.

The comparison is complicated further if the programmers at the two hypothetical companies write code at different rates (as would be expected even if they have the same fundamental abilities). Because of the different languages used, each staff member at the first firm may be able to deliver 500 lines of code each month, whereas the comparable number for the second company might be 360. Even so, the second company would be able to develop the application faster—1,100 staff-months versus 2,000—because fewer lines need to be written and because programs in high-level languages typically require less debugging, among other reasons. As a result, the total cost of the program for the first company would be $20 million, and the corresponding expense for the second firm would be $11 million. Yet each line of code at the first company costs $20, as opposed to $27.50 for the second firm. So it might at first glance appear that the programmers in the first company are more productive even though the second company is able to develop the same application faster and more cheaply. Thus, a low cost per line of code does not necessarily indicate economic efficiency.

An Alternative to LOC: Function Points and SNAP Points

Software can be categorized into two types using IFPUG. The first type represents the flow and storage of data through the application. This flow and storage of data is the software's functionality. One standard unit of this functionality is called the function point. According to Tichenor (2015, p. 14), "A function point can be thought of as one standard unit of software data processing capacity. It is analogous to a 'gallon' of gasoline, a 'cord' of wood, or a 'meter' of length. An application of 1,000 function points has twice the data processing capability of an application having 500 function points."

IFPUG function points consider that data flow and storage is measured by the impact of the following five aspects of software: (1) inputs; (2) outputs; (3) internal data files; (4) external interface files; and (5) queries. More specifically, function points look at each aspect from a logical perspective. For example, function points consider internal data files from a logical standpoint rather than a physical standpoint. It is really called an internal logical file (ILF) because one or more physical data tables are grouped together to compose a single logical grouping of data per ILF. From a logical perspective, this grouping eliminates sizing confusion due to programming language of the data or style of the programmer. The user wants a single logical group of data regardless of how it is programmed. Depending on the number of fields (data element types [DETs]) and subgroupings of data, the ILF is valued at 7, 10, or 15 function points. External interface files belong to another application and are used in a "read only" method. These are logically viewed and are worth 5, 7, or 10 function points.

Inputs cross the boundary of the application to eventually load ILFs. The methodology only considers inputs that cross the application boundary. Therefore, they are called external inputs (EIs). Each EI is a logical packet or group of fields (DETs) and associated control information (such as the ENTER key). One EI can encompass an entire input screen, multiple screens, or partial screens. The way that it is programmed is not material. Depending on the number of DETs in each EI and the number of ILFs referenced, the size of the EI will be 3, 4, or 6 function points.

Outputs and queries represent data crossing the application's boundary from the ILFs (and EIFs) to the outside. They are termed external outputs (EOs) and external inquiries (EQs). An EO example is a weekly sales report with calculations. Depending on the number of DETs and files from the original data, the EO is valued at 4, 5, or 7 function points. While the EQ is like the EO, it does not contain calculations. Without calculations, these are less valued at 3, 4, and 6 function points. See Figure 1.

Figure 1. Function point view of data flow and storage (or data processing capacity)

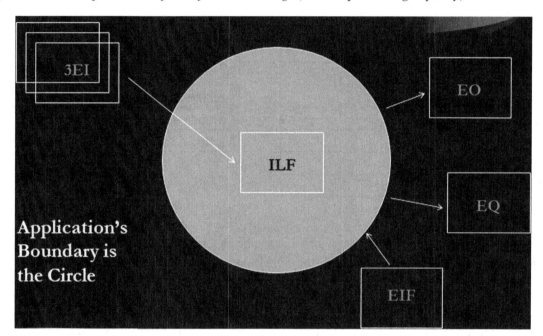

Equation 4 shows the total function points for an application with three EIs, one ILF, one EIF, one EO, and one EQ (all with low complexity, IFPUG, 2009):

$$(3 * 3) + 7 + 5 + 4 + 3 = 28 \tag{4}$$

This function point methodology has some advantages over LOC methods. Function point size is based on the user's viewpoint rather than the programmer's viewpoint. Therefore, the data processing capacity of 28 function points does not depend on the programming language, style, or LOC count (which is the way it should be viewed). Given the standards in the IFPUG Function Points Counting Practices Manual (2009a), different software metrics analysts will examine the software and arrive at nearly the same data capacity volume measurement. Therefore, the process is repeatable. In addition, function points provide an economic incentive for software developer efficiency since they paid by functionality delivered instead of LOC.

Non-functional software does not represent data processing capacity. It is measured by the SNAP point. There are 14 subcategories of non-functionality recognized by IFPUG (see Figure 2).

Figure 2. SNAP subcategories of non-functionality

Data Operations
Date entry validations
Logical and mathematical calculations
Data formatting
Internal data movement
Delivering added value to users by data configuration

Technical Environment
Multiple platforms
Database technology
Batch processes

Interface Design
User interface methods
Help methods
Mulitple input methods
Multiple output methods

Architecture
Component based software
Multiple input / output interfaces

SNAP size is counted like function points. Each subcategory has its own description, definitions, examples, and sizing matrix. For example, the SNAP Assessment Practices Manual subcategory 1.1 "Data Entry Validations" contains the following definition: "Operations that are performed either to allow only certified (predefined) data or to prevent the acceptance of uncertified data." If a data entry external input required data validation using one or two nesting levels, then the corresponding number of SNAP points would be two times the number of fields needing validation (DETs). If there were three to five nesting levels, the corresponding number of SNAP points would be three times the number of DETs. If there were more than five nesting levels, the corresponding number of SNAP points would be four times the number of DETs (IFPUG, 2015).

Comparing LOC and Function Points

Jones (2010) developed a scoring method to measure the effectiveness of numerous software project management practices. He scaled the effectiveness from +10 (most favorable having a productivity improvement of 25% and a quality improvement of 35%) to -10 (most harmful having a productivity improvement of -25% and a quality improvement of -35%). It was scaled so that a "0" score represented a neutral impact on the effectiveness of project management.

In order to evaluate the effectiveness or harm of these numerous and disparate factors, a simple scoring method has been developed. The scoring method runs from +10 for maximum benefits to -10 for maximum harm.

The scoring method is based on quality and productivity improvements or losses compared to a mid-point. The midpoint is traditional waterfall development carried out by projects at about level 1 on the Software Engineering Institute capability maturity model (CMMI) using low-level programming languages. Methods and practices that improve on this midpoint are assigned positive scores, while methods and practices that show declines are assigned negative scores.

The data for the scoring comes from observations among about 150 Fortune 500 companies, some 50 smaller companies, and 30 government organizations. Negative scores also include data from 15 lawsuits. The scoring method does not have high precision and the placement is somewhat subjective. However, the scoring method does have the advantage of showing the range of impact of a great many variable factors. This article is based on the author's book Software Engineering Best Practices published by McGraw Hill at the end of 2009.

In relation to this chapter, IFPUG function points (adjusted) scaled in as a benefit of 7.37 (a "very good practice"), and LOC yielded a harm factor of -4.5 (an "unsafe practice").

Backfiring: Converting LOC Into Function Points

Some practitioners employ the practice of converting LOC into function points. This provides the economic incentive to inexpensively size software by automatically counting LOC. Then, it applies a published conversion factor to calculate equivalent function points. This process is called backfiring. For example, research may have found that, on average, there are 38 LOC per function point for the hypothetical programming language ALPHA. If an application written in ALPHA had 10,000 LOC, then the backfired number of function points would be calculated as:

$$10,000 / 38 = 263 \tag{5}$$

At this point, the organization's metrics program would log in 263 function points as the size of the application in question. Next, it would apply functional metrics (quality, cost, productivity, etc.).

This backfiring process and the corresponding backfiring language ratios are largely based on tables developed by Software Productivity Research (SPR), a management consulting company. This company gives average numbers of LOC per function point for a variety of languages. These practitioners advertise that their results are based on function point counts. The margins of error associated with these averages are typically so huge that backfiring is considered malpractice. In January 2002, SPR issues an e-mail statement regarding the backfiring practice (Brindley, e-mail communication, January 2002).

This is the SPR strategy going forward for supporting and publishing the backfiring table on the web:

1. *Because backfiring at its very best is an extremely high-order estimation technique, we strongly discourage its use in virtually every conceivable circumstance.*
2. *Nevertheless, people seemingly will do anything to avoid counting function points properly, which raises the fundamental point: if you don't have any desire to count, and you have faith in your LOC data, why bother to translate the LOC count (assuming the LOC were actually counted and not guessed at—a lot of people don't want to count anything at all) to FPs? But that's a rhetorical question; I'll return to it in a moment.*
3. *Our website is under a complete reconstruction. All of the content is being redone, as well as the look and feel. However, we continue to receive numerous inquiries about the table.*
4. *So, in early January, we will put the table back online, accessible from the home page. It will be as it was. We plan to keep it there indefinitely, even as we discourage its use.*

5. *Many of those who tell us they want to use the table also complain that we never update it anymore, either with new languages (which proliferate daily, it seems) or with new ratios for old languages.*

6. *The cost of maintaining the table in such a way (updating it with new data) has become prohibitive, since all of the folks who are so upset with its disappearance from the website want to use it for free. Still, if it's going to be out there, it should be updated. This is our dilemma.*

7. *At a point in the near future, probably early second quarter 2002, we will do a thorough update of the table. The updated table will go on the website, but at that point in time, we will begin to charge a small fee for access. The exact details have not been worked out, but the cost will not be great.*

8. *Very likely, subscriptions will be available for extended periods of time, say for a year's worth of unlimited access. Something like that. Also, I imagine that current SPR customers of our products and services will get a free pass. Again, these details are still being ironed out, but that is the broad outline.*

9. *Finally, let me reiterate something you've heard me say before: The reason function points were invented in the first place those many years ago at IBM was that the LOC metric was becoming less and less useful as a reliable, portable, apples-to-apples software sizing metric. That was in the late 1970s. Nothing has happened since then to make LOC more universally meaningful. In fact, if anything the idea of a "line of code" itself has become virtually meaningless. So, if a synthetic metric not based on LOC was needed in the 1970s, why would anyone – anyone—use LOC metrics today? More astonishing, though, is that if one has faith enough in one's LOC metrics, why would one bother to convert them to function points? That person is still just using the LOC count by another name. Makes you wonder if maybe people aren't trying to hedge in on the scientific "cachet" of function points without really doing the work.*

Let this be your mantra as a metrics consultant: You get what you pay for.

Game Theory

Game theory is a mathematical approach to modeling relationships. According to Rasmusen (1997, p. 9), "Game theory is concerned with the actions of decision makers who are conscious that their actions affect each other."

As an introduction, assume that two players enter a relationship. The players can be people, companies, countries, a person, nature, etc. The entrance can be voluntary or imposed. One can hire a new employee (a voluntary relationship); when one assumes a new employment, co-workers represent an involuntarily relationship. The relationship can be friendly, warlike, or competitive. Regardless of how the relationship begins, the resulting relationship dynamics use game theory.

During the relationship, each player acts in an economically rational manner. In this chapter, rational refers to acting in a way to obtain personal utility. Personal utility is a rational person gaining economic benefit from the relationship's interactions. This may mean striving for financial gain, striving for personal gain (a friendship), or giving up financial or material gain to achieve a higher level of personal integrity (for example, returning a wallet to its owner). The following text is a form of a popular game in game theory literature.

Two suspected criminals are arrested by the police soon after a local convenience store robbery. The police believe that both are equally responsible for the robbery. They interrogate the suspects in separate rooms to get confessions. The first suspect is offered a deal in return for a confession. If he confesses first, then he will go free and the partner will get five years. However, if the partner (in the other room) confesses first, then the partner will get the deal. If neither suspect confesses and they are found guilty, then they will both get two years. If neither suspect takes the deal, then they will both get three years.

This situation can be modeled as shown in Table 1. The rows represent prisoner 1's actions. The columns represent prisoner 2's actions. The cells represent the payoff each suspect will receive based on their actions.

Table 1.

		Prisoner 2's Courses of Action	
		Cooperate: shut up	Defect: take the deal
Prisoner 1's	Cooperate: shut up	2,2	5,0
Courses of Action	Defect: take the deal	0,5	3,3

For example, if prisoner 1 cooperates by keeping quiet and prisoner 2 defects by taking the deal, then prisoner 1 will receive five years in jail. Prisoner 2 will receive zero years in jail.

The game theory can model many angles of human behavior. Moral hazard occurs when one person takes more risks than (s)he would normally take because someone else bears the burden of those risks (adapted from Wikipedia, 2015). As an example, a family needs their new teen driver to get himself to school, get to work, and assume household errands. Since the teen cannot afford car insurance payments, the parents choose to pay. However, the teen may take driving risks because the parents are paying for the insurance. If the teen causes an accident, then the parents' insurance rates will increase. The parents assume a moral hazard by allowing their teen to drive.

A car insurance company may also assume a moral hazard. For example, a dishonest driver may deliberately leave their keys in an old car with hopes that it will be stolen. In turn, the dishonest driver could make an insurance claim, pocketing more money for the car than if it had been traded. By offering the insurance, the insurance company assumes a moral hazard.

Another example of moral hazard is when an employer hires a new employee. The employer is less than 100% certain that the new employee will work honorably. Therefore, the employer assumes a moral hazard that the new employee is somewhat dishonest and the organization may suffer consequences.

Moral hazard also exists in software project management. Software development project managers want to use function points. With an economic demand for such a metric, the values include:

- What is the cost per function point?
- How many days to build a function point?
- Are costs and schedule forecasts within industry benchmarks?
- Can we document its value to the organization in terms of cost control and other metrics?

Moral hazards arise in software development when the software team is presented with an economic incentive to behave contrary to the goals of the organization. The goals of an organization's software development program include: delivering software at the agreed-upon cost; schedule; and quality.

However, team members are often incentivized to miss these goals. Many experience or self-generate opposite and, in many cases, will get away with it.

Moral Hazard 1: Software Project Managers and CIOs Refuse to Use Function Points and SNAP

- They do not want to be measured based on content.
- They do not want to be measured against industry benchmarks.
- They do not want to be held accountable for meeting measurable budgets.
- They know that LOC metrics have huge margins of error. Therefore, they "cannot" be responsible for the error.

The outcome of such refusal is that numerous software projects go overbudget and overschedule (more than 50%). Their uninformed upper management "has no idea why." Project managers repeatedly hide the cost and schedule overruns. However, contractors who bid on these projects may not use function points. They may overbid projects knowing that the customer is unaware of reasonable bid prices. It important to beware of software contracts with an excessive line of bidders.

Moral Hazard 2: Deliberately Using LOC Instead of Function Points and SNAP

Many managers and organizations implement a software metrics program to quantitatively forecast and control cost, schedule, and quality. However, they use the LOC metric.

A senior analyst for an organization (perceived as the local metrics guru) recommends LOC to an uneducated senior manager. The analyst does not explain the function point alternative. Senior management approves the LOC method for their software metrics program. It takes years (generations of senior management) to realize that their IT subordinates and acquisitions contractors have been taking advantage of them. IT subordinates kept their jobs and were rewarded by complying with the metrics program although their organization experienced cost and schedule overruns.

Moral Hazard 3: Software Quality

A related moral hazard looks at how software quality is determined. Software quality can be measured using the following metric (IFPUG, 1991):

defects found/ function point   (6)

For example, it appears that Project A (defect ratio of 20 defects / 200 function points) has better quality than Project B (defect ratio of 20 defects / 100 function points).

Following this reasoning, if the quality standard was 20 defects / 200 function points and a contractor's work for a 200-function point project was found to have 23 defects, then the contractor would need to remove three defects before the software was released and they received payment. The contractor removes three defects to meet the contract requirement. The contractor could sue for payment because the contractor met the quality standard.

The moral hazard builds around the notion that there are various levels of serious defects. Level 1 defects may introduce a virus or security violation into the software. With just one Level 1 defect, software cannot be used. Level 2 defects may be a mistake in key calculations or algorithms. A Level 2 defect example is miscalculated paychecks. With just one Level 2 defect, software cannot be used. Level 1 and Level 2 defects can be expensive to correct. Level 5 defects may be a misspelled word on a report or the wrong color on a screen. Level 5 defects do not affect the software functionality of the software; they are cheap to correct. Level 3 and Level 4 defects are scaled between Level 2 and Level 5, according to an organization's standards.

The following is an example related to the third moral hazard. What if the contractor, having 23 defects in its 200-function point software, removes three cheap Level 5 defects and retains three expensive Level 1 defects to meet the contract obligation of no more than 20 defects? The contractor has an economic incentive to do this since it is the least expensive fix. The contractor could meet the terms of the contract, deliver an unusable product, sue for payment, and win.

SOLUTIONS AND RECOMMENDATIONS

IFPUG published the following solutions and recommendations in its 2016 issue of *MetricViews* (Tichenor, 2016).

Moral hazard may arise in software development when software development project teams are presented with some form of economic incentive or reward to "behave" in a way which is contrary to the goals of the organization. The goals of an organization's software development program include delivering software at the forecast cost. For whatever reason, not all in software development are incentivized to try to reach those goals; many either experience or self-generate just the opposite.

One way to reduce these moral hazards is to have senior management ensure economic incentives point in the same direction as the ethical incentives. In my opinion, an organization may need one or more "honest brokers" that can educate and sell senior management on a function point-based metrics program and ask senior management to install the discipline and resources to maintain it. Here are some suggestions that seem to work for me.

- *The boss must understand the basics of the methodology and direct its institution. It would be good to put this decision in writing and place metrics procedures into the organization's operating manual.*
- *The metrics team must either directly report or have an unobstructed avenue to either the boss or the deputy. They must not be placed deep into the organization so that their work product and requests for support are filtered by intervening layers of management.*
- *The software development organization needs to be trained in the function point-based metrics methodology.*
- *The metrics team must generate success after success in metrics program implementation.*

FUTURE RESEARCH DIRECTIONS

Graduate schools of business often teach business forecasting methods in their quantitative analysis courses. Introductory algorithms lay the groundwork for mathematically-sophisticated algorithms. Future research could focus on whether economic incentives provided by business school forecasting algorithms will positively or negatively affect an organization's behavior of the organization, especially in terms of moral hazard.

CONCLUSION

Forecasting software development costs should be understood by all levels of project management, including supervisors, project managers, CIOs, and senior leadership. The two purposes of software should be understood: (1) to provide for data flow and storage (the data processing capacity) required by the user and (2) to provide for other aspects of software required by the user. Function points measure the amount of data processing capacity required by the user. SNAP points measure the amount of other aspects of software required by the user. Methods that can be gamed and do not directly relate to fulfilling user requirements should not be utilized. While LOC metrics may have been the best technology in prior software development, they provide an economic incentive for the introduction of moral hazard in an organization's financial system.

REFERENCES

DeHaven, T. (2010, October 25). *Cost overruns for FBI's 'Sentinel.'* Retrieved from https://www.downsizinggovernment.org/cost-overruns-fbis-sentinel

docplayer.net. (n.d.). *ORSA fundamental principles, techniques, and applications*. Retrieved from http://docplayer.net/14272590-Operations-research-systems-analysis-orsa-fundamental-principles-techniques-and-applications-a-publication-by.html

Force multiplier. (2016). Retrieved from www.thefreedictionary.com/Force+multiplier

International Function Point Users Group (IFPUG). (1991). *Function points as assets*. Princeton Junction, NJ: International Function Point Users Group.

International Function Point Users Group (IFPUG). (2009a). Function point counting practices manual v. 4.3. Princeton Junction, NJ: International Function Point Users Group.

International Function Point Users Group (IFPUG). (2009b). Software non-functional assessment process (SNAP) assessment practices manual v. 2.3. Princeton Junction, NJ: International Function Point Users Group.

Jones, C. (1998). Sizing up software. *Scientific American*, 279(6), 104–109. doi:10.1038cientificamerican1298-104 PMID:9648306

Jones, C. (2010). *Scoring and evaluating software methods, practices, and results, version 3.1.* Capers Jones & Associates LLC.

Mills, E. E. (1988). *Software metrics. (SEI Curriculum Module SEI-CM-12-1).* Pittsburgh, PA: Carnegie Mellon University. This work was sponsored by the U.S. Department of Defense. Retrieved from http://www.sei.cmu.edu/reports/88cm012.pdf

NASA.gov. (2017). *Shuttle computers navigate record of reliability.* Retrieved January 14, 2017, from https://www.nasa.gov/mission_pages/shuttle/flyout/flyfeature_shuttlecomputers.html

opm.gov. (n.d.). Retrieved from www.opm.gov/policy-data-oversight/classification-qualifications/general-schedule-qualification-standards/1500/operations-research-series-1515/

Rasmusen, E. (1997). *Games and information: An introduction to game theory* (2nd ed.). Malden, MA: Blackwell Publishers Inc.

Rudin, S., Kimmel, S., Karsch, A., & Bakshi, M. (2016). *Moneyball* [Motion picture]. United States: Sony. Retrieved October 17, 2016, from http://www.sonypictures.com/movies/moneyball/

Tichenor, C. (2015). How function points and Snap work together. *MetricViews*, *9*(2), 14–16.

Tichenor, C. (2016). Industry best practices v. moral hazard in software development. *MetricViews*, *10*(2), 15–16.

This research was previously published in Information Technology as a Facilitator of Social Processes in Project Management and Collaborative Work; pages 124-143, copyright year 2018 by Business Science Reference (an imprint of IGI Global).

Chapter 50
Software Maintainability Estimation in Agile Software Development

Parita Jain
Amity University, Noida, India

Arun Sharma
IGDTUW, New Delhi, India

Laxmi Ahuja
Amity University, Noida, India

ABSTRACT

Agile methodologies have gained wide acceptance for developing high-quality products with a quick and flexible approach. However, until now, the quality of the agile process has not been validated quantitatively. Quality being important for the software system, there is a need for measurement. Estimating different quality factors will lead to a quality product. Also, agile software development does not provide any precise models to evaluate maintainability. Therefore, there is a need for an algorithmic approach that can serve as the basis for estimation of maintainability. The article proposes an adaptive neuro-fuzzy inference system (ANFIS) model for estimating agile maintainability. Maintainability is one of the prominent quality factors in the case of agile development. The proposed model has been verified and found to be effective for assessing the maintainability of agile software.

1. INTRODUCTION

In the engineering of software systems, agile development approach is becoming a popular approach for many software projects day by day. Agile practices are becoming attractive due to faster development approach while maintaining a level of customer satisfaction. Over the past several years, agile methodologies have gained wide acceptance, with maintaining standards and execution approach for develop-

DOI: 10.4018/978-1-6684-3702-5.ch050

ment. The practice promotes continuous iteration of development and testing throughout the software engineering process, accommodating rapid changes as given by Abrahamsson (2017). The agile software development lifecycle starts with requirement elicitation as shown in Figure 1, identifying functional requirements which are fragmented into the set of user stories that are further disintegrated into a smaller task if required. The agile methodology includes an idea of iterative cycles of multiple releases. The benefits arise from improved customer collaboration, responding to change and refactorization of codes, daily standup meetings, retrospection meet after each sprint release.

With the success of agile development on small to medium scale projects where agile methods prove to be a best practice for software development, has led to an intended expansion for large scale and complex projects. Various studies provide evidence for successful completion on small-scale software development projects also. For large scale projects, the problem exists with the quality of the product. Researchers are still not able to prove quality development for such type of projects in a holistic manner.

Quality being an important concern nowadays, the relevant software development process is a necessity. From different developers, it has been observed and found that if the quality of the process is as per the standards then the high quality of the product can be expected as high. While adopting a quick and flexible approach like agile practices is a good option, with the proof that it will lead to a quality product development (Jain et al., in press).

Software process quality used for engineering software systems significantly affects the value of customer satisfaction. Hence, more importance must be given to software process quality rather than software product quality. However, an ample number of studies show that still, researchers are in a way to prove agile practices as a quality development process quantitatively founded by Jain et al. (2016). Quality of the product depends on various different factors. With the identified quality factors for agile development process given by Jain et al. (2016) based on ISO 9126-1 quality model using the ISM approach, the foremost quality factor is maintainability. In the development of software development, maintenance is considered an important activity for software capabilities enhancements and optimization.

The formal definition of software maintenance' given by IEEE (1998) is "Modification of a software product after delivery to correct faults, to improve the performance or other attributes, or to adapt to a modified environment." Maintainability, in general, refers to how these operations can be carried out effectively. For the whole development life cycle, it has been observed that up to 60–70% of effort and time is utilized in the maintenance of the product, making it the most expensive activity in the development lifecycle of software given by IEEE (1993). Marco (1986) suggested that we can control this cost only by measuring it. Influential critical factors have to be determined for measuring the software product. However, measuring these factors is a bit tough to get the final value of maintainability.

In today's era, an ample number of software companies use the agile methodology for the development of software products as it allows efficient software maintenance. With the rise of agile software products, there is a need for effective maintenance aspect. Researchers are constantly trying to devise a method to forecast the maintainability of any software in prior phases of software development life cycle (SDLC) by measuring the characteristics of its design. Agile Software Development does not provide any precise model basis to evaluate estimation. Therefore, there is a need for an algorithmic approach that can serve as the basis of estimation.

The present work propounds an adaptive neuro-fuzzy inference system (ANFIS) model for estimating maintainability of the agile software product. Based on experts' opinion fuzzy if-then rules are constructed in the fuzzy inference system. Although, this will lead to time consumption. ANFIS has an advantage over FIS systems that is, for solving a problem ANFIS combines fuzzy logic with the neural network (NN) learning capabilities. The focus of our research work is to propose a model that integrates the most significant characteristics of fuzzy logic (FL) and neural network (NN) in an agile maintainability estimation model. The results show that how maintainability of software product gets minimized by using agile as a development process.

Figure 1. Agile software development life cycle

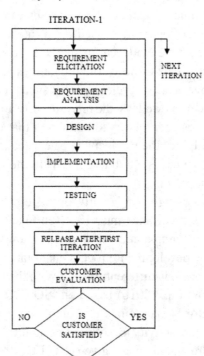

2. RELATED WORK

A rigorous review is conducted on the topics including agile development, maintainability and quality for various software development approaches especially for the agile approach. Research findings up to 2018 published in reputed conferences and journals including IEEE, ACM, and Elsevier, etc., have been considered to analyze the existing work in this direction. All the research papers reviewed are classified in two parts: one is traditional approaches for predicting maintainability and other is soft computing-based approaches for predicting maintainability and other quality aspects.

Various methods have been propounded for the estimation of maintainability in the past to reduce the efforts required and cost of software maintenance based on distinct dimensions and criteria. Fioravanti and Nesi (2001) presented a model for effort evaluation and forecasting adaptive maintenance. In their work different metrics like understanding, modification in system code portions and insertion and deletion of facts have been taken from various different software projects and ratified for foretelling maintenance. The results showed that the proposed model performs well in comparison to other models. Bandini et al. (2002) predicted the maintenance performance of object-oriented systems by considering three independent factors, named as; design complexity, maintenance task, and programmers' ability. Four metrics are considered for measurement based on these three factors and correlation was found between these factors to predict maintenance.

2.1. Traditional Approaches for Predicting Maintainability

Kajko et al. (2006) proposed two models, one for product maintainability and other for process maintainability. The model solves the problems related to maintainability by considering common characteristics and variable characteristics of the product and software process aspects to maintain the software throughout the development cycle. Another model for measuring software maintenance and effort estimation has been proposed by Ahn et al. (2003). The function point measures and 10 different maintenance productivity factors were taken to propose the model and survey method was used to validate it. Ardimento et al. (2004) made an assessment regarding project maintenance that if the project is difficult to understand then it is also difficult to maintain it. Also, the authors suggested using the software project as on trial basis first before adopting it.

Khairuddin and Elizabeth (1996) proposed a model for evaluating the maintenance of software systems considering various factors such as programming language, level of validation and verification, complexity, traceability and many more. Kumar (2012) describe maintainability measure with the understanding of the code. According to the author if the code is understandable it is easy to maintain the product otherwise, it is intractable to maintain the software product, leading to higher maintainability risk. For software maintenance, development team skills and experience also matters a lot which in general are ignored as suggested by (Banker, 1993; Kitchenham, 1999).

Three factors namely functionality, software complexity, and development practice were identified that significantly affect the maintainability of the software as given by McCabe (1976). Other authors, named Shen et al. (1985) illustrate that the age of the developers and size of the development team straightly affects the software maintenance. Whereas, Niessink et al. (1997) stated that the size of the module plays a major role in estimating maintenance effort. Also, for maintaining software systems, program comprehension is a critical factor given by Yau and Collofello (1980). Broy et al. (2007) introduced a model for software maintainability in which all the other activities of software development are strictly separated from the maintenance activities. The model represented by a hierarchical structure defining which activity influence the other activity.

Coleman et al. (1994) propounded a maintainability index to measure software maintainability based on the source code of the software product. It is a conglomeration depending upon different metrics of the software system. The higher this maintainability index, more the software systems are considered to be maintainable. Based on the Halstead Volume (HV) metric, the maintainability can be also measured as given by Halstead (1977). Oman and Hagemeister (1992) proposed different maintainability metrics to form maintainability index to measure software maintainability. Hayes et al. (2004) in their research stated that using two factors LOC and the total number of operators; adaptive software maintenance can be evaluated.

Polo et al. (2001) estimated maintainability using the number of modification requests, which type of correction required to maintain and mean effort per modification request. Hayes and Zhao (2005) proposed a model for software maintainability, categorizing software components into two types. One is the software components that are easy to maintain and other the components that are not easy to maintain.

2.2. Soft Computing Based Approaches for Predicting Maintainability and Other Quality Aspects

To forecast the maintainability time of the software product Aggarwal et al. (2005) used a fuzzy-based approach. The authors have taken total 81 rules as fuzzy if-then rules and to vindicate the proposed work, they have taken the data set of 10 different projects based on procedure-oriented methodology and maintenance time was measured. Jamimi and Ahmed (2012) in their paper captured uncertainty to predict maintainability using fuzzy logic and proposed a prediction model for the maintenance of software systems considering object-oriented metrics for prediction. Pratap et al. (2014) also proposed a software maintenance model using a fuzzy system. The authors have used different object-oriented metrics for prediction of maintainability.

The fuzzy logic approach used by Sharma et al. (2009) for the prediction of maintainability of component-based systems have taken maintainability as one of the important quality factor and identified related factors, making different rules to validate it. Although the validation has not been performed on large data sets but using analytical hierarchy process (AHP) authors have validated on small-scale classroom project data sets.

Grover et al. (2007) also proposed an approach using fuzzy if-then rule approach to estimate the maintainability of the component-based systems by extended the ISO 9126 model and adding one more sub-attributes, track-ability under software maintainability. A total of 243 rules were taken up to get the output and the proposed model was applied to different classroom-based projects to validate it. Pizzi and Pedrycz (2006) used a fuzzy integration approach, combining fuzzy logic with classification outcomes for the judgment of complexity and maintainability of software systems. The results showed enhancement of 15% while estimating the complexity of the software and a enhancement of 29% in estimating maintainability of the software. Jianhong et al. (2010) propound an approach for the prediction of the seriousness of faults in a software application based on the neural network. With the proposed model they are able to detect the most crucial areas where faults can occur and with an immediate action, they can be resolved, improving the quality of the software product.

Kaur et al. (2010) discuss four different aspects of object-oriented metrics for software systems. Using neural networks maintenance effort prediction models was proposed and the predictive accuracy was obtained. The results were compared with the outcomes coming using a radial basis function. Singh et al. (2004) consider a backpropagation algorithm to measure the maintainability of software systems providing 91.42% of prediction quality for software systems.

Ardil and Sandhu (2010) presented a neuro-fuzzy based approach for predicting maintenance of software applications. The results conclude that neuro-fuzzy based implementation gives better results in comparison with the fuzzy inference system (FIS). Kumar and Rath (2017) developed a model with the notion of parallel computing and neuro-fuzzy for estimating maintainability of the software products. For validation of the model, the authors take the input of 10 different static source code metrics, revealing that neuro-fuzzy approach can be used efficiently for prediction and with the integration of parallel computing concept the training time required in NN gets decreased to a notable amount.

An ample number of various other researchers has conducted experiments for prediction different quality factors for the overall improvement of the software product. It's not only maintenance that provides the overall quality, but other factors are also important from the different perspective. Kumar et al. (2013) provide a critical and exhausted review on quality aspects of the component-based systems proving reusability as one of the important factors for software quality and with the review the author also concluded that not much work has been explored in this area using soft computing techniques. Sedehi and Martano (2012) discuss two methodologies, GQM & PSM which focus on selecting critical metrics for agile software development. Rashid et al. (2012) also discuss different machine learning algorithms and case-based reasoning approaches to software error patterns for defining the overall quality of the software systems.

Shiva Kumar et al. (2016) propounded a method to estimate software development effort using neuro-fuzzy approach. But the limitation of the proposed method is that it is not suitable for large dataset. Another method is proposed by Sharma & Verma (2010) to estimate the cost of software systems by using function points. They used Gaussian membership function for validation and produced very good results.

Baisch et al. (1995) proposed a model that provides a prediction of changes using a neuro-fuzzy approach. They used the similar type of historical data to build a neuro-fuzzy model and claims that if the maintenance data of each module can be collected then the proposed approach can also be used for predicting maintainability but with the defined metrics. Nachiappan and Thomas (2005) provided an analysis of the general regression models and based on the similar concept a model with a relative measure has been proposed that predicts the defect density in software systems. Also, a framework for complex software has been proposed by Georgios (2009) to predict the defects and quality of the software product.

There are multiple heuristic methods for estimation of different factors based on their various sub-factors. Various researchers have already provided efficient results with these heuristic methods but still, there is a scope for improvement as the sub-factors always change. Also, it has been found that for agile software development there is no precise algorithmic basis to evaluate estimation. So, there is a need for an estimation model for different factors of it.

3. OBJECTIVES

For the present work, in total there are three objectives:

1. To ascertain the current state of research regarding the assessment of the quality factors for the agile approach;
2. To propose a novel approach to assess the maintainability aspect for the agile approach;
3. To empirically evaluate and validate the proposed approach.

4. PROPOSED MODEL

The research work proposes an adaptive neuro-fuzzy inference system (ANFIS) model for estimating maintainability of an agile software product developed using agile methodology on the basis of software defects. With a great success, the fuzzy logic approach previously been used in different fields of engineering for evaluations. The if-then rules in FIS are fired in parallel such that, whenever if conditions get true, the resultant of those defined rules get fired to the degree to which its antecedents of the rules are met as given by Bih (2006). The major challenge in developing a FIS is to find out the fuzzy sets and fuzzy inference rules used by the system to get the output. As a solution, it is better to use FIS with the learning capabilities of NN's as a combination, resulting in ANFIS.

4.1. Adaptive Neuro-Fuzzy Inference System (ANFIS)

Adaptive neuro-fuzzy inference systems were firstly proposed in 1992 by Jang (1993). The function of these systems is similar to FIS but they are adaptive in nature. It integrates the best features of both FIS and NN's. Providing the integrated feature, the ANFIS system provides a network that allows nodes with directional links and associate if-then rules allow learning to these networks. ANFIS allows simulating and analyzing the mapping relationship between inputs and outputs through an algorithm that provides the learning mechanism so as to optimize FIS parameters. The system can learn by itself that is, without any involvement of expert person typically needed for designing of the fuzzy if-then inference system. There are two different inference models; one is the Sugeno type and Mamdani type. The ANFIS system uses only Sugeno type fuzzy if-then inference model. The Sugeno style FIS gives crisp outputs using the weighted average technique.

An estimation model for agile maintenance is proposed using ANFIS system in the work done. The system provides an adaptive network which is alike to fuzzy if-then inference systems. The work done is divided into different steps.

4.2. Factor Identification

Agile being a lightweight methodology considered as one of the most used approaches for software development. It is a people-based approach rather than plan based. It promotes continuous iteration of development and testing throughout the software development. While using an agile approach for software development the process of development flows in a different manner as in traditional approaches used for software development.

In this, firstly the product backlog list is created by the product owner where all the necessary details are entered to get the final deliverable product. Each and every functionality of the system is known as a user story and individual iterations in which these user stories get developed is known as a sprint. During each sprint, top listed user stories from product backlog are selected and turned into sprint backlog. The development team works on the sprint backlog and delivers the product functionality at the end of the sprint. The overall time for each sprint to get complete is about 2-4 weeks. And within each sprint daily meetings are to be called to get the details about each sprint in progress (Hsu, (2018); Lacerda, (2018)).

By analyzing the agile approach in depth along with its terminologies which makes it different from other traditional approaches, the proposed model considers the four essential factors for predicting agile maintainability. The four factors are user stories, story points, pre-defects, and post-defects:

1. **User Stories:** Every time a user asks for some features to be implemented or development of an entire product a new user story is created. The number of stories is a simple value or count weighted by the story complexity;
2. **Story Points:** Story points are a very abstract concept for estimation. It does not indicate the time required to complete a task, but the task size. Scales used for story points are t-shirt sizes, Fibonacci sequences, etc. This leads to better results in terms of uncertainty and number of user stories to be implemented in an iteration;
3. **Pre-Defects:** Iteration may or may not have defects. It is these defects which need to be identified and prevented from occurring in subsequent iterations;

4. **Post-Defects:** Post defects are the total defects that occur once the product has been delivered to customers. It is the customer which notifies the defects that occur on his site.

4.3. Data Set Collection

The data set got cumulated from different industry sources working in the development of software using agile methodology. In total 93 different live projects data set collected from the chosen parameters. The software projects chosen are from different categories some are complex agile projects while some of them are simple agile projects. Mainly three input factors are used for the research work named as, user stories, story points, pre-defects and one output factor namely, post defects. For a Sugeno type fuzzy inference model, the rule set with fuzzy if-then rules is formed with the collected data set. It was first normalized and then categorized into LOW, MEDIUM and HIGH for the input set and output set both as described in Figure 2.

Figure 2. Rule base for Sugeno Fuzzy Model

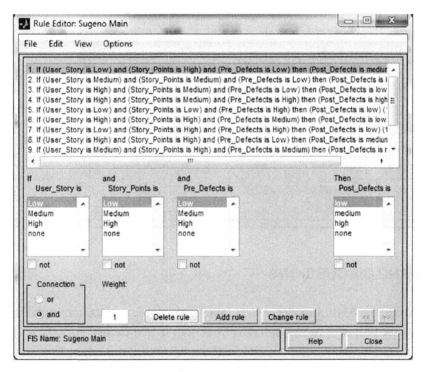

4.4. Experimentation and Evaluation of the Model

For experimentation purpose, an ANFIS system that is, a Sugeno style fuzzy inference system is designed. The adaptive neuro-fuzzy inference system was first trained with some training inputs to the network so that the network gets generalize and adapts the trends to provide the output in the presence of inputs that are already given. After that ANFIS system was tested using the testing data set again determined from these cumulated agile software projects. A total of 93 different live projects data set collected from the chosen parameters. Data from 70 projects were used for testing the network and then 23 were used for testing purpose.

Figure 3. Training error window

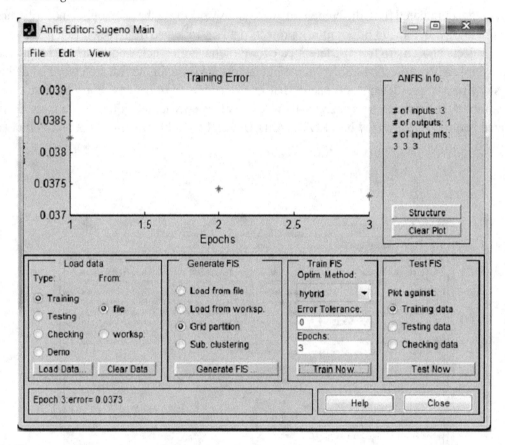

5. RESULTS AND DISCUSSIONS

In this research work, the ANFIS model is used for evaluating the maintainability of the agile software project. To assess the proposed model, the ANFIS system is first trained with the agile software projects data available as shown in Figure 3, and then the network got training with the testing data set. The models get validated when the inference system plotted the testing error predicting the output, as shown in Figure 4. Performing this process for the entire collected agile data set, on the whole, the average error is calculated and the efficiency of the network gets verified. The result shows an accuracy of approximately 85% which gives a confidence that the proposed approach may be used effectively for predicting the post defect for agile development. Assessment of Post Defect is a clear indication of the maintainability prediction during the development phase.

Figure 4. Testing error window

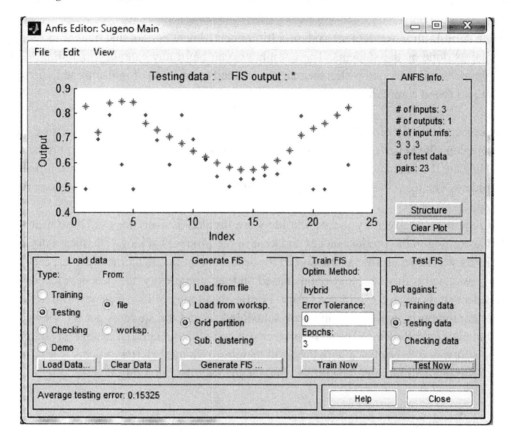

6. VALIDATION OF THE PROPOSED MODEL

To validate the proposed model, we considered another 4 classroom-based projects. These projects were developed by the undergraduate students which they developed during their final semester projects. These projects were web-based solutions for various University activities and developed using Java language. The projects are as follows:

1. **Attendance monitoring system:** It is a software system that monitors the attendance of the students online. The faculties have to upload the attendance in the system which further get stored in the database and can be further accessed by concerned faculties for later use at any point of time;
2. **End semester result preparation system:** Based on the marks of the students they get in their subjects, the system calculates the percentage of every student. The final result of the students gets displayed by using the software system. Also, the ranks of the students were calculated to identify the highest marks year wise;
3. **Fee module software system:** In today's era as all the things are getting digitalized, the students also pay their fees through various online gateways. The software developed generates a fee receipt automatically when the respective student fees get paid and also maintains the record for the same.

The fee can include either the tuition fees or bus fee or any other type of fees for various other activities in the university;

4. **Online complaint management systems:** It's a management system that maintains records of the complaints done by the students. The complaints can be of any category including food-related complaints that is provided within the campus, related to any kind of indiscipline issue or any type of lost and found complaint, etc.

These projects were developed using the agile approach where University authorities' i.e. faculty mentors were consulted after every small development. The faculty mentors act as a product owner to the team. They are the final authorities for the acceptance of the software that gets developed. They are the stakeholders. The team includes 5-6 members comprising of the developers, testers, scrum master and the product owner.

All the requirements given by the stakeholders are divided as user stories. These user stories are prioritized according to the product owner and kept in the product backlog. The user story having the highest priority was taken up first and analyzed for development one at a time. Further, each and every user story is assigned with some story points based on their complexity and gets developed in a sprint. The team selects how much to do in one sprint. For the development its necessary to interact with the stakeholder continuously, daily meetings were scheduled so that the students get the viewpoints from the faculty mentor (stakeholder). The students are provided with the agile environment so that they can develop the software in accordance with the agile manifesto. In total all the projects were developed in a span of one to one-half months. The project details are described in Table 1.

Table 1. Project details

Projects	User Stories	Story Points	Pre-Defects	Actual Post-Defects
Attendance Monitoring System	18	31	35	2
End Semester Result Preparation	12	28	18	4
Fee Module System	10	21	25	6
Online Complaint Management System	19	33	15	3

The metric values for all the inputs and final output i.e. post defect were determined over a period of one month after the implementation. We applied our proposed model on these four projects and compared the results with actual output i.e. the post defects using the tool. The predicted post-defect values obtained were normalized values. These values were first de-normalized and then using a round off function we got the predicted post-defect values as 3,3,7,5 respectively for all the projects. The comparative analysis of the proposed and actual metrics clearly proves a good correlation which indicates the acceptance of the proposed approach.

7. CONCLUSION AND FUTURE WORK

The paper presents an adaptive neuro-fuzzy inference system (ANFIS) model for estimating maintainability of the agile software product. The result shows an accuracy reasonably of 85% which gives a confidence that the proposed approach may be used effectively for predicting the post defect for agile development. Assessment of post defect demonstrates how maintainability of the software product can be predicted on the basis of post defect prediction in the agile development process. Also, the approach gets validated using 4 classroom-based projects and compared the results with the actual output values i.e. actual post-defects. The comparative analysis proves a good correlation of 0.76. The constraint on the proposed model is the data set collected from agile projects. As the data set was not very exhaustive, it may be possible that results may vary if the dataset gets increased. Also, the data set collected are not from very complex projects or for a specific domain so, the rules and output may result differently depending upon the complexity of the dataset. In the future, we are working on collecting a large amount of data set from industry working on agile development so that more generic and better results may be obtained. We also did not consider the severity of the defects, however, the same can be considered to estimate the efforts needed for maintainability of the software product.

REFERENCES

Abrahamsson, P., Salo, O., Ronkainen, J., & Warsta, J. (2017). *Agile software development methods: Review and analysis.* VTT Technical Research Centre of Finland.

Aggarwal, K. K., Singh, Y., Chandra, P., & Puri, M. (2005). Measurement of Software Maintainability Using a Fuzzy Model. *Journal of Computational Science, 1*(4), 538–542. doi:10.3844/jcssp.2005.538.542

Ahn, Y., Suh, J., Kim, S., & Kim, H. (2003). The Software Maintenance Project Effort Estimation Model Based on Function Points. *Journal of Software Maintenance: Research and Practice, 15*(2), 71–85. doi:10.1002mr.269

Ai-Jamimi, H. A., & Ahmed, M. (2012). Prediction of Software Maintainability Using Fuzzy Logic. In *Proceedings of 3rd International Conference on Software Engineering and Service Science (ICSESS),* Beijing, China (pp. 702-705).

Ardil, E., & Sandhu, P. S. (2010). A soft computing approach for modeling of severity of faults in software systems. *International Journal of Physical Sciences, 5*(2), 74–85.

Ardimento, P., Bianchi, A., & Visaggio, G. (2004). Maintenance-oriented Selection of Software Components. In *Proceedings of 8th European Conference on Software Maintenance and Reengineering,* Tampere, Finland (pp. 115 –124).

Baisch, E., Bleile, T., & Belschner, R. (1995). A Neural Fuzzy System To Evaluate Software Development Productivity. In *Proceeding of IEEE International Conference on Systems, Man and Cybernetics,* Vancouver, Canada (Vol 5, pp. 4603-4608). . 10.1109/ICSMC.1995.538521

Bandini, S., Paoli, F. D., Manzoni, S., & Mereghetti, P. (2002). A support system to COTS based software development for business services. In *Proceedings of the 14th International Conference on Software Engineering and Know ledge Engineering, 27,* 307–314.

Banker, R. D., Datar, S. M., Kemerer, C. F., & Zweig, D. (1993). Software complexity and maintenance costs. *Communications of the ACM, 36*(11), 81–94. doi:10.1145/163359.163375

Bih, J. (2006). Paradigm shift—an introduction to Fuzzy logic. *IEEE Potentials, 25*(1), 6–21. doi:10.1109/MP.2006.1635021

Broy, M., Deissenboeck, F., & Pizka, M. (2007). Demystifying Maintainability. *Paper presented in Fourth International Workshop on Software Quality Assurance (SOQUA 2007).* NY: ACM.

Coleman, D., Ash, D., Lowther, B., & Oman, P. (1994). Using metrics to evaluate software system maintainability. *Computer, 27*(8), 44–49. doi:10.1109/2.303623

Fioravanti, F., & Nesi, P. (2001). Estimation and Prediction Metrics for Adaptive Maintenance Effort of Object -Oriented Systems. *IEEE Transactions on Software Engineering, 27*(12), 1062–1084. doi:10.1109/32.988708

Georgios, L. (2009). Software Metrics Suites for Project Landscapes. In *Proceeding of 13th European Conference on Software Maintenance and Reengineering (CSMR'09),* Kaiserslautern, Germany (pp. 317-318).

Grover, P. S., Kumar, R., & Sharma, A. (2007). Few Useful Considerations for Maintaining Software Components and Component -Based Systems. *Software Engineering Notes, 32*(1), 1–5. doi:10.1145/1290993.1290995

Halstead, M. H. (1977). *Elements of Software Science (Operating, and Programming Systems Series).* NY: Elsevier Science.

Hayes, J. H., Patel, S. C., & Zhao, L. (2004). A metrics-based software maintenance effort model. In *Proceedings of 8th European Conference on Software Maintenance and Reengineering,* Tampere, Finland (pp. 254-258).

Hayes, J. H., & Zhao, L. (2005). Maintainability Prediction: a Regression Analysis of Measures of Evolving Systems. In *Proceedings International Conference on Software Maintenance,* Budapest, Hungary (pp. 601-604). 10.1109/ICSM.2005.59

Hsu, H. J., & Lin, Y. (2018). How Agile Impacts a Software Corporation: An Empirical Study. In *Proceedings of 42nd Annual Computer Software and Applications Conference (COMPSAC)* (pp. 20-25). 10.1109/COMPSAC.2018.10197

IEEE. (1993). *IEEE Standard: 1219-1993_IEEE Standard for Software Maintenance, INSPEC Accession No. 4493167.* IEEE Computer Society.

IEEE. (1998). *IEEE Standard: 828-1998_IEEE Standard for Software Configuration Management Plans.* IEEE Computer Society.

Jain, P., Ahuja, L., & Sharma, A. (2016). Current State of the Research in Agile Quality Development. In *Proceedings of the International Conference on Computing for Sustainable Global Development,* Delhi, India (pp. 1877-1879).

Jain, P., Sharma, A., & Ahuja, L. (2016). ISM Based Identification of Quality Attributes for Agile Development. In *Proceedings of the 5th International Conference on Reliability, Infocom Technologies and Optimization (Trends and Future Directions) (ICRITO),* Noida, India (pp. 615-619). 10.1109/ICRITO.2016.7785028

Jain, P., Sharma, A., & Ahuja, L. (in press). A Customized Quality Model for Software Quality Assurance in Agile Environment. *International Journal of Information Technology and Web Engineering.*

Jang, J. S. R. (1993). ANFIS: Adaptive-network-based fuzzy inference system. *IEEE Transactions on Systems, Man, and Cybernetics, 23*(3), 665–685. doi:10.1109/21.256541

Jianhong, Z., Sandhu, P. S., & Rani, S. (2010). A Neural network based approach for modeling of severity of defects in function based software systems. In *Proceedings of International Conference on Electronics and Information Engineering (ICEIE),* Kyoto, Japan (pp. 568-575). 10.1109/ICEIE.2010.5559743

Kajko-Mattsson, M., Canfora, G., Chorean, D., Van Deursen, A., Ihme, T., Lehmna, M., . . . Wernke, J. (2006). A Model of Maintainability – Suggestion for Future Research. In Proceedings of International Multi-Conference in Computer Science & Computer Engineering (SERP'06) (pp. 436-441). Nevada, USA.

Kaur, A., Kaur, K., & Malhotra, R. (2010). Soft Computing Approaches for Prediction of Software Maintenance Effort. *International Journal of Computers and Applications, 1*(16), 69–75.

Khairuddin, H., & Elizabeth, K. (1996). A Software Maintainability Attributes Model. *Malaysian Journal of Computer Science, 9*(2), 92–97.

Kitchenham, B. A., Travassos, G. H., Mayrhauser, A. V., Niessink, F., Schneidewind, N. F., Singer, J., & Yang, H. (1999). Towards an ontology of software maintenance. *Journal of Software Maintenance, 11*(6), 365–389. doi:10.1002/(SICI)1096-908X(199911/12)11:6<365::AID-SMR200>3.0.CO;2-W

Kumar, B. (2012). A Survey of Key Factors Affecting Software Maintainability. In *Proceedings of International Conference on Computing Sciences (ICCS),* Phagwara, India (pp. 261-266). 10.1109/ICCS.2012.5

Kumar, L., & Rath, S. K. (2017). Software maintainability prediction using hybrid neural network and fuzzy logic approach with parallel computing concept. *International Journal of System Assurance Engineering and Management, 8*(2), 1487–1502. doi:10.100713198-017-0618-4

Kumar, V., Sharma, A., & Kumar, R. (2013). Applying Soft Computing Approaches to Predict Defect Density in Software Product Releases: An Empirical Study. *Computer Information, 32*(1), 203–224.

Lacerda, L. L., & Furtado, F. (2018). Factors that help in the implantation of agile methods: A systematic mapping of the literature. In *Proceedings of 13th Iberian Conference on Information Systems and Technologies (CISTI)* (pp. 1-6). 10.23919/CISTI.2018.8399406

Marco, T. D. (1986). *Controlling Software Projects: Management Measurement and Estimation*. Prentice-Hall, Yourdon Press.

McCabe, T. J. (1976). A complexity measure. *IEEE Transactions on Software Engineering*, 2(4), 308–320. doi:10.1109/TSE.1976.233837

Nachiappan, N., & Thomas, B. (2005). Use of Relative Code Churn Measures to Predict System Defect Density. In *Proceeding of 27th International Conference on Software Engineering (ICSE '05)*, St. Louis, MO (pp. 284-292). .

Niessink, F., & Van Vliet, H. (1997). Predicting maintenance effort with function points. In *Proceedings of International Conference on Software Maintenance*, Bari, Italy (pp. 32-39). 10.1109/ICSM.1997.624228

Oman, P., & Hagemeister, J. (1992). Metrics for assessing a software system's maintainability. In *Proceedings of Conference on Software Maintenance*, Orlando, FL (pp. 337-344). 10.1109/ICSM.1992.242525

Pizzi, N. J., & Pedrycz, W. (2006). Predicting Qualitative Assessments Using Fuzzy Aggregation. In *Proceedings of Fuzzy Information Processing Society* (pp. 267–272). Montreal, Canada: NAFIPS.

Polo, M., Piattini, M., & Ruiz, F. (2001). Using Code Metrics to Predict Maintenance of Legacy Programs: a Case Study. In *Proceedings of International Conference on Software Maintenance*, Florence, Italy (pp. 202-208). 10.1109/ICSM.2001.972733

Pratap, A., Chaudhary, R., & Yadav, K. (2014). Estimation of Software Maintainability using Fuzzy Logic Technique. In *Proceedings of International Conference on Issues and Challenges in Intelligent Computing Techniques (ICICT)*, Ghaziabad, India (pp. 486-492). 10.1109/ICICICT.2014.6781331

Rashid, E., Patnayak, S., & Bhattacherjee, V. (2012). A Survey in the Area of Machine Learning and Its Application for Software Quality Prediction. *Software Engineering Notes*, 37(5), 1–7. doi:10.1145/2347696.2347709

Sedehi, H., & Martano, G. (2012). Metrics to evaluate & monitor Agile based software. In *Proceedings of Joint Conference of the 22nd International Workshop on Software Measurement and the Seventh International Conference on Software Process and Product Measurement*, Assisi, Italy (pp. 99-105). 10.1109/IWSM-MENSURA.2012.22

Sharma, A., Grover, P. S., & Kumar, R. (2009). Predicting Maintainability of Component-Based Systems by using Fuzzy Logic. *Communications in Computer and Information Science*, 40(11), 581–591. doi:10.1007/978-3-642-03547-0_55

Sharma, V., & Verma, H. K. (2010). Optimized Fuzzy Logic Based Framework for Effort Estimation In Software Development. *International Journal of Computational Science*, 7(2), 30–38.

Shen, V. Y., Yu, T. J., Thebaut, S. M., & Paulsen, L. R. (1985). Identifying error-prone software-an empirical study. *IEEE Transactions on Software Engineering*, 11(4), 317–324. doi:10.1109/TSE.1985.232222

Shivakumar, N., Balaji, N., & Anathakumar, K. (2016). A neuro Fuzzy Algorithm to Compute Software Effort Estimation. *Global journal of Computer Science and Technology, 16*(1), 1-6.

Singh, Y., Kaur, A., & Sangwan, O. P. (2004). Neural Model for Software Maintainability. In *Proceedings of International Conference on ICT in Education and Development (AISECT)* (pp. 1-11).

Yau, S. S., & Collofello, J. S. (1980). Some stability measures for software maintenance. *IEEE Transactions on Software Engineering, 6*(6), 545–552. doi:10.1109/TSE.1980.234503

This research was previously published in the International Journal of Open Source Software and Processes (IJOSSP), 9(4); pages 65-78, copyright year 2018 by IGI Publishing (an imprint of IGI Global).

Chapter 51

The Moderator of Innovation Culture and the Mediator of Realized Absorptive Capacity in Enhancing Organizations' Absorptive Capacity for SPI Success

Jung-Chieh Lee
International Business Faculty, Beijing Normal University Zhuhai, Zhuhai, China

Chung-Yang Chen
National Central University, Jhong-Li, Taiwan

ABSTRACT

Software process improvement (SPI) is critical to information system development. In the context of successful SPI, this research focuses on a firm's dynamic learning ability to see how it facilitates an effective means of acquiring and utilizing external SPI knowledge in responding to changing software development environments. Specifically, the authors propose a research model to investigate how two mechanisms of absorptive capacity are incorporated with innovation culture as a contextual factor to enable successful software process improvement. A survey was conducted including 125 SPI certified firms in China and Taiwan to examine the model. The findings indicate that a firm's potential absorptive capacity significantly influences realized absorptive capacity, which has a significant impact on SPI success and acts as a partial mediator between potential absorptive capacity and SPI success. Moreover, the results suggest that the mediating effect of potential absorptive capacity on SPI success via realized absorptive capacity is amplified when innovation culture is imposed.

DOI: 10.4018/978-1-6684-3702-5.ch051

1. INTRODUCTION

Software process improvement (SPI) is particularly important for firms and business units because it enhances and sustains their competitive advantage in the business market (Lee et al., 2016). Software development is knowledge intensive in innovation and mutual learning and often takes advantage of external sources to advance software development processes (Matusik and Heeley, 2005). Therefore, SPI implementation often relies on SPI knowledge, skills, expertise, experience, methodologies, technical support from external sources – e.g., external mediating institutions, such as SPI consulting firms and vendors – and external knowledge bodies, such as the Capability Maturity Model Integration (CMMI) and the International Standards Organization (ISO), to address challenges that arise during implementation (Feher and Gabor, 2006; Meehan and Richardson, 2002).

Based on organizational learning theory (March, 1991), SPI is commonly recognized as an organizational learning process because the exploration of external process knowledge and the exploitation of existing process knowledge in organizations play critical roles in SPI implementation (Rus and Lindvall, 2002; Dyba, 2005; Lee et al., 2017). However, successful SPI relies on how effectively a firm can internalize these external lessons (Mathiassen and Pourkomeylian, 2003; Alagarsamy et al., 2008). Furthermore, software processes are executed in dynamic development and turbulent business environments (Xu and Ramesh, 2007). Thus, SPI requires continual endeavours in order for firms to maintain their competence. However, the existing literature does not fully grasp how to address a firm's learning ability to internalize external SPI knowledge nor addresses how organizational learning continually supports changing SPI needs under dynamic environments.

This study focuses on dynamic capabilities theory to address continual learning ability in SPI. Dynamic capabilities refer to a firm's abilities to adapt, renew, and reconfigure internal and external competences to address rapidly changing environments (Teece et al., 1997; Zahra et al., 2006). Zahra and George (2002) extended dynamic capability to include absorptive capacity (AC), which represents a firm's dynamic ability to acquire, assimilate, and apply knowledge from external environments. AC enables a firm to renew or reconfigure its existing knowledge stock, creating new knowledge, processes, or products to better match rapidly changing environments (Jansenet al., 2005; Volberda et al., 2010). It can be considered a specific organizational learning process for learning, implementing, and disseminating external knowledge internally in order to strengthen, complement, or refocus the firm's knowledge mechanisms (Zahra and George, 2002; Lane et al., 2006; Volberda et al., 2010; Sun and Anderson, 2010; Roberts et al., 2012). Peng et al. (2014) showed that firms with greater AC can quickly and precisely recognize and assimilate the value of external knowledge and information, which then allows them to adopt ad hoc information technology more quickly.

To gain a better understanding of a firm's ability to acquire and utilize external SPI knowledge, this study adopts the two categories of AC developed by Zahra and George (2002) – potential AC (PAC) and realized AC (RAC) – and investigates how these types of AC influence SPI success. PAC represents a firm's ability to identify, acquire, embrace, and assimilate external knowledge, while RAC refers to its ability to leverage newly acquired knowledge and incorporate transformed knowledge into the development of innovation processes and operations (Fosfuri and Tribo, 2008). In the existing information systems (IS) literature, Saraf et al. (2013) indicated that PAC helps a focal firm acquire and understand external knowledge that is specific to the enterprise's information systems, such as enterprise resource planning (ERP), while RAC provides a firm with the ability to exploit the absorbed knowledge to facilitate greater ERP usage. In the context of SPI, a firm's AC is expected to be the enabler that continually turns external SPI knowledge into internal development processes to reflect the environmental changes in software development. Accordingly, insight into a firm's PAC and RAC is essential to understand how SPI knowledge acquisition and utilization affects SPI success.

The knowledge-based view (KBV) suggests that contextual factors, i.e., corporate culture, impact how knowledge is acquired and employed in firms (Abubakre et al., 2017; Alavi and Leidner, 2006; Lee et al., 2011; Castro et al., 2013) and play an essential role in a firm's knowledge-intensive software development (Jones et al., 2006; Leidner and Kayworth, 2006; Ke and Wei, 2008; Moreno et al., 2012). Nonaka and Takeuchi (1995) considered innovation culture (IC) to be the most important contextual factor influencing a firm's knowledge mechanisms. IC has been shown to enhance the acquisition and application of new knowledge, to improve a firm's knowledge stock and to help achieve organizational objectives (Castro et al., 2013). However, in the context of SPI, little research investigates how IC might be associated with PAC or RAC.

Therefore, we address the following research questions:

1.   How do the mechanisms of AC in terms of PAC and RAC help a firm achieve SPI success?
2.   How does IC influence the contexts of PAC and RAC?

We propose a research model that links PAC, RAC, IC, and SPI success by using a quantitative empirical survey of SPI certified firms in the Asia-Pacific region and emphasizing Taiwan and mainland China as the primary data source. Specifically, this study adopts partial least squares (PLS), a structural equation modelling approach, to test the proposed model empirically, analysing 125 samples of organizations with the specific SPI program Capability Maturity Model Integration (CMMI) (CMMI Institute, 2010). The rest of this study is organized as follows. Section 2 reviews relevant research studies on SPI, AC, and IC, and proposes corresponding research hypotheses. Section 3 provides details on the data collection, including population and sampling. Section 4 examines the proposed research model and explores relationships between the hypotheses. Section 5 summarizes the findings and discusses the outcomes. Finally, we describe the limitations of this study and outline directions for future research in Section 6.

2. THEORETICAL BACKGROUND AND HYPOTHESES DEVELOPMENT

2.1. Software Process Improvement Success

SPI helps firms integrate traditional organizational functions and sets process improvement goals and priorities that update existing process systems to improve organizational performance (Shih and Huang, 2010; Lee et al., 2016). SPI has played a critical role in helping firms achieve various business benefits, e.g., improving product quality, reducing time to market, improving productivity, and reducing costs. To realize these benefits, effective SPI implementation requires time, careful scheduling, resources, and knowledge (Meehan and Richardson, 2002; Mathiassen and Pourkomeylian, 2003; Niazi et al., 2006). Decisions about SPI implementation are influenced by organizational factors, and several studies have analysed the critical success factors for SPI (Rainer and Hall, 2002; Dyba, 2005; Niazi et al., 2006; Sulayman et al., 2014). Specifically, Dyba (2005) empirically investigated software organizations to examine the influence of organizational factors on successful SPI implementation and discussed six organizational factors, including the exploitation of existing knowledge and the exploration of new knowledge. Several recent studies have also proposed similar findings to explain the importance of SPI knowledge in an SPI context. For example, Larrucea et al. (2016) indicated that firms should gather useful knowledge and the experiences of others to help them deploy appropriate processes to best meet their needs. Uskarci and Demirors (2017) stated that employees must possess satisfactory knowledge regarding SPI activities to support them and participate in teams working to improve organizational processes.

Dyba (2005) validated a theoretical model of SPI success factors and proposed an operational definition of variables for this success. The study suggested that SPI success was defined by two indicators: improved organizational performance and the perceived level of SPI success, including cost reduction, decreased cycle time, and increased customer satisfaction. Dyba's theoretical model has been applied in various studies. Sulayman et al. (2014) used Dyba's work to develop a specialized framework of SPI success factors for small web companies. Winter and Ronkko (2010) investigated product usability metrics, adopting Dyba's (2005) SPI success factors. Based on Dyba's (2005) work, Egorova et al. (2009) evaluated the effect of software engineering practices for industrial projects. In this study, we adopt Dyba's (2005) definition of SPI success as the dependent variable in the proposed model.

2.2. Absorptive Capacity

AC has played a critical role in investigations of IT and IS (Roberts et al., 2012; Sharma et al., 2012; Saraf et al., 2013). While AC was originally defined as a firm's ability to recognize the value of, assimilate, and apply new external information to commercial ends (Cohen and Levinthal, 1990, p. 128), it also implies learning and acting in discovering scientific and technological activities outside the organization's limits (Zahra and George, 2002; Lee et al., 2018). Therefore, AC enables firms to achieve superior organizational performance, innovation capability, and competitive advantage (Jansen et al., 2005; Lane et al., 2006; Lee et al., 2017). Generally, AC is treated as a dynamic capability that affects a firm's ability to reconfigure its existing substantive capabilities (Zahra and George, 2002; Jansen et al., 2005). Thus, AC helps firms flexibly generate new valuable knowledge in turbulent environments by reshaping and renewing its existing knowledge stock (Pavlou & El Sawy, 2006; Roberts et al., 2012). Zahra and George (2002) further distinguished four dimensions of AC: acquisition, assimilation, transformation, and exploitation. Each dimension is considered a capability that helps to produce the organizations' dynamic capabilities (Sun and Anderson, 2010), and these dimensions explain how AC influences a firm's knowledge mechanisms when the opportunity or need arises (Camisón and Forés, 2010; Lee et al., 2017).

Specifically, acquisition refers to a firm's ability to identify, acquire, and value external knowledge that is critical to operations, while assimilation refers to a firm's ability to analyse, process, interpret, and understand the acquired knowledge. According to several studies, knowledge acquisition and assimilation combine to form PAC, a type of AC that enables a firm to identify, filter and then acquire new valuable external knowledge for future use and application (Lee et al., 2017; Zahra & George, 2002). Transformation is a firm's ability to combine existing knowledge and newly acquired and assimilated knowledge for future use, while exploitation refers to its ability to integrate acquired, assimilated, and transformed knowledge into its operations to develop new processes, routines, operations, and systems. After implementing PAC, a firm's RAC transforms and exploits the absorbed knowledge by utilizing and applying it to support innovation (Lee et al., 2017; Zahra & George, 2002).

PAC and RAC represent two separate yet complementary roles of AC to facilitate the use of new external knowledge (Zahra and George, 2002). According to Saemundsson and Candi (2017), PAC is critical because it allows firms to acquire and assimilate externally generated knowledge and helps them recognize opportunities in a business environment. However, RAC is an essential foundation for firms to leverage the absorbed knowledge to develop new products, services or processes (Fosfuri & Tribo, 2008; Leal-Rodríguez et al., 2014). As Leal-Rodríguez et al. (2014) stated, firms cannot take advantage of knowledge without first acquiring it. Conversely, firms may possess the capability to acquire and assimilate knowledge but may not transform and exploit this knowledge for profit generation.

The literature has shown the importance of AC in IT/IS deployment and implementation. For example, Harrington and Guimaraes (2005) indicated that AC establishes an external communication channel to gather useful knowledge that influences implementation of new technologies. Sharma et al. (2012) showed that AC acts an important facilitator to help ensure effectiveness and efficiency during the highly customized and learning-intensive process of ERP systems adoption. Bharati et al. (2014) noted that a higher level of AC contributes to a greater assimilation of social media technologies. Wei et al. (2015) indicated that AC can help organizations perceive the commercial potential of technological breakthroughs. Thus, strong AC is critical for organizations' successful technological adoption.

2.3. Absorptive Capacity and SPI Success

During SPI implementation, the acquisition capability of PAC first enables a firm to identify and gather relevant SPI information and knowledge, such as best practices, methodologies, and technical support, from external sources (i.e., SPI consulting firms and vendors; Lee and Chen, 2017). Knowledge acquisition helps the firm recognize, value and capture adequate and useful SPI knowledge to meet and satisfy the firm's SPI demands, depending on its specific characteristics, such as technology, systems, people, and processes (Lee et al., 2018). In the next stage of PAC, the assimilation function addresses the acquired SPI knowledge by converting the knowledge into a comprehensible and meaningful format for the company and then disseminating it across the firm to ensure effective SPI implementation.

Nevertheless, acquiring knowledge alone is not enough for complete SPI implementation. The firm may need further RAC to exploit and embed this knowledge when implementing ad hoc process improvement situations (Albort-Morant et al., 2018; Joshi et al., 2010; Leal-Rodríguez et al., 2014). Regarding the contextual effect between PAC and RAC, Joshi et al. (2010) demonstrated that a firm's PAC can help strengthen its RAC because PAC gathers considerable amounts of external knowledge to be filtered, harvested and analysed into local formats to prepare RAC to take effect. In other words, for the absorption of external SPI knowledge, PAC helps a firm to acquire and assimilate suitable external knowledge that can be used and applied to a firm's operations via its RAC. Thus, we hypothesize the following:

H1: Potential absorptive capacity has a positive influence on realized absorptive capacity.

In the context of this study, RAC is reflected in the transformation and exploitation of SPI knowledge. Specifically, in the first stage of RAC, knowledge transformation aims to combine a firm's existing knowledge and its newly absorbed SPI knowledge. Transformation acts by integrating the newly acquired knowledge about SPI practices into the firm's software development operations. As a result of transformation, internal and existing SPI knowledge may be synthesized through the addition or elimination of knowledge or the conversion of external knowledge (Lee & Chen, 2018, p. 24). Knowledge exploitation not only helps the firm leverage the transformed SPI knowledge into its software development routines but also renews and rearranges the software processes that are meant to increase the effectiveness of the development. Thus, RAC can provide support for SPI activities and upgrade the firm's software engineering competence by increasing the efficiency of software development and customers' satisfaction with the result. As such, RAC seems to be critical for SPI success. Thus, we hypothesize the following:

H2: Realized absorptive capacity has a positive influence on SPI success.

Zahra and George (2002) argued that external knowledge may not be transformed and exploited until it has been acquired and assimilated. Further, SPI is often aided by external knowledge (Ravichandran and Rai, 2003). As discussed above, AC development could enhance SPI knowledge acquisition and utilization, and the implementation of SPI first requires the effective acquisition of external knowledge (i.e., PAC). However, external knowledge cannot affect SPI success if the mechanism to transform and embed the absorbed knowledge into the firm's real processes, operations, and routines is not established (i.e., RAC). Thus, PAC is the first step to acquire external SPI knowledge and RAC is the next logical step to exploit this new SPI knowledge. This argument is logically consistent with Albort-Morant et al.'s (2018) study, which indicated that an organization's competence in acquiring and exploiting external valuable knowledge is essential in the new product development context. They revealed a full meditation relationship between PAC, RAC and new product development performance and further confirmed that even if PAC exists, RAC is necessary to further utilize the acquired external knowledge and achieve greater new product development performance. Based on these arguments, we assume that RAC may act as a full mediator between PAC and SPI success. Accordingly, we hypothesize the following:

H3: Realized absorptive capacity fully mediates the relationship between potential absorptive capacity and SPI success.

2.4. The Moderating Role of Innovation Culture

According to the literature, IC refers to organizations that are predisposed to learning continuously and that are open to new knowledge or breakthrough solutions to detect and fill gaps between what the market desires and what the firm currently offers (Brettel & Cleven, 2011). When an organization has IC, organizational behaviours facilitate the creation and development of new products, services, or process innovations to address business and environmental challenges and needs (Castro et al., 2013; Ali and Park, 2016). Olmospeñuela et al. (2017) and Aksoy (2017) indicated that IC spurs organizational learning, helps organizations accept new knowledge, technologies, and markets, and determines how they tolerate failure. In addition, IC strengthens organizational cohesion and departmental relationships, which increases the organization's innovation capacity for the adoption of new processes (Nemeth, 1997). An organization's contextual factors also influence its AC mechanisms (Van den Bosch et al., 1999; Harrington and Guimaraes, 2005; Volberda et al., 2010). Specifically, IC enables a firm to increase its openness to external knowledge (Brettel and Cleven, 2011) and helps increase the firm's external learning capacity for knowledge acquisition and assimilation, thereby strengthening high PAC levels (Harrington and Guimaraes, 2005; Winkelbach and Walter, 2015).

In the context of SPI, process improvement may also be viewed as innovation since it encourages a new approach to developing software (Agarwal and Prasad, 2000). During SPI implementation, IC establishes an organizational social environment that facilitates engaging in SPI more creatively, opening the firm to external SPI knowledge. Under a stronger IC, a firm's PAC more aggressively absorbs and filters knowledge to obtain more suitable external SPI knowledge, even when it comes in unfamiliar forms. IC also helps firms better interpret and comprehend the acquired SPI knowledge, which more efficiently and effectively stimulates RAC (Joshi et al., 2010). IC activates an organization's knowledge mechanism to smooth the flow from acquiring external SPI knowledge to utilizing internal SPI knowledge. In this regard, as the level of IC increases, the relationship between PAC and RAC for innovative process improvements strengthens because IC helps the collaboration between PAC and RAC, which better integrates external SPI knowledge into the organization's intelligence. PAC works in conjunction with RAC to improve the efficiency of SPI knowledge transfer, shortening the time to internalize external SPI knowledge and contributing to SPI success. Thus, we suggest that the mediating effect of PAC on SPI success through RAC is moderated by IC and that this effect is stronger for firms with stronger IC. Therefore, we hypothesize the following:

H4: IC positively moderates the relationship between PAC and RAC.
H5: IC moderates the mediating effect of RAC on the relationship between PAC and SPI success.

We propose a theoretical model that integrates PAC, RAC, IC, and SPI success, as shown in Figure 1, and we conducted an empirical investigation to test the proposed research model and hypotheses.

Figure 1. Proposed research model

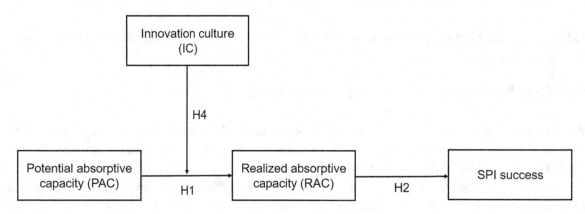

<Descriptions>
H3: RAC fully mediates the relationship between PAC and SPI success.
H5: IC moderates the mediating effect of RAC on the relationship between PAC and SPI success.

3. RESEARCH METHODOLOGY

3.1. Data Collection and Sample

A survey method was adopted to empirically examine the proposed model. Since this study was conducted in Taiwan and China, the questionnaire was prepared and administered in traditional Chinese (for Taiwan) and simplified Chinese (for China), and then, a back-translation procedure was employed to translate the original English versions of the instrument into traditional and simplified Chinese for this paper. To ensure reliability and validity, the traditional and simplified Chinese questionnaires were examined by three IS scholars who are familiar with both the traditional and simplified Chinese language to ensure the survey items were clear, understandable and consistent in meaning. A pilot test was conducted with 10 IS managers from different organizations in China and Taiwan to ensure that the survey questions were understandable.

The organizations that participated in the survey had adopted the CMMI-based SPI program and received official certification from the CMMI institute (see https://sas.cmmiinstitute.com/pars/pars.aspx). We can observe that organizations that had obtained CMMI certification were either software organizations or the software development functions/departments of organizations in different industries. By using the website mentioned above, we first contacted these CMMI-certified organizations by e-mail or telephone and then explained the study's purpose to them to ensure that they understood and agreed to participate. This process was also done to ensure that the participants were serious about answering the questions. As an incentive, the participating organizations were told that they would be provided with our research reports. A total of 200 organizations were willing to participate in the survey. The survey participants were senior and middle management representatives and were directly involved in CMMI implementation at their firms. An electronic mail survey was used for the sample from October to December in 2016, and a total of 200 questionnaires were sent to the CMMI-certified organizations. Since the unit of analysis in this study was at the organizational level, survey participants were asked to answer on behalf of their respective organizations. The respondents returned 125 usable questionnaires (62.5%). Table 1 in the Appendix shows the demographics of the respondents and organizations.

To check the sample's representativeness, we tested the nonresponse bias using the method of Armstrong and Overton (1977). We conducted t-tests to compare the sample attributes (job position, education, and work experience) of the first 25% and last 25% respondents – that is, those who had replied during the first and last seven days. There was no significant difference between these two groups on these items, which indicates that the non-response bias was not significant, and that the representativeness of the samples was supported. Moreover, we performed independent-sample t-tests to compare the means of the same variables for the samples of Chinese firms and Taiwanese firms. The results showed no significant differences between the groups; thus, we can aggregate the data from these two groups.

3.2. Measures

Constructs were adapted from those developed and validated in previous studies. All the variables were measured based on a seven-point Likert scale ranging from "strongly disagree" to "strongly agree," as shown in Table 2 in the Appendix. PAC represented a reflective construct including four items that were used to estimate external knowledge acquisition and acquired knowledge assimilation to process newly obtained knowledge. RAC represented a reflective construct comprising four items that were used to estimating knowledge transformation, to combine external knowledge with existing knowledge, and to subsequently apply the new organizational knowledge to achieve a firm's objectives. The items for PAC and RAC were adapted from Pavlou and El Sawy (2006). IC was measured using three reflective items adapted from Castro et al. (2013): (1) our firm encourages creativity, innovation, and new ideas in software development processes; (2) our firm encourages experimentation and innovation in improving software development processes; and (3) a common system of values, beliefs, and objectives are related to innovation.

SPI success was measured using a second-order reflective construct formed from two first-order reflective constructs derived from Dyba (2005). The first-order reflective constructs comprised the software organization's perceived SPI success (abbreviated PS) and organizational performance (abbreviated OP). PS was measured as the extent to which SPI was able to (1) substantially increase a firm's software engineering competence and (2) improve a firm's overall performance. The OP construct was measured using three items: (1) the reduction in firm costs, (2) the reduction in the firm's software development cycle time, and (3) the increase in the firm's customer satisfaction. In using these two constructs (i.e., OP and PS), it is worth mentioning that the measurement, particularly the OP in Dyba's (2005) study, was provided with reliability (Cronbach's alpha) to check the internal consistency of the construct, which implies that the study considered cost, cycle time and customer satisfaction to be similar content/ indicators that share a common theme: SPI success. This common theme considers that, according to his earlier study (Dyba, 2003), all software processes are expected to help organizations deliver a quality product on schedule and on budget for the ultimate purpose of achieving customer satisfaction. In other words, SPI success is anticipated to help increase OP. In this respect, the construct may serve as a reflective measurement. Based on Jarvis et al. (2003) and Petter et al. (2007), the direction of causality is from construct (i.e., the OP of SPI success in this study) to items (i.e., cost, cycle time and customer satisfaction in this study). Accordingly, we operationalized the OP construct as a reflective construct in this study. For the data analysis in his study, Dyba (2005, p.413) addressed the SPI success construct by averaging the ratings of the two performance dimensions (OP and PS) to form a "single" measure of overall SPI success. Nevertheless, this study used another method to operationalize the second-order construct of SPI success by using two first-order reflective constructs (OP and PS) instead of simply averaging them. The method in this study had a better explanatory power (R-square value) for the model.

Two variables (i.e., firm size and industry types) were controlled in this study. Firm size was regarded as a control variable because large firms may have high-level competencies in software development and can command extra resources (Lee and Chen, 2017, p.7). Therefore, firm size was included in the research model since it may impact organizational SPI success, and it was measured as the natural logarithm of the number of employees. Industry types were controlled because they may produce differences in management and strategies for SPI implementation (Staples et al., 2007).

4. DATA ANALYSIS AND RESULTS

The data were empirically examined using PLS structural equation analysis, which is commonly used in the IS literature. PLS is distribution-free, i.e., the estimation is not affected by the complexity of the model, a small sample size, or non-normality in the data; it is orthogonal and overcomes multicollinearity problems (Hair et al., 2013; Lee and Chen, 2017). Analysing a PLS model requires a two-stage approach. The measurement model is first examined to assess reliability and validity, and the structural model is then evaluated to test the relationships among the latent constructs and hypotheses. SmartPLS 3.0 software (Ringle et al, 2015) was employed for the analyses.

4.1. Measurement Model

To validate the measurement model, internal consistency, convergent validity, and discriminant validity were assessed. Internal consistency was examined using composite reliability (CR). Table 3 in the

Appendix shows that all CR > 0.7, with a range of 0.789 to 0.885, which satisfies common acceptable levels, as recommended by Fornell and Larcker (1981). Thus, CR was reliable. Convergent validity was assessed by two criteria (Fornell and Larcker, 1981; Hair et al., 2013): all factor loadings should be significant and greater than 0.7; and average variance extracted (AVE) for each construct should exceed 0.5, as it indicates that 50% or more of the variance was explained by the indicators of the latent variable (Chin, 1998). Table 3 shows that all factor loadings exceed 0.7 and the AVE range was 0.582–0.687, i.e., all AVE were above the recommended level. Thus, the factor loadings and AVEs support convergent validity of the constructs. To confirm discriminant validity, the square root of AVE of a construct should be greater than the correlations between the construct and other constructs in the model (Fornell and Larcker, 1981), as shown in Table 4 in the Appendix. This study also adopted the heterotrait-monotrait ratio of correlations (HTMT) to examine the discriminant validity. All HTMT values were below the accepted value of 0.90; hence, discriminant validity has been established between the two variables (Henseler et al., 2015; see Table 4). Tables 3 and 4 show that convergent and discriminant validity are empirically supported, demonstrating the sufficient construct validity of the scales.

The survey data were self-reported, which means common method bias (CMB) may have occurred (Lee and Chen, 2017). To examine CMB, we conducted Harman's one-factor test (Harman, 1967) by performing an exploratory factor analysis (principal components analysis) with all manifest items. All produced factors had eigenvalues greater than 1, and the first factor accounted for only 29.8% of the total variance. No single factor explained the majority of the variance. Thus, CMB was not significant in this study.

4.2. Structural Model

The proposed hypotheses were tested using the bootstrapping technique, and the significance of all hypotheses was examined via 5000 bootstrap runs (Henseler et al., 2016). The test of the structural model included path coefficients and coefficients of determination (R-square). The path coefficients displayed the strength of the associations between the dependent and independent constructs, and the coefficient of determination (R^2) indicated the amount of variance explained by the independent constructs, representing the predictive power of the model (Lee et al., 2018). Figure 2 shows the main effects, including standardized path coefficients among the constructs, t-value and the variance explained. The positive effect of PAC on RAC is significant ($\beta = 0.651$, $p < 0.001$), supporting H1. Additionally, a positive relationship exists between RAC and SPI success ($\beta = 0.336$, $p < 0.001$), supporting H2. R^2 for SPI success was 0.312, suggesting 31.2% of the variance, which exceeded 10%, indicating substantive explanatory power (Bock et al., 2006).

Based on Ajamieh et al.'s (2016) study, we examined the mediating effect by linking the relationship between PAC and SPI success in the research model (see Figure 2). Then, we followed Hair et al. (2013)'s approach to examine H3. We calculated the variance accounted for (VAF), which determined the size of the indirect effect in relation to the total effect, i.e., direct + indirect effects. Therefore, the VAF = (0.651 * 0.336) / [(0.651 * 0.336) + 0.319] = 0.407, i.e., 40.7% of PAC's effect on SPI success is explained via mediation by RAC. Since 20% < VAF < 80%, this effect can be characterized as partial mediation (Hair et al., 2013).

Figure 3 shows that IC positively enhanced the PAC–RAC relationship ($\beta = 0.311$, $p < 0.01$), supporting H4. Since the proposed model confirmed IC as a moderator of the path from PAC to RAC, the first stage of the mediated effect of PAC on SPI success, a test of moderated mediation is required (Edwards and Lambert, 2007). Accordingly, we conducted Edwards and Lambert's (2007) moderated mediation path analysis. We used Table 5 in the Appendix to illustrate the moderated mediation analysis. Table 5 shows that the indirect effect of PAC on SPI success via RAC was stronger for high IC ($\beta = 0.214$, $p < 0.01$) than for low IC ($\beta = 0.129$, $p < 0.01$). Overall, the differences in the indirect effect were significant ($\triangle\beta = 0.085$, $p < 0.05$), supporting H5. Therefore, IC moderated the mediating effect of RAC on the relationship between PAC and SPI success.

Figure 2. PLS analysis without moderating effect

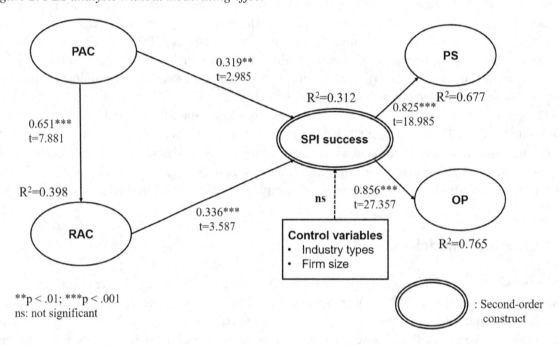

We also examined predictive relevance (Stone-Geisser Q^2). All the cross-validated redundancy Q^2 was greater than 0 (Hair et al., 2013), showing that the constructs of our model possessed predictive relevance. Finally, we used the standardized root mean square residual (SRMR), a measure of the goodness of structural model fit measure for PLS estimations. SRMR = 0.065, demonstrating that the proposed model was rational (Henseler et al., 2016).

5. DISCUSSIONS AND CONCLUSION

5.1. Theoretical Contributions

Our findings offer several important theoretical contributions. First, dynamic capabilities theory and KBV are combined to explain how a firm achieves SPI success through AC and IC. SPI is an organizational learning process (Rus and Lindvall, 2002; Dyba, 2005) and is often aided by external knowledge to support the needs of processes innovation (Ravichandran and Rai, 2003). In the current SPI literature, Dyba

(2005) adopted organizational learning theory as a theoretical basis and indicated that a firm's successful SPI implementation depends on the effective exploration of new software development knowledge and the exploitation of existing knowledge. This study extends to further questions and explores how a firm's learning ability internalizes external SPI knowledge. The nature of software development is dynamic, but the organizational learning and related literature does not address this characteristic (e.g., Lee et al., 2016; Mathiassen & Pourkomeylian, 2003; Niazi et al., 2006; Rus & Lindvall, 2002; Sulayman et al., 2014), leading to the need for AC to advance our understanding of constant learning and the internalization of externally acquired knowledge.

Figure 3. PLS analysis of the moderating effect

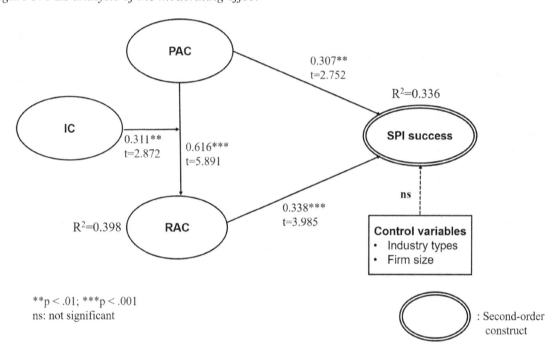

**p < .01; ***p < .001
ns: not significant

In determining the influence of dynamic capability on SPI results, Lee et al. (2017) examined AC in terms of PAC and RAC and studied the mechanisms of SPI success. This study further answers and explains the contextual relationship between PAC and RAC. Strengthening the PAC-RAC linkage is important for firms in dynamic software development environments because this knowledge-intensive linkage helps firms increase their efficiency when acquiring and internalizing SPI knowledge by addressing changing development needs and the need to expedite this development. Regarding the enhancement of the PAC-RAC relationship, Zahra and George (2002) stated that the use of social integration mechanisms (e.g., offering incentive feedback for the donation and application of ideas or knowledge) can promote the connection between PAC and RAC, increasing the efficiency of AC. Leal-Rodríguez et al. (2014) showed that relational learning plays a moderating role by reinforcing the PAC-RAC link. This study focuses on IC and investigates how it, as a contextual factor, boosts the PAC-RAC association during this attempt. Our empirical results demonstrate that PAC significantly influences RAC, which has a positively significant impact on SPI success and partially mediates the effects of PAC on SPI success. Furthermore, IC positively amplifies the relationship between PAC and RAC.

Second, our empirical results demonstrate that PAC acts as a significant antecedent of RAC. Specifically, PAC enables a firm to prepare for and expose itself to external environments to better gather useful external knowledge; then, RAC is based on PAC to further make use of the absorbed knowledge by addressing and implementing similar SPI needs. Furthermore, RAC operates as a partial intermediary in the relationship between PAC and SPI success, as evidenced by the following empirical situation. In the CMMI-based SPI context, the CMMI reference model provides distinct specific goals (SGs) for process areas (PAs) and recommends corresponding specific practices (SPs) that firms may implement to accomplish the required SGs (SEI, 2010). With PAC, the firm can obtain practical external knowledge (e.g., from consulting firms or exchange conferences) regarding the implementation of SPs. With RAC, the firm can integrate and combine external know-how with the firm's own existing methods to improve and customize practices that meet the firm's goal and accommodate the firm's characteristics. PAC and RAC have different natures and involve distinctive behaviours but are complementary in constructing AC as a whole, which helps the firm to learn and use external SPI knowledge to accomplish SPI in accordance with a CMMI's goals and practices.

Additionally, the findings of this study do not indicate the expected full mediation between PAC, RAC and SPI success (i.e., H3), which may be because PAC can be seen as a catalyst to induce a firm's intention to engage in behaviour that initiates SPI-related learning activities, a critical premise for a firm aiming to achieve successful SPI implementation. Without PAC, participating firms that conducted SPI by implementing CMMI were unable obtain and select useful external references when learning how to implement the improvement goals and practices specified in the model. This factor may also be critical to SPI success. In addition, the empirical evidence implies that PAC possesses the capability to individually foster SPI success. Nevertheless, if firms aim to widely realize and sustain SPI success, RAC is still needed, as it helps the firm to extensively transform and exploit SPI knowledge for similar and future SPI actions.

Finally, compared to a prior study (Lee et al., 2017) that explored and established the relationship between PAC, RAC and SPI success, this study not only further determines the causality of PAC and RAC but also discovers the determinant (IC) to amplify their contribution to SPI success. Specifically, our results show that IC has a critical contextual role to reinforce the path from PAC to RAC. Thus, while the effectiveness of a firm's RAC generally depends on its PAC, this dependence becomes stronger when a higher IC level is present. In software development, which is innovative in nature, process improvements often involve innovative changes or breakthroughs, such as a shift in the development process from a traditional waterfall to an agile approach, which requires the entire organization to buy in. Firms with stronger IC are characterized by intensive communication, embrace of change and a high degree of openness to new or unconventional thoughts or practices (Aksoy, 2017; Olmospeñuela et al., 2017). This situation spurs the firm's propensity toward a dynamic external business environment, helping it become more active in accepting and accommodating external SPI knowledge, which may appear conflicting or inconsistent to the firm. This situation triggers the firm to strengthen the transfer, diffusion and utilization of the newly absorbed SPI knowledge, thus reinforcing RAC mechanisms in terms of transformation and the ability to evolve more effectively. In other words, when a firm has a high level of IC, the synergetic relationship between PAC and RAC is further promoted.

Moreover, stronger IC also amplifies the indirect effect of RAC on the relationship between PAC and SPI success, which implies that IC encourages firms to become actively involved in the quest for external knowledge while simultaneously tightening the link between PAC and RAC, providing greater potency for SPI. This study extends KBV to empirically confirm the conceptual argument of Volberda et al. (2010) that a firm's AC mechanism strengthened under suitable contextual factors, i.e., IC as investigated here, and higher dynamic capability levels, i.e., AC, can be achieved. Thus, a firm with higher AC has relatively efficient SPI knowledge absorption, leading to more positive SPI implementation.

5.2. Practical Implications

This study has major managerial implications. First, AC is an interactive process between learning and applying knowledge to improve and enhance organizational capability, and human resources are at the centre of this process (Valentim et al., 2016). A firm's AC resides in employees and can be activated with effective human resource practices. Firms should invest in employees by offering more education and enriching the job design to foster greater AC and should promote advanced competence to keep pace with the dynamic and changing business environment. For example, firms could encourage and sponsor employees to take part in external educational venues, such as conferences, workshops, and professional exhibitions. Effective human resource practices should include job rotation, multi-skill training, and broadly designed jobs in order to broaden employee knowledge in software development and process improvement (Chang et al., 2013) and enable them to absorb knowledge that is not limited to the job scope, which in turn contributes holistically to SPI implementation. In the SPI context, learning from outside the organization requires more than just the acquisition and exploitation of external SPI knowledge. Firms need to update and reconfigure their knowledge stock for superior implementation outcomes. To achieve this, a firm should share its own SPI knowledge with other organizations and thereby receive valuable knowledge feedback. This process will extend a firm's AC to include outside firms' learning abilities.

Second, firms should provide informal means or venues to support the organizational process of implementing acquired SPI knowledge. For example, firms should establish innovative ways to participate more actively in informal knowledge exchanges, e.g., conversations in the cafeteria or social media (Facebook, etc.), to stimulate SPI knowledge flows throughout the organization. Social media makes it easier for relevant employees to acquire and understand SPI knowledge. Ooms et al. (2015) showed that social media enables multi-directional and interactive knowledge exchange, which contributes to AC. Thus, encouraging employees to be involved in social media communities helps synthesize acquired SPI knowledge into current organizational knowledge and broadens the utilization of new knowledge when implementing SPI.

Finally, the effect of a firm's PAC on its RAC can be increased by IC since knowing how to apply knowledge to various work domains or different projects requires creativity and imagination. An important role of organizational leadership is to reinforce an active IC, e.g., reward systems must be designed to encourage innovation. Furthermore, assigning activity ownership and giving employees the authority to make decisions regarding trying new things are also encouraged. Firms should embrace divergent thinking, listen to employees, be open to new ideas, and provide employees with appropriate resources in turning new ideas into action. Firms with greater IC will achieve a better response from the dynamic software development environment and consolidate positive SPI implementation outcomes.

6. LIMITATIONS AND FURTHER RESEARCH

Despite the above contributions, the current study has several limitations and opportunities for further research. This study included only SPI-certified firms in the Asia-Pacific region; hence, the findings lack generalizability, which is an opportunity for future work. While the CMMI-based SPI-certified samples were appropriate for the research design, this study did not distinguish SPI success in terms of different CMMI maturity levels, i.e., levels 2-5, and the purpose of this study was to investigate the distinct impacts of PAC, RAC and IC on SPI success. Thus, future research should replicate these empirical results for different maturity levels. Finally, because the data in this study are cross-sectional in nature, future research should perform a longitudinal study to better establish causality for the hypothesized relationships.

ACKNOWLEDGMENT

We would like to thank the associate editor and the four reviewers for their constructive comments and suggestions regarding the earlier drafts of this study. The research is supported by the Program for Research Development of Beijing Normal University Zhuhai.

REFERENCES

Abubakre, M., Coombs, C. R., & Ravishankar, M. N. (2017). The impact of salient cultural practices on the outcome of IS implementation. *Journal of Global Information Management*, 25(1), 1–20. doi:10.4018/JGIM.2017010101

Agarwal, R., & Prasad, J. (2000). A field study of the adoption of software process innovations by information systems professionals. *IEEE Transactions on Engineering Management*, 47(3), 295–308. doi:10.1109/17.865899

Ajamieh, A., Benitez, J., Braojos, J., & Gelhard, C. (2016). IT infrastructure and competitive aggressiveness in explaining and predicting performance. *Journal of Business Research*, 69(10), 4667–4674. doi:10.1016/j.jbusres.2016.03.056

Aksoy, H. (2017). How do innovation culture, marketing innovation and product innovation affect the market performance of small and medium-sized enterprises (SMEs)? *Technology in Society*, 51, 133–141. doi:10.1016/j.techsoc.2017.08.005

Alagarsamy, K., Justus, S., & Lyakutti, K. (2008). Implementation specification for software process improvement supportive knowledge management tool. *IET Software*, 2(2), 123–133. doi:10.1049/iet-sen:20070086

Alavi, M., & Leidner, D. E. (2006). An empirical examination of the influence of organizational culture on knowledge management practices. *Journal of Management Information Systems*, 22(3), 191–224. doi:10.2753/MIS0742-1222220307

Albort-Morant, G., Leal-Rodríguez, A. L., Henseler, J., & Cepeda-Carrion, G. A. (2018). Potential and realized absorptive capacity as complementary drivers of green product and process innovation performance. *Sustainability*, *10*(2), 381. doi:10.3390u10020381

Ali, M., & Park, K. (2016). The mediating role of an innovative culture in the relationship between absorptive capacity and technical and non-technical innovation. *Journal of Business Research*, *43*(4), 1680–1687.

Armstrong, J. S., & Overton, T. S. (1977). Estimating nonresponse bias in mail surveys. *JMR, Journal of Marketing Research*, *14*(3), 396–402. doi:10.2307/3150783

Bharati, P., Zhang, C., & Chaudhury, A. (2014). Social media assimilation in firms: Investigating the roles of absorptive capacity and institutional pressures. *Information Systems Frontiers*, *16*(2), 257–27. doi:10.100710796-013-9433-x

Bock, G. W., Kankanhalli, A., & Sharma, S. (2006). Are norms enough? the role of collaborative norms in promoting organizational knowledge seeking. *European Journal of Information Systems*, *15*(4), 357–367. doi:10.1057/palgrave.ejis.3000630

Brettel, M., & Cleven, N. J. (2011). Innovation culture, collaboration with external partners and NPD performance. *Creativity and Innovation Management*, *20*(4), 253–272. doi:10.1111/j.1467-8691.2011.00617.x

Camisón, C., & Forés, B. (2010). Knowledge absorptive capacity: New insights for its conceptualization and measurement. *Journal of Business Research*, *63*(7), 707–715. doi:10.1016/j.jbusres.2009.04.022

Castro, M. D., Delgado-Verde, M., Navas-López, J. E., & Cruz-González, J. (2013). The moderating role of innovation culture in the relationship between knowledge assets and product innovation. *Technological Forecasting and Social Change*, *80*(2), 351–363. doi:10.1016/j.techfore.2012.08.012

Chang, S., Gong, Y., Way, S. A., & Jia, L. (2013). Flexibility-oriented FRM systems, absorptive capacity, and market responsiveness and firm innovativeness. *Journal of Management*, *39*(7), 1924–1951. doi:10.1177/0149206312466145

Joshi, K. D., Chi, L., Datta, A., & Han, S. (2010). Changing the competitive landscape: Continuous innovation through it-enabled knowledge capabilities. *Information Systems Research*, *21*(3), 472–495. doi:10.1287/isre.1100.0298

CMMI Institute. (2010). *CMMI for development quick reference*. Retrieved from https://cmmiinstitute.com/getattachment/6807c668-a92d-405a-894d-014876dcafb9/attachment.aspx

Cohen, W. M., & Levinthal, D. A. (1990). Absorptive capacity: A new perspective on learning and innovation. *Administrative Science Quarterly*, *35*(1), 128–152. doi:10.2307/2393553

Dyba, T. (2003). A dynamic model of software engineering knowledge creation. Managing software engineering knowledge. Springer Berlin Heidelberg. 95-117.

Dyba, T. (2005). An empirical investigation of the key factors for success in software process improvement. *IEEE Transactions on Software Engineering*, *31*(5), 410–424. doi:10.1109/TSE.2005.53

Edwards, J. R., & Lambert, L. S. (2007). Methods for integrating moderation and mediation: A general analytical framework using moderated path analysis. *Psychological Methods*, *12*(1), 1–22. doi:10.1037/1082-989X.12.1.1 PMID:17402809

Egorova, E., Torchiano, M., & Morisio, M. (2009). Evaluating the perceived effect of software engineering practices in the Italian industry. In *Trustworthy Software Development Processes* (pp. 100–111). Springer Berlin Heidelberg. doi:10.1007/978-3-642-01680-6_11

Feher, P., & Gabor, A. (2010). The role of knowledge management supporters in software development companies. *Software Process Improvement and Practice*, *11*(3), 251–260. doi:10.1002pip.269

Fornell, C., & Larcker, D. F. (1981). Evaluating structural equation models with unobservable variables and measurement error. *JMR, Journal of Marketing Research*, *18*(1), 39–50. doi:10.2307/3151312

Fosfuri, A., & Tribó, J. A. (2008). Exploring the antecedents of potential absorptive capacity and its impact on innovation performance. *Omega*, *36*(2), 173–187. doi:10.1016/j.omega.2006.06.012 PMID:18680889

Grant, R. M. (1996). Toward a knowledge-based theory of the firm. *Strategic Management Journal*, *17*(S2), 109–122. doi:10.1002mj.4250171110

Hair, J. F., Hult, G. T. M., Ringle, C., & Sarstedt, M. (2013). *A primer on partial least squares structural equation modeling (PLS-SEM)*. SAGE Publications.

Harman, H. (1967). *Modern factor analysis*. Chicago: University of Chicago Press.

Harrington, S. J., & Guimaraes, T. (2005). Corporate culture, absorptive capacity and it success. *Information and Organization*, *15*(1), 39–63. doi:10.1016/j.infoandorg.2004.10.002

Henseler, J., Hubona, G., & Ray, P. A. (2016). Using PLS path modeling in new technology research: Updated guidelines. *Industrial Management & Data Systems*, *116*(1), 2–20. doi:10.1108/IMDS-09-2015-0382

Henseler, J., Ringle, C. M., & Sarstedt, M. (2015). A new criterion for assessing discriminant validity in variance-based structural equation modeling. *Journal of the Academy of Marketing Science*, *43*(1), 115–135. doi:10.100711747-014-0403-8

Jansen, J. J. P., Bosch, F. A. J., & Volberda, H. W. (2005). Managing potential and realized absorptive capacity: How do organizational antecedents matter? *Academy of Management Journal*, *48*(6), 999–1015. doi:10.5465/amj.2005.19573106

Janz, B. D., & Prasarnphanich, P. (2003). Understanding the antecedents of effective knowledge management: The importance of a knowledge-centered culture. *Decision Sciences*, *34*(2), 351–384. doi:10.1111/1540-5915.02328

Jarvis, C. B., Mackenzie, S. B., & Podsakoff, P. M. (2003). A critical review of construct indicators and measurement model misspecification in marketing and consumer research. *The Journal of Consumer Research*, *30*(2), 199–218. doi:10.1086/376806

Jones, M. C., Cline, M., & Ryan, S. (2006). Exploring knowledge sharing in ERP implementation: An organizational culture framework. *Decision Support Systems*, *41*(2), 411–434. doi:10.1016/j.dss.2004.06.017

Ke, W., & Wei, K. K. (2008). Organizational culture and leadership in ERP implementation. *Decision Support Systems*, *45*(2), 208–218. doi:10.1016/j.dss.2007.02.002

Ko, D. G., Kirsch, L. J., & King, W. R. (2005). Antecedents of knowledge transfer from consultants to clients in enterprise system implementations. *Management Information Systems Quarterly*, *29*(1), 59–85. doi:10.2307/25148668

Lane, P. J., Koka, B. R., & Pathak, S. (2006). The reification of absorptive capacity: A critical review and rejuvenation of the construct. *Academy of Management Review*, *31*(4), 833–863. doi:10.5465/amr.2006.22527456

Larrucea, X., O'Connor, R. V., Colomopalacios, R., & Laporte, C. Y. (2016). Software process improvement in very small organizations. *IEEE Software*, *33*(2), 85–89. doi:10.1109/MS.2016.42

Leal-Rodríguez, A. L., Roldán, J. L., Ariza-Montes, J. A., & Leal-Millán, A. (2014). From potential absorptive capacity to innovation outcomes in project teams: The conditional mediating role of the realized absorptive capacity in a relational learning context. *International Journal of Project Management*, *32*(6), 894–907. doi:10.1016/j.ijproman.2014.01.005

Lee, J. C., & Chen, C. Y. (2017). Exploring the determinants of software process improvement success: A dynamic capability view. *Information Development*, *2017*. doi:10.1177/0266666917724194

Lee, J. C., Chen, C. Y., & Shiue, Y. C. (2017). The moderating effects of organisational culture on the relationship between absorptive capacity and software process improvement success. *Information Technology & People*, *30*(1), 47–70. doi:10.1108/ITP-09-2013-0171

Lee, J. C., Hsu, W. C., & Chen, C. Y. (2018). Impact of absorptive capability on software process improvement and firm performance. *Information Technology Management*, *19*(1), 21–35. doi:10.100710799-016-0272-6

Lee, J. C., Shiue, Y. C., & Chen, C. Y. (2016). Examining the impacts of organizational culture and top management support of knowledge sharing on the success of software process improvement. *Computers in Human Behavior*, *54*, 462–474. doi:10.1016/j.chb.2015.08.030

Lee, W. T., Hung, S.-Y., & Chau, P. Y. K. (2011). Influence of knowledge management infrastructure on innovative business processes and market-interrelationship performance: An empirical study of hospitals in Taiwan. *Journal of Global Information Management*, *19*(2), 67–89. doi:10.4018/jgim.2011040104

Leidner, D. E., & Kayworth, T. (2006). Review: a review of culture in information systems research: toward a theory of information technology culture conflict. *Management Information Systems Quarterly*, *30*(30), 357–399. doi:10.2307/25148735

March, J. G. (1991). Exploration and exploitation in organizational learning. *Organization Science*, *2*(1), 71–87. doi:10.1287/orsc.2.1.71

Mathiassen, L., & Pourkomeylian, P. (2003). Managing knowledge in a software organization. *Journal of Knowledge Management*, *7*(2), 63–80. doi:10.1108/13673270310477298

Matusik, S. F., & Heeley, M. B. (2005). Absorptive capacity in the software industry: Identifying dimensions that affect knowledge and knowledge creation activities. *Journal of Management, 31*(4), 549–572. doi:10.1177/0149206304272293

Meehan, B., & Richardson, I. (2010). Identification of software process knowledge management. *Software Process Improvement and Practice, 7*(2), 47–55. doi:10.1002pip.154

Moreno, V., Pinheiro, J. R. M., & Joia, L. A. (2012). Resource-based view, knowledge-based view and the performance of software development companies: A study of Brazilian SMEs. *Journal of Global Information Management, 20*(4), 27–53. doi:10.4018/jgim.2012100102

Mueller, J. (2014). A specific knowledge culture: Cultural antecedents for knowledge sharing between project teams. *European Management Journal, 32*(2), 190–202. doi:10.1016/j.emj.2013.05.006

Nemeth, C. J. (1997). Managing innovation: When less is more. *California Management Review, 40*(1), 59–74. doi:10.2307/41165922

Niazi, M., Wilson, D., & Zowghi, D. (2010). Critical success factors for software process improvement implementation: An empirical study. *Software Process Improvement and Practice, 11*(2), 193–211. doi:10.1002pip.261

Nonaka, I., & Takeuchi, H. (1995). *The knowledge-creating company: how Japanese companies create the dynamics of innovation*. New York: Oxford University Press.

Olmospeñuela, J., Garcíagranero, A., Castromartínez, E., & D'Este, P. (2017). Strengthening smes' innovation culture through collaborations with public research organizations. do all firms benefit equally? *European Planning Studies*. doi:10.1080/09654313.2017.1279592

Ooms, W., Bell, J., & Kok, R. A. W. (2015). Use of social media in inbound open innovation: Building capabilities for absorptive capacity. *Creativity and Innovation Management, 24*(1), 136–150. doi:10.1111/caim.12105

Pavlou, P. A., & Sawy, O. A. E. (2006). From it leveraging competence to competitive advantage in turbulent environments: The case of new product development. *Information Systems Research, 17*(3), 198–227. doi:10.1287/isre.1060.0094

Peng, G., Dey, D., & Lahiri, A. (2014). Healthcare it adoption: An analysis of knowledge transfer in socioeconomic networks. *Journal of Management Information Systems, 31*(3), 7–34. doi:10.1080/074 21222.2014.994672

Petter, S., Straub, D., & Rai, A. (2007). Specifying formative constructs in information systems research. *Management Information Systems Quarterly, 31*(4), 623–656. doi:10.2307/25148814

Rainer, A., & Hall, T. (2002). Key success factors for implementing software process improvement: A maturity-based analysis. *Journal of Systems and Software, 62*(2), 71–84. doi:10.1016/S0164-1212(01)00122-4

Ravichandran, T., & Rai, A. (2003). Structural analysis of the impact of knowledge creation and knowledge embedding on software process capability. *IEEE Transactions on Engineering Management, 50*(3), 270–284. doi:10.1109/TEM.2003.817278

Ringle, C. M., Wende, S., & Becker, J. M. (2015). SmartPLS 3. Boenningstedt: SmartPLS GmbH. Retrieved from http://www.smartpls.com

Roberts, N. H., Galluch, P. S., Dinger, M., & Grover, V. (2012). Absorptive capacity and information systems research: Review, synthesis, and directions for future research. *Management Information Systems Quarterly*, *36*(2), 625–648.

Rus, I., & Lindvall, M. (2002). Guest editors' introduction: Knowledge management in software engineering. *IEEE Software*, *19*(3), 26–38. doi:10.1109/MS.2002.1003450

Saemundsson, R. J., & Candi, M. (2017). Absorptive capacity and the identification of opportunities in new technology-based firms. *Technovation*, *64*, 43–49. doi:10.1016/j.technovation.2017.06.001

Saraf, N., Liang, H., Xue, Y., & Hu, Q. (2013). How does organisational absorptive capacity matter in the assimilation of enterprise information systems? *Information Systems Journal*, *23*(3), 245–267. doi:10.1111/j.1365-2575.2011.00397.x

Sharma, S., Daniel, E. M., & Gray, C. (2012). Absorptive capacity and ERP implementation in Indian medium-sized firms. *Journal of Global Information Management*, *20*(4), 54–79. doi:10.4018/jgim.2012100103

Shih, C. C., & Huang, S. J. (2010). Exploring the relationship between organizational culture and software process improvement deployment. *Information & Management*, *47*(5), 271–281. doi:10.1016/j.im.2010.06.001

Staples, M., Niazi, M., Jeffery, R., Abrahams, A., Byatt, P., & Murphy, R. (2007). An exploratory study of why organizations do not adopt CMMI. *Journal of Systems and Software*, *80*(6), 883–895. doi:10.1016/j.jss.2006.09.008

Sulayman, M., Mendes, E., Urquhart, C., Riaz, M., & Tempero, E. (2014). Towards a theoretical framework of SPI success factors for small and medium web companies. *Information and Software Technology*, *56*(7), 807–820. doi:10.1016/j.infsof.2014.02.006

Sun, P. Y. T., & Anderson, M. H. (2010). An examination of the relationship between absorptive capacity and organizational learning, and a proposed integration. *International Journal of Management Reviews*, *12*(2), 130–150. doi:10.1111/j.1468-2370.2008.00256.x

Teece, D. J., Pisano, G. P., & Shuen, A. (1997). Dynamic capabilities and strategic management. *Strategic Management Journal*, *18*(7), 509–533. doi:10.1002/(SICI)1097-0266(199708)18:7<509::AID-SMJ882>3.0.CO;2-Z

Uskarci, A., & Demirors, O. (2017). Do staged maturity models result in organization-wide continuous process improvement? insight from employees. *Computer Standards & Interfaces*, *52*, 25–40. doi:10.1016/j.csi.2017.01.008

Valentim, L., Lisboa, J. V., & Franco, M. (2016). Knowledge management practices and absorptive capacity in small and medium-sized enterprises: Is there really a linkage? *R & D Management*, *46*(4), 711–725. doi:10.1111/radm.12108

Volberda, H. W., Foss, N. J., & Lyles, M. A. (2010). Absorbing the concept of absorptive capacity: How to realize its potential in the organization field. *Organization Science*, *21*(4), 931–951. doi:10.1287/orsc.1090.0503

Wei, J., Lowry, P. B., & Seedorf, S. (2015). The assimilation of RFID technology by Chinese companies: A technology diffusion perspective. *Information & Management*, *52*(6), 628–642. doi:10.1016/j.im.2015.05.001

Winkelbach, A., & Walter, A. (2015). Complex technological knowledge and value creation in science-to-industry technology transfer projects: The moderating effect of absorptive capacity. *Industrial Marketing Management*, *47*, 98–108. doi:10.1016/j.indmarman.2015.02.035

Winter, J., & Rönkkö, K. (2010). SPI success factors within product usability evaluation. *Journal of Systems and Software*, *83*(11), 2059–2072. doi:10.1016/j.jss.2010.04.066

Xu, P., & Ramesh, B. (2007). Software process tailoring: An empirical investigation. *Journal of Management Information Systems*, *24*(2), 293–328. doi:10.2753/MIS0742-1222240211

Zahra, S. A., & George, G. (2002). Absorptive capacity: A review, reconceptualization, and extension. *Academy of Management Review*, *27*(2), 185–203. doi:10.5465/amr.2002.6587995

Zahra, S. A., Sapienza, H. J., & Davidsson, P. (2006). Entrepreneurship and dynamic capabilities: A review, model and research agenda. *Journal of Management Studies*, *43*(4), 917–955. doi:10.1111/j.1467-6486.2006.00616.x

This research was previously published in the Journal of Global Information Management (JGIM), 27(4); pages 70-90, copyright year 2019 by IGI Publishing (an imprint of IGI Global).

APPENDIX

Table 1. Characteristics of the samples (N=68 from Taiwan, N=57 from Mainland China)

Industry type	Frequency	Percentage
Characteristics of the Organizations		
Information technology	70	56.0%
Manufacturing	36	28.8%
Research institute	8	6.4%
Finance	6	4.8%
Education	3	2.4%
Health care	2	1.6%
Number of employees		
Below 50	30	24.0%
50–100	36	28.8%
100–500	32	25.6%
500–1000	17	13.6%
Above 1000	10	8.0%
Characteristics of the Respondents		
Job Position		
CEO	5	4.0%
Vice/Assistant president	9	7.2%
General manager	36	28.8%
Manager	75	60.0%
Education		
Bachelor's degree	42	33.6%
Master's degree	64	51.2%
Doctorate	19	15.2%
Work Experience		
1–5 years	16	12.8%
6–10 years	61	48.8%
11–15 years	31	24.8%
16–20 years	10	8.0%
Above 21 years	7	5.6%

Table 2. Measurement instrument

Construct	Items	Adapted From
Potential absorptive capacity (PAC)	(PAC1) We are able to identify and acquire internal and external knowledge.	Pavlou and El Sawy (2006)
	(PAC2) We have routines to identify, value, and import new information and knowledge.	
	(PAC3) We have adequate routines to analyse the information and knowledge obtained.	
	(PAC4) We have adequate routines to assimilate new information and knowledge.	
Realized absorptive capacity (RAC)	(RAC1) We can successfully integrate our existing information into new knowledge.	
	(RAC2) We are effective in transforming existing information into new knowledge.	
	(RAC3) We can successfully exploit internal and external information and knowledge into concrete applications.	
	(RAC4) We are effective in utilizing knowledge into new products or services.	
Perceived level of SPI success (PS)	(PS1) Our SPI work has substantially increased our software engineering competence.	Dyba (2005)
	(PS2) Our SPI work has substantially improved our overall performance.	
Organizational performance (OP)	(OP1) Over the past three years, we have greatly reduced the cost of software development.	
	(OP2) Over the past three years, we have greatly reduced the cycle time of software development.	
	(OP3) Over the past three years, we have greatly increased our customers' satisfaction.	
Innovation culture (IC)	(IC1) Our company encourages creativity, innovation and/or the development of new ideas in software development processes.	Castro et al. (2013)
	(IC2) A common system of values, beliefs and objectives exists in our company, directed towards innovation.	
	(IC3) Our company encourages experimentation and innovation in order to improve software development processes.	

Table 3. Measurement model results

Construct/Indicator	Factor Loadings	AVE	CR
Potential absorptive capacity (PAC)		0.582	0.847
PAC1	0.712		
PAC2	0.731		
PAC3	0.788		
PAC4	0.815		
Realized absorptive capacity (RAC)		0.658	0.885
RAC1	0.786		
RAC2	0.830		
RAC3	0.812		
RAC4	0.815		
Level of perceived SPI success (PS)		0.651	0.789
PS1	0.836		
PS2	0.777		
Organizational performance (OP)		0.584	0.808
OP1	0.719		
OP2	0.758		
OP3	0.812		
Innovation culture (IC)		0.687	0.868
IC1	0.785		
IC2	0.876		
IC3	0.823		

Table 4. Correlation of the constructs, the square root of AVEs and the HTMT

Construct	OP	PAC	PS	RAC	IC
OP	**0.764**				
PAC	0.468 (0.522)	**0.763**			
PS	0.412 (0.758)	0.372 (0.228)	**0.807**		
RAC	0.489 (0.558)	0.539 (0.605)	0.351 (0.209)	**0.811**	
IC	0.377 (0.309)	0.455 (0.511)	0.568 (0.612)	0.365 (0.217)	**0.829**

Note: Square root of AVEs on diagonal in boldface. The values in parentheses are the HTMT.

Table 5. Moderated mediation path analysis

Moderating Variable	PAC (X) → RAC (M) → SPI Success (Y)				
	Stage		Effect		
	First (P_{MX})	Second (P_{YM})	Direct (P_{YX})	Indirect $(P_{YM}P_{MX})$	Total $(P_{YX} + P_{YM}P_{MX})$
High levels of innovation culture	0.625***	0.342***	0.317**	0.214**	0.531**
Low levels of innovation culture	0.392**	0.330***	0.302**	0.129**	0.431**
Differences	0.033*	0.12*	0.015	0.085*	0.10*

Note: N = 125; * $p < 0.05$; ** $p < 0.01$; *** $p < 0.001$ (two-tailed test); PAC = potential absorptive capacity; RAC = realized absorptive capacity; SPI = software process improvement. P_{MX} = path from PAC to RAC; P_{YM} = path from RAC to SPI success; P_{YX} = path from PAC to SPI success; Tests of differences for the indirect and total effect were based on bias-corrected confidence intervals derived from bootstrap estimates.

Chapter 52
Metaheuristic Techniques for Test Case Generation:
A Review

Rashmi Rekha Sahoo

ITER College, Siksha 'O' Anusandhan University, Bhubaneswar, India

Mitrabinda Ray

ITER College, Siksha 'O' Anusandhan University, Bhubaneswar, India

ABSTRACT

The primary objective of software testing is to locate bugs as many as possible in software by using an optimum set of test cases. Optimum set of test cases are obtained by selection procedure which can be viewed as an optimization problem. So metaheuristic optimizing (searching) techniques have been immensely used to automate software testing task. The application of metaheuristic searching techniques in software testing is termed as Search Based Testing. Non-redundant, reliable and optimized test cases can be generated by the search based testing with less effort and time. This article presents a systematic review on several meta heuristic techniques like Genetic Algorithms, Particle Swarm optimization, Ant Colony Optimization, Bee Colony optimization, Cuckoo Searches, Tabu Searches and some modified version of these algorithms used for test case generation. The authors also provide one framework, showing the advantages, limitations and future scope or gap of these research works which will help in further research on these works.

INTRODUCTION

Generation of test cases is one of the key steps of software testing task. Automatic test case generation can reduce the time of the testing process. Nature inspired algorithms play an important role in automatic/semi-automatic generation of suitable test cases for a software. The main aim of evolutionary testing is to achieve high degree of automation with quality tests in low cost (Kumar et al., 2011). Exhaustive

DOI: 10.4018/978-1-6684-3702-5.ch052

testing is impossible as the solution domain (number of possible test cases for a software under test) is very huge or may be infinite. So, it is required to select the test cases that find out maximum faults with greater coverage and minimum cost. An optimization problem means to find a best solution from all possible solutions. To avoid the so-called problems of time, cost and efficiency, test suite with minimum number of test cases should be designed to achieve maximum coverage (code / requirements coverage), maximum fault detecting capability/ mutant killing score with minimum execution efforts and cost. So, test cases optimization can be defined as a multi objective optimization problem (Roshan et al., 2012). It cannot be solved in combinatorial time and hence it is a Np-hard problem (McMinn, 2011). These types of problems are solved satisfactorily using metaheuristic searching techniques. Some of the optimization techniques that have been successfully applied to test data generation are Genetic Algorithm, Tabu Search, Ant Colony Optimization, Particle Swarm Optimization, Cuckoo Search, Hill Climbing, Simulated Annealing etc. (Harman et al., 2015). In this paper, the strengths and weaknesses of the existing work in the said methods have been identified and future research directions has been suggested.

This paper is organized as follows: This paper provides a Section on the background study of several existing metaheuristic techniques and some widely used test case generation techniques. Next Section presents a systematic review on various search based testing methods. After systematic review, there is a Section containing comprehensive outline of our review. Then, the conclusion is presented in the end Section.

BACKGROUND

Meta Heuristic Search Based Techniques

A metaheuristic is a higher-level procedure to find a heuristic to provide a sufficiently good solution to an optimization problem, especially with incomplete or imperfect information or limited computation capacity (Harman et al., 2007). According to search strategies, it can be classified as local search and global search methods. Global algorithms make balance between exploration and exploitation of the search space by providing globally best solution. These algorithms terminate when a user defined stopping criteria is met. Unlike global search algorithm, local search algorithms do not give emphasis to exploration. They try to find a good solution among the neighbouring solutions. These algorithms terminate when they do not get any better neighbour solution and hence becomes locally optimal (Leonora et al., 2009) (see Figure 1).

In this section, some most widely used local search algorithms like Hill Climbing (HC), Tabu Search (TS) and Simulated Annealing (SA) and global search algorithms like Genetic Algorithm (GA), Particle Swarm Optimization (PSO), Ant Colony Optimization (ACO), Artificial Bee Colony (ABC) and Cuckoo Search (CS) are discussed. Also, their advantages and disadvantages and their application in suitable problems are mainly focused.

Local Search Methods

Hill Climbing is an iterative algorithm that starts with a random solution to a problem, then attempts to find a better solution by incrementally changing a single element of the solution (Ali et al., 2010). The major disadvantage is its maximum probability of getting stuck at a poor local optimum. An alternative to Hill Climbing is Simulated Annealing. Searching process in Simulated Annealing is similar to Hill Climbing, except movement around the search space is less restricted. This is guided by the probability value of 'temperature' parameter (Pirim et al., 2008). The major disadvantage is that it depends on the logic that a slow descent will lead to a local optimum that is closer to a global one. Tabu Search is based on the iterative improvements like Simulated Annealing. To overcome the limitations of local optimality it uses many methods, such as linear programming algorithms and specialized heuristics. TS is the only heuristic search having the memory property and maintains a search list, called as *tabu list* (Pirim et al., 2008). *'History'* data structure is maintained in TS to avoid local optima problem in which the last created solutions (moves) are recorded. The major advantage of TS is the avoidance of stagnation of memory at local optimum due to the use of data structure, history.

Figure 1. Search based methods

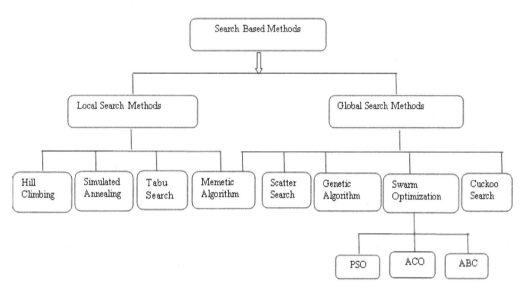

Global Search Methods

Genetic Algorithm mimics the process of biological evolution. It uses two genetic operators named mutation and crossover (Glover, 1995). Smaller mutation rate is taken to generate different solutions and to explore different areas of the search space (Glover, 1994). GA suffers from large number of iterations and premature convergence. Particle Swarm Optimization imitates the behaviour of bird flocking. Unlike GA, it has no cross over and mutation operator. Here particles are the candidate solutions and they move through the solution domain by following a current optimum solution (Selvi et al., 2010). PSO has fewer parameters in comparison to GA. PSO is applicable for the problems which are fuzzy in nature. It is not applicable for the problems which are crisp in nature. Ant Colony Optimization is a probabilistic technique to solve optimization problem. Combinatorial optimisation problems can be solved using ACO. It is more applicable where the source and destinations are predefined and specific. It can be applied for the problem which needs crisp result (Selvi et al., 2010). In this algorithm ants represent the stochastic solution construction procedures (Talbi, 2009). Its convergence is guaranteed but time to convergence is uncertain. It is prone to falling in the local optimal solution. Exploration may not be sufficient (Gunavathi et al., 2014). It is not so efficient for multimodal and multivariable problems. Artificial Bee Colony Optimization (ABC) algorithm produces better results on multimodal and multivariable problems than other algorithms considered in this paper. This algorithm mimics the foraging behaviour of honey bees and their work distribution skill to collect sufficient amount of honey for their survival. In ABC, employed and onlooker bees do local search, scout bees do the global search and they maintain a balance between exploration and exploitation process (Karaboga, 2009). Cuckoo search (CS) is based on the brood parasitism of some cuckoo species. In addition, this algorithm is enhanced and could perform efficient search by the use of Levy flights (Karaboga, 2009). It requires a very few parameters to be adjusted in comparison to other algorithms discussed in this paper. CS is a very simple algorithm and easy to implement, it outperforms other evolutionary algorithms such as GA, PSO, Tabu Search and ABC (Yang et al., 2009). Based on the experimental results, CS also improves the performances such as computation and time, convergence rate and cost.

AUTOMATIC TEST CASE GENERATION TECHNIQUES

There are several techniques available for automatic test case generation. In this section, we briefly discuss some widely used techniques like random testing, symbolic execution, model based testing and combinatorial testing and pros and cons of these techniques. Random Testing is the simplest test case generation technique among all the techniques. Random input test data are generated to test the software (Anand et al., 2013). As it is generated randomly, many of the test data are redundant which incur wastage of time. Though some variants like adaptive random test case generation techniques and its extensions are proposed still, for complex software it remains a problem for generating efficient test data. Symbolic Execution (King, 1975) is a data analysis technique. Instead of concrete values, symbolic values are taken as program input. This approach is widely used because it is able to solve complex constraints. But it not possible to solve all types of constraint with symbolic execution as test case generation is an undecidable problem. It suffers from three major problems; path explosion, path constraint and complex constraints (Anand et al., 2013). Though many researches tried to solve these problems still, these are the open problems for future research. In Model Based Testing test cases are generated from the model. It is a much-demanded technique as it can find faults at early stage of software development. But the major drawback with model based testing is model designing is too difficult for large and complex software and there are ample scope to miss bugs with generated test data (EI-Far et al., 2001). Combinatorial Testing considers all variable's values pairwise for test case generation to find flaws. Though the test cases generated from this technique give maximum coverage but the time and number of test case requirement increase exponentially (Anand et al., 2013).

These techniques for automatic test case generation is constrained by the size and complexity of software. As test case generation is also an undecided problem, these approaches cannot challenge to provide effective and efficient test cases. But metaheuristic search techniques show much potential regarding these problems.

SYSTEMATIC REVIEW ON TEST CASE GENERATION USING SEARCHING TECHNIQUES

In this section, we discuss the use of most widely used metaheuristic algorithms in software test case generation. Algorithm wise the section is organized into subsections. This gives an insight into pros and cons of using the algorithms and a direction for further research in various testing methods.

Testing Based on Genetic Algorithm

In most of the papers, GA and its extensions have been applied as one of the search based testing techniques. Jones et al. (1996) have developed a library of GA and applied successfully to generate a set of test cases for the software under test to ensure all branch coverage. The fitness function is based on the predicate associated with each branch and in case loops; fitness function is based on number of iteration required. High quality test data are produced which reveal maximum faults. It is important to ensure that the diversity of the population of test sets is maintained; otherwise the global optimum in terms of high quality tests will not be located. Srivastava and Kim (2009) enhanced the work of Jones et al. (1996) by identifying the most critical path clusters in a program to be tested. They have used weighted Control Flow Graph (CFG) to find the critical path. The fitness function is defined as the summation of weights of path traversed by a given input data in CFG. They are able to generate an optimized test suite. But while the numbers of test cases are reduced at the same time it suffers from a number of iterations to generate test cases for a small program. Singhal et al. (2012) have applied GA to generate test cases for a model which can accept 5 integers as inputs and generates one output. They have found non-redundant and minimum set of test cases as compared to the test cases generated by the decision coverage technique.

Researchers have considered data dependencies and/or control dependencies for automatic test case generation. Andreou et al. (2007) have proposed an approach for automatic test case generation based on data flow coverage criteria. They combined a data flow graph module with an existing testing framework and used the specially designed GA. The proposed method is implemented on a number of sample programs of different size and complexity. The experiments give significantly better result incomparision to existing dynamic data flow-oriented test data generation methods. To fulfil the all-uses criterion, S.Varshney et al. (2014) have also considered data flow dependencies in the program to search for test data whereas earlier work (Andreou et al., 2007) was only on covering def-use paths. The GA based technique used in later one accepts the list of def-use paths to be covered, the number of input variables and the domain and precision of each input variable as input. At the time of coverage calculation, manually identified def-use paths are not considered with respect to all-uses criterion. The outputs of the algorithm are a set of test cases, set of def-use paths covered by the test suite and a list of uncovered def-use paths, if any. The performance of proposed approach outperforms random testing in test data generation and optimization. Khan et al. (2016) proposed a novel approach for all du-path coverage using GA. They have used probabilistic based fitness function and achieved 100% path coverage. Hybridized or modified GA (Liu et al., 2013; Garg et al., 2015) are used to overcome the problem of large iteration time and low efficiency in test case generation. Liu et al. (2013) have proposed modified GA by adding delaunay triangulation network in program generation. The algorithm uses real number coding and the principles of logic coverage with genetic - oriented control. Result shows that modified GA has faster convergence speed and higher test data generation efficiency compared with traditional GA. But such improved algorithm is not quite ideal in time efficiency and the generation of special test case. Therefore, further studies are also needed in this field. Garg et al. (2015) proposed a new fitness function named Extended Level Branch fitness function (ExLB) with Simple GA (SGA) and Hybrid GA(HGA) i.e., Hill Climbing with selection operator for basis path testing. They have combined Branch Distance Based Fitness Function (BDBFF) and Approximation Level Based Fitness Function (ALBFF) and multiplied a large constant to make the magnitude of ALBFF high, so that it will be distinguishable of different path executed by different test cases from the target path. One more modification they have done, when all branching nodes are covered instead of taking zero as ALBFF value they have assigned half of the parent branching node. They have got better result than existing ALBFF and BDBFF fitness function with GA. But ExLB has given best result with HGA.

Observations and New Direction

From the above studies, it is concluded that Genetic Algorithm is an efficient method for automation of software testing. It outperforms the exhaustive search and local search techniques. But at the same time, it suffers from large number of iterations and premature convergence. For basis path coverage, GA is not able provide promising result. In this work (Garg et al., 2015), the researchers have not covered a target path. It is suggested that their proposed fitness function may generate efficient test cases with Adaptive PSO and Cuckoo Search as it balance exploration and exploitation well or their algorithm may require higher mutation rate. GA is good at global search and SA is good at local search. So, the combination of GA and SA may give better path coverage.

Testing Based on Particle Swarm Optimization

Test case generation and optimization using PSO and variants of PSO are claimed to be better than GA based test data generation (Windisch et al., 2007; Zhu et al., 2010; Singla et al., 2011).

Windisch et al. (2007) have used a novel approach i.e., Comprehensive Learning Particle Swarm Optimizer (CL-PSO). In their learning strategy, each particle learns from different neighbours of each dimension separately dependent on its assigned learning rate. Both PSO and GA are used to automatically generate test cases for the same set of test objects. The experimental results show that PSO is equivalent, even outperforms for complex cases in comparison to GA. Though GA gives faster test case coverage than PSO in some cases, but in the majority of the cases PSO is much faster than the GA. This result indicates that PSO is a better alternative to GA as it is better than genetic algorithms in terms of effectiveness and efficiency. In the traditional PSO constant inertia weight coefficient does not reflect properly the fact of the search process. To improve the efficiency of automatic test data generation, Zhu et al. (2010) have proposed an improved PSO algorithm i.e., Adaptive PSO (APSO), in which inertia weight is adjusted according to fitness value. It is observed in APSO algorithm, when particle is far away from the optimum solution, convergence speed is quickened, when particle is near to the optimum, convergence speed becomes slower. Experimental results show that, APSO not only more efficient than GA, but also perform better than PSO in automatic test data generation. Huang et al. (2014) proposed a parallel thinking concept for single and multi-path fitness function structure by introducing group self-activity feedback (SAF) operator and Gauss mutation (G) changing inertia weight. It gives better results with respect to the iteration time in single path test and more efficient in multi-path test case generation. Singla et al. (2011) have developed an algorithm integrating the power of GA and PSO, called GPSCA i.e., Genetic Particle Swarm Combined Algorithm with a new multi objective fitness function for generating test cases. The proposed GPSCA consists of a new operator called 'enhancement' along with the crossover and mutation operator. GPSCA is better than GA and PSO in terms coverage, number of test cases and number of generations required. Jiang et al. (2015) proposed a novel approach of Reduced Adaptive Particle Swarm Optimization (RAPSO). They have reduced the particle swarm evolution equation without using velocity and make an adjustment on inertia weight. Though it enhances convergence speed and solve the problem of easily falling into the local optima and low search accuracy, the average evolutionary generations and the total evolutionary time by their approach are less in comparison to APSO (Harman et al., 2007) and GPSCA (Singla et al., 2011).

There are some problems observed in Basic Particle Swarm Optimization algorithm (BPSO) like easily stuck up at local optimum, difficult to come out of local optimum and when the particles in the population are relatively spread over the solution space early, the algorithm cannot fully explore the search space and wastes a lot of time on repeated invalid iterations. By observing various populations in nature, Ming et al. (2015) have found that close association among various particles make the population strengthen. So, they have proposed PSO algorithm based on clustering thought (Cluster PSO) with fast convergence. The validity of the algorithm has been verified by applying it to generate test cases for path coverage of some typical applications and the results has been compared with that of RAPSO (Jiang et al., 2015). ClusterPSO can effectively jump out of local optimum by ensuring the complete coverage. Souza et al. (2011) have used PSO for multi-objective test case selection. They implemented two different algorithms: a Binary Multi-Objective PSO (BMOPSO) and a modified version, known as BMOPSO-CDR (which uses Crowding Distance and Roulette Wheel). These algorithms provide a set of solutions (test suites) with different values of requirements' coverage versus execution effort to the user. BMOPSO-CDR gives maximum coverage of the search space that are not covered by BMOPSO and the Random method. PSO algorithm has also been tested on regression testing. Tiwari et al. (2013) have proposed a variant of PSO algorithm called modified time varying acceleration coefficients (PSO-TVAC) to create new test cases for modified code. The performance is measured on five benchmark test functions and compared with other existing PSO algorithms. Experimental result shows that PSO-TVAC algorithm is better than PSO-Time Varying Inertia Weight (PSO-TVIW) and PSO-Random Inertia Weight (PSO-RANDIW). Hence, they compared the proposed algorithm with only PSO-TVAC algorithm. The proposed modified PSO-TVAC algorithm have greater code coverage capability over the initial test cases. The experiments show that the proposed algorithm has better performance over the existing algorithms and has been utilized in generation process of new test cases on the basis of changed code coverage analysis. Jatana et al. (2016) used PSO algorithm for mutation testing. The proposed approach is called PSO-MT. The fitness function of the proposed approach returns the number of mutant killed by each test case and it proves its significance in killing a notable amount of mutants. Prasad et al. (2016) have proposed two PSO based algorithm for generating pairwise test cases. Their algorithms are based on one-test-at-a time strategy and IPO-like strategy respectively and give efficient result.

Observations and New Direction

A lot of work has been done on structural testing using PSO and its variant and it gives good result. In Cluster PSO (Ming et al., 2015) stuck into local optima successfully avoided but the cost may further be reduced by applying fuzzy concept to each cluster. Some PSO variants like Emotional Particle Swarm Optimization (Ge and Rubo, 2005), Fuzzy Particle Swarm Optimization Algorithm (Tian et al., 2009) have not been explored with test case generation.

Testing Based on Simulated Annealing

Latiu et al. (2012) have used Simulated Annealing for solving the path testing problem. In their work, GA, SA and PSO algorithms have been used to generate suitable test data for covering the target path and to reduce execution time. The metric used in this method calculates the difference between the selected path to be traversed, and the actual path traversed by the input values. Experimental results show that Simulated Annealing is the best evolutionary algorithm for path testing. Because it can generate test data which cover the target path quickly. The proposed approach has been applied on a subset of some of the most commonly used benchmark programs. Goal oriented test data generation has been done by Mann et al. (2016) using GA and SA with branch distance based fitness function. They have compared the efficiency of both the algorithm basing on number of generation required to reach the target goal and time required to generate the test cases. In both criteria, they have found GA is better than SA.

Observations and New Direction

To the best our knowledge, enough work on SA has not been done on test case generation. Scopes are there to work on SA for other coverage criteria like branch coverage, MC/DC coverage, Data flow testing etc.

Testing Based on Tabu Search

Simulated annealing getting stuck in the local minima when the number of local minima is larger and the cooling is not very slow. The study shows that this problem is overcome by existing work using Tabu Search which claims for obtaining 100% branch coverage. Diaz et al. (2003) have created an efficient testing technique that combines Tabu Search with Korel's chaining approach. Their technique automatically generates test data in order to obtain branch coverage in software testing. Tabu Search technique searches inside the neighbourhood of a solution and remembers the best solutions. The experimental results say that TS is an effective technique for obtaining very high branch coverage. But they have not achieved 100% coverage. They extended their work (Diaz et al., 2008) and proposed Tabu Search Generator (TSGen). It is an automatic generator of software tests for a given program. In this approach, the Current Solution (CS) is selected taking into account the chaining approach. Fitness function measures how close a test is in order to make a branch decision true. They have introduced a backtracking process that able to detect bad CS and unfeasible nodes. Unlike SA, the approach avoids TSGen to getting stuck in the local minima. TSGen has been evaluated using benchmark programs for which it is very difficult to find a test that covers branches. The experimental results show that TSGen achieves 100% branch coverage for all the programs and executes in a reasonable time.

Observations and New Direction

TABU Search is effective in achieving 100% branch coverage. More research work are required for test case generation basing on other different coverage criteria using Tabu Search. As Tabu Search is having the memory property, it may give better test case generation for regression testing. Tabu search may limit in test case generation for large and complex problem as it is lack of sufficient and long-term memory. So Improved memory strategy can be proposed.

Testing Based on Ant Colony Optimization

ACO is mainly used for automatic test data and test pattern generation. Li and Lam (2007) have proposed to generate test data for UML State chart diagrams using ACO. This approach deals with Automatic Test Pattern Generation (ATPG) for large and complex combinatorial circuit which is a challenging task. Advantages of this approach is that it directly uses the standard UML artefacts designed in design phase and it generate feasible and non-redundant test sequences which achieves all state coverage criterion. Farah and Harmanani (2008) have proposed a novel approach based on ACO. Test vectors generated by this method achieve maximum fault coverage in minimum time for several benchmark circuits than other simulated-based ATPGs. Sebastian Bauersfeld (2011) has used ACO for test sequence generation for Graphical User Interface (GUI) applications. Fitness function is formulated based on the Call Tree Size criterion [MM08]. The lacuna of this proposed approach is that it can only generate a single input sequence. Yang et al. (2014) have introduced four improved ACO algorithms for test case generation to overcome the traditional ACO drawbacks. They have worked on local pheromone update strategy, pheromone volatization coefficient, global path pheromone update strategy and improved the search efficiency, restrain precocity, maximum statement, branch and modified condition/decision coverage with minimum number of iterations.

Observations and New Direction

ACO gives good result in test pattern/sequence generation. But in case of long sequence generation redundancy occurs. Also it is difficult to generate multiple sequence with ACO due to its pheromone updation strategy. As the testing based on ACO is mainly a sequential process, selection of the solution is done only at the end. ACO may give better result when it will be combined with other metaheuristic techniques.

Testing Based on Artificial Bee Colony Optimization

Unlike ACO, ABC based testing is a parallel process and selection of solution is done in each increment. In ABC, computational overhead and memory limit problems are well balanced in comparison to ACO. Lam et al. (2012) proposed a novel search technique deals with automatic generation of feasible independent paths and software test suit. It also provides an approach for the automated generation of feasible independent test path based on the priority of all edge coverage criteria. Generation of feasible independent paths and software test suite optimization become faster by the parallel behaviour of these three bees. Dahiya et al. (2010) have proposed ABC based approach using static symbolic execution method. The result is quite satisfactory for most of the program under test except the programs having large solution domains and many equality-based path constraints. Suri et al. (2012) have presented a hybrid technique based on GA and BCO for test case reduction where for regression testing. It yields optimum results in minimum time. GA and BCO are also used to generate test cases from Unified Modelling Language (UML). S. Dalal et al. (2013) have proposed a hybridized technique by combining GA and BCO to generate test case from UML diagram. They aim to minimize test suite which ensure the maximum coverage. Stratified Sampling is used for test case selection and minimization. It identifies all possible faults by covering all possible paths of the system. BCO-mGA (Bharati et al. (2015)), a modified BCO-GA gives maximum coverage in minimum time by executing the minimized test suite. The hybridization of BCO and GA provides satisfactory result in terms of maximum coverage and minimum execution time compared to using individual BCO and GA.

Observations and New Direction

ABC approach has some advantages over TS, GA and ACO as follows.

In ABC based approach, local optima problem does not occur. The main disadvantage in Tabu search is the requirement of remembering all test cases for the current search which creates a big problem but ABC does not require remembering all test cases. Increasing mutation rate is a major problem itself in GA based approaches. It yields unstable result as it suffers from premature convergence. ABC steadily improves the efficiency of test cases in terms of their path coverage measure. Pheromone updating is a substantial overhead in ACO based approach. In ABC, there is no overhead of pheromone updating. Though ABC has several advantages over other metaheuristic algorithms, but it limits the search space by initial solution. For more efficient test case generation normal distribution sample may be used.

Testing Based on Cuckoo Search

As cuckoo search has proven its better efficiency than the other search algorithm like GA, PSO, ACO and ABC etc., it becomes a demanding search technique for researchers of testing field. This section discusses some work on cuckoo search and hybridized cuckoo search. Nasser et al. (2015) have discussed the design and implementation of a new pairwise strategy based on Cuckoo Search, called Pairwise Cuckoo Search strategy (PairCS). The result with PairCS has been promising, as they have managed to obtain good test sizes for most of the considered configurations. Their results, in most cases outperform the existing nature-inspired-based as well as other computational based strategies. Ahmed et al. (2015) have presented combinatorial optimization technique to minimize the number of test cases in configuration-aware structural testing. For further optimization, the generated test suite is filtered based on an adaptive mechanism by using a mutation testing technique. The technique proves its effectiveness through the conducted case study. The paper also shows the application of combinatorial optimization and CS to the software testing. Srivastava et al. (2012) have presented a heuristic method for automation of test data generation using cuckoo search along with Lévy flight and tabu search. It combines the cuckoo algorithm's strength of converging to the solution in minimal time along with the tabu mechanism of backtracking from local optima by Lévy flight. This approach uses cuckoo algorithm for selection and generation of candidate solutions guided by Control Dependency Graph to obtain path coverage criterion. The results from the experimental study supports the fact that the proposed algorithm performs better than the other meta-heuristic approaches such as GA, ACO, ABCs, etc. in terms of node coverage, number of iterations and number of parameters. Thus, test data can be generated efficiently and optimally. However, by using efficient data structures for tabu lists and Lévy flights, the time complexity can be reduced in the proposed approach for high value range integers (16, 32 bits).

Observations and New Direction

CS performs better than the other metaheuristic algorithms in testing but still, it has not been tested for multi objective purpose for test case generation.

COMPARISION STUDY

In this Section, a clustered view of the metaheuristic based test case generation techniques has been represented and further it is sub clustered based on the objective and coverage criteria used. Table 1 shows various metaheuristic approaches used for test case generation/ optimization, the intermediate graph used to implement the algorithm and the result obtained. The table helps the reader to get idea for further research direction at a glance.

Table 1. Clustered view of search based test case generation techniques

	Objective	Work	Intermediate Graph Used	Conclusion
GA based SBT	Optimised test set generation for code coverage.	Jones et al., 1996; Singhal et al., 2012	CFG	The quality of test data produced is high.
	To find the most critical path	(Srivastava, P.R. and Kim, T. 2009)	Weighted CFG	Refine effort and cost estimation in the testing phase.
	Test case generation based on data flow coverage criteria.	Andreou et al., 2007; Varshney & Mehrotra, 2014; Khan et al., 2016	Data Flow Graph	100% coverage achieved
	Overcome the problem of premature convergence and large iteration times using Modified GA.	Liu et al., 2013	NA	Faster convergence speed and higher test data generation efficiency but not quite ideal in time efficiency and the generation of special test case.
	Test Case generation for basis path coverage	Garg et al., 2015	CFG	HGA gives better result than SGA with ExLb fitness function but cannot cover the target path.
PSO based SBT	To achieve efficient Code coverage	Windisch, et al., 2007; Zhu et al., 2010	NA	CL-PSO and APSO outperforms GAs for most code elements to be covered in terms of effectiveness and efficiency.
	Generating test data automatically to improve efficiency.	Singla et al., 2011); (Ziang et al., 2015); (YueMin et al., 2015); (Tiwari et al., 2013)	CFG	Cluster PSO is superior to APSO, GPSCA, RAPSO and MARPSO in iteration times, and has a greater advantage on the convergence speed.
	To improve the performance of PSO using Group self-activity feedback operator and Gauss mutation changing inertia weight	Huang et al., 2014	NA	It is more efficient in multi-path test case generation than standard PSO.
	maximize requirements coverage while minimizing test case execution effort	Souza et al., 2011	NA	BMOPSO-CDR approach outperformed BMOPSO and the Random method
	Test case generation for pair wise testing	Prasad et al., 2016	NA	Gives efficient result
	Test case generation for mutation testing	Jatana et al., 2016	NA	Significant amount of mutant killed
Simulated annealing Based SBT	To generate test data automatically for path testing using GA, PSO and SA.	Latiu et al., 2014; Mann et al., 2016	NA	Simulated Annealing is best for path testing

continues on following page

Table 1. Continued

	Objective	Work	Intermediate Graph Used	Conclusion
Tabu Search based SBT	Generate test data in order to obtain branch coverage in software testing using Tabu Search with chaining approach	Diaz et al., 2003; Diaz et al., 2008	CFG	Effective technique for obtaining very high branch coverage.
ACO based SBT	Test data generation using ACO	Li et al., 2007	State chart diagram	Feasible, non-redundant test data are generated which achieved all state coverage criteria.
	ACO approach for test pattern generation	Farah et al., 2008; Yang et al., 2014	NA	Set of test cases generated which achieve high fault coverage in minimum time.
	Test sequence generation for GUI	Bauersfeld, 2011	NA	Single sequence generated efficiently. Improvement required for multi sequence generation
ABC based SBT	Automatic independent paths generation and test suite optimization	Lam et al., 2012	NA	ABC is better in comparision to Tabu search, GA and ACO
	Symbolically generate test case	Dahiya et al., 2012	CFG	Satisfactory performance achieved for most of the programs except programs with large solution domains and many equality based path constraints.
	Regression Test Suite Reduction and generation of test cases using a Hybrid Technique Based on BCO And Genetic Algorithm.	Suri et al.,2012; Dalal et al., 2013	NA	Optimum results achieved in minimum time.
Cuckoo Search Based SBT	A Cuckoo Search based Pair wise strategy for combinatorial testing problem	Naseer et al., 2015; Ahmed et al., 2015	NA	Outperform the existing nature-inspired-based (SA, Ga, PSO) as well as other computational-based strategies.
	Automated Test Data Generation Using Cuckoo Search and Tabu Search (CSTS) Algorithm	Srivastava et al., 2012	CDG	Performs better than the other meta-heuristic approaches such as GA, ACO, ABCs, etc. in terms of node coverage, number of iterations and number of parameters.

CONCLUSION

Though a lot of work has been done on test case generation using metaheuristic techniques still, a vast scope is there to further research. This paper gives a review with new research direction on test case generation using search based methods in which various metaheuristic techniques are implemented. The merits and demerits adhered to metaheuristic techniques and test case generation techniques has been discussed here. The authors have tried to justify the main objective i.e., limitations and gaps in test case generation based on metaheuristic approaches. This survey paper helps the reader in choosing appropriate metaheuristic technique for search based testing. To the best of our knowledge, accurate result cannot be derived and no one has achieved the best result for a piece of code based on search based testing. So, scope is there to use some more metaheuristic optimization techniques to achieve better results. Though, enough work has been done on structural testing but a few works have been done on behavioural testing using metaheuristic techniques. Test case optimization is a multi-objective task but a few work is done in that direction. Scatter Search, Differential Evolution, Fish Schooling, Spider Monkey algorithm etc. have not been used for automation purpose yet. Some more hybridization techniques are possible to overcome the deficiency of individual algorithms.

REFERENCES

Ahmed, B.S. (2015). Test case minimization approach using fault detection and combinatorial optimization techniques for configuration-aware structural testing. *Engineering Science and Technology, an International Journal.*

Ali, S., Briand, L. C., Hemmati, H., & Kaur, R. (2010). A Systematic Review of the Application an Empirical Investigation of Search-based Test-case Generation. *IEEE Transactions on Software Engineering*, *36*(6), 742–762. doi:10.1109/TSE.2009.52

Anand, S., Burke, E., Chen, T. Y., Clark, J., Cohen, M. B., Grieskamp, W., ... McMinn, P. (2013). An Orchestrated Survey on Automated Software Test Case Generation. *Journal of Systems and Software.*

Andreou, A. S., Economides, K. A., & Sofokleous, A. A. (2007). An automatic software test-data generation scheme based on data flow criteria and genetic algorithms. In *Proceedings of the Seventh International Conference on Computer and Information Technology* (pp. 867-872). 10.1109/CIT.2007.97

Bauersfeld, S. (2011). A Metaheuristic Approach to Automatic Test Case Generation for GUI-Based Applications.

Dahiya, S. S., Chhabra, J. K., & Kumar, S. (2010). Application of Artificial Bee Colony Algorithm to Software Testing. In *Proceedings of the Software Engineering Conference (ASWEC), Proceeding of 21st Australian IEEE Conferences* (pp. 149-154). 10.1109/ASWEC.2010.30

Dalal, S., & Chhillar, R. S. (2013). A Novel Technique for Generation of Test Cases Based on Bee Colony Optimization and Modified Genetic Algorithm (BCO-mGA). *International Journal of Computers and Applications*, *68*(19), 12–17. doi:10.5120/11687-7359

Díaz, E., Tuya, J., & Blanco, R. (2003). Automated Software Testing Using a Metaheuristic Technique Based on Tabu Search. In *Proceedings of the 18th IEEE International Conference on Automated Software Engineering (ASE '03)* (pp. 310–313). 10.1109/ASE.2003.1240327

Diaz, E., Tuya, J., Blanco, R., & Javier Dolado, J. (2008). A Tabu Search Algorithm for Structural Software Testing. *Computers & Operations Research*, *35*(10), 3052–3072. doi:10.1016/j.cor.2007.01.009

El-Far, I. K., & Whittaker, J. A. (2001). Model-Based Software Testing. In Encyclopaedia on Software Engineering. Wiley.

Farah, R., & Harmanani, H. M. (2008). An Ant Colony Optimization Approach for Test Pattern Generation. In *Proceedings of the Canadian Conference on Electrical and Computer Engineering (CCECE)* (pp. 1397 – 1402). 10.1109/CCECE.2008.4564771

Garg, D., & Garga, P. (2015. Basis Path Testing Using SGA & HGA with ExLB Fitness Function. In *Proceedings of the 4th International Conference on Eco-friendly Computing and Communication Systems* (pp. 593-602). Elsevier.

Glover, F. (1994). Genetic Algorithms and Scatter Search Unsuspected Potentials. *Statistics and Computing, 4*(2), 131–140. doi:10.1007/BF00175357

Glover, F. (1995). Tabu Thresholding: Improved Search by Nonmonotonic Trajectories. *ORSA Journal on Computing, 7*(4), 426–442. doi:10.1287/ijoc.7.4.426

Gunavathi, C., & Premalatha, K. (2014). A Comparative Analysis of Swarm Intelligence Techniques for Feature Selection in Cancer Classification. *Scientific World Journal*.

Harman, M. (2007). The Current State and Future of Search Based Software Engineering. In *Proceedings of the International Conference on Future of Software Engineering* (pp. 342–357). 10.1109/FOSE.2007.29

Harman, M., Jia, Y., & Zhang, Y. (2015). Achievements, Open problems and challenges for search based software testing. In Proceedings of the *IEEE 8th International Conference on Software Testing*.

Harman, M., Lakhotia, K., & McMinn, P. (2007). A Multi-objective Approach to Search-based Test data Generation. In *Proceedings of the International conference on Genetic and evolutionary computation* (pp. 1098–1105). ACM.

Huang, M., Zhang, C., & Liang, X. (2014). Software Test Cases Generation Based on Improved Particle Swarm Optimization. In *Proceeding of 2nd International Conference on Information Technology and Electronic Commerce (ICITEC)* (pp. 52-55). 10.1109/ICITEC.2014.7105570

Jatana, N., Suri, B., Mishra, S., Kumar, P., & Choudhury, A. R. (2016). *Particle Swarm Based Evolution and Generation of Test Data Using Mutation Testing.* doi:10.1007/978-3-319-42092-9_44

Jiang, S., Shi, J., Izhang, Y., & Han, H. (2015). Automatic test data generation based on reduced adaptive particle swarm optimization algorithm. *Neurocomputing, 158*, 109–116. doi:10.1016/j.neucom.2015.01.062

Jones, B. F., Sthamer, H. H., & Eyres, D. E. (1996). Automatic Structural Testing using Genetic Algorithms. *Software Engineering Journal, 11*(5), 299–306. doi:10.1049ej.1996.0040

Karaboga, D., & Akay, B. (2009). A comparative study of Artificial Bee Colony algorithm. *Applied Mathematics and Computation, 214*(1), 108–132. doi:10.1016/j.amc.2009.03.090

Khan, R., Amjad, M., & Srivastava, A. K. (2016). Optimization of Automatic Generated Test Cases for Path Testing Using Genetic Algorithm. In *Proceedings of the Second International Conference on Computational Intelligence & Communication Technology* (pp. 32-36). 10.1109/CICT.2016.16

King, J. C. (1975). A new approach to program testing. In Programming Methodology, LNCS (Vol. 23, pp. 278–290). doi:10.1145/800027.808444

Kumar, M., Sharma, A., & Kumar, R. (2011). Optimization of Test Cases using Soft Computing Techniques: A Critical Review. *WSEAS Transactions on Information Science and Applications, 8*(11), 440–452.

Lam, S. S. B., Raju, M. L. H. P., M, U. K., Ch, S., & Srivastav, P. R. (2012). Automated Generation of Independent Paths and Test Suite Optimization Using Artificial Bee Colony. *Procedia Engineering, 30,* 191–200. doi:10.1016/j.proeng.2012.01.851

Latiu, G. I., Cret, O. A., & Vacariu, L. (2012). Automatic Test Data Generation for Software Path Testing using Evolutionary Algorithms. In *Proceedings of the Third International Conference on Emerging Intelligent Data and Web Technologies.* 10.1109/EIDWT.2012.25

Leonora, B., Marco, D., Gambardella, L. M., & Gutjahr, W. J. (2009). A Survey on Metaheuristics for Stochastic Combinatorial Optimization. *Natural Computing: an international journal, 8*(2), 239–287.

Li, H., & Lam, C. P. (2007). Software Test Data Generation using Ant Colony Optimization. *International Journal of Computer, Electrical, Automation, Control and Information Engineering, 1*(1), 137–140.

Liu, D., & Wang, X., & Wang, j. (2013). Automatic Test Case Generation based on Genetic Algorithm. *Journal of Theoretical and Applied Information Technology, 48*(1), 411–416.

Mann, M., Tomar, P., Sangwan, O. P., & Singh, S. (2016). Automatic Goal-oriented Test Data Generation Using a Genetic Algorithm and Simulated Annealing. In *Proceedings of the 6th International Conference - Cloud System and Big Data Engineering* (pp. 83-87). 10.1109/CONFLUENCE.2016.7508052

McMinn, P. (2011). Search-Based Software Testing: Past, Present and Future. In *Proceedings of the IEEE Fourth International Conference on Software Testing* (pp. 153-163). 10.1109/ICSTW.2011.100

Nasser, A. B., Sariera, Y. A., Alsewari, A. R. A., & Zamli, K. Z. (2015). A Cuckoo Search Based Pairwise Strategy For Combinatorial Testing Problem. *Journal of Theoretical And Applied Information Technology, 82*(1), 154–162.

Pirim, H., Bayraktar, E., & Eksioglu, B. (2008). Tabu Search: A Comparative Study.

Prasad, M. L., Nikhitha, M., Divya, G., & Reddy, Y.K. (2016). A Particle Swarm Optimization Technique for Generating Pairwise Test Cases. *International Journal of scientific engineering and Technology Research, 5*(7), 1358-1362.

Roshan, R., Porwal, R., & Sharma, C. M. (2012). Review of Search based Techniques in Software Testing. *International Journal of Computers and Applications, 51*(6), 42–45. doi:10.5120/8050-1387

Selvi, V., & Umarani, R. (2010). Comparative Analysis of Ant Colony and Particle Swarm Optiization Techniques. *International Journal of Computers and Applications, 5*(4), 1–6. doi:10.5120/908-1286

Singhal, A., Chandna, S., & Bansal, A. (2012). Optimization of Test Cases Using Genetic Algorithm. *International Journal of Emerging Technology and Advanced Engineering, 2*(3), 367–369.

Singla, S., Kumar, D., Rai, H. M., & Singla, P. (2011). A Hybrid PSO Approach to Automate Test Data Generation for Data Flow Coverage with Dominance Concepts. *International Journal of Advanced Science and Technology, 37,* 15–26.

Souza, L. S., de Miranda, P. B. C., Prudencio, R. B. C., & Barros, F. A. (2011). A Multi-Objective Particle Swarm Optimization for Test Case Selection Based on Functional Requirements Coverage and Execution Effort. In *Proceeding of 23rd IEEE Int'l Conf. Tools with Artificial Intelligence* (pp. 245-252). 10.1109/ICTAI.2011.45

Srivastava, P. R., Khandelwal, R., Khandelwal, S., Kumar, S., & Ranganatha, S. S. (2012). Automated Test Data Generation Using Cuckoo Search and Tabu Search (CSTS) Algorithm. *Journal Intelligent System, 21*(2), 195–224. doi:10.1515/jisys-2012-0009

Srivastava, P. R., & Kim, T. (2009). Application of Genetic Algorithm in Software Testing. *International Journal of Software Engineering and Its Applications, 3*(4), 87–95.

Suri, B., Mangal, I., & Srivastava, V. (2012). Regression Test Suite Reduction using an Hybrid Technique Based on BCO And Genetic Algorithm. *International Journal of Computer Science & Informatics, 2*(1, 2), 165-172.

Talbi, E. (2009). *Metaheuristics from Design to Implementation (2nd ed.).* Wiley.

Tiwari, S., Mishra, K. K., & Misra, A. K. (2013). Test Case Generation for Modified Code using a Variant of Particle Swarm Optimization (PSO) Algorithm. In *Proceeding of 10th International Conference on Information Technology: New Generations* (pp. 363-368). 10.1109/ITNG.2013.58

Varshney, S., & Mehrotra, M. (2014). Automated Software Test Data Generation for Data Flow Dependencies using Genetic Algorithm. *International Journal of Advanced Research in Computer Science and Software Engineering, 4*(2), 472–479.

Windisch, A., Wappler, S., & Wegener, J. (2007). Applying Particle Swarm Optimization to Software Testing. In *Proceedings of the 9th annual Conference on Genetic and Evolutionary Computation (GECCO '07)* (pp. 1121–1128).

Yang, S., Man, T., & Xu, J. (2014). Improved Ant Algorithms for Software Testing Cases Generation. *The Scientific World Journal.* PMID:24883391

Yang, X., & Deb, S. (2009). Cuckoo Search via L'evy Flights. In *Proceeding of World Congress Nature Biologically Inspired Computing* (pp. 210–214). 10.1109/NABIC.2009.5393690

YueMing., D., YiTing, WU. & DingHui, WU. (2015). Particle Swarm Optimization Algorithm For Test Case Automatic Generation Based On Clustering Thought. In *Proceeding of 5th Annual IEEE International Conference on Cyber Technology in Automation, Control and Intelligent Systems* (pp. 1479-1485).

Zhu, X., & Yang, X. (2010). Software Test Data Generation Automatically Based on Improved Adaptive Particle Swarm Optimizer. In *Proceedings of the International Conference on Computational and Information Sciences* (pp. 1300-1303). 10.1109/ICCIS.2010.321

This research was previously published in the Journal of Information Technology Research (JITR), 11(1); pages 158-171, copyright year 2018 by IGI Publishing (an imprint of IGI Global).

Chapter 53
Software Testing Under Agile, Scrum, and DevOps

Kamalendu Pal

ⓘ https://orcid.org/0000-0001-7158-6481
City, University of London, UK

Bill Karakostas
Independent Researcher, UK

ABSTRACT

The adoption of agility at a large scale often requires the integration of agile and non-agile development practices into hybrid software development and delivery environment. This chapter addresses software testing related issues for Agile software application development. Currently, the umbrella of Agile methodologies (e.g. Scrum, Extreme Programming, Development and Operations – i.e., DevOps) have become the preferred tools for modern software development. These methodologies emphasize iterative and incremental development, where both the requirements and solutions evolve through the collaboration between cross-functional teams. The success of such practices relies on the quality result of each stage of development, obtained through rigorous testing. This chapter introduces the principles of software testing within the context of Scrum/DevOps based software development lifecycle.

INTRODUCTION

The world is witnessing a tremendous influence of software systems in all aspects of personal and business areas. Software systems are also heavily incorporated in safety-critical applications including manufacturing machinery, automobiles operation, and industrial process controls. In these applications, software failure can cause injury or loss of life. The correct behaviour of software is crucial to the safety and wellbeing of people and business. Consequently, there is an increasing requirement for the application of strict engineering discipline to the development of software systems.

DOI: 10.4018/978-1-6684-3702-5.ch053

The human being, however, is fallible. Even if they adopt the most sophisticated and thoughtful design techniques, erroneous results can never be avoided *a priori*. Consequently, software products, like the products of any engineering activity, must be verified against its requirements throughout its development.

One fundamental approach to verification is experimenting with the behaviour of a product to see whether the product performs as expected. It is common practice to input a few sample cases *(test cases)*, which are usually randomly generated or empirically selected, and then verify that the output is correct. However, it cannot provide enough evidence that the desired behaviour will be exhibited in all remaining cases. The only testing of any system that can provide absolute certainty about the correctness of system behaviour is exhaustive testing, i.e., testing the system under all possible circumstances.

In addition, new improved methods and tools for software development are the goals of researchers and practitioners. The procedure of software development has evolved over the decades to accommodate changes in software development practice. Many methods and modelling techniques have been proposed to improve software development productivity. Also, software engineering has gone through an evolution in its conception by the business world in the 1960s to recent day application development methodologies (Pal, 2019).

Software practitioners employ software development methodologies for producing high-quality software, satisfying user requirements, effectively managing the software development cost, and ensuring timely delivery. In this way, software development methodologies play an important role to provide a systematic and organized approach to software development (Sommerville, 2019). According to Kevin Roebuck (Roebuck, 2012), a traditional Software Development Life Cycle (SDLC) provides the framework for planning and controlling the development or modification of software products, along with the methodologies and process models are used for software development.

According to researchers such as (Beck et al., 2001), the Waterfall Modell (Royce, 1970) was proposed to the information processing industry, as a way in which to assess and build for the users' needs. It starts with an end-user requirements analysis that produces all required input for the next stage (software system design), where software engineers collaborate with others (e.g. database schema designers, user interface designers) to produce the optimal information system architecture. Next, coders implement the system with the help of specification documents, and finally, the deployed software system is tested and shipped to its customers (Beck, 1999).

This process model (work practice) although effective from a theoretical perspective, did not always work as expected in real life scenarios. Firstly, software customers often change their minds. After weeks, or even months, of gathering requirements and creating prototypes, users can still be unsure of what they want – all they know is that what they saw in the produced software was *not* quite "it". Secondly, requirements tend to change mid-development, however, it is difficult to stop the momentum of the project to accommodate the change. The traditional process models (e.g. Waterfall, Spiral) start to pose problems when change rates of requirements are relatively high (Boehm, 2002) because coders, system architects, and managers need to introduce and keep up to date a huge amount of documentation for the proposed system, even for small changes (Boehm, 1988). The Waterfall software process model was supposed to fix the problem of changing requirements once and for all by freezing requirements and not permitting any change once the project starts. However, it is a common experience that software requirements cannot be pinned down in one fell swoop (Beck, 1999).

In recent decades, the software industry has moved its production mechanism from traditional software development practice to agile methodologies, to mitigate the ever-increasing software complexity and globalization of software design and development business. Many industries have started to adopt new software development methodologies, known as *Agile methodologies*, for their software development purpose (VersionOne, 2011). Agile methodologies are premised on the values expressed in the Agile Manifesto (Cunningham, 2001), a statement from the leaders of the agile movement. In short, Agile methodologies are a reaction to traditional ways of developing software and acknowledge the "need for an alternative to documentation driven, heavyweight software development process" (Beck et al., 2001). The main purpose of these methodologies is to keep close customer collaboration, to provide business value as quickly as possible in an incremental manner, and to respond promptly to changing customer requirements (Barlow et al., 2011) (Cockburn, 2003).

However, large software projects are more problematic to tackle and often fail to satisfy stakeholders' expectations. While agile methods have been received with interest in the software industry, there is insufficient investigative research regarding their architecture and their mode of adoption within a large scale environment involving outsourcing, multiple programs, projects and methodologies – currently seen as a major challenge in the industrial problem-solving context (Rodriguez et al., 2012) (Lee & Young, 2013). It is widely agreed that there can be no single methodology that can be universally applied to all projects; thus, all agile and non-agile methodologies need to be tailored and integrated to support software development (Mahanti, 2006) (Boehm & Turner, 2003) (Gill, 2014). Hence, the trend to adopt agility in non-agile elements for architecture context-aware hybrid adaptive methodologies.

Scrum is one of the most widely used Agile methodologies in the industry (VersionOne, 2011). Scrum provides a lightweight process framework that can be described in terms of *roles* (product owner, scrum master, team), *process* (planning, iteration, review), and *artefacts* (product and sprint backlogs, burndown charts) (Schwaber & Sutherland, 2009). Scrum projects progress through a series of definitive (e.g. 30 days long) time-based iterations called *sprints*. At the start of each sprint, the team determines the amount of work it can complete during that sprint. Work is selected from a prioritized list called the *product backlog*. The work the team believes it can complete during the sprint is moved onto a list called *sprint backlog*. A brief daily meeting, the *daily scrum*, is held to allow the team to inspect its progress and to adapt any change, as necessary. Software testing is part and parcel of all Scrum activities.

In addition, contemporary software development is complex, and all the manual operations are moving towards automated solutions. The accelerated software delivery is a key to success in business. The increased business demand for continuous software delivery and the interwinding of development and operations has resulted in the concept of DevOps. DevOps has been adopted by prominent software and service companies (e.g. IBM) to support enhanced collaboration across the company and its value chains. In this way, DevOps facilitates uninterrupted delivery and coexistence between development and operation facilities, enhances the quality and performance of software applications, improve end-user experience, and help to the simultaneous deployment of software across different platforms.

Moreover, software testing is a very costly part of the software development process, estimated to make fifty per cent of the whole process development cost (Pal, 2020). In addition, testing in Scrum projects is different from traditional testing because of the continuous and integrated nature of testing in the project lifecycle from the very beginning (Crispin & Gregory, 2009) (Lindvall et al, 2004) (Talby et al, 2006). Furthermore, because every iteration aims to deliver a "potentially shippable" product, the development functionality within every iteration should be tested and validated to assure that risks are covered. Although the conceptual differences between Agile testing and traditional testing are several, the test types and techniques that are applied in Agile testing are not different from those applied in traditional testing (van Veenendaal, 2010) (van Veenendal, 2009), as after all, the goal of testing in Scrum is still to verify that requirements are met.

This chapter examines the importance of effective testing strategies in the context of the aforementioned paradigms of agile software development/Scrum and DevOps, for efficient software delivery. The chapter focuses on the importance of software testing in Agile methodologies such as Scrum, often practised in a DevOps environment.

The rest of this chapter is structured as follows. Section 2 describes background information on software design, agile methodologies, and particularly Scrum-based application development practice. Section 3 explains the basic concepts of testing in the software development process. Finally, Section 4 concludes the chapter with final remarks and future research plans.

AGILE/SCRUM BASED SOFTWARE DEVELOPMENT

This section describes Scrum, an Agile methodology, for software development business processes. Scrum was conceived by Ken Schwaber and Jeff Sutherland in the early 1990s, who published a research paper (Schwaber & Beedle, 2002) to describe the processes. The term "Scrum" is borrowed from the game of rugby to stress the importance of teams, and illustrates some analogies between team sports like rugby, and being successful in the game of product development.

As discussed in the previous section, the demand for rapid delivery of software is booming, due to stiff competition in the business domain and the premise that accelerated deliver the key to success. Many organisations believe that the solution to rapid delivery is DevOps. DevOps focuses on the long run of the software with shorter feedback, quick integrations, and rapid deliveries.

The literature suggests that Scrum is the best methodology to be used as an Agile practice. The success of Scrum is based on the integration of the flow throughout the software development process. Scrum, however, does not place a priority on the quality of all produced artefacts. As a result, one drawback of Scrum is that the developers may have not delivered the most optimal implementation, focusing for example on 'quick and dirty' solutions.

An incremental process is one in which software is built and delivered in real-world applications. Each piece or increment represents a complete subset of functionality. The increment may be either small or large, perhaps ranging from just a system's login screen on the small end to a highly flexible set of data management screens. Each increment is fully coded and tested, and the assumption is that the work of an iteration will not need to be revisited. In the Scrum world, instead of providing complete detailed descriptions about how everything is to be done on a project, much of it is left up to the software development team. This is because it is assumed that the team will know better how to solve any problem they are presented with. The approaches to projects that agile teams pursue are diverse. A team can be dedicated to a single project or be part of another larger project. Every project, every team and sometimes every iteration is different. How a software development team solves problems depends on the requirements, the people involved, and the software tools that the team will use.

Today, agile approaches promising rapid delivery and time to market have started to dominate the software industry, removing traditional approaches such as Waterfall from the mainstream (Schwaber & Beedle, 2002). Agile introduces key four principles i.e:

(1)   Individuals and interactions over processes and tools.
(2)   Working software over comprehensive documentation.
(3)   Customer collaboration over contract negotiation.

(4)   Responding to change over following a plan.

The above concepts do not directly fit to the conventional software development lifecycle which include deriving the specification, design and development evaluation and evolution. As a result, several methodologies have been evolved from the basic principles of the Agile concept, with Scrum, Extreme Programming, Lean, Kanban the main examples. Scrum is used as an Agile software development practice (Schwaber & Beedle, 2002) (Hneif & Ow, 2009). It comprises project management as part of its practices. Scrum creates a product backlog about the pending development.

Scrum is both an iterative and an incremental process-based development methodology. An iterative process is one, which makes progress through successive refinement. A development team takes the first approach at a system, knowing it is incomplete or weak in some (perhaps many) areas. They then iteratively refine those areas until the product is satisfactory. With each iteration, the software is improved through the addition of greater detail. For example, in a first iteration, a search screen might be coded to support only the simplest type of search. The second iteration might add additional search criteria. Finally, a third iteration may add error handling.

Scrum is one of the more widely used Agile methodologies in the industry (VersionOne, 2011). Scrum provides a lightweight process framework that can be described in terms of roles (product owner, scrum master, team), process (planning, iteration, review), and artefacts (product and sprint backlogs, burndown charts) (Schwaber & Sutherland, 2009). Scrum projects progress through a series of definitive (e.g. 30 days) time-based iterations called sprints. At the start of each sprint, the team determines the amount of work it can complete during that sprint. Work is selected from a prioritized list called the product backlog. The work the team believes it can complete during the sprint is moved onto a list called sprint backlog. A brief daily meeting, the daily scrum, is held to allow the team to inspect its progress and to adapt, as necessary.

Scrum relies on a self-organizing, cross-functional team. The Scrum team is self-organizing in that there are no overall team leaders who decide which person will be doing which task and how the problem will be solved. In other words, Scrum is a project management framework that applies to any project with aggressive deadlines, complex requirements, and a degree of uniqueness.

When describing the Scrum framework, it is easy to split it into three main areas. They are:

- Roles, which include the product owner, Scrum Master, and Scrum team.
- Ceremonies, which include the sprint planning meeting, sprint review, and sprint retrospective meetings.
- Scrum artefacts, which include the product backlog, sprint backlog, and the burndown chart.

The product owner is a project's key stakeholder and represents the users for whom the developers are building the solution. The product owner is often someone from the product management, a key stakeholder, or a user of the system. It is quite common for a business analyst with the domain experience to take on the product owner role of the development team who will engage regularly with the customers.

A diagrammatic representation of a Scrum-based software life cycle is shown in Figure 1.

The Scrum Master is responsible for making sure the team is as productive as possible and achieves this by removing impediments to progress, by protecting the team from outside, and so on. Their role is very much facilitating the team to steer their product to completion, and they act very much as a servant leader, fulfilling the needs of the team. The typical Scrum team has between five and nine people. A

Scrum project can easily scale into the hundreds; however, Scrum can easily be used by one-person teams and often is.

Figure 1. Diagrammatic representation of the Scrum process

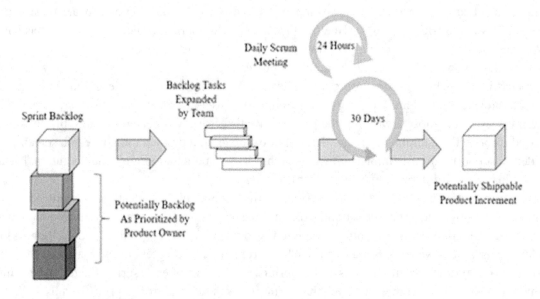

The Difference Between Agile and Scrum

Agile is a concept comprised of principles that guide through the iterative approach for software processes. Agile management is a set of methodologies for software development that are incremental and iterative. Agile management apart from Scrum includes the rational unified process (RUP), extreme programming (XP). Agile processes result in need and outcome evolution made possible because of the collaboration between teams. Agile teams are cross-functional and self-organizing. The analysis, documentation, and development of a new project go hand in hand. Advancement occurs with every iteration. This approach offers ease of accommodation of changes. It also results in better scalability. The flexibility of operations and processes increases. There are certain rules that testers must follow in an agile environment. This set of rules is called Scrum, therefore, Scrum needs to be part of an Agile framework, as a technique used to address complex issues and deliver high-quality products simultaneously.

Scrum with DevOps

Typically, a software development process addresses the following activities: (i) Requirements Analysis and Specification, (ii) Software architecture and Implementation, (iii) Testing and Documentation, and (iv) Training, Support and Maintenance. Software maintenance was considered as a separate subprocess and developers focus on the rest of the process activities. This has created a crucial gap between the developers, the production, and operations staff, which is leading to challenges such as process cost overheads.

However, the pressure derived from the ever-changing business environment (e.g., competition, technology, market conditions), an increasing number of software companies are adopting (or considering adoption) the 'Development and Operation' (DevOps) practice that is supposed remove the barriers between the development people and operation people and continuously deliver services to the customers. According to an international survey (Puppet Labs, 2015), the DevOps could support high performance for software development (e.g. sixty per cent less failures in IT organization and two hundred percentage faster deployment) and stability of service (up to one hundred and sixty-eight percentage faster recovery from failure). The survey mentioned above also confirmed the increased adoption of the DevOps in all types of organizations regarding size and industrial field (Puppet Labs, 2015).

DevOps reduces the gap between the developer, operation, and the end-user (Boehm & Papaccio, 1988) which leads to detect problems early. As in Scrum, though the system developed according to specification it may not get validated by end-users. DevOps support continuous development and integration to avoid those pitfalls.

The term DevOps is a combination of 'Development' and 'Operation', which may have various definitions under a different context. Jens defined DevOps as three inter-supported elements – i.e., Capabilities, Cultural Enablers, and Technological Enablers (Smeds et al., 2015), and argued that the Capabilities is the main DevOps aspect, which includes capabilities such as continuous planning, collaborative and continuous development, continuous integration and testing, continuous release and deployment, continuous infrastructure monitoring and optimization, continuous user behaviour monitoring and feedback and service failure recovery without delay, etc. To strengthen these capabilities requires process improvement in various aspects. However, process improvement usually means different things to different companies due to the unique issues they are facing. To this end, a relatively thorough understanding of the performance of the current process and effective guidance for future process improvement is thus needed.

However, DevOps, does not incorporate a software development framework or process (Boehm & Papaccio, 1988). To become stable DevOps should have a complete software process model, which supports specification, design and development, evaluation, and evolution phases. The deployment flow between Scrum and DevOps cannot be achieved without addressing the missing components. To identify gaps, it is needed to check the role and the requirements of Scrum and DevOps in different stages of the software lifecycle. The Scrum methodology covers the first three stages of the software lifecycle, i.e., up to the development and release stages only. The final stages of (i) Planning (ii) Execute (iii) Inspect and adapt, and (iv) Operation and support, are not covered at all by the Scrum process.

DevOps cannot therefore be combined directly with the current Scrum. To understand the gaps and missing components, first, it is required to understand the industry need to minimize the time to market while maintaining the stability of the product. in addition, the industry needs to attend the production issues as fast as possible to achieve customer satisfaction and retention.

SOFTWARE TESTING

Software Testing is the execution of code using selected combinations of input and state, to reveal bugs. Software testing can be viewed as a systems engineering activity, i.e. as the design and implementation of a special kind of software system: one that exercises another software system with the intent of finding errors (Binder, 2000). In software testing, a program with well-designed input data is run to observe errors (Ipate & Holcombe, 1997; Mall, 2006; Jalote & Jain, 2006). In other words, software testing addresses the problem of effectively finding the difference between the expected behaviour given the system specification, and the observed behaviour of the implemented system (Binder, 2000). Testing of software also helps to find errors, gaps, or missing requirements. This can be done either manually or with automated tools.

The testable artefacts can be requirements and design specifications, modules of code, data structures, and any other objects that are necessary for the correct development and implementation of the software.

Software testing, on average, accounts for a large percentage of total development costs and increases in accordance with the size and complexity of software (Myers, 2004). As systems grow larger and more complex, testing time and effort is expected to increase. Therefore, the automation of software testing has become an urgent practical necessity to reduce test cost and time. Also, defining complete test case sets plays an important role in software testing, and the generation of test cases has generally been identified as an important research challenge. In recent years, researchers presented the results of an informal survey in which researchers in testing were asked to comment on the most notable achievements of the research effort and the open challenges in the field. The most common keywords in the experts' answers are the word "generation", which, together with a few other terms such as "tools" and "practice", confirms the importance of the topic of test generation approaches, which must be accompanied by good tool support to cover practical needs.

Modern software development is a knowledge-intensive activity. Process models, development methods, technologies, and development tools are part of the toolbox of the modern software designer, which includes several toolkits, configuration management tools, test suites, standards, and intelligent compilers with sophisticated debugging capabilities, just to name a few. The software engineer's vision of carefully crafting language statements into a work program is outdated and gives way to the use of a variety of tools and techniques that support the coordination of work and the creation of systems that conform to the complexity of the concept demanded by users of modern software.

Much of the development cycle is spent on debugging, where the programmer performs a long, failure trace and tries to locate the problem in a few lines of source code to clarify the cause of the problem. In this way, testing among software quality assurance techniques is one of the commonly used techniques in practice. Consequently, testing is also extensively studied in research. An important aspect of testing that is receiving a lot of attention in the issue of generating reusable test cases.

Software testing has been the most widely used software quality assurance technology for many decades. Due to its successful practical application, considerable research effort has been made to improve the effectiveness of tests and to scale the techniques for dealing with increasingly complex software systems. Therefore, automation of test activities is the key factor for improving test effectiveness. Automation involves four main activities: (i) generating tests, (ii) performing these tests on the system under test, (iii) evaluating the results of test procedures, and (iv) managing the results of test executions.

Software Testing Types

Below are the main types of software tests addressing different stages of the software development lifecycle:

- Collaborative testing involving developers, testers, and other QA professionals
- User acceptance testing- involving actual software users test the software to make sure it can handle required tasks in real-world scenarios, according to specifications
- Exploratory testing- an approach that involves simultaneous learning, test design and test execution

- Usability testing- evaluating a product or service by testing it with representative users
- Pairwise testing- a test case generation technique that is based on the observation that most faults are caused by interactions of at most two factors

Testers test performance, data migration, infrastructure, stress, and load. Other aspects include security to ensure authentication. The product should have preventive measures for hacking and attacks. Scalability is another factor tester undertake.

Automatic Test Case Generation

The software industry needs to perform testing by a systematic and practical approach and to address complete test coverage. This testing criterion attempts to group elements of the input domain into classes such that the elements of a given class behave in the same way. This way, the software testing group can choose a single test case as representative of each class. If testing group divide the input domain into disjoint classes, they say the classes constitute a partition or an equivalence partitioning of the domain, then there is no particular reason to choose one element over another as a class representative. As in any other engineering disciplines, it is important to document the design of software products, from the initial development through the maintenance period that follows. Documentation is used in design reviews, to guide the programmers, to guide the users and to save cost when the software must be extended or modified. The software development team needs to perform testing on developed software product to provide quality assurance to the ultimate users of the software. In this way, testing needs to be a systematic and practical approach that cover all aspects of the software product and commonly known as complete coverage principle.

This testing principle tries to group elements of the input domain into classes such that the elements of a given class behave in the same way. This way, one can choose a single test case as representative of each class.

Test case generation is a critical step in testing. A test case species the pretest state of the product under test and its environment, as well as the test inputs or conditions. A test suite is a collection of test cases, typically related by a testing goal or implementation dependency.

The test case generation can generate not only input to exercise the software, sometimes the properties of the corresponding output can be specified too. In this thesis, only the generation of input data is concerned. However, the method and algorithm, as well as the tool developed in this chapter, can be easily extended to determine whether an <input, output> pair satisfies the relation described by the specification.

An analysis of black-box testing techniques is described in, such as boundary-value analysis. Later binomial method was proposed, and a tool based on this method was developed. While our method is selecting test cases randomly within a partition, they select test data according to rules-based upon certain assumptions. Both of these are complementary to but different from, the work described in this chapter.

The equivalence partitioning is usually regarded as black-box testing. However, because tabular expressions can be used to document all the software documentations involved in all stages of software life cycle, including software requirements as well as module internal design and implementations, this method can also be used to test system specification, i.e., consistency, and to test module internal design.

A recent survey (Anand et al., 2013) covers test-case and test data generation techniques that include various techniques like symbolic execution, model-based testing, combinatorial interaction testing, adaptive random testing, and search-based testing. Relevant work includes that of Mayrhauser's (Mayrhauser et al, 2000), approach is an attempt to design a system that can use the idea of test case generation. In their work, a new method of test case generation is proposed to improve the reuse of test cases through domain analysis and domain modelling. Also, research into the reuse of test cases has been proposed, mainly divided into two categories: the generation of reusable test-cases and the management of reusable test cases.

Xu and colleagues (Xu et al., 2003) advocated a theoretical model for generating and executing patterns, making the test cases independent of the software under test and achieving the goal of reusing tests. Wang has focused on a test-case generation approach based on ontology. To describe the test case precisely and accurately, Guo and his colleague (Guo et al., 2011) pointed to an ontology-based method widely used as the basis for the sharing and reuse of knowledge in information science. Xiao-Li and collaborators (Xiao-Li et al., 2006) developed a test case library and discussed the model of test case management. To aid effective reuse of tests, Shao and collaborators (Shao, Bai & Zhao, 2006) proposed a software test design model based on the analysis of reusable test assets and their relationships.

Comparison of Traditional and Agile Software Testing

Traditional software development uses a phased approach (e.g. requirement elicitation, specification, coding, testing, and release). Testing takes place at the end of the software development, shortly before the release. This is shown schematically in the upper part of Figure 2. The diagram describes an ideal situation because it gives the impression that there is just as much time for testing as for coding. However, this is not the case with many software developments projects. Testing is 'squeezed' because coding takes longer than expected and the teams end up going through a code-and-fix cycle. Traditional testing was the mainstream, but efficiency increases when an enterprise makes a shift from traditional to agile testing.

Traditional testing aims to understand user needs and develop a product. After development, testers test the product and report bugs before deployment. The development team then works on them and fixes any errors using the best possible solution. Traditional testing works on the assumption that the processes are repetitive and predictable.

The concept is that the team can get the processes in control during the SDLC. A hierarchy ensures stability at different levels. It standardizes procedures by allotting different tasks to people according to their skills. But while the traditional model seems clear, it lacks flexibility. The procedure is time-consuming as the team completes tasks in a fixed sequence.

In contrast, Agile testing seeks to correct the rigidity of traditional testing. It is a team-based approach that, unlike traditional testing, is interactive and dynamic. As a result, the delivery time shortens. Agile testing is iterative and incremental. This means that the testers test each code increment as soon as it is complete. An iteration can only take a week or a month. The team builds and tests a bit of code to make sure it is working properly, and then proceeds to the next part that needs to be created. Agile software development is shown in the lower part of Figure 2. The label 'A', 'B', 'C', 'D', 'E', and 'F'- represent block or unit of code in a software system.

In comparison, in the Waterfall model, the testing process is more structured and there is a detailed description of the testing phase. Agile testing is well suited for small projects. On the other hand, Waterfall testing can be adopted for all sorts of projects. As testing begins at the start of the Agile project, errors can be fixed in the middle of the project. In the waterfall model, however, the product is tested at the end of the development. For any changes, testing must start from the beginning.

There is very less documentation required for agile testing. In contrast, the testing in the waterfall approach requires elaborate documentation.

Figure 2. The difference between traditional software development model and agile model

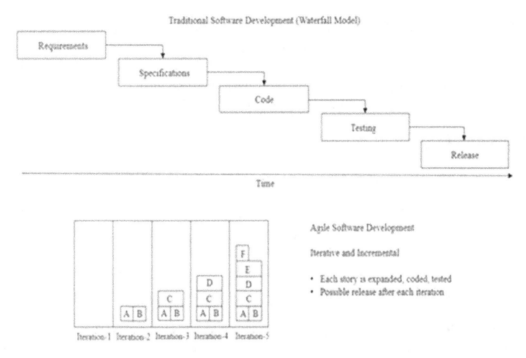

In the Agile approach, every iteration has its own testing phase. The regression tests can be run every time new functions or logic are released. In the waterfall approach, testing begins only after the completion of the development phase.

In agile testing shippable features of the product are delivered to the customer at the end of an iteration. In the waterfall approach, however, all features developed are delivered altogether after the implementation phase.

While testers and developers work closely in Agile testing, they work separately under a waterfall approach. User acceptance is performed at the end of every sprint but can only be performed at the end of the project in waterfall projects.

While in Agile, the testers need to establish communication with developers to analyze requirements and planning, developers are not involved in analyzing the requirements and planning process under a waterfall approach

Agile testing, therefore, is characterized by the following:

- *Testing is continuous*: Agile team tests continuously because it is the only way to ensure continuous progress of the product.
- *Continuous feedback*- Agile testing provides feedback on an ongoing basis and this is how your product meets the business needs.

- *Tests performed by the whole team*: In a traditional software development life cycle, only the test team is responsible for testing but in agile testing, the developers and the business analysts also test the application.

The resulting benefits can be summarized as:

- *Decreased time of feedback response*: Because the business team is involved in each iteration feedback is continuous and the time of feedback response is shortened.
- *Simplified & clean code*: All the defects which are raised by the agile team are fixed within the same iteration, which helps in keeping the code clean and simplified.
- *Less documentation*: Agile teams focus on the test instead of the incidental details.

Agile Testing Methods

There are various agile testing methods as follows:

- Behavior Driven Development (BDD)
- Acceptance Test-Driven Development (ATDD)
- Exploratory Testing

Behavior Driven Development (BDD)

Behavior Driven Development (BDD) improves communication amongst project stakeholders so that all members correctly understand each feature before the development process starts. There is continuous example-based communication between developers, testers, and business analysts.

The examples are called Scenarios that hold information on how a given feature should behave in different situations with different input parameters. These are called "Executable Specifications" as it comprises of both specification and inputs to the automated tests.

Acceptance Test-Driven Development (ATDD)

ATDD focuses on involving team members with different perspectives such as the customer, developer, and tester. Meetings are held to formulate acceptance tests incorporating perspectives of the customer, development, and testing. The customers focus on the problem that is to be solved, while the developers focus on how the problem will be solved, whereas testing is focused on what could go wrong. The acceptance tests are a representation of the user's point of view and they describe how the system will function. It also helps to verify that the system functions as it is supposed to. In some cases, acceptance tests are automated.

Exploratory Testing

In this type of testing, the test design and test execution phase go hand in hand. Exploratory testing emphasizes working software over comprehensive documentation. The individuals and interactions are more important than the process and tools. Customer collaboration holds greater value than contract negotiation. Exploratory testing is more adaptable to changes. In this tester identify the functionality of an application by exploring the application. The testers try to learn better determination of issues through daily meetings.

Test Plan for Agile

In agile testing, the test plan is written as well as updated for every release. A test plan in agile includes:

- The scope of the testing, consolidating new functionalities to be tested
- Types of testing/Levels of testing
- Performance & load testing
- Consideration of infrastructure
- Risks Plan
- Planning of resources
- Deliverables & Milestones

Iterative Testing Cycle in Agile Methods

The agile testing life cycle includes the following 5 phases:

- Impact assessment
- Agile Testing Planning
- Release Readiness
- Daily Scrums
- Test Agility Review.

The iterative cycles make changes according to consistent customer communication and feedback.

The first step is to check the quality of the code. The testers give immediate feedback. Then, based on the feedback, the developers carry on with their tasks. These tasks include unit testing and component architecture testing. The former refers to checking a coding unit to see if it fulfils the requirement, which is often done by the developers. The latter is to ensure that the pieces of code work when integrated.

Both the testers and developers get the requirement. Both carry out their respective tasks keeping business objectives in mind. That includes testing possible scenarios. Testers must perform prototype and wireframe testing while keeping user experience in mind.

Automation testing evaluates the product usage. Despite the product development being incomplete, tests are run. The scheduled demos ensure that development is going on according to business goals. These are the five stages the third quadrant covers:

Challenges of Agile Testing

Since the methodologies are different in traditional and agile testing, there are many challenges testers must face. These include:

- Sharp deadlines

- Learning the development procedure and programming languages
- Sudden changes requested from the stakeholder
- Need for impeccable coordination between teams

However, these challenges are counteracted by huge learning opportunities for the testers.

Agile Testing Automation Tools

Test automation is software that automates any aspect of testing of an application system. It includes capabilities to generate test inputs and expected results, to run test suites without manual intervention, and to reveal pass/no pass. The aim is to run the tests in a timely and efficient manner.

The aim is to automate testing as much as possible. Automated testing offers many significant advantages such as (Binder, 2000):

- Every time the software is changed, the automated test can be generated accordingly. On the other hand, manual testing is not repeatable, and rewriting is time consuming, tedious and errors prone.
- The test process information produced by manual testing is often inconsistent and fragmentary.
- An automated test is the only repeatable way to generate a large quantity of input and to evaluate a large quantity of output.
- The randomly generated test can greatly improve tester productivity.
- The cost of test automation is typically recovered after two or three projects from increased productivity and the avoided costs associated with buggy software.

Regression testing. automation tools to speed up testing include **Selenium WebDriver**, **HP UFT**, and **Appium**. **JUnit**, **Cucumber**, **Pytest**, **JBehave**, are some testing tools relevant to Agile testing.

Additionally, Project Management Tools such as **Slack**, **JIRA**, and **Mantis** can be used, apart from identifying bugs, for efficient collaboration and project management.

CONCLUSION

This chapter has addressed the important challenge of testing in a Scrum/DevOps software development environment. The adoption of agility at a large scale often requires the integration of agile and non-agile development elements in a hybrid adaptive methodology. The challenge is to determine which elements or components (agile and non-agile) are relevant to develop a hybrid adaptive testing methodology and framework. Making a move from traditional to agile testing can be overwhelming for testers at first, however, it offers potential for broadening the learning scope and an opportunity for enhancing their skills and professional growth. In agile processes like Scrum/DevOps, strong customer involvement demands techniques to facilitate the requirements acceptance testing. Additionally, test automation is crucial, as incremental development and continuous integration require high efforts for testing. In test-driven development, tests are written before the code, with developers adopting a short cycle of test-code-test-code and so on. During the test phase, the rule is that no operational code may be written except in response to a failing test.

The benefits of the agile testing approach can be summarized as follows: (i) it saves time and money, (ii) agile testing reduces documentation, (iii) it is flexible and highly adaptable to changes, and (iv) it provides a way for receiving regular feedback from the end-user.

As the size of developed software systems increases, agile testing will need to increasingly rely on software testing tools to solve challenges and speed-up the release of feedback from stakeholders. Such test tools and environments will need to incorporate collaboration features, automated and customized reporting and ways to avoid repeated efforts. Additionally, such tools will need to co-exist and integrate with other Agile lifecycle development environments.

REFERENCES

Ananda, S., Burke, E. K., Chenc, T. Y., Clark, J., Cohene, M. B., Grieskampf, W., Harmang, M., Harrold, M., Phil, J., & McMinn, P. H. (2013). An orchestrated survey of methodologies for automated software test case generation. *Journal of Systems and Software, 86*(8), 1978–2001. doi:10.1016/j.jss.2013.02.061

Barlow, J. B. (2011). Overview and Guidance on Agile Development in Large Organizations. Comm. of the Ass. for Inform. *Systems, 29*(1), 25–44.

Beck, K. (1999). Embracing change with extreme programming. *Computer, 32*(10), 70–77. doi:10.1109/2.796139

Beck, K. (2003). *Test-Driven Development: By Example*. Pearson Education.

Beck, K., Cockburn, A., Jeffries, R., & Highsmith, J. (2001). *Agile manifesto*. http://www.agilemanifesto.org

Binder, R. V. (2000). *Testing Object-Oriented Systems: Models, Patterns, and Tolls*. Addison-Wesley.

Boehm, B. (1988). A spiral model of software development and enhancement. *IEEE Computer, 21*(5), 61–72. doi:10.1109/2.59

Boehm, B. (2002). Get Ready for Agile Methods, with Care. *IEEE Computer, 35*(1), 64–69. doi:10.1109/2.976920

Boehm, B., & Papaccio, P. (1988). Understanding and controlling software costs. *IEEE Transactions on Software Engineering, 14*(10), 1462–1477. doi:10.1109/32.6191

Boehm, B., & Turner, B. (2003). *Balancing Agility and Discipline: A Guide for the Perplexed*. Addison Wesley Pearson Education.

Boehm, R., & Turner, B. (2003b). Using risk to balance agile and plan-driven methods. *Computer, 36*(6), 57–66. doi:10.1109/MC.2003.1204376

Cockburn, A. & Williams, L. (2003). Agile software development: it's about feedback and change. *IEEE Computer, 36*(6), 39–43.

Crispin, L., & Gregory, J. (2009). *Agile Testing: a Practical Guide for Testers and Agile Teams*. Addison-Wesley Professional.

Cunningham, W. (2001). *Agile Manifesto, 2001*. http://www.agilemanifesto.org

Gill, A. Q. (2014). Hybrid adaptive software development capability: An empirical study. *Journal of Software, 9*(10), 2614–2621. doi:10.4304/jsw.9.10.2614-2621

Guo, S., Tong, W., Zhang, J., & Liu, Z. (2011). An Application of Ontology to Test Case Reuse. *International Conference on Mechatronic Science, Electrical Engineering and Computer.*

Ipate, F., & Holcombe, M. (1997). An integration testing method that is proved to find all faults. *International Journal of Computer Mathematics, 63*(3-4), 159–178. doi:10.1080/00207169708804559

Jalote, P., & Jain, G. (2006). Assigning tasks in a 24-hours software development model. *Journal of Systems and Software, 79*(7), 904–911. doi:10.1016/j.jss.2005.06.040

Jilin, C., Hneif, M., & Ow, S. H. (2009). Review of Agile Methodologies in Software Development 1. *International Journal of Research and Reviews in Applied Sciences, 1*(1), 2076–73. doi:10.1109/MEC.2011.6025579

Labs, P. (2015). *State of DevOps 2015 Report.* IT Revolution Press. https://puppet.com/resources/white-paper/2015-state-of-devops-report

Lee, S., & Young, H. (2013). Agile Software Development Framework in a Small Project Environment. *Journal of Information Systems, 9*(1).

Lindvall, M., Muthig, D., Dagnino, A., Wallin, C., Stupperich, M., Kiefer, D., May, J., & Kahkonen, T. (2004). Agile Software Development in Large Organizations. *IEEE Computer Society, 4*(12), 26–34. doi:10.1109/MC.2004.231

Mahanti, A. (2006). Challenges in Enterprise adoption of agile methods – a survey. *Journal of Computing and Information Technology – CIT*, 197-206.

Mall, R. (2006). *Fundamental of Software Engineering* (2nd ed.). Prentice Hall.

Mayrhauser, A., France, R., Scheetz, M., & Dahlman, E. (2000). Generating test-cases from an object-oriented model with an artificial-intelligence planning system. Reliability. *IEEE Transactions on., 49*, 26–36. doi:10.1109/24.855534

Myers, G. J. (2004). *The Art of Software Testing* (2nd ed.). John Wiley & Sons.

Pal, K. (2019). Markov Decision Theory Based Crowdsourcing Software Process Model. In Crowdsourcing and Probabilistic Decision-Making in Software Engineering: Emerging Research and Opportunities. IGI Publication.

Pal, K. (2020). Framework for Reusable Test Case Generation in Software Systems Testing. In Software Engineering for Agile Application Development. IGI Global Publication.

Rodriguez, P., Markkula, J., Oivo, M., & Turula, K. (2012). Survey on agile and lean usage in finnish software industry. *Proceeding of ACM-IEEE international symposium on Empirical software engineering and measurement*, 139-148. 10.1145/2372251.2372275

Roebuck, K. (2012). *System Development Life Cycle (SDLC): High-impact Strategies – What You Need to Know: Definition, Adoption, Impact, Benefits, Maturity, Vendors.* Emereo Publishing.

Royce, W. W. (1970). Managing the Development of Large Software Systems. *Proceedings of IEEE WESCON*, *26*(August), 1–9.

Schwaber, K., & Beedle, M. (2002). *Agile Software Development with SCRUM*. Prentice-Hall.

Schwaber, K. & Sutherland, J. (2009). Scrum guide. Scrum Alliance, Seattle. *Journal of Mini-Micro Systems, 27*, 2150-2155.

Sommerville, I. (2019). *Software Engineering*. Addison Wesley.

Talby, D., Keren, A., Hazzan, O., & Dubinsky, Y. (2006). Agile Software Testing in a Large-scale Project. *Software*, *23*(4), 30–37. doi:10.1109/MS.2006.93

van Veenendaal, E. (2009). Scrum & Testing: Back to the Future. *Testing Experience, 3*.

van Veenendaal, E. (2010). Scrum & Testing: Assessing the risks. *Agile Record, 3*.

VersionOne. (2011). State of Agile Survey 2011 - The State of Agile Development. *Journal of Computational Science, 33*, 290–291.

Xu, R., Chen, B., Chen, B., Wu, M., & Xiong, Z. (2003). Investigation on the pattern for Construction of Reusable Test Cases in Object-oriented Software. *Journal of Wuhan University*, *49*(005), 592–596.

KEY TERMS AND DEFINITIONS

Agile Software Methodology: An evolutionary and iterative approach to software development with focuses on adaption to changes.

Critical Software Systems: Software whose failure would impact safety or cause large financial or social losses.

DevOps: Development and operations (DevOps) has been adopted by prominent software and service companies (e.g., IBM) to support enhanced collaboration across the company and its value chain partners. In this way, DevOps facilitates uninterrupted delivery and coexistence between development and operation facilities, enhances the quality and performance of software applications, improving end-user experience, and help to simultaneous deployment of software across different platforms.

Scrum: An agile process framework for managing knowledge work, with an emphasis on software development.

Software Engineering: The application of engineering to the development of software in a systematic method.

Software Life Cycle Processes: It provides a framework for the sequence of activities to be performed for software projects.

Software Process Standards: It presents fundamental standards that describe activities performed as part of the software life cycle. In some cases, these standards also describe documents, but these represent plans for conducting activities.

Software Quality: Software engineering standards, if sufficiently comprehensive and if properly enforced, establish a *quality system*, a systematic approach to ensuring software quality, which is defined as (1) the degree to which a system, component, or process meets specified requirements; and (2) the degree to which a system, component, or process meets customer or user needs or expectations.

Software Quality Assurance: Software quality assurance is defined as follows: (1) a planned and systematic pattern of all actions necessary to provide adequate confidence that an item or product conforms to established technical requirements; and (2) a set of activities designed to evaluate the process by which products are developed or manufactured.

Software Testing: Software testing provides the mechanism for verifying that the requirements identified during the initial phases of the project were properly implemented and that the system performs as expected. The test scenarios developed through these competitions ensure that the requirements are met end-to-end.

Verification and Validation: The process of determining whether the requirements for a system or component are complete and correct, the products of each development phase fulfil the requirements or conditions imposed by the previous phase, and the final system or component complies with specified requirements.

Waterfall Model: A sequential design, used in software development processes, in which progress is seen as flowing steadily downwards (like a waterfall) through the phases of Requirements, Specifications, Coding, Testing, and Release.

This research was previously published in Agile Scrum Implementation and Its Long-Term Impact on Organizations; pages 114-131, copyright year 2021 by Engineering Science Reference (an imprint of IGI Global).

Index

F

G

H

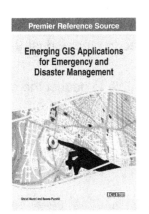
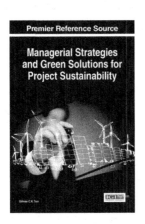

IGI Global Author Services

Providing a high-quality, affordable, and expeditious service, IGI Global's Author Services enable authors to streamline their publishing process, increase chance of acceptance, and adhere to IGI Global's publication standards.

Benefits of Author Services:

- **Professional Service:** All our editors, designers, and translators are experts in their field with years of experience and professional certifications.

- **Quality Guarantee & Certificate:** Each order is returned with a quality guarantee and certificate of professional completion.

- **Timeliness:** All editorial orders have a guaranteed return timeframe of 3-5 business days and translation orders are guaranteed in 7-10 business days.

- **Affordable Pricing:** IGI Global Author Services are competitively priced compared to other industry service providers.

- **APC Reimbursement:** IGI Global authors publishing Open Access (OA) will be able to deduct the cost of editing and other IGI Global author services from their OA APC publishing fee.

Author Services Offered:

 English Language Copy Editing
Professional, native English language copy editors improve your manuscript's grammar, spelling, punctuation, terminology, semantics, consistency, flow, formatting, and more.

 Scientific & Scholarly Editing
A Ph.D. level review for qualities such as originality and significance, interest to researchers, level of methodology and analysis, coverage of literature, organization, quality of writing, and strengths and weaknesses.

 Figure, Table, Chart & Equation Conversions
Work with IGI Global's graphic designers before submission to enhance and design all figures and charts to IGI Global's specific standards for clarity.

 Translation
Providing 70 language options, including Simplified and Traditional Chinese, Spanish, Arabic, German, French, and more.

Hear What the Experts Are Saying About IGI Global's Author Services

"Publishing with IGI Global has been *an amazing experience* for me for sharing my research. The *strong academic production* support ensures quality and timely completion." – **Prof. Margaret Niess, Oregon State University, USA**

"The service was *very fast, very thorough, and very helpful* in ensuring our chapter meets the criteria and requirements of the book's editors. I was *quite impressed and happy* with your service." – **Prof. Tom Brinthaupt, Middle Tennessee State University, USA**

Learn More or Get Started Here:

For Questions, Contact IGI Global's Customer Service Team at cust@igi-global.com or 717-533-8845

www.igi-global.com

Printed in the United States
by Baker & Taylor Publisher Services